THE PERSON

His Development

The Person
throughout the Life Cycle

by THEODORE LIDZ

PROFESSOR AND CHAIRMAN
DEPARTMENT OF PSYCHIATRY
Yale University
School of Medicine

BASIC BOOKS, INC. *Publishers*   NEW YORK   LONDON

To Ruth, my love

Preface

During the eighteenth century many leading biologists were convinced that the person existed completely preformed within the ovum as a microscopic homunculus. A number of eminent scientists disagreed. They insisted that the animalcule resided in the spermatazoa and not in the ovum. The inordinately intricate step-by-step differentiation of the organism from the fertilized germ cell could not be grasped, nor even observed, because of rationalistic and religious judgments of what made sense. The understanding of personality development and integration has been deterred by similar preconceptions. An individual's personality traits were long ascribed primarily to his ancestry. Aberrant behavior could readily be attributed to inheritance, for it clearly runs in families. One of my teachers could lightly dismiss an unmarried mother or a mentally retarded child as being made of "poor stuff." Constitutional psychopathic inferiority was a proper diagnosis but a few decades ago, when delinquents were born and not made. Currently most psychiatrists accept as axiomatic that persons suffering from schizophrenic disorders are genetically blighted.

Appreciation of the complexity of personality development has emerged slowly. Even the most dynamic orientation to the study of personality functioning and malfunctioning, psychoanalytic psychology, long assumed that the infant would develop into a well-integrated and highly adaptable individual unless an inherent defect, a childhood emotional trauma, or gross maternal neglect induced a fixation of libidinal investment during childhood. The many factors that enter into personality development and the many requirements that must be supplied by the nurturing persons and the enveloping social system could be overlooked because all viable societies must provide for the essential needs of their offspring and, because the family is so essential that it is universal, many of its critical functions were taken for granted.

This book presents a psychodynamic description and conceptualization of personality development and functioning from birth to death. After presenting the fundamentals of the biological and cultural endowments with which the infant enters the world, we shall carefully consider each phase of his life cycle, the individual's capacities, and the cardinal issues and the tasks he must surmount to be properly prepared to enter into and accept the challenges and opportunities of the next phase that comes with the inevitability of the passage of time. The mastery of the tasks of each developmental phase of childhood is not simply an end in itself but is directed toward the attainment of a cohesive identity and a workable integration by the end of adolescence. The course of the life cycle will be followed past adolescence, for each period of adult existence requires reorientation and reorganization of the personality. We shall be following the person, not as an isolate, but within the interpersonal, social, and cultural settings in which he lives and from which he gains support and direction.

My purpose in writing this book has been to provide medical students with a guide for learning about the persons who will be their patients. Many other professions require a similar comprehensive understanding of people, and I believe this book can serve equally well the needs of those training to become clinical and social psychologists, social workers, counselors, college-trained nurses, and even attorneys. I have sought to reorganize current knowledge to achieve a conceptualization which is not only internally consistent but which is also compatible with both the biological and the behavioral sciences with which personality theory must interdigitate. Insofar as the book succeeds in formulating a coherent and consistent approach to the study of personality development and functioning, it may also be of interest to those who are seeking to bring order to the current confused and confusing state of the theory. Further, I hold some hope that the book may be of value to persons who are simply interested in "the proper study of mankind."

The developmental psychology of dynamic psychiatry and medicine has arisen relatively independently of the remainder of psychology. Indeed, many academic psychologists and psychiatrists approach the study of personality so differently that they can scarcely communicate with one another and some have virtually ceased trying. Medical psychology developed out of therapeutic needs and has had strong leanings toward seeking the origins of disturbed behavior in how the genetically endowed infant unfolds in interaction with his interpersonal environment. It has been interested in learning how emotionally disturbed persons came to be the way they are, how such adverse developments might have been prevented or modified, and how personality functioning can be altered therapeutically. It has not been as interested in basing its theories on experiment or in obtaining statistically significant findings as it has been in gaining meaningful insights from work with patients and in achieving therapeutically useful knowledge.

This psychodynamic psychology received much of its impetus, its concepts, and its hypotheses from the genius of Sigmund Freud, who, by linking various psychiatric syndromes to repressed unconscious motivations and residual influences of childhood sexuality, directed attention to the critical importance of childhood experiences to mental illness. A new grasp of personality development and functioning arose out of the study of the pathological, for only when the smooth flow of normative development is disrupted can many of its intricacies be appreciated. Although long neglected in medical as well as in academic psychology circles, Freud's insights gradually gained wide attention not simply because of their therapeutic value but because they provided new depths to understanding humans and to human understanding.

It may have been advantageous for psychoanalysis to develop as it did, outside of the universities, free of the academicians who need to deal with measurable data; or who might prefer to experiment with rats because of the relative simplicity of such subjects and then make generalizations about human psychology, forgetting that man is not a monkey and even much less a rat; or who wish to avoid the complexities of human motivation and decision making even though they are of the essence of human psychology. Although psychoanalysis now permeates the thought and art of Western man, serious difficulties have arisen within psychoanalysis as a science and in relationship to other sciences where clarity and precision of concepts are necessary.

Under attack for many years because of the emphasis of psychoanalysis upon infantile sexuality and the importance of the sexual drive and unconscious motivation, analysts closed ranks and rightly regarded most of the attacks upon Freud and themselves as due to efforts to deny the pertinence of these topics. Many continued to believe that later criticisms by persons who were just as interested as they in unconscious processes and in infantile sexuality were still basically resistance rather than attempts at constructive criticism. Gradually the advantages of freedom from the academician were lost in a domination by a kind of scholasticism—a limitation of the search for knowledge and truth to within the confines of concepts that had been transformed into tenets or axioms. The world's resistance to accepting Freud's discoveries led to a counter-resistance by psychoanalysts[2] to the inclusion of the findings of other sciences and scientists into psychoanalytic psychology.

As a result, no general theory of psychoanalysis exists that is internally consistent or adequately compatible with the remainder of science, but only an array of more or less related theories.* This is not the place to examine the various inconsistencies between these part-theories, particularly as I consider that many of them derive directly or indirectly from some fundamental deficiencies in understanding the nature of man and human adaptation.†

Any developmental psychology must appreciate and give due consideration to the unique nature of man's adaptive capacities—his ways of coping with his environment and surviving its hazards. The emergence of man depended upon the evolution of a brain and neuromuscular system capable of using tools, and particularly that tool of tools—language. The nature of the consequences of the development of language will be set out in the first two chapters and developed throughout the book. As the orientation emphasizes the central position of language and thought in understanding human development and behavior, it rests upon Meyerian psychobiology as well as psychoanalytic observation and theory. Adolf Meyer taught that man can be properly understood only as integrated at a symbolic level because what he thinks and feels influences his functioning down to the cellular and biochemical levels of integration.[4] To incorporate language and thought into the description and conceptualization of the person's development, the studies of Jean Piaget as well as those of M. M. Lewis and others have been utilized. Meyer did not, however, consider how the communicative aspects of symbolic activity led to the development of cultures and social institutions, as required to formulate an adequate "field" theory or comprehensive working theory for the study of human development and maldevelopment.

* Careful study of the monumental labor of the late David Rapaport, who was among the foremost psychoanalytic scholars, clearly reveals his inability to achieve a satisfactory integration of psychoanalytic theories.[5] Similarly, the efforts of Merton Gill,[3] one of the most brilliant contemporary psychoanalysts, to achieve an integrated theory did not, I believe, turn out felicitously; and a related effort by J. Arlow and C. Brenner[1] has added as many problems as it has managed to clarify.

† It might be useful to some readers, however, if I noted briefly how the book differs from various widely accepted psychoanalytic concepts. The purpose of the book, however, is not to offer a divergent or a modified theory, but rather an internally consistent approach that is in accord with established findings of both the biological and the behavioral sciences. Several salient differences will, however, be noted. (1) Those aspects of psychoanalytic theory that depend upon Lamarckian concepts of the genetic transmission of acquired characteristics, as also those that invoke a closed energy system for a biological organism, can, of course, have no place in a contemporary approach. (2) Libido theory is omitted except as metaphor that can occasionally be useful. No evidence of a

Some aspects of personality development are common to all humans, reflecting the basic similarities in their biological structure and functioning. The prolonged helplessness and dependency, the late puberty, the dependence upon language and upon learning adaptive techniques, the need to provide prolonged care for offspring, and many other such factors tend to lead to common features in all peoples and also set a sequential pattern of the phases in the life cycle. All societies must take into account the same basic needs of man and the human ways of survival and adaptation. Nevertheless, there is considerble leeway in how man's essential needs can be satisfied and even greater latitude in how human abilities can be utilized. Different ethnic groups essentially reflect the evolution of different cultural heritages—that is, of different sets of adaptive techniques for coping with the environment. Thus, some aspects of the presentation of personality development in this book can have pertinence to all persons, some aspects to many peoples, but other portions are relevant primarily to middle- and upper-class Americans. The limitations will usually be apparent to the thoughtful reader.

In closing the prefatory remarks, I wish to note some of the major

---

displaceable sexual energy has been found; it has led to an unnecessary complexity of theory and probably nothing has done more to confuse psychoanalytic thinking. It explains nothing that is not more readily understood in other ways. The renunciation of libido theory does not mean neglect of the importance of sexual drives in human motivation, though it leads to a different approach to infantile sexuality. (3) The conflict between the topographic and structural hypotheses—that is, between considering psychic organization in terms of levels of consciousness as against conceptualizing it in terms of an id, ego, and superego—is resolved simply by considering that levels of consciousness pertain to mental functioning whereas the id, ego, and superego are constructs concerned with the structure and functioning of the personality. (4) The oedipal situation is considered in terms of the critical transition during which the essential erotized attachments of the small child to the mother must be frustrated and transcended. (5) The "secondary process" of reality-oriented conscious thought is given more importance—as in psychoanalytic ego psychology—and "primary process" thinking is considered neither to be present in early infancy nor to be a constant precursor of rational thinking, but rather is regarded as a different type of mental process that goes on under different conditions.

The most significant differences concern, first, the concept of man as a social being whose development into a person depends upon his growth into and his internalization of the instrumentalities of a culture and the institutions of a structured social system as well as upon identification with and internalization of significant persons who themselves have made such assimilations; and second, the emphasis upon cognitive development, which has been largely neglected in psychoanalytic theory.

influences entering into the book's orientation. The confluence of psychoanalytic and psychobiological approaches reflects my psychiatric training. I entered medicine in order to become a psychoanalyst after first reading Freud in 1928. My training in psychoanalysis was delayed by two circumstances that were not without benefit. I was directed for my residency training to Adolf Meyer at the Henry Phipps Psychiatric Clinic of the Johns Hopkins Hospital, who strongly discouraged concomitant psychoanalytic training. However, because of my prior interests in language and aphasia and in the philosophies of James and Dewey, Dr. Meyer's approach to psychiatry was particularly meaningful to me. Then, four years of military service intervened during which I assumed responsibility for extremely severe psychiatric casualties and took care of several thousand patients who formed a cross section of American youth. Concomitantly, I was brought into contact with two preliterate societies and a decadent culture. These experiences have had a pervasive influence upon me. Immediately after the war, I entered upon my psychoanalytic training. My clinical and investigative interests in psychosomatic disorders and in schizophrenic patients have required major theoretic reconceptualizations of theories based primarily on studies of neurotic patients.

Aside from Adolf Meyer, John Whitehorn, and Lewis Hill, my major teachers have been persons whose writings I have studied rather than persons under whom I studied. The influences within psychoanalysis and psychiatry are many, and those outside of psychiatry even more numerous. A number of such influences will be apparent in the text, which is, of course, the product of such teachings as filtered through my own experiences and integrated into a new entity.

The preparation of this book was supported in part by the National Institute of Mental Health through my Career Investigator grant. I wish to take this opportunity to thank the Commonwealth Fund for the support of a sabbatical year during which a preliminary draft of this book was prepared; and to the Center for Advanced Study in the Behavioral Sciences for providing a haven where most of the book was written, and to the various members of its staff who helped make the year highly rewarding as well as pleasant, particularly to Miss Joan Warmbrunn, who cheerfully typed various versions of chapters. I wish to express my warm appreciation to Mrs. Harriette D. Borsuch, who devotedly and speedily prepared the manuscript for publication and assumed a variety of responsibilities in the process which lightened my work considerably. I am much indebted to Kenneth Keniston, who read most of the manuscript with unusual care and thoughtfulness and who made many valuable suggestions which are incorporated in the text; and I wish to thank my friend and colleague Stephen Fleck, who assumed my departmental responsibilities for several months to enable me to write the last chapters. Ruth Wilmanns Lidz, my wife, co-investigator, colleague, sometime informal therapist, and much besides, to whom the book is dedicated, has been a direct and indirect source of a great deal contained in this volume.

References

1. Jacob Arlow and Charles Brenner, "Psychoanalytic Concepts and the Structural Theory," *Journal of the American Psychoanalytic Association,* Monograph Series No. 13 (New York: International Universities Press, 1964).
2. John Benjamin, "Methodological Considerations in Validation and Elaboration of Psychoanalytical Personality Theory," *American Journal of Orthopsychiatry,* 20 (1950), 139–156.
3. Merton M. Gill, "Topography and Systems in Psychoanalytic Theory," *Psychological Issues,* Vol. 2, No. 2, Monograph 10 (New York: International Universities Press, 1963).
4. Theodore Lidz, "Adolf Meyer and the Development of American Psychiatry," *American Journal of Psychiatry,* 123 (1966), 320–331.
5. David Rapaport, "The Structure of Psychoanalytic Theory," *Psychological Issues,* Vol. 2, No. 2, Monograph 6 (New York: International Universities Press, 1960).

THEODORE LIDZ

Yale University,
New Haven, Connecticut
July 1968

Remarks to the Reader—If a Medical Student

This book concerns the normative development, structure, and functioning of man. Its focus, however, does not fall upon his tangible structure as learned by dissection or by peering through a microscope, or primarily upon the unity of his physiological processes and the homeostasis of his internal environment, but upon man as the person to whom the physician relates in treating him—man as a total person with an individual life history and with relationships to others that provide meaning to his existence. It deals with the intangible matters of thoughts and feelings and the continuity of personality over time. It will seek to follow his development from a helpless animal infant into a specific individual with relationships to himself, to others, and to events that influence his physical make-up, his physiological responses, and his state of health. Our concern, then, will be with those attributes of man that are essentially human rather than simply animal and with his integrated behavior within the world in which he lives, a human social world as well as a physical environment.

Although concerned with matters that are essential to the study of psychiatry, this book seeks to provide some fundamentals required for the practice of modern medicine in which the patient rather than the disease is the focus of attention, and to prepare for the trained use of the doctor-patient relationship which enters into all treatment and, more often than is realized, forms the core of it. No book, no course, no individual tutelage can seek to convey all that a physician needs to know about people in order to be a good physician. The doctor learns from his patients and the task can never be completed in a lifetime. Still a person learns more readily if directed toward what is pertinent and if provided a conceptual framework for organizing his experiences.

The good physician has always known that the majority of his patients come to him because of emotional difficulties. People turn to physicians, clergymen, and attorneys for help with problems with which they cannot cope alone, but the physician is in a particularly difficult position. Patients come to him with physical complaints derived from emotional difficulties and problems in living of which the patient is unaware, which he seeks to banish from consciousness in order to retain his equanimity, but for which substitute physical symptoms appear. It is safe to say that the majority of errors committed by physicians involve failures to recognize the emotional origins of symptoms, and when it is a failure to recognize a serious depression it can be as fatal as a failure to diagnose a still-operable malignancy. However, medicine and medical science have changed and entered an era in which the understanding and study of personality problems has become essential to scientific advance in many areas. The virtual conquest of infectious diseases through antibiotics and immunization has directed attention to other types of illness and has also created new problems. Medicine has been left with many conditions that do not kill but also cannot be cured, and with a number of serious diseases that are often termed "diseases of stress" because emotional factors contribute notably to their origins. Whereas infectious diseases could often be studied and mastered by work with laboratory animals, the utility of animals in studying diseases of stress, such as peptic ulcer, essential hypertension, hyperthyroidism, ulcerative colitis, and rheumatoid arthritis, is far more limited. It is not quite possible to reproduce in rats or even in anthropoids conflicts involving marital discord, frustrated ambitions, "turned-on" hippie daughters, or discrepancies between ethical standards and sexual drives. The resolution of many of these conditions would seem to require an ability to work with emotionally disturbed patients and to become able to understand what can cause such disturbances and how they can be ameliorated. Thus, it is not only the care of patients but also the proper scientific study of their diseases that requires an understanding of psychodynamics.

Students enter medical school for a wide variety of reasons, and often for reasons of which they never become fully aware. One identifies with his physician father whom he admires; another is simply following the expectations of his parents; a student may be setting out to combat cancer that had robbed him of his mother, or is determined to solve the problem of schizophrenia that has incarcerated his sister in a mental hospital; he may be following his religious beliefs, "of the most high cometh healing"; or he has decided that if he cannot be great he can at least be useful. These and other such motivations are acceptable reasons for studying medicine, but among these manifold reasons there must be an interest in people and a desire to help them, a wish to stand with the patient against his fate and help him avert tragedy, and when one cannot, to help provide the strength to bear it. If there is no such interest in people, a student cannot properly become a physician. He can still become a medical scientist, for which there is great need, and become very helpful to mankind, but not a physician.

Almost all medical students enter medical school with such interests in people, usually avid interests in patients as individuals, and are keenly sensitive to suffering and reactive to the drama, the often tragic drama of the hospital. Yet, as has been documented, during the four years in medical school this dominant interest in people often declines. Some claim that medical schools inadvertently teach their students to become indifferent and even cynical.[1] Others insist that the student simply becomes more realistic in his understanding of people and the expectations he holds for them. There is, of course, an important difference between the two words: "cynical" connotes a disillusionment; "realistic," an ability to see man as he is, a human, and because he is human often with selfish and even brutal motivations. The physician, however, is involved with human weaknesses and requires an ability to take care of people despite their frailties—or even because of them.

There is some truth to the charge that the medical student becomes indifferent to patients. He enters medical school to learn to treat people. He is immediately confronted by a person—a dead person called a cadaver, which he dissects. For variety, he peers at very thin slices of another body through a microscope. In the second year the student progressses to study pathology; his subject is no less dead, simply more recently alive. He soon becomes accustomed to a patient who is, indeed, very passive. He may consider that the only good patient is one who is anaesthetized or, at least, does not disrupt the study of him by talking, and certainly does not disagree with the physician and express an opinion about what is being done to him. The physician's sensitivity to suffering and a constant awareness of what illness means to a patient and his family cannot but cause him pain. He has need for defenses against too great an involvement. The construction of such defenses starts on the first day of school, when he calls the body he dissects a "stiff," as if to deny that it had once been a person, when he utilizes "dissecting room humor" to blunt the grimness of the task and the place. Such defenses are proper, necessary, and valuable, but they become deleterious to the development of a physician when the protective shell turns to callus and the student withdraws from learning what is meaningful in the lives of patients. The study of patients and their personalities can be hampered by just such needs to erect and maintain defenses.

Withdrawing or becoming indifferent or callous is not the most useful way to withstand the stresses and pain that are inherent in the practice of medicine. Here, as elsewhere, a little knowledge may cause hurt, whereas broader knowledge brings strength. With trained understanding of people and their ways of reacting, the physician can serve as a guide to the patient who is confronted by unfamiliar experiences and new stresses and is lost among his concerns and involvements. The physician can learn to realize how much illness and misfortune mean to a patient and still not become personally caught up in the patient's troubles. He cannot become too involved personally and yet maintain the perspective and judgment he requires to help the patient. When he can help, and he can often help simply by listening and understanding, he is not likely to become resentful to the patient because he can do nothing to cure the illness or save his life: the patient will in some way be better off for having been under the physician's care.

The adage "Know thyself" is intimately related to "The proper study of mankind is man." The medical student is in a privileged position, for he will be given the opportunity to learn about man more intimately than persons in any other profession; and not simply as a spectator but as an active participant in the drama of people's lives. Self-knowledge is fostered and even provoked by knowledge of others and comparisons of the self with them. One cannot come to know very much about others, however, without learning to know oneself, how one's life fits together and how one defends against experiencing insecurities and anxieties. Such learning about the self is bound to produce some discomfort in anyone who dares be sensitive. All students of people, of personality, of themselves, must recognize that "norms" by which to measure and judge the self do not exist. There is no proper standard of normality, no proper way of life, but rather different types of workable integrations. Everyone has defects, weaknesses, hidden shames and guilts, but they are usually offset if not balanced by assets. There is ample room in society for difference and divergence, and few persons are capable of understanding others who have not been made alert because of their own shortcomings and insecurities. Tolerance of others may well start with tolerance of the self. The only way to be completely stable is to become inert, and there is ample time for that. The processes of development, accomplishment, and creativity, the pursuit of goals and the involvement in the lives of others, are all stabilizing forces that serve to integrate and protect against the effects of personality deficiencies that may become disturbing when development and involvement with matters beyond the self come to a halt.

Reference

1. Leonard Eron, "Effect of Medical Education on Medical Students' Attitudes," *Journal of Medical Education,* 30 (1955), 559–566.

Contents

PART I

The Setting

CHAPTER 1

The Human Endowment

WHEN THE INFANT EMERGES into the world from his mother's womb, a loud wail marks the entry of air into his lungs and the shock of exposure to the world. Without being asked, he is committed to the world and the life that lies ahead of him. If he is reluctant, the obstetrician holds him by his heels and raps them sharply, for this is the moment of decision. The baby has given up his symbiotic existence within his mother, where he was fed through the placenta by filtration of the mother's blood. Now the umbilical cord is cut and tied. The neonate, or newborn, appears puny and he is helpless—among the most helpless of all creatures born into this world—and he will require total care for a long time. Still, he is a member of the human species that has inherited the earth and is master of it: the most far-ranging and adaptable species that has ever existed—a creature who increasingly changes his environment to suit his needs and his desires.

This is an awesome moment, and it is a rare obstetrician who, despite the hundreds of similar deliveries he has performed, has not marveled at the process of the unfolding from the fertilized ovum that has taken place, and wondered what the future will hold for this particular infant whom he has ushered into the world. After the cord is cut, the obstetrician, with his practiced eye, will examine the infant to see if he is properly equipped for the task that lies ahead. At this point of transition we too shall pause to review what the human child brings into the world with him, considering certain essentials of what he acquired during the ten dark lunar months in the womb and then what he must acquire in order to survive and develop into an individual.

Man's Dual Heritage

The neonate is just sufficiently complete to survive with the help of a mothering figure. Despite his relatively poor equipment at birth, he possesses a great deal. His body contains an inborn directedness for further growth and the potentiality for the very special type of adaptation that man acquired at the end of a billion or so years of evolution from a unicellular organism. Within his mother's uterus the fetus recapitulated in a token fashion the emergence of man through his many prior evolutionary forms and his preparation, through evolutionary trial and error, for survival. Although man attained his present physical structure some thirty thousand years ago and his genetic make-up has changed little in essentials since then, his way of life and his adaptive capacities have altered enormously—to an extent that makes his pre-Stone Age progenitors seem closer to the anthropoid apes than to the astronaut.

The infant can grow up to become a contemporary man because he has a second heritage that he acquires after birth from those with whom he will live. It is a heritage that has accumulated over countless generations, and which had been made possible by the uniquely human capacity to use words to communicate and think. The infant will acquire an organized filtrate of the ways his forebears had learned to cope with their environment and live together—that is, a culture and its instrumentalities. He will learn these ways slowly as he grows up, for the ability to acquire them is an essential part of his physical endowment and he cannot even survive and grow into adulthood without them. Not only is the newborn infant physically immature and incomplete, but man's method of adaptation, in contrast to that of all other animals, rests upon learning essential techniques of adaptation during the long period of immaturity that is a necessary correlate of the development of the complicated cerebral cortex which permits thought, learning, and decision making to supplant inborn patterns of behavior essential for survival. The infant, then, is born with two endowments, or, more properly stated, with one and into one. He possesses at birth a genetically determined biological endowment which is both common to all mankind and also uniquely individual and which has already been modified by interaction with the intrauterine environment. He will grow into and assimilate a cultural heritage that is a product of the cumulative experiences of the particular ethnic group into which he is born but which also will be somewhat different for him than for any other individual. The two will be inextricably intertwined as the child matures and develops. Unless both endowments and their fusion in the individual are taken into account, human development and integration can never be understood properly. All dynamic psychologies have been concerned, either explicitly or implicitly, with the growth of the biological organism in its interpersonal setting, varying in emphasis on the importance of the genetic endowment and environment in shaping the personality. Neglect of one or the other has led to gross distortions of understanding, and unawareness of the problem has led to many of the grievous errors that have plagued psychology and psychiatry.

Evolutionary Considerations

Questions concerning why man is constructed as he is, why his physiological processes function as they do, why his adaptation depends upon his capacities to use tools and language, why and how he developed a "mind" or "psyche," can be answered only in evolutionary terms— through an understanding of man's emergence from a unicellular organism through countless forms of animal organization by means of innumerable genetic mutations. We can ask such questions as "What for?" and "What purpose does it subserve?" without embarrassment over teleological implications. The process of evolution promoted survival through selecting out through mating those mutations or recessive genes that permitted a new or improved means of adaptation to a segment of the environment. We can assume that a structure or process found in the organism subserves the preservation of the individual or species and is a modification of something found in prior evolutionary forms, or that it is vestigial from a structure that had been useful in a prior form.

When our post-simian ancestors climbed down from their arboreal habitat to give up their monkey business and keep their feet on the ground—clutching a stick as a club instead of hanging to it as a branch, and calling to one another with words instead of through interjectional sounds of warning or passion—a new phase in the history of our planet had its primordial origins some million or more years ago. Once the value and superiority of the new form of adaptation were established, man emerged by successive modifications over approximately another million years. Then, within the brief thirty thousand years of his existence *Homo sapiens* has changed the order of nature radically, interposing the switching system of the human brain into the sequence of events and even the selection of species until eventually—now—the question of how long life in any form may continue on this planet depends more upon what transpires in men and between men than upon the eventual dimming of the sun.

Let us note in summary fashion what is distinctive about human evolution and adaptation. All forms of life are variations of a single theme. They are different means of assuring survival and reproduction of the fundamental unit of life, the cell. The cell contains chromosomes composed of genes—chemical templates that reproduce themselves and then control the development, structure, and organization of the organism. Single-celled organisms can survive and reproduce only under very specific conditions and are dependent upon the immediate availability of essential chemicals in the environment in order to function, if not to survive. Increasingly complex organisms evolved which could exist under more varied conditions and with longer periods of self-sufficiency. Each new form of life had a somewhat different structure suited to interacting with a different segment of the environment. Changes in structure that permitted such changes in adaptation depended upon utilization of mutations in the germinal cells—chance failures of the genes to reproduce themselves precisely, so that the new genes gave rise to an organism that was different from the parents. Stated succinctly, at least as far as higher animals are concerned, there can be no question about the answer to the age-old riddle—the egg preceded the hen. For the hen to have attained attributes different from its non-hen parents', a change had to have occurred in the chromosomes of the fertilized egg from which it emerged.

Let us shift from a chicken to a finch—to take a classical example. Darwin's finches, which played an important role in the evolution of the theory of evolution, comprise a number of varieties of finches, all of which emerged from common ancestors who happened into the Galápagos Islands. They flourished and competed for the available food supply—they might occasionally peck a bug from the bark of a tree, but they could not survive only by eating bugs from beneath the bark. Some underwent an accidental mutation of the genes that provided a longer and sharper beak—and could now enjoy a diet other finches could not reach—and as the trait aided survival, it was retained by means of the mating of finches with this characteristic. Other finches gained an advantage from other modifications in structure—such as permitted them to suck nectar from flowers or to eat insects in flight. Each structure permitted a different way of competing and a better use of a different segment of the environment and fostered the ability to survive and produce eggs. Birds that lived in and used the same environmental niche tended to mate with one another, and eventually the new mutant traits replaced former physical characteristics and thus changed the finch into a new variety.

While the emergence through such means of the millions of different forms of life that have inhabited the earth may seem highly improbable, we must remember that mutations are very common, that a billion years is a long time, particularly for rapidly reproducing simple organisms, and that, as Simpson,[33] the renowned geneticist, has pointed out, selective mating is a means of achieving a high degree of improbability.

Selective Mating and Evolution

The emergence of a new species—at least in more complex forms of life—does not occur by the selecting out of a single mutation through mating. It results by selecting out in mating those specific mutations, from among the myriads that occur by chance, which improve some particular attribute or set of attributes that bestows a greater chance of survival in a given environment as mutations improve this attribute over thousands or hundreds of thousands of generations. In herbivorous mammals, for example, increased neck length allowed a mutant group to eat leaves competitors could not reach—and continuing selecting out of improvements in neck length permitted better use than competitors of a different segment of the environment. Another line fed in the open plains and its chances were increased by developing the fur that permitted ranging northward—combined with strength and horns to defend itself in the open country. The mutation that gave rise to a trait that permitted moving into a different environment led to selecting out further improvements in this trait that increased chances of survival and reproduction in that environment.

Although this summary of the evolutionary process is a gross and perhaps a brazen oversimplification, I believe it will suffice for our purposes.

The Evolution of Human Attributes

The human species, of course, emerged in the same gradual way. We cannot here trace the many fascinating phases in our evolution, but it is essential to note that man with his inordinately complex brain could have emerged only from an arboreal ancestor who had developed an opposable thumb to aid in climbing; who could nurture only one offspring at a time because the infant had to cling to its mother while she jumped from tree to tree, and thereby was more amenable to education by example; who lived in groups that were dependent upon the exchange of vocal signals for defense; and who lived by its wits and was already rewarding through selective mating increases in brain size and intelligence as means of survival.

Tools and Language

When for some reason our ancestors returned to live on the ground, and left the protection of the rain forest, the direction of future evolutionary selection had been established. Out of the trees, this ape man must have been highly vulnerable. He had little in the way of physical characteristics to safeguard his existence: no body armor, horns, tusks, claws, or massive strength, special fleetness of foot, or protective coloring. But he was endowed with a brain that, even in its relatively rudimentary form, bestowed new attributes that were worth the sacrifice of other characteristics. He could use tools: the stick that his ancestors had grasped for about fifty million years now became an extension of his physical structure—a disposable and replaceable extension that could be used as a club or throwing stick, and later as a digging tool to root out foods; as material for a shelter, as a bit of fuel for his fire; and as charcoal for drawing pictures. It was an extension of himself—but also one object with many uses, and many objects with the same use, and thereby something that had a symbolic connotation.*

The ability to use tools depended upon the evolutionary acquisition of a brain and neuromuscular system capable of exquisite voluntary move-

---

* The chimpanzee dips a stick into an insect hole and then eats the insects that collect on the stick.[16,17] This is a primitive use of a tool, but only for one specific purpose. Anthropoid apes are highly social animals, teaching a great deal to their offspring through example.

ments that could be learned. It was a brain that also made possible the fine coordination of movement of lips, tongue, larynx, and facial and respiratory muscles that permitted the acquisition of another tool, that less tangible tool that faded into thin air as its waves spread out in widening circles—the word. Upon the importance of this abstract tool grown into language rested the further evolution of the prehominid into the human—that is, upon the word which permitted protoman to communicate explicitly in order to direct others, and eventually to direct himself by reflective thinking.

The Human Brain

Over the ensuing million years many changes in prehominid physical structure took place. Many varieties of protohuman species developed until one became dominant or the more successful lines fused. But the important characteristics selected out of the mutations that occurred were those which had to do with the increasing development of the cerebral cortex and particularly of those several areas of the brain essential for language development and with the accompanying increase in nerve pathways that permitted inborn or instinctual patterns to be supplanted by learned ways, and permitted complex choice and decision. In these hundreds of thousands of years—comprising over more than four million generations—through the selecting out of the proper mutations the brain tripled in size, and about thirty thousand years ago the human species came into existence. It is a species whose newborn are among the most helpless of all animals, depending upon parental protection and nurturance for a dozen or more years, and who have little capacity for survival anywhere without being taught—that is, without learning the techniques of adaptation—and yet who spread out and flourished almost everywhere on earth, from tropic to pole, from beneficent islands nurtured by green plants to harsh brick and concrete canyons nourished by green paper.* Yet, despite this increase in the range of environments, the many changes in man's techniques of adapting to them have occurred with very little, if any, basic alterations in his physical structure, including his brain. This is in complete contrast to all other living things. We can say that although man as an animal has remained unchanged,

* That man is born "to live in an average expectable environment" is a notion which has gained wide popularity but which misses the essence of man's adaptive capacities[19]—namely, his ability to adjust the environment to meet his inborn physiological capacities.

man as a person changes constantly. In contrast to other animals in which changes in adaptive techniques await changes in physical structure, man continues to evolve without such changes. The completion of the human brain through genetic mutations did not imply the completion of the human mind. Indeed, it was only after the emergence of the human brain that man's mind really began to develop. It is, I believe, through the contemplation of how this evolution without genetic change could take place that we may gain an understanding of human adaptation and of what we mean by the human mind.

What then was so valuable about this ability to manipulate tools, both tangible and symbolic, that it was selected out as a superior means of assuring survival, and led to the development of man and to a new type of evolution?

Some are skeptical that man could evolve from a pre-Stone Age specimen to his present heights without incurring changes in his brain capacity. But consider, we can observe a transition of almost this magnitude occurring today in but one or two generations. While living in a remote country, I worked with a well-trained physician and enjoyed conversing with his brother, a colonel who was skilled in the civilized techniques of killing with a tommy gun and bazooka—and yet their grandfather had gained prestige and position by his skill in wielding a solid club of wood and showed his good manners by using a specially carved fork rather than his fingers when eating the men he killed with his club. As the sons of the chief, my friends had been educated in England. But one need only wander about most sheltered university campuses to encounter scholars whose parents or grandparents lived in Stone Age fashion in Africa or New Guinea as had countless generations of their ancestors.

Let us, for purposes of clarity, examine separately two sets of consequences of the acquisition of language, even though they are in actuality inextricably linked: those derived from verbal communication and those arising from its internal counterpart, mentation.

Language, Communication, and Culture

All animals communicate through actions and odors, if not through sound. Communication is a major adaptive attribute. Two animals who can cooperate through communicating have abilities that far exceed the sum of their individual capacities. They can warn one another, signal the presence of food, mark out areas against intruders, inform the opposite sex of their presence at appropriate times, etc. Apes that live in bands—such as baboons—depend greatly upon group organization for protection and survival. Indeed, the young and injured adults have little chance of surviving for a day if separated from the band.

Further, all higher animals depend upon learning from their mothers to supplement inborn patterns of behavior. Even a squirrel must be taught how to run properly along a branch, and how to scurry for cover upon jumping to the ground; but such learning depends upon following direct and tangible examples. Man, in contrast, could, by means of the language he gradually constructed, communicate the fruits of his experience to others without having to resort to direct illustration. He could convey what he had learned to the next generation and across generations. He might, for example, prepare his grandchildren to survive a flood by telling them to take to high ground when certain signs of danger had appeared, or give directions where to find game in years of scarcity. Methods of coping, adapting, means of surmounting crises—experience in general—became cumulative. Gradually, each group of persons living in the same area built up sets of ways of coping with their environment and of living together cooperatively that formed their culture and its instrumentalities. These included the language itself and ways of perceiving, thinking, and experiencing, as well as the tangible tools they created to work upon nature.

A body of information, customs, sentiments became part of the human heritage. The newborn no longer started life from scratch, acquiring knowledge of ways of surviving through what he could learn during his lifetime, but rather he assimilated the ways of the people who reared him through the long years of his immaturity. The language itself is a central part of these acquisitions, for after infancy a person's learning depends largely upon language.

Unless we understand clearly that the human infant is born with a dual heritage, we can never understand human behavior rightly. He has a biological inheritance that is transmitted through the genes from generation to generation, and a cultural heritage into which he grows and which he must assimilate to become a person. These cultural and social institutions form a new environment that engulfs each individual as much as does the air he breathes, entering into the child and nourishing him into a person rather than an animal, teaching him how to live and how to survive, as an Aleut or Zulu according to where he happens to be born.

This assimilation of ways of living transpires so naturally that we are apt to accept much of it as part of the unfolding of man's physical endowment. We may laugh when we read in Herodotus[21] of how the Pharaoh Psammetichos learned to his chagrin that the Phrygians rather than the Egyptians were the original race. Unable to find out through inquiry from the sages, Psammetichos gave two infants to a herdsman and instructed him that they be fed by goats and that no one ever speak a word in their presence. Herodotus' informants specifically denied the canard that Psammetichos had the children raised by women whose tongues he had cut out. He wanted to learn what word the children would first articulate after the babblings of infancy were past. After two years both children clearly enunciated and then frequently repeated the single word "Becos," which, as we well know, is the word for bread in Phrygian. At least one ignorant commentator on Herodotus observed that if there were any truth whatsoever in the story, the children were probably imitating the bleating of goats.*

Yet, many of us are apt to believe in inborn ethnic or national personality characteristics. We may even have to check our credulity when we read of an infant who grew into manhood reared by apes, and who eventually became their leader by dint of his human intelligence; and of how, when a young and beautiful white woman inevitably was cast up by the sea, he revived her and gently carried her to his treehouse where he served her tea—for, after all, he was really a scion of English nobility and would not have done otherwise. Such childish credulity is scarcely greater than that of a biologist who wrote an article suggesting that we might soon be able to send fertilized embryos to colonize other planets and thus conserve space and weight in rocket ships. Apparently this scientist expects the offspring to emerge like Pallas Athena from the head

* Salimbene, a medieval chronicler, narrates in more detail a similar story about Frederick II, the scientifically curious despot who ruled the Holy Roman Empire in the thirteenth century. Frederick "wanted to find out what kind of speech and manner of speech children would have when they grew up if they spoke to no one beforehand. So he bade foster mothers and nurses to suckle the children, to bathe and wash them, but in no way to prattle with them, or to speak to them for he wanted to learn whether they would speak the Hebrew language, which was the oldest, or Greek, or Latin, or Arabic, or perhaps the language of their parents, of whom they had been born. . . . But he laboured in vain because the children all died. For they could not live without the petting, and joyful faces and loving words of their foster mothers." [31] Although this is very likely a legend repeated about various kings, we have recently learned that Frederick's findings could have been accurate. Spitz found that infants raised in an orphanage under good hygienic conditions but impersonally and without stimulation gradually wasted and died, or became irrevocably mentally defective.[35] (See Chapter 5.)

of Zeus, fully educated and capable of perpetuating the human species on some distant planet.*

What would the natural child be like—the child unaffected by a cultural and interpersonal environment? There are many tales of feral children aside from those of Romulus and Remus. None are definitely substantiated. The most plausible account is found in Arnold Gesell's *Wolf Child and Human Child*,[15] which contains the diary of an Indian, Reverend Singh, recording how he raised two girls saved in early childhood after having been reared by a wolf. According to the account, Kamala, the girl who survived for some years, remained more animal than human: she continued to crawl on all fours; ate only from the floor; and could never be taught to speak. We cannot advocate belief in the report, for most authorities contend that a child could not survive if mothered by an animal. However, in India infant girls are sometimes abandoned because they impose a grave financial liability upon a family. Still, the children simply may have been congenital idiots found soon after abandonment.†

The Cultural Endowment

A culture, then, has become an essential part of the human endowment. To examine the influence of the culture upon personality development is not to continue an old conflict concerning the importance of cultural versus biological factors in personality formation, but simply to recognize that the biological nature of the human organism is such that it depends upon the assimilation of cultural instrumentalities to make possible survival and development into a person. The culture in which the child is raised serves as a mold to shape the rough outlines of his

---

* *Life* for September 10, 1965, in an article entitled "Control of Life," shows Dr. E. S. E. Hafez of Washington State University holding a set of vials, which he says "could contain 'the barnyard of the future complete with the farmer.'" Hafez believes that his techniques are particularly suited to the space age, as a means of colonizing the planets. "When you consider how much it costs in fuel to lift every pound off the launch pad," he says, "why send fully grown men and women aboard spaceships? Instead why not ship tiny embryos in the care of a competent biologist who would grow them into people, cows, pigs, chickens, horses—anything we wanted —after they got there?" Why not, indeed? Perhaps because we might confuse the resultant humans with the pigs.

† It is of interest, however, that the measurements of the long bones of the arms and legs of these children did not conform to those of children who walk; the difference would be expected in children who only crawled, as the length of these bones is regulated to some extent by muscular usage. The inclusion of such details requires unusual sophistication from a person perpetrating a fraud.

personality, delimit his drives, and provide organization to the manifold ways of adapting to the environment permitted man by his physical endowment. Although the repressive and limiting influences of society have been bemoaned,* delimitation is essential to the realization of potential. Man cannot develop into a harmonious entity without it. Indeed, without the skills and customs provided by society, he cannot be anyone at all.†

Culture and Human Adaptation

The accumulation of abilities to work upon nature; to control fire; to make clothing, tools, and shelters; to cultivate plants; to domesticate animals, diminished the sway that natural forces held over man. Such acquisitions increased, far beyond limits permitted by his innate physiological capacities, the range of environments in which man could live. The control of the temperature of his body, for example, no longer rested solely upon the physiological mechanisms of regulating heat loss through the dilatation and constriction of peripheral blood vessels, and upon sweating, shivering, and muscular activity: these physiological mechanisms were augmented and often obviated by the use of fire, clothing, and housing. Eventually, the body's thermostatic control could be abetted by a man's sleeping under a thermostatically controlled blanket within a thermostatically controlled house. Through man's interference with the process of natural selection by selecting to his purposes, a minute wild grain was transformed into hybrid corn which, together with the domestication of the hog and cow, provides some groups of people with a constant surplus of food which they must be cajoled into buying lest the economy fail and some persons go hungry. While the fundamental needs for the sustenance of life have not altered, the means of satisfying them have.

The culture influences physiological functioning in a great variety of ways. What stimulates or abolishes appetite depends on the culture more than on physiology; swallow nest soup, ancient eggs, grasshoppers, termites, human flesh are all considered delicacies by some, and yet none of these is apt to arouse American appetites. Anger and fright are innate emotional states, but what enrages and what frightens varies greatly.

* See S. Freud, "Civilization and Its Discontents," 14 and the radical and untenable extension of the thesis in the book of Norman Brown, *Love's Body*.6
† "The vast proportion of all individuals who are born in any society always, and whatever the idiosyncrasies of its institutions, assume the behavior dictated by the society. Most people are shaped to the form of their culture, because of the enormous malleability of their original endowment"—Ruth Benedict5

Physique may be affected by preferred activities: the high-status Greek in ancient times cultivated his physical prowess, whereas the Talmudic scholar of eastern Europe was rarely of muscular athletic build.

The ways of reacting to life situations vary profoundly and affect the total functioning of the person. The Hopi Indians, for example, believe that thinking and concentrating bring about manifestation—that is, cause something to happen.[38] Thus relatives and friends beseech a sick person to forgive any slights they may inadvertently have given, to have positive thoughts about living, to wish to live for their sakes. They seek to save his life by having affectionate thoughts about him and by collectively wishing for his recovery. Should the patient perversely persist in remaining ill and worsen, those around him become enraged and start berating him for being mean and disregarding their needs and wishes. Eventually they may even beat him to make him change his attitude.* Further, in our society we feel sorrow or are supposed to feel sad when a friend or relative dies; we rarely feel rage, and if we do we try to repress such feelings. Tears are accepted if not expected. If, however, a Hopi is found crying when a relative is dying, he is stigmatized as a "witch," for he would be crying only if he had purchased his own life at the expense of the life of the relative.

Culture and Personality

It becomes increasingly clear that the manner in which children are raised in a society influences their personalities. The Balinese mother, for example, customarily indulges the child during the first two or three years of his life while he is nursing, but then she purposefully frustrates and teases him when he is older and seeks affection from her and she fosters envy of younger siblings: the schizoid aloofness of the Balinese can virtually be seen developing in response to such treatment.[4] Hopi parents also indulge their children and avoid antagonizing them by punishment but rather threaten that the supernatural Kachinas will come and beat them if they are not obedient. Then if a child misbehaves, the parents act as if they are protecting the child, whereas in reality they have summoned relatives to come in disguise and whip the child, sometimes very severely. It is a case of Santa Claus in reverse. The children are deeply disillusioned when they eventually learn the truth, and this

* Such ideas and behavior may seem ridiculous to us, and yet they involve insights and wisdom usually absent from our medical practice and concepts of the etiology of illness. Many psychologically minded medical researchers now appreciate how depressive feelings, wishes to die, and states of helplessness and hopelessness contribute to the onset and the worsening of disease. (See G. Engel [12] and Chapter 20.)

disillusionment helps foster the suspiciousness of the motives of others that is so characteristic of the Hopi. This character trait is also fostered by the Hopi belief that any close relative, including the mother, might be a malevolent witch who will trade the child's life for hers. The relationship between a society's belief systems and child-rearing methods forms an extremely complex topic that extends beyond the scope of this book.*

The ways in which different ethnic groups have patterned their lives and the customs they pursue are amazingly diverse, and some are almost beyond the imagination of persons from other cultures. Still, amidst these extremely varied patterns there are some requisites that all cultures must fulfill. No society can long survive without taking into account the biological make-up of its members. It cannot, for instance, neglect the total dependency of its newborn, or the sequence of the biological maturation of the child, or the presence of two sexes. Some small societies have placed a ban on all sexual relationships but they have not lasted for long, somehow finding but few recruits from the outside. A society is not only essential to its members but it has an existence of its own, and its culture is its heart, which its members will defend with their lives because without it they are rootless and lost. As all societies must fill certain identical needs for their members, including preserving the society itself, some features are common to all cultures, so common that they are often taken for granted and their critical nature overlooked. Families and language are of the essence and will be examined in greater detail below.

This, then, is one of the advantages bestowed by the capacity for verbal communication. It enables the gradual acquisition of a cultural heritage that becomes an essential part of the human endowment. It enables children to be born into very divergent environments and acquire from those who raise them the techniques essential for survival and for adaptation to the physical and social environment in which they will live.

Language and Thought

We must now examine another consequence of the acquisition of symbolic capacities—that internal counterpart of communication that we term thought or mentation.

Words make reflective and conceptual thinking possible. Even though

* The reader is referred to E. Erikson,[13] A. Kardiner,[22] B. Whiting,[37] D. Aberle,[1] and M. Carstairs.[8]

we think with visual symbols as well as with other sensations and perceptions, words are the switching points—the symbols that we can manipulate in order to shift from one associational trend to another. They are
our symbolic tools. Thought and language are inseparable. The autobiography of Helen Keller and the accounts of her remarkable teacher,
Anne Sullivan, make it clear that even this person with her extraordinary
intellectual potential remained imprisoned in a world of diffuse impressions and feelings until she was released by the word, and particularly
until she grasped that each word her teacher spelled into her hand meant
something.* Even the congenitally deaf who use sign language are impaired intellectually unless they learn to use words. Efforts are made to

---

* After a month of intensive work Miss Sullivan had taught her seven-year-old deaf-
blind pupil to spell some twenty words. Still, these spelled-out words had not attained the status of symbols. Miss Sullivan was seeking desperately to convey that
these finger signs represented a category of things. Like a very young child, Helen
Keller confused "mug" and "water" and could not learn that "doll" stood for a new
doll as well as for an old one. Miss Keller wrote of the critical day in her childhood
when she passed across the barrier: "Miss Sullivan had tried to impress it upon me
that 'm-u-g' is mug and that 'w-a-t-e-r' is water, but I persisted in confounding the
two. In despair she had dropped the subject for the time, only to renew it at the first
opportunity. I became impatient at her repeated attempts and, seizing the new doll,
I dashed it upon the floor. I was keenly delighted when I felt the fragments of the
broken doll at my feet. Neither sorrow nor regret followed my passionate outburst. I
had not loved the doll. In the still, dark world in which I lived there was no strong
sentiment or tenderness. . . . She brought me my hat, and I knew I was going out
into the warm sunshine. This thought, if a wordless sensation may be called a
thought, made me hop and skip with pleasure. . . . Someone was drawing water
and my teacher placed my hand under the spout. As the cool stream gushed over
one hand she spelled into the other the word water, first slowly and then rapidly.
I stood still, my whole attention fixed upon the motions of her fingers. Suddenly I
felt a misty consciousness of something forgotten—a thrill of a returning thought:
and somehow the mystery of language was revealed to me. I knew then that 'w-a-t-e-r'
meant the wonderful cool something that was flowing over my hand. That living
word awakened my soul, gave it light, hope, joy, set it free! There were barriers still,
it is true, but barriers that could in time be swept away. . . . Everything had a
name, and each name gave birth to a new thought. As we returned to the house
every object which I touched seemed to quiver with life. That was because I saw
everything with the strange new sight that had come to me. . . . It would have
been difficult to find a happier child than I was as I lay in my crib at the close of
that eventful day and lived over the joys it had brought me, and for the first time
longed for a new day to come." 24
The account is not a retrospective idealization. From that moment Helen Keller
learned with avidity, her disposition changed profoundly, and her teacher's task
changed from an ordeal of striving to break through a wall to one of teaching the
words and supplying a picture of the world around Helen so that she could readily
learn what the words meant. It may be important to note that "water" was one of
the two words Miss Keller had retained of what she had learned before meningitis
left her blind and deaf at the age of twenty months.

insist that they use an alphabet and preferably learn to lip read, not because it is esthetically and socially superior but because the sign language does not contain symbols that are sufficiently abstract for higher intellectual functioning. If, as occasionally happens, a child is born with damage to one of the areas of the brain essential to symbolic activity—areas necessary for the comprehension of words rather than simply for hearing them and for the expression of words as symbols—the child remains an idiot.

Let us return to that protohuman and the stick he was grasping so that we may examine the functions of words in thinking. The stick he was wielding as a club was important because it was a tool—a disposable, interchangeable extension of himself. The word "stick" was also important, for it not only meant that specific piece of wood used as a club but it also denoted other pieces of wood used for fuel, for building shelters, for making arrows, for charcoal with which to draw mastodon, for "digging sticks." The word had acquired an abstract meaning or categorical usage designating pieces of wood of a certain approximate shape. It was abstract in another related context: pivoting about the word were all of the individual's many experiences with sticks—those he tossed into the river and watched float, those he saw break off the branches of a tree as it crashed to earth, those turning into flame, the feel of various sticks, their weight, their odor when freshly peeled or after a rain. These various experiences could shift back and forth, one leading to another, connecting a variety of experiences that were dissimilar except in that they involved sticks.

Man could think about sticks: their use in the past, a current need, and a potential use for them in the future. He could fragment his memories and utilize them selectively, drawing upon past experiences to construct a hypothetical future. He could anticipate that something he was told was made of "wood" would burn; that something he had not seen but was termed an "arrow" could be used for shooting from a bow. The word contained a predictive value that helped him direct his behavior. We shall return to consider the importance of the categorizing and predicting functions of words when we consider the child's linguistic development and how it relates to his "ego" functioning (Chapters 5 and 6).

As John Dewey pointed out, by means of verbal tools man can "act without acting." [11] He can go through trial-and-error performances imaginatively, without committing himself to the consequences of the actual deed. He could consider whether a certain stick would suffice to kill an animal or whether it would be better not to risk the encounter until he obtained a better weapon. He is freed from the need to act in order to learn whether an action will be advantageous or disastrous to him. He can select between alternatives upon the basis of what the imagined outcomes will be.

By the use of symbols, man can select out appropriate fragments of his past and project converging lines through the momentary present into an imagined future. Herein lies a momentous change from animal behavior that greatly increases the chances for survival. He is no longer bound to the impulsion by his immediate past and his present impulses, drives, and wishes. He can strive to achieve future gains and objectives that he keeps in mind. We can say that man is goal-directed as well as drive-impelled. Any increase in his ability to plan toward the future greatly enhances his chances of surviving. Much of human behavior is directed toward a consciously projected future—to provide for needs of the morrow, the next year, or for a future generation. With such potentialities, man gains a sense of free will; for when we leave theological matters out of consideration, this is what we mean by free will: the ability to select from among alternative paths into the future on the basis of past experiences.*

We cannot attempt to consider the many ramifications of man's capacity to symbolize, primarily through the use of words. This capacity enables him to create a symbolized internal version of reality which he manipulates imaginatively in order to increase the predictability of events, to find means of controlling them, and to be prepared in advance to meet them—but also to create and re-create worlds of his own that have no existence except in his own mind. According to Greek mythology, civilization started when Prometheus stole fire from the Olympians and bestowed it upon man—a first harnessing of nature to his ends. Prometheus means "forward thinking" or foresight. With this attribute came an awareness of contingency and death that bred anxiety—perhaps

---

* As Freud noted, the sway of instinctual drives and unconscious memories upon the determination of behavior is great, and an individual is not as "free" as he believes when making decisions on the basis of remembered experiences. However, such considerations do not settle the problem of determinism versus free will, and in no way prove that all human behavior is "determined" by the past. The complexity of the neuronal switching systems and the memories "programmed" therein is so great that perhaps little more is meant by free will than that all factors involved in a decision can never be traced and numerous contingencies may be involved. In essence it is a theological problem that does not concern us here.

like the vulture pecking at the liver of the enchained Prometheus—but also the ability to eradicate imaginatively the ultimacy of death if man so wished.

These then are the characteristics—stated in bare outline—that permitted man to survive, flourish, spread out over the earth, and become master of it; altering nature to serve his ends rather than simply living in his natural environment. Man can utilize symbols in order to think and plan ahead, and he does so by imaginatively creating a symbolized version of his world that he can manipulate; and he learns new techniques of mastering his environment which he transmits to others so that learning becomes cumulative, and each new generation can possess the knowledge of its forebears.

The Human Mind

Man thinks and meets the future, anticipating what will come. But what does he think with? The possession of a human brain is, of course, the sine qua non of abstract thinking, but the structure and functioning of this brain determines only in part *how* we think, and virtually nothing of *what* we think. True, the body, through the mediation of the brain, demands that we direct attention to the basic needs for survival of ourself and our species. If we lack oxygen, water, food, warmth, sleep, salts, or sexual outlets, or if we are endangered, primitive drives—mechanisms that antedated the human species—direct us toward seeking relief and influence our thinking. A starving man can think of little other than food and dreams of food pervade his sleep. But how we set about stilling such needs will vary with time and place. One hungering individual picks up a crossbow and seeks water buffalo; another picks up a harpoon, finds a hole in the ice, and waits for a seal; another balances his checkbook and drives off to a supermarket. Then, too, man because of his foresight may have long periods during which he can be occupied with other matters, relatively free from the direct dictation of basic drives.

We say, rather, that we think with our minds. Mind! The concept of "the mind" carries varying degrees of purposeful vagueness. It refers to something so complex and intangible that we prefer not to be pushed into a definition that we may be expected to defend. We speak constantly about the "unconscious mind" but are not clear at all what we mean by either conscious or unconscious mind. The term contains residues of countless variant philosophies and psychologies that continue to haunt us. Ever since man started to ponder about himself, he has puzzled over that intangible attribute that permits him to direct his behavior; that distinguishes him, at times, from the beast; bestows the godlike ability to reorder nature; and enables him to surmount the dull or aching reality through soaring fantasy, or to note the poignancy of his experience in poetry or song. He has been apt to consider his mind as separate from his body, and even as distinctive from matter. Descartes strengthened the mind-body dichotomy and achieved a long but restless peace with the church by considering the mind an attribute bestowed by God and influenced by the soul that funneled into the brain via the pineal gland; he claimed the body and matter for science and left the soul and the mind to the church and to philosophy.

During the past half century, the scientists of the mind, the psychologists, envious of the tangible physical and chemical foundations of the biological sciences, have sometimes insisted that the functioning of the mind could be understood in terms of the neural impulses in the brain. Some have convinced themselves that the mind and brain are synonymous. Some have studied man through the examination of lower animals and found no place for a "mind." Some have sought to solve the problem by maintaining that we have simply been caught up in antiquated prescientific religious and philosophical speculations in seeking to locate and define the mind. The very word "mind" disseminates a decadent odor, and any respectable scientist who uses the term must be out of his mind. We can outlaw the word; we can use other terms; we can chant daily in unison that "the body and the mind are one" so as to exorcise the dichotomy from our thinking, but somehow none of these maneuvers quite comes off. "Mind" is not an archaism; we have need for such a concept, whatever we may term it; and no serious thinker can encase the mind within the skull as part of the brain. We can well envy that nineteenth-century pundit who managed to make short shrift of the problem: "What is Mind? No matter! What is Matter? Never mind!" *

Of course, in writing a book about the personality it would be possible to evade the issue by avoiding the term. Still, as a psychiatrist who spends his days and years contemplating the mind, I should know what it is I study. I can say, like Humpty-Dumpty speaking to Alice on the other side of the looking glass, "When I use a word—it means just what I choose it to mean—neither more nor less." [7] This state of affairs may

* T. H. Key.

have been all right for Humpty-Dumpty, even though it left Alice some-what perplexed, but on this side of the looking glass meanings are meas-ured in terms of how they foster communication. If we wish to join hands in a scientific effort to learn about the nature of man and his development, we require a common understanding of what we are scru-tinizing.

Surprisingly or not, I think I do know what we mean when we speak of "the mind." By means of our brains we manipulate symbols, and without these symbols we cannot think. What we term "mind" includes both the complex neural apparatus and the symbolized material gained from experience that it utilizes. As we have been noting, the na-ture of the brain is determined genetically, but the nature of the sym-bolic material varies widely. How we think is established partly by the structural organization and physiology of our brains and bodies. We can-not, for example, utilize supersonic vibrations as does the bat, or carry out calculations for hours as does an electronic computer; but how we think also depends upon our education. Scientific thinking, to take one exam-ple, is a relatively recent phenomenon, a disciplined method of thinking that has been utilized for only a few hundred of the tens of thousands of years of human existence.

The brain is the apparatus with which we think, but it must be pro-grammed to become a mind even as an electronic brain must be pro-grammed. There are, of course, vast differences between the brain and the most complex electronic computers aside from the size and rigidity of the machine. Among the many differences is the fact that the brain is part of a living person and is not passive but seeks out and takes in according to its drives, needs, desires. It programs itself to a large extent. The brain as part of an organism is influenced by passions and desire; and as part of a person it partakes of character. Still, there are interesting similarities. The machine also utilizes a language. It stores memories that can be recovered only by the appropriate symbol. It can serve as an exec-utive organ which utilizes insignificant amounts of energy to direct and control activities expending vast quantities of energy—as when a com-puter directs a foundry. But it must be programmed, and it is incapable of learning:* the programmers must learn for it.

Enculturation—Programming the Brain

In the human mind, the basic programming is the process of encul-turation—the child's assimilation of the ways of the society in which

---

* The point is debatable, depending on what is meant by learning.

he grows up. He is taught and learns the verbal symbols essential for thinking, but he must also have experiences for which the words stand. He thinks with the memories of his experiences, but his experiences include what he has learned from others. He has available to him that collectivity of experiences which is his cultural heritage and which, even though it is the product of human minds, has an existence outside of any single brain. In literate societies a large segment of the experience and knowledge of the culture is recorded in print and conserved in books which are repositories of other minds. An individual may tap these repositories in order to add to his experiences and to expand the information with which he thinks. The particular mind which has assembled a particular set of experiences and utilizes a unique way of perceiving and understanding the world ceases to exist with the death of the individual. Books such as *The Making of the Modern Mind* [29] or *The Mind in the Making*[30] are not treatises on the development of the brain, but upon the gradual emergence of the body of ideas and the ways of thinking of contemporary man. The existence of brains, or rather of persons with brains capable of carrying on the tradition, is taken for granted. In the sense in which I am using the word "mind" the content alone is insufficient, for the word also encompasses the brain which utilizes the material.

A basic part of the process of enculturation concerns the acquisition of ways of thinking. Man does not simply accumulate sensations or even experiences but requires ways of perceiving and thinking about what he experiences. Each cultural group has evolved its own system of meanings and logic, and how people think and feel about events affects their physiological processes. The experiences that a person lives through, or which impinge upon a person, can be categorized and understood in countless ways. Each culture perceives its environment somewhat differently; and even the language we use, with its specific vocabulary and rules of grammar, sets limits and guidelines for our thinking.* One difference be-

---

* A person cannot pay attention to everything that transpires about him but must be able to focus his attention. Each culture directs its members to what that particular ethnic branch of mankind considers important, what pertinent, and what can be neglected and what must be ignored. One important method by which such filtering and sorting is carried out is through language. The flow of experience must be divided into categories to be thought about, talked about, and even to be perceived. Each culture categorizes experience somewhat differently, and very divergent cultures categorize experience very differently. The vocabulary of a language is, in essence, a catalogue of the culture's categories—which the child learns as he learns to speak. There are other filtering devices and techniques. A neurophysiologic system,

tween English and German philosophy—indeed between the English and German mind—would appear to result from the linguistic sanction in German for the coinage of new words to fit approximate nuances, whereas in English we are disciplined to fit our thoughts to the common vocabulary. We can also note that scientific efforts in the Western world had to remain limited until contact with the decimal system invented in India and until abstract algebraic thought introduced through Moslem culture brought release from cumbersome numerical systems and concrete geometric conceptualizations. While man's mind has always been his cardinal instrument for adaptation, a new era of human existence opened when he consciously recognized that through the use of the mind as a tool to understand nature he could begin consciously to alter nature for his purposes. This revolution in the use of the mind, which was first specifically promoted by Francis Bacon,[3] was more basic than either the industrial or atomic revolutions which were but outgrowths of it. The possession of a mind (at least what I—using my Humpty-Dumpty prerogatives—mean by the mind) is a human attribute dependent upon the genetic evolution of a brain with a unique structure that permits the use of symbols as tools for communication and thinking. These are distinctively human capacities that make possible an extraordinarily useful method of adaptation and assurance of survival. This brain with its large cerebral cortex allowed less rigid patterns of living, by replacing built-in instinctive patterns with learned ways of coping with the environment. Men's ability to live in many different ways in vastly different environments depended upon the cumulative transmission of what men had learned, their ability to plan for the future, and to work upon nature and alter it to their ends. The mind consists of the internalized, symbolized representation of man's world and the techniques for living in it which his brain enables him to assimilate and manipulate. We cannot understand the mind in terms of the physiological functioning of the brain any more than we can seek to understand a telephone conversation in terms of the telephone system: though some garbled phone conversations are due to defects in the apparatus, and others to the confusion of the speakers.

---

the *reticular activating system*, has much to do with helping an individual maintain focal attention. The individual also acquires filtering techniques in accord with his own experiences and emotional needs. As will be examined in some detail in later chapters, he learns not to perceive, to alter perception, to repress feelings and drives and memories in order to avoid anxiety. The topic leads into the consideration of cultural taboos and unconscious mentation.

To understand the mind, we must understand the capacities afforded man by his anatomic structure and his physiological processes; and we must understand how his unique brain enabled him to symbolize, communicate, and build up social systems and their cultures, and also to communicate with himself by utilizing the verbal symbols that his progenitors had gradually developed as their language. It becomes apparent that men's minds could increase in complexity as the culture and its language became enriched by the accumulation of experiences and learning. Mind, culture, and language are intimately related.

Biological Drives

We have been considering the essentially human capacities of adaptation that permitted man to survive, spread out over the globe and become master of it. Although it is necessary to recognize that man is not a monkey and to study his development and behavior as integrated through the capacities bestowed by symbolization, it is equally important to realize that man is an animal and is directed and impelled by biological drives that often hold sway over his intellectual capacities and that his survival as an individual and a species depends upon biological processes that were firmly established even before his emergence as man.

Although we cannot review all of the inborn genetic endowment that influences man's personality development, we shall consider briefly the nature of his basic drives and the biological bases of his emotions. The basic drives can be divided into three, and perhaps four, groups: those deriving from the tissue needs indispensable to life; the sexual drives; the defensive drives; and somewhat less clearly, the impulsions to stimulation and activity. All furnish primary directives in personality development.

The Homeostatic Drives

As noted earlier in this chapter the continuation of life in the simplest unicellular organism depends upon maintaining its composition constant within the relatively narrow limits that permit the chemical processes fundamental to life. No living thing is a closed system but carries out a constant interchange with its environment, from which it obtains nutriment for its development and its vital processes and into which it excretes waste products. Simple organisms can exist only under fairly specific environmental conditions, and the evolutionary process involves providing new ways of assuring the chemical transactions essential to life in the face of competition and environmental change. More complex and highly integrated organisms became less dependent upon the immediate constancy of the external environment. Higher organisms developed an "internal environment" of tissue fluids that surround the cells with a relatively constant environment despite the changes that take place in the external world. Maintenance of the internal constancy of the cells of the organism provides a major motivating force in all living things. "Homeostasis," the term used to designate this maintenance of constancy, is a key word in the study of physiology and behavior. It refers to several things. The internal environment is highly buffered chemically, and filled with checks, balances, and feedback systems that resist change; the organism is provided with various means of regulating its interchange with its surroundings that help maintain its constancy; there is an impulsion to activity that furthers the necessary assimilation and excretion. Such activities are automatic in lower systems of integration but include volitional activities in higher forms.

With the increasing complexity that permitted ever greater freedom from reliance upon the constancy of the external environment, organisms required more involved systems for interchange with the environment and for inner regulation to assure the proper milieu for every cell.* The chemical processes essential for the existence of the unicellular organism are no less vital to the most complex forms of life, whose intricate integrations are, in essence, only a means of maintaining the environment necessary for the occurrence of these processes in the cells. However, when a brain that permitted decision making developed, those functions that are indispensable to the preservation of the animal and the species were not left simply to choice or chance.

In man the executive system involving the cerebral cortex, which is concerned with the choice of alternatives and decision making, remains subject to powerful persuasion that directs attention to homeostatic needs. Centers sensitive to such needs are located in the hindbrain,

---

* Special systems evolved for respiration, assimilation and digestion of food, and for excretion; a circulatory system for the internal transport of chemicals; sensory organs and systems for gaining information about the environment; metabolic organs for the breakdown and manufacture of essential chemical compounds and for the transformation of food, water, and oxygen into a variety of forms of energy—for example, heat, kinetic, bioelectric. To gain information as well as to integrate the bodily functioning, chemical messengers transported in the body fluids were abetted by nerve fibers that transmitted messages with great rapidity. The development of an integrative executive organ in the form of a brain permitted unity of action of the complex organism. This fragmentary sketch only seeks to remind the reader of the inordinately involved integration of any higher form of life.

which developed early in vertebrate evolution; these centers send out signals in response to chemical changes in the blood and to neuronal stimuli which, when necessary, can virtually dominate the thought and activity of the individual. The person becomes preoccupied with the need to alleviate a state of tension or discomfort produced by the chemical imbalance in the tissues—and, in some instances, to gain a sense of pleasure achieved by supplying the need that restores the requisite balance.

The most imperative need is for oxygen. Man lives in air and cannot survive for more than a few minutes without it. A diminution of oxygen in the tissues* reflexly produces increased respiration; but cutting off the air supply, as by strangulation, sets off immediate frantic efforts to free the air passages. Thirst can be withstood longer; but as tissue fluids become depleted, a craving for water dominates thought, feelings, and dreams, and virtually forces a person to direct his energies to obtaining water. Lack of food does not create an impelling need as rapidly, for stored reserves in the body can be mobilized but hunger preoccupies; and the need for food and the efforts to be secure that food supplies are always available forms a major motivation of man, individually and collectively. The force that starvation can exert in directing a life and upon the mood can readily be overlooked or forgotten in a land of abundance, but even existence on a semi-starvation diet can seriously influence the ethics and emotional health of the individual.† It is not clear whether a deficiency of specific chemical elements or compounds other than water produces a drive to obtain them. Lack of sodium, which is vital to maintaining a proper fluid balance, causes animals to make long migra-

---

* Actually an increase in carbon dioxide which is usually synonymous with a need for oxygen.

† Schiele and Brozek[32] in a postwar study of nutrition placed a group of university student volunteers on a twelve hundred calorie diet. After a few weeks they quarreled over the number of peas they received and became very irritable. Some broke the diet in minor ways and suffered severe guilt feelings, and several had to be withdrawn from the experiment because they had become emotionally disturbed, probably because they hungered in a setting where the major barriers to eating were their own pledges to maintain the diet. Soldiers starving to death in Japanese prisoner-of-war camps were likely to lose their usual ethical standards, and a man needed a buddy to guard his food when he was too ill to feed himself. Knut Hamsun's *Hunger*[18] and Gottfried Keller's *Der grüne Heinrich*[23] present excellent portrayals of the emotions and motives of a starving man.

However, chronic gradual starvation may elude the drive as apathy intervenes. Persons suffering from the psychogenic emaciation termed "anorexia nervosa" may not experience hunger and refuse to eat even when reduced to living skeletons.

tions to salt licks, and groups of people living in areas where salt is sparse set up complicated trade channels to obtain it regularly. Children's craving for candy may be due to, or at least reflect, their need for large quantities of carbohydrates to supply their lavish expenditures of energy.* However, it is well to remember that human beings are so constituted that despite the intensity of hunger as a drive, persons have starved themselves to death amid plenty for political or religious convictions.

The maintenance of an internal body temperature very close to 98.6°F. is essential for the bodily chemistry; and although the regulation of temperature is carried out reflexly, there are limits to the body's ability to dissipate and generate heat. The search for warmth, and sometimes for relief from excessive heat, can also become an imperative drive that takes precedence over almost everything else. When a person is freezing to death, apathy—as in starvation—may finally intervene and replace the drive.

Although the functions of sleep are still poorly understood, the need for it can become a dominant motivation. Though it seems difficult to think of the urge to sleep as a drive, it can also preoccupy, but usually it simply will occur despite efforts to remain awake. Prolonged sleep deprivation can lead to mental confusion. An army unit which I studied in the South Pacific, after fighting for eight days and nights with almost no sleep, suffered from mass hallucinosis.

The excretion of urine and feces also is vital and the need to urinate can also be an impelling preoccupation. However, the problems are somewhat different from those of the tissue needs, for prolonged delay in satisfying the urge is a product of social requirements.

In fulfilling the body's needs for food and sleep and to excrete wastes, the individual is not only motivated by a need to relieve tension or pain but also because the alleviation of the imbalance can be pleasurable. People enjoy eating and sleeping, and many gain some erogenous pleasure from urinating and defecating, as will be discussed in later chapters.†

---

* The question has arisen whether a person will somehow eat the foods that contain the essentials he requires provided they are available. Vitamin deficiencies can occur in well-nourished persons, but they are uncommon. C. M. Davis[9] believes that babies will select a satisfactory diet. She presented a variety of foods to fifteen infants of weaning age in a manner that permitted the baby to eat any quantity of any combination of foods. Although their choices were temporarily unbalanced, all gradually selected well-balanced diets.

† The theory that pleasure could be equated with tension release was accepted by Freud and has played a critical role in psychoanalytic theory. Although "parsimo-

Indeed any of the vital activities of breathing, drinking water, eating, seeking or avoiding heat, sleeping, and excreting can sometimes become perversions in the sense of being carried to excess for emotional reasons rather than because of bodily need, and some clearly become erotized through becoming connected to the sexual drives.

The Sexual Drive

In the post-Freudian world it seems unnecessary to emphasize the pervasive importance of sexuality in human behavior, or to draw the attention of the young adult reader to how sexual impulsions furnish the themes around which fantasies are woven, or how desire populates the dream world and inserts itself between the pages of books one studies, seeking to replace the dull facts recorded on them, or how it heightens sensitivity and at times would seem to provide invisible antennae with which a person can detect the feelings and cravings of another person.

The reasons why the evolutionary process led to the elaboration of strong sexual drives seems apparent. All higher forms of life are divided into two genders. The need for a union between two germinal cells for propagation permits opportunity for the selecting out of favorable mutations and assures a constant reshuffling of genes that lessens the influence of harmful mutations. As the perpetuation of the germinal cells is the essence of life, after the separation into two genders the act of mating could not be left to chance or entirely to choice; a drive to procreate exists in some form in all creatures. In some species instinctive patterns almost completely control mating behavior. The life cycle may lead to procreation and then death as in some fish. In most mammals a rutting period exists when the sexual drives become dominant and may even take precedence over self-preservative drives. In response to the sexual impulsion, the male may neglect almost all else and even court death in combat for the female. Anyone who has seen the torment of a male beagle (about the most "highly sexed" canine, I am informed) if confined when a female nearby is in heat; or watched two otherwise docile and domesticated tomcats turn into miniature tigers and slash and bite one another for priority with a female feline who acts as if nothing con-

---

nious" it does not fit the facts, and the investigations of Olds[28] and of Delgado *et al.*[10] practically force us to accept the concept that evolutionary selection set a premium on reward through pleasure as a separate factor from release from tensions. Stimulation of certain areas in the brain evoke positive responses, and an animal will learn to press a lever or carry out an action in order to have the area stimulated.

cerned her less than which of her two overardent suitors triumphed—
must be impressed by the power of the sexual drive. Anthropoids and
humans do not have rutting seasons, even though sexual drives may well
be influenced by the season. Humans can delay gratification of the drive
and forgo the pleasurable reward indefinitely, perhaps aided by the capacity for masturbatory release from compelling tensions. But the drive
toward sexual union is denied only with difficulty. The sexual act is impelled both by the need for relief from tissue tensions and by the reward
of positive sensual pleasure: the pleasure is accompanied by heightening
of tension that further impels, and the climactic orgasm becomes a goal
and reward in its own right. Sexual union between people is often further motivated by desires for the interpersonal closeness and sharing involved in love, and these include recrudescences of "attachment behavior" that will be discussed in Chapter 5. Nature has created strong
impulsions and rewards to assure the continuity of the species.

Although sexuality exerts one of the most compelling forces in the
lives of humans, it does not have the inexorable power over human behavior of the homeostatic drives. Only persons leading relatively sheltered lives in which water, food, and warmth are readily available and in
which sexual drives are impeded by social conventions can consider sexuality more compelling.* Indeed, upon consideration we can realize that
it is because sexual gratification is not vital to life and satisfaction of the
drive can be delayed, displaced, and sublimated into other types of outlets that sexuality forms a critical lever in the educational process and
forms a significant force in shaping the personality. The topic will be
discussed in subsequent chapters.

Sexuality and aggression are crucial forces in human motivation and
personality development, not because they are the most fundamental
drives but because they are modifiable and subject to socializing influences and also because both sex and aggression must be controlled and
channeled lest they become disruptive of the family and the community
upon which man depends so greatly for his survival and well-being. Aggression is one of another set of essential drives.

---

* The author, who studied survivors immediately after their release from three years
of starvation in a Japanese prisoner-of-war camp in the Philippines, gained a lasting
impression of the force of hunger and starvation as a drive. It was somewhat surprising, however, to observe that soldiers on isolated islands who were deprived of sexual
partners for two or three years and lived on a monotonous but adequate diet regularly
reported that gradually their "bull sessions" shifted from talk of women and sex to
long discussions of the meals they would eat after returning home, and that dreams
of food became more common than overt sexual dreams.

Defensive Drives

An array of physiological defenses against danger that concomitantly arouse fear or aggression can also dominate the organism's motivations and behavior. These built-in automatic defenses against danger, which arose early in the evolutionary process to implement the capacity to fight enemies, flee danger, and mobilize resources in emergencies, are only slightly less important to the preservation of the animal than the drives arising from tissue needs. As soon as danger is sensed the bodily processes alter almost instantaneously to prepare for flight or fight without the intervention of conscious decision. Such defenses are crucial to survival in a world filled with enemies and inanimate hazards. The shifts in the physiological processes convey an ability to run faster, jump farther, fight beyond the limits of endurance; and to sense more keenly, react more rapidly, and think more alertly; as well as to minimize the effects of injury. Man is heir to these physiological responses, even though they may be an impediment as often as they help in dealing with dangers in civilized societies; but, as we shall see, these defensive drives continue to exert a profound influence on both behavior and mental activities.

Fear and aggression are potent drives, either of which can change a man's life in a split second, sweeping aside resolve, training, plans, judgment, and careful reasoning. The dreams of glory of many a youth have vanished and turned into self-hatred with the first bombardment by the enemy; or the tensions of pent-up hostility suddenly unleashed have carried persons into conflicts in which they were hopelessly outclassed. The two behaviors are intimately related both physiologically and emotionally: fear is not synonymous with cowardice, and aggression is one means of overcoming the dysphoria of fear*—and there is an old adage about him who fights and runs away.

The automatic physiological changes may be initiated in response to some signal of impending danger that is not even consciously recognized.

---

* An essential part of the indoctrination of United States soldiers prior to their entering jungle combat during World War II consisted of impressing them that being fearful did not mean they were cowards and that even the most heroic men were likely to experience fear but managed to surmount the fear and its often very distressing physiological accompaniments. They also had to learn not to break the tension by becoming aggressive and giving away their positions by firing their weapons or dashing out of their foxholes. The "banzai" charges of the Japanese that were often so disastrous to them may well have been related to an inability on their part to withstand the need to do something to alleviate anxiety in the face of continuing danger.

The autonomic nervous system and particularly the adrenal-neural system is most clearly involved in these changes and employs many of the
same mechanisms utilized in the preservation of the homeostatic needs,
and can even interfere with the homeostatic functioning, as will be discussed in Chapter 20. The animal or person is first alerted and then
prepared to save itself by fighting or fleeing; which of these responses
will predominate varies with the species and the total development of its
means of survival—a tiger is primarily prepared to fight and a doe to flee.
In some forms, such as man, it is possible that lesser stimuli to the adrenal-neural mechanisms prepare for flight while more intense and prolonged stimulation prepares for fighting. Epinephrine secretion tends to
heighten fear, which increases alertness to danger; and norepinephrine
secretion helps prepare for action, particularly aggressive action, and thus
helps induce feelings of hostility. We will not, at this point, discuss the
complexities of these automatic preparations for self-defense. They are
not only dysphoric feeling states from which the individual seeks to free
himself, but they are accompanied by immediate pervasive changes in
the physiological functions, such as speeding of the heart, sweating,
changes in respiration and distribution of blood flow, as well as
numerous less apparent alterations.

The capacity or proneness to experience fear and aggressive impulsions
is born into man, but aggressivity is not a quantity that must find an
outlet. It is a type of response to danger that can dissipate when danger
passes and the physiological processes resume their non-emergency functioning. Some persons may be innately more prone to aggressive feelings
than others, but chronically aggressive individuals are more usually
persons who grew up under conditions that trained them to respond
readily to certain circumstances or people—such as authority figures—
with defensive aggressivity.*

* I am specifically emphasizing that aggression is not a genetic characteristic that
makes murder and warfare an expected characteristic of mankind and therefore to
some an acceptable state of affairs because it is inevitable. Two recent books that
express such views, Konrad Lorenz's recent On Aggression,[26] which considers aggression a human instinct, and Robert Ardrey's The Territorial Imperative,[2] have gained
widespread acceptance even though their conclusions are unwarranted. Lorenz's work
on "imprinting" phenomena in ground nesting birds[25] has rightly won him a position
as one of the world's leading scientists, but much of the material in On Aggression is
outside his field of special competence, and he has chosen to omit an enormous
amount of data and evidence that controverts his thesis. Ardrey's book concerning
territoriality in animals and the idea that humans defend their national territory in-
stinctively also omits much evidence that many mammals and anthropoids behave

In humans, anxiety is a derivative of fear and is accompanied by its physiological manifestations. Anxiety is largely concerned with unconscious dangers, particularly those that could result from one's own impulses, and it is also concerned with anticipated future dangers rather than tangible matters that can be coped with through action. Aggression has the derivatives of hostility and resentment, which like anxiety are not usually relieved by overt action. These derivative drives or emotions play major roles in motivation and behavior, as will be discussed in various contexts throughout the book.*

---

very differently; and, in addition, misses the point that peoples defend their culture, their way of life, and right to live it rather than primarily their territories.

I lived for a time among the Fijians, who with their taboo against ambition, self-advancement, and individual possessions were among the friendliest persons I have ever encountered. They could easily live off their bountiful volcanic soil and the fish that teemed in the ocean. These friendly and happy people—for I became convinced that as a people they were unusually happy—had not always been such. Just about one hundred years ago they lived in terror and were terrifying and treacherous. They were known among sailors as the most bloodthirsty, flesh-craving cannibals in the world, their islands to be avoided. The people themselves feared to venture alone into the bush, lest they be clubbed by members of a neighboring village and end up at a feast. They were savage and cruel in their constant internecine warfare. To the missionary the Fijis were no paradise, but rather a brief stopover en route to paradise via the cooking pot—a much sought-after assignment by the zealous as a certain route to martyrdom and heaven. Eventually, however, the Fijians were converted to Western medicine and the Christianity the medical missionaries taught. An enlightened British government, to whom the Fijian chief ceded his authority, put an end to interisland warfare and soon induced the Fijians to abolish cannibalism. Then, for the first time, the natives could enjoy their blessed islands. No longer fearing their neighbors, they could live in peace and became men of peace. If the accounts of the early missionaries and travelers can be trusted, a remarkable change in the Fijian mentality occurred over the past few generations. They are now fully trustworthy rather than treacherous; they show no suspiciousness of others; they live and let live as only people of dignity and pride can; and they are sure of their enormous strength, enjoying both work and play—and perhaps not clearly differentiating between them. Their ferocity—easy to regard as the untamed ways of the savage—disappeared within two or three generations.

If the fearsome cannibals could change rapidly, once they no longer needed to fear their fellow man, when in fact their dictum was no longer eat or be eaten, there is a chance, at least, that we too may learn to enjoy the bounty available to us—not that from a teeming ocean or a productive volcanic soil, but from our teeming and productive minds.

* Aggression and hostility are so clearly defensive and protective drives or affects that it is difficult to understand how psychoanalytic theory has, at times, connected them with an inborn "death instinct" or self-destructive instinct. However, in humans hostility can readily turn against the self and become self-destructive, even as it can fuse with sexual impulses to become sadism. These theoretic problems need not be dis-

Assimilatory Drives

The group of phenomena that we shall consider under this heading concerns the innate impulsions of the infant and child to seek stimulation and to carry out motor activity. Proper physical and intellectual development of the child appears to rest upon such needs to assimilate new experiences; and, as we shall see, a new type of experience in itself serves as a stimulus to the individual to seek its repetition. There is now ample evidence that the basic motivations of animals, including humans, arise not only from needs to reduce physiological tensions, but that the organism requires arousal for its well-being. The organism requires stimulation and seems motivated to seek it. The infant requires stimulation beyond his own capacities to obtain it, and failure to provide it leads to the disastrous consequences that the Pharaoh Psammetichos and the Emperor Frederick II reputedly found. Absence of stimulation is also almost unbearable to the adult who may lose his hold on reality when kept in solitary confinement or when he is a subject in a sensory deprivation experiment[34] in which he is shielded as completely as possible from any stimulation.

We shall also note that an impulsion to the use of the neuromuscular system seems to be a built-in part of the organism's means of survival. The child enjoys movement for its own sake, including the use of vocalizations. Such more or less spontaneous activity seems essential for gaining mastery over the sensori-motor apparatus and for explorations of the environment.* Consideration of such innate motivation for assimilation of experience is fundamental to Piaget's theory of cognitive development which will be discussed throughout the early chapters of the book.

Emotions

When mental activity and ways of relating to others are being considered, fear, aggression, sexual feelings and their related states such as anxiety, anger, and love are often regarded as emotions or affects rather than "drives." It is difficult to isolate emotions in pure form, to separate them from drives, or even to analyze their nature.

Emotions are diffuse combinations of physiological states and mental

cussed at this juncture. The reader is referred to Robert Waelder's discussion of both sides of the question in *Basic Theory of Psychoanalysis*, pp. 130–153.[36]
* How far this extends to an impulsion toward gaining mastery over tasks, thereby giving rise to a fundamental "drive for mastery," remains an open question.[20]

sets that pervade thinking and influence relationships and an individual's satisfaction with himself and his sense of well-being. The list of human emotions is almost endless. The study of emotions has ever been highly controversial, and a discussion of emotions must remain unsatisfactory at the present time. Attention here is simply being directed to the fundamental role of emotions in behavior, to their relationship to the preservation of the individual and the species, and to their diffuse and pervasive character.

Emotions do not simply develop through experience. They have a physiological basis;* but what arouses various emotions, how emotions combine, and which are most readily and frequently aroused in an individual depend largely upon experience, and to a large extent the childhood experiences with parents and family that color the attitudes a person has and the ways in which he feels about life.

Aside from emotional states that relate to drives, several others require mention. Euphoria, a feeling of well-being, balances between depression and elated feelings, and all three can be either appropriate or inappropriate to the circumstances.† Other emotional states mix with these rather basic moods. Depressive states may be due to loss of love of the self or of self-esteem, or to resentment toward a loved person. Such states relate to the feelings of the small child when deprived of the mother. A sense of well-being and even elation may relate to the infant's pleasurable responses to closeness to the mother and proper nurturance. The infant's smile and pleasurable gurgling have a positive evolutionary value because they elicit positive maternal feelings that help assure the infant the necessary nurturant care (see Chapter 5). Elation may also accompany un-

* Certain diffuse states are organized into physiologic patterns in the limbic system of the brain which MacLean has termed the "visceral brain." [27] It is the oldest portion of the cortex and the part which may well have directed a primitive animal to partially organized behaviors on the basis of olefaction, olefactory memory, and the arousal of drives. Oral drives (concerned with food and its acquisition), attack and defense, and sexual stimulation have centers of organization in the limbic cortex with connections to the hypothalamus, neocortex, reticular activating system, and other centers. The close neuroanatomical connections between centers concerned with sex, aggression, and orality are worth noting. Continuing studies of the "visceral brain," together with those of the areas that arouse feelings of "pleasure" or "unpleasure" when stimulated, are currently clarifying some of the fundamental neuroanatomical and physiological problems connected with drives and emotions.
† Euphoria is sometimes improperly used for elation. Euphoria is pathological only when inappropriate; thus persons dying of tuberculosis or of multiple sclerosis sometimes are euphoric, despite their miserable states of health. In the case of multiple sclerosis the euphoria reflects the severe damage to the frontal lobes of the brain.

expected success which brings a heightened evaluation of the self or of those with whom one identifies—as when a team is victorious or a school is cited for an achievement: it also occurs as part of a pathological effort to deny misfortune or loss that more properly should evoke depressive feelings.

Apathy, which is often related to depression, is a means of withdrawal from stimulation when efforts to reduce tension or, in the child, the need for the mother, are chronically frustrated; it provides a way of conserving bodily resources rather than squandering them in futile, frantic, and repetitive efforts to gain relief.

Among the elementary affects we may include fear, anxiety, anger, rage, elation, depression, apathy, attachment feelings, and sexual erotic feelings. These blend with pleasure and unpleasure feelings, and with pain, a sensation that signals trauma. Other emotions may be derivatives or combinations of these, also combining in many ways with thoughts, memories, and values derived from relationships. An analogy may be drawn to the sense of taste, which rests upon the four basic sensations of sweet, bitter, sour, and salt which are modified by odors into an infinite variety of tastes. Various emotions, such as anxiety, disgust, shame, guilt, depression, will be discussed in some detail in appropriate places in subsequent chapters.

We have been focusing upon some of the fundamentals of animal organisms that assure the continuity of the germinal cell and its carrier. The need to preserve the constancy of the cell in a changeable environment, the impulsion toward union of the germinal cells for procreation, the automatic preparations to defend against danger, attachment behavior that helps the animal infant secure nurturant care—all these persist to exert compelling influences in the highest mammalian forms. They continue to direct attention to fundamentals amid the extremely complex processes of adaptation that man carries out while living in a society. A dynamic adaptive approach to human personality development requires recognition of such basic motivating forces underlying behavior.

The Sequence of Maturation and Decline

At least one other genetic factor requires mention. The organism has a predetermined sequence of development and decline: a period of growth when assimilation prepares for maturity; a period of maturity when metabolic processes primarily subserve maintenance, repair, and procreation;

a period of decline when metabolic exchange lags behind the needs for renewal and leads to death. Death, which we tend to consider the negative of life, makes much life and variety of life possible. It permits evolutionary change by the sorting out of mutations. Because of the sequence of development, decline, and death, all living things possess a time factor and a directedness in time as well as in space. Experience is not repeatable, for any experience that may seem a repetition occurs at a different time in the life cycle and affects an organism that has been changed by the earlier experience. The time factor, including the inevitability of death, profoundly influences the behavior and motivations of man, who alone among animals is ever aware of it (see Chapter 18).

The Racial Physical Endowment

Within the endowment of characteristics common to the human species, each infant has racial traits and a specificity of structure that depend upon the genes carried by his parents. The influence of biological racial differences upon adaptation and personality development is difficult to assess. The direct influence of racial differences on personality development was formerly overemphasized because of the tendency of every group to regard outsiders as barbarians as well as to justify its mistreatment of other races while bolstering its own self-esteem. It seems likely that contemporary man developed from a single type of protoman; and if divergent types of protoman survived, they were absorbed in the more dominant strain that gained supremacy. Groups which were cut off from interbreeding produced separate races, all of which are equally human. The minor differences that may have arisen through the selection of genetic variation were virtually wiped out through the later migrations of people and the blending of their genes. Obviously differences in the appearance of the races and their skin color persist. However, all races have blended with others, and gradations exist that do not permit the definition of clear boundaries of where one race starts and another leaves off.

In some instances a genetic mutation that was advantageous to the survival of persons living in a specific environment spread among them. The "sickling trait" of red blood cells found in a small percentage of African Negroes provides a concrete example. These cells become deformed, fragile, and may fragment when the oxygen tension in the capillaries is low; persons who have this trait are susceptible to a serious anemia, but it renders them more resistant to malaria, which formed a much greater threat to their survival. A few groups which have remained relatively isolated, such as the Australian primitives and the African pygmies, maintain distinctive characteristics. However, anyone who has not specifically been interested in human dispersion may have difficulty in appreciating the extent of the migrations that brought a reblending of divergent strains.*

The Family Biological Endowment

Traits of both parental lines clearly show in the child's physical structure, often with features of one or the other parent dominating at different phases of his maturation. The genetic endowment of each person is unique, differing from all others except an identical twin. These individual physical characteristics influence the child's reactivity to his environment, including his interaction with others, and thereby the personality he develops.† As the parents usually raise the child as well as conceiving him, it is often impossible to differentiate the relative importance of their chromosomes and their interpersonal influence upon the personality traits that the child develops.

The precise physical structure of the person does not depend upon his genetic make-up alone. The chromosomal structure directs, patterns, and

* It may be useful to cite some examples. The Polynesians left India in the remote past, picked up and left influences in Indochina, Indonesia, and New Guinea; eventually they reached Tahiti and then spread out across the expanse of the Pacific in their double canoes. They fused with the Japanese (who had already mingled with the Ainu and later with the Mongols) in Micronesia; with the Melanesians who had migrated from Africa across the Indian Ocean into the South Pacific; with the Maorori (wherever they had come from) in New Zealand; with the Eskimo (who had crossed the Bering Sea from Siberia into Alaska); and probably with the Incas and other Amerindians on the coasts of America and in the islands of the Pacific. We might also note the sweep of the Mongols across all of Siberia into Europe, Asia Minor, China, the periphery of India, and over into Japan; or of the Semite Mohammedans into Spain, Sicily, and Italy, and their further intermingling across the trade routes of the Indian Ocean that lasted from the early centuries of the Christian era until the sixteenth century (with Indians, Chinese and the inhabitants of cities on the east coast of Africa); and eventually into Indonesia and beyond. In recent times, of course, the union of races has gained increasing momentum through improvements in transportation and through global wars.
† The inheritance of certain mutant genetic traits, such as Amaurotic family idiocy or Huntington's chorea, virtually seals the infant's fate. Others, such as limitations in the ability to metabolize sugar as in the diabetic, can present serious impediments that influence his way of life and the attitudes he develops. Other hereditary characteristics, such as an unusually short or tall stature, an unusually long nose, an inability to perceive red and green or to recognize the pitch of sounds, may influence his personality development, depending on where and how he is brought up.

sets limits within which the organism can develop as it grows in an environment. The phenotype of some insects will vary widely according to the locale in which they develop. A relatively constant environment during the critical phases of the unfolding of the fertilized germ cell is assured all mammals, but the newborn has already been influenced to some extent by his specific uterine environment. Disruption of the placental circulation or the occurrence of viral diseases such as German measles in the mother may, for example, produce anomalies. Abnormalities of the mother's metabolism can affect fetal development, as when a lack of iodine in her serum causes the infant to be a cretin; and her emotional state during pregnancy may influence the infant's reactivity even before birth. Even identical twins differ at birth, for the uterine environment is not identical for them. The environment continues to exert an influence after birth. Genetic endowments may set limits for the height or intelligence that an individual can attain but his actual height or intelligence also depends upon how he is raised. The increasing height of the American population over the past several generations reflects the change in living conditions and probably the diminution in childhood illnesses rather than a genetic selection.

Whatever the person's specific genetic endowment, it is a human endowment and forms the foundation upon which his personality characteristics will develop through interpersonal experience. As with all biological phenomena each physical attribute will vary from person to person, and if graphically represented will be scattered along a bell-shaped distribution curve. Persons have different ranges of tone perception, lengths of arm, sensitivity to touch, rates of metabolizing glucose, pepsin secretion, visual acuity, and so on. The range of variance is slight for some attributes, marked for others. Most traits in a person will be close to the median of the distribution curve, perhaps with an occasional attribute falling toward the more extreme ranges of the curve. Many divisions of persons or their attributes into distinct groupings, such as into hyperactive, average and placid babies, or into asthenic, athletic, and pyknic physiques, are simply means of stressing placement along distribution curves. However, some attributes, such as iris color and skin color, have multimodal distribution curves. Little is known about the distribution curves for many human attributes and even less about the importance of the interrelationships of such curves for various attributes within a single individual.

The significance of such differences for personality development is more a matter of conjecture than of knowledge at the present time; but they clearly have importance. One mother will be more at ease mothering a placid baby, whereas another will gain more satisfaction from a lively, active infant. A parent's lifelong fantasies may be shattered by the birth of a brunet child rather than a blond one. A girl who starts to menstruate at nine will have a different early adolescence than a girl whose menarche occurs at sixteen. Such influences can vary with differing cultural settings. In the United States even twenty or thirty years ago, if a boy was shooting upward in adolescence past the six-foot-six inch mark, his parents were very likely to be concerned and may well have taken him to an endocrinologist because of his abnormal growth. His life may have been made miserable by the teasing and jibes of confreres, and girls may have avoided the "freak." Today the parents of such a boy may hope he will grow another inch or two to be assured of free college tuition, and girls may eagerly eye this high school basketball star. A person's precise shade of color is extremely significant on the island of Jamaica, where it forms a cornerstone of a social class system; whereas in the southern United States it is not so much the shade of color but the presumption of colored ancestry that has importance. Various life settings may foster or lead to the neglect of certain inborn potentialities. Innate perfect pitch perception will have a different influence upon a child depending on whether he is born into a musical or nonmusical family, or into a society devoid of music. The developing personality will depend to a greater or lesser extent, in ways that can only be surmised at present, upon these innate physical differences.

Summary

In this chapter we have considered the evolution of man through the selection out by mating of mutations that improved capacities for tool bearing and symbolic communication until modern man emerged, sufficiently capable of modifying his environment to suit his needs, and of altering his own adaptive capacities through thinking, foresight, learning, and the transmitting of what he learned to subsequent generations, so that further marked genetic change was no longer necessary to enable him to spread out over most of the earth and dominate it.

Through his abilities to think and communicate verbally, he acquired a culture and a mind, and increasingly came to live in a social and interpersonal environment. It is apparent that both the ability to think and the development of a cultural heritage are facets of the same human attribute, and that they had to emerge gradually in conjunction with one another. In the evolution of man, the changes in the brain that permitted increasing reliance upon decision and less upon inborn patterns could occur only gradually as prehominid forms slowly acquired a heritage of learned ways of coping with the environment that could be taught to their descendants.

Although man's particular and essential techniques of adaptation rest upon his capacities to choose between alternatives and to utilize foresight, the needs of his body critical to survival, his defenses against danger, and the assurance of the perpetuation of the species are not left entirely to his judgment, decision, and possible neglect, but gain his attention and even dominate his activities through the force of the basic drives.

Whereas the physical equipment essential for living, including the brain that enables man to acquire a mind, is assured by the chemical code of the genes, the cultural heritage does not and cannot depend upon any such biological device. The transmission cannot be rigid and yet it cannot be left to chance. The welfare of the individual and the continuity of the culture which is essential to man depend upon his having satisfactory means of indoctrinating the members of the new generation into the mores, sentiments, and instrumentalities of the society, and to assure that they, in turn, will become satisfactory carriers of the culture. The major task of indoctrination devolves upon the family, even though the members of the family often do not know that they have the task. It is essential that we scrutinize the family as a basic social institution and as the primary nurturing and socializing agency, for it is a major part of the newborn child's heritage. It is in the family that the various elements of his genetic and cultural heritages converge.

References

1. David F. Aberle, *The Psychosocial Analysis of a Hopi Life-History*, Comparative Psychology Monographs, Vol. 21, No. 1, Serial No. 107 (Berkeley: University of California Press, 1951).
2. Robert Ardrey, *The Territorial Imperative. A Personal Inquiry into the Animal Origins of Property and Nations* (New York: Atheneum, 1966).
3. Francis Bacon, "The Great Instauration" (1625), in *Selected Writings of Francis Bacon* (Modern Library ed.; New York: Random House, 1955).
4. Gregory Bateson and Margaret Mead, *Balinese Character: A Photographic Analysis* (New York: New York Academy of Science, 1942).
5. Ruth Benedict, *Patterns of Culture* (New York: Penguin Books, 1934), p. 235.
6. Norman Brown, *Love's Body* (New York: Random House, 1966).
7. Lewis Carroll, *Through the Looking-Glass* (1871) (London: Macmillan Co., 1963), p. 114.
8. Morris G. Carstairs, *The Twice Born: A Study of a Community of High-Caste Hindus* (London: Hogarth Press, 1957).
9. C. M. Davis, "Self-Selection of Diet by Newly Weaned Infants," *American Journal of Diseases of Children*, 36 (1928), 651–679.
10. José M. R. Delgado, Warren Roberts, and Neal Miller, "Learning Motivated by Electrical Stimulation of the Brain," *American Journal of Physiology*, 179 (1954), 587–593.
11. John Dewey, *Experience and Nature* (London: Open Court Publishing Co., 1925).
12. George L. Engel, *Psychological Development in Health and Disease* (Philadelphia: W. B. Saunders, 1962), pp. 72–304.
13. Erik H. Erikson, *Childhood and Society* (New York: W. W. Norton, 1950).
14. Sigmund Freud, "Civilization and Its Discontents" (1930), in *The Standard Edition of the Complete Psychological Works of Sigmund Freud*, Vol. XXI (London: Hogarth Press, 1961).
15. Arnold Gesell, *Wolf Child and Human Child* (New York: Harper & Bros., 1941).
16. Jane Goodall, "My Life among Wild Chimpanzees," *National Geographic*, 124 (1963), 272–308.
17. Jane Goodall, "New Discoveries among Wild Chimpanzees," *National Geographic*, 128 (1965), 802–831.
18. Knut Hamsun, *Hunger*, trans. Robert Bly (New York: Farrar, Straus & Giroux, 1967).
19. Heinz Hartmann, *Ego Psychology and the Problem of Adaptation* (1939), trans. David Rapaport (New York: International Universities Press, 1958).
20. Ives Hendrick, "The Discussion of the 'Instinct to Master,'" A Letter to the Editor, *Psychoanalytic Quarterly*, 12 (1943), 561–565.

21. Herodotus, *Euterpe*, Book II, Chapter 2.
22. Abram Kardiner, *The Psychological Frontiers of Society* (New York: Columbia University Press, 1945).
23. Gottfried Keller, "Der grüne Heinrich," in *Gesammelte Werke* (Zurich: Rascher & Co., 1918).
24. Helen Keller, *The Story of My Life* (1902) (New York: Dell Publishing Co., 1964).
25. Konrad Lorenz, *King Solomon's Ring: New Light on Animal Ways*, trans. Marjorie K. Wilson (New York: Thomas Y. Crowell, 1952).
26. Konrad Lorenz, *On Aggression*, trans. Marjorie K. Wilson (New York: Harcourt, Brace & World, 1966).
27. Paul D. MacLean, "The Limbic System ('Visceral Brain') in Relation to Central Gray and Reticulum of the Brain Stem," *Psychosomatic Medicine*, 17 (1955), 355–366.
28. James Olds, "Self-Stimulation of the Brain," *Science*, 127 (1958), 315–324.
29. John Randall, Jr., *The Making of the Modern Mind* (rev. ed.; Boston: Houghton Mifflin, 1940).
30. James Robinson, *The Mind in the Making* (New York: Harper & Bros., 1921).
31. Salimbene, cited in James B. Ross and Mary M. McLaughlin, *A Portable Medieval Reader* (New York: Viking Press, 1949), p. 366.
32. B. C. Schiele and Josef Brozek, " 'Experimental Neurosis' Resulting from Semistarvation in Man," *Psychosomatic Medicine*, 10 (1948), 33.
33. George Simpson, *The Meaning of Evolution. A Study of the History of Life and of Its Significance for Man* (New Haven: Yale University Press, 1950).
34. Philip Solomon, Philip E. Kubzansky, P. Herbert Leiderman, Jack H. Mendelson, Richard Trumbull, and Donald Wexler (eds.), *Sensory Deprivation* (Cambridge, Mass.: Harvard University Press, 1961).
35. René A. Spitz, "Hospitalism: An Inquiry into the Genesis of Psychiatric Conditions in Early Childhood," *The Psychoanalytic Study of the Child*, Vol. 1 (New York: International Universities Press, 1945), pp. 53–74.
36. Robert Waelder, *Basic Theory of Psychoanalysis* (New York: International Universities Press, 1960), pp. 130–153.
37. Beatrice Whiting (ed.), *Six Cultures: Studies of Child Rearing* (New York: John Wiley & Sons, 1963).
38. Benjamin L. Whorf, "The Relation of Habitual Thought and Behavior to Language" (1939), in John Carroll (ed.), *Language, Thought and Reality: Selected Writings of Benjamin Lee Whorf* (New York: M.I.T. Press and John Wiley & Sons, 1956).

Suggested Reading

Ruth Benedict, *Patterns of Culture* (New York: Penguin Books, 1934).

Roger Brown, *Words and Things* (Glencoe, Ill.: Free Press, 1958).

Theodore Lidz, "The Family, Language and Ego Functions," in *The Family and Human Adaptation: Three Lectures* (New York: International Universities Press, 1963).

Edward Sapir, *Selected Writings of Edward Sapir in Language, Culture and Personality* (Berkeley: University of California Press, 1949).

Sol Tax (ed.), *Evolution After Darwin*. Vol. II of *The Evolution of Man: Mind, Culture and Society* (Chicago: University of Chicago Press, 1960).

Lev S. Vygotsky, *Thought and Language,* ed. and trans. Eugenia Hanfmann and Gertrude Vakar (New York: M.I.T. Press and John Wiley & Sons, 1962).

CHAPTER 2

The Family

THE INFANT, as we have shown, must acquire the adaptive techniques handed down by his society's culture to supplement his inborn endowment. Acquiring them cannot be left to chance, nor can it be haphazard, for these instrumental techniques must fit together into a workable pattern. The child also needs prolonged nurturant care; and his innate potentialities require structuring, directing, and delimitation in order to become capabilities and to enable him to develop into an integrated individual capable of living in the society and transmitting its ways to subsequent generations.

The child does not grow up in the general society, but within the shelter of a family, or some substitute for it. The prolonged helplessness and dependency of the child dictate that he be reared by persons to whom his welfare is as important, if not more important, than their own; and his dependent need for them and his attachment to them serve as major motivations and directives for his development into a member of the society. The family is knowingly or unknowingly entrusted by every society with the task of providing for the child's biological needs and simultaneously with indoctrinating the society's new recruits—to nurture and at the same time enculture the child and structure his developing personality.

The family is a universal phenomenon because it is an essential correlate of man's biological make-up and the basic institution that permits his survival by augmenting his inborn adaptive capacities. It forms a shelter for its members within the society and against the remainder of the society; and it mediates between the child's biological needs and the societal directives. It is an institution for which no workable substitute has been found except in very special instances.* The structure and functioning of the family must everywhere meet two determinants: the biological nature and needs of man, and the requirements of the particular society of which it forms a subsystem and in which its offspring must be prepared to live. Therefore, families everywhere will have certain essential features in common while also having some very discrepant ways of handling similar problems. But everywhere the family is part of the child's endowment, and any attempt to describe and study personality development as an autonomous process, independent of the family matrix in which it transpires, distorts as much as it simplifies; it is bound to error for such abstractions can be made only by virtually destroying the essence of the topic.

The family forms the earliest and most persistent influence that encompasses the still unformed infant and small child for whom the parents' ways and the family ways are *the* way of life, the only way he knows. All subsequent experiences are perceived, understood, and reacted to emotionally according to the foundations established in the family. The family ways and the child's patterns of reacting to them become so integrally incorporated in the child that they can be considered determinants of his constitutional make-up, difficult to differentiate from the genetic biological influences with which they interrelate. Sub-

* The Israeli kibbutz method of raising children collectively in nurseries and then in special children's units is a means of making it possible for the pioneer women to work, as required by the circumstances, without its affecting the children deleteriously. However, very careful attention is paid to providing adequate mothering and individual attention by substitute mothers. No effort is made to minimize the importance of the biological parents, who spend considerable time with the child after work each day, perhaps giving the child more of their undivided attention than parents do in most societies. There is some reason to doubt that the kibbutz method will become a permanent child-rearing system rather than one suited to the temporary needs of a period.

sequent influences will modify those of the family, but they can never undo or fully reshape these early core experiences.

Child Rearing for Membership in a Society

Let us first consider in very general terms how the family shapes the child to the societal patterns and conveys the culture's instrumental techniques as an integral part of providing the essential nurturant care before we examine various aspects of the process separately.*

The infant is fed on a more or less regular schedule and may be left to cry if he becomes hungry before feeding time; his mother dresses and feeds him at the same time each morning, and places him in his own crib in his own room for naps at about the same time each afternoon, and prepares him for bed according to schedule each evening. As a toddler, he spends time in his playpen and soon learns what he can touch and what he must leave alone, and which toys are his and which are his siblings'. In most Western societies the infant or child is already being prepared to live in time, for scheduled living, and for existence as an independent individual with his own possessions and for eventual auton-

* It has taken social scientists a long time even to begin to gain an appreciation of the many critical functions carried out by the family for the spouses, the society, and children because the family is omnipresent and therefore has often been taken for granted—sometimes even as an outmoded institution that did little other than cause trouble. Indeed, the family is so vital that it has unknowingly been carrying out its complex tasks since the emergence of man, and some even long before protoman appeared on the scene. As the parents who usually provide the family environment also by and large transmit the genetic heredity, the child's personality traits have traditionally been attributed to heredity. It was obvious enough: intelligent parents usually had intelligent children; the ruling class provided most governmental leaders; artisans bred artisans; and laborers supplied most of the laborers. Children did not always live up to expectation, but that was due to some fault in the ancestral line of the spouse. Perhaps it required the opening of the New World for such obvious truths to be questioned, for in the gigantic reshuffling children en masse began to differ from their parents in many significant ways, and even more distinctively in Australia, where, I understand, few boast of traits handed down from their ancestral settlers at Botany Bay. True, some children were raised in institutions and most of these did not turn out particularly well; but after all, with rare exceptions, these were children of the poor and little more could be expected of them. It has required the comparisons of the influence of child-rearing procedures in widely different societies, the study of children raised in institutions,[10,19] the gradual realization that individuals who are seriously disturbed emotionally were almost always raised in very faulty family settings,[2,15] and even more recently the understanding that the child's cognitive development rests heavily on family influences[4,14] to draw attention to some of these essential functions of the family and to pose the proper questions that are always required before proper answers can be found.

omy from his family of origin. But other little children are being prepared for a different way of life. Let us look at our friends the Hopi in
considering the education to live in a time-oriented scheduled world.
The Hopi child, in contrast, grows up in a relatively timeless world that
traditionally was encompassed by the horizon that surrounded the mesa
on which he lived. In this small world, which his ancestors had inhabited
for countless generations, little changes from day to day or from year to
year. The child does not learn to hurry lest something be missed or an
opportunity neglected; or to make every minute count on his way to
amounting to something. He does not learn to do things to bring about
innovations because there can be no innovation; the Hopi believe that
everything already exists. Everything already exists, but some things have
not yet become manifest. He learns that wishing and thinking for something, particularly collective concentration such as occurs during rituals,
are means of having things become manifest. Thus, thought and wish
have greater pragmatic value than activity, and among the Hopi the
child's wishful thinking and daydreaming are not likely to be derogated
as escape mechanisms that supplant effort. He does not grow up being
oriented to do things to try to improve himself and his world. The language he imbibes along with his mother's milk not only is suited to this
orientation but prevents him from considering matters very differently
because there are no tenses in the Hopi language.* He has no way of
talking about the past, present, and future but can talk simply about
what has and what has not become manifest—and to say that something
is not yet manifest is the same as saying it is subjective; that is, it exists
only in the mind, which of course is the only place we experience the
future. He also does not think or talk about tomorrow or the day after
tomorrow, but rather about when day will return again or return for the
second time. Such differences are more than different ways of expressing
something; they reflect a divergent orientation to the nature of the universe and human experience.†

* This does not necessarily make the Hopi language the ideal of language students
who may be bothered by the many tenses in Latin, Hebrew, or English. The complexity comes about in other ways, such as in the change in the form of the verb
to tell how something is known—for example, because it is seen, or heard, or because
someone has said so, or because it customarily happens.[23]
† The illustrations are not necessarily accurate and should be taken as symbolic
illustrations (as the author is not an ethnologist). See D. F. Aberle, *The Psychosocial Analysis of a Hopi Life-History;*[1] L. W. Simmons, *Sun Chief: The Autobiography of a Hopi Indian;*[18] and B. L. Whorf, "The Relation of Habitual Thought
and Behavior to Language." [24]

We might also consider the plight of the benighted Fijian child who is brought up without gaining any notions of attaining possessions or amassing wealth, or of outstripping his peers in achievement and preparing to gain power in order to bring prestige and pleasure to his parents. Little wonder that he continues to live in grass huts and plays neither golf nor bridge. He does not learn in early childhood that if his father does not work the family will go hungry, be dispossessed, or go on relief and lose their self-esteem. There is no cajoling or tacit threat of loss of love if he does not exert himself to learn enough to gain entry into the proper nursery school that will assure admittance to the private school that will open the gates to the college that will prepare him for graduate school to make it possible for him eventually to occupy a prestigious position in society. Indeed, the Fijian child does not even know the meaning of private possessions except in the limited sense of a few personal necessities. What the others in his village possess, is his.* Food is generally available without requiring much effort to grow or catch and is freely shared. When the hut is rotted by termites, the villagers gather and collectively build a new one. Aspirations are limited because there is a taboo on ambition and self-advancement. The infant and small child gains a basic trust (see Chapter 3) in his world and those who people it because he is well nurtured during these early years and free from rivalry with his father or close siblings because of the taboo on sexual intercourse between his parents for two years after his birth. The Fijians may, like some other peoples, believe that if a nursing mother has sexual relations her milk will become diluted—which may be an implicit recognition that the mother's libidinal investment of her baby may be diluted.

Social Class and Ethnic Influences

In the United States child rearing and the process of enculturation are far from homogeneous. They vary with social class and ethnic origins, and are affected by the personality of the parents even more than in most societies because the parents and their children are so often isolated from the extended family of kin, and because of the admixture of ethnic backgrounds and the rapidity of social change.

No society is homogeneous and its component families reflect its sub-

* The Chinese have owned the trading posts near Fijian villages because traditionally, at least, if a Fijian ran a store his extensive "relatives" felt free to help themselves to whatever they needed.

divisions in their structure and functioning. Subdivisions exist according to social class, ethnic-religious groupings, and race. Although social class divisions are not so striking in the United States as in many other countries, they are still very significant; and the admixture of ethnic groups that have immigrated to America has resulted in a wide variation in family forms and practices. Children are raised very differently according to the social position of the parents and according to ethnic origins, particularly in families that have not yet been assimilated.

A conventional way of dividing the population according to social class is to subdivide each of the usual upper, middle, and lower class groupings into upper and lower subclasses. Families can be allocated into the six categories adequately according to a scale based on place of residence and the occupation and education of the parents. Although such categorization divides up a continuum, clear-cut differences in living patterns and child rearing typify the social class groupings; and the differences are fairly sharp between groups that are not adjacent in the scale; for example, the lower-upper class and the lower-middle class mores are notably different. The traditions taught, the expectations held, the role examples provided, and the intellectual atmosphere afforded the child vary from class to class. Even though greater opportunity for upward social mobility exists in the United States than ever existed elsewhere, the classes tend to perpetuate themselves through the differing ways in which they rear their children. The lower-class family child will, in general, complete twelve years of schooling with reluctance and will have virtually finished his personality development by his mid-teens. The upper-middle and upper class families will expect children to gain at least a college degree and continue to expand their horizons into their twenties, permitting them to remain more or less dependent upon parental support. Sexual mores also differ notably, as Kinsey [12] pointed out; delay of gratification being less common in lower socio-economic classes than in upper, and with very different concepts of what are acceptable and unacceptable sexual practices. Although the topic cannot be pursued here, the influences are far-reaching—affecting, for example, the prevalence of different types of physical and emotional illness in each social class.[11]*

* The difficulties in verbal communication of persons in the lower socio-economic groups is of particular pertinence to those occupied with their physical and emotional welfare. Communication between persons of differing social class backgrounds often presents difficulties because of the dissimilarities in the ways of thinking and in the value standards, and such difficulties are aggravated by the poor verbal skills of many lower-class persons. The poor verbal abilities of the lower socio-economic

Ethnic Differences in Families

A relationship often exists between ethnic groupings and social class, as when one ethnic group is subjugated by another, whether it be the Anglo-Saxons by the Normans or the African Negro by the slaveholder, or when a displaced group finds a humble refuge in a new country. However, ethnic groups tend to perpetuate themselves because of their adherence to customs that afford their members a feeling of identity. The methods of child rearing which are unconsciously accepted as proper and which are the only spontaneous methods that the parents know, promote the continuity. The peoples of the United States comprise an agglomerate of ethnic groups which are gradually shedding their prior cultural heritages to assume an American way of life—a culture of somewhat indefinite characteristics which is in the process of formation or constant re-formation as it assimilates characteristics of different groups and seeks ways of suiting its members to live under rapidly changing conditions. Some ethnic groups seek to guard against assimilation and try to maintain a strict hold over each new generation in order to preserve a separate identity, such as the Hutterites, the Mennonites, Hassidic Jews, and certain Greek Orthodox communities. The customs of such groups are notably divergent from those of the general community. Other groups seek to become assimilated while maintaining some separate identity, whereas many immigrant groups tend to lose the desire for separateness after one or two generations.

However, even after considerable assimilation has taken place, the way in which the family is structured and functions frequently contains many elements of Old World patterns which the parents continue to carry within them without knowing it. The understanding of the child's

---

groups have many other far-reaching consequences. The children do not gain ample mental equipment to compete in school. Ability to delay gratification for future rewards also relates to verbal and intellectual ability. Conceptualization is impoverished and imagination may be stunted.

The lower-lower class has particular importance to the medical and socially oriented professions because it includes a large proportion of persons who have sedimented out, so to speak, because of the emotional instability of the homes in which they were raised, and many members are no longer capable of forming families that can properly rear a new generation. Perhaps too little attention has been paid to the difference between lower-class families that have not yet had an opportunity to raise their positions, such as immigrant families or Negro families recently migrated northward, and those lower-class families that have fallen back or remained lower-lower class because of chronic emotional instability over several generations.

development and the tasks he encounters requires recognition of such ethnic and religious differences. The Irish-American child may grow up influenced by the mother's tendency to treat her husband like a grown-up child, pretending to believe the fabricated tales he tells and admiring his ability to tell them; and while she seems to defer to her husband's authority she holds the family reins tightly in her own hands, at the same time ceding to the church a superordinate authority which must not be questioned. The boys and girls in such families grow up with very different ideas and feelings about their respective roles and responsibilities, and with different reactions to male and female authority figures from those of children in a German-American family which retains the strict discipline of a stern father who is almost unapproachable to the child, but in which the mother acts as a go-between, knowing how to circumvent her husband by being deferential and concerned with his comfort while swaying him to yield to a child's wishes. The child with parents of southern Italian origins may be influenced by the expectation that he maintain strong ties to his extended family, and may be puzzled about his parents' seeming irreligiosity, for their attitude to the church is much more relaxed than that of the Irish children in the neighborhood and that of the Polish priest who is so rigid in his expectations of children. Jews, even after several generations in the United States, may be surprised to learn that some of their attitudes concerning health and education as well as a variety of family customs are not idiopathic to the family but clearly derive from customs of eastern European Jews.*

Acculturation and Personality

Problems arising from acculturation are well recognized in America and do not require elaboration here beyond a reminder that at times certain child-rearing techniques, personality traits, or prejudices are attributed primarily to idiosyncrasies of the individual when they are

* The anthropological and sociological reconstruction of the East European Jewish communities wiped out by the Nazis, Life Is with People,[26] shows that even though separated for several hundred years, these communities in different countries had preserved identical customs, many of which are reflected in contemporary American-Jewish practices, value systems, and attitudes. A comparison of this volume with Thomas and Znaniecki's classic study, The Polish Peasant in Europe and America,[20] offers a striking contrast of two cultures occupying the same physical environment— as striking as comparisons of the Navajo and Hopi, or the Fijians with the Indians living in Fiji. Italian-Americans can gain an appreciation of the origins of many of their family patterns by reading the novels and short stories of Varga[22] or such books as Italian or American? The Second Generation Conflict.[6]

residues of ethnic differences, or characteristics of social class differences. Let us note several such examples in somewhat simplified fashion. A husband relates that he has never seen his wife in the nude, and the physician takes this to indicate extreme inhibition on the part of the wife, whereas the lower-class husband of Polish origin would be shocked if his wife ever undressed in his presence. A young woman from a Greek Orthodox family becomes profoundly withdrawn and stops eating after a diagnosis of tuberculosis has been established; her family acts as if they are in mourning when they visit her and can offer her little emotional support. The patient had long sought to escape from her patriarchal family, which refused to let her date unchaperoned, but she knew that even a "touch" of tuberculosis made her completely unacceptable in the close-knit community, and now she will never marry unless she makes a complete break with her family, her community, and their traditions.

The American Negro Family

The situation of the American Negro presents some very special problems. In general, the lower classes are comprised of the most recent impoverished immigrants, the majority of whose families emerge from lower-class status within one or two generations in the United States. The Negro, because of his color and earlier slave status as well as other factors, has not been able to become upwardly mobile as readily, to an extent that anomie and permanent lower-class status threatens a large portion of the Negro population. Many of the ways of life and of rearing children that are considered typically Negro are, rather, lower class. Relative lack of concern for the future, high rates of broken homes, premature reliance on older siblings to care for the young child are common among other lower socio-economic segments of the population. However, other factors also require consideration. The Negro, brought to the United States as a slave, was to a very large extent cut off from the cultural traditions of his forebears in Africa. He brought customs totally unsuited to life in slavery; he was separated from his kin and his ethnic group; he was left without ideal figures after whom he could shape himself, etc. Then, very frequently the slave owner paid little attention to family formation among slaves: couples were separated; women were used for breeding a new generation of slaves; they were taken as sexual objects by masters. The children were commonly raised without fathers, and child rearing became the sole responsibility of women, but not always of the mother. The man had relatively little responsibility for a family. Matriarchy, or at least the mother-centered family, became a pattern that tends to persist, affording the boy an inadequate role pattern to follow into manhood. Because of meager economic opportunities the man has difficulty in achieving or maintaining adequate self-esteem. Problems such as these continue to aggravate those created by poor education and economic deprivation, and they obviously seriously influence the children's development.*

Parental Personality and the Family

The family and the child rearing it provides obviously also vary with the personalities of the parents; and how the child's enculturation is carried out depends greatly upon how the parents grew up and internalized the societal patterns and the culture which became part of their personalities. They transmit the cultural ways to their offspring through the language they use, their ways of relating, the taboos which they unconsciously hold, their value systems, and their role assumptions and expectations more than through what they consciously teach to their children. Differences reflecting the individuality of the parents and how they interrelate transcend ethnic, religious, and social class origins. One child may, for example, grow up in a home filled with talk; his mother happily recites nursery rhymes to her totally uncomprehending infant, gives him a cloth picture "book" as one of his first playthings, and later reads him a story each night as part of the bedtime ritual; and he may have a father who takes him on trips and patiently responds to endless questions. Another child has a mother who cannot be close and is annoyed when her child interrupts the fantasy life that sustains her; and has a father who like the child feels excluded by his wife and has found refuge in his profession and rarely relates to the child. Such differences will be referred to repeatedly in subsequent chapters.

The Family's Requisite Functions in Child Rearing

The family, however, has other functions in respect to the child's development than enculturation. In order for the infant to develop into an integrated and reasonably independent adult, he must not only be adequately nurtured and enculturated, but his development into an inte-

---

* An excellent presentation of the situation can be found in E. F. Frazier's *The Negro Family in the United States*.[9] See also the *Daedalus* issue on "The Negro American" [7] and the U.S. Department of Labor report on *The Negro Family: The Case for National Action*.[21]

grated person must be directed by the family in which he is reared. The family and its influence upon its children cannot be understood simply in terms of the personalities of its members and the interactions between them.

The family forms a true small group in that the action of any member affects all, producing reactions and counterreactions in them; its members must find reciprocally interrelating roles or the personalities of one or more members becomes distorted; and the weal of the group requires some degree of precedence over the wishes and even the needs of its individual members. Such requirements for group functioning are heightened by the prolonged intimate relationships of its members, by their interdependence, and the erotized aspects of their relationships; but also because of the biologically determined nature of the family's composition, organization, and purposes. For the child the family constitutes the primary social group upon which all subsequent group and interpersonal relationships have their foundations.

Let us now turn to examine in greater detail how the family carries out its essential functions with respect to its offspring. We shall discuss these requisite and interrelated functions under four headings. These are: (1) the parental nurturant functions which must meet the child's needs and supplement his immature capacities in a different manner at each phase of his development. (2) The dynamic structure of the family which forms a framework for the structuring of the child's personality or, perhaps stated more correctly, channels and directs him into becoming an integrated individual. (3) The family as the primary social system in which the child learns the basic social roles, the value of social institutions, and the basic mores of the society. (4) The task of the parents and the family they create of transmitting to the child the essential adaptive techniques of the culture, including its language. The child requires these positive directive influences of the family in order to grow into an integrated and functioning individual, and we must examine the nature of these essential contributions to the shaping of the personality as we follow its emergence from infancy through adolescence.*

---

* The family subserves other major functions aside from child rearing, of course, and these other functions can, and to some extent always do, conflict with the child rearing to a greater or lesser extent. The nuclear family is formed by the marriage of a man and woman who seek from it fulfillments that had to be frustrated in their families of origin and a completion of the incompleteness that comes of being a man or woman—which involves far more than sexual gratification (see Chapters 13, 14). The demands of the spouses upon one another can obviously

Parental Nurturance

The nurture of the infant and child forms a major topic of much of this book. Here we shall consider only a few principles that are germane to the topic of the integrated functioning of the family; and these will be elaborated in subsequent chapters.

Nurturance concerns more than filling the child's physical needs, it involves his emotional needs for love, affection, and a sense of security; it includes providing the opportunity for utilization of new capacities as the child matures. Proper nurturance requires parents to have the capacity, knowledge, and feeling to alter their ways of relating to the child in accord with his changing needs. The degree of protective constraint provided a nine-month-old is unsuited for a toddler, and the limits set for a fifteen-month-old would restrain the development of a two-and-a-half-year-old child. The capacity to be nurturant or for a mother to be maternal is not an entity. Some mothers can nurture a child properly as long as he is a helpless and almost completely dependent infant, but become apprehensive and have difficulties in coping as soon as he becomes a toddler and can no longer be fully guarded from dangers inherent in his surroundings.

The mother is the primary and major nurturant figure to the child, particularly the small child. She is, so to speak, the family expert in child-rearing techniques. Although the child's nurturance can be studied in terms of the mother-child relationships, it involves more than this twosome. The father is also an important nurturant person and becomes increasingly important as the child grows older. Further, the mother also requires support in order to invest her infant properly with her love and attention. In giving of herself to her child or children, she also needs to feel supported and to have her own emotional needs replenished, and in many contemporary families there is none other than the husband from whom she can gain such physical and emotional sustenance.

The attachments of the child to his parents that arise as a concomitant

interfere with child rearing, as when a husband is competitive with a child for his wife's attention, but, as we shall note, the spouses' needs for one another also play an important positive function in child rearing. The family also fills societal functions other than child rearing: it forms a grouping of individuals that the society treats as an entity; families are part of kinship networks that help structure and stabilize the society; the family provides incentives, roles, and statuses for its members within the society. Societal demands can interfere with child rearing, as when the father is called to military duty, or when his seeking of higher economic status for the family leads to neglect of the child, etc.

of their nurturant care provide major directives and motivations for his development into a social being, and furnish the parents with leverage with which to channel their child's drives. The child's wishes and needs for his parents' love and acceptance and his desire to avoid rebuff and punishment lead him to attempt to conform with expectations. Indeed, the infant's first movement toward rescinding immediate gratification of his own bodily needs may well result from his unknowing efforts to gain the reward of the comfort of a tension-free mother (see Chapter 5). Further, the child, in wishing both to be loved by a parent and to become someone like a parent, gains a major developmental directive through seeking to emulate one parent or the other, and he gains organization by internalizing and assimilating their characteristics.

The quality and nature of the parental nurturance which the child receives will profoundly influence his emotional development—his vulnerability to frustration, and the aggression, anxiety, hopelessness, helplessness, and anger he experiences under various conditions. As Erikson[8] has pointed out, it affects the quality of the basic trust he develops—the trust he has in others, and in himself. It influences his sense of autonomy and the clarity of the boundaries established between himself and the parental persons. It contributes to the child's self-esteem as a member of his own sex. It lays the foundations for trust in the reliability of collaboration and the worth of verbal communication as a means of problem solving. The child's physiological functioning can be permanently influenced by the manner in which the parental figures respond to his physiological needs. Hilde Bruch[5] has pointed out, for example, that the child needs to learn that the physiological phenomena that occur with hunger are signs of *hunger* that can be satisfied by eating—something which may never occur if the mother feeds the child whenever he cries for any reason, or in response to her own hunger rather than the child's. It is, of course, apparent from this brief summary of topics that will be discussed in later chapters why so much attention has properly been directed to the parental nurturant functions and how profoundly they influence personality development.

The Family Structure and the Integration of the Personality

Let us now consider the relationship between the dynamic organization of the family and the integration of the personality of the offspring. Although the family organization varies from culture to culture and with social class within a society, it seems likely that the family everywhere follows certain organizational principles that are established by its biological make-up. The nuclear family not only is a true small group with distinctive features dictated by the prolonged and intense nature of the relationships and its specific functions, but also its structure is partly determined by the fact that it is composed of two generations and two genders.[17] The division into two generations and two sexes minimizes role conflict and tends to provide conflict-free areas into which the immature child can develop and directs him into the proper roles. Any group needs unity of leadership, but the family contains two leaders—a father and a mother. Unity of direction and organization requires a coalition between the parents that is possible because of the different but interrelated functions of a father and a mother. *In order for the family to be conducive to the integrated development of the offspring the spouses must form a coalition as parents, maintain the boundaries between the generations, and adhere to their respective sex-linked roles.*[18]

The Parental Coalition

The mother, no matter how subjugated, is the expressive-affectional leader of the family, she is concerned with maintaining a stable home and with the emotional well-being of the children, and she is the specialist in child rearing. The father is the instrumental leader, the protector and provider who usually establishes the family's position in the broader society. A *coalition* between the parents is necessary not only to give unity of direction but also to provide each parent with the emotional support essential for carrying out his or her cardinal functions. Any small group tends to divide up into dyads—a tendency which creates rivalries and jealousies but which is diminished if the parents can maintain a unity in relating to their children. The coalition helps direct the child by frustrating his fantasies of dividing the parents and possessing one and redirects him to the reality that requires repression of such wishes. The child properly requires two parents: a parent of the same sex with whom to identify and who provides a model to follow into adulthood; and a parent of the opposite sex who becomes a cardinal love object and whose love and approval is sought through identification with the parent of the same sex. However, a parent can fill neither role effectively for the child if denigrated by the spouse, and even less if despised or treated as an enemy. In actuality, directives from both parents are internalized and each child identifies to a greater or lesser extent with each parent. If the parents are irreconcilable the child will be subject to conflicting motivations, directives, and standards that interfere with his achieving an integrated personality.

The Generation Boundaries

The nuclear family is divided into parental and childhood generations. Each generation has different prerogatives and responsibilities. The parents, having been raised in different families, unite in seeking to form a permanent union, whereas the children must be so raised that although dependent upon their parents they can eventually emerge into the broader society and form families of their own. The parents are the guiding, nurturing, teaching generation who must give of themselves so that the children can grow. They may be dependent upon one another but should not be dependent upon immature children. The children must be dependent upon parental figures and be free to invest their energies in their own development. While a sexual relationship between the parents is not only permitted but expected, all overt sexual behavior between a child and other members of the family is prohibited, which helps assure that the child will seek fulfillment beyond the family.[16] Parents can inappropriately breech the generation boundaries in a number of ways; for example, by utilizing a child to fill needs unsatisfied by the spouse; by a mother's failing to establish boundaries between herself and a son whom she expects to live out the life closed to her because she is a woman; by a father's behaving more like a child than a spouse and offering his wife little except satisfaction of her needs to mother, and so on. Such a father, for example, provides a weak figure for a son to emulate and he is someone who can be displaced rather than a figure whose prerogatives must be recognized.

The Sex-Linked Roles

Perhaps no other factor is so important a determinant of personality characteristics as the sex of the child, and nothing as important to attaining a stable personality as security of gender identity (see Chapter 6). However, identity as a member of one's own sex is not an inherent accompaniment of anatomy. A major factor in establishing gender identity derives from identification with a parent of the same sex who fills his or her proper sex-linked role. Role reversals in parents can obviously distort the child's development, as when a father is overtly homosexual or blatantly feminine in behavior; but the inability of the mother to fill an affectional-expressive role or of the father to provide instrumental leadership for the family also creates difficulties. Either a cold and unyielding mother or a weak and ineffectual father is apt to distort the family structure and a child's development. As Parsons and Bales[17] have pointed out,

a cold and unyielding mother is more deleterious than a cold and unyielding father, and a weak and ineffectual father more harmful than a
weak mother. Perhaps it is also pertinent to note that a cold and aloof
mother can be particularly detrimental to a daughter who requires childhood experience with a nurturing mother to attain the maternal characteristics she will need as a woman; and an ineffectual father who is
overtly dependent upon his wife creates problems for a son who must
overcome his initial dependency upon his mother and learn to feel capable of providing instrumentally for a wife and children.

In considering the relationship between the family structure and the
integration of the offspring's development, we have been indicating a
new and important parameter in the study of personality development
that has scarcely been explored. Still, a little consideration leads us to
recognize that the provision of proper models for identification and motivation toward the proper identifications, security of sexual identity, the
frustration of the child's desire to pre-empt one parent, the repression of
erotic cravings for a parent before the onset of adolescence and many
other factors essential to proper development are affected profoundly by
the family structure. Unless the parents can form an adequate coalition
and maintain boundaries between the generations and provide the appropriate gender-linked models by their behavior, chronic and profound
conflict will interfere with the proper channeling of the child's drives,
energies, and role learning.

The Family as a Social System

The form and functions of the family evolve with the culture and
subserve the needs of the society of which it is a subsystem. It is the first
social system that the child knows and into which he grows, and from it
he must gain such things as a familiarity with the basic roles as they are
carried out in the society in which he lives: the roles of parents and
child, of boy and girl, of man and woman, of husband and wife, and how
these roles impinge upon the broader society and how the roles of others
impinge upon the family and its members. Although roles can be regarded as units of a social system, they also become part of the personality through directing behavior to fit them and by giving cohesion to personality functioning. Individuals do not learn patterns of living entirely
from scratch but in many situations learn roles and then modify them to
the specific individual needs.

Within the family the child also learns about basic institutions and
their values, such as the institutions of the family, marriage, extended

family systems, institutions of economic exchange. Within the family
social system values are inculcated by example, teaching, and interaction.
The wish to participate in or avoid participation in such institutions is a
major directive in personality development. It is the function of the family to transmit to the offspring what the prescribed, permitted, and pro-
scribed values of the society are and what are the acceptable and unacceptable means of achieving goals. Within the family's social system a
child is involved in a mutiplicity of social phenomena that leaves a permanent imprint upon him that is difficult to define; for example, the
value of belonging to a mutually protective unit; the rewards of renounc-
ing one's own wishes for the welfare of a collectivity; the hierarchies of
authority and the relationship between authority and responsibility. The
family's value systems, role definitions, patterns of interrelating enter
into the child through the family's behavior far more than through what
he is taught or even what is consciously appreciated by the family.

The Family and Enculturation

We have been considering the family's critical role in transmitting the
culture's adaptive techniques to its children in a general way. Here we
shall be concerned with the process of enculturation separately from the
process of socialization. It concerns that which is transmitted symbolically from generation to generation rather than through societal organizations, but there is obviously considerable overlap. Enculturation of the
young cannot be considered discretely from socialization, for social roles
and social institutions are also part of the cultural heritage. It is a topic
that has received increasing attention in antipoverty programs in which
it is becoming apparent that the cultural deprivation of the children
is almost as important as their social and economic deprivations. They
cannot learn readily because they have not been provided with the
symbolic wherewithal for abstract thinking and with the breadth of experience to reason adequately to guide their lives into the future. Further, there is increasing consideration that a significant proportion of
mental deficiency derives from cultural deprivation rather than from biological inadequacy.*

* An example, more amusing than malignant, of the handicaps imposed upon a
child by cultural deprivation is provided by the following essay written by a London
slum child evacuated to the country during World War II.

BIRDS AND BEASTS
The cow is a mammal. It has six sides, right and left and upper and below.
At the back it has a tail on which hangs a brush. With this he sends flies

   In a complex industrial and scientific society such as ours the family
obviously can transmit only the basic adaptive techniques to its offspring, and many of the instrumentalities of the culture must be conveyed by schools and other specialized institutions. Among the most crucial tasks performed by the family is the inculcation of a solid foundation
in the language of the society. Language is the means by which man
internalizes his experience, thinks about it, tries out alternatives, conceptualizes a future and strives toward future goals rather than simply seeking immediate gratifications. After infancy a person's ability to acquire
almost all other instrumental techniques depends upon language, and
most cooperation with others, which is so vital to human adaptation,
depends upon the use of a shared system of meanings. Indeed, the capacity to direct the self into the future, which we shall term "ego functioning," depends upon a person having verbal symbols with which he
constructs an internalized symbolic version of the world which he can
manipulate in imaginative trial and error before committing himself to
irrevocable actions.
   To understand the importance of language to ego functioning, we
must appreciate that in order for anyone to understand, communicate,
and think about the ceaseless flow of his experiences, he must be able to
divide his experiences into categories. No one can start from the
beginning and build up his own system of categorization. Each child
must learn his culture's system of categorizing, not only in order to communicate with others in the society, but also in order to think coherently. Each culture is distinctive in the way in which its members
categorize their experiences and its vocabulary is, in essence, the catalogue of the categories into which the culture divides its world and its
experiences.[25]
   The proper learning of words and their meanings and of the syntax of

---

   away so they don't fall into the milk. The head is for the purpose of growing
   horns and so his mouth can be somewhere. The horns are to butt with and
   the mouth to moo with.
      Under the cow hangs milk. It is arranged for milking. When people milk,
   milk comes and there never is an end to the supply. How the cow does it I
   have not yet realized, but it makes more and more. The cow has a fine sense
   of smell and one can smell it far away. This is the reason for fresh air in the
   country.
      A man cow is called an ox. The ox is not a mammal. The cow does not
   eat much but what it eats it eats twice so that it gets enough. When it is
   hungry it moos and when it says nothing at all it is because its insides are
   full up with grass.

the language is essential to human adaptation, but there is no assurance that it will be taught or learned correctly. The correctness and the stability of the child's learning rests upon his teachers, primarily upon the members of his family. It depends upon their meaning systems and the way in which they reason but also upon the consistency of their use of words and of their responses to the child's usage.* The topic of how the child learns language and its importance to his development will be amplified extensively as we follow the course of his development.

The enculturation of boys and girls differs in all societies. Each sex is taught a somewhat different array of skills and knowledge according to the society's gender-role divisions of the tasks of living. Raising vegetables, the priesthood, teaching in grade schools, for example, may be predominantly male activities in some societies and female activities in others. However, child rearing and the maintenance of the home are female functions in virtually all societies, and hunting and warfare are rarely part of the female role.

The Family Type and Child Rearing

Within the limits set by the biological make-up of man that divides the nuclear family into two generations and two genders and imposes certain functions upon the family, families exist in an endless number of forms, varying with the culture and subserving differing functions for the parents and children. Families can be classified in different ways; as patrilinear or matrilinear, patriarchal or matriarchal, patrilocal or matrilocal; as monogamous, polygynous, or polyandrous; as nuclear or extended; or according to various rules of exogamy that help direct the choice of partners. Here, we shall draw attention to two general types of family organization that we commonly encounter in order to highlight some contemporary problems of family life.

The extended family with strong kinship ties will be contrasted with the more self-contained isolated nuclear family of parents and their children that is becoming increasingly prevalent in an industrial and highly mobile society.

* We know, for example, from direct observation of family interaction and tests of family members individually and collectively that the styles of communication and meanings in families with schizophrenic offspring are strikingly vague and idiosyncratic. The verbal and nonverbal cues, punishments, and rewards of one parent are apt to be inconsistent and those of the two parents conflicting.

The Extended Kinship Family

We shall first take a model, an approximate model that is not specific to any society, of an extended kinship system common in societies with essentially nonmigratory populations. It may be applied to some very different types of families such as the Mexican village family, the Hopi, and the Sicilian peasant. However, it is of importance to us because many immigrant or second-generation families are emerging from this form of family life and continue to have values based upon it. Indeed, in modified form, extended families remain fairly common in contemporary urban populations. In the extended kinship system, the nuclear family is not clearly demarcated from the larger network of relatives. The various functions of a family are shared by the relatives. The parents have help in raising their children, who, reciprocally, have many surrogate parents. The influence of the eccentricities and deficiencies of the parents is minimized, and the impact of the individuality of parents upon children is also lessened. Advice and support are readily available to the parents. As at least one of the parents remains close to his or her family of origin, the couple are not completely dependent upon one another for tangible support and emotional complementation. Indeed, the husband and wife tend to carry out parallel functions rather than interacting in carrying out shared functions. In a study of London families, Bott[3] found that the women in modified extended families tended to spend much of their time with female relatives—sisters, sisters-in-law, mothers-in-law—whereas the men spent very little time in the home, making the pub the center of their nonoccupational activities. Persons who grow up in extended families have ample opportunity to observe and practice child-rearing techniques. Little girls often are assigned to care for children of relatives. Further, in communities where both parents are reared in a similar type of family and observe a number of other similar families intimately, the spouses enter marriage with relatively compatible ideas of the roles of husbands and wives and of how children are to be raised. Particularly in nonindustrial rural communities, few new influences accrue to change the family pattern and parental roles from generation to generation. The family here is an organization which places emphasis upon the transmission of traditional ways of adaptation to the environment and upon the ways of living together that evolved slowly with the culture.

The extended family tends to provide security through furnishing clear patterns of how to live and relate to others. It has the disadvantage of retarding changes in adaptive techniques as required in a rapidly changing scientific era. The extended family breaks down as industrial societies demand that the participants, both labor and management, follow opportunities for employment. It would be erroneous to consider that the modified extended family is found only among the lower socioeconomic groups. The strength and power of some wealthy industrial and banking families has been heightened by the kinship loyalties.*

The Isolated Nuclear Family

For an ever increasing number of American families the extended kinship ties have been broken by social and geographic mobility. A family pattern has evolved in which the couple is often on its own very soon after marriage. Marriage, for many, marks the final achievement of independence from parents, and the marital partners are expected to be the heads of their own family. Marriages, particularly in cities, often cross ethnic and religious lines. This rapid reshuffling of ethnic influences and the fracturing of kinship ties contribute to the unprecedented social mobility and scientific progress that has occurred. This pattern enables each generation to raise its children differently rather than according to set patterns that become unsuited to changing needs.† However, a gross admixture of mores results which impinges upon the children.

There is little assurance that a family which arises from the joining of two dissimilar backgrounds, rather than through the trial and error of many generations, will be suited for rearing stable children. The isolated family is subject to many strains, and often the insecurities provoked by the rapidly changing society lead to a pursuit of conformity due to a need for standards that are no longer inherent in the customs and values of the family.‡

The atomization of family life into isolated nuclear families has placed

* The family of the late President Kennedy offers a particularly clear example of the advantages that can come from the unified purposes and mutual support of members of an extended family.
† Differentiating so sharply between extended and isolated nuclear families serves to accentuate some of the problems confronting the family as an institution in the United States at the present time. In actuality a large proportion of families do not fit clearly into either category but are parts of modified extended families in which the father is the head of his nuclear family but can expect support from his and his wife's parents and siblings, particularly in emergencies.
‡ Overt and clear communication of needs, wishes, and expectations becomes increasingly important to intrafamilial harmony as roles and role expectations become

many additional strains upon the family and its members. As Parsons[17] has properly pointed out, the high divorce rates and even higher incidence of marital conflict do not bespeak a diminishing importance of the family as has been so often assumed. Indeed, despite the frequency of divorce a larger proportion of the American population is married now than at any period in the past. The increasing disruptions of the family, aside from reflecting a greater ease in obtaining divorce, are a result of the greater importance of the family, the increased number of functions subsumed by the family, and the greater dependency of the spouses upon one another for meeting their essential needs. Without the help of relatives, the wife must often be mother, housekeeper, laundress, cleaning woman, and cook; she is also supposed to provide the major companionship for her husband, and be a stimulating sexual partner or consider herself a failure as a woman. In her spare time (what spare time?) she may be expected to be a good bridge player, golfer, and auxiliary teacher for her children. Her training for household tasks and raising children is often meager, as her education had been directed primarily toward earning a living or pursuing a career. The husband, in turn, finds that in addition to earning a living he is required to be an auxiliary nursemaid, a general handyman, gardener, playmate for his children, companion for his wife. In most societies many of these functions are carried out by persons other than the spouses; couples do not necessarily expect companionship or even sexual gratification from one another. In the contemporary American family there have been notable shifts in the roles of husband and wife and in the division of functions between the couple; such changes have created new strains on the marital relationship and caused disturbances in child-rearing patterns and insecurities in parental roles and functions. Exogamy is not only important to assure a constant reshuffling of genes and to avoid the perpetuation of harmful mutations, but also to prevent cultural inbreeding that can lead families to become too idiosyncratic in terms of the larger society to rear children for life in the society. However, currently the admixture of family backgrounds sometimes becomes so marked that a workable family pattern does not evolve, and the two parents inculcate divergent social and cultural mores and concepts.

---

less definite and less implicitly understood by the family members. What had been implicitly understood in the family of origin may be misunderstood in the marital family. Such considerations enter into the efforts of psychiatrists and marital counselors to improve verbal communication between couples.

A mature and workable personality integration is not achieved simply through nurturance of inborn directives and potentialities but requires positive direction and guidance in a suitable interpersonal environment and social system. The positive molding forces have been largely overlooked because they are built into the institutions and mores of all societies and into the omnipresent family which everywhere has unknowingly been given the task of carrying out the basic socialization and enculturation of the new generation. Man's biological make-up requires that he grow up in a family or a reasonable substitute for it, not only for protection and nurturance during his immaturity but in order to be directed into becoming an integrated person who has assimilated the techniques, knowledge, and roles he requires for adaptation and survival. It requires that he grow into and internalize the institutions and roles of structured social systems as well as identify with persons who themselves have assimilated the culture. He acquires characteristics through identification but also by reactions to parental objects and through finding reciprocal roles with them. His integration is guided by the dynamic structure of the family in which he grows up and which channels his drives and guides him into proper gender and generation roles and provides a space relatively free from role conflict in which the immature child can develop and be secure. His appreciation of the worth and meaning of both social roles and institutions is affected by the manner in which his parents fill their roles, relate maritally, and behave in other contexts. The capacities to have the verbal tools necessary for collaborative interaction with others, to think and to direct the self, depend greatly upon the tutelage within the family and upon the parents' styles of communicating.

It becomes clear that numerous sources of deviant personality development open before us when we consider the implications of this concept of the nature of man and his adaptation. It is apparent, of course, that theories which hold that man could be free of neurosis and other emotional problems if only he were rid of the repressions required by society are not only fallacious but sources of considerable harm. Without a social system and its directives and the delimitations they set, there can be no individual freedom and, indeed, no human could develop into a person, and probably could not even survive.

References

1. David F. Aberle, *The Psychosocial Analysis of a Hopi Life-History*, Comparative Psychology Monographs, Vol. 21, No. 1., Serial No. 107 (Berkeley: University of California Press, 1951).
2. Nathan Ackerman, *The Psychodynamics of Family Life* (New York: Basic Books, 1958).
3. Elizabeth Bott, "Urban Families: Conjugal Roles and Social Network," *Human Relations*, 8 (1955), 345–384.
4. Roger Brown, "Language: The System and Its Acquisition," in *Social Psychology* (New York: Free Press, 1965).
5. Hilde Bruch, "Transformation of Oral Impulses in Eating Disorders," *Psychiatric Quarterly*, 35 (1961), 458–481.
6. Irvin Child, *Italian or American? The Second-Generation Conflict* (New Haven: Yale University Press, 1943).
7. *Daedalus*, Journal of the American Academy of Arts and Sciences, issue on "The Negro American," Fall, 1965.
8. Erik H. Erikson, *Childhood and Society* (New York: W. W. Norton, 1950).
9. E. Franklin Frazier, *The Negro Family in the United States* (Chicago: University of Chicago Press, 1939).
10. Anna Freud and Dorothy Burlingham, *Infants Without Families* (New York: International Universities Press, 1944).
11. August B. Hollingshead and Fredrick C. Redlich, *Social Class and Mental Illness* (New York: John Wiley & Sons, 1958).
12. Alfred C. Kinsey, Wardell Pomeroy, and Clyde Martin, *Sexual Behavior in the Human Male* (Philadelphia: W. B. Saunders, 1948).
13. Theodore Lidz, "Family Organization and Personality Structure," in *The Family and Human Adaptation: Three Lectures* (New York: International Universities Press, 1963).
14. Theodore Lidz, "The Family, Language, and Ego Functions," in *The Family and Human Adaptation: Three Lectures* (New York: International Universities Press, 1963).
15. Theodore Lidz, Stephen Fleck, and Alice R. Cornelison, *Schizophrenia and the Family* (New York: International Universities Press, 1965).
16. Talcott Parsons, "The Incest Taboo in Relation to Social Structure and the Socialization of the Child," in *Social Structure and Personality* (New York: Free Press, 1964).
17. Talcott Parsons and Robert F. Bales, *Family, Socialization and Interaction Process* (Glencoe, Ill.: Free Press, 1955).
18. Leo W. Simmons, *Sun Chief: The Autobiography of a Hopi Indian* (New Haven: Yale University Press, 1945).
19. René A. Spitz, "Hospitalism: An Inquiry into the Genesis of Psychiatric Conditions in Early Childhood," *The Psychoanalytic Study of the Child*, Vol. 1 (New York: International Universities Press, 1945), pp. 53–74.

20. William Thomas and Florian Znaniecki, *The Polish Peasant in Europe and America* (New York: Alfred A. Knopf, 1927).
21. United States Department of Labor, Office of Policy Planning and Research, *The Negro Family: The Case for National Action* (Washington, D.C.: U.S. Government Printing Office, 1965).
22. G. Varga, *Little Novels of Sicily* (New York: Grove Press, 1953).
23. Benjamin Lee Whorf, "Discussion of Hopi Linguistics" (1937) in John Carroll (ed.), *Language, Thought, and Reality: Selected Writings of Benjamin Lee Whorf* (New York: M.I.T. Press and John Wiley & Sons, 1956).
24. Benjamin Lee Whorf, "The Relation of Habitual Thought and Behavior to Language" (1939), in John Carroll (ed.), *Language, Thought, and Reality: Selected Writings of Benjamin Lee Whorf* (New York: M.I.T. Press and John Wiley & Sons, 1956).
25. Benjamin Lee Whorf, *Language, Thought, and Reality: Selected Writings of Benjamin Lee Whorf*, ed. John Carroll (New York: M.I.T. Press and John Wiley & Sons, 1956).
26. Mark Zborowski and Elizabeth Herzog, *Life Is with People: The Jewish Little-town of Eastern Europe* (New York: International Universities Press, 1952).

Suggested Reading

Norman Bell and Ezra Vogel (eds.), *A Modern Introduction to the Family* (Glencoe, Ill.: Free Press, 1960).
Gerald Handel (ed.), *Psychosocial Interior of the Family* (Chicago: Aldine Publishing Co., 1967).
Theodore Lidz, *The Family and Human Adaptation: Three Lectures* (New York: International Universities Press, 1963).
Talcott Parsons and Robert F. Bales, *Family, Socialization and Interaction Process* (Glencoe, Ill.: Free Press, 1955).
George Simpson, *People in Families* (New York: Thomas Y. Crowell, 1960).

CHAPTER 3

❦ ❦ ❦

The Life Cycle

IN THE ENSUING CHAPTERS we shall follow the child through his life cycle, his course from his emergence from his mother's womb along the circuitous route until, weighted by years and with dimming memory, he returns to the earth, the mother of all living things. No two persons are alike, and the path one follows is never the same as another's, for we are part of the infinite variety of an inexhaustible nature. The course of life that we intend to follow will be an abstraction that is no one's, but that of Everyman containing the essentials of all.

Despite the uniqueness of each individual and the different ways and varied environments in which they are raised, all persons are endowed with physical make-ups that are essentially alike and with similar biological needs that must be met. In common with all living things their lives go through a cycle of maturation, maturity, decline, and death. In common with all human beings each person goes through a prolonged period of dependent immaturity, forms intense bonds to those who nurture him, and never becomes free of his need for others; and he matures sexually relatively late as if the evolutionary process took into account his need to learn how to live himself and how to raise offspring. Each individual requires many years to learn adaptive techniques and become an integrated person, and he depends upon a culture and a society to provide his essential environment; he relies upon thought and foresight to find a path through life and therefore becomes aware of the passage of time and his changing position in his life cycle. From an early age he knows that his years of life are numbered; at times he bemoans the fact and at times he is glad of it; but in some way he learns to come to terms with his mortality and the realization that his life is a one-time venture in a very small segment of time and space. These and many other such similarities make possible the generalizations and abstractions necessary for the scientific study of personality development.

The Phasic Nature of Personality Development and the Life Cycle

The development of the personality* and the course of the life cycle unfold in phases, not at a steady pace. The process is not like climbing up a hill and down the other side, but more akin to a Himalayan expedition during which camps must be made at varying altitudes, guides found, the terrain explored, skills acquired, rests taken before moving up to the next level, and the descent is also made in stages. The child goes through periods of relative quiescence and then undergoes another marked change as he moves into a new phase of life, which opens new potentialities, provides new areas to explore, and poses new challenges for him to master that require him to learn new sets of skills and abilities. Thus, when the infant learns to crawl and can move toward objects that attract him, a new world opens before him that enables him to channel his ebullient energy in a new way, permits a new zest to become manifest, and opens up opportunities for new learning. But it also alters his mother's life and the relationship between mother and child, and he will have to learn to relate differently, expect rewards for different types of performance, and gain greater control of his own behavior before achieving a new relative equilibrium. Whereas his parents had always been delighted with any display of new activities, now they seek to restrain or somehow limit his behavior, and the child has difficulty in ad-

* In discussing the life cycle we follow a convention whose purpose is to lessen confusion by using the word *maturation* when referring to biological unfolding and physical growth, and *development* when referring to personality functions.

justing to such changed attitudes. Similarly, a child may have settled down into a reasonably stable relationship with his family and peers, and found his pace and place in his school world, when the sudden spurt of growth that precedes puberty alters the proportions of his body, almost making it unfamiliar to its owner, and then the surges of sexual feelings aroused by hormonal changes must be managed; and a period of relative calm and security has ended.

The phasic nature of the life cycle derives from several interlocking factors.

1. Physical maturation obviously plays a major role. The acquisition of certain abilities must wait upon the maturation of the organism. No amount of training can teach a child to walk until the nerve tracts that permit voluntary discrete movements of the lower limbs become functional. However, even after maturation permits the acquisition of a new attribute, gaining the skills and knowledge needed to develop it is a very lengthy procedure, but is amenable to specific training and education. The amount of practice required before a child can properly use his hands and learn to measure space three-dimensionally is enormous; but because much of it seems random movement or play, the quantity is rarely appreciated. Adequate mastery of simple skills must precede their incorporation into more complicated activities.

Then, there are changes produced by shifts in physical equilibrium that come with phasic changes in the process of maturation. The metamorphosis of puberty furnishes a prime example of how new inner forces provoke change without regard to prior developmental progress: the menopausal "change of life" also tends to force a basic reorientation.

2. The society, through the child's parents, through his peer groups, and through the roles it establishes for persons of differing ages, sets expectations that promote shifts in life patterns. At the age of five or six, for example, a child is moved into the role of the schoolchild which includes many new demands as well as new privileges. Becoming a married person involves socially set expectations such as an ability and willingness to rescind areas of independence to care for and consider the needs of a spouse. But, in order for any society to remain viable, the expectations and roles it establishes must be compatible with people's capacities and needs at each period of life.*

* Differences in societal institutions and role allocations create differences in some aspects of the life cycle in each society and even in subsystems of the same society—including differences in just when some phasic shifts occur in the life cycle. Thus,

3. The passage of time is, in itself, a determinant of phasic changes, not only because there is a need to move into age-appropriate roles, but also because changes in physical make-up require changed attitudes and self-concepts, as when people reach middle life and realize that their life story is approaching a climax.

4. The individual's cognitive development and decline play a significant role in creating phasic shifts. The capacity to assume responsibility for the self and the direction of one's own life depends upon the increasing abilities to think, to communicate, and to know the nature of the world and of the people with whom one lives. Yet the capacity to think is very limited before the child can speak; and, as we shall see, the child's cognitive development does not progress at an even pace, for qualitatively different capacities emerge in rather discrete stages.

5. The child gains attributes, capacities, roles, and, particularly, capacities for self-control and self-direction by internalizing parental characteristics. The little child clearly needs a "surrogate ego" in the form of one or both parents to direct his life. The internalization of these directive influences also takes place in stages in relationship to his physical, intellectual, and emotional development and the expectations established for him.

Progression, Fixation, and Regression

The course of any life contains a series of inevitable developmental crises that arise out of the need to meet the new challenges that are inherent in the life cycle. Through surmounting these crises the individual gains new strength, self-sufficiency, and integrity. The avoidance of challenge leads to stagnation. Each person meets each developmental crisis somewhat differently but similarities exist in the ways people meet similar developmental problems, and there is a repetitive pattern in how the same individual is likely to surmount various crises in his life.

There is often a pause before a child achieves the confidence and vitality to venture into the strange uncertainties of a new phase of life. The need for emotional security sets limits upon the pace of development.

---

the Okinawan child is expected to have very little capacity for self-direction before the age of five, but is given considerable responsibility, particularly for siblings, soon thereafter.

Adolescence is different in societies in which sexual intercourse occurs freely at or before puberty, and initiation rites lead rather directly into adult status and responsibilities. Old age differs from the period in the United States in societies where people are aged at forty-five and very few live beyond fifty or sixty.

The child constantly faces in two directions and is prey to opposing motivations. There is an inner impetus to expansion and the mastery of new skills and situations, a desire for greater independence and new prerogatives, and a wish to become more grown up like the parental figures he seeks to emulate; but movement into new areas brings insecurity, inability to manage the new situation creates frustrations, and independence means giving up dependency. The ensuing anxieties tend to direct the child toward regaining the security of shelter and dependency and to renounce for a time further developmental movement.

The child needs support and guidance in order to progress properly. In some instances, he may need to be restrained from unbridled and untutored use of new capacities, as when he first walks or when he becomes sexually mature; whereas in other circumstances he may need help or even some prodding to move into the next phase, as when he is reluctant to leave his mother to attend school, or timid about assuming the responsibilities of marriage. The developmental hazards lie on both sides: too much support can lead the child to become overly dependent; too little can leave the child stranded or struggling to keep afloat.

The failure to cope with the essential tasks of a developmental phase leaves the child unprepared to move forward into the next phase. Emotional insecurity, lagging physical maturation, and premature pressures upon the child to cope before he has the necessary skills and emotional mastery are among the major reasons for such failures. The child gives up and tries to remain where he is developmentally; or, more usually, he moves ahead in some spheres but continues to make repetitive efforts to master what he has failed to surmount. Energies are squandered in coping with old problems. A child who does not receive enough gratification during infancy may continue to suck his thumb, seeking the gratification he needed then; or a school-age child who never gained adequate security in the home continues to seek maternal protection when his peers are secure when with one another. Such developmental arrests are termed *fixations*. The movement backward to an earlier developmental phase in which the individual felt secure is termed *regression;*[*] and paradoxically

---

[*] Regression is said to occur to points or levels of fixation. Freud [7] used the analogy of an advancing army leaving troops at strongholds along its line of march; this "fixation" of troops at the strongpoints progressively weakens the advancing contingents but provides a secure line to which to retreat if the army experiences a setback. However, it seems more suitable to consider fixation as repetitive attempts to resolve old unsolved problems or tasks, and regression as the gaining of relief from anxiety by returning to a period of security or to former ways that do not arouse anxiety.

regression is part of developmental progress, for every child will, at times, regress in order to regain security. He may fall back to regain stability after a forward thrust or when some external threat upsets his equilibrium and makes him anxious. The small child progresses with security when he feels that parental protection can be found when he needs it at the center of his expanding world.

Although fixations and regressions are means of maintaining or regaining security, they almost inevitably create insecurities in turn. The child remains improperly prepared to meet the developmental tasks of the next stage of the life cycle; the adult cannot accept the opportunities and challenges that await him. He remains securely attached to his mother, for example, but his mother cannot provide security in the workaday world; he does not achieve interdependence with a spouse; his mother's protection becomes fragile and her advice is no longer that of an omniscient figure but only that of an aging adult; she becomes dependent and the reversal of the dependency is resented by the adult child who has never achieved security as a self-sufficient adult.

Even though the child is pulled in two directions and the desires to remain secure can be powerful, the motivations to move forward are greater. He is carried along by his growth, by the impulsions for stimulation and new experiences, by his drives, by his need for approbation and affection from the persons significant to him, by the desire for companionship with peers, by the yearning of his body for another, by the needs of survival, by the roles provided by the society, by his desire for progeny, by awareness of his mortality, and by other such influences which we shall examine in the ensuing chapters.

The Divisions of the Life Cycle

The division of the life cycle into developmental stages in this book follows fairly clear lines of demarcation. *Infancy* approximates the first fifteen months of life when the baby can neither properly walk nor talk and requires almost total nurturant care both for survival and for the stimulation necessary for his emotional and cognitive development. The *toddler* stage starts with the ability to ambulate and take initiative which outruns the child's capacities to comprehend, speak, and delimit himself: the ensuing essential control by parental figures leads to critical conflicts over control and initiative. In the *preschool* or *oedipal* period the child finds his place as a boy or girl within his family: he must rescind his erotized attachments to his mother as well as his egocentric view of his relationship to her, and internalize parental directives sufficiently to move into peer groups. The *juvenile* moves beyond his family into peer groups and school where he gains acceptance and position on the basis of his achievements and his personality gains new coherence through the impact of how others relate to him and help him define himself. *Adolescence* involves the discrepancy between sexual maturation and incomplete physical maturity, and between the upsurge of sexual impulsions and the unpreparedness for adult responsibilities and parenthood. Adolescence will be divided into three substages: the period around puberty starting with the sudden spurt of prepubertal growth; mid-adolescence with its expansive strivings and the revolt against adult standards and controls and its conformity to peer-group values; late adolescence, when delimitation and the achievement of an ego identity are central issues and yearnings for intimacy become major motivations. In the *young adult* period the personality undergoes marked modifications through the choice of an occupation, in relation to marital choice and adjustment, and the reorientation required by parenthood and its responsibilities. *Middle age* concerns the changes that follow upon the person's moving toward and away from the peak years of his life: when children usually are no longer a central preoccupation and the declining physical capacities often lead to stock taking. In *old age* the physical abilities become increasingly limited; men retire, mental capacities decline, and persons again become more or less dependent upon others for the provision of essential needs.

The description and study of the salient features of these developmental stages evolve from three rather different approaches to understanding the phasic emergence of essential attributes of the personality: those of Freud, Erikson, and Piaget. The orientations and the essential contributions of each of these investigators and theorists will be included in the presentation of each developmental stage even when they differ or run counter to the conceptualizations of the writer. Familiarity with these approaches is essential to understanding the literature and language of personality development and psychopathology. In the ensuing paragraphs only brief orienting material will be offered so as to provide an overview of these orientations and a perspective concerning the emergence of the phasic and epigenetic approaches to personality development.

Freud's Phases of Psychosexual Development

Consequent to his epoch-making studies of childhood sexuality, but based primarily on his analytic studies of adults, Freud conceptualized five phases of psychosexual development between birth and maturity: the oral, anal, phallic or oedipal, latency, and genital phases.

The *oral* phase is virtually equivalent to infancy, when the child's needs and energies focus upon nursing and close relatedness to the mother. It is a time of almost complete dependency, with intake at first largely passive but shifting to more active and aggressive incorporation as the infant matures. The lips and mouth are highly erotized and a primary source of sensuous gratification. Either too much or too little oral gratification or some innate predisposition to orality can supposedly cause fixation and unpreparedness to move into the subsequent phases.

The *anal* period follows, and attention was directed to it by the frequency of problems related to bowel functioning, by anal erotic practices in adults, and by certain character traits connected to withholding and letting go. Bowel training was considered a primary developmental task of the second year of life, and the anal zone a primary source of erotic gratification during the period. Fixations at the anal phase have been related to various character traits such as obsessiveness, stubbornness, miserliness, a perduring sense of shame, and many other related characteristics as well as lasting erotization of the anal orifice.

In the *phallic* or *oedipal* period the primary erogenous zone has been considered to shift to the penis in the boy and the clitoris in the girl with an upsurge of sexual feelings toward the parent of the opposite sex. The boy's wish to possess the mother and be rid of the rival father, and the girl's desire for the father and jealousy of the mother—the oedipal situation—comes in conflict with reality, creates fear of retribution from the hated parent, and leads the child to repress his sexual feelings and his possessiveness of the desired parent. Instead, the boy pursues the more realistic goal of ultimately becoming a person like his father who can possess a person like his mother, and the reverse occurs in the girl with variations and differences that will be elaborated in the presentation of the oedipal phase. The child gains strength by identifying with the previously hated and feared parent, internalizes parental controls, and becomes more oriented to reality.* The oedipal situation is considered a

* The oedipal complex was named by Freud after the mythical king of Thebes who unknowingly fulfilled his predicted fate by killing his father, Laius, and marrying his mother, Jocasta, after solving the famous riddle of the Sphinx. When eventually the incestuous nature of the marriage was revealed, Jocasta hanged herself and Oedipus blinded himself. Freud considered that the myth symbolized an unconscious wish in all men that had to be overcome in their lives, and that unresolved residua created problems for everyone but serious problems for some that explained

central event in personality development and critical to the patterning of all subsequent interpersonal relationships.

Following the resolution of the oedipal conflicts the child enters the *latency* period—a period when sexual impulses are supposedly latent, either because of a biological subsidence of libido or because of the repression of the sexual impulses that seemed to the child to endanger him.

The *genital* phase starts with the upsurge of puberty, with an erogenous reinvestment of the phallus in the male but supposedly with a shift from the clitoris to the vagina in the girl. If the individual has passed through all previous phases without undue fixations, he becomes capable of mature sexuality. The capacity for genital sexuality was originally equated with the achievement of emotional maturity.

In a strict sense Freud was not proposing stages in personality development but tracing the vicissitudes of the sexual energy which he termed *libido* and deemed a prime motivating force in all human behavior. He considered that the libidinal investment (cathexis)* of the oral, anal, and phallic zones in turn was an inherent part of physical maturation. The origins of these concepts are significant because as foundations of psychoanalytic theory they continued—and continue—to exert profound influence upon the subsequent development of the theory.†

---

much psychopathology. Freud did not invent the oedipus complex; he discovered it. The story of Oedipus is the myth of the hero found (in one variant or another) in virtually all parts of the world: the tale of the child supposedly put to death lest he eventually kill his father or some father-substitute but who grows up in a foreign land and returns unknowingly to kill his father and marry his mother. Among the most primitive versions are the very ancient myths of Uranus and Kronos, and among the most sophisticated variants that of Shakespeare's Hamlet.

Perhaps it should be noted that the Oedipus myth proper concerns a father who feared the rivalry of his son (reflecting his own feelings to his father) and a mother who was willing to commit infanticide for her husband's sake. Some myths also hold that Laius introduced sodomy into Attica.

* The German word *Besetzung* was unnecessarily translated by a neologism created from the Greek—*cathexis*—which has come into common usage not only in psychoanalysis but in many related fields. "Cathexis" connotes the charge that attaches the libidinal energy to something, analogous to a positive or negative charge in electricity. Actually, *Besetzung* can properly be translated by the term *investment*, in the sense of an army investing a stronghold, and "invest" or "investment" will be used in this book. The use of the word "cathexis" has become somewhat loose in much of the psychoanalytic literature.

† A theory, like a child, is permanently influenced by its early developmental phases, particularly if such early influences are relegated to the unconscious lest parental figures be offended. Freud had been considering that anxiety states were caused by

Freud also used the phases of psychosexual development in a broader sense, and when the concepts of the various postulated phases of childhood development were divested of such metaphysiological speculations, or when less attention was given to these concepts of energetics, they served to draw attention to important aspects of child development and the parent-child interaction. Thus, to note but a few examples, the critical importance of proper maternal nurturance during infancy to all future emotional security; the relationship between harsh and rigid bowel training to the development of obsessive-compulsive personality traits; the origins of certain adult sexual incompetencies in fixations during the oedipal phase—devolved from appreciation of the phasic nature of childhood development and a focusing upon the critical issues of each phase.

The Epigenetic Principle

Freud's introduction of the *genetic* or *epigenetic principle* has served as a major guide to dynamic studies and theories of personality functioning ever since. In brief, the epigenetic principle maintains that proper developmental progress requires the meeting and surmounting of the distinctive critical tasks of each developmental phase at the proper time and in the proper sequence. The concept was derived from embryology, in which the proper unfolding of the embryo depends upon each organ's arising out of its anlage in the proper sequence and at the proper time, with each development depending upon the proper unfolding of the preceding phase. If something happens that causes a disturbance of development of one aspect of the sequence, a series of maldevelopments will follow in chain. Some such aspects of personality development are obvious and have already been noted in our discussion of the life cycle: a child who cannot stand cannot progress to walking and to experiences in the broader environment he needs in order to develop greater initiative and autonomy. Personality development is not, however, so rigidly set as embryonic maturation; and it is apparent that even though development is impeded or altered, compensations are possible, and deficiencies can even be turned into strengths, which is not the case with the embryo.

---

a damming up of sexual fluids by inhibition or repression of sexual activity, and that neurasthenia was a resultant of excessive sexual activity. The idea of a sexual fluid playing a major role in the production of certain neuroses continued in the modified form of a libido that cathected the various erogenous zones, and that was at first autoerotically invested in the self and then in one or another external object.

We once again recall Helen Keller, who did not learn to use language and remained very immature emotionally until she was seven, as an outstanding example of such plasticity in personality development.*

The Orientations of Sullivan and Erikson

The modifications of psychoanalytic developmental theory formulated by Harry Stack Sullivan[14] and by Erik Erikson[3] have particular pertinence to the orientation of this book.

Sullivan emphasized the importance of the interpersonal transactions between parents and child and the child's development in a social system; and he thus became an important influence in bringing psychoanalytic theory into a working relationship with the behavioral sciences. He also directed attention to the importance of the juvenile period, instead of permitting it to remain the "latency phase," to the significance of the juvenile and youth peer relationships, and to the crucial events of adolescence.

Psychosocial Phases of the Life Cycle

Erikson also opened new approaches by superimposing an epigenesis of psychosocial development upon the psychosexual phases, and by designating the critical psychosocial task of each phase that the individual must surmount in order to be prepared for the next stage. A developmental crisis, so to speak, is inherent in each phase, for the sequence of maturation and development presents new essential problems with which the person must cope. Erikson also went beyond the traditional psychoanalytic psychosexual phases that end with the "genital phase." He emphasized the critical moment of late adolescence, when the personality must gel and a person achieve an ego identity and a capacity for intimacy, and then continued to consider the critical tasks of adult stages of the life cycle. He has formulated eight stages of psychosocial development, focusing upon the specific developmental tasks of each phase and how the society meets the needs by providing essential care, promoting independence, offering roles, and having institutionalized ways of assuring the child's survival, his proper socialization, and his emotional health. The critical tasks of each phase are handled more or less differently in each culture.

* Perhaps Helen Keller was enabled to reach her unusual emotional and intellectual capacities because she had the brilliant Miss Sullivan constantly interpreting the world to her—a compensatory advantage that perhaps no other person has ever had.

As Erikson's paradigms will be discussed when we consider the specific developmental periods, only a résumé will be presented here. In the oral phase of psychosexual development the psychosocial task concerns achievement of a *basic trust* in the self and others, with failures leading to varying degrees of *basic mistrust;* the "basic" is emphasized to convey that the task is not particularly conscious but blends into and forms an inherent component of the total personality. Emphasis in the second year of life is upon the attainment of muscular control in general rather than upon bowel control in particular. In learning self-control the child properly gains a lasting sense of *autonomy,* whereas loss of self-esteem and shaming in the process leads to a pervasive sense of *doubt* and *shame.* In the phallic period the resolution of the oedipal crisis leads to a heightening of conscience, and it is the time when the child needs to develop the prerequisites for masculine or feminine *initiative* or become prey to a deep and lasting *sense of guilt.* The latency period moves the child to school, where the gaining of admiration, approval, and affection depends upon achievement, and now the child must acquire a capacity for *industry* or become subject to an enduring sense of *inferiority.* Erikson then departs from emphasizing the relationship between genital sexuality and emotional maturity and focuses upon the attainment of an ego synthesis by the end of adolescence that affords a sense of *ego identity,* "the accrued confidence that one's ability to maintain an inner sameness and continuity is matched by the sameness and continuity of one's meaning for others";[4] and if this is not attained the person is subject to *identity diffusion.* After achieving a sense of identity, the young adult can move on to achieve a true *intimacy* with another with the concomitant capacity to *distantiate* the self from forces or people whose essence is dangerous to his own; failure almost inevitably leads to *self-absorption.* Then, an interest in producing, guiding, and laying the foundations for the next generation makes the capacity for *generativity* the critical issue in the next phase of adulthood, with *stagnation* the negative outcome. The final phase in the schema concerns the achievement of mature dignity and *integrity* through acceptance of "one's own and only life cycle" and responsibility for how it has turned out, whereas *despair* involves the feeling that this one chance has been wasted and has, in essence, been worthless.

The approach takes cognizance of the fact that the child grows into a social system and must assimilate its institutions and roles, and helps eliminate the untenable concept that civilization through requiring repression is inimical to man's freedom. The specific dichotomies utilized to characterize the critical issues of each phase sharpen the appreciation of the need to cope with tasks rather than simply to pass through a phase free of traumatic influence.* Still, the critical issues selected neglect other personality attributes that seem just as vital, and some that are more important.

Piaget's Approach to the Study of Cognitive Development

Another extremely important approach to the study of the child's development is found in the monumental work of Jean Piaget and his school. The child's cognitive development forms the core of these studies. Piaget has sought to trace and conceptualize how each new capacity develops through the reorganization and expansion of prior capacities by means of the assimilation of new experiences and skills. The epigenetic development of intelligence, language, reasoning, concepts of nature, and the emergence of the categories of time, space, causality, etc., have been scrutinized; but studies of the child's moral development and of the child's play and dreams have also provided new insights and stimulation. Piaget has given but passing attention to the child's emotional development and to interpersonal and social influences upon development, which leaves some serious deficiencies in his observations, explanations, and theory.†

Piaget has developed a complex system to direct his detailed observations of children's cognitive development and to conceptualize them. He traces the ever increasing scope of the child's abilities by the constant process of adaptation of the existing state of the organism to new experiences. The child cannot utilize experiences which his cognitive capacities

* The orientation, however, remains attached to a system of psychosexual phases based on libidinal shifts, even though it places minimal emphasis upon libidinal concepts and more upon the observable unfolding of the individual in his cultural setting, somewhat in contrast to the formulations of the psychoanalytic ego psychology of Hartmann, Kris, Loewenstein,[11] and others. Hartmann's important contributions are not discussed in this chapter, as they have greater importance to efforts to reorganize and revitalize psychoanalytic theory than to developmental psychology.[9, 10]

† Piaget has been interested primarily in epistemology and set out to investigate how man learns to know and the psychological foundations of knowing. His studies led to the discovery and description of a vast amount of knowledge about child development. In evaluating Piaget's work, we must realize his intentions and not criticize him for not studying what we wish he would have studied. However, Piaget follows the French intellectual tradition and Ariès has commented in his book *Centuries of Childhood* [1] that until recently child development meant to the French the child's intellectual development.

are not yet ready to assimilate. The foundations for experiencing develop step by step through the expansion and reorganization of existing capacities as they take in new experiences, and thereby become prepared to react to and utilize more complex experiences. The process of cognitive development is thus understood as a very active process in which the organism is, in a sense, ever reaching out to incorporate new experience within the limits permitted by its capacities and organization at that moment in its development. Piaget's theory posits a constant cognitive reorganization that is more dynamic than either associational psychology, learning theory, or operant conditioning psychology.

Piaget's general orientation cannot be presented succinctly. He and his collaborators have been carrying out their studies for more than forty-five years, and have published hundreds of articles and numerous books, of which a dozen or more have now been translated into English. It is difficult for the uninitiated to begin to find his way into the vast fund of data, and even more difficult to grasp the conceptualizations which are often presented as universals but which sometimes are unsuited to other aspects of the material, and which few readers find as lucid and compelling as Piaget seems to believe them to be. However, as this book will be primarily concerned with his observations rather than with the ramifications of his theory, only a very cursory introduction to his ideas and terminology will be presented in the following paragraphs.*

The reader is likely to be puzzled and even discouraged by the unfamiliar terminology that is an inherent part of Piagetian psychology. Terms such as "aliment," "assimilation," "accommodation," "schema," and "egocentricity" have specific and rather idiosyncratic meanings, and other terms such as "circular reactions" and "decentering" are unique to the system. They do not, however, pose too formidable a barrier. The *aliment* is new experiential food which furnishes the nutriment for cognitive growth. The aliment is *assimilated* by the cognitive processes insofar as they are prepared to do so, and the cognitive processes *accommodate* to include what has been assimilated, reorganizing and expanding in the process. The term *schema* is used primarily in describing the first developmental period, that of sensori-motor development.† A schema is

---

* The reader is referred to J. H. Flavell's *The Developmental Psychology of Jean Piaget*,[6] which provides a fairly comprehensive and highly useful introduction that permits the serious student to read meaningfully in Piaget's various works; and particularly to pages 41–67 for an introduction to the basic theory.
† Schemata are, so to speak, the preverbal sensori-motor equivalents of a system of relations and classes. See Piaget, *The Origins of Intelligence in Children*,[13] p. 385.

a cognitive structure to which experiences are assimilated, and which reorganize in the process. There are "sucking" schemata, "visual," "grasping," "hearing," and other schemata. The organism seeks, so to speak, to repeat schemata that produce new experiences, setting up *circular reactions* in order to gain the reward of new aliment until the aliment is thoroughly assimilated into the schema that has accommodated to it. The development of the child's cognitive abilities through increasingly complex circular reactions will be described in subsequent chapters, which, it is hoped, will help clarify these basic concepts of Piaget's system.*

Piaget's Developmental Periods

Piaget has divided cognitive development into four major periods, which in turn are subdivided into a number of stages and substages. The *sensori-motor* period, which lasts from birth through the first eighteen to twenty-four months, essentially covers preverbal intellectual development. The development of the child's ways of interacting with the world is traced, step by step, from the primitive reflex sucking, hand movements, and the random eye movements of the neonate to the stage when the child uses internalized visual and motoric symbols to invent new means of solving problems at a very simple level. The *preoperational* period follows and lasts until about the time the child enters school. The child becomes capable of using symbols and language. He does not yet have the ability to appreciate the role of another and adapt what he says to the needs of the listener, to note contradictions, or to construct a chain of reasoning. During the period he moves away from his egocentric orientation and from his static ways of thinking as he gains experience and as words become symbols of categories.† The period of *concrete*

---

* One other major aspect of Piaget's orientation requires mention. The newborn is completely egocentric, apprehending only in terms of how a new sensation meets an existing built-in reflex. Development involves a progressive *decentering* until sometime in adolescence the individual places himself in his universe and time in history, and can fit his ideas into abstract systems of logic and thought. However, in each period the child must learn to decenter from an "egocentric" use of his new capacities. The preschool child gradually learns that others see things from a different perspective. The adolescent learns that the manipulation of ideas in his own fantasy is not the same as convincing others who have differing orientations and convictions.
† Piaget's studies of the early phases of the preoperational period are sparse, limiting their usefulness for clarifying the early development of language, but his studies of the later phases of preoperational development contain some of his most significant work.

operations approximates the years between the start of schooling and the onset of puberty and is similar in time to the latency phase. The child has acquired a coherent cognitive system with which he can understand his world and work upon it, and into which he can fit new experiences. The period of *formal operations* starts early in adolescence when the youth becomes capable of conceptualizing, of thinking propositionally, and of using hypotheses. Not all individuals achieve the stage of formal operations, which, as we shall show, may depend upon the extent of a person's formal education.

In following the life cycle we shall focus on the critical aspects of each phase of development, noting how the biological process of maturation provides much of the pattern by opening new potentials and setting limits for the child's capacities, but also on how the culture, through the society and particularly the child's parents, provides expectations, and how the child develops other expectations for himself that help establish the sequence of phases and the crucial issues of each phase. Although attention will be given to the epigenetic concept as a cornerstone of developmental theory, room for compensations and later restitutions will be included. The phases, as in Erikson's approach, are not simply important in themselves, but as part of the larger pattern of how the child grows into an integrated adult.

Panphasic Influences on Personality Development

However, other factors in the developmental process that are not phasic must also be taken into account. Persistent attitudes and styles of the parental figures, and indeed of the social system, pervade all phases of the child's developmental years. It is true that a parent may be more capable of relating adequately to the child in one phase than another because of problems in the parent's own development, but many such influences are panphasic. The obsessive parent not only exerts a deleterious influence upon the child by perfectionistic and rigid efforts to over-control the child's life when he is starting to ambulate and control his bowels, but continues to teach a specific way of coping with life and its anxieties that helps shape the child's personality. The mother who needs to find her own completion through her son is not only likely to interfere with his individuation and need to establish boundaries between himself and her during the second year of life, but also impedes his gaining a sense of autonomy during the oedipal transition, when he leaves her to attend school, in adolescence, and when the youth seeks to gain intimacy with another early in adulthood.

We must also note that *identifications* that are a major factor in shaping the personality also transcend specific periods; and although major patterns of identification may be set during the oedipal transition, later shifts in identification can be of paramount importance. Then, as we mentioned in the chapter on the family, there are the crucial intrafamilial influences involving the parents' relationships with one another, the nature of the family they establish, the structuring influence of this family, and the enculturating capacities of the parents that impinge throughout childhood and transcend any single phase.

The approach taken specifically differentiates from those that explicitly or implicitly consider that the infant will unfold into a mature and well-integrated person as a concomitant of his physical maturation unless there is something innately wrong with him, or unless he is deprived of proper maternal nurture in the first years of life or is seriously traumatized emotionally. Such factors are, of course, critical, but we must also consider the positive influences that go into inculcation of emotional stability, stable integration, coherent identity, intellectual development, and that provide familiarity with roles and institutions, and instill the instrumental techniques required for successful adaptation. Some of the fundamentals of this orientation were introduced when we discussed the family's requisite functions of nurturing, structuring, and enculturating the developing child.

Conscious and Unconscious Mental Processes

As part of the description of the dynamics of the child's development we shall trace the slow organization of his mind, which is part of his personality but not synonymous with it. We shall note the intricate development of the foundations of his concepts of the world during his first few years of life, and his gradual progression to conceptual thinking,[2, 6, 12, 15] and how this epigenesis of his cognitive development intermeshes with his total personality development. But attention will also be directed to the importance of unconscious mentation: how the unconscious processes differ from the conscious in the solving of problems; how they contribute to breadth of experience, and how they utilize unverbalized and diffuse factors in decision making; and how they permit the dreams and fantasy without which men are scarcely human. We shall also examine how drives and impulses that must be denied direct expression lest they provoke punishment or loss of self-esteem continue unconsciously to influence behavior and thought in various subtle ways.

The Id, Ego, and Superego

We shall also note the emergence of what is usefully termed an *ego*, a construct used to designate the decision-making, self-directing aspects of the self or of the personality. Ego functions depend upon the use of language to construct an internalized representation of the world which can be manipulated in trial-and-error fashion to weigh potential outcomes and to contain gratification of wish, drive, and impulsion in order to cope with "reality" and the pursuit of ultimate objectives. The ego has been conceived as mediating between *id* impulses—the pressure of the basic drives and their pleasure-seeking or tension-releasing derivatives*—and the *superego*, a construct that designates the internalized parental directives and, to some extent, also the internalized parental figures who continue to seem somewhat outside of the self. The superego, like the parents in childhood, can provide conscious and unconscious support to the ego in its struggle against pressures from id impulsions and can also punish as would imagined parental figures. The id pressures can oppose the superego sufficiently to force the ego to allow adequate gratifications.† It is essential, at this point, to indicate that these are simply highly useful ways of conceptualizing the structure of the personality, to clarify conflicts and to help explain why certain motives and thoughts are repressed and kept out of consciousness. There are other useful ways of

---

* Freud considered the *pleasure principle* a major directive in development and behavior. The organism is motivated to seek pleasure and avoid unpleasure (*Unlust*). Pleasure was, at times, equated with tension reduction, and tension—such as that created by uncathected libido—was equated with unpleasure. However, Freud also recognized that some pleasure was not simply the reduction of tension. The *id* seeks to follow the "pleasure principle," but the ego must modify its strivings in keeping with the demands of the superego and reality, or the "reality principle," for purposes of adaptation.

† The superego is often called the *ego ideal*. However, "ego ideal" is a term used in several different contexts and is no longer safe to use without specifying just what is meant by it. Freud tended to endow the id with all of the attributes of his unconscious regions of the mind. Id impulses are clearly often all too conscious. It seems better to use the id, ego, and superego constructs as divisions of the personality, or the self, and not of mental processes. The ego has been termed an "organ" of the mind—which is a highly misleading concept. It might be considered a function of the mind, ego functions depending upon language and the internalization of experiences. The reasons for this partial departure from custom will be clarified after the proper foundations have been established (see Chapter 8).

conceptualizing the structure of the personality,* and grave difficulties arise if these abstractions are reified and considered as clearly differentiated parts of either the mind or the personality. These concepts will be presented in greater detail in Chapter 8 after more adequate foundations for their consideration have been established.

Now, as we are about to start the infant on his course through life, observing rather than guiding the process, we must be prepared for the countless dangers that beset his path. He is sturdy, the product of millions of years of trial and error. During the first years, when he neither knows the way nor possesses the necessary strength or skills, he will be guided by persons who cherish him, and predecessors have trodden trails for him to follow. None traverse the life cycle unscathed. A smooth passage through each developmental phase is neither possible nor even an ideal. It provides a conceptual pattern against which to measure the actual. Parents and the society strive to provide a nontraumatic passage; they do not foster deviance because they know that it comes unbidden and despite all efforts to avert it. Overprotection or development in an extremely stable and homogeneous setting is likely to produce colorless individuals.† As everyday experience often shows, difficulty can strengthen one; trauma can produce defenses that can serve well in later emergencies; deprivation can harden. It is not a matter of adhering to a norm, but one of balance and integration. A seed bedded in but a handful of soil on a boulder can sometimes grow into a large tree by sending roots down to the earth, roots that firmly wedge it onto the rock: and the sequoia, the greatest of trees, grows best when forest fires periodically threaten its existence; they often scar it deeply but assure the proper composition of the soil.

* As, for example, in Fairbairn's psychoanalytic "object-relations" theory, which does not utilize concepts of the id, ego, and superego in this fashion. See W. R. D. Fairbairn, *Psychoanalytic Studies of the Personality*.[5]
† See the study of R. Grinker *et al.* of middle-class, midwestern students at a Y.M.C.A. college, whom he has designated as "homoclites," persons who are unimaginative and uninterestingly average.[8]

References

1. Phillipe Ariès, *Centuries of Childhood* (New York: Alfred A. Knopf, 1962).
2. Jerome Bruner, Jacqueline Goodnow, and George Austin, *A Study of Thinking* (New York: John Wiley & Sons, 1956).
3. Erik H. Erikson, *Childhood and Society* (New York: W. W. Norton, 1950).
4. Erik H. Erikson, "Growth and Crises of the 'Healthy Personality,'" *Psychological Issues*, Vol. 1, No. 1, Monograph No. 1 (New York: International Universities Press, 1959), p. 89.
5. W. Ronald D. Fairbairn, *Psycho-Analytic Studies of the Personality* (London: Tavistock Publications, 1952).
6. John H. Flavell, *The Developmental Psychology of Jean Piaget* (Princeton, N.J.: Van Nostrand, 1963).
7. Sigmund Freud, *A General Introduction to Psychoanalysis* (New York: Boni & Liveright, 1916–1917).
8. Roy Grinker, Sr., Roy Grinker, Jr., and James Timberlake, " 'Mentally Healthy' Young Males (Homoclites)," *Archives of General Psychiatry*, 6 (1962), 405–453.
9. Heinz Hartmann, *Ego Psychology and the Problem of Adaptation* (New York: International Universities Press, 1958).
10. Heinz Hartmann, *Essays on Ego Psychology: Selected Papers on Psychoanalytic Theory* (New York: International Universities Press, 1964).
11. Heinz Hartmann, Ernest Kris, and R. Loewenstein, "Comments on the Formation of Psychic Structure," in *The Psychoanalytic Study of the Child*, Vol. 2 (New York: International Universities Press, 1946).
12. Jerome Kagan and Howard Moss, *From Birth to Maturity* (New York: John Wiley & Sons, 1962).
13. Jean Piaget, *The Origins of Intelligence in Children*, trans. Margaret Cook (New York: W. W. Norton, 1963).
14. Harry Stack Sullivan, *The Interpersonal Theory of Psychiatry* (1946–1947), ed. Helen Perry and M. Gawel (New York: W. W. Norton, 1953).
15. Lev S. Vygotsky, *Thought and Language*, ed. and trans. Eugenia Hanfmann and Gertrude Vakar (New York: M.I.T. Press and John Wiley & Sons, 1962).

Suggested Reading

Erik H. Erikson, "The Problem of Ego Identity," *Journal of the American Psychoanalytic Association*, 4 (1956), 56–121.
Erik H. Erikson, "Growth and Crises of the 'Healthy Personality,'" *Psy-*

chological Issues, Vol. 1, No. 1, Monograph No. 1 (New York: International Universities Press, 1959).

John H. Flavell, "Basic Properties of Cognitive Functioning," in *The Developmental Psychology of Jean Piaget* (Princeton, N.J.: Van Nostrand, 1963).

Sigmund Freud, *New Introductory Lectures on Psycho-Analysis* (New York: W. W. Norton, 1933).

PART II

The Life Cycle

CHAPTER 4

❀ ❀ ❀ ❀

The Neonate and
the New Mother

THE BIRTH OF THE BABY marks a long awaited moment. The expectant mother has spent long hours daydreaming about the fetus growing within her; daydreaming about whom the child will resemble, its future accomplishments, and what the child will mean in her life and her husband's. Her reveries have recaptured the crucial turns in her own life that led to her marriage and her pregnancy, and her fantasies reach into the distant future of the life waiting within her. She awaits the affection she will give and receive; and her daydreams, now as always, seek to evoke compensations for the frustrations and disappointments in her own life. Days of comfort and expectant hope are interrupted by periods of discomfort and anxiety. Although the first-born are in a minority, they require our attention for they usually present a more critical experience to the mother, profoundly altering her life, bringing new sensations and awareness, and creating problems and questions for which she seeks more guidance from the physician.

The Expectant Mother

"Morning sickness," with nausea and occasional vomiting, has often disturbed the first few months of the pregnancy; but if the woman is mature and happily married, the pregnancy soon turns into a period of blooming when she experiences a sense of completion and self-satisfaction. If the mother has come to terms with being a woman, which includes some lingering regrets at not having been born a boy, she feels that her pregnancy is fulfilling her fate, completing her life as a woman, and she knows a creativity that compensates for past restrictions and limitations. She finds a new sense of closeness and sharing with her husband that forms a new and strong bond between them. An appearance that reflects such happiness and contentment augurs well for the course of the pregnancy and for the child. Gradually, however, the expectant mother usually turns inward, often from the moment when she first feels the fetus move and she knows that she has a living being in her womb. She experiences a self-sufficiency because the most important thing to her is within her, and her own life and her own needs have become secondary to perpetuating herself and the species through the baby. Her husband may feel excluded and neglected, for he is no longer the primary recipient of her emotional investment. Yet he is more important to his wife than ever, for she can relax properly and invest her emotions in the fetus only when she feels secure, protected, and supported by her husband.

As much as the woman may enjoy her pregnancy, she eventually grows impatient. Her increasing girth makes her feel awkward; her balance becomes insecure; often she tires more readily; the movement and kicking of the fetus are annoying; and after the baby's head descends and engages her pelvis, she must urinate more frequently. She wants to know how it will turn out, properly experiencing some concerns—not so much for herself, for maternal deaths have become a rarity, but wishing to know that the baby will be normal. Anomalous developments are sufficiently common to justify some concern. She has also been limited in her fantasies, for she cannot know the sex of the child. As many mothers feel disappointed if the child turns out to be of the opposite sex from that awaited, they tend to hold their imaginations in check, or are willing to consider both alternatives until they are certain.

The obstetrician reassures the mother and informs her of the baby's sex immediately after the delivery, without waiting for any questions.

Despite such reassurance, many mothers must stifle some feelings of disappointment when they see their babies, and hesitate to express concerns that a newborn's appearance may arouse in an inexperienced mother. The newborn is not very prepossessing, and it may take all of the mother's maternal love not to be disappointed with the creature to whom she has just given birth. The infant possesses the many endowments and assets that have been reviewed in the preceding chapters, but most of them are not yet apparent. Let us, now, take a more careful look at the infant who has just started his life in the world.

The Newborn's Appearance

The average baby born at term weighs seven and one-fourth pounds and is twenty to twenty-one inches long. With its knees flexed and body curled in its familiar fetal position, it seems very tiny indeed, particularly when the obstetrician or nurse skillfully holds it on a hand and wrist. Somewhat wizened, the baby may appear more like an elderly denizen of the world than a newcomer; for there is little fat, and particularly the fat pads that will fill out the cheeks are missing, and the jaws are unsupported by teeth. The hair may be dark and straight, coming low over the forehead and conveying a hairy appearance that deprives the infant of resemblance to any known relative within the last few thousand generations. Such hair, when present, will soon be replaced by hair so fine that some babies appear bald to casual observation. The vernix caseosa, a cheesy material which covers the body, provides a protective coating for the skin. The skin is reddened, moist, and deeply creased. The "caput," or swelling formed by pressure during the passage through the birth canal, may have temporarily deformed the nose, caused a swelling about one eye, or elongated the head into a strange shape. The skull is incomplete, for the bones have not joined in two areas called the "fontanelles" where the brain is covered only by soft tissues. The external genitalia in both sexes are disproportionately large due to stimulation by the mother's hormones and will regress in size. The breasts may be somewhat enlarged for the same reason and secrete a watery discharge discouragingly termed "witch's milk." The irises are a pale blue, which does not indicate a resemblance to either parent, for the true eye color develops later. The head, even though its contents are not fully developed, is very large in proportion to the body, and the neck cannot support it; whereas the buttocks are tiny, creating an appearance that is very disproportionate in comparison with adult dimensions.

The Neonate's Physiological Instability

The baby is arbitrarily termed a "neonate" for the first several weeks when control of the physiological processes remains unstable. The regulation of the body temperature is imperfect and requires particular attention. The neonate's breathing is often irregular. The eyes wander and cross, and most babies are unable to fixate on an object and can perceive only vague sensations.* The newborn can hear little during the first twenty-four hours until air enters the Eustachian tubes. The neonate seems to prefer its former home and acts as if it resents any stimulation. It will sleep about twenty hours a day, its slumber broken primarily by signals of hunger that provoke a reedy crying, and it needs milk from six to eight times a day. The infant's needs are sleep, warmth, and milk to continue maturing outside the mother. It is still parasitic but sucks in nutriment rather than receiving it through the umbilical cord by filtration from the mother's blood.

His Capabilities and Reactions

The baby still is not a social creature, but he possesses a few important ways of interacting with the world about him. He can suck and will start to suck when a nipple or anything else is placed in his mouth. At birth, or within the first few weeks, the baby reflexly turns his head to the side of a stimulus to his lips and starts to suck. He cannot yet properly grasp the nipple with his mouth unaided. The lips and mouth are all-important to the neonate, and the oral area is highly sensitive, richly endowed with tactile sensory receptors. A fetus will respond reflexly to stimulation of the oral zone long before birth. The baby's existence centers on his ability to incorporate nourishment and fluids; and if unable to suck and swallow reflexly, he can survive only with the help of considerable medical attention. The neonate's hands tend to be held closed, and if something rubs the palm, particularly if the area between thumb and forefinger is stroked, the hand reflexly clenches it and holds on with a strength that suffices to support the baby's weight if both hands are grasping. This innate "grasp reflex" serves no apparent purpose in the human infant but was of utmost importance in the last prehuman phase of evolution when the infant had to cling to its mother's hair. The grasp reflex

---

* About a quarter of infants can fixate gaze almost immediately after birth and about 95 per cent by ninety-six hours after birth.[5] Gazing at the mother often elicits a very positive response from the mother.

lasts from four to six months until the forebrain matures and the nerve fibers that conduct impulses to the upper extremities are covered by a sheath of myelin which permit the baby to begin to use his hands to make voluntary discrete movements. If the baby is dropped, or is suddenly jerked downward, or is startled by a loud noise, an immediate reflex change from the usual curled posture occurs as all four extremities are flung out in extension and the infant starts to cry. This "startle" or "Moro" reflex may have served to help a simian mother catch a falling infant by causing it to spread out to a maximal extent. Playful dropping motions that excite and please an older child terrify the young infant.

Several other reflexes require note. For some weeks after birth, if the baby is held erect with his toes touching the ground, he will make reflex stepping movements. However, they do not indicate that he is an extraordinary youngster, prematurely ready to learn to walk, any more than the swimming movements he makes when properly suspended warrant a try at swimming. Stroking the outer side of the sole of the foot to test the "plantar" reflex causes a fanning out of the toes and an upward movement of the big toe, termed a "Babinski" response or reflex. It is an abnormal response in adults but indicates in infants that the pyramidal tracts of nerve fibers, essential for voluntary muscular control, are not yet covered by the myelin sheaths necessary for their proper functioning. Until the Babinski response disappears toward the end of the first year of life, the baby cannot voluntarily control the lower parts of his body. The, upper extremities can be controlled sooner than the lower, and the infant will be able to start practicing finger control before he is six months old. Thus the infant's ability to handle things, to maintain his balance, to talk, to walk, to control his sphincters, awaits the maturation of his nervous system, rather than practice and training alone.

Differences among Newborn Infants

Even casual observation of the newborns assembled in a hospital nursery reveals that they differ a great deal. Some are fairly well fitted out and others appear somewhat premature. They are actually of differing ages at birth, for the exact periods of gestation and the rates of maturation vary. The neonates differ in temperament—showing differences that are genetically innate but also some that result from divergent intrauterine environments. Some infants are naturally "cuddly" and easy to hold, whereas others are loose and sprawling, or rigid, when held. Some are placid, sleeping most of the time, and others are sensitive to stimuli and their needs are not so easily satisfied. Newborns, therefore, require some-what different management of their needs, and start to experience the world on a somewhat different basis.[4]

Some developmental defect, usually relatively trivial, exists in about one out of every sixteen infants. Some will create difficulties sooner or later and influence the course of personality development. Cardiac anom-alies may require surgery during the first months or chronically impede physical development and activity. A prominent birthmark may have in-fluence through parental attitudes and later through provoking self-consciousness in the child. The first weeks of life remain somewhat pre-carious, for even though infant mortality has been cut almost in half over the past thirty years, the death rate among neonates has declined only slightly. However, much of the danger to life arises because a cer-tain number of babies are born without the essential equipment for sur-vival. The properly formed and adequately mature neonate will survive without difficulty in contemporary civilized societies unless something untoward occurs.

The infant's physiological processes become considerably more stable by the end of his first month. His breathing becomes regular, his body temperature fluctuates less, and he sucks with vigor when fed. The movements of his limbs are more or less symmetrical, but still random, though some infants can get their thumbs into their mouths to pacify themselves. The intervals between feelings of hunger have usually be-come more regular, but they are still brief and the infant requires five or more feedings every twenty-four hours. He enjoys his bath, its warmth, and the handling that goes with it, but protests if clothing is drawn on over his head—something to which infants seem to have an inborn aver-sion. His impressions of the sensations that he feels seem dim and diffuse, and feelings of hunger are the most dominant. These weeks are a time of stabilization primarily spent in sleep, with the calories consumed directed largely toward physical maturation.

Total Dependency

Despite the diffuse and unorganized nature of the neonate's feelings, which we can, of course, only surmise through observation of his reac-tions, these first weeks of life receive much emphasis in the study of personality development—perhaps more because of how the mother's attitudes toward her child are established than because of the direct im-pact of events upon the infant. The neonate is virtually helpless, not even, as are other animals, capable of finding the nipple himself, which must carefully be placed in his mouth. He is helpless and passively omnipotent; his needs are all provided for by others. His comfort and well-being depend upon the ability of the mother or of a mother substitute to understand his needs and satisfy them. The baby's future emotional security rests to a very great extent upon the development of a mutuality between him and the mother that permits them to interact on a non-verbal basis during the first year and provides the mother with empathic feelings for his needs. The neonate has little tolerance for frustration and can do little toward directing his mother's efforts except to signal discomfort, and it is up to the mother to adjust to the infant. The ability to give birth to a baby does not assure the ability to nurture and properly care for one. Maternal feelings may be stimulated hormonally, and inborn responsivity may be stirred by certain activities of the infant, but such feelings do not provide the necessary skills, nor are they adequately pervasive to overcome the emotional problems aroused in many women by the tasks of mothering.

The Family Matrix

The birth of a child, particularly the first child, produces a change in a woman's life. Her life and well-being are bound to the child's life for many years to come. The family unit undergoes a reorganization in order to provide room for the infant, and the roles of husband and wife alter to embrace the roles of father and mother. The woman fills the pivotal position in the emotional relatedness of family members and usually must make the greatest shift in her emotional attitudes to enable a new equilibrium to be established within the family. Although the arrival of the baby is usually a time of happiness, it also can bring anxiety-provoking frustration and confusion that the mother communicates to the infant by the manner in which she handles him. A good start is so important to the new life that considerable effort has been expended in recent years to prepare mothers properly, taking into account the relative inexperience of the majority of new mothers with the care of infants and the paucity of help available to her from others.

The Mother's Ability to Nurture

Even though the mother's fundamental emotional attitudes toward her baby involve her own personality development, her maturity as a woman, her happiness in her marriage, and other such factors that can scarcely be influenced by direct instruction, her insecurities over every-day, seemingly trivial matters of child care can create despair in her con-cerning her ability properly to care for her infant and satisfy him. The mother must learn new techniques that sound so rudimentary and are so often taken for granted that she feels ashamed to admit her ignorance and seek help. She must, for example, learn how to get her nipple into the baby's mouth and how to hold the infant securely. If the baby is bottle-fed, she must prepare a formula and test the temperature of the milk. She does not know without instruction how long the baby should nurse, or when he is satisfied, or how frequently to feed. Diapering, cleaning, bathing, deciding how much the baby should be handled and how much left alone, and many other such items can provoke indecision. Nothing may seem to go right, usually because of the uneasiness and anxiety that security concerning her techniques and abilities can dissi-pate. The turmoil can involve her mother and mother-in-law, start fam-ily frictions, and lead her husband to doubt his choice of a wife. Instruc-tion in the elements of child care and making advice available to the young mother are particularly important in contemporary life, as tradi-tional techniques are poorly conveyed and often mistrusted as old-fash-ioned and unscientific.*

In keeping with the general cultural trend, young people look to sci-ence for guidance in rearing their children—an orientation that is often accentuated by the divergent cultural backgrounds of the two parents and their dissatisfaction with the ways in which they were raised accord-ing to Old World traditions. But scientific concepts of infant care also change, causing additional confusion. During the third and fourth dec-ades of this century the teachings of behaviorist psychology dominated the scene and formed one of the first major scientific challenges to tradi-tional child-rearing procedures. This outgrowth and modification of Pav-lovian psychology sought to "condition" the child's responsivity almost from birth in order to inculcate proper training of character and sociali-zation. The teaching ran beyond actual scientific experiment and experi-ence, and self-assured psychologists were surprisingly certain of the valid-ity of the theory. As in many such instances, the person who does not know how little he knows can gain credence by his certainty and dogma-

---

* The millions of copies of Benjamin Spock's *Baby and Child Care* sold in many languages attest to the need. This excellent book, with which every physician should be familiar, has become the contemporary mother's "bible"—according to which much of the generation now entering maturity has been reared.

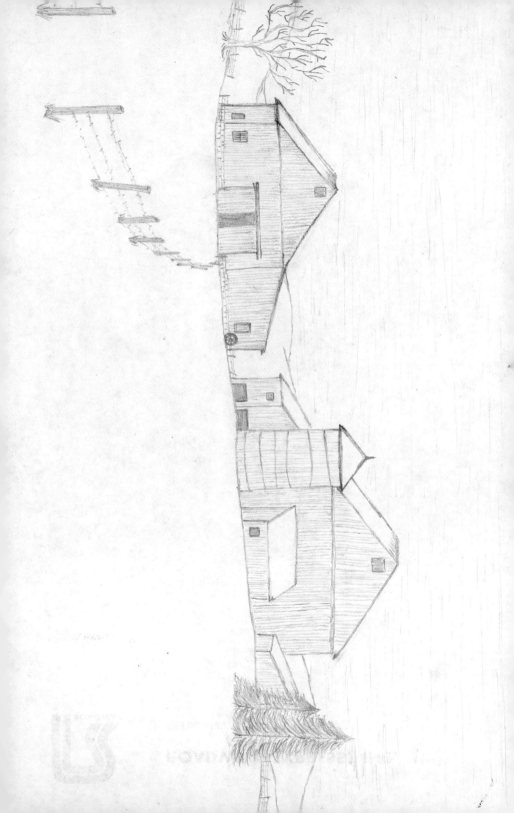

ROADWAY EXPRESS, INC.

DEDICATED TO BETTER SERVICE

tism. The infant's needs were considered in relatively mechanistic terms. The baby was fed according to a rigid schedule and maternal cuddling and handling kept to a minimum. The baby's cries for food were to be ignored. Implicitly, even though it was not expressed in these terms, the infant was considered to be wily, seeking to gain attention and control over his parents by unnecessary behavior which could be overcome by parental firmness. Following such teachings, a good mother was supposed to squelch her own concerns and much of her maternal feelings if she would properly care for her child. Many mothers found this unnatural task difficult, but only the more independent and secure mothers could flout the authorities and accept the guilt of raising their children improperly. Toward the end of the 1930's, a major shift in policy occurred under the growing impact of psychoanalytic teachings. Repression was considered the source of most emotional disturbances, but the advice to avoid unnecessary repressive measures was often misunderstood to mean abandonment of guidance and consistent firmness. The more recent teachings have urged parents and teachers to seek to meet the child's maturational needs at each phase of his development—neither to place demands before the child is capable of meeting them, nor, on the other hand, to restrain the child from utilizing his abilities when he is ready either by continuing to do for him or by unnecessary restrictiveness.

Although differences of opinion exist concerning the older child's capacities and what might be expected of him, virtually all experienced persons agree that the neonate can do almost nothing for himself other than carry out his essential physiological processes, and that attention must be focused upon the mother's handling of her infant. The neonate has virtually no tolerance for frustration of its needs, and if he is born normally developed there is no need for him to experience any frustration, as the essential problems of the physical care of the newborn have been worked out.

Whereas the neonate has but recently entered the world, his mother's relatedness to him was developing throughout her pregnancy, and her attitudes toward the child reflect her own personality development, her marital adjustment, and her conscious and unconscious feelings about having a baby and being a mother. Therefore, obstetricians, pediatricians, and psychiatrists have become interested in the mother's attitudes toward pregnancy and during it, recognizing also that her emotional state can influence both the course of the pregnancy and the delivery.

Mutuality between Mother and Child

The mutuality between mother and child which seems essential for the mother properly to empathize with the infant's needs and feelings, and to bestow love and tenderness, usually develops during the pregnancy rather than appearing suddenly after the birth. The fetus is part of the mother, and the love of the infant is properly partly a narcissistic love—not fully distinguishable from the woman's love and concern for herself and her pride in what she can produce and achieve. The pregnant woman's life, the investment of her thoughts and emotions encompass the fetus which gives a new and expanded meaning to her own existence. When properly developed, such investments of herself continue to enfold the helpless infant, who continues to develop through her care almost as completely as when he was within her womb. The differentiation of mother and child is a lengthy process for both, continuing progressively over many years.

• All sorts of interferences with the development of proper maternal preoccupation with the developing infant can arise. Thus, a young and immature woman had married on the rebound and considered her husband inferior to her. She became infuriated when he did not idolize her and cater to her adolescent whims but expected her to assume responsibility for their household. She had never really accepted the finality of the marriage, daydreaming that her former boy friend would realize his error, divorce his wife, and return to her. Her resentments welled up when she believed that her husband had purposefully impregnated her in order to hold her in the marriage. As the pregnancy progressed, unable to accept the reality, she spent more and more time lost in a fantasy of an imaginary life with her true love. She scarcely thought of the fetus within her and became annoyed by every movement or kick that encroached upon her daydreams, irritable and antagonistic to her baby before it was born. Another woman greatly desired a baby, and felt pride and fulfillment in being pregnant. Since early adolescence she had been concerned about her femininity, considering herself boyish in build and masculine in her intellectual interests, and her pregnancy allayed conscious fears that she might not be properly constructed as a woman. Her early happiness was, however, disturbed as childhood fantasies, long repressed, emerged and filled her dreams and daydreams with fears of the delivery as a sadistic attack by a man inserting instruments of torture into her; and with fears of the fetus itself conceived as a parasitic growth devouring her insides. More tangibly perhaps, a woman already harassed by the care of six young children—a task amplified by her perfectionism and her concerns when they were out of her sight—finds that she cannot make room, emotional room within her, for the coming baby. While the more serious emotional problems can be helped only by psychotherapy, many lesser problems can be alleviated and their impact upon the child blunted by provision of emotional support and guidance to the insecure and troubled expectant mother. •

Prenatal Influences

The emotional problems of the pregnant woman can affect the course of the pregnancy and the fetus. The influence of emotional turmoil in causing spontaneous abortions and serious physiological disturbances in the mother, such as pernicious vomiting or toxemia, is beyond the scope of this book except as an indication that the fetus is not totally protected from physiological imbalances of the mother. The baby's development does not start at birth but with conception. It is responsive to its fetal environment. If the mother bleeds seriously or if there is a marked disturbance in her metabolic equilibrium, the fetus may develop an anomaly through interference with its maturation. If the mother contracts German measles early in her pregnancy, the virus can affect the development of the fetus's brain. Marked thyroid or iodine deficiency in the mother can lead to the production of a cretin, a child with deficient thyroid development. Diabetic mothers tend to give birth to unusually large babies. The course of labor can be influenced by the mother's fears; and a difficult prolonged labor requiring considerable anesthesia can cause anoxia in the emerging fetus or interfere with his breathing immediately after birth, thereby influencing the infant's start in life. It has become clear, particularly through the studies of Sontag and his coworkers,[7, 8] that the mother's emotional state can influence the fetus. We are not concerned with superstitions that a child develops a harelip because the mother saw a rabbit, or that Annie Oakley's mother was frightened by a shotgun. Even though no direct nerve connections exist between the mother and the fetus, there is a neurochemical bond through the placental circulation. The mother's internal secretions can produce changes in the fetal heart rate, in its bodily movements, and perhaps in its intestinal activity. Spelt's studies have shown that during its last two months the fetus not only responds to loud noises but that its heart rate can probably be conditioned.[9] There is evidence that the newborn of disturbed mothers may tend to be hyperactive in their responsivity to stimuli, and have more labile heart action and gastrointestinal functioning.[7, 8, 9] However, any tendency to consider such newborn as neurotic at birth constitutes a very dubious extrapolation of known facts. While reasonable evidence indicates that undue sensitivity in the neonate is partly related to the mother's emotional state during the pregnancy, we must also realize that such mothers are also likely to remain upset after the delivery when the baby's well-being depends upon her conscious and unconscious attitudes toward him rather than directly upon her physiological processes.

Measures to Foster Mutuality

During the past several decades, obstetricians and pediatricians have initiated various measures to improve the mother's security and to foster the development of a satisfactory mutuality between mother and infant.[10, 11]

Prenatal Courses

Expectant mothers, particularly those awaiting a first child, and often the fathers as well, are often offered *prenatal courses*. The parents are taught the essentials of the physiology of pregnancy, of fetal development, and of childbirth so that they may overcome misconceptions and fears arising from ignorance. Here, too, parents learn about the infant's physical and emotional needs and how to provide for them. Many normal aspects of pregnancy and of infant behavior can upset young parents, who may consider them unusual or abnormal. Such instruction, which usually includes an opportunity for free discussion, can help prevent mishandling of the baby as well as foster greater security in the parents. These courses also establish, even before the baby is born, a relationship between the mother and an expert, to whom she can turn if problems arise during the pregnancy or in caring for her baby.

Natural Childbirth

Many obstetricians promote the practice of "natural childbirth"—the conduct of the labor and delivery without anesthesia, or with minimal anesthesia—to permit the mother who is awake to participate in a process that properly constitutes one of the most important experiences in her life. The movement was started by an English obstetrician, Grantly Dick Read, whose book *Childbirth Without Fear*[6] has exerted wide in-

fluence upon the practice of obstetrics. Read considered that most of the
pain of labor is a product of civilization and that childbirth was simple
and relatively painless among primitive peoples. Useful techniques can,
upon occasion, derive from faulty assumptions. Indeed, many, if not
most, preliterate peoples fear childbirth, the women experience considerable pain, and the high maternal and infant mortality rates can lead to
reliance upon elaborate rites that may be almost as painful to an observer
as to the mother because of their inefficiency. However, if the woman
can relax during the labor and delivery and maintain the muscles of her
pelvic floor in a reasonably relaxed state, labor is easier and less painful
than when she is tense. Pain itself is bearable and often can be virtually
ignored when it is not accompanied by fear. The woman who has gained
confidence in her obstetrician and in herself, and who has been prepared
by exercises that teach her to relax properly, can often cope with the pain
experienced during a normal delivery without requiring narcotics and
anesthesia. In a sense, "natural childbirth" has become feasible because
of the advances of modern obstetrics that permit the mother to feel
secure. She knows that her life is not in danger, and that if she should
suffer severe pain she can obtain relief. When the mother is awake, par-
ticipates in the delivery, and can see her baby immediately, it helps foster the essential bond between her and the infant. She can feel more
keenly that this is her baby whom she has brought into life, rather than
needing to overcome a hiatus in her consciousness, perhaps awakening
only after the infant has been placed in the nursery. Most women who
deliver "naturally" are extremely pleased to have participated and enjoy
seeing or even handling the infant immediately after the birth. Remaining awake, the mother can share the situation with her husband. Perhaps
the effect upon the baby is almost as important, for not having absorbed
a narcotic and anesthetic from the mother he is active and responsive,
which fosters the establishment of a bond with the mother.

Rooming-In
   During the last few decades the vast majority of babies have been born
in hospitals. Various efforts to promote childbirth in the home have
failed because of the superior facilities available in hospitals; and now
that infections in the newborn and in mothers have been curbed, such
efforts have virtually ceased. Until fairly recently, the newborn customarily were kept together in an impersonal nursery until the mother left the
hospital. They were fed at regular intervals by nurses, and their crying

was largely ignored as neonates are not disturbed by the crying of others. The infants were taken to visit their mothers once or twice a day for brief periods—unless the mother nursed the baby, a practice that had been growing more and more uncommon in the United States. Indeed, many obstetricians and nurses discouraged breast feeding because it upset hospital routines. The infant, very much a stranger wrapped in blankets, was deposited on the mother's bed for her to look at or to hold gingerly. The mother gained the impression in the hospital, though perhaps inadvertently, that her newborn child was so fragile that only a specially trained nurse could care for him properly, an impression that increased her concerns when she took her infant home and was on her own. In "rooming-in" programs, the newborn is kept in a bassinet alongside the mother's bed, where she can watch and take care of the baby herself. In some hospitals, mothers are urged to share rooms rather than have single rooms in order to permit discussion with other new mothers. As women are now usually permitted to get up within twenty-four hours of the delivery, they can take charge of their babies, feed, diaper, and cleanse them, under guidance if necessary. The rooming-in experience fosters early contact and responsibility for the child, and permits guided practical experience in baby care. Mothers can often relax better with their babies close to them, secure that they are well. However, the routine use of such practices, rather than consideration of the individual mother's needs, can cause difficulties. Some women, particularly those tired out from the last stages of pregnancy while caring for other children, may well prefer a respite from all responsibilities and enjoy a few days of attention while others provide for their babies.

Breast Feeding

There is an increasing trend to induce mothers to breast feed their babies. Breast feeding has many advantages.[1] The mother's milk is only rarely unsuited to the infant; it contains antibodies that help protect the infant from various infectious diseases; the suckling promotes contractions of the mother's uterus, aiding its reduction to normal size following the delivery. There are other practical advantages, such as freeing the mother from the need to prepare bottles; and contrary to expectation, breast feeding often permits greater freedom of movement, for the baby's food goes along with the mother. However, we are here interested in its promotion of a relatedness between mother and child. It is, for example, difficult to nurse a baby at the breast without holding it closely and providing the stimulation and the comfort of body contact, the mother's odor, and the mother's face upon which the baby fixes his eyes as soon as he is able. Suckling also properly stimulates genital sensations in the mother which helps establish an erotic component to the mother's attachment and can add to the pleasure of nursing. Unfortunately, some mothers become uneasy because they are sexually stimulated and believe that something is wrong with them and cease breast feeding. All in all, breast feeding assures that the infant will receive a reasonable amount of maternal attention and contact and during the first months spend much of the intervals between sleep in his mother's arms.

Some women, however, have a deep aversion to nursing, experiencing it as if a parasite were suckling at them, and others may have a strong sense of shame about its animal-like character. A baby can thrive very well if bottle-fed, and the mother may relate to her infant better while giving a bottle. Pressures toward breast feeding can be injurious if they make a mother feel guilty or unworthy because she is not for it. Indeed, the same danger holds for natural childbirth. Today many young matrons, particularly many from well-educated groups, feel obligated to have babies without anesthesia and consider themselves failures if they cannot do so. A firmer start might have been made if anesthesia had been sought and used. Fortunately with breast feeding the problem often takes care of itself, for fairly reliable studies indicate that mothers who do not really desire to nurse, or have unconscious blocks about it, do not succeed and must wean the child after a brief trial (see Chapter 5).

Well-Baby Clinics

The pediatrician seeks to provide guidance for the mother in childrearing practices. Efforts are made to establish regular contacts even when the child is well and thriving. The physical development of the infant and young child is followed, prophylactic measures such as inoculation recommended and provided, and discussions of any problems stimulated. The mother learns that she can discuss her own emotional difficulties which might interfere with the care she provides her offspring. The interest of the personal pediatrician, or of the clinic, lies in the total well-being of the child and in the mother-child relationship rather than in the child's physical health alone.

These various measures can all be effective and have been very worthwhile when they do not contain moralistic implications that set expectations, spoken or unspoken, beyond the mother's capacities, and provoke in her feelings that she is inadequate or rejecting of her baby.

The mother's security and spontaneity of feeling for her baby are usually more important than the precise techniques used in delivering and nourishing her infant. If the mother is happy during her pregnancy, if she consciously and unconsciously wants the baby and has become caught up in the feeling of the miracle going on inside of her, and if she feels completed by the process, everything else is relatively secondary. Although she may experience difficulties, the chances are great that she will learn to overcome them and her positive feelings will win out over fears of labor, dislike of breast feeding, or her inexperience in caring for an infant.

A good start is important, for absence of a good relationship can make the new infant fretful, and the mother's inability to satisfy him can nullify the enjoyment of having a baby and establish a pattern that may be difficult to overcome. Still, the baby's primary needs during the first few weeks of life are food, sleep, and warmth, and he is not extremely sensitive to the mother's inexperience. The atmosphere established is probably more important than the precise details of management. Babies are handled in very divergent ways in different cultures and in some places in a manner that to us would seem deleterious, and yet the infants survive and flourish. Of late, increasing attention has been directed toward inculcating security in the mother concerning her capacity to care for her baby properly. Her assurance is helped by training and instruction and the various measures outlined that can, at least, modify or blunt the edge of anxiety-ridden handling and cover difficulties in accepting the baby. Fortunately, a mother's anticipated rejection of her baby often fails to materialize, because babies in their helplessness are very seductive and difficult to resist.

The Unwanted Infant

Although one likes to believe that the birth of a child is a happy event for the parents, it would be unrealistic if physicians did not recognize that the baby is often unwanted and that one or both parents are emotionally incapable of welcoming it. Such situations are important to physicians, even though they constitute a minority of instances, because it is among such children that difficulties in physical and emotional health are more likely to arise. About 70 per cent of pregnancies are unplanned, but this does not mean that most of these babies are unwanted or unwelcome. Many were simply not wanted at the specific time; and others, though undesired, are well-accepted after the fact. Maternal rejection of a child and its serious effects have received much consideration in recent years. A variety of emotional and psychosomatic disturbances have been somewhat uncritically attributed to "maternal rejection" as if it were an entity. Whereas occasional mothers neglect their infants physically and emotionally and clearly do not respond to them properly, the matter is usually not this simple, for the mother's difficulties are less global and more specific. Some women fear pregnancy and labor because of residual childhood fears; often these are fears that have been banished from consciousness since childhood rather than having been re-evaluated and overcome, such as ideas that the baby is born by an operation, or through the navel or the anus, and that they will be mutilated through childbirth. Some are fearful of being caught in a situation over which they have no control, such as the growth of the fetus within them and its birth. Some are ashamed of being pregnant, with its visible testimony of a sexuality that they still consider forbidden and shameful. Yet they may desire and very much love the baby. On the other hand, a woman may enjoy being pregnant because of the attention and care she receives during it but have difficulties in being maternal to the baby because she seeks to be cared for as a child herself. Another does not wish to be tied to the marriage by the baby, or resents being kept from her occupation and the relationships at her job that are more important to her than her marital life. Some women deeply resent their femininity, and can accept neither the pregnancy nor the baby which definitively challenge and destroy fantasies and self-deceptions of not being a woman. There are a wide variety of reasons, conscious and unconscious, why a woman can have problems with one or another phase of pregnancy, with childbirth, or with child rearing. Some who fear pregnancy or childbirth and have sought to avoid them may make excellent mothers after the child is born, having lived through their fears and found release from them. As we shall see later, some women can accept a child during one phase of his development and feel at ease, whereas she may have grave difficulties with the child at some other developmental period.

Emotional Incapacitation for Motherhood

More deep-seated emotional problems exist that involve the entire personality development of the mother; these are little influenced by instruction or techniques of improving the mother's relatedness to her child, and may even resist intensive psychotherapy. Let us consider an example. A young woman had little difficulty during her first pregnancy. Her mother, who lived in another part of the country, had remained with her during the last months of her pregnancy, taking over the household duties and then the care of the infant during its first ten days of life. Within a few days of her mother's departure, the young woman became seriously ill with ulcerative colitis, a serious disease that many authorities consider to be related to severe emotional problems. The patient, as soon as her mother had left her, had been filled with doubts and intense feelings of inadequacy. She became indecisive, frustrated, and fearful over trivia. She felt uncertain that she had prepared the formula correctly, fearful that a diaper pin would injure her baby, incapable of holding the infant correctly, perplexed about when and how long to feed him. She became sorry that she had ever had the baby, feeling deserted and unsupported, and guilty over increasing feelings of rage at the baby and hostility toward her husband for expecting her to know how to care for their child. She had never felt secure. Her own mother had directed and supervised every aspect of her life until she had married. She had been confined to the back yard when young and forbidden to cross streets alone until she entered high school. Her mother had selected her clothing, chosen what she should wear each day, and reviewed just what she should do and then what she had done on dates. She had passively acquiesced in her mother's choice of a husband for her. She had grown up feeling incapable of caring for herself, and certain that she would never attain her mother's abilities and wisdom. Fortunately, after some psychiatric help, she could discuss her dilemma with her mother; and she learned, much to her surprise, that her mother had been so controlling because of her own uncertainties and anxieties rather than because of lack of trust in her daughter. With treatment, both psychiatric and physiological, this patient's illness remitted and she remained well for several years, only to suffer a fulminating relapse on the day she realized that she had again become pregnant. Although we are not here concerned with such serious and somewhat unusual pathology, the case illustrates how emotional problems tend to be transmitted from one generation to the next, and can start to exert their influence even before the new infant is born. •

Intrafamilial Problems

The mother-infant relationship is often regarded as if the two were living in a vacuum rather than as part of a family. The concentration of attention upon the mother and her child provides a useful focus, but often leads to neglect of highly significant influences affecting the relationship. The birth of a child, particularly the first, is a time of trial for many marriages. The marriage turns into a family unit that must include and find room for a third member. Anger and irritation with the infant frequently reflects unhappiness in the marriage as hostility is deflected from the spouse onto the child. The father must be able to share the mother with the infant and not feel left out, and the mother cannot exclude her husband from her life and the child's. A couple who had purposely remained childless for five years in order to enjoy their own lives unhampered by parental responsibilities finally had a baby at the wife's insistence. The husband was a person who required constant bolstering of his self-esteem by admiration from women, and although promiscuous demanded his wife's complete attention. Soon after the baby was born, the mother found herself in a dilemma. When her husband was at home, each time she went to feed her son or paid attention to his cries, her husband would voice an imperative need and throw a tantrum if the infant's needs took precedence over his. He refused to forgo any social activities, and when babysitters were not available insisted that his wife bring the neonatal infant along to noisy drunken parties. As the son grew older, the father's jealousy and rivalry increased, and he constantly belittled his son's abilities while holding himself up as an unattainable model of masculine achievement. This mother could have provided adequate mothering only if she had broken off her marriage. Fathers can be just as immature as mothers, and some behave even more immaturely, particularly when they have married primarily in order to regain a mothering figure to care for them and then cannot share their wives with their children and accept parental responsibilities.

Fortunately, the infant usually creates new ties between the parents. They are united in their common product and become involved in experiences with their child that no one else can really share with them. The baby gives their lives new purpose and direction, and a sense of continuity with a new generation. The influence of children upon the lives of their parents will be discussed in Chapter 15.

When the new infant is not the first-born, brothers and sisters are not only affected, but their reactions impinge upon the neonate both directly and through the impact of their altered needs upon the parents. They are supposed to welcome the new sibling but almost always feel that he is an intruder who pre-empts the mother's attention and affection. The older child frequently regresses, unconsciously seeking the benefits of greater dependency, and requires more care and demonstrations of love than previously. The mother may become perplexed and frustrated in her efforts to provide for her infant while she is caught up in the obvious unhappiness of her older child.* Many contemporary parents, aware of the jealousies aroused, seek to prepare the older children for the birth, consider their needs, permit verbal expression of hostility, and seek to compensate for the attention they give the infant and try to find ways of making the advent of the new child advantageous to the older children.

The mother, soon after her child is born, adjusts not only to having a baby but also to the specific characteristics of her infant. A mother who may previously have interacted very well with a calm and docile first child may grow anxious when confronted with the care of a hypersensitive infant; or, on the other hand, a woman may grow concerned or even dissatisfied with a baby who is quiet and relatively unresponsive, needing greater reactivity in the child to stimulate and satisfy her. The innate characteristics of the baby can start a chain of interactional responses which may persist and greatly influence his development, or which may alter either as the infant changes as he matures or in response to the mother's handling.

The Infant's Sex

The sex of the child is one of the most important factors that influence the parents' ways of relating to the child, regardless of whether they wanted a child of the given sex, are disappointed because of it, or whether they truly had no preference. Even though boys and girls are cared for in the same way while neonates, except for the method of

---

* De Saussure cites an interesting though rather extreme example from the reports of Descuret, a physician who practiced in the middle of the last century. Descuret writes of how he diagnosed the reason why a seven-year-old boy began to fail physically and become seriously withdrawn. These symptoms were the effects of his intense jealousy of his nursing infant brother. Descuret then proudly told of his treatment. He had the parents send the infant to live with a wet nurse for a year and the older brother soon recovered. When the baby was permitted to return home, he had the parents chide the baby frequently to prove to the older son that they did not prefer the baby to him.[2] After all, why be concerned about the trauma to the baby!

diapering, the child's gender stimulates subtle differences in parental handling and responses that are part of the covert training of the child to behave as a boy or a girl.* Often enough, the sex of the child evokes disappointment—more commonly the birth of a daughter. Sometimes the mother's personality structure leads her to wish strongly for a son who will compensate for her disappointments in being a woman and live out her fantasies of what life would have been like for her if she had been a boy. Envy of the penis she lacks, often prominent at some phase of the girl's development, becomes lessened by her ability to produce a boy who possesses the desired genitals. A woman may also feel disappointed in a girl primarily because she knows or believes that her husband wanted a son. She may feel that the birth of a daughter reflects her own inadequacy, even though she may consciously know that it is the husband's chromosomes that determine the sex of the offspring. She has such examples as the shah of Iran, who, despite the availability of excellent medical advice, divorced a wife because she produced daughters rather than the needed male heir. However, the birth of a son may also be disappointing when sons are already present, or when the mother envisions a daughter who will provide her with feminine companionship in the home.

The nature of the neonate's world can only be reconstructed imaginatively. It seems to be dominated by the need for a quiet comfort that permits growth and sleep and is disrupted primarily by sensations of hunger. The mouth and lips—sucking and taking in—are central to the baby's relatedness to the world in which it lives. The neonate does not distinguish between himself and the remainder of the world, including the nipple, whether flesh or latex, that comes and satiates and then disappears. Still, the baby is alive and responsive and in its undifferentiating way takes in sensations as well as milk—a satisfying closeness to the mother, her warmth, her feel, and her smell. He is cleaned gently or roughly, bathed with confidence or trepidation, is satiated or left tense and vaguely unhappy. Nurses familiar with neonates believe that they can often differentiate within the first weeks between babies who are content and those who are fretful in response to their mother's attitudes

* Boys and girls tend to behave somewhat differently even as neonates; boys tend to be more active from the start, probably because the androgen secreted *in utero* sets off a neural organization in the brain conducive to masculine activity[3, 12] (see Chapter 7).

and handling. Many authorities believe that the mother's tensions are clearly conveyed to the neonate. Still, there are reasons to consider that the newborn infant is not unduly sensitive to the manner in which he is handled, and provided that his essential needs are met, the mother's emotional attitudes are important largely because of the patterns established and their consequences to the continuing mother-child relationship.

The neonate possesses an omnipotence that he will never again possess. He but raises his voice and his needs are served. It is an omnipotence of helplessness; but he is fed, cleaned, cuddled, and kept comfortable. His energies are used for growth, and the disturbances to his equilibrium are rapidly corrected. The feelings of undisturbed nirvana-like calm remain dimly within him, and may serve as a retrogressive goal toward which he strives to return as he grows from it into a more demanding and disturbing world. All ill persons have a tendency to regress in order to regain care and protection, and the fetal position adopted by some schizophrenic patients is considered to derive from unconscious and unformed memories of the only period of bliss the patient has known. The neonate's helplessness diminishes gradually and the period blends into the remainder of infancy, but for many months the vital issues will continue to focus upon the mother's capacities to provide the total care that the young infant requires.

References

1. C. Anderson Aldrich, "The Advisability of Breast Feeding," *Journal of the American Medical Association*, 135 (1947), 915–916.
2. Raymond De Saussure, "J. B. Félix Descuret," in *The Psychoanalytic Study of the Child*, Vol. 2 (New York: International Universities Press, 1946), pp. 417–424.
3. Milton Diamond, "A Critical Evaluation of the Ontogeny of Human Sexual Behavior," *Quarterly Review of Biology*, 40 (1965), 147–175.
4. Sibylle Escalona, "The Study of Individual Differences and the Problem of State," *Journal of the American Academy of Child Psychiatry*, 1 (1962), 11–37.
5. G. W. Greenman, "Visual Behavior of Newborn Infants," in Albert J. Solnit and Sally A. Provence (eds.), *Modern Perspectives in Child Development* (New York: International Universities Press, 1963), pp. 71–79.
6. Grantly Dick Read, *Childbirth Without Fear: The Principles and Practice of Natural Childbirth* (New York: Harper & Bros., 1944).
7. Lester W. Sontag, "The Significance of Fetal Environmental Differences," *American Journal of Obstetrics and Gynecology*, 42 (1941), 996–1003.
8. Lester W. Sontag, "Differences in Modifiability of Fetal Behavior and Physiology," *Psychosomatic Medicine*, 6 (1944), 151–154.
9. David K. Spelt, "The Conditioning of the Human Fetus in Utero," *Journal of Experimental Psychology*, 38 (1948), 338–346.
10. Celia Stendler, "Sixty Years of Child Training Practices," *Journal of Pediatrics*, 36 (1950), 122–134.
11. Clark E. Vincent, "Trends in Infant Care Ideas," *Child Development*, 22 (1951), 199–209.
12. William Young, Robert Goy, and Charles Phoenix, "Hormones and Sexual Behavior," *Science*, 143 (1964), 212–218.

Suggested Reading

Therese Benedek, "Psychological Aspects of Mothering," *American Journal of Orthopsychiatry*, 26 (1956), 272–278.

Grete L. Bibring, Thomas F. Dwyer, Dorothy S. Huntington, and Arthur F. Valenstein, "A Study of the Psychological Processes in Pregnancy and the Earliest Mother-Child Relationships: Some Propositions and Comments," in *The Psychoanalytic Study of the Child*, Vol. 16 (New York: International Universities Press, 1961), pp. 9–72.

Sylvia Brody, *Patterns of Mothering: Maternal Influence During Infancy* (New York: International Universities Press, 1956).

Benjamin Spock, John Reinhart, and Wayne Miller, A *Baby's First Year* (New York: Duell, Sloan & Pearce, 1955).

Herbert Thoms, *Childbirth with Understanding* (Chicago: Charles C Thomas, 1962).

Peter H. Wolff, "The Courses, Controls, and Organization of Behavior in the Neonate," *Psychological Issues*, Vol. 5, No. 1, Monograph 17 (New York: International Universities Press, 1960).

CHAPTER 5

❀ ❀ ❀ ❀ ❀

Infancy

WE SHALL CONSIDER the first fifteen months as the period of infancy, a definition that is somewhat arbitrary, for the rates of both maturation and development vary from child to child. In these months the helpless neonate, who spends most of his time sleeping and can do little but suck milk reflexly and signal his discomfort or pain by diffuse crying, turns into an alert toddler whose verve is fascinating, who actively explores his world, and who is learning how to gain some mastery over it by incessant experimentation. At some time around fifteen months of age, his development leads to a focus on new tasks both for the child and his parents; he becomes ambulatory and can pursue objectives; he begins to try to direct his own behavior and yet does not have the capacities or the experience to do so, and the nurturing persons must set limitations for him.

These are a very long fifteen months. During no other period of life is the person so transformed both physically and developmentally. Yet what happens lies beyond the individual's recall, buried in the oblivion of wordlessness. At most some vague feeling, some amorphous recollection that eludes conscious memory may upon occasion flit in and out of an adult's awareness, perplexing or troubling as might a fragment of a dream. The inability to recollect our infancies sets limitations on our capacities properly to understand or depict the period. We depend largely upon observation and making presumptive connections between occurrences in infancy and characteristics that develop later in life. Considerable impetus for the study and understanding of infancy came from psychoanalytic reconstructions of what might have happened in the infancy of adult patients. Still, because we recall nothing, there has been a tendency to discuss infancy in very global terms; sometimes primarily in terms of the infant's need for maternal love and of disturbances that ensue from lack of proper maternal nurturance or from frustration of oral needs. Yet these are the months when the foundations are laid, not only for future emotional stability, but also for basic though global character traits and for intellectual development. No part of his life experience will be as solidly incorporated in the individual, become so irrevocably a part of him, as his infancy.

The clarification of how the many developments occur and how the profound transformation from neonate to toddler transpires has awaited direct, skilled, and detailed observations of infants.* Such direct observational studies, and particularly longitudinal studies that relate the events of infancy to subsequent personality functioning, are vital to assessing the importance of various influences affecting the infant and to clarifying the essentials of infant care.

* Planned, scientific study of the infant's development has been carried out only during the past three or four decades. It has not always been obvious that the infant's personality development is a topic for scientific study. Direct observation of infants and children over the course of time probably started with Gesell's careful studies of maturation that established landmarks for comparison, and with Piaget's studies of the cognitive development of his own children in the service of epistemology. Currently, a variety of direct studies are expanding our knowledge of the period. Longitudinal studies through infancy and childhood are difficult to carry out, and many of them tend to focus on some specific facet of the problem to avoid a complexity that cannot be handled with scientific rigor. Only an occasional study is conducted in the infant's natural habitat, the home. The longitudinal studies of the infant and his family being carried out at the Yale Child Study Center are unique in their efforts to combine direct observation with psychoanalytic study, and to consider the essential data despite its inordinate complexity because simplification is possible only at the price of considerable error. These studies seek to consider the child's make-up at birth, his particular attributes, the mother's personality and problems, the child-rearing patterns, the influences of other family members, etc., and seek to relate the interplay of such factors during infancy to later personality development and characteristics.[25, 28]

During infancy profound maturational changes take place. The baby's weight triples by the end of the first year, and at fifteen months he may weigh close to twenty-five pounds. With six teeth and the buccal pads filled, his face has rounded out. The nerves of the pyramidal tracts of the spinal cord that transmit motor impulses from the cortex have been covered by myelin sheaths and become functional, enabling the child to learn to stand, walk, and begin to gain sphincter control. The buttocks that were minuscule at birth have filled out, and body proportions have changed so that the head, while still relatively large, is balanced by the trunk and extremities.

The Need for Total Nurturance

When we scrutinize the infant's developmental progress carefully, we find that so much occurs over fifteen months that we may doubt the wisdom of considering this span collectively as a single period. Indeed, so profound a shift in behavior takes place some time between the sixth and eighth months that we might well divide infancy in half. However, infancy is unified by the extent of the child's dependency on others, by his inability to walk or talk except in halting and rudimentary fashion, and by the limitations of his intelligence.

Throughout infancy the child is dependent upon the nurturant care provided by others. During the first several months when the predominant portion of his energy goes into growth and he can survive only under carefully controlled conditions, the physical aspects of nurturant care are most important. The young infant requires the food, warmth, diapering, bathing, and care of his delicate skin that permit the long periods of sleep during which the organism matures to become prepared for survival with better physiologic homeostasis than at birth. Then, as we shall discuss, the infant increasingly requires stimulating and socializing experiences to provide "nutriment" for his development into a person. The lack of adequate physical care means death, wasting, or ill health; failure of socializing nurturance means distortion of emotional development and stunting of intellectual growth. The two aspects of nurturant care are obviously related: the infant whose basic physiologic needs are not, or cannot, be satisfied remains in a state of tension that impedes his absorption of environmental stimuli, and it appears as if many infants make "friends with death for lack of love alone." *

During the first half of infancy, particularly during the first four months, the physical nurturance is of dominant importance and neglect

* Edna St. Vincent Millay, "Love Is Not All."

of socializing and affectional attention can probably be largely neutralized by subsequent efforts; but disregard of such needs in the second half of infancy leaves permanent impairments that can later be ameliorated but never completely undone. Whereas the infant still requires careful attention to his physical needs in the latter part of infancy, he is more resilient, which permits greater leeway in the manner in which physical care is provided. Still, it is a relative matter, for the socializing care provided during the first four months is probably very important even though not so essential as later. The mother who is pleased with herself and with having a baby brings a great deal of socialization to her small infant almost without realizing it. She cuddles her baby while she nurses him, whether from breast or bottle; she holds him closely for a moment after lifting him from the bassinet; she smiles at him, talks to him, croons, while holding him in her lap or changing his diaper. She shakes her head up and down at him, shuttles him about gently as she raises him into the air to admire him at arm's length; she swishes him about in the bath, drips water from the cloth onto his chest, scoops handfuls of warm water over him; she kisses his feet and holds his face to hers. Indeed, the mother is very likely to carry out a great deal of play, stimulation, and interaction with the infant simply as tangible expressions of her feelings toward her infant, her delight with him, and of her satisfaction with herself for having produced him.

Mutuality between Mother and Child

The provision of nurturance that fills the infant's needs is not always simple. Instruction and even firm tradition cannot take into account the marked differences among infants, or provide the mother with the "feel" that seems so important to establishing the proper mutuality between infant and mother. Although infants at a given stage of maturation are much alike, they also vary markedly within the range and patterns common to all. It is obvious that they look different and act and react diversely. Infants suck more vigorously or quietly; they take in different amounts of food and are satiated for longer or shorter periods; they are cuddly, sprawling, or resistant when held; their thresholds of alertness and sensitivity to discomfort vary; they vary from being very placid to hyperactive. Less apparent but just as surely, infants' physiological processes vary and influence their needs and how they mature and develop.

We assume, with considerable certainty, that the infant's inborn characteristics will influence the sort of person he will become; but it is often difficult to know just which of such observed traits come into the world within the infant and which appear in response to the type and quality of the nurture provided. In any case, the interweaving of inborn and environmental influences starts in the uterus and becomes increasingly complex during birth and thereafter. Some infants would present difficulties to any mother, but some mothers would create difficulties for any infant. At different periods in history or in different social settings the infant or the mother is more likely to be blamed: the baby is just impossible, or the mother is rejecting or emotionally unsuited to being a mother. We know that the young infant can do nothing about his part in establishing a proper symbiosis with his mother; and although we like to think that the mother could be other than she is if she would only try, the most pertinent matters concern feelings and attitudes that are not readily influenced by conscious decision. We must try to accept both infant and mother as they are, hoping that support, advice, or psychotherapy can help the mother, and that improved nurturance, perhaps more suited to the infant's specific needs, will make him more satisfied and easier to manage.

One mother may find it easier to enjoy a placid infant, another a baby who is more alert and responsive or even hyperactive. One mother will feel more maternal because her infant has difficulties in nursing, but another will feel frustrated, tense, and angry. Problems can be compounded by the great changes which occur as infancy progresses and which require constant shifts in how the mother relates to her baby. To serve properly as a custodial ego and meet the child's needs, the mother must be able to empathize or identify with her child; but it is not a diffuse feeling state or a static condition that is required but rather an ability to shift her identification with a child who is changing more rapidly than he will at any other time of his life. Such shifts are made particularly difficult because he can tell her nothing; and she must grasp how he feels, what he needs, what he may be able to do, and what exceeds his abilities today but may not next week. It is a task that can be helped by conscious knowledge and decision making, but it is carried out largely intuitively.

The creation and development of a mutuality in which the mother is perceptive—unconsciously or empathically perceptive—and responsive to her infant's needs must depend upon the mother and not the infant. Some mothers, presumably because of their own experiences during infancy and early childhood, have an earthy sensuous attachment to the infant; some have gained security, ease and knowledge from having helped raise younger siblings; and some simply gain so much pleasure from caring for their babies that the proper feelings follow. The care of the child is burdensome to some mothers, for it seems like a very one-sided proposition with little reward. Many mothers, in contrast, feel that their infants give them a great deal: a sense of completion as a woman; relief from engorged breasts and the pleasure of having them sucked; focus to their lives; a source of interest and pride; a new bond to their husbands. Although the unit of mother and child is of primary importance throughout infancy, the pair are not living in isolation, and the mother's capacities to feel herself in a unity with the infant and the pleasure she gets in so doing reflect her relations to her husband and her other children as well as her own personality.

A proper empathy permits a consistency in responding to the infant's changing needs and ways which permits a type of nonverbal communication to become established between mother and child that eases the first year of life and can help greatly to keep his discomforts and tensions minimal. But it also serves other important purposes. The mother's relaxation and comfort, and also her tensions and irritability, are conveyed to the infant through her handling of him. The relief of a mother's tensions may well be almost as important to the infant as relief of his own needs. Perhaps the first leverage in having the infant rescind instinctual efforts to gain immediate relief of tensions produced by hunger or thirst comes when he delays or modifies his behavior in order to have the comfort of a relaxed mother. Such responsiveness on the part of the infant can arise only when his mother's ways of relating to him are sufficiently consistent to enable him to become conditioned to, or otherwise learn, signals and cues. Further, such responsivity to felt and observed cues by both mother and child provides the foundations upon which more clear-cut communicative signals will develop, and provides assurance that the infant will gain trust in the value of communication—including verbal communication—as a means of solving problems.

Of course, not all infants are cared for by their mothers. An older sibling may gain little pleasure from the activity, carrying it out in cursory, impatient, or even angry fashion. Not all mothers are able to invest the baby adequately. A mother may be stiff, perfunctory, and silent in handling the child, particularly if she is depressed following the birth, as occurs commonly enough. The infant may be nurtured more salubriously by an experienced, secure, and interested nurse than by the mother. Indeed, although the practice of leaving the essential care of the infant and small child to a nursemaid, once common among the well-to-do, has diminished greatly, many children are still raised in this manner. The mother's influence can then be reserved for interactions and for periods of childhood for which she has greater competence and security.

Basic Trust

A critical task and a central theme of infancy concerns the establishment of feelings of confidence in the world. While completely dependent upon the care of others, the child needs to gain a sense that those upon whom he unknowingly depends, and who comprise his world, are dependable. As Erikson has aptly put it, the child attains a *basic trust* in others which will form the nucleus for achieving trust in himself, or he is left with an enduring distrust.[11] If essential needs are met when he is unable to provide anything for himself, he gains a feeling that the world is trustworthy and adequately consistent to enable him to live in it with security. The provision of a firm foundation during infancy permits the child to move into the next phase and invest his energy and attention in solving its basic tasks. He will have experienced and have established at the core of his personality the security that when he was helplessly dependent unbearable tensions had not been permitted to mount within him to provoke rage, nor had neglect led to the establishment of a pattern of apathy to defend against untenable tensions, nor had parental fears and anxieties been transmitted to him through his parents' ways of handling him and responding to him. In contrast, deprivations during infancy interfere with progression as energy continues to be expended in a repetitive seeking after the satisfactions and security that were lacking. Such frustrations pave the way for tendencies toward regressive strivings for dependency and a hungering for affection in later life; or engender proclivities toward pessimistic hopelessness and to resentful rage when the individual is deprived.

A basic *trust in the self*, a pervasive sense of confidence that becomes an inherent characteristic in later life, rests upon *trust in others* during infancy because during much of infancy there is no clear boundary between the self and the remainder of the world, and the infant cannot differentiate between how he feels and what the mother does that influences his feelings. How the infant feels, particularly during the early months, rests largely upon the satisfaction of his hunger and upon a comfortable satiety that permit relaxation and rest. The need for nourishment to supply the demands of his growth dominates his life.

Infancy as the "Oral" Phase

Psychoanalytic psychology has termed infancy the *oral phase* of psychosexual development, thus emphasizing that the infant's life centers upon his taking in nutriment through sucking and that his first critical relationships with others form while he is completely dependent upon them and receiving the vital nourishment from them.* In the process, a firm and enduring connection is established between affection and feeding, between a need for others and oral activity, and a basis is laid for later wishes, when overwhelmed by life's difficulties, to return or regress to such oral dependency. The infant is born prepared to maintain life by sucking and swallowing, which are the only coordinated movements he can make and his only organized way of relating to anything outside of himself. The lips and their mucocutaneous junction areas are highly sensitive, and their stimulation sets off the sucking reflex. They are not only sensitive but a source of sensuous pleasure which serves to assure—in evolutionary terms—that the infant will seek the stimulation that sets off sucking. The oral zone and the act of sucking are erotized in that sucking is pleasurable for its own sake, as is obvious if one watches a child suck his thumb with lustful avidity, and because of the generalized gratification that accompanies nutritional and also non-nutritional sucking. Other types of sensual pleasure will be related to these oral satisfactions and connect orality to sexuality.

The period is "oral" also in the broader sense that the infant's development rests upon the taking in of stimuli from the environment to start the organization of his cognitive processes, and because his emotional security rests upon the assimilation of feelings of security and well-being from those who nurture him.

The concept of orality, however, must not be taken too literally† as

* Originally the concept of the oral phase, as noted in Chapter 3, connoted that the lips and mouth were the area in which the libido was primarily invested during the first year of life. It is not necessary to utilize this concept of a displaceable sexualized energy to explain the importance of orality in infancy and the erotization of the oral zone.

† Such literal concern with "oral libido" has led some to discuss problems of the period virtually in terms of the relationship between the mother's breast and the child's mouth. Melanie Klein and her followers have made significant contributions by drawing attention to the intensity of the infant's primitive feeling states and their influence on development, but they have neglected the state of the infant's cognitive development and attributed perceptions and concepts to it that are impossible at this period of life. The notions of the "good" and "bad" breast can be considered only metaphorically. See M. Klein, *The Psychoanalysis of Children*.[18]

implying that how the child is fed is almost all that matters. Other sensations are also very important to the very young infant. Tactile sensations and skin erotism, as well as the totality of the handling, are significant in providing a sense of comfort and security in the infant when he is held by the mothering person.* The oral relatedness properly includes the relationship through touch, odor, body position, warmth, and the visual connections to the mother's eyes and face that are an important aspect of nursing. The security, tenderness, and conviction with which the mother carries out her many maternal tasks enter into conveying the sense of inherent trust that is a cardinal task of the period. However, the very young infant's sense of well-being rests largely on his proper nourishment, and we shall return to discuss feeding shortly.

Other Major Developmental Tasks

Although the attainment of an inherent sense of trust is a crucial task of infancy and critical to the future emotional well-being of the individual, it is far from the only fundamental task of infancy. The neonate is amorphous, still undifferentiated from his mother except in the literal sense—even unaware of a self and a mother; he is incapable of directing his movements, of perceiving his environment, of communicating except through crying. At the end of the period he is still far from a self-sufficient person but he has gained considerable stability and organization. He can control his body fairly well, relate to much of his environment and manipulate it meaningfully, and his emotional reactions have become more discrete and interrelate with those of others. His mind is developing rapidly and he can communicate verbally; and he has become very much of a person. Boundaries between the self and his environment and particularly between himself and his mother are being established; and he has learned something of the difference involved in controlling the self, others, or inanimate objects. Though his tolerance is limited, he can brook delay in having his needs met, and he can begin to

---

* Harlow, in a classic experiment,[15, 16] demonstrated the importance of skin erotism in the infantile "oral" behavior of monkeys. He had rhesus infants nursed by artificial mothers of two types: one was constructed of wire and contained a bottle and nipple; the other was covered with terry cloth and did not contain a feeding device. The monkeys fed from the "wire mother"; but when frightened by a snakelike device that set off an inborn fear reaction, they ran to the "terry cloth mother" and clung to it, very much as baby monkeys cling to a real mother when frightened. Thus, the feeding did not lead the baby monkeys to turn to the wire device as a mother; the tactile quality of the terry cloth was more important. We shall refer to these experiments again for other important, though serendipitous, findings.

delay his own responses and actions to permit trial and error and some
degree of intention.

As we shall note, the infant traverses a great distance and establishes
the foundations for many developmental accomplishments; and it is imperative that a great deal be gained besides a sense of basic trust. However, such abilities and characteristics are potentials permitted by the
process of physical maturation which the infant acquires under reasonable environmental conditions with greater or lesser facility, but they are
not an inherent part of maturation. As careful studies of seriously deprived children have taught, without suitable nurturant care if not affection, and without environmental stimulation and an opportunity to use
limbs and sense organs, very little developmental progress may take place
—as will be discussed later in the chapter.

Even without considering the catastrophic results of gross neglect, it is
apparent that what a baby will be like by the end of infancy depends
upon the interplay of many factors. Erikson has stated that "while it is
clear what must happen to keep a baby alive and what must not happen
lest he be physically damaged or chronically upset, there is a certain leeway in regard to what may happen." [11] This leeway permits different
societies to utilize differing child-rearing procedures, each of which the
members of the society consider to be the only proper method. Different
societies may prescribe letting an infant scream until it is the scheduled
time for feeding; or carrying the baby in a sling, positioned so that he
can nurse at his mother's breast when he desires; or swaddling and leaving the infant in a covered cradle; or giving the infant to an experienced
wet nurse to raise for the first year or two. Each method works but leaves
its imprint on the developing personality. Indeed, the varying techniques
are part of the way in which each society unknowingly prepares its offspring to become proper members. The essential tasks of the mother are
simplified in societies with definitive traditional directives for infant
care. The mother can carry out her functions with a conviction and security that help impart an innate sense of trust to her child,* particularly
since in such societies little if any connection between the child-rearing
procedures and the child's future personality is appreciated.

* This does not imply that the traditional techniques are always suited to instilling
a basic trust; there are indications that the Balinese techniques described elsewhere
in this book (see also G. Bateson and M. Mead [4]) prevent the development of such
trust, and sometimes a workable child-rearing pattern no longer exists—as perhaps
during the Middle Ages after the Black Death and the Crusades so disrupted the
structure of European society that in some localities only one out of every ten babies
reached adulthood.

The situation of the contemporary American mother is apt to be very different. She may mistrust the traditional and be very much on her own; and she is often burdened by an awareness that just what she does, how she feels, her own neurotic problems, etc., may be influencing her child's future. In considering the infant's development and the importance of the mother, it should be realized that an infant has considerable resiliency.

The Nurture of the Young Infant

During the first few months the infant's eating and sleeping are of central importance to him; and the mother's sleep as well as the child's depends greatly upon his feeding. The mother seeks to furnish ample nourishment, to keep the baby clean and warm, to provide suitable conditions for sleeping. The infant can in these first months survive and even flouish without any socializing activities; but after the first few weeks, the stimulation, the cuddling, the being talked at makes a difference. Even in neonates a relationship exists between the amount of crying and the amount of nursing care provided.* Because of the critical importance to the infant of proper nutrition, but also to help foster a proper mutuality between mother and child, breast feeding has been encouraged by many pediatricians and obstetricians during recent years, as has been discussed in the preceding chapter. However, we must realize that only a minority of mothers in the United States nurse their babies. When a mother breast-feeds willingly and without conscious conflict, breast feeding is very likely to be the most satisfactory method for both mother and baby; but there is nothing inherent in the process to insure gentleness, restfulness, or intimacy.† When a woman nurses from a sense of obligation or to prove to herself that she is a good mother, it is of dubious value. Indeed, it is likely that a mother who does not really wish to nurse will not have sufficient milk.‡ An impression has long existed that the milk of anxious or tense mothers may cause gastrointesti-

---

* In a systematic study the crying of neonates was reduced by 50 per cent by increasing nursing care from 0.7 to 1.9 hours a day for each infant.[3]

† Brody found by experimental observation that neither breast feeding, nor demand feeding, nor holding the baby while it was being fed would separately or collectively assure satisfaction in feeding.[8]

‡ Newton and Newton[22] found that 74 per cent of ninety-one mothers with a positive attitude about nursing before they delivered had enough milk by the fifth postnatal day, as against 26 per cent with negative attitudes. Newton also reported a correlation between preference for breast feeding and the avoidance of rigid feeding schedules.[21]

nal upsets—which may be the reason a leading dairy firm advertises "milk from contented cows." However, the mother's tensions may be conveyed through the manner in which she handles the baby rather than through her milk. In any event, the manner in which the infant takes his food and how he digests it often reflects the mother's handling,* and it is a matter that concerns attitudes and feelings that are not easily overcome by conscious effort or direct instruction, though instruction that serves to reassure and promote confidence can be very helpful.

Demand Feeding

The desire of pediatricians to see that their young patients receive adequate nourishment and oral gratification, and their recognition of the deleterious effects of frustration, have led many of them to recommend the practice of "self-demand feeding." † [2] According to this regimen, the infant is fed when he cries or otherwise shows his hunger. The practice follows upon the realization that infants differ both in how much milk they can take at a feeding and also in how long it meets their needs. Little is gained by making the child wait for a scheduled feeding when he is becoming upset. A seriously frustrated and enraged baby has difficulty in nursing, and an upset child's gastric functioning may not be suited for digestion. The infant is incapable of learning to wait for a scheduled time during the first several months of life, and even later has little tolerance for delay. "Demand feeding" is a sensible approach, particularly when the mother can be adaptable in using it. If the mother can anticipate when her baby will become hungry and is not overly con-

---

* Escalona, in a study of infants of mothers in a reformatory, found that infants' refusals of food, sudden changes in preferences, and digestive upsets occurred in relation to the attitudes and behavior of the person who was feeding them, or to such factors as separation from the mother. In eight of ten infants who refused to take the mother's breast, the mothers were clearly high-strung and excitable; and six infants accepted a formula from another feeder on the same day on which they refused the same formula when offered by their mothers.[12]

† "Self-demand" also arose in reaction to the rigid scheduling that had been foisted upon mothers by pediatricians under the influence of behaviorist psychologists in the 1920's and 1930's. By this approach, a baby was to be trained—conditioned—almost from birth, and a mother who gave in to a child's needs for food at an unscheduled time was considered a bad mother who spoiled the child. Only reasonably self-sufficient mothers were likely to follow their own feelings and defy the authorities. A comparison of the 1938 and 1948 editions of the United States Children's Bureau bulletin *Infant Care*, published by the United States Government Printing Office, provides striking evidence of the vast change that occurred in these ten years concerning the child-rearing procedures advocated.

cerned about letting the child cry for a short time, a satisfactory feeding pattern can usually be established within a few weeks as the infant gains in physiological stability. Some mothers, however, who are insecure and overly conscientious interpret "self-demand" to mean that the baby must be fed only when he cries and then as soon as he cries; a mother then can become enslaved to the task, often confusing the infant in the process, and her aggravation disrupts the mother-child harmony.* When, as has been observed, a mother tries to nurse twenty or thirty times a day, a consistent signaling system cannot be established.

The Mother's Security

In general, the precise techniques for caring for the baby and handling him are less important than having a secure and consistent mother who can enjoy her infant and achieve a close mutuality with him. An overemphasis on the benefits of breast feeding or of prolonged breast feeding has at times been as brash as the behavorist strictures of an earlier period.† And warnings of the dire consequences of relatively minor deficiencies in handling the young infant have been based upon theory and conjecture rather than definitive knowledge.‡ Fortunately, the infant seems very capable of tolerating the awkwardness of new and well-intentioned mothers. Although mothers do not always know best, provoking guilt in a mother because her needs sometimes take precedence

* S. Brody, *Patterns of Mothering*,[8] p. 320.
† Thus a psychiatrist who noted the paucity of anxiety states and combat neuroses among the Okinawans during the intense fighting for their island in World War II attributed their emotional stability to the fact that Okinawans were habitually breast-fed for three years.[20] He did not take other potential factors into account or realize that although Okinawans might be unusually mentally healthy on Okinawa, Okinawans living in Hawaii had mental illness rates as high as or higher than the remainder of the population, even though they too had been breast-fed for several years.
‡ There is no evidence that childhood schizophrenia, severe apathy, or serious mental retardation can be related to deficiencies in maternal child rearing alone, unless it is a matter of severe neglect, maternal apathy, or brutality; and certainly there is no reason to believe that lack of cuddling, faulty holding, or inadvertent frustration lead to any such dire consequences.
Margaret Ribble's widely read book, *The Rights of Infants*,[27] though properly drawing attention to the relief of tensions that can be accomplished by proper handling, feeding, etc., seems to have overstated the case to the extent of frightening some mothers and inadvently creating the tensions in handling their babies that the author sought to have them overcome. Hilde Bruch's *Don't Be Afraid of Your Child*[9] sought to reassure mothers of the sturdiness of their infants' emotional balance in order to offset such influences.

over her baby's, or because her personality difficulties make her anxious in caring for the baby, helps neither mother nor child. Personality problems are not solved by admonition or through warnings of dire consequences. Fostering security is usually far more important; the care of the baby can and should provide pleasure and become neither a chore that wears out the mother nor a source of constant concern.

Attachment Behavior

The mere fact that a woman has become a mother provides no assurance that she will be maternal. The capacities to be properly nurturant involve basic factors in her own development which will be discussed in subsequent chapters. Still, there are biological factors that help establish an attachment between mother and child. One potential benefit of breast feeding is that the pituitary hormone prolactin which stimulates the flow of milk may help foster feelings of receptive passivity and contentment in the mother.[5] Bowlby has suggested that several forces induce "attachment behavior" between mother and child which he relates to "imprinting" phenomena in ground-nesting birds and the attachment of baby ungulates to their mothers.[6] Although Bowlby may overstate the situation by the analogy, several factors of potential importance should not be neglected. Greenman reports the mother's pleasure and excited interest when her neonate fixes his gaze on her, and considers that this early fixation of the eyes may serve the infant in a biological sense by enhancing the care the pleased and responsive mother gives him.[14] We have noted that both the infant's lips and the mother's nipples are erogenous zones: sucking gratifies the baby independently of the satisfaction derived from food intake; and the baby's sucking properly provides the mother with sensuous pleasure, including genital stimulation. It has been suggested that the infant's crying may arouse some inborn response in adults. Whether the response is innate or not, most adults find the baby's wails sufficiently unpleasant to induce them to try to stop the crying. The mother's odor may, as in many animals, form a basic linkage between the baby and his own mother or the mothering person.* Then, in the older infant, the verbalizations of adults stimulate him to babble, which in turn leads adults to talk more to the infant.

* The hypothesis is difficult to test in infants. However, older children can be noted to gain comfort and pleasure by inhaling the mother's odor, perhaps her genital odor, when they stand with head in the mother's skirt and sniff or breathe deeply. The relationship of the mother's odor to certain types of fetishist behavior and renifleur activities comprises a complex and inadequately studied topic.

The Smiling Response

The baby's smile, which first appears between the fourth and twelfth week, forms a significant developmental landmark that has been carefully studied. It clearly serves to promote the mothering person's attachment to the infant. The baby smiles on seeing his mother's face, which leads the mother to feel that her baby now recognizes her. Wolff has documented [35] the observation that there is a noticeable rise in the amount of attention that the mother gives her child after he begins to smile at her. We must examine this slight but important event that so fosters the mother's attachment to her infant.

The infant starts taking in his environment orally, and then, as he gains control of his oculomotor muscles and before he can use his hands, he starts to explore his surroundings visually—even before he can bring objects to his mouth to explore them orally. As he nurses he stares at his mother's eyes and face, not at her breast or the bottle. He stares and begins to follow with his eyes. Aside from such following, the smile is the first clear indication of a relationship to another person. However, Spitz has shown that the baby does not really recognize the mother.* Any face will do, provided it is seen in full face, for a profile will not elicit the smile. According to Piaget, a singing and nodding full face will be most successful in eliciting the response at first. Spitz further found that the region of the forehead, eyes, and nose is the inducer of the response; it does not matter if the mouth is covered, but the smile is not elicited if any portion of the upper face is covered. Actually, it does not require a face; a crudely formed mask resembling the forehead, eyes, and nose suffices to elicit the smile when moved up and down. Spitz's studies indicate, then, that the baby is innocently perpetrating a fraud upon his mother by inducing her to believe that his smile is one of personal recognition. It may take another six months for the child to know his own mother—that is, to distinguish her as an individual;† though long before that he will be responding to her presence differently than to others.

---

* René Spitz, who has carefully investigated the smiling response, finds that it appears between two and six months of age in almost all infants, and that only 2 per cent smiled at an earlier age.[33] Others find it appears at four to six weeks in many children. Piaget, for example, definitely records the appearance of smiling responses at six weeks in his own children. Perhaps most of the children Spitz studied were seriously deprived and thus late in forming the reaction.

† It is possible that the early smiling response is an inborn response to a specific "releaser," the "releaser" consisting of a pattern resembling a human forehead, eyes, and nose, even as certain birds respond to a fixed pattern in the mother's coloring

Cognitive Development during the First Four Months

The infant's development starts slowly but accelerates during the third and fourth months. When he is about four months old the period of diffuse existence in which maturation and growth predominate is coming to an end, and the infant shows evidence of becoming more of a social creature. He has doubled his birth weight and is far more sturdy than he was at birth. His life no longer consists primarily of sleeping and eating, and he now is awake for fairly long periods, playing with his hands, looking and listening, and making cooing and gurgling sounds. He can now be propped into a sitting position and with the grasp reflex gone he can clutch at things and play with his fingers, and he seems intrigued by dangling toys. He watches and listens and is alert to cues that signal what may happen next. His life has gained regularity through a pattern of an unbroken sleep of ten to twelve hours at night and reasonably regular feedings three to five times a day. When we study him closely he has gained many capacities and skills since he was born.

The slow start reflects not only the dominance of maturational needs during the first several months, but also the building of a foundation to which experiences can be assimilated. The branches must spread out from the seedling and the roots must branch out to obtain nourishment. The newborn's mind may not be a "tabula rasa" (for it has a predetermined structure and organization), but it is bereft of experience with which to perceive its surroundings and it has only some simple reflex motor patterns built in. As explained in Chapter 3, Piaget has sought to trace how the motor skills, sensory perceptions, and cognitive abilities are acquired in a steplike process of assimilation of new experiences to pre-existing schemata that are modified by what is assimilated, and how through such modifications of schemata the infant becomes capable of assimilating new experiences and carrying out increasingly complex activities. Let us consider some of Piaget's observations of how the infant acquires the abilities of a four-month-old baby.

Piaget's First Stage

Piaget terms the first two years *The Period of Sensori-Motor Development*. Its first stage, which approximates the first month, is sim-

---

or in the appearance of a hereditary enemy—the smiling response here having an evolutionary survival value through fostering proper nurturant care.

ply called *The Use of Reflexes*, in which the innate sucking and grasp reflexes and the eye movements are modified slightly.* However, there is little, if any, accommodation to sensory "aliments," and therefore little expansion in what can be assimilated by the infant. Sucking is set off by an increasing variety of different stimuli to the lips; the head reflexly turns to the side on which the lips are stimulated; and some discrimination between non-nurturant and nurturant objects develops in that when the infant is hungry he is apt to reject his fingers or any thing other than the nipple as an object for sucking.

The Second Stage

The second stage of sensori-motor development starts at the age of a few weeks and continues approximately through the fourth month. It is *The Stage of First Acquired Adaptations and the Primary Circular Reaction*. Now the innate reflex patterns begin to be modified. The changes start with the sucking schema, and it is worth examining these seemingly trivial alterations, as they form the simplest example of the pattern of assimilation and accommodation that forms the core of Piaget's conceptualization of cognitive development. The tongue in the sucking schema accidentally licks the lips and thus receives a new type of sensation or stimulation—new sensory aliment. The sensori-motor schema repeats the activity that provided the new aliment and becomes circular in "seeking" to regain it. The innate reflex schema of sucking is now altered by the experience; the sensation of lips on tongue has been assimilated and the sensori-motor sequence accommodates to include it. It is in such fashion that the child begins to modify reflex patterns, build up schemata, and start his intellectual development and knowledge of the world.

The infant soon begins to bring his thumb to his mouth, originally by accident, but the behavior develops into a firm schema after frequent repetition as a circular reaction; it is rewarded by relief of tension through sucking and by the erogenous pleasure of the act. The child follows light and then objects that fall within his visual field during the first month, and he soon spends much waking time staring at objects. He is not perceiving as yet,† but simply looking and assimilating, gradually organizing

---

* J. Piaget, *The Origins of Intelligence in Children*,[24] p. 23.
† Studies of congenitally blind persons whose sight was operatively restored in adolescence or adult life indicate how visual perception must be organized through experience. Patients reported that at first they experienced only new strange sensations or diffuse light. It took days to discriminate any differences between objects. These were

his visual schemata. Through a blending of visual schemata with sucking schemata, he will respond to the sight of the bottle by opening his mouth or by stopping his crying. Soon, aside from crying, the child shows a tendency to repeat sounds he makes—blowing noises, little laughing sounds, etc.—and the sounds themselves serve as stimuli for their reproduction in circular reactions. Then some distinctions that begin to signal differing needs may be noted in his cries. Such differentiation will depend upon the mother's consistency in responding to different sounds, which then leads the child to repeat the sound which is the first part of the circular reaction that leads to the effect. These simple accommodations of the vocalizing muscles to repeat sounds heard are important preliminaries of learning to speak. The schemata of hearing and vision begin to interpenetrate and accommodate to one another, and soon the baby listens to what he sees, and looks at sounds.

Sucking activities are, of course, very much the center of the infant's life. The mouth, at first, is virtually his organ of prehension, and through it many things are sampled and experienced. However, starting in this second period, the grasp reflex diminishes and manual prehension develops rapidly. Piaget has studied the changes in prehension, carefully considering five substages that lead from the simplest circular reactions to the ability to look at what is grasped and to try to grasp what is seen.* This coordination between grasping and vision forms a notable step toward differentiating objects and relating to the world. Sucking and the visual-sucking schemata diminish in importance, whereas vision and the coordination of vision and handling increasingly gain importance as a means of relating to and understanding the environment. Then, at about the end of the third month the child begins to coordinate vision, per-

---

persons who, in contrast to the infant, had already organized their surroundings through nonvisual perception—had an object concept and names for objects.

* The sequence is as follows: (1) The innate grasp reflex is modified by primary circular reactions that lead to repetitions of touching and grasping of various parts of the body: bringing the hand to the mouth to suck, and a simple staring at the hands in the visual field. (2) The child not only carries whatever he grasps to the mouth, but also grasps whatever is placed in his mouth—a prelude to the future dominance of prehension over mouthing. (3) Looking at the hand in the visual field leads to an increase in hand movements, which suggests that causing a new sensation in the visual field leads to a circular reaction of repeating the hand movement that changed the visual sensations. Now, when the hand happens into the visual field, it can be held there. (4) The infant can grasp objects in his visual field. At about four months, for example, if the rattle and hand are *both* in the visual field, the infant can grasp the rattle. (5) The child looks at what he grasps and tries to grasp what he looks at, a tendency that can cause the mother considerable difficulty.

hension, and sucking. Thus a child, looking at his mother's hand, grasps it, and draws it toward his mouth while looking at it.*

The Very Young Infant's World

In these first months of life, then, the infant is occupied with physical maturation, including physiological stabilization, and with the assimilation of his own movements, with learning the feel of his body, gaining control over his hand movements, and coordinating them with his sucking and vision. His mother is not yet a person, for there are no persons. There is still no proper distinction between himself and the environment, or between what is internal and external, or with objects as distinct from the sensori-motor patterns through which the infant interacts with them. Nevertheless, as discussed earlier, the mother is distinguished from others by the fourth month, as is apparent from the infant's anticipations of her actions; and she or some nurturing person is of utmost importance to him. She seeks to provide for her baby's physiological needs and keep his physiological tensions minimal while bringing some new stimulation to him. The infant can do little about reducing drive tensions except signal his discomfort. The mother is not only providing conditions that will enable the child to gain a sense of confidence in his world, but promotes conditions under which he can best learn. The infant does not advance by resolving conflicts or learning how to rid himself of tensions, for he has no such capacities. He learns because of an innate urge to assimilate new experiences. He is so constituted, his central nervous system is so constituted, that new experiences, including his own bodily movements, are rewarding sources of stimulation.

The mother's attempts to satisfy her child's needs are not always effective: indeed, the difficulties encountered lead some mothers to the verge of despair. An occasional child is hypersensitive and difficult to satisfy. An illness may disturb the equilibrium of another. A satisfying feeding schedule or method of feeding cannot be established. Holding and cuddling do not seem to comfort another. Colic or bowel movements cause the child pain. The sleep of the child and that of the parents is intermittent. Most difficulties are short-lived and are resolved—perhaps with the aid of the pediatrician. How much derives from something in the child and how much from the nature of the nurturing care may remain unanswered. This is the time when disturbances in the mother-

* J. Piaget, The Origins of Intelligence in Children,[24] pp. 89–121. See also P. H. Wolff, The Developmental Psychologies of Jean Piaget and Psychoanalysis.[36]

child relationship are apt to be reflected in physiological dysfunctions, particularly in feeding disturbances and gastrointestinal functioning.

From the Fourth to the Eighth Month

After the first four months there begins a period of transition, during which the infant's interests move away from himself into his surroundings, and which leads up to the critical shift that takes place some time around the seventh month when the mother clearly becomes a specific person to the child and the baby becomes much more of a social being— the time when the second major subphase of infancy starts.

During the middle third of the first year a great deal occurs as the baby increasingly becomes a lively character with a distinctive personality whose activities adults can find intriguing. By about the seventh month, he sits comfortably and without effort and can use both hands to hold things at the same time and perhaps pound them on the table or floor, enjoying both the movement and the noise. He can handle things, for the grasp reflex is virtually gone. In sitting he has gained a new perspective on the world and greater freedom to use his hands. When prone, he begins to make crawling movements and may even manage to move a bit: he will not remain static much longer. He has found his feet and explores them with his hands and even with his mouth. He can occupy himself by using almost any object as a toy to manipulate, to wave, or to bang. He likes to sit and watch his mother and is likely to enjoy sorties beyond the house—gazing and learning. Now he babbles endlessly, stimulated both by his own voice and by others talking to him. He is making sounds that prepare for almost any language, but soon they will move toward sounds of the language he hears. Certain noises he makes have become rudimentary signals of needs and wishes. Some frustration can be tolerated, and delays in signaling needs through crying can be noted, as when the child waits until he hears the mother in an adjacent room to convey his hunger by crying. There is one new source of discomfort. His first teeth—the two lower incisors—are cutting through his gums. They cause pain and may provoke sudden outbursts of crying. He bites on his gums seeking relief. The discomfort may interfere with sleep or eating, and the biting sometimes interferes with breast feeding.

Piaget's Third Stage of Cognitive Development

This midportion of the year is the time of Piaget's third stage of sensori-motor development to which he has given the interesting title *The*

Stage of Secondary Circular Reactions and Procedures Destined to Make Interesting Sights Last.* It follows upon the achievement of the ability to guide manual activities visually and upon the increasing importance of visual-motor schemata that direct the child toward explorations of the environment. As with the primary circular reactions, the infant repeats actions that accidentally produce a new experience, but these experiences are now primarily changes produced in the environment rather than changes related to bodily activities as in the earlier stage. Thus, a hand movement accidentally sets a hanging toy in motion and the infant then repetitively makes the hand movement that strikes the toy and swings it. Through such circular reactions the child begins to explore the world around him and gains means of influencing it. He assimilates the sensori-motor unit, for actions and objects are not yet clearly distinguished but remain part of a unified schema. In watching the child strike a swinging toy, one can note gradations in the intensity with which the toy is hit, and he slowly gains control over the amplitude of the swings. Eventually, a further modification occurs. A familiar object or situation may no longer set off the movement required for its activating the circular reaction, but the infant seems content to carry out only a fragment of the movement. It seems as though "the child were satisfied to recognize these objects or sights . . . but could not recognize them except by working, instead of thinking, the schema helpful to recognition . . . [that is] the secondary circular reaction corresponding to the object in question." † These are precursors of purely contemplative recognition and symbolization.

The infant now also tends to assimilate new objects into old patterns or schemata. A new doll, for example, is put through the baby's repertoire of sensori-motor schemata set off by such objects: it is sucked, waved, fingered, rubbed against the bars of the crib, dropped to the floor. An interesting aspect of these secondary circular reactions is the use of "procedures for making interesting sights last." The child's behavior may seem very puzzling. The child sees something happen at a distance and then in order to get it to recur will go through a set of movements as if he is attempting to control the distant object by magic—through waving his arms, kicking his feet, shaking himself; but he is simply providing the first portion of a circular reaction that may have accidentally preceded the "sight," and then goes on to use his repertoire of sensori-motor sche-

* J. Piaget, *The Origins of Intelligence in Children*,[24] pp. 122–180.
† *Ibid.*, pp. 185–186.

mata to try to activate the "sight." It is behavior that is semi-intentional; it is really still aimed at bringing about a repetition of something that happened accidentally. A significant aspect of these "procedures" concerns the substitution of sounds for actions, as when the baby smiles and says "aah!" when his door opens. The sound may be considered as an indication of recognition that someone is about to appear, or it may be understood as part of a secondary circular reaction—the first part of the procedure for making the "interesting sight" of a person appear again. In any case, it is part of the preparation for language.

The Second Half of Infancy

In the second half of the first year a new major subphase of infancy starts. Psychoanalytic psychology has emphasized a shift to an oral aggressive phase with teething, when the infant seeks actively to incorporate rather than assimilating more passively.*

Piaget has demonstrated that the infant now gains a more discrete concept of objects, including the mother; and Spitz emphasizes that a new organizing principle occurs when the infant relates to his mother as a specific individual.† In any event, the infant now needs his mother in order to feel secure, and he is becoming much more of a social creature for whom deprivation of interpersonal stimulation becomes a serious handicap to his emotional and intellectual development. We shall consider the nature of this change.

The Mother as a Separate Object

Ever since A. Freud and D. Burlingham's pioneering observations of the traumatic impact on babies of separation from their mothers during World War II[13] and Spitz's studies of institutionalized infants[33] a great deal has been written about the importance to the small child of a con-

* The pain of teething may stimulate tensions and conceivably aggressive feelings. The breast-fed infant may be weaned because he bites the nipple, and weaning can engender frustration with marked aggressivity—as can clearly be observed in older children when abrupt weaning is enforced. However, at this time the infant can begin to go after things and becomes less passive.
† As we have noted, the infant has a special relationship to his mother that is apparent after the age of four or five months. Many of the child's sensori-motor schemata have been developing in relation to the mother, her ways of handling her infant and reacting to him. The infant is more relaxed and comfortable when the mothering person takes care of him. Although separation from the mother causes the baby to be upset, before he is seven or eight months old she can be replaced by another competent person without serious consequences.

tinuing mothering person, and of how the loss of the mother disrupts the child's development and leads to depression and apathy. Although the evidence is not conclusive as yet, it appears that deprivation of the mother becomes particularly significant and highly traumatic some time between the ages of six and eight months. When younger infants are placed in a hospital they show strange behavior *after* they return home or when they are shifted to a new setting within the hospital. Schaffer has termed this the "global syndrome." [29] On returning home the infant seems preoccupied with his surroundings, raising his head and scanning objects without focusing on anything, and even ignoring his mother. The blank expression or frightened look is naturally very disturbing to the mother, who finds her child very changed. However, such behavior lasts only for a few hours or occasionally for a few days.

But by seven months of age the development of the essential interaction with the mother culminates in what Spitz has termed "eight-month anxiety" but which may appear any time after six months.* Instead of responding to a stranger's smile with a smile, the baby shows evidence of apprehension, tends to turn away and may start crying. The response is not to the mother's leaving but to the stranger's approach. It is as if the infant were upset at the dissonance from the familiar. Now strangers are best introduced when the child feels safe by being close to his mother or some other very familiar person. The mother has now become a specific source of comfort to the child, and her presence, as we shall see, seems essential to his well-being.

Even more important, during the second half of infancy separation from the mother produces far more drastic results than those described by Schaffer in the younger infant. The baby is stricken with a reaction similar to grief or depression which can progress to continued weeping, clinging, and disinterest, and to virtual loss of contact, apathy, and retardation, depending upon the duration of the separation and the quality of the substitute care that is provided.† It is difficult to sort out the differential impact of loss of the mother, loss of social stimulation, duration of the loss, and the quality of the substitute care. After the child and mother are reunited, the child displays a marked overdependence with excessive crying when his mother leaves him, a clinging to the

* See R. Spitz, *The First Year of Life*,[33] pp. 150–162. Here, as elsewhere, Spitz may have fixed the onset of a phenomenon late because a large portion of his studies were conducted with deprived infants.
† See also J. Bowlby, "Grief and Mourning in Infancy," [7] and subsequent discussions by Anna Freud, Max Schur, and René Spitz, pp. 53–94.[7]

mother, and a heightened fear of strangers; this behavior lasts for several weeks or longer. Spitz in his study of infants of prison inmates noted that those children whose mothers had been more involved with them suffered more than those whose mothers had not related well and who, in addition, were able to accept substitute mothers more readily.*

We should also note that the retardation and lack of verve shown by infants who are institutionalized soon after birth become pronounced during the second half of infancy. Of course, the mother does not become more important to the infant when he becomes seven months old. The difference is that the baby now recognizes that objects, and particularly the mother, are separate entities and not part of his schemata. He now reacts to her loss, rather than simply experiencing the diffuse uneasiness or the physiologic upset that absence of the mother provoked at an earlier age.

Piaget's Fourth Stage of Cognitive Development

Piaget has clearly demonstrated that by seven or eight months of age the infant has an idea of an object as against the earlier inclusion of the object as part of a sensori-motor schema. The fourth stage of sensori-motor development has much to do with the differentiation of objects. It is termed *The Coordination of Secondary Schemata and Their Application to New Situations*. The circular reactions begin to coordinate with one another and form new patterns of behavior that are clearly intentional. The idea of the object and intentionality are related. Thus, in seeking after an object, the baby retains the image or knowledge of the object even though it is partially hidden from view, and he combines schemata in obtaining it. A child will push away a pillow placed between him and a ball (one schema) and then grasp the ball (a second schema). His actions are now moving away from modifications of reflex acts to the pursuit of ends-in-view. He will begin to explore objects carefully, turning them over to look at the other side, feeling their shapes and looking

* This indicates that the benefits of good maternal care can turn into a disadvantage if the child loses the mother. An experiment of Seitz furnishes similar evidence that what is advantageous depends on the conditions. He deprived some of the kittens in a litter of adequate nursing experience, leaving the remainder to nurse freely. The orally deprived kittens did not flourish as well as the others and were less placid. After weaning, he conducted a test in which the kittens, in order to obtain food, had to cross a platform on which they were shocked. The orally deprived ignored the shock and obtained food regularly, whereas the normally nursed kittens became upset, could not gain food, and developed rather typical animal neuroses.[31]

at them from various angles. The objects seem to present him with a problem, and to some degree he recognizes that there is an objective reality to which he must adapt himself. As the period progresses, the infant is less bound to testing procedures "destined to make interesting sights last." If he sees a person ring a bell, he will push the person's hand toward the bell rather than going through his own repertoire of sensorimotor schemata. An object is no longer something simply to be used as part of one of his schemata, or for purposes of activity for activity's sake, but something to be mastered. This new relationship to his environment helps explain why separation from the mother becomes so traumatic at this phase of his development.*

The Start of Locomotion and Speech

As the infant moves toward and past his tenth month, he is not only much more active but interacts with members of his family, drawing them into his life. When his mother enters his room in the morning she is apt to find him standing holding on to the side of his crib, babbling away, and with his toy animals tossed on the floor. He begins to crawl and moves around his play pen. He may even be able to walk in tottering fashion if held by both hands. His babbling has moved toward the sounds of the language, and he may well please his parents by saying "da-da" or "ma-ma." These reiterative syllables are not yet real language, as will be discussed when we focus on early language development in the next chapter. He may also have learned to imitate waving "bye bye" and awkwardly clap his hands. There are still difficulties in using some of his newly gained skills: he may pull himself up to standing position but have difficulty getting down to the floor again, hesitant of landing with a thud; he may enjoy rolling or throwing a ball but be unable to release it at will.

The Response to "No!"

The "mama" and "dada" are scarcely words and do not yet designate specific persons, but sometime during these last months of the first year a

---

* Another important development in the child's ways of relating involves his response to signals. Although he has shown recognition of anticipatory signals earlier, anticipatory responses now become much more consistent. He may start to cry when he sees his mother putting on her coat. Many such responses are conditioned, but they are merging with intentional behavior. It seems quite intentional when a child will open his mouth for the spoon when it comes from the fruit bowl but not when it comes from the cereal bowl.

significant step takes place in the child's language development and, indeed, in his ways of relating when he begins to respond to "no!"* Perhaps it is a major step away from the unblemished innocence of childhood. At first the sharp "no-no!" of a parent simply frightens the infant and causes a pause in his activity, or causes him to cry, but soon the interjection stops him from what he is doing. The control is limited, but it is control through verbal communication that can be carried out from a distance; and it forms a sign that the child can internalize. It merges with the child's growing awareness that displeasure in the parent causes discomfort in him. However, it will be another five or six months before the child uses "no" himself. At this time of childhood he is becoming capable of sufficient independent activity to mobilize parental efforts to restrain him. The problems engendered by his mobility and incessant exploratory curiosity will reach their crisis later and will be discussed in the next chapter. During the remainder of infancy, the baby is consolidating and improving his skills. He practices through endless play at gaining dexterity as well as at learning to judge size and distance. At about a year he may toddle if held by one hand and cruise by holding on to furniture; but he is most mobile on all fours, perhaps often hoisting his rear end into the air and dashing along on hands and feet rather than really crawling. The number of words he knows increases, and their use is becoming more specific.

Self-Gratification

The child may have adopted a favorite blanket, sweater, or stuffed animal as a transitional object[34] and begin to display the phenomenon that Linus in the comic strip "Peanuts" has made so famous. It is a tactilely pleasant object that provides comfort and a sense of security in the mother's absence. It is a reflection of the skin sensuality that forms a part of the child's "oral" behavior. The child will clearly express his displeasure when the transitional object is missing, particularly at bedtime. As he grows somewhat older it becomes increasingly difficult if not impossible to provide a substitute without provoking a serious upset. Thumb sucking, genital play, the need for a transitional object are all means of providing for the self and of gaining comfort when the mothering person is not available. They are expected behaviors, and absence of genital play or thumb sucking may be as much a reason for concern as their presence. Efforts to deprive the infant and young child of such gratifications will

* R. Spitz, The First Year of Life,[33] pp. 174–195.

result in frustration and increased insecurity. However, many parents are seriously concerned by these "habits" and are apt to take stringent measures to stop them.*

Weaning

Weaning, which often occurs between the tenth month and the end of infancy, may increase the frequency and intensity of thumb sucking. The infant needs to gratify his oral sucking impulsion and there is evidence that insufficient sucking during feeding increases finger sucking, but too brief periods of nursing or too easy a flow of milk may also lead to intensive finger sucking. The determinants are not always clear and studies of the topic are in some respects contradictory.[17,19,30] Weaning traditionally has been considered a major frustration and potential source of emotional trauma. Abrupt weaning, particularly when accompanied by separation from the mother, can have serious consequences, but currently weaning does not usually cause notable frustration. If the baby is more than a few months old, additional foods including semi-solids have been added to the diet and he has become accustomed to taking food from a spoon or cup. If the child is weaned from the breast, a bottle may be substituted, and if the mother or nurse continues to hold the baby and cuddle him, the shift from breast feeding can proceed smoothly. The desire to satisfy the oral needs of the child properly had led some to delay weaning from a bottle until the child is older, but ideas that prolonging breast feeding into the second or third year makes weaning easier have no clear foundation.†

* Even the leading pediatric texts of twenty-five to thirty years ago advocated the use of arm braces to keep a baby from sucking his thumb, and various physical restraints to stop masturbation in both male and female children. There is little, if any, evidence that thumb sucking causes irregular dentition. The common belief that masturbation leads to mental deficiency, insanity, or neurasthenia dies slowly and continues to be held by many parents. It is probable that the erotic quality of thumb sucking and the use of transitional objects as well as masturbation is disturbing to many adults, partly because it reawakens their own childhood fears, guilt, and shame.

† The interesting studies of Sears and Wise[30] indicate that weaning frustration increases with the duration of breast feeding. However, many variables require further attention and study. It seems possible that weaning came to be considered so traumatic because of the difficulties in weaning older children, as well as the manner in which it had been done before the practice of gradually introducing other foods early. Even in primitive societies the process can be so difficult that it is sometimes carried out with the help of such procedures as anointing the nipple with a bitter substance, or by painting the breast to make it look frightening. In some societies the mother leaves the community for several weeks, thus forcing the weaning process but adding

Twelve to Fifteen Months

As the child's first birthday forms a major occasion to the parents, there is a tendency to consider that the period of infancy or the "oral phase" terminates at this turn of the calendar. It seems more appropriate, however, to include the first fifteen months in infancy, for at about fifteen months the child is no longer just tottering but usually can toddle about; and the phase of sensori-motor development is drawing to a close, for the use of words and the greater comprehension of language is markedly changing the child's intellectual potential and permitting increases in his ability to direct himself.

Piaget's Fifth Stage

It is worth scrutinizing some of the senior infant's techniques more closely in order to appreciate the limitations as well as the capacities of his mind as he is about to be graduated into the next phase of life. Piaget terms the fifth period of sensori-motor development that extends from about the twelfth to the sixteenth month *The Tertiary Circular Reaction and the Discovery of New Means by Active Experimentation.** The child now clearly differentiates himself from the object, and the object from the act. The exploration of objects that had occupied him earlier now turns into explorations of how objects act and how they can be manipulated. The child is now experimenting, so to speak, to see what happens, rather than simply repeating experiences. The experimental trial and error still begins with something that happens by chance; it is still a "circular reaction" but of a higher type. The difference between repeating the fortuitous and active experimentation is narrow. The child drops an object accidentally, repeats the action, and continues noting the deviations that occur each time, and thus experiments with different ways of dropping an object. And now the object is differentiated from the action, and thus the action can be tried with different objects. A child may, for example, learn to pull a string in order to get a toy attached to it by means of numerous trial-and-error experimentations

problems caused by loss of the mother's presence. It may be simpler to wean from the breast before the mother becomes a highly significant object to the child or before the child develops a conscious memory.

Bowel training commonly is started toward the end of the first year and can create many difficulties, but is better deferred until later in life. This topic will be discussed in the next chapter.

* J. Piaget, *The Origins of Intelligence in Children*,[24] pp. 263–330.

which started with the chance appearance of the toy after the cord was pulled. Once the child has learned with one toy, the schema or knowledge rapidly becomes generalized. From here it is only a small step to the next stage when foresight based on a related experience leads to insightful action without trial and error.*

If an object the child wants is placed under a cushion where the baby finds it and it is then placed under a different cushion, he will now look directly under the second cushion rather than repeat his previously successful act as he would when somewhat younger. Nevertheless, limitations of the senior infant's cognitive powers can be noted in the way in which an object is still apt to be tied to the circular reaction of which it had been a part. Thus, a thirteen-month-old rolls his ball under a chair and successfully retrieves it. Then he rolls it under the sofa where he cannot see it and cannot reach it. After trying unsuccessfully to reach under the sofa he returns to the chair and seeks the ball under it. He is repeating the act that had previously been rewarded by retrieval of the ball, and seems to expect to find it even though he has seen the ball roll under the sofa.†

Piaget's Sixth Stage

Piaget's sixth and final stage of sensori-motor development is not part of infancy, extending as it does from the sixteenth or eighteenth to the twenty-fourth month, though some manifestations of the stage may be present at fifteen months. The child becomes capable of inventing new means for solving problems through mental combinations without requiring tangible trial and error. Such behavior requires the use of symbols and the internalization of symbolic acts. Piaget notes that verbal

---

* Thus one of Piaget's daughters at just thirteen months of age, upon seeing an orange peel, turns it upside down and makes it rock; apparently she was able to foresee the possibility from the shape. (See J. Piaget, *Origins of Intelligence in Children,*[24] p. 328.) It is of interest that this same child who could use foresight to this degree still employed a much more primitive *secondary* circular reaction some five months later. After obtaining a toy by dislodging it by shaking the chair on which it was resting, after it had been removed to another part of the room she continued to try to get the toy by shaking the chair.

† Similarly one of Piaget's daughters at fifteen months of age sees her father approaching in the garden and smiles at him; but when her mother asks, "Where is Papa?" she turns and points at his office window, carrying out a customary (and probably an emotionally rewarded) response to the mother's question. Even when this child was over two years old, when she was walking with her father in the garden and heard a noise in his office, she said to him, "That is Papa up there." (See J. Piaget, *Construction of Reality in the Child,*[23] p. 59.)

symbols may not be necessary at this level of complexity, for the child may use motoric "signifiers" in carrying out such acts. For example, the child uses the gesture of opening his mouth wider and wider to help master the opening of a matchbox. However, as the child now understands many words, it is difficult to assess just how much the child is using verbal symbols even though he does not speak them. While this sixth stage forms the culmination of the sensori-motor period in which familiar sensori-motor schemata are applied to new circumstances, it also marks the beginning of a new major phase in which the child begins to use the human attributes of verbal symbols and foresight in solving problems.*

Early Determinants of Personality Traits

As the child reaches and passes his first birthday, he has assumed certain more definite and distinctive characteristics—some of which seem to foreshadow what sort of person he may become. Still, there will be time for many revisions and time for significant changes in the way in which parents relate to him as he grows older, and time for exigencies of trauma, illness, or for months or years of fair weather to alter radically the way in which development is progressing.

However, careful observation may reveal to an experienced observer that the child is beginning to favor and develop certain adaptive mechanisms and may also be utilizing some precursors of specific defensive mechanisms. He may, perhaps, be making the most of some innate attribute such as particularly good intellectual endowment or motor coordination; or he may unknowingly be reacting to some particular way in which the parents have responded to him. It is difficult to differentiate between innate tendencies and those that develop in response to the nurturant care, and virtually impossible unless the child had been studied carefully since shortly after birth. We might consider, however, an infant who displayed superior motor coordination in his first months of life. His mother and father, both of whom are athletically inclined, take pleasure in his motor activity. They play with him by swinging him by his arms, turning him in somersaults, encouraging swimming and stepping movements. However, when he begins to throw things from his crib and will not desist, his mother considers him contrary and disobedient and slaps his hands; when he crawls and knocks over a lamp, she smacks him sharply. "No's" punctuate the air and startle the active baby into

* J. Piaget, *The Origins of Intelligence in Children,*[24] pp. 328–330.

inactivity. The mother is afraid he is becoming wayward like her brother who is in a reformatory. Her impulsive slapping of the child starts loud quarrels with her husband, which in turn cause the baby to cry frantically. His movements become more crude and the anticipated excellent motor coordination fails to develop. Instead, he seems to become perplexed and given to more impulsive actions. In contrast, another child's motor dexterity may develop into coordination of fine movements as his parents spend time with him playing with simple puzzles and construction toys, and enjoy seeing him use crayons. In similar fashion, we can note children develop verbal skills either because of a particularly keen ability to discriminate sounds, or through being with older persons who talk with them or at them a great deal, or because their mothers like to sing to them and stimulate responsive recitation. •

The child may also be showing more diffuse patterns of reactivity, such as a geniality that reflects the developing innate sense of trust; or, in contrast, something of a disinterest in people, turning from them to play with toys, which may seem to reflect his mother's preoccupation with other matters when with the child, or the mother's compulsive ways of handling her child,* or, as in the case of another child, in reaction to her mother's need not to have her flow of fantasies disrupted by her child's moves toward companionship.

These more subtle relationships between inborn capacities, parental interests, parents' emotional problems, and the family atmosphere are now first coming under careful scrutiny; and the long-term influences upon the emerging personality are still somewhat conjectural. Currently, we can only consider some of the grosser and more obvious influences, and even then it becomes increasingly apparent that the number of variables is so great that they are difficult to assess clearly.

Some Developmental Disturbances

The child approaching fifteen months can be, and usually is, a being filled with vitality, curiosity, and with a push toward exploring his expanding universe and finding ways of mastering it. Frustrations are inevitable and cause outbursts of anger, but they are short-lived. His need for familiar persons, and particularly for a mothering person whose ways he knows and who knows his ways, is great. He gives affection and responds

---

* See S. A. Provence, "Some Aspects of Early Ego Development," [25] for an example of the infantile precursors of the use of intellectualization as a major adaptive technique.

to it; he has become sensitive to his parents' likes and dislikes, and their affectionate approval is a great reward. However, not all children flourish in this manner. Some have become quiet, apathetic, and do not emit any glow; many others show evidence of being troubled; and some have not reached anticipated levels of intellectual capacity. Even though we are not concerned with pathology in this book, it seems useful to consider some of these less fortunate outcomes in order to demonstrate and accentuate the importance of the interpersonal environment to the developmental process, even during infancy.

The Effects of Emotional and Social Deprivation

The observations made by Spitz of children raised in a foundling home are among the most dramatic and tragic.[32] * The babies had been breast-fed by their own mothers or by substitute mothers for three months. During this period they developed normally. Then the mothers were removed and the babies retained in the foundling home, where they received adequate physical care, good food and medical attention, and lived under very hygienic conditions. Each nurse took care of from eight to twelve infants who were left in cribs separated by opaque partitions almost all of the time where they received little handling or personal attention. The infants soon showed a progressive deterioration and by six months were notably retarded, lying supine and almost immobile, unable to turn themselves over, in contrast to the usually active ways of the child at this age. Gradually their faces became vacuous and their expressions imbecilic. They developed bizarre, uncoordinated movements. Despite the food provided, some developed marasmus—a wasting from malnutrition—and about 30 per cent died within the first year. Of the survivors many—or most—were unable to stand, walk, or talk at the age of four. These children had not only been deprived of affectionate care and the attention that usually goes with it, but they had received extremely little stimulation of any type, being thus deprived of the fundamental experiences required as "aliment" for learning.

While there are no other reports of *series* of children who did as badly as those reported by Spitz, other studies, and notably those of Provence and Lipton,[26] have documented the severe retardation of institutionalized infants that grows progressively worse during the second half of infancy. The children studied by Provence and Lipton were seriously impaired in their motor control; and their interests and interactions with

* See also A. Freud and D. Burlingham, *Infants Without Families*.[13]

people and toys as also their language development were impoverished; even self-exploration and autoerotic activities such as thumb sucking and genital manipulation became minimal. Moreover, they were dull and disinterested, "the light had gone out," or, as an observer remarked about the child that stood out as being the least handicapped, "If you crank his motor you can get him to go a little, he can't start on his own." *

The effects of maternal deprivation are complicated, even during infancy.† They vary with the time of onset of the separation, the duration, the quality of the mother's care prior to the separation, the individual endowment, and the quality and quantity of the substitute care provided, so that various difficulties and deficiencies can result. At present, relatively little is known about the interplay of these various factors. Now, raising an infant in the family does not, of itself, insure against emotional and social deprivation. Indeed, a pediatrician is apt to see some children who are not just deprived and neglected but grossly mistreated, occasionally an infant that has been beaten and battered for crying and thereby disturbing the immature and unstable parent. Even some well-intentioned parents can provide little because of economic necessity when the baby is left in the care of a completely disinterested sibling or incompetent child. Immature parents with little self-control are likely to be very impatient with their babies. One encounters depressed or apathetic mothers who cannot do anything for or with the child beyond providing food and hygienic care accompanied by little if any fondling, play, or talk. Such situations, particularly after the first four to six months, can create serious impairments and emotional disturbances.

* Provence and Lipton's comparisons of the best endowed and best cared-for institutionalized child in the study with an average child who was reared by his parents at home is very much worth reading.

The follow-up studies of some of these children who had been placed in families when they were about a year and a half old showed that they improved very rapidly and made up for much of the lost time, but careful examination revealed that they continued to suffer serious deficiencies, such as impairments in the capacity to delay when frustrated that interfered with their abilities to solve problems; a failure adequately to generalize what they learned; an undue concreteness in thinking; and failure to expect and seek help from adults that limited learning; and a continuing superficiality in their relationships to others. It appeared unlikely that certain attributes that should be acquired in the first year of life can be properly acquired later, which provides further evidence of the importance of the ontogenetic sequence during the first year that has been emphasized by Piaget.

† For evaluative efforts of such studies see M. S. Ainsworth, *Deprivations of Maternal Care: A Reassessment of Its Effects.*[1]

The full effects of infantile deprivation on personality functioning in later life are still unknown. Thus, when Harlow raised baby monkeys on "wire" and "terry cloth" mothers, it seemed at first that they did well on such impersonal mothering. However, they later became asocial in various ways, and eventually it became apparent that they were uninterested in mating and did not know how to mate. However, some of the females were successfully impregnated, but after giving birth to offspring they were completely lacking in maternal behavior, refused to permit the baby to approach and cuddle against them, and often attacked the baby so that it sometimes became necessary to remove the offspring from the mother's cage lest she kill it.[15, 16]

The Hospitalized Infant and Small Child

Such studies have forcefully drawn attention to the necessity of providing for the infant and small child's emotional and social needs when they are hospitalized for illness or surgery. Indeed, it is only during the past few decades that hospitals have considered that the baby has critical needs other than strictly medical attention.* The young child needs his mother with him a good deal of the time or good substitute care must be provided. The disturbances caused by separation have often been confused with the effects of an illness or with difficulties in recovering from an operation. Most modern hospitals now realize the importance of providing for the emotional needs of the young child as well as his physical care. Surgeons have recognized that speed of recovery and even postoperative mortality rates can depend upon the emotional climate of the unit. With more prolonged hospitalization the child's intellectual and social needs require attention, and pediatric services now tend to have nurses who play with the children and maintain nursery school-like playrooms in which the children spend their time whenever feasible.

The Influences of Infantile Patterns on the Adult Personality (Oral Traits)

The long-term problem has received attention in psychoanalytic literature through consideration of the "oral" character and the effects of

---

* Twenty-five years ago in one of the foremost pediatric centers, babies were tied down when they were about a year old, lest they fall out of the cribs; and mothers could not stay with the baby at night, and were even treated as nuisances who interfered with the nursing routine when permitted to visit during the day.

fixations at the oral stage of development. The term "oral character" is loose and has varied connotations that cannot be defined too closely. Psychoanalytic theory has tended to divide "oral" characters into two major types which supposedly reflect frustrations in the two halves of infancy. The "oral incorporative" character consistently seeks to get from others passively, wishing to be cared for as a dependent child. He fears being abandoned and starved and has little faith in the world unless he has someone to feed and care for him, and lacks confidence in his ability to manage for himself. The "oral aggressive" character retains strong needs for care from others but does not feel he can obtain what he needs without being grasping and hurting others in the process. In adult life he may drive himself intensely while exploiting others to obtain security. Another dichotomy that has been formulated concerns excessive indulgence as contrasted with deprivation in infancy. Those indulged excessively as infants acquire a lasting and inappropriate optimism that prevents them from providing for themselves as they feel certain that others will look out for them. Those who have been deprived and frustrated have a deep-seated pessimism, becoming hostile and resentful when their needs are not met, and they tend to give up easily.

However, these are oversimplifications of a complex problem. The longitudinal studies starting with the birth of an individual and continuing into his adulthood, such as those being carried out at the Yale Child Study Center, which are willing to consider the inescapable complexity of such investigations hold promise of uncovering far more sophisticated relationships. Further, few adults can be characterized in terms of oral tendencies that are the resultants of infantile experiences alone. Other developmental periods will be affected by whatever gave rise to the oral problems, and the child is usually raised by the same parents who contributed to the oral problems of infancy. It seems more useful to speak of oral characteristics that enter into the shaping of the personality. Such oral characteristics may be of such dominant importance that they prevent the development of a mature person, or may simply consist of traits that can sometimes be turned into assets as well as create handicaps. The term "oral traits" need not be an epithet but simply a useful term to help describe a personality. Oral characteristics can be highly useful, as in the case of some authors who boundlessly take in and then pour forth words. Thomas Wolfe, for example, could not contain his "orality" but incorporated vast chunks of life and had difficulty limiting the flow of words in his writings, and had a prodigious love of food. Indeed, in one short story he has the hero make love to his girl in terms of food, with his passion centering on the girl's ability to cook and provide food. A more aggressive type of orality may be considered evident in the love of words shown by George Bernard Shaw, who displayed a "biting wit" that contained considerable hostility.

"Oral" Character Traits in an Adult

The relationship between food and affection is often very noticeable. Of course, many mothers consider providing food as an essential manifestation of their love, and some offer food as a substitute for affection.* The relationship between affectional needs and food requires consideration when a physician prescribes a diet; for when a person addicted to food is placed on a stringent diet, he may become seriously depressed. The striving to amass wealth because of the fear of being left without resources can motivate industrialists. Indeed, the comic strip "Dick Tracy" sometimes contains a tycoon named "Diet Smith," who is portrayed as sitting at his desk surrounded by four or five telephones while eating baby food from jars. The interrelated "oral" problems of love, food, insecurity, dependency are apparent in the history of a man suffering from a peptic ulcer: it will also demonstrate some of the difficulties inherent in any attempt to sort out the salient factors in their development.

• A man in his mid-thirties was flown to a medical center because of a recurrence of bleeding from a peptic ulcer. He had never previously left his home town and the vicinity of his mother. The first episode of ulcer symptoms and bleeding had occurred while he was awaiting induction into the army and was apprehensive about leaving home. He was a highly intelligent man who worked at a job far below his intellectual capacities. It was a secure job in which he could not easily be replaced; and on the several occasions when he had made plans to take a job of greater interest and potentiality, he would start to overeat markedly, become apprehensive, and decide that the risk of changing positions was too great. He would then become resentful because he was not properly appreciated within his firm, feel like telling off his employer, but could never dare to show his hostile feelings. He would then suffer from indigestion, which led him to believe that he was not healthy enough to assume greater responsibility in a new job. He had married at the age of thirty, finding a widow who was not only a mothering sort of person but

* The relationship of such maternal traits to obesity in the offspring has been studied and documented by H. Bruch and G. Touraine.[10]

who also had sufficient independent income to allay his concerns about his ability to support a wife. Indeed, he realized that he had married only because his mother was growing old and might soon die.

Although his infancy and early childhood could not be reconstructed accurately some thirty-five years later, it was known that his mother had been a very apprehensive woman who sought to remedy her son's supposed frailty by pouring food into him. Food had been important to her as a token of security. The patient had become obese in childhood. When the patient was four years old his father lost his job and could not find another, as it was during the economic depression of the 1930's. The family ran out of food; the mother baked a cake with the remaining flour and told the patient to eat well as she did not know when they would be able to buy food again. He became acutely anxious, fearing that the family would starve to death. The father soon found employment and the family was never again in such desperate straits. The patient considered that this traumatic experience had a lasting effect on him.

Although the patient felt that his parents were unusually devoted and kind to him and had provided for him as well as they could, his wife disagreed. She told the social worker that her husband's parents had brainwashed him into believing in their beneficence by telling him of their many sacrifices for him. She found them penurious people, chronically fearful of the future, who transmitted their insecurities to their son and who had discouraged him from attempting to seek better employment. As an example, she told of an episode that had occurred when the patient was a young adolescent. He had very much wanted a bicycle and worked hard all summer to earn the money to purchase one. His parents encouraged him to work and save; but when he had enough money, they insisted that he buy a new suit instead of the bicycle. Although he had considered leaving home to find employment in a city, he developed severe motion sickness when he rode on a train, or even when riding in an auto beyond his town limits.

It seems very likely that this man's distrust of the world and his own capacities started in infancy, but later experiences certainly contributed to it, amplifying rather than helping him overcome his lack of confidence and reflecting the attitudes of both of his insecure parents. Indeed, it is possible that an inborn pattern of gastric functioning made him difficult to satisfy, which increased his insecure mother's insecurities and led her to focus on efforts to satisfy his oral needs. Peptic ulcer occurs primarily in individuals with high rates of pepsin secretion; however, in this instance the relationship of the patient's lack of basic trust to his parents' insecurities seems unusually clear. ●

The concepts of oral fixation and regression have been highly useful despite their diffuseness. However, as we have seen, they are not fully sufficient to explain the personality problems and deficiencies that follow upon infantile deprivations. The emotional, social, and cognitive deficiencies leave gaps in basic action patterns or schemata upon which later interpersonal, intellectual, emotional, and motor coordination patterns develop. As these foundations need to be laid down in association with the physical maturation of the child, later experiences can never fully compensate for the deprivations experienced in infancy.

The first fifteen months of life have a unity as a developmental period because throughout them the child is completely dependent on others for his nurture: for the food and bodily care essential for survival and healthy physical maturation; for the affectionate attention he requires for security and freedom from untenable tensions; for the experiential stimulation that is necessary for his cognitive development. The infant undergoes a profound physical transformation during these months and the foundations are laid down upon which his future personality development will rest. If his essential needs are filled and untoward tensions do not repeatedly arise within him, he will have established at the core of his being a basic trust in his world and those who inhabit it upon which a confidence in himself and in his capacities to care for himself can develop. A great deal more than gaining a basic trust and the satisfaction of oral needs must take place during infancy if the person is to develop properly. We have followed the infant's slow emergence from the symbiotic state in which he started life, and his preverbal cognitive development from the use of simple innate reflex responses through six stages of sensori-motor development to gain increasing control over his movements, to differentiate himself from his environment, and to interact meaningfully and intentionally with it. We have noted how, as the infant differentiates, he has a greater need for a specific mothering figure and how deprivation of such care can have disastrous effects upon him.

Now, as the child enters the new phase, walking, chattering a jargon mixed with words, more definitely understanding language, moving about on his own, exploring and getting into things, his mother's tasks in caring for him also change. She can no longer be concerned only with satisfying his needs and wishes, providing experience and socialization, but must now also limit his activities so as to assure his safety and the integrity of the household. The child, in turn, now must learn self-control and delimitation to be capable of exercising some sovereignty for the self.

References

1. Mary Satter Ainsworth, *Deprivations of Maternal Care: A Reassessment of Its Effects*, Public Health Papers No. 14 (Geneva: World Health Organization, 1962).
2. C. Anderson Aldrich and Edith S. Hewitt, "A Self-Regulating Feeding Program for Infants," *Journal of the American Medical Association*, 135 (1947), 340–342.
3. C. Anderson Aldrich, M. Norval, C. Knop, and F. Venegas, "The Crying of Newly Born Babies. IV. Follow-up Study after Additional Nursing Care Had Been Provided," *Journal of Pediatrics*, 28 (1946), 665–670.
4. Gregory Bateson and Margaret Mead, *Balinese Character: A Photographic Analysis* (New York: New York Academy of Sciences, 1942).
5. Therese Benedek, "The Psychosomatic Implications of the Primary Unit: Mother-Child Relatedness," *American Journal of Orthopsychiatry*, 19 (1949), 642–654.
6. John Bowlby, "The Nature of the Child's Tie to His Mother," *International Journal of Psycho-Analysis*, 39 (1958), 350–373.
7. John Bowlby, "Grief and Mourning in Infancy and Early Childhood," *The Psychoanalytic Study of the Child*, Vol. 15 (New York: International Universities Press, 1960), pp. 9–52.
8. Sylvia Brody, *Patterns of Mothering: Maternal Influence during Infancy* (New York: International Universities Press, 1956).
9. Hilde Bruch, *Don't Be Afraid of Your Child: A Guide for Perplexed Parents* (New York: Farrar, Straus & Young, 1952).
10. Hilde Bruch and G. Touraine, "Obesity in Childhood: V. The Family Frame of Obese Children," *Psychosomatic Medicine*, 2 (1940), 141–206.
11. Erik H. Erikson, "Growth and Crises of the 'Healthy Personality,'" in Milton J. E. Senn (ed.), *Symposium on the Healthy Personality*, Vol. 2: *Problems of Infancy and Childhood* (New York: Josiah Macy, Jr., Foundation, 1950).
12. Sibylle Escalona, "Feeding Disturbances in Very Young Children," *American Journal of Orthopsychiatry*, 15 (1945), 76–80.
13. Anna Freud and Dorothy Burlingham, *Infants Without Families* (New York: International Universities Press, 1944).
14. G. W. Greenman, "Visual Behavior of New-born Infants," in Albert J. Solnit and Sally A. Provence (eds.), *Modern Perspectives in Child Development* (New York: International Universities Press, 1963).
15. Harry F. Harlow, "The Nature of Love," *American Psychologist*, 13 (1958), 673–685.
16. Harry F. Harlow and Margaret Harlow, "Learning to Love," *American Scientist*, 54 (1966), 244–272.
17. G. Klackenberg, "Thumbsucking: Frequency and Etiology," *Pediatrics*, 4 (1949) 418–424.

18. Melanie Klein, *The Psycho-analysis of Children,* trans. Alis Strachey (London: Hogarth Press, 1937).

19. D. M. Levy, "Fingersucking and Accessory Movements in Early Infancy: An Etiologic Study," *American Journal of Pediatrics,* 7 (1928), 881–918.

20. James Clark Moloney, "Psychiatric Observations in Okinawa Shima: The Psychology of the Okinawan," *Psychiatry,* 8 (1945), 391–399.

21. N. R. Newton, "The Relationship Between Infant Feeding Experience and Later Behavior," *Journal of Pediatrics,* 38 (1951), 28–40.

22. N. R. Newton and M. Newton, "Relationship of Ability to Breast-Feed and Maternal Attitudes Toward Breast Feeding," *Pediatrics,* 5 (1950), 860–875.

23. Jean Piaget, *The Construction of Reality in the Child,* trans. Margaret Cook (New York: Basic Books, 1954).

24. Jean Piaget, *The Origins of Intelligence in Children,* trans. Margaret Cook (New York: W. W. Norton, 1963).

25. Sally A. Provence, "Some Aspects of Early Ego Development: Data from a Longitudinal Study," in Rudolph Loewenstein, Lottie Newman, Max Schur, and Albert J. Solnit (eds.), *Psychoanalysis: A General Psychology* (New York: International Universities Press, 1966).

26. Sally A. Provence and Rose C. Lipton, *Infants in Institutions: A Comparison of Their Development with Family-Reared Infants during the First Year of Life* (New York: International Universities Press, 1962).

27. Margaret A. Ribble, *The Rights of Infants: Early Psychological Needs and Their Satisfaction* (New York: Columbia University Press, 1943).

28. Samuel Ritvo, Audrey McCollum, Eveline Omwake, Sally A. Provence, and Albert J. Solnit, "Some Relations of Constitution, Environment and Personality as Observed in a Longitudinal Study of Child Development: Case Report," in Albert J. Solnit and Sally A. Provence (eds.), *Modern Perspectives in Child Development* (New York: International Universities Press, 1963).

29. H. R. Schaffer, "Objective Observations of Personality Development in Early Infancy," *British Journal of Medical Psychology,* 31 (1958), 174–183.

30. Robert S. Sears and George W. Wise, "Relation of Cup Feeding in Infancy to Thumb-Sucking and the Oral Drive," *American Journal of Orthopsychiatry,* 20 (1950), 123–138.

31. Philip F. D. Seitz, "Infantile Experience and Adult Behavior in Animal Subjects: II. Age of Separation from the Mother and Adult Behavior in the Cat," *Psychosomatic Medicine,* 21 (1959), 353–378.

32. René A. Spitz, "Hospitalism: An Inquiry into the Genesis of Psychiatric Conditions in Early Childhood," in *The Psychoanalytic Study of the Child,* Vol. 1 (New York: International Universities Press, 1945), pp. 53–74).

33. René A. Spitz, *The First Year of Life: A Psychoanalytic Study of Normal and Deviant Development of Object Relations* (New York: International Universities Press, 1965).

34. D. W. Winnicott, "Transitional Objects and Transitional Phenomena: A Study of the First Not-Me Possession," *International Journal of Psycho-Analysis*, 34 (1953), 89–97.
35. Peter H. Wolff, "Observations on Newborn Infants," *Psychosomatic Medicine*, 21 (1959), 110–118.
36. Peter H. Wolff, "The Developmental Psychologies of Jean Piaget and Psychoanalysis," *Psychological Issues*, Vol. II, No. 1, Monograph No. 5 (New York: International Universities Press, 1960).

Suggested Reading

John Bowlby, *Child Care and the Growth of Love* (Baltimore: Penguin Books, 1953).
Sylvia Brody, *Patterns of Mothering: Maternal Influences during Infancy* (New York: International Universities Press, 1956).
Arnold Gesell, *The First Five Years of Life: A Guide to the Study of the Preschool Child* (New York: Harper & Bros., 1940).
Julius B. Richmond and Bettye E. Caldwell, "Child-Rearing Practices and Their Consequences," in Albert J. Solnit and Sally A. Provence (eds.), *Modern Perspectives in Child Development* (New York: International Universities Press, 1963).
René A. Spitz, *The First Year of Life: A Psychoanalytic Study of Normal and Deviant Development of Object Relations* (New York: International Universities Press, 1965).

CHAPTER 6 ¹⁴

❀ ❀ ❀ ❀ ❀ ❀

The Toddler:
Ambulation, Speech, and
Primary Socialization

Challenges and Tasks

As THE BABY EMERGES from infancy and starts to walk and talk, he enters a phase in which the crucial problems involve the imbalance between his new-found motor skills and his meager mental capacities. He is driven by an impulsion to use his new abilities and to explore his surroundings, but his verbal and intellectual abilities lag far behind his motor development. Limits must be placed upon his activities for his own safety and for the preservation of his family's possessions. He has little if any ego of his own; the past and future are nebulous, and a mothering person must now, more than at any other time, function as a surrogate ego for him. But the child does not understand; he is only beginning to tolerate delay and frustration; it is not possible to talk things over with him. The child now finds himself in a different relationship with his mother than previously. During his infancy she had nurtured him, provided for his needs, and encouraged his expansiveness: now she must delimit him. She expects him to respect limits and renounce immediate gratifications in order to maintain a satisfactory relationship with her. She now sets expectations for him to meet. It is not a simple transition for an unreasoning and unreasonable baby to make.

The baby has emerged from the passivity of infancy, and now seems both driven by an inner impulsion to activity and pulled by the attraction of new stimuli in his surroundings—by a need to gain mastery over his body and to explore his environment. Whereas during his first year much of his food intake went into his physical maturation, now an increasing amount goes into fuel for the physical activity that reaches prodigious proportions by the middle of his second year. Gains in height and weight slow down markedly. The annual increments in weight are less between two and five than at any other time before the attainment of adulthood.

The baby is moving away from his need for complete care and his symbiotic existence with his mother. It is a phase that is critical to the establishment of a basic *trust in the self* and a *sense of initiative*. The child is in the process of establishing boundaries between himself and his mother, both physical boundaries and a sense that he can do things as a separate individual and begin to take care of himself. He now needs to gain a sense that he can learn to master himself and his environment.

The dangers, as always, lie on both sides. He cannot yet really be responsible for himself, and he is far from independent. Indeed, his venturesomeness depends upon his having close at hand the shelter of his mother's arms and lap to which he can retreat when he overreaches himself. A mother who finds too anxiety-provoking those activities of her child that lead him into a world full of very real dangers—stairways, gas vents, lamps that topple, car-filled streets—may overly limit the child, surrounding him with gates, fences, and a barrier of "no's" that stifle initiative and self-confidence. Mothers who have little confidence in their ability to guide and control the child are apt to project such feelings and magnify the child's incapacity to care for himself. Mothers who cannot tolerate disorder, or who overestimate the baby's capacities to conform and regulate his impulses, can convey a sense of his "being bad" to the child, and thereby provoke a sense of guilt or shame that undermines his feelings of worth and self-trust. The child may be led into an overconformity that satisfies the parents but covers hostile resistance and stubbornness.*

* Erikson[6] considers this period in the child's life vital to the development of *autonomy*, with the negative trend being the development of a lasting sense of shame and

In psychoanalytic theory, this period of life is the *anal phase* of psychosexual development in which the investment of the child's libido has shifted from the oral zone to the anal region. The child now gains erogenous pleasure from passing or withholding bowel movements that stimulate the libidinized anal mucosa. Giving or withholding, compliance or stubbornness, and related behaviors become important and influence character formation. For many children in Western societies, the conflicts that arise because of the need to conform and comply with the wishes of others, in contrast to infancy when needs were satisfied by parental figures, can focus on bowel training, particularly on premature bowel training. The demands for bowel control can epitomize all of the requirements imposed by early socialization—the need to rescind gratification and the freedom to give in to impulsions and accept a need to control the self. Ever since Freud published his essay, "Character and Anal Erotism," [7] * it has been recognized that there is a clear connection between anal erotic gratification, conflicts over bowel training, and certain configurations of personality traits. However, bowel training need not take place during the second year; it is neither a biological nor a social necessity. Certain of the problems conventionally associated with anal erotism and bowel training seem more clearly related to the developmental tasks pertaining to conflicts between initiative and conformity.† Therefore, the anal aspects of the period will be discussed after the broader developmental characteristics have been considered.

---

doubt, and he considers "initiative" vital to the subsequent phase. The child is clearly beginning to establish autonomy, but I believe the problems of autonomy reach their zenith in the next developmental phase, and that the achievement of initiative precedes the capacity really to move toward autonomy. The difference is partly a matter of word meanings as well as of emphasis. There is always a danger in using single phrases to epitomize the involved tasks of a complex developmental period. The reasons for my not focusing on "autonomy" will become apparent (I trust) in the way we shall consider the oedipal period. However, I wish to stress that other, crucial tasks arise and require resolution in this stage of life—particularly certain aspects of language learning and their impact on cognition and ethical development.
* See also K. Abraham, *Contributions to the Theory of Anal Character*,[1] pp. 376–392.
† Erikson's observations of the Yurok Indians cannot be passed over casually. The Yuroks place great emphasis upon the acquisition of wealth, holding on to possessions, rituals for controlling nature obsessively, etc., which, according to psychoanalytic theory, would carry with it an expectation of unusual emphasis on anality and rigid bowel training. Yet there seems to be only the most casual type of bowel training. On the other hand, there are ritualized regulations about eating and obtaining food that demand premature self-control from the child.

The period will terminate toward the end of the third year when the child has gained sufficient vocabulary and adequate syntax to comprehend much of what is said to him. His linguistic abilities and knowledge will help him brook delays because he can anticipate future goals and benefits. He will have internalized enough of his world to understand expectations, to begin to reason, and to listen to reason.

Although a smooth passage from fifteen to thirty-six months is not an impossibility, it is certainly a rarity. The toddler's developmental situation almost inevitably creates difficulties for him and his parents. The extent and nature of the problems, and just when they arise, vary with the child, the parents' sensitivities, and the child-rearing practices they utilize. Although the more manifest problems usually involve difficulties in control and the expectations for self-control of some form of behavior—bowel training, eating, or physical initiative—and the child's reactive temper outbursts, resistance, and negativism, another critical task of the period that has received far less attention in the literature demands attention. It concerns the child's linguistic development—how it is influenced by his interaction with his mother and how parental and cultural value systems become involved in the process. There is a contrapuntal-like development of these two themes—the increasing physical capacities and the slower acquisition of language. Both involve the child's expanding abilities. The developmental phase ends when a reasonable equilibrium between the two is established.

We shall note how the child's physical development leads him into difficulties; how the limits that must be set arouse conflict; how his domestic socialization, particularly bowel training, can become a paramount issue; and we shall also trace in broad outline the baby's linguistic and intellectual development, noting, in particular, how the child requires a mediator or interpreter in order to acquire the meanings of words and the syntax of the language—a role that only a mothering figure can properly fill.

The Toddler's Capacities and Behavior

Sometime before fifteen months the baby really walks, even though in a stumbling, wobbly manner. Although his skill increases rapidly, it will take more than a year for his walking to become fully automatic. As he progresses through his second year into his third, the toddler can be a delight to watch as he moves with earnest intent from one activity to another. He is a source of constant interest as new abilities and skills follow one another rapidly and he becomes increasingly responsive to verbal exchange. His babyish speech is still amusing, for no more is expected from him. He is venturesome and ventures constantly but still remains a baby who enjoys giving and receiving demonstrable affection. He is unfolding to become an individual with ways of acting and expressing himself that are distinctively his own. As he approaches two the pace quickens and, typically, he is into everything. Anything precious or potentially harmful must be kept out of his way. While intriguing to watch develop, he can also readily become a source of despair to his mother, whose energy and wits are taxed to the limit as she tries to keep up with him and find ways either to control him or to arrange the surroundings for him. He can be highly exasperating in his innocence, for in the flash of an unguarded moment he can light into something forbidden, turn the living room into a shambles, or vanish from sight. The impulsion to activity outruns not only mastery of the body but even more the knowledge of what he can do or may do.

Motor Skills

The toddler is a strange admixture of grace and awkwardness; the graceful and well-proportioned body somewhat comical in its rapid stumbling movements, body tilted slightly forward, ankles somewhat stiff, and both arms waving in extraneous movements. Until the child is well past two, arm movements are apt to accompany many of his activities, and when one hand is used the other accompanies it until unilateral differentiation of muscular control is well established. When the small child pounds on a pan with a block held in one hand, both arms will be in movement. The gross movements of the arms and legs are mastered long before fingering, which requires a great deal of practice. He is apt to carry small objects tucked under his arm rather than in his hand. It takes practice to time the release of objects, as in throwing or rolling a ball, perhaps to the annoyance of the father who wishes to start training his son to be a ball player as soon as he emerges from the cradle.

Through play which appears to be so random, the child is gradually learning muscular coordination and is exploring one item after another as is necessary for organizing his world. Even movements that seem completely natural to adults require lengthy practice before they can be carried out automatically and without concentration. The child of two sitting down in a chair appropriate for his size takes care and expends effort. He may climb into it laboriously and then let his feet down, or he may carefully measure the distance by sighting through his legs and then let down his rump while still watching himself. His skills do not come simply through maturation but through countless repetitions that go on day after day and which are required for him to learn coordination and to measure the space in which he lives.

Cognitive Capacities

Similar considerations apply to perceptual and cognitive development. He is endowed with organs that register sensations, but he must learn to organize the sensations that impinge upon them, utilizing the concordance of various sense modalities and sensori-motor schemata to build the sensations into perceptions, and then with the help of words learn what constitutes entities. He is distractable as his attention shifts from one stimulus to another, taking his body along with it. To some observers his naïveté seems surprising. The young toddler will, for example, try to grasp the line made by a crack in the floor, and he reaches for things well beyond his range. It is a very new world that is distracting to any continuity of effort. He leaves a toy to touch a kitten only to move toward the sound of his mother in the next room, but he may be waylaid by the carpet sweeper in the hall that demands his attention. Still, he learns very rapidly and as he gains skills he will be fascinated by repeating over and over again what he is mastering. The circular reactions of the sensorimotor period are still his major means of learning (see Chapter 5). He will place one block on another and repeat it, and can keep amused piling colored rings on a stick until such tasks are thoroughly assimilated and become so simple that they are meaningless, and then are part of the schema that is ready to assimilate more complex activities. His attention becomes firmer, bringing with it a period of relative calm until still greater skills lead him more rapidly about the house and to a wider range of exploration. The mother unconsciously becomes alert to the sound of his activities and to his chatter; she learns that silence must be investigated because it may well indicate that something new has attracted and held his attention and he is likely to be exploring something that is potentially dangerous to him, or to which he is a danger.

Routines can become time-consuming and try the parents' patience. The child develops his own ideas about what should be done, his own interests, his own pace. He can refuse to be hurried as he messily feeds himself and becomes more interested in play than in food. His hands may be too occupied to be lifted into the armholes of an undershirt or sweater. The mother must exert ingenuity to keep him either interested or distracted while he is eating, bathing, and dressing. He is attentive to songs and soon likes to listen to simple stories, even though he may not understand them. The crib ceases to be confining as he learns to clamber out of it by himself; and even though everyone else in the house may be thoroughly fatigued by his bedtime, the child may be reluctant to end the day. On the other hand, if things have gone well he is usually delighted and full of laughter when others pay attention to him and participate in some activity.

Gradually he keeps himself occupied for longer periods, but preferably with someone close at hand. He may happily play with a couple of pots, listen to a phonograph record repeat itself, or page through a picture book, occasionally glancing at his mother while she works in the kitchen. Water often holds a particular fascination for the toddler, and he can keep busy pouring it from pot to pot, filling containers in the sink, or playing with the contents of his tub. He imitates more and more, and likes to "help" his mother with household chores if she can good-naturedly and appreciatively accept his interfering aid. He not only imitates his mother but both boys and girls identify with the mother at this stage, picking up her ways of doing things, her intonations, and her likes and dislikes. Of course, the child will also enjoy being with his father and share his work of tinkering with the car or gardening. Less alert than the mother to the child, a father may suddenly realize that the child is no longer at his side and become shaken when he locates the two-year-old climbing a tree, or stumbling along carrying a pruning knife, oblivious to the danger.

Control and Conflict

As the child's motor abilities and his urges to use them have temporarily outrun his comprehension and experience, the parents must provide the guidance and set the limits. The parents' own security and contentment, the prerogatives of other children in the family, and the preservation of the household must be taken into account along with concern for the child's safety. Providing the proper guidelines always presents problems to parents. The baby's logic at eighteen months is composed largely of his impulse to carry out his desires, which direct him toward release of tensions; his life consists of the present, and he is bereft of foresight. His response to others is based largely upon their intonation and expression. As we have seen, "no" is learned before "yes," and it can become a major tool in his effort to preserve his prerogatives. He takes over from his parents their use of "no" to refuse to comply with demands. Too much limitation, too frequent negations deprive him of his sense of initiative and enjoyment, and can lead him to become negativistic.

There are ways of avoiding collisions of wills and frequent clashes of temperament without having the family become enslaved to the baby's whims and without squelching the child. Insofar as possible an area of the house is cleared for action with all dangerous and valuable things removed but with enough left to permit interesting exploration. The child's energy is channeled into nondestructive activities. He is highly distractible, and drawing his attention to some new activity can often serve better than a "don't" or a physical restriction. The parents are bolstered by a realization that the phase will pass. Still, this is not a time for offering explanations or alternatives. Later he can be given choices, but at this stage firm, pleasant, and patient guidance free from indecision solves the important matters, whereas latitude is permitted in areas that do not matter.

Now, as throughout early childhood, the mutuality between mother and child forms a major guide. It requires the indefinable judgment of a person who knows the child well and empathizes with him. It involves permitting the child to use his abilities as they develop but not setting demands beyond his capacities. It requires a consistency from the parent that enables the child to learn how to have a pleased parent. The need for a comfortable parent, as has been noted, serves as a major directive to the child and a reward for which he relinquishes immediate gratification. Still, the most devoted mother is human and has her limits and moods. The young dynamo wears out his mother faster than himself and she cannot always be wise, consistent, and pleased.

Any attempt to consider the process of child development only in terms of an unattainable ideal is unrealistic. The parents' moods and limits require recognition as well as do the child's needs. Just as in infant feeding, the trend in setting controls has shifted from early training in obedience and conformity to a "permissiveness" that has sought to minimize frustration and the repression of self-expression. "Permissiveness" has too often been interpreted by educators as well as by parents to connote that any restriction of the child will distort his personality development. Mothers have often had the notion that restricting a child indicates the presence of rejecting qualities in the mother derived from unconscious hostility to the child. The ensuing inhibition of self-expression in the mother, who often cannot admit her frustration and weariness even to herself, can produce an unnatural atmosphere in the home and a false front that has a more deleterious influence in the end. The general atmosphere created, the comfort and security of the mother in feeling that what she does is correct, and the meaningfulness of the restrictions that must be imposed are far more important than temporary maternal upsets and losses of patience. Somehow the child can usually accept what the mother is convinced is proper.

Family Membership

The home is the center of the toddler's world and in this sheltered environment he is trying himself out, gaining the feel of his body and how to use it and acquiring confidence in himself. It is a moving away from the symbiotic union with the mother while still having her close to provide for his needs. He is slowly becoming a member of the family rather than primarily a member of a mother-child unit. Before he emerges from the home he must first learn to relate to others through experiences with members of his family. Even within the home he is constantly moving against the limits that are safe and into conflicts with the rights of others. The essential delimitations of his behavior are properly learned under the aegis of parents who seek to foster his welfare and cherish him, who know his ways and can tolerate his trespasses, and who comfort him when he overreaches himself. His intense bond with his mother and his need for her meliorates the restrictions that are placed on him tolerantly and lovingly. The onus of delimitation is offset by the satisfaction of pleasing the mother. Theoretically, at least, he lives in a tolerant and understanding world in which the consistency of the parents leads to consistency in himself. Behavior that would produce a rebuff from outsiders is not only acceptable but is expected within the home. Here his temper outbursts need cause no lasting shame and his tears no loss of face as they will when he moves into the world of his childish compeers.

Although the home and the family are the center of the child's life, he is increasingly moving into contact with new places and persons. He goes walking with his mother and gets into things on the way. They are important things that he cannot resist exploring and examining until he learns to anticipate the more intriguing goal of a playground or store. While he may refuse to ride in his stroller, feeling grown up enough to walk just like his mother, he can, at first, use the support of pushing the stroller along and he is glad to have it as a vehicle when he tires.

Peer Relationships

In one way or another he meets other children and at first may simply regard them as objects to be explored, and he feels, pats, and pushes them. Even later he will not play with them but go about his own activities in their company, enjoying their presence. The solitary play of several two-year-olds in the same room or yard will be broken by sudden, silent tugs of war or outbursts of screams and tears as the child encounters the outrage of someone else wanting to use what he wishes for himself. At home unless he has siblings close to his age, toys are his possession. In another few months he will engage in parallel play with other children in which two or more play at the same thing but still not with one another. The presence of other children of the same age is important to the child as he passes the age of two. He will watch another child play, enjoying observing briefly, and may then imitate the other. The boundaries of the self are still far from clear, emotionally as well as physically, and the exuberance, laughter, or tears of another child may become infectious to him.

Activities with other children provide a new essential experience through which he learns the role of a child. He gains a new perspective of himself through seeing other children, and, eventually he begins to see himself through the eyes of other children, which is a very different matter from seeing himself only as a child in an adult world in which he is small, relatively helpless, and unequal to what others can accomplish.

As the child approaches three he is beginning to move beyond the confines of the home, where he is the center of attention, and into the world with others. Even though it will be a very protected world for another few years, his ease and security in it will rest upon his definition of himself, the limits he has learned, and his ways of interacting as an autonomous child within his family group. A basic trust in himself provides the foundation for relating to other children, including the freedom he feels to express and assert himself and the tacit assumptions of finding friendliness.

The baby is rapidly expanding his range of activities and his knowledge of the world, but his expansion has necessitated delimitation by the parents. Learning what is permissible and what is forbidden, what pleases and what displeases his parents, is part of the process of socialization. The child is becoming more of a social creature through the limitation of his drives and desires. There is an unfortunate element of confusion in the process. Some activities are prohibited simply because they are dangerous to a baby and not because they are otherwise unacceptable, whereas some behaviors are banned because they are contrary to the mores.

Learning Language

Concomitantly the baby is learning to talk. He is now acquiring the adaptive technique which is uniquely human. It constitutes a major expansion of his capacities and a major aspect of the process of enculturation, but it also presents difficulties and frustrations as well as pleasures to the baby. The delimitations in using language that the parents impose upon the child are not so apparent as the bounds they set upon his actions, and they are not so likely to create feelings of frustration, but they are very real.

During his first year and a half, the baby's cognitive capacities develop essentially by progressive expansion of his sensori-motor schemata, as has been outlined in the preceding chapter. The nurturing persons play a part primarily through keeping the child's tensions and emotional upsets minimal and by supplying gratifying stimulation and opportunities for new experiences. Learning to use language, however, is a very different matter.* It involves the acquisition of an existing complex system of sounds, meanings, and syntax through interaction with tutors, primarily the family members. Although it depends upon the prior elaboration of sensori-motor schemata, it is not a direct continuation of this earlier type of cognitive development. The development of verbal communication requires a new start, so that language will at first play a relatively small part in directing the baby's behavior.

In learning language, the baby is not only learning to communicate verbally but he is also assimilating the culture's system of meanings and its ways of thinking and reasoning. As noted in an earlier chapter, each society categorizes experience somewhat differently, and the vocabulary of its language forms a catalogue of the categories it uses in perceiving, thinking, and communicating. We have also noted that the family is the society's major enculturating agency. The baby is extremely dependent upon parental tutors, particularly his mother, to mediate between him and the language of the society. The mother, as we shall see, interprets

---

* We may consider that learning language requires the assimilation of schemata that have been built up by others. It is not a more or less spontaneous elaboration of experience through assimilation to existent schemata.

the baby's primitive words into words of the language and also interprets the language to the child. It is a lengthy and involved process and we shall only be able to touch upon some of the highlights. Thus, at this phase of life when the baby is gaining greater initiative and strives to do more and more things for himself, he becomes very dependent upon his mother for verbal comprehension. In order for the baby to gain the language facility essential for the development of good intelligence, he needs someone who is thoroughly familiar with his behavior, and who can interpret his needs, gestures, and primitive usage of words with reasonable accuracy and teach him, albeit often unknowingly, how these things can be conveyed linguistically, patiently working with the child to build up his language. The consistency of the tutor's interaction with the child is extremely important, as also is his ability to suit the teaching to the child's capacities. More is involved than the speed and fluency of linguistic development; the child must now develop a trust in the utility and reliability of verbal communication and thereby a trust in the value of rationality. We will amplify this topic in the next chapter. As we examine a few salient aspects of the process by which the child acquires language, the importance of the mothering person or persons will become apparent.*

The Origins of Words

The foundations upon which the acquisition of language is built are laid down in the first year along with the mutual understanding between child and parents of needs, wishes, feelings, and intentions. The capacity to develop speech is an innate human attribute and all infants start to babble. However, the babbling must be reinforced by his hearing it, and the deaf child soon stops babbling. The sounds that the child makes stimulate him to repeat them and then to vary them. In Piaget's terms the sounds are aliments that stimulate circular reactions (see Chapter 5), and the vocalizations of others also stimulate the child's babbling

---

* Piaget can be followed only in part. Piaget's studies of intellectual development between the end of the sensori-motor period and the later preoperational period when the child is three and a half or four are very meager. His studies also seem deficient because of his tendency to consider the period very much as he did the sensori-motor period, with a relative lack of appreciation of words as carriers of categories developed by the culture and of the interactional nature of the learning process. His theories of the period of preoperational intelligence are more suited to the later portions of the period when the child is between three and seven. Fortunately, M. M. Lewis has collated many of the studies made of children's language between one and three years and has furnished numerous observations of his own.[11]

and vocal experimentation. The infant's babblings gradually shift to re-semble the sounds used in the language being spoken to him and around him. However, M. M. Lewis believes that there are six archetypal nursery words—a type of basic baby language—that are used everywhere, varying but slightly from place to place. These are repetitions of the vowel "ah" with different consonants—"dada," "nana," "mama," "baba," "papa," and "tata." * The baby repeats these or closely related sounds as circular reactions to his own sounds and to his parents' modi-fied imitations of him.† Certain of the repetitive sounds such as "mamama" or "dadada" are selected out and repeated by parents and are thus reinforced. The persons around the child respond to given sounds when they are used under certain circumstances, which lead to their repetition as part of particular action patterns or circular reactions. Still, the child's early use of "mama" is far from giving a name to his mother. Its use creates a situation somewhat analogous to that brought about by the smiling response at six weeks, in which the baby unknow-ingly deceives his mother into being more responsive through seeming to make a personalized appeal to her.

The word "mama" begins to fill an instrumental function for the child when he is about eleven to twelve months old. When, for example, he drops an object from his crib, fails to reach it, and says "mama" while reaching for it, his mother sizes up the situation and hands him the object. It also has a declarative value; after being fed he gazes at his mother and contentedly says "mamama," which induces his mother to hug him. The repetition of the syllable thus produces a response. Now we find that a generalization of the "word" occurs and it is used in a wide variety of manipulative and affective contexts. It will require an-other ten to twelve months until "mama" is gradually limited to a desig-nation for the mother. Thus, Piaget recorded that his son said "mummy" at fourteen months in surprise or appreciation when his mother was swing-ing her body; at fifteen months he used it to indicate that he wanted something, even when appealing to his father; and at sixteen months to get his father to light a lamp, when he saw his mother's clothing in a closet, and also when his mother gave him something. Eventually, the

* See M. M. Lewis, *Language, Thought and Personality in Infancy and Childhood*,[11] p. 33.

† Although just how the drift toward the sounds used in the language occurs is not completely clear, the parents induce some of it by their imitations of the baby's bab-blings which they distort in the direction of the language. Imitation by the child is, of course, another factor.

child learns the meaning because of the consistency of the mother's response to the word, because she and others apply the term to her, and because of other such social interactions.

The baby's speech starts with the archetypal sounds used by infants everywhere that are reinforced by the parents and made to denote something by them. The baby's language is then expanded by "words" that form a transition between the "basic baby language" and conventional words. They are two-syllable repetitions such as "tata" for "good-bye," "nana" for nurse or grandmother, etc., and then "bye-bye," "bow-wow," and other such words that the baby learns from adults who are adapting their speech to the baby's capacities.* He cannot learn to say "mother" but only "mama" or some such similar simple utterance. "Mom" or "mommy" can then be assimilated to "mama," etc. The parents, then, are speaking baby language to the child as if they were aware that the baby can at first only imitate and learn words that they have transformed into two simple syllables. Then, in accord with the child's development, they gradually move toward using sounds that more closely approximate the real word.

The Origins of Meanings

It seems likely that each new word the child learns during this period goes through a phase of expansion before it becomes narrowed down to a usage that is approximately appropriate. Thus, Piaget found that soon after his thirteen-month-old daughter learned "bow-wow," she pointed to a dog while standing on her balcony and said "bow-wow," and thereafter the word was used for anything seen from her balcony—including horses, baby carriages, cars, and people; and not until three months later was "bow-wow" reserved for dogs.†

Let us look further at the process of expansion and contraction of word meanings. Expansions are difficult to follow. "Wawa" meaning water may be learned for a glass of water and then be used for the glass as well as the water, and then for all shiny objects, before being narrowed down to the fluid; and it may go through other such false expansions at the time it is applied to running water in a bath, and again when water is seen in an ocean. Lewis has provided an example of how the expansion and limitation of a word occurred.‡ The child when twenty

* The child is not only learning meanings but also to accommodate his vocal sensori-motor schemata to pronouncing words.
† J. Piaget, *Play, Dreams and Imitation in Childhood*,[13] p. 216.
‡ M. M. Lewis, *Language, Thought and Personality in Infancy and Childhood*,[11] pp. 50–57.

months old said "Tee" (Timmy) for the household cat and then, at twenty-one months, for a small dog. Soon thereafter he used "Tee" for a cow and then for a horse. At twenty-two months he learned "goggie" for his toy dog and soon also used this word instead of "Tee" for a small dog. Then he learned "hosh" for horse, and stopped using "Tee" for cat as he had learned "pushie," but he continued to use "Tee" for cow until he learned "moo-ka" when a little over two years old. A St. Bernard dog was rather understandably termed a "hosh" until he learned that it was a "biggie-goggie." Thus, over a period of about three months, the "Tee" which had been used for a variety of animals was replaced by words that classified animals in a manner that was reasonably similar to that used in the culture. He learned such differentiation through experiments in establishing communication by extending and contracting the applications of these sounds under the "responsive guidance of those who share in his experiences." *

The word gradually gains a discrete meaning and becomes a symbol as it comes to designate the unity and identity of the object as perceived from different perspectives and in differing situations; and also when different objects with the same critical attributes are categorized together by being denoted by the same word. The first of these ways of achieving a stable meaning is obviously simpler for the child. When the child at about a year and a half of age says "mama," he is symbolizing his mother's identity for him under various conditions. It is much simpler to use "bow-wow" for his toy dog under all circumstances than to learn what objects are properly denoted by the word. The meanings of words continue to develop, narrowing to precision of meaning and broadening to include an ever increasing number of experiences with the word and whatever it designates. Although the meanings of common words become fairly definite during childhood, they will continue to change throughout life. The word "mother" has different meanings for a person when he is a small child and when he is a college student, and a still somewhat different meaning after he has become a psychiatrist.†

Early Syntactical Development

The single word used by the baby at eighteen or twenty months has a diffuse meaning, and in its diffuseness it often expresses a sentence

* *Ibid.*, p. 57.
† Miss Sullivan's major concern in teaching Helen Keller was to convey the knowledge that words stood for categories of things and not single objects. The reader may also be interested in the ingenious manner in which Dr. Itard in 1797 taught the wild boy "Victor" that words stood for categories, and the limited success he attained.⁹

which the mother who knows her child can understand. His "mama" can mean, "I am hungry," or "Give me my ball," or "I love you, Mother"; and the mother, sizing up the situation, responds as if a complete sentence had been expressed. In the process, she will often also expand the child's verbalization by saying, "Tommy hungry" or "Tommy want ball?" which is part of the lengthy process of teaching language to the child, even though she knows that it may be months before the child will be able to use the expanded expression.

Then when the child is about two years old, he begins to use two- to four-word expressions which, despite their simplicity, greatly increase the specificity of the communication. These are expressions such as "Mommy come," "Papa go bye-bye," "Nice doggie." The words are almost always in the proper sequence.[3] It is not clear whether the child can "program" only such simple expressions because of the immaturity of his nervous system or because they are a step in gradual assimilation and accommodation.* Here again, the parental persons are in a position to guess the meaning from the situation, or they know how to behave or question the child in order to find out. The communication is between child and parent and not between child and any person in the community. Outsiders can understand only a small fraction of what the child seeks to convey. Brown has observed that mothers will, virtually without realizing it, expand the two- or three-word sentences for the child by adding a few crucial words. They do not usually expand them into complicated sentences but judge how far the child's comprehension may exceed his capacities for expression. For example, the child says, "Mama lunch," and the mother judges whether he means "Mother, give me lunch," "Mother is eating lunch," "Mother is making lunch," etc. She then adds the words that make the distinction and, in the process, is teaching the rudiments of syntax.

Questions and the Naming Game

Sometime during the third year, varying from child to child, the baby begins to ask questions, and then if he has proper respondents his vocabulary and comprehension expand rapidly. The questions are of several general types, each reflecting increases in the child's intellectual capacities. Perhaps most notable are the naming questions that mount to a

---

* As Brown points out, the words used are "contentives"—that is, words with content that can be used to designate things or actions; and the words left out are "functors" —articles and prepositions, and perhaps forms of "to be." [2]

crescendo that strains the patience of many parents. The "What's this?"
or "What's that?" may be stimulated by the parent's questions. Some of
the questions are a game; it is a game that the child can play as well as
adults. Some questions are asked about names he knows in order to have
the adult turn the question back and permit the child to have the pleasure of answering correctly. Sometimes it is a means of gaining attention;
sometimes a search for confirmation that the name applies to another
object of the same category. It appears as if the child now realizes that
everything has a name that he must learn and starts seeking this important knowledge. It will be recalled that the moment Helen Keller
learned that objects have names constituted the turning point in her life.
Knowing the name actually bestows a new power upon the child. He
needs the names in order to begin to learn through talking rather than
through action and to internalize his environment symbolically so as to
make possible its imaginative manipulation. Even at this early age the
names permit a degree of predictability about his small world. Whereas
he may be able to learn simply by playing with them that all balls roll, he
cannot know from their appearance what objects are "toys" and can be
played with, as toys come in very varied shapes; nor will he know before
tasting them what foods are "sweet"—but the words let him know in
advance.[5]

The child developed some appreciation of the constancy of the object,
illustrated in his searching for it after it disappeared, during the period
of sensori-motor development. Such knowledge is often fostered by
adults, who hide objects and ask the child where it has gone. At first
such questions only produce action responses—the child seeks the missing ball or block—but eventually they produce verbal responses, such as
"there," or even "stairs" meaning "upstairs in my room." The baby now
clearly holds visual images of absent objects in his memory, and from
here it is not a very large step to references to the past and future. As the
notion of the future is based upon expectations derived from past experiences, the child for some time remains somewhat confused about what is
past and what future. He may, at times, refer to yesterday when he
means tomorrow, even when he is considerably older.

As the child approaches his third birthday, the questions are apt to
include inquiries about reasons, "Why?" and "What you doing?" The
child does not have any real concept of cause and effect, as Piaget has
pointed out, and even when he learns to reply to questions with "because" responses, he is only designating spatial or temporal juxtaposi-

tions.[12] Still, it is a start, and, after all, the entire problem of causality is confusing even to philosophers and scientists.

By means of such step-by-step development as we have considered only in fragmentary form, the child's linguistic and intellectual growth gains momentum during his third year of life. By his third birthday, and perhaps even by the age of two and a half, he has acquired hundreds of words, and some children know more than a thousand by then. According to Brown,[2] he may use nearly all of the syntactical forms of the language in sentences of twelve to fifteen words. He is really conversing, and it is sometimes difficult for adults to realize the limitations with which the words are used. Nevertheless, he can now begin to reason, to reason with himself, to project a simple future, to play imaginatively, and to fantasy. With such mental abilities he passes into a new phase of development.*

We have seen that the child's language development depends greatly on the parental tutors, particularly the mother who can understand the child's nonverbal communication and who interacts so constantly with him. However, not all mothers understand intuitively, not all are patient or even interested, and many mothers nurture their babies in relative silence. It appears as if paucity of interchange affects the child's linguistic and perhaps his intellectual development, but the topic is just now

* The child spends time practicing using language very much as he repeats motor activities over and over until they are mastered and can be incorporated into more complex schemata. The linguist Ruth Weir studied the speech of her son while he was alone in his bedroom prior to falling asleep by making tape recordings of his productions at about two and a half years of age.[14] The child's language development was somewhat precocious, as might be expected of the child of a linguist who was particularly interested in language development. As Roman Jakobson notes in the introduction to Ruth Weir's book, "Many of the recorded passages bear a striking resemblance to . . . exercises in text books for self-instruction in foreign languages: 'What color—What color blanket—What color mop—What color glass . . . Not the yellow blanket—The white . . . It's not black—It's yellow . . . Not yellow—Red . . . Put on a blanket—White blanket—and yellow blanket—Where's yellow blanket . . . Yellow blanket—Yellow light . . . There is the light—Where is the light—Here is the light.' "[10] The recordings reveal many fascinating aspects of linguistic development.

Of course, some children say very little until they are two years old, or occasionally even older, and yet their language usage is not retarded when they start to speak. Such development is likely to occur most frequently when there are other young children in the family and the child hears a great deal of simple speech. One such child, who had clearly comprehended a great deal but said very little, announced soon after his second birthday, "I can talk now," and soon showed that he had assimilated a fairly extensive vocabulary and proper syntactical forms.

coming under scientific scrutiny. The child's dependency upon his mother for verbal understanding is great, for no one else is likely to be able to communicate as effectively with the baby. It is one reason why removal of the child of two and three from the mother is so traumatic to him, for the child now needs his mother for many such reasons. He exists in a state of dependency—he may be establishing boundaries between his mother and himself but he is far from autonomous. He is not yet really separate from her, and when a child is separated from his mother for a period of long duration, he loses much of his capacity for initiative and even for survival.

The Struggle for Mastery

The struggle for mastery and control often reaches a peak between the ages of two and two and a half, when the child is struggling with conflicting impulses within himself as well as against parental controls. In some instances, the increase in a child's verbal ability at this time when he communicates in two- to four-word expressions leads parents to overestimate his comprehension and his capacities for being reasonable. Often it seems high time for the child to be toilet-trained. The child has now learned a good deal about the household rules and regulations but is either not yet motivated to rescind his impulses or still incapable of complying as much as is expected of him. The child may be heard muttering "no" to himself as he begins to internalize parental rules. There may be temper outbursts when he can neither decide to conform nor tolerate loss of affection. Periods of negativistic behavior occur when he does not wish to comply with anything and when he may also regress to more infantile behavior.

This is often a time of notable *ambivalence*—that is, an admixture of opposing feelings toward the same person. However, as the two-year-old cannot really contain opposite feelings at the same time, he vacillates from one to the other, often to the bewilderment of his parents. At this age, the child is apt to consider the mother who gives and bestows love as the "good mother" and the frustrating mother as another person—the "bad mother." Similarly, he is apt to consider himself as two children: a good, pleasing child and a naughty, contrary one. The "good child" may wish to renounce responsibility for the "bad child." He has difficulties with his unity and with accepting responsibility to the same parents, for all of his behavior. At about this time one may hear the child say, "Now you my mommy," when the mother becomes pleasant after a set-to; or the "good child" will insist that not he, but the bad boy or a toy doll, had pushed his plate off the table. After all, the notion of the conservation of objects is not yet firm, and a person or object may not be recognized after changing a characteristic.*

Toilet Training

Many of the cardinal problems of this developmental phase may focus upon the process of toilet training, particularly when premature training imposes demands that the child cannot readily master or even understand before the age of two and a half or three. Toilet training places paradoxical demands upon the puzzled child who sometimes must give in order to please while at others he must hold back in order to please. Continence and control are demanded just when conflicts over self-control are at a height. The struggle over who is to be the master, the mother or the child, can reach an impasse on this battlefield. Like the proverbial horse who can be led to water, the child can be sat on the toilet but he cannot be made to defecate. Here is one aspect of interaction in which the child can stubbornly have his way—well, can almost have his way, for some mothers will resort to suppositories and enemas, "for the sake of the child's health," and thus win the struggle on this front, usually only to lose it elsewhere.†

Actually, there is no reason why bowel training should be attempted before the age of two and a half, or why it must present anything of a problem at all. Many mothers have found that if they can be patient and

---

* We can note, for example, that Piaget's daughter, J., at two years and seven months, upon first seeing her younger sister, L., in a new bathing suit and cap, asked, "What's the baby's name?" Her mother explained that it was a bathing costume but J. pointed to L. herself and said, "But what's the name of that?" and repeated the question several times. As soon as L. had her dress on again, J. exclaimed very seriously, "It's L. again," as if her sister had changed her identity with her clothes. (See J. Piaget, *Play, Dreams and Imitation in Childhood*,[13] p. 224.) At two years and four months in looking at a picture of herself as a younger child she asked, "Who is it?" When told it was she when she was small, she said, "Yes, when she [J.] was L."

† A young woman of eighteen, for example, was admitted to the hospital because of serious fecal impaction and for study of why she was unable to move her bowels. She related that she had never defecated spontaneously in her life. Soon after her birth her mother had used suppositories and, when these became ineffective, enemas. Enemas are likely to lead to other types of difficulties. For most children they are more painful than pleasurable and can stimulate sadistically toned fantasies of being controlled and attacked; others find the sensuous quality of the stimulation, and being controlled while passive, highly seductive.

unmoved by the condescension of neighbors who believe that their own children were perfectly trained at the age of a year or eighteen months, the child will eventually start going to the toilet himself following the example of the other members of the family or upon the suggestion of the mother. Children trained in this manner may never know that having bowel movements can raise a significant issue or even that such a thing as constipation exists. It is also clear that when a child is trained before he is one and a half years old there will often be recrudescences of soiling behavior later. Further, virtually all children are bowel-trained by the age of three, the difference being that those who have been trained strictly will continue to have preoccupations and difficulties if not certain of the characterologic problems that will be discussed below.

Anal Erotism

Still, our culture virtually dictates that sometime during the second year, if not even earlier, the process of bowel training must be started. The ensuing conflicts can then epitomize the developmental period and provide very ample reasons why psychoanalytic theory has termed this the *anal phase* of development. Paradoxically, virtually all of the literature on child rearing emphasizes the problems of toilet training in discussing the period, even though the major problems for which mothers seek help concern feeding and temper tantrums.

Psychoanalytic theory has hypothesized a shift of libidinal investment from the oral to the anal zone toward the end of the first year of life. The area is highly sensitive, and its stimulation can produce erotic gratification. After weaning increased attention may be given to the pleasurable stimulation provided by the mother when she cleans the soiled child. The process provides the child with another source of intimate relatedness to the mother in which she is simultaneously caring for the child and providing him with sensory stimulation of a pleasurable nature. In addition, cleaning the child often requires cleansing and stimulating the genitalia.

Eventually the child must renounce obtaining this care and pleasure from his mother. Actual control of defecation can be attained only after muscular control of the sphincters becomes possible through maturation of the nerve tracts in the spinal cord, and even then the achievement of coordination takes time. However, many infants are more or less conditioned to have bowel movements at a given time, perhaps after meals when the gastro-colic reflex that tends to produce evacuation after eating is activated. Perhaps it is more accurate to say that the mother is trained to set the baby on the pot when he is apt to have a movement until he becomes conditioned to doing so. However, the child finds that all satisfaction derived from anal eroticism need not be relinquished. He can gain pleasure from holding on to the feces until the release of the bolus stimulates the mucosa. He can stimulate himself while cleaning himself, or wait until he is given enemas. In general, it has been considered that early bowel training with its premature demands and deprivation of gratification leads to a fixation at an anal level of psychosexual development and to perseverance of "anal" problems. It seems more in keeping with known facts that undue erotization of the anal area follows upon excessive maternal interest in the problem and stimulation of the region. Many mothers continue to place considerable emphasis on proper evacuation throughout childhood and even into adolescence.* Some aspects of the problems attributed to anal fixation are more clearly reflections of the more general struggle concerning initiative and control that so often focuses on bowel training.

When training is carried out in a relaxed and noncompulsive manner, the child comes to feel that he can care for these essential needs by himself. He gains a sense of trust in himself and in his bodily equipment. The parents who distrust the child's capacities to care for himself and his use of initiative in play are likely to be parents who cannot trust his body to function properly unaided, and those who are upset by the disorder the child creates in the house are likely to be disturbed by soiling and seek early bowel training.

Early Ethical and Aesthetic Influences

Now, bowel training is particularly likely to contain ethical and aesthetic implications that will influence character structure. The child is learning basic meanings which can be influenced by the process. Whereas a soiled diaper does not disturb the infant or small child who seems to value his product and even enjoy its odor and feel, the mother regards it differently. Usually, the mother's behavior in cleaning the soiled child is very different from her behavior when nursing or bathing him. She is not likely to gain pleasure from the act, and at best her

* A set of seriously disturbed adolescent twins claimed that whenever one had a fight with their mother, she gave them both enemas simultaneously, insisting that they were contradictory because they were constipated. The procedure was carried out in a highly ritualized and erotized manner. Both twins insisted that they had believed that "constipation" meant "being angry at mother."

attitude is ambivalent. She is apt to show disgust in her facial expression; and as the child begins to understand, words such as "dirty boy," "shame," and "smelly baby" may accompany her discovery that the child is soiled. Before long the child will call himself "dirty" or say "shame" at such times. These are among the earliest aesthetic and ethical evaluations. Soiling and matters associated with defecation are considered shameful, dirty, and bad; and, by contrast, clean and good are equated. When the child in a negative mood toward his mother soils himself, he is "bad" and he feels ashamed of himself—and such feelings spread to other contrary behaviors. He learns to defend against such feelings by being overly clean—at least externally, particularly if he is feeling hostile and dirty inwardly.

"Anal" Characteristics

The problems arising from parental restrictiveness of the child's initiative, and paradigmatically from bowel training and the renunciation of anal erotism, transcend this developmental phase and influence character formation. Various groupings of traits related to the problems that are paramount during this critical stage of early socialization have been designated as *anal characteristics.* For example, it has been repeatedly noted that persons who are constipated may also be stubborn, showing covert hostility through withholding from others in a silent and determined fashion. Not infrequently there will also be varying degrees of miserliness, pettiness about details, meticulousness, and pedanticism. A person who is meticulously clean externally may be dirty or messy underneath, or perhaps meticulous in the way his possessions are arranged on the surface while those things that are out of view are disordered. Such persons have problems about holding on and letting go, and about keeping for oneself or sharing with others both possessions and information about the self. There is ambivalence about love and hate which must be concealed and is clearly connected to obsessive-compulsive character disorders. The traits may be present in various combinations as well as hidden from the self and others by reaction formation—that is, by a tendency to undo such trends by going to opposite extremes. Such characteristics are, of course, not necessarily pathological unless they dominate the total personality, and some such trends exist to a greater or lesser degree in almost everyone. In moderate degree they can have very positive value as when they contribute to perseverance, thoroughness in work, and ability to save.

As these traits develop in relationship to the all-important parental figures when basic attitudes are first being established, they are likely to permeate later interpersonal relationships. Some persons who are "anal characters" may feel that others are always trying to get something from them, or that others will shame them if they express their natural feelings or needs. They learn to keep things to themselves and cannot be open or trusting. Paranoid individuals who fear attack from others often have strong anal characteristics. The essence of the matter seems to be that a child who has been overcontrolled at this critical phase is likely to become a person who must hide the hostilities and aggression engendered and who unconsciously feels that if his true feelings are found out he will be rejected, hated, and in danger. He develops devious ways of preserving initiative or autonomy, but it is usually a constricted and withholding way of maintaining a semblance of self-assertion.

An "Anal" Character

One often sees persons much of whose way of life seems to have been determined by the events of this period but whose anal characteristics are not altogether pathological. For example, an excellent physicist who has made significant contributions to science has never been incapacitated by such characteristics but has turned them into assets that balance his limitations. Although a fine physicist, he is very slow in his work, carrying out his experiments with meticulous precision. Fortunately he had moved into a sphere of study concerned with physical measurement where such characteristics are highly advantageous. His colleagues know very little about what he does and his chief is often frantic because nothing seems to emerge from months of effort. If rushed, he becomes anxious and a negativistic streak appears which leads him to waste his time in unnecessary checking and endless recalculations. However, slowly and carefully his researches become productive. He is a tight-lipped man with a very pedantic manner, and even his wife knows little about what he thinks or does. At home he is constantly concerned about money, insisting upon paying the bills himself but in a manner that makes his wife frantic, as his tardiness embarrasses her with various shopkeepers. He spends hours going over his accounts and he has difficulty in making out checks. Quarrels in the home arise about matters of waste, for he insists that his wife never throw out any food, claiming that he prefers eating stale bread and drinking leftover coffee. He examines the refrigerator each night to make certain that nothing that might possibly have been used has been discarded. While he appears very neat in his dress, his wife complains that "his drawers are a mess." These words unconsciously conveyed one of her reasons for being aggravated with him. She feels that despite his oversolicitous concern about her health and welfare, he is hostile to her in many little ways, never giving or really sharing; and responding to complaints by becoming more silent and withdrawn.

Feeding Problems

Problems of "orality" and difficulties with feeding are not confined to infancy. Feeding problems are a major reason why mothers consult pediatricians about their two- and three-year-olds. The contemporary emphasis upon the child's vitamin, mineral, and protein intake, particularly in television commercials, abets such concerns. However, mothers commonly unconsciously relate feeding with bestowing love and care. Food is something tangible that they can give that enters into the child and fosters his growth. The child is very likely to learn very early that eating is a function that also enables him to assert his independence. He can stubbornly refuse to open his mouth, avert his head, spit out food, and even vomit what has been put into him. If he has felt neglected, his dawdling or fussing about eating can provoke his mother and hold her attention. Feeding can become the arena in which the struggle for mastery and initiative takes place. Such conflicts are, of course, unnecessary. The hungry child seeks relief from the tensions produced by hunger, and soon learns to eat sufficiently if the food is removed when he begins to dawdle unduly or when he becomes negativistic. However, the mealtime is usually a social occasion for both child and mother, a time when they can relate happily and the child cannot be expected to consume his meal in a playless mechanical routine.

When a mother conveys to her child that he will eat if he loves her, or must eat to show that he loves her, difficulties are very likely to ensue. Such patterns often last into late childhood, and mothers who continue to feel that an adult offspring is still a child may try to show their affection and concern through insisting that the child eat all she provides.* Occasionally, serious disturbances arise because a mother does not follow the child's needs but her own emotional needs or insecurities in feeding her child. Hilde Bruch points out that the child must learn the relation-

---

* Such attributes are often considered to epitomize the Jewish mother, but, of course, a mother does not have to be Jewish to be a Jewish Mother. See D. Greenberg, *How to Be a Jewish Mother*.[8]

ship between the physiological indication of hunger and the ability of food to still such sensations. If a mother feeds her infant whenever he cries, and continues to act as if any unhappiness of the small child can be allayed by food, the child may never learn to recognize hunger, or learn that food is a means of satisfying hunger feelings rather than a way of coping with his own or his mother's unhappiness or anxieties.[4]

The Influence of the Parents and Their Relationships

A mother's basic attitudes toward her child reflect her own personality and upbringing and not simply her acceptance or rejection of the child. They are affected profoundly by her relationship with her husband, by the satisfaction gained from her marriage and her sexual fulfillment in it. Her husband's behavior as a father cannot but influence her behavior as a mother: must she protect the child from his father's jealousy or annoyance with him; must she "cover up" for the child, or begin to cover up for the father to his children? The father is essentially the first intruder into the mother-child entity. He is probably always resented to some extent, but he can also be welcomed as someone who adds enrichment and enjoyment to the child's life.

The mother's ways of relating to her child and her basic attitudes about child rearing extend across the years rather than being limited to a single developmental phase—though almost all mothers are likely to be more concerned about some developmental tasks and have greater problems in coping with one developmental phase than with others. A mother who could not feel that her milk would properly nourish was also afraid to bathe her son lest she drop him, later thought he needed frequent enemas to move his bowels, and could rarely let him play outside of a fenced enclosure; and when he was a schoolboy, she constantly sought additional help for him from teachers. However, some mothers who feel very insecure in handling a helpless, frangible infant become more relaxed with an older child; but, perhaps more commonly, mothers who are at ease as long as they can care for a child completely become apprehensive when he begins to venture on his own. For such reasons the essential mother-child harmony is often disrupted during the period of early ambulation, and the anxieties provoked in the mother concerning the child's initiative and the dangers of the world are conveyed to the child. The anxieties may lead to regressive trends toward the securities of the oral phase accompanied by fears of venturing beyond attachment to a feeding and protecting mothering figure.

Some parents limit the child excessively not because of anxieties concerning physical harm but because they cannot tolerate the child's unknowing infractions of rules, as they consider his expressiveness an indication of his being "bad." The baby is not only limited but is surrounded by a wall of evil. Many generations of persons in our society have been raised on the assumption that the basic evil in man must be countered by discipline and prayer. Such indigenous belief systems have tended toward the production of a somewhat guilt-laden child who must either achieve salvation or demonstrate that he is one of the elect who will be saved through good deeds or achievement. In general, a moderate sense of guilt commensurate with the Protestant ethic is deemed desirable in our society. However, some parents because of ignorance or impatience either seriously constrict the child or foster undue hostility in him by reinforcing a barrier of "don'ts" with impatient grabs, slaps, and glances.* Aggression is mobilized, but as the child cannot win in overt conflict he finds covert means of combat; but as he is still closely identified with his mother, hostility and aggression toward a parent is always also aggression toward the self. As he needs his parents and seeks to love them, it is also often better to feel guilty and turn the hostility against the self.

A child's innate tendencies to be particularly active and explorative may aggravate such problems when a parent can cope well only with a quiet and conforming child. If boys are inherently more active than girls, the difficulties of the male toddler and his parents may be greater unless the parents enjoy a child's outgoing activity.

In discussing the child's development between the ages of fifteen and thirty-six months, we have emphasized the problems that arise because of the imbalance between the toddler's motor skills and his abilities to

* The author recently interviewed a working-class mother who sought advice concerning her six-year-old who stammered severely. She brought her two-and-a-half-year-old with her, as he could not be trusted to remain in the waiting room with his older brother. The child sat quietly in her lap for ten minutes and then wiggled to get up. The mother shook him and impatiently exclaimed, "Can't you stop fussing about?" A few minutes later she apologized and put him down. As he walked to look out of the window, she called, "Stay away from the radiator, you'll burn yourself." When he put his hand on my desk to pick up a ruler, "Why do you always have to be a nuisance?" stopped him. Then his thumb went into his mouth, but his mother pulled it out saying, "Aren't you ashamed to let the doctor see you suck?" Then, as he climbed into a chair, she smacked him on his rear with a "Why can't you be still for a moment?" It seemed clear why his older brother stammered.

communicate verbally, to understand, and to think. The parents must set limits on the child's impulsions to be active, to explore, and gain mastery over his world. The cardinal tasks of gaining a sense of initiative and of confidence in his own competence are likely to be countered by the manner in which the child is controlled, which can foster inhibition of action and lack of self-confidence. Some struggle between child and parents over control is almost inevitable and often focuses on bowel training or feeding. The child's overt compliance and conformity is often accompanied by suppressed anger, heightened ambivalence to parental figures, covert resistance and stubbornness that can exert lasting influences upon the personality. The child is simultaneously acquiring the ability to use language, and we have sought to outline the beginnings of the complex process that will enable the child to communicate his needs and wishes verbally, to acquire new knowledge from others, and to gain the cognitive abilities he needs to direct and control his own behavior. At the end of the period a relatively good equilibrium has been established between the child's motor and linguistic abilities, and he is ready to gain a more definite autonomy from his mother and find his place as a member of the family. At this toddler stage his life interdigitates so closely with his mother's that prolonged separation from her affects him profoundly, causing physiological and depressive disturbances, very much along the lines discussed in the preceding chapter. The reader may have noted that we have scarcely differentiated between the two sexes in this chapter; the differences between boys and girls have not been forgotten or disregarded. Indeed at this age the differentiation of the genders is becoming very clear. The topic has simply been skirted to permit a more focused discussion in the next chapter.

References

1. Karl Abraham, "Contributions to the Theory of Anal Character" (1923), in *Selected Papers of Karl Abraham* (London: Hogarth Press, 1942).
2. Roger Brown, "Language: The System and Its Acquisition. Part I. Phonology and Grammar," in *Social Psychology* (New York: Free Press, 1965).
3. Roger Brown and Ursula Bellugi, "Three Processes in the Child's Acquisition of Syntax," in Eric H. Lenneberg (ed.), *New Directions in the Study of Language* (Cambridge, Mass.: M.I.T. Press Paperback, 1961).
4. Hilde Bruch, "Transformation of Oral Impulses in Eating Disorders: A Conceptual Approach," *Psychiatric Quarterly*, 35 (1961), 458–481.
5. Jerome S. Bruner, Jacqueline Goodnow, and George Austin, *A Study of Thinking* (New York: John Wiley & Sons, 1956).
6. Erik H. Erikson, *Childhood and Society* (New York: W. W. Norton, 1950).
7. Sigmund Freud, "Character and Anal Erotism" (1908), in *The Standard Edition of the Complete Psychological Works of Sigmund Freud*, Vol. 9 (London: Hogarth Press, 1959).
8. Dan Greenberg, *How to Be a Jewish Mother* (New York: Price, 1965).
9. Jean-Marc-Gaspard Itard, *The Wild Boy of Aveyron*, trans. George and Muriel Humphrey (New York: Century, 1932).
10. Roman Jakobson, Introduction to Ruth Weir, *Language in the Crib* (The Hague: Mouton & Co., 1962).
11. Morris M. Lewis, *Language, Thought and Personality in Infancy and Childhood* (New York: Basic Books, 1964).
12. Jean Piaget, *Judgment and Reasoning in the Child*, trans. Marjorie Warden (New York: Harcourt, Brace, 1928).
13. Jean Piaget, *Play, Dreams and Imitation in Childhood*, trans. C. Gattengo and F. M. Hodgson (New York: W. W. Norton, 1962).
14. Ruth Weir, *Language in the Crib* (The Hague: Mouton & Co., 1962).

Suggested Reading

Roger Brown, *Words and Things* (Glencoe, Ill.: Free Press, 1958).
Sigmund Freud, "Three Essays on the Theory of Sexuality" (1905), in *The Standard Edition of the Complete Psychological Works of Sigmund Freud*, Vol. 7 (London: Hogarth Press, 1953).
Mabel Huschka, "The Child's Responses to Coercive Bowel Training," *Psychosomatic Medicine*, 4 (1942), 301–308.
Morris M. Lewis, *Language, Thought and Personality in Infancy and Childhood* (New York: Basic Books, 1964).
Dorothea McCarthy, "Language Development in Children," in Leonard

Carmichael (ed.), *Manual of Child Psychology* (New York: John Wiley & Sons, 1946).

Robert R. Sears, Eleanor Maccoby, and Harry Levin, *Patterns of Child Rearing* (Evanston, Ill.: Row, Peterson & Co., 1957).

U. S. Children's Bureau, *Your Child from One to Six* (Washington, D.C.: U. S. Government Printing Office, n.d.).

CHAPTER 7 ²³

❀
❀ ❀ ❀ ❀ ❀ ❀

The Oedipal Period

The Basic Developmental Tasks
SOMETIME AROUND THE AGE of two and a half or three, the child ceases to be a baby and becomes a preschool child. During the next two or three years the child passes through one of the most decisive phases of his journey. As a baby and very young child he has required a close relationship with the mother, and it has been a reciprocally erotized attachment. Now, to free his attention and energies for investment beyond the family and for learning, he must relinquish the erotic aspects of the relationship, albeit reluctantly and often painfully. This is a critical phase in the eventual achievement of autonomy. How this essential transition transpires depends upon the child's preparation in the previous developmental phases and upon the mother's ability gradually to frustrate her child's attachment, but it is fostered by other changes which accompany maturation and which require careful scrutiny. The child's movement toward increasing independence involves his gaining the experience and the tools needed for reality testing and self-guidance. He must not only develop improved cognitive capaci-

ties but gain a basic trust in the utility and validity of verbal communication. His ego functioning—his ability to guide himself into a future—progresses considerably and gains support and guidance from his ability to internalize the directives of others—that is, from superego dictates. By the end of the period he will have learned the lessons of primary socialization, and id impulses are better contained and delayed. The child will have attained considerable organization of his personality, and the major lines of his future development will have been established. The start of coming to terms with reality as a specific individual in a social system takes place within the family, which forms a microcosm in which a patterning of ways of relating to others and of reacting emotionally is laid down. Here the child must gain an appreciation and acceptance of himself or herself as a boy or girl and achieve a firm gender identity. He finds his place as a member of the childhood generation with its limitations as well as prerogatives; he adjusts to the competition of siblings for attention and affection; and he gains some realization of his family's position in society. A great deal must happen in these years to make possible the shift in his emotional relatedness to his parents, the oedipal transition, and to prepare him for schooling and peer-group participation.

Psychoanalytic theory has focused upon the hypothesized shift in libidinal investment from the anal to the genital or phallic area, specifically to the penis in the boy and the clitoris in the girl, and on the far-reaching consequences of the upsurge of phallic sexuality with its attendant desires to possess the parent of the opposite sex. These oedipal strivings with the ensuing guilt which creates anxiety over punishment by castration, abandonment, or death, and the nature of the eventual resolution of the problem form a major directive to personality development as well as a potential source of various types of developmental disturbances. The nature of this oedipal transition will be examined carefully after the necessary foundations for understanding it have been considered.

Erikson considers the basic issues of the period to involve the balance between initiative and guilt: the initiative being concerned with the seeking of a parental love object and to become a person like a parent through identification with the father or mother; the guilt derives largely from rivalry with the father and siblings for the mother. From the ensuing anxiety over retribution, a conscience or superego develops that serves to regulate initiative, and by making the child dependent upon himself makes him dependable. These developments are fostered by the expansion of the child's imagination permitted by his increased locomotor and linguistic capacities.* The reversal in this book of the periods in which the issues of initiative and autonomy are crucial does not indicate a basic difference concerning the essential tasks of these periods, but rather a difference in the use of terms as well as a somewhat different orientation concerning the nature of the transition the child is making. The use of an eponym to signify the crucial issues of these years has serious limitations; but if a summary term is useful, the central task of the oedipal phase involves achievement of autonomy from the mother. It is at this period that the child crosses a narrow defile between his earlier need for a close and erotized attachment to his mother and his beginning capacities to care for himself beyond his family and home and to free his attention and energy for learning.

The child of three is beginning to emerge from the protected but confining shelter of his mother's care, but it will require time and experience before he has the mental tools and emotional stability properly to comprehend his still small world and become able to guide himself. Piaget has forced upon us an awareness of the striking limitations of the preschool child's language, reasoning, comprehension, and moral judgments. It seems essential to understand something of the child's cognitive abilities and limitations to be able to grasp properly the tasks confronting him and his means of coping with them.

There are many aspects of this complex and crucial developmental period that require attention, each clamoring, so to speak, for priority. To bring order to the presentation, we shall adhere to the following sequence: a general description of the oedipal child's capacities and behavior; his cognitive development; development of gender identity, including the impact of fantasies about childbirth; sibling rivalries; the oedipal problem and its resolution. Last, we shall consider the influence of the nature of the oedipal transition upon personality functioning and malfunctioning.

The Capacities of the Three- and Four-Year-Old

If the child's development has gone reasonably smoothly, the three-year-old is usually a source of pleasure to those who watch and listen to him. Difficulties arise if one attempts to give a brief and coherent description of what the child of three and four is like, not only because

* See Erik Erikson, "Growth and Crises of the 'Healthy Personality.' " [5]

rates of maturation and development vary, but also because boys and girls can no longer be encompassed by the same description. By the age of three and even more by the time he is four the child becomes more of a companion and less someone to take care of, but his desire to participate in activities with his parents can sometimes become more trying to them than were their efforts to contain and control him. The simple motor schemata that the child acquired so laboriously now become increasingly automatized and coordinated, and slowly but steadily become subordinated to more integrated and purposeful uses which permit satisfaction from more sustained activities. Even the early stages of language mastery lead to a major inner reorientation. The parent and child can increasingly give directions to one another, and the child is learning to direct himself, in part, by talking to himself. He gains a modicum of self-control, some orientation toward a proximate future rather than simply toward gratification of present needs and wishes, and he can use fantasy as a means of gratification and amusement. Increasing periods of delay can be interposed between the stimulus and the response, and simple alternatives can be taken into account. Alertness to reward and punishment, even if they are only a matter of parental approval or disapproval, tempers behavior. The child becomes much more of a participant in social interaction. However, his tolerance remains limited and frustrations can produce sudden outbursts of temper and aggression, which can pass as quickly as a cloud on a windy day unless the parent prolongs the storm.

The mother has someone to converse with during the day, though perhaps primarily as a listener to the increasingly lengthy monologues in which the child talks of his imagined activities and tells her what he is going to do for her when he grows up. At three and four years of age both the boy and the girl will participate with the mother as she works around the house. There is considerable movement toward behaving grown up in real activities as well as in play, both through imitation of the behavior of elders. The child at three builds blocks just to make towers or piles that he can demolish, but at four he will laboriously make constructions that need not resemble very closely what he intends them to be. As he works at his play he carries on a monologue, even when no one is present. He is, in essence, thinking aloud and telling himself what to do: "a block—one there—one there—a boat—boat—make a boat—Mommy will go in boat—another block," and so on. This inner or *synpractic* speech will gradually be internalized, but will still be vocalized occasionally even after the child starts school.[33] At three, the child's imagination can transform almost anything into the object needed for play. A block becomes a boat in the bathtub, a train on the carpet, a hammer when he is imaginatively constructing something. Having achieved sufficient motor control, the child is usually not so interested in tasks of body mastery as in carrying out activities. He will enjoy finger painting for the outlet it affords for smearing, but also for the pleasure of creation. He is still free from the need to make a picture of something. A four-year-old responded to a parent's question of what he was painting: "How should I know, I haven't finished it yet!" but the younger child need not have anything other than the colored lines when he is finished. He is likely to admire his production, praising himself and seeking the praise of an adult. Modesty is not yet part of his vocabulary or his behavior, but self-aggrandizement seems to come naturally.

Even a father who has shown little interest in babies is now likely to find enjoyment in the child. He is an object of admiration; the son perhaps more than the daughter now wants to be with him and do things with him, and boasts of *his* father to other children. Whereas the child invokes authority with "My mommy says—" he seeks status and prestige with "My daddy can—." The girl, even before three, learns alluring ways of endearing herself to her father, who finds it easier to be tender and affectionate with a daughter than with a son. The father will, reciprocally, usually enjoy spending time with the child who provides such gratifications. The patterns of father-child interaction vary greatly from culture to culture, but in ours there has been an increasing tendency for the father to become an important figure to the child at an early age.

Social Behavior

The child has by now gained control over his bowels, and accidents are rare; but although urination is controlled by day, the child may still wet at night, or needs to be picked up to urinate without actually waking. When preoccupied with play, he may occasionally wet himself, much to his shame; and the parent or nursery teacher is alert to the little boy holding his penis or the girl wriggling though perhaps unaware of her discomfort. The boy is likely to enjoy urinating and now stands up and imagines that he is shooting a machine gun—"ack-ack-ack"—or hosing out a fire, gaining a feeling of masculine power. The girl who has watched boys may now also wish to stand up to urinate and expresses feelings of deprivation.

The two sexes are beginning to separate; more clearly in the neighborhood than in nursery school. Their interests and behavior become increasingly different. In family games the four-year-old boy becomes reluctant to fill a maternal role, even though the mother may be the more
important and powerful parent. It is the boy who tends to exclude the
girls as part of his way of overcoming his dependency on females, a trend
that becomes more marked during the next developmental phase. The
girl spends more time in the house and in her mother's company, and
when she is with her friends, more time talking than doing. The types of
activities and games in which the two sexes engage are already diverging.

Play with Peers

The child's world is expanding even when he does not go to nursery
school. He can care for himself sufficiently to play with other children in
their yard, or in the park under supervision. He enjoys riding his "bike,"
gaining a sense of masculine power from his ability to race along on it.
He enjoys swings and jungle gyms, where he demonstrates his prowess
with pride. A few props help the four-year-old with his imaginative play;
a six-shooter turns him into a cowboy and a space helmet into an astronaut. The child has entered that wonderful period when fantasy need
not yield too much to reality, and his dilemmas can be solved simply by
his altering the way he imagines the world. He begins to play with other
children; at first it is parallel play but it gradually shifts into imaginative
role taking. Naturally, playing "house" and "family" predominates, for
these are roles and activities the child knows best; this play often innocently reveals family characteristics that parents prefer not to recognize.
Television has, of course, increased the range of activities that even very
young children can initiate and elaborate upon. At this age, the child
may suddenly shift from being a space pilot to become a snake wig-
gling along the floor; or, when fatigue mounts, he may even turn into a
baby sucking an imaginary bottle.

If we listen to children conversing when they are sitting together idly,
or when they are engaged in some sedentary activity, we find that although the talk has the form of conversation it is very likely to be a dual
or *collective monologue*. One child says something to the other and
waits for a reply, then the other child speaks but what he says has no
connection with what the first child said, and so they continue, each
voicing his own preoccupations or fantasies in turn. Many children at
four virtually crave the company of other children, at least of another

child. The child awakens in the morning filled with energy and with plans of what he will do with his friend, impatient to be finished with breakfast and off on his adventures. Some must be satisfied with imaginary companions, or prefer them as they are more amenable to direction and are less aggressive and competitive. An imaginary comrade may be quite fleeting, imaginary even to the imagining child, or he may have the force of reality that must be taken into account in planning the day's activities. A mother may sometimes feel desperate when she must not only set the table for two but even serve food for two rather than one. One such child enjoyed playing catch with older boys but, unable to catch as yet, became very fond of Joe, invisible to others, with whom he could play flawlessly with an equally invisible ball. Transitional objects, dolls, or fuzzy toy animals are favored companions and may virtually be endowed with life, even as Christopher Robin shared his adventures with Pooh Bear;[24] and the child cannot go to bed and face the dark and lonely night without them.

Family Behavior

The child is now clearly a member of the family rather than simply his mother's child, and he is having difficulty finding his place in it. He is envious of older siblings and jealous of younger ones, and he may resent the father's prerogatives with the mother. Nevertheless, in relationship to outsiders he has a sense of belonging to his family. He has two names: his first name identifies him within the family and his last name identifies him with his family. A four-year-old refused to return to nursery school on the day after his three-year-old brother first attended: it turned out that it was not a matter of rivalry or jealousy, but of his intense shame because *his* brother had made a puddle on the nursery school floor.

Anxieties

The period is not without blight. The greater independence brings insecurity in its wake. Thumb sucking is more common at four than at two or three and there are other regressive behaviors toward babyish ways and former security. As we shall presently see, the ability to anticipate and to fantasy brings new sources of anxiety. Concerns over death may begin; these are extensions of separation anxiety: his death and the mother's are almost equally anxiety provoking to the child, who does not and cannot understand what death really means. Rivalry with a sibling and wishes to be rid of him may lead to fears of kidnappers who could, after all, kidnap him as well as his brother. Concerns over retribution from the father, whom the child ambivalently wishes were dead, bring wolves or lions into the bedroom at night. Dreams and reality are not readily separable. A three-and-a-half-year-old girl who was afraid to sleep because of nightmares was assured that the tigers were not real but just pictures in her head. A few days later she started to cry when a fire engine with siren screaming stopped outside of the house, but she immediately reassured herself, saying, "Sissy [her younger sister] is having a bad dream about a fire engine." Many children now seek the comfort of the parents' bed in the middle of the night in order to feel safe; they feel secure from all harm as long as the omnipotent parents are tangibly close. Such concerns usually heighten as the child approaches five and the oedipal feelings become more intense, and we shall later note how the development of means of handling the anxiety will be a major force in directing personality development.

Cognitive Development

We followed the child's early acquisition of language until the age of two and a half or three, by which time he had acquired a sizable vocabulary and had mastered the essentials of syntax. It is essential to the understanding of the oedipal or preschool child to recognize the limitations of his intellectual capacities and his comprehension of his world. As we followed the child's emergence from the period of sensori-motor intelligence to the age of about three, his limitations were apparent; but after he becomes able to speak fairly fluently and begins to lead an active life with a fair degree of self-direction and control, his capacities are readily overestimated. Indeed, as one reads Piaget's many studies and experiments one is apt to be surprised again and again at the limitations on the child's ways of thinking and conceiving of reality well into the school years.

Verbal Communication and Fantasy

Even as understanding of the child's intellectual abilities is essential for following his emotional and psychic development, we must also appreciate the impact of his interpersonal and emotional life upon the development of his intellect. One of the crucial aspects of the transition from infancy to school age, or from the oral to the latency periods, concerns the attainment of a fundamental trust in the utility and validity of verbal communication. In order to direct his own life and to relate to others comfortably and effectively, the child increasingly depends upon language: the meanings of words, and the logic with which they are used. It will take many years before his words acquire any real fullness of meaning and he is able to think logically. During these years he also learns from his interaction with others, primarily with his parents, whether words and communication help solve problems and provide a knowledge of the reality with which he must cope, or whether language is used to mask feelings, to alter reality to suit emotionally determined needs, to conceal, to deceive, to justify the self, and, in general, to become a means of manipulating others; or perhaps largely to spin fantasy that may attract attention or provide substitute gratifications but has little relationship to reality.[22] The child may learn that what he says is more important than what he does. This is the time when the child has difficulty in differentiating fantasy from reality, and although fantasy need not yet yield to implacable reality, a gradual transition must be made in the ensuing years. There is danger, on the one hand, that the child will continue to gain major satisfaction from fantasy, and on the other that he can become unimaginative, constricted, pedantic. If communication does not help the child solve problems and relate to those he needs, or if the child's world becomes too anxiety provoking, or if the gratifications provided by the real world are sparse, he can and may need to find refuge in fantasy and neglect the social, communicative meanings of language.

Reality and Fantasy

When the child acquires language he gradually becomes freed from the tangible sensori-motor schemata and the concrete present. He can internalize visual symbols, recall them, rearrange them and recombine them imaginatively with the aid of verbal signs or symbols.* He becomes able to fragment his past in order to select appropriate memories and

---

* Piaget considers that the child can learn to use language only after becoming capable of forming discrete stable motoric and visual symbols that can be recalled and "imitated." Words or verbal signs can then be attached to these symbols. These aspects of his theory are far from satisfactory. Piaget has had difficulty in considering how the child learns the existing language that directs his perception and conceptualizing. However, I wish only to call attention to such problems; they need not be discussed or argued here. Piaget discriminates between *symbols*, which always remain bound to the tangible experience and are therefore personal, and verbal *signs*, which are socially learned and capable of communication, and eventually (but not in early childhood) become freed from the more concrete and specific symbols. However, in keeping with more common usage, in this text "symbols" will also be used to mean words, except when we are specifically discussing Piaget's concepts.

project a future toward which he can direct himself. Ultimately such attributes will permit intelligent reflective behavior. However, the internalization of the environment symbolically also permits the development of imagination and fantasy, which need not be referred back to reality. For a time, at least, this capacity to manipulate symbols imaginatively will interfere with problem-solving behavior.* It is patently simpler to solve problems in fantasy than in reality. The child whose oral and anal drives have been frustrated, and who cannot gain the solace and personal attention he would wish, and who finds that he cannot compete with elders, or control his world, can gain or regain in fancy what he cannot in reality. Indeed, as we learn from patients in analysis, the three- and four-year-old is very likely to regress in fantasy to recapture oral and anal gratifications, particularly when he is going to sleep or in conjunction with masturbatory play. Such fantasies are usually deeply repressed and can be recovered only with difficulty. However, fantasy also serves other ongoing and more reality-oriented needs.

After all, it is difficult for the child to know what is reality and what is imagination. His experience is very limited and he hears about things that he can grasp but vaguely. He can go exploring for the North Pole at the end of his street—that is a very distant place where he has seen a pole, a laundry pole, sticking through the snow. Let us consider the tales of a four-year-old whose father has been overseas in World War II for over three years. His mother has a great investment in this unknown figure whom he knows only by hearsay, and she constantly attracts attention by telling friends and relatives—and even the boy—about his father's experiences in the war. After a time, the child also has his "boys," his sons, overseas who are in and out of battles, in and out of hospitals, and who lose legs and regain them from day to day. These "boys" (all soldiers were "boys") were just as real to him as a father he had never known and who existed only in his mother's talk. Another four-year-old heard a great deal from his grandmother about how things were done in her native land. Soon he has his own Cocaigne, his Utopia, where he goes almost any night and which has the appropriate name of "Milkins." There, things are done properly, his way: the family has one very large bed in which they sleep together; he has his own automobile which he can drive, and when his mom is nice to him she can come to Milkins with him, sleep in the big bed, and he will give her a new car. Is "Mil-

* We shall see that a similar problem arises in the young adolescent when he becomes able to organize and reorganize ideas in the abstract (see Chapter 10).

kins" any less real to him than Europe, or even New York, which he has never seen?

The child is not at all certain that he cannot change the world to suit his needs, or even change himself. Many little girls have believed they would turn into a boy, like the three-and-a-half-year-old Piaget reported who said, "I think the mountain [the mons] hanging here grows and turns into a little long thing with a hole in the end for water to come out, like boys have,"* or like another girl who decided that she would go back inside of her father and when she came out she would be a boy. Naturally, mothers give birth to girls and fathers to boys. After all, her mother can grow a large tummy and even a new baby. It will take years before the facts are sorted out, and before the child learns that although fantasy can give pleasure and dampen the pain of frustrations, it does not change reality, or at the most can be but a prelude to acting upon reality.

Limitations of the Child's Comprehension

Words are the carriers of categories and contain a predictive value (as has been presented in Chapter 1), but when the child first learns names for things they are almost only empty shells into which the members of the category or class will be fitted as the child gains experience. They are like labels on empty filing folders. The categorizing function of words is not a matter that can be pushed and rushed very much: mere instruction in word meanings and in the relationships between words divorced from experience or from a need to solve problems serves little. Meanings keep developing throughout life, and it is not until the age of six or seven that the child has learned enough to abstract from the tangible image and to form the superordinate and subordinate categorizations that are necessary for logical thinking—and even then it is still at a rather concrete and limited level. The child of four or five may well know that dogs, cats, and cows are animals, but is his stuffed bear an animal? Do animals think and talk? After all, in the stories that are read to the child, animals understand. Christopher Robin goes walking with Pooh, who does not say very much but is very understanding.[24] The "Little Engine That Could" thinks and has a very determined will that permits it to pull much harder than anyone thinks it can because it thinks it can.[29] In some respects, just as the mother modified sentences for the younger child's comprehension, parents and people who write stories for

* J. Piaget, *Play, Dreams, and Imitation in Childhood*,[28] p. 173.

children fit the stories to the child's conception of the world. The successful writer for children, such as A. A. Milne, properly grasps how the child thinks and views the world. The process tends to be circular. The child does relatively little thinking for himself about the nature of the world. He relies upon the authority of his elders. If they talk about what animals think, why then animals must think. However, as we shall see, there are other reasons why the child endows animals with language and thought and the inanimate world with feelings. The adult who reads or tells imaginative tales that depart from reality is not perverting the child's notions of truth and falsehood, or of reality and fantasy. Usually, he is stimulating fantasy that can serve the child well. The child's manipulations of a fantasy world and its people in accord with his own needs constitutes a prelude to coping with the reality that cannot be so readily manipulated. It is an important stage in the process of mastery through the manipulation of symbols. A reality orientation will come to the child in time through his sorting out of his own tangible experiences of what works and what leads to further frustration, and in terms of how useful his communications are in establishing a workable interaction with others.

Another difficulty arises because the child has no organized frame of reference into which he can fit what he learns. He has only his own limited experiences and the authority of his elders as to what constitutes reality and truth. He does not yet have the various systems developed by his culture, its measures of time and space, its ways of categorizing, its ethical code, and its value systems into which to fit and organize his experiences, and which provide him with bases for comparison and standards of evaluation. He does not know what his society considers worthy of attention and what can, or should be, ignored.* No one can pay attention to all of the stimuli that encroach upon him, and each culture varies in what it finds significant.†

---

* An interesting approach to the subject of how a culture establishes taboos in order to differentiate between things categorized as separate entities, and the functions of language in the process, is found in E. Leach, "Anthropological Aspects of Language: Animal Categories and Verbal Abuse." [21]
† Stating the matter more in Piaget's terms, the child has not built up schemata to which many of his experiences, particularly those imparted to him verbally, can be properly assimilated, and the processes of accommodation and assimilation are temporarily out of balance.

Egocentricity

The preschool child's orientation, as Piaget repeatedly points out, is markedly *egocentric*. The use of the term has often been misunderstood, sometimes being confused with narcissism, another notable trait of early childhood. The child can see things only from his own limited view and from his narrow perspective. He does not realize or appreciate properly that other persons see things differently. For a time, he cannot even grasp that a person seated in another part of the room does not have the same view of things. If asked what the other person sees, he is very likely to describe what he himself sees. Even a seven- or eight-year-old has notable difficulties in explaining something to another child, or in repeating a story so that another can understand it. He cannot grasp properly what needs to be explained, and may omit things he visualizes in thinking of the story. Thinking is also egocentric in that the child believes that other persons, and also animals and inanimate objects, are motivated or activated in the same way in which he and his parents are. For example, the clouds move because they want to hide the sun; the water in a stream flows because oars push it; didn't the train (that was missed) know we weren't in it?*

Preoperational Intelligence

The child from about two and a half to six or seven is in Piaget's *preoperational* period of intellectual development. It constitutes a prolonged transition from the sensori-motor period to the period of concrete operational intelligence, and retains marked residues of sensori-motor behavior, with language and thought remaining tied to concrete and specific visual images. The linguistic signs or symbols are not yet adequately abstracted from the specific and examples of the categories they designate. Piaget has carefully analyzed the nature of preoperational intelligence, but his explanations of it are intricate and perhaps unnecessarily involved because he seeks to explain the child's development of symbolization as a direct extension of sensori-motor development and minimizes the interpersonal and social aspects of language development.† The

---

* J. Piaget, *Play, Dreams, and Imitation in Childhood*,[28] pp. 245–291.

† The period is sometimes subdivided into two stages at about the age of four to five; the first stage is that of *preconceptual* thought, and the second that of *intuitive* thought.

The preconcept is characterized by incomplete assimilation since it is centered on a typical sample of a set rather than including all the elements of a set (which

transition to the stage of *concrete operations* and the ability to deal with categories is gradual, and school-aged children are often thinking preoperationally—to some extent even up to the start of adolescence. Indeed, in many respects the changes in how the child thinks and conceptualizes his world seem to reflect his increased experience and what he learns from his tutors.*

Let us consider some of the oedipal child's ideas and ways of thinking. We have already noticed the *animism*. Piaget's daughter J., when she was three years old, remarked that the clouds moved to hide the sun; and when she was five and a half that "the moon was hiding in the clouds, it's cold." † She not only bestows upon the moon the power to hide but also a motive. The child is apt to believe that a tree hurts when it is cut and may be reluctant to pick a flower and hurt it. Aspects of nature are explained by *artificialism*. "Mountains are little stones that have grown bigger," ‡ or at three, "I think the sky is a man who goes up in a balloon and makes the clouds and everything." § Names are an inherent part of an object and not something bestowed by man. At four Piaget's daughter L. was certain that the name of a mountain was "Soleve" and not "Saleve," insisting she could tell by looking at it; ‖ and when over five and a half his daughter J. asked, "How did they find out the name of [the mountain] the Dent Blanche?" ¶ Dreams are puzzling. The child believes that they have a tangible existence in the room, outside of himself;

---

requires a further abstraction from concrete reality and visual symbols) and also by incomplete accommodation which is limited to evocation of the image of the individual example. The child cannot yet grasp transformations but only a series of static states, and these are irreversible—that is, the child cannot hold the original state in memory so as to refer back to it and follow the transformation (J. Piaget, *Play, Dreams, and Imitation in Childhood*,[28] p. 284). Reasoning is *transductive*, neither inductive nor deductive but proceeding only from the particular to the particular (A = B; B = C; therefore A = C) and not generalizing from classes or developing class generalizations—that is, categories (*ibid.*, p. 234). *Intuitive thought* shows evidence of less "centration" on the image, a diminution of egocentric confusion between what is subjective and what objective, and movement toward concrete operations. The reader is referred to Chapter 10 of Piaget's *Play, Dreams, and Imitation in Childhood*.[28]

* Studies of the concept formation of adults by means of the Object Sorting Test show that the concept formation of many persons with less than a high school education remains very limited.[36]

† J. Piaget, *Play, Dreams, and Imitation in Childhood*,[28] p. 251.

‡ *Ibid.*, p. 248.

§ J. Piaget, *Play, Dreams, and Imitation in Childhood*,[28] p. 248.

‖ *Ibid.*, p. 256.

¶ *Ibid.*, pp. 255–256.

and may be uncertain whether or not someone else in the room might be able to see the dream, and is puzzled how he sees it with his eyes closed. Causality is also considered in animistic terms. An eight-year-old child studied by Piaget still believed that she could make the clouds move by walking, that everybody could; and when asked if the clouds also moved at night, said that the animals walking about at night made them move. At an earlier age, the child may become involved in circular reasoning such as that the wind makes the trees move, and the moving trees make the wind that moves the clouds. As we might anticipate, rules of games are, like their names, something inherent in the game, or perhaps rules that God or the parents once made. The child of four or five may be able to understand and try to adhere to the rules, but is very likely to change them to suit his needs. Thus one four-year-old invented his own game and insisted that his brother and father play it with him, but they could not follow his rules until they grasped the one fundamental rule: that the four-year-old must always win.

It is apparent that the child's ways of reasoning are very loose. Before the age of seven his use of "because" is rare, and when it occurs in response to "why" questions it usually precedes an animistic or artificialistic explanation. The child is likely to join ideas together by using " 'n-then" as a conjunction, relying upon sequence as a cause. Actually, it is difficult to analyze the child's reasoning at this age because of its global, syncretic nature which is related to the absence of adequate categories or classes. When pushed the child can usually find some reason to connect things together. As he approaches school age, he increasingly uses *transductive* reasoning.

In describing the child's abilities we have noted the various characteristics of preoperational thought. It is egocentric as a result of the child's limited experience, absence of reference systems, and difficulties in differentiating the subjective from the objective. Fantasy and reality are intermingled, and reality gives way to fantasy in face of the child's needs. As word meanings are limited they do not supply the categories required for logical thinking. Thought is still tied to internalized visual symbols, and the child is apt to *center* on a single aspect of the object and neglect other attributes and so distort his reasoning: he also centers on a typical example of a category rather than a true abstraction. The child's thinking tends to be static because he cannot take into account the transformations from one state to another. It suffers from being irreversible because the child cannot maintain an original premise while reasoning;

and, similarly, there is difficulty in remembering the image with which he started and which he needs for comparison with the end result.* Piaget stresses in many different ways the imbalance between assimilation and accommodation during this period of life.†

Piaget's analyses of the child's intellectual processes and ways of experiencing during the preoperational stage are highly intriguing.‡ However, for our present purposes it may suffice to understand something of the child's capacities and limitations and how he understands the world about him. Many of his limitations would seem to be understandable in terms of his inexperience, which means that he will be egocentric; in terms of the fact that even though he has words it will take time and experience before they really designate categories; and that he has not yet gained the culture's ways of reasoning and systematizing. How much depends upon the immaturity of his nervous system, and how much upon the slow process of organizing the "mind," is not yet known.

There is some danger that emphasis on the limitations of the young child's mental processes and his egocentric view of the world can lead to gross underevaluations of the child's potentialities. The child's abilities and grasp of reality vary with his intelligence level and the social and intellectual milieu in which he is raised. After all John Stuart Mill, as well as other childhood prodigies, could manage the syntax of Greek and Latin by the age of four to five. Far less remarkable children can manifest a strange admixture of primitive and complex thinking. The four-year-old who seemed to believe in the reality of his fantasy country "Milkins" could at the same time readily distinguish various makes of cars, including the models from different years under the proper brand names, and also categorize them according to the body style, irrespective of brand names. This constitutes a rather high level of category forma-

* See Chapter 9 for further discussion of these concepts.
† Piaget notes that in contrast to the sensori-motor period the child not only assimilates current experiences but must also try to handle internalized imagistic symbols and assimilate to these schemata as well as current ones. I believe this does not differ greatly from saying that the child must deal with material he can recall from memory as well as with ongoing experiences. It is also essential to bear in mind that he does not yet have the schemata to which he can properly assimilate what he simply hears about. Piaget considers the imbalance between assimilation and accommodation to account for the child's pervasive use of *imitation*, in which there is a primacy of accommodation over assimilation; and of *symbolic play*, in which there is primacy of assimilation over accommodation. The reader must again be referred to Chapter 10 of *Play, Dreams, and Imitation in Childhood*,[28] pp. 273–291.
‡ Studies of preoperational intelligence may serve to clarify many aspects of the thinking of schizophrenic patients.

tion, and was related to a dominant interest and the presence of an adult companion who went to considerable effort to help him learn the differentiations.

With experience and education the child will move beyond preoperational thought. With increasing socialization and under the subtle pressure to conform in order to gain acceptance, as well as to find relief from anxieties, the child will begin to repress unacceptable wishes and the fantasies and thoughts that accompany them. Much of the material will become unconscious and interfere less directly with reality-directed and reflective thinking. The nature of the unconscious processes and how they continue to influence behavior will be considered in the next chapter.*

The Development of Trust in Verbal Communication

The child of three or four is starting to assemble his major resources for conducting his life through his ability to communicate and manipulate symbols. The child's reality testing will depend upon the slow sorting out of his experiences and the learning of what works and what does not that started during infancy; but this will, in turn, also depend upon the consistency and reliability of the behavior of his tutors, primarily the members of his family. Verbal communication assumes increasing importance as the child emerges from his family. Members of the family had, through long experience, been able to understand and even anticipate many of his needs without his verbalizing them. Still, the child's trust in language—and what can be conveyed verbally and what responses his words will elicit—develops in the home setting. Here he learns how effective words will be: whether they concur with the unspoken communications; whether they are apt to match the feelings that accompany

---

* The movement beyond preoperational thinking does not depend upon maturation alone. In various primitive societies persons depend upon animistic and artificialistic explanations of causality throughout life and tend to think in syncretic, "precausal" ways;[34] or have very different systems of logic.[35] In the absence of a scientific approach peoples tend to depend upon various types of magical thinking in order to try to exert some control over the contingencies of life. One need not venture among primitive peoples to find adults who manifest similar phenomena. Palmists, astrologers, and faith healers abound in localities where the law does not forbid them. Magic potions, amulets, and love charms are readily available in most large cities. Physicians who take care of persons from the lower socio-economic sectors and from various minority ethnic groups are likely to become aware that some of their patients are not placing all of their eggs in one basket and are relying upon various types of white magic as well as upon the physician.

them; whether they subserve problem solving or are just as often a means of masking the existence of problems. The child's trust in verbal communication depends upon whether the words of the persons who are essential to him help solve problems or confuse, whether they provide more consistent signals than nonverbal cues, and whether the child's use of words can evoke desired responses. Difficulty can arise when parents' words contradict their nonverbal signals, as, for example, when the mother's words of affection are accompanied by irritable and hostile handling of the child; or when the mother's instructions for the child to obey his grandmother are accompanied by her obvious delight when the child disobeys and becomes a nuisance to the grandmother. The value of words is also diluted or negated when erroneous solutions are habitually imposed, as when the child who cries because he wants attention is told that he is hungry and is fed. Predictive values of communication are undermined when promises rarely materialize. A disturbed youth told how very early in life he had ceased to trust what his mother said, and virtually stopped listening to her incessant talk, for he had learned that her tales of the wonderful things they would do together never materialized. It took him many years to learn that his mother was simply sharing with him the fantasies that sustained her.*

Interference with the child's efforts to explore his world and solve problems by himself can also impede the development of language. Children who have been treated as passive objects for whom almost everything must be done have little need to speak. Discouragement of verbal play also hinders. The child needs to try out words and expressions in a multitude of contexts and he learns from the responses elicited. He often repeats what a parent says and does, imaginatively exchanging roles with the parent. "You are tired, Mommy; sit here, Johnny reads you a story." Through filling the reciprocal role in play, the child expands his comprehension and use of words as well as developing

* Persistent denial of the correctness of the child's perceptions and understanding of what transpires about him can have a particularly malignant influence in promoting distrust of language and fostering distortions of meanings. The child is repeatedly placed in a "bind" because the obvious is negated, and he is threatened with loss of approval or love if he does not see things the way in which his parents need to have him see them. A mother keeps telling a little boy that he must love his father as she does, that Father is very good to them; but Father comes home drunk every other night, beats his wife, and usually gives his son a whack or two. Perhaps, less malignantly and more commonly, the child is punished if he does not tell the truth, but cannot avoid hearing his mother falsify why she cannot attend a church meeting or his father boast of how he concealed the truth in selling the old family car.

through such identifications. Parents who cannot participate in such play, and who insist upon firm adherence to reality, discourage such exploratory problem solving. Sometimes, parents consider the child's "make-believe" to be lying, reprimand the child severely, and cut off all his expressions of fantasy. The parents of an adolescent delinquent related that they were not surprised that he was in serious trouble, for he had been a difficult child from the start, already given to lying at the age of three—he had told them about playing with another boy when no one had been about, and of how he had helped mow the lawn when he could not yet push the lawnmower. They felt that they had been forced to make strenuous efforts to change his ways, but their punishments could not alter his inherent nature.

Discouragement and disparagement of a child's questions also limit language experience and the verbal explorations essential for learning. Children's incessant questions can become a test of parental patience and provoke: "Why can't you shut up for a while?" "Be quiet! Can't you see I'm reading?" "What difference does it make what it is called?" "It doesn't mean anything at all!" Sometimes punishment for what is simply the conveying of needs can lead to a vicious cycle of creating greater needs, more pressing attempts to communicate, and eventually to despair. A little girl of four who imparted her wish to be rid of her baby brother was told that she was wicked and severely admonished never to hurt the baby. Fearful of rejection, she called for her mother at night, only to be threatened that she would be sent off to a school for bad girls if she didn't let her mother sleep. The child stopped calling her mother at night because of her fears, but instead developed a severe pain in her head. The severe headaches then led to her hospitalization, which caused the girl to suffer acute separation anxiety. Parents can impede and distort the development of linguistic abilities in a great variety of ways. The examples presented should suffice to indicate how the child can fail to develop trust in the usefulness of language for communicating and as an instrument for solving problems.*

Gender Identity

Whether the child is born a boy or girl is perhaps the single most important determinant of personality characteristics. The difference is more than a matter of anatomy. The two sexes have different ways of

* Disturbances in the child's language development are increasingly being related to impoverished self-control in childhood and to the development of serious psychopathology such as schizophrenia and delinquency in later life.[2, 22, 30, 31, 37, 38]

relating and reacting, different perspectives and interests, different tasks and roles. The human species is divided into two sexes, and in every culture the males and females have different tasks and functions though the division varies from place to place. As Freud said, "Male and female is the first differentiation that you make when you meet another human being, and you are used to making that distinction with absolute certainty." [10] Even though, since the time when Freud wrote, it has become increasingly difficult to make an immediate distinction, the difference remains of the essence of human relationships. The child's gender will determine much of the future pattern of his or her life.

Gender and Personality Characteristics

The influence of the child's gender is so pervasive and develops so naturally that usually little attention is paid to the dynamics of the personality differentiation of the two sexes. Again, it is the study of pathology, in which a gender identity appropriate to the physical sex is not attained or where physical sex is ambiguous, that has opened the way for careful scrutiny of the process. Achievement of a firm identity as a member of one's own sex is basic to emotional stability and to the eventual development of a cohesive ego identity. Even though it is possible to come to terms with strivings to be a member of the opposite sex, and even to live out a life as if a member of the opposite sex, or to be attracted sexually primarily by members of one's own gender, such adaptations usually are fraught with problems and are manifestations of other personality difficulties. We are not concerned here with aberrations of sexual behavior but with how the child achieves an identity as a boy or girl and then gains security and comfort in that identity. The topic requires discussion before we turn to the oedipal transition proper, for the nature of the oedipal strivings and the way in which they are resolved depends upon the child's gender and the firmness of his gender identity. Conversely, it is the proper resolution of the child's oedipal problems which solidifies the child's gender identity, but which can, at times, augment conflicts or even create new problems.

Determinants of Gender Identity

The child's sex is genetically determined, but biological factors only influence the gender identity. Freud tended to explain problems of homosexuality through recourse to an innate bisexuality in all animal organisms, pointing out that the male and female sex organs differentiate from the same embryonic rudiments. Freud, however, also recognized and considered the influence of interpersonal factors impinging upon the child and their fusion with biological determinants in directing him toward various types of sexual gratification and the choice of sexual objects. Psychoanalysis has also emphasized that the way in which the child moved through the earlier oral and anal phases influences his sexual identity by establishing basic attitudes of passivity or activity, fostering masochistic or sadistic tendencies, and feelings of mastery or wishes to be mastered, all of which enter into the development of male or female traits. The sexual organs in themselves also contribute to a basic orientation as a male or female. Erikson considers that a boy, in response to the presence of his penis and the feelings it engenders, tends to become intrusively active, whereas a girl, responding to her external and internal sexual organs, feels receptive and even ensnaring. He considers that the girl develops feelings and ideas of an inner space, a creative space that profoundly influences her way of relating and her feelings about herself.[5] The sexual hormones may have influenced the fetus *in utero* and will affect behavior later but do not impinge upon the young child.

Despite the importance of various biological factors, the gender assigned the child by the parents and the ensuing interactional patterns within the family can outweigh all other considerations. Naturally, the assigned sex concurs with chromosomal and anatomical sex except under unusual circumstances. Still, children have occasionally grown up fairly firmly identified as members of the sex opposite to that indicated by their genitalia. The parents' overt acceptance of the child as a boy or a girl is not always in accord with their emotional attitudes. As parents neither treat a child completely in accord with his or her sex, nor themselves provide fully consistent models as males or females, nor consistently reward masculinity in a boy or femininity in a girl, no child grows up to be purely masculine or feminine, which designations are, after all, only relative. As every psychiatrist knows, some of the most aggressive masculine behavior often covers intense feminine strivings or homosexual tendencies; and among the most ensnaringly seductive women are some who are incapable of attaining any sexual gratification. The Greeks in their mythology of the heroic and unconquerable Heracles included an episode in which he exchanged roles with Queen Omphale and lived with her as a woman.

BIOLOGICAL FACTORS

Let us now review very briefly some of the salient aspects of gender determination and what it may have to do with gender identity in humans. Whether the child is male or female depends upon the presence of an X or a Y chromosome in the fertilizing sperm that joins with the X chromosome in the ovum. The presence of the Y chromosome usually assures that at a critical phase in fetal development the testes secrete androgen which influences the anlage of the genito-urinary tract to develop male internal organs and later to develop male external genitalia. There is now fairly clear evidence that in mammals, including monkeys, the hormone acts upon the undifferentiated brain to organize certain circuits in male rather than female patterns.[4, 39] The androgen acts upon the fetal brain to direct young males after birth to show more active and aggressive play and a tendency to sexual mounting behavior; and the absence of such an androgen leads to female trends of interest in babies and greater interest in grooming behavior. The duration of such influences in primates is unknown, but they last for at least two years and start the baby in the proper gender role. Indeed, in Jane Goodall's studies of chimpanzees in their natural habitat,[12, 13] a young immature female was observed to try repeatedly to take a baby away from her mother to care for it herself: such behavior was not observed and would not be anticipated in young males.

Recent studies have shown that when androgens are given to pregnant monkeys, the female offspring of such pregnancies tend to show the male rather than the female behavior patterns in childhood. Pregnant women might secrete sufficient androgens from the adrenal cortex in response to emotional stress to affect the fetus, but studies of such phenomena cannot as yet be generalized to humans, who depend so much more on learning than primates. It seems unlikely that androgen secretion in the mother would induce such *patterned* male behavior in human infants, but it might well increase the readiness of males and females to learn behaviors appropriate to their gender.* There are also indications, though they are still far from clear cut, that chromosomal abnormalities may influence gender-linked behavior in a very general way. Thus, men with Klinefelter's syndrome, an anomaly due to the presence of two X chromosomes and one Y chromosome, are not only

* See D. Hamburg and D. Lunde, "Sex Hormones in the Development of Sex Differences in Human Behavior" [15] for an excellent review of the literature on this topic.

sterile and weakly motivated sexually, but may tend toward confusions in gender identity. In contrast, men with two X and two Y chromosomes tend toward outbursts of aggressive behavior as well as being very tall, eunochoid, and mentally deficient.[11] Current evidence indicates that because of prenatal genetic and hormonal influences, humans are pre-disposed at birth to a male or a female gender orientation, but that such influences only predispose to a pattern that can be modified greatly by subsequent life experiences.*

GENDER ALLOCATION

The studies by Hampson, Hampson, and Money of seventy-six pseu-dohermaphrodites and hermaphrodites of almost every known type require thoughtful assessment in any theory of gender role determina-tion.† In these individuals various combinations of discrepancies existed between the assumed gender in which the person had been raised and the external genitalia, the internal organs, the chromosomes, and the hormonal secretions after puberty. In only four of the seventy-six sub-jects was there any notable inconsistency between the sex in which the person had been raised and the gender role established despite the obvi-ous developmental difficulties created for many of them by the uncer-tainties about their actual gender and by various physical abnormalities. Thus, chromosomal males with gonadal agenesis had almost always been thought to be girls, at least till puberty, and they were clearly feminine in behavioral characteristics. In some diagnostic categories some children had been raised as boys and others as girls. It is also significant that in twenty-five of the series there was a marked contradiction between the appearance of the external genitalia and the assigned sex, and yet all but a few had come to terms with the anomalous situation and established a gender role consistent with the assigned sex and rearing. The topic is

* "Life experiences most likely act to differentiate and direct a flexible sexual disposi-tion and to mold the prenatal organization until an environmentally (socially and culturally) acceptable gender role is formulated and established." [4]
† The cases studied include females with virilizing adrenal cortical hyperplasia, simu-lant females with testes, chromosomal males with gonadal agenesis and female physical morphology, cryptorchid males reared as females, and others. There were contradictions between chromosomes and the gender in which the child was reared in nineteen cases; between the gonads and the gender in which the child was reared in twenty; between hormonal sex and the gender in which the child was reared in twenty-seven. postpubertal cases; between appearance of external genitalia and the gender in which the child was reared in twenty-three; and between internal accessory organs and gender rearing in eighteen.[16, 25, 26]

extremely complex but the results of the study seem sufficiently definitive to warrant the conclusion that the gender assigned and in which the child is reared can outweigh chromosomal and hormonal influences and the appearance of the genitals in determining gender identity, even though there seems reason to modify the investigators' tentative conclusions that the human is born psychosexually neutral: that is, with gender-linked sexual behavior developing only in accord with the way in which the child is reared.

While such investigations are important in helping sort out the factors determining sexual identity as well as sex-linked behavioral traits, confusions concerning a child's gender are rare, and with occasional exception the physical appearance, chromosomes, hormonal secretions, and the assigned gender are in harmony. By the age of two or two and a half the identity of the child as a boy or girl is already well ingrained in the child's awareness and behavior. Indeed, the Hampsons and Money, on the basis of their experience with children whose gender assignment had been changed, believe that such changes after the age of two and a half are very likely to create serious problems for the child.[26] Although neonates seem to be treated in very much the same way whether they are boys or girls, parental attitudes are very likely to differ according to the child's sex from the time of birth and influence the child's emerging behavior in many subtle ways. It is difficult to tell whether the boy usually becomes more active in response to a pattern evoked *in utero* by androgen secretion or in response to the manner in which he is treated. Many mothers relate more actively with a son than with a daughter.[3] The father may often play as crucial a role as the mother in fostering gender-linked attributes. Whereas the mother may fill her nurturant role with the young child in very much the same way whether it is a boy or girl, the father may have a more active physical interaction with a little son and feel freer to display affection and softness with a daughter. He wants the boy to be boyish and the girl to be feminine more decisively than many mothers.

IDENTIFICATIONS

Although the child knows its gender by the age of two or three, the matter is not so clear cut as one might imagine. If we remember the way in which the child thinks and fantasies between the ages of three and five, it becomes apparent that many inconsistencies can exist in the child's concept of himself. The boy, as well as the girl, tends to identify with the mother who is the important person in his life. Many boys of three or four will openly express their belief or wish that they will grow up to be a mommy. The boy, as the girl, starts life in symbiosis with the mother and gradually differentiates from her. His love of the mother is accompanied by a desire to be like her. She is the source of security and affection, and he wishes to become the strong and capable person. The "I'm going to become a mommy like you" reflects his fantasies and is a normal aspect of development. Then, the child knows what he is, but knows not what he may become: both boys and girls may fantasy as well as fear that they may change sex when they grow up. It is necessary to appreciate the boy's initial identification with his mother to understand the foundations for many sexual aberrations and related psychopathological conditions.

Awareness of Sex Differences—Penis Envy

What makes children boys or girls may not be obvious to the child. Some do not have an opportunity to ascertain the physical differences till later in childhood, but ignorance of the difference is more often due to an inability to see or to remember what has been seen and is upsetting. Children may pay more attention to the clothing than to the genitalia. A five-year-old, when asked while he was looking at a nude baby if it were a boy or girl, replied, "I don't know—it's hard to tell with the clothes off." The discovery that a boy has a penis and a girl does not marks a critical turn in the lives of many children. The impact is apt to be more severe on the girl. Indeed, the girl's feeling that she has been deprived, or that she was born with a penis which has been removed, forms a common trauma in women. Freud believed that the psychoanalysis of women could not progress beyond recognition and acceptance of such feelings of deprivation.[7] The universality of penis envy has been a topic for considerable debate. Some psychoanalysts insist that a woman's feelings of being a second-class citizen derive from the social role in which she is placed rather than from feelings of castration or physical deprivation.* In any event, the little girl can become very much concerned or preoccupied with the absence of the handy little tool that she observed on a boy. Some will rebel and try to change the situation either in reality or imaginatively. The girl may insist on standing up to urinate and on wearing pants; or the parents may merely note references to her fantasies. Thus, a four-and-a-half-year-old had been a happy child until the birth of

* See, for example K. Horney, "Feminine Psychology," [17] pp. 101–119.

her brother. She was not only jealous of the attention the infant received but properly attributed the parents' delight with the baby to his sex. She began to stand up to urinate and insisted on wearing blue jeans, refusing to wear dresses. Her mother sought to ease the situation by explaining the advantage the girl had in being able to have a baby. The explanation included some information about how babies are made and grow in the mother. The girl then developed a severe phobia of contamination and refused to eat many foods, fearing she might ingest a "seed" and have a baby grow in her "stomach." As will be shown later, the girl may feel that her mother is to blame for her shortcoming and such feelings may lead her to turn away from her mother.

The little girl usually comes to terms in one way or another with the absence of the desired penis. The crisis is surmounted best when the girl can appreciate that the mother has self-esteem as a woman, and also that the father has esteem and affection for his wife as a woman. Femininity can be sufficiently advantageous to offset feelings of deprivation. The manner in which the girl comes to terms or compensates will have a very important and lasting influence upon the course of her development. A period of tomboy behavior is very common and often lasts until shortly before the onset of puberty, and it is usually accompanied by unexpressed fantasies of being a boy. Obviously, not all girls will accept their femininity. Some will simply enter masculine occupations, but some will seek to act out and live a male role, including a sexual role. The eventual solution of the problem may hang in balance until some time in adolescence; but a proper resolution of the oedipal situation usually consolidates the acceptance of a feminine identity. The identification with the mother, fortified by the father's pleasure in having a daughter, usually wins out, directing the girl into feminine ways and satisfactions.

Masculine Pride

The little boy usually takes considerable pride in his penis, particularly when he has sisters. Such feelings are often enhanced by his mother's obvious or unconscious admiration of the penis she produced. Masturbation develops naturally, often before the child can remember. It is not only a source of erotic pleasure but a means of gaining solace when the boy is upset. The penile sensations stimulate fantasies of an erotic nature, which in the little child are rather naturally connected to the mother and the bodily care she provides. Masturbation tends to continue unless the child is severely admonished or threatened with dire

consequences unless he stops. However, the connection between masturbation and fantasies about the mother may eventually lead to severe
conflicts and guilt feelings which force the child to suppress his autoerotic play and repress memories of early masturbation. Erections are not
always pleasurable; the child may become disturbed at the behavior of an
external organ that is outside of his control, and even become concerned
about his erections. They are likely to contain an admixture of pain
along with the pleasurable sensations: a forerunner of the arousal of tension that requires ejaculation for relief, but which also stimulates masochistic fantasies. Whereas little girls also masturbate, it is not so common or so frequent; and the difference may have a bearing on the greater
intensity and erotization of the boy's attachment to his mother.

Castration Anxiety

The discovery that there are persons without visible external genitalia
can also be extremely upsetting to the boy. He may conclude that girls
have had their penises cut off, and fear for his own intactness and male
identity. Concern that the penis can disappear may be augmented by the
fluctuations in its size. The concern may be so anxiety-provoking that
the boy seeks to deny the potentiality, refusing to perceive or remember
having seen anyone without a penis. He may imagine that his mother has
simply hidden hers, or that his baby sister has not yet grown one. Such
ideas and concerns were brought home to a mother very vividly when
her five-year-old son asked where she kept her penis. She reminded him
that she had told him that boys and men have penises but girls and
women do not, that they have other organs instead. The boy then said,
"Yes, I remember now, that's where someone axed you one!"

Freud considered castration anxiety to be a universal and a critical
aspect of all male development, one that plays a major role in the oedipal
transition. It seems likely that in homes where matters concerning sex
and genitals are taken more casually than in Victorian times, anxiety
over castration may not occur or, at least, be less of a central issue. However, the existence of castration concerns is very apt to be minimized
because of the tendency to repress the childhood fear after the problem
has been resolved. In any event, when castration anxiety becomes a severe and enduring problem, it is likely to reflect the individual's wish to
be rid of the penis. Although such wishes might seem unlikely, a boy
may fantasy retaining his identification with his mother, or he may
become envious of the prerogatives of sisters and feel burdened by the

demands placed upon him for achievement because he has a penis. Severe anxiety here, as elsewhere, is very often related to fear that an ambivalent wish might materialize.*

Although psychoanalysis has focused attention on the woman's penis envy, probably as many men wish that they were women as vice versa, but such desires are far less acceptable—or at least have been until very recently.

The little boy may also become concerned over the difference in the size of his father's genitals and his own. The size and urinary power of his father's genitals may symbolize to him the father's strength and potency; and he has difficulty in understanding that his genitals will grow. Of course, the child, particularly when he wishes to retain his childhood dependency, can manage to forget that he is going to grow up into a man.

Gradually, the consolidation of gender identity in the boy means modeling himself after his father. It is a shift in identification not required of the girl. It is fostered by the mother's admiration of her husband and the culture's evaluation of the male role. The transition will gain impulsion from the oedipal resolution. However, by the age of four, boys and girls are beginning to move apart. Boys may already show indications of being contemptuous of girls. Such attitudes have been considered to reflect scorn of the "castrated" sex, but evidence indicates that it is part of boys' needs to emancipate themselves from feminine influence and dominance. For boys to be independent and feel free, women and girls must be kept out of the play.

Security of Gender Identity

A child's comfort and security as a member of his or her own sex depends very greatly upon parental attitudes. Is there room for a child of the given sex in the family and in the parents' affections? Parents who have had their hearts set upon having a child of a given sex may be unable to absorb their disappointment when the newborn turns out con-

---

* A young man with severe castration anxiety, who could have his hair cut only by a woman barber and his teeth repaired by a female dentist because of unconscious derivatives of such fears, also had mild transvestite tendencies. He was markedly envious of his older sister, not because she enjoyed a favored place with their mother, but rather because his mother had such inordinate expectations that he live out the life she would have wished for had she been a male, and also that he recoup for her the position in select society that her father had lost for her family by being an alcoholic and a wastrel.

trary to their hopes. Girls are more likely to feel unwanted, and are probably less often of the sex that the parents wanted. In an effort to make up to her father for having disappointed him (as if it were her doing and not his) the girl may strive to become a boyish companion for her father.* Some mothers are unable to relate properly to a daughter, and may more or less consciously encourage the development of masculine traits. A husband may treat his wife so contemptuously that their daughter sees little advantage in a feminine role. Boys can also disappoint their parents and feel that they should have been girls. The male role may be dangerous in a home where an aggressive and dominant wife constantly belittles and cuts off her husband. An occasional mother may have her heart so set on having a daughter to provide companionship, or to whom she can give all the things that she lacked in childhood, that she feminizes the boy. A marine who suffered a combat neurosis after displaying exceptional heroism confided that he had joined the service to bolster his inadequate feelings of masculinity: he had been dressed as a girl until he was five, and had never been able to believe that he was really a male.

When the development goes well, the emerging gender-linked roles fuse with the biological directives. The culture, just like the evolutionary process, has a vital interest in seeing that they do. The girl who is to become a mother, and who will have a vital interest in preserving the integrity of her family, is already becoming more interested in people and how they relate to one another. She is not as physically active as the boy. She is spending more time playing house and caring for her dolls. She is quieter and more passive, waiting upon the action of others, but she is also very likely to know how to make herself attractive to her father. The boy, who is to become a husband upon whom a wife and children can be dependent, is beginning to deny his dependency upon his mother and manifest feelings of superiority to girls. He will eventually move out into the world to gain a livelihood and he is already moving out into the neighborhood and into a male competitive world. The trends start early; they need to be deeply rooted.

Since the gender identity and its accompanying roles are so dependent upon the ways in which parents relate to the child, interact with one another, and regard themselves, it becomes apparent that all sorts of variations in gender identity and in the security and stability of the gender identity can develop. Because the entire pattern of a person's

* A classic example of an extreme outcome can be found in Radclyffe Hall's novel, *The Well of Loneliness*.[14]

relationships will be carried out in accord with his sex, the gender identity will have far-reaching repercussions, but here we must be concerned
primarily with how it influences the oedipal transition.

Knowledge and Fantasies of Conception and Childbirth

Sooner or later, often in conjunction with the birth of a younger sibling, the child puzzles about the origin of babies. Stories about storks are
likely to stretch the credulity of even a young child, particularly in a
country where there are no storks. Simple explanations that the child
grows within the mother and comes out through a special opening may
satisfy for a time. Detailed explanations are beyond the child's comprehension and do not decrease misapprehension. The child usually develops or expands theories on his own. The mystery of the origin of
babies is one of the primal mysteries of childhood.

The young child is likely to believe that the seed is placed in the
mother's mouth, or that it comes from eating a seeded food. The baby
before birth may be envisioned as sitting in his mother's stomach with
open mouth, ingesting the food she eats. How the baby gets out of the
mother is an even greater puzzle. Obviously, the child is likely to believe
that it emerges from the anus; but the navel, which appears to serve no
other good purpose, is often selected. As mothers go to hospitals, the
doctor may remove the baby by an operation. There are many potential
sources of anxiety to the child, particularly to the little girl who cannot
conceive of how she could produce a baby without incurring disastrous
consequences to her body. However, in this regard as in many others, the
child's attitude reflects the parents'; and if he is not given reasons to feel
discomfort or concern, the child usually accepts the parents' explanation
and asks when he wishes to know more. The child's reasoning may be
difficult to follow, as in the case of the four-year-old boy who, after puzzling over an explanation of how the baby grows in the mother, asked,
"Now, before the baby is born, is the baby in the mother or the mother
in the baby?"

Sibling Relationships

Although it is simpler to consider the development of a single child
growing up in relation to his parents, it is unrealistic as the interactions
between siblings are among the major formative influences. If a child
does not already have siblings, he is very likely to gain a brother or sister
before he completes his oedipal phase. Sibling relationships are not only

almost as important as the oedipal situation in directing and crystallizing a child's early development, but the oedipal transition is usually greatly influenced by the presence of other children. Even though a discussion of siblings will complicate an already complicated subject, it will permit a more rounded and realistic presentation.

Sibling Rivalry

Sibling rivalry has probably received far more attention than the advantages of sibling relationships. The hostility of brothers receives attention in the opening pages of the Old Testament in which Cain's fratricide—a crime relating homicidal impulses to fraternal jealousy—is considered second immediately after the original sin of Adam and Eve. The rivalry between brothers for a father's blessing led Jacob to drive a hard bargain with the starving Esau and cheat him, albeit with their mother's help. Jacob, in turn, was deprived of his favorite son when his ten oldest sons united to rid themselves of the precocious Joseph. The Greeks also placed sibling rivalry in central positions in their mythology. In the myths of the curse of the house of Tantalus, for example, Thyestes seduces the wife of his brother Atreus, who gains revenge by killing Thyestes' sons and feeding them to him at a banquet.*

Jealousy of the New Baby

The arrival of a new baby naturally provokes a small child's intense jealousy. His entire life is changed. He is no longer the major recipient of the mother's attention and the baby usually has priority. Still, he is often expected to take delight in the new arrival and share the parents' enthusiasm. If he had been awaiting the child with happy anticipation he now feels that he had been deceived: the little brother can't play with him, doesn't talk, and is little more than a nuisance. The child is not joking when he asks if the parents can't give the baby back, or comments that a new puppy would have been preferable. Despite the parents' attempts to prepare the child and make him feel that the baby is his as well as theirs,

---

* Which led the son of Thyestes, Aegisthus, to gain vengeance on Agamemnon the son of Atreus. Aegisthus was aided by Agamemnon's wife Clytemnestra, who was enraged because her husband had sacrificed their daughter Iphigenia to the gods to help his brother recover his wife, Clytemnestra's sister Helen, from the Trojans. Clytemnestra had reason to be hostile to her ship-launching sister, whose beauty attracted such attention. In another series of Greek myths, the sons of Oedipus fight over the succession to the rule of Thebes and kill one another. Clearly sibling rivalries caused the Greeks considerable trouble.

this is a time of tribulation during which most children can be expected to show regressive behavior. The child may insist on returning to the bottle, or start soiling again. Being a baby and unable to care for oneself clearly has advantages. He may develop tics or a stammer, symptoms that reflect efforts to control aggression toward the baby.

Parents often sigh with relief after the baby is several months old and the older child has accepted the situation without obvious difficulties. However, problems are even more likely to occur when the infant emerges from the crib or playpen and gets into the older child's possessions. The mother must now divide her attention between two active children. The older child's aggressivity toward the baby or toddler may provoke the first real conflict with the parents, who must protect the younger child and cannot practice their customary tolerance. The child learns to conform in order to maintain the parents' approval but may do so by *reaction formation* in which hostility is repressed and he is overly good or overly demonstrative toward the baby. The defense does not always work and the child may develop a disturbing slyness in which he appears accepting of the baby when the parents are about but may pinch, hit, or otherwise provoke the baby when alone with it.

Envy of Older Siblings

Whereas the older child is given to jealousy of the younger, the younger child is usually envious of the older who has many prerogatives and gains attention through his accomplishments. The envy may spur the child to activities beyond his capacities and lead to frustration. When the young child can somehow identify with the older and take pride in his abilities, things can go well; but if he feels defeated and constantly left out because of them, he may stop trying to emulate the older sibling and simply resent him. Here again, the older child is very likely to follow the parental example of being helpful to the younger if he does not feel deprived or constantly reprimanded because of the younger.

The rivalrous conflicts that are almost bound to occur, particularly among closely spaced siblings, create turmoil; and the noise of the friction, like a squeaking wheel, gains attention from the parents who seek means of lubrication to restore quiet and calm. The regressions of the older child, the turn from carefree happiness to sullen discontent, the hyperactive strivings to regain the center of the stage, cannot but disturb the parents. Their efforts to mediate and provide justice are not

always compatible with the child's emotional needs. Punishment for
attention-seeking tactics can readily leave the child feeling misunderstood and lead to new infractions.

Affection and Identification between Siblings

The positive feelings between siblings and the great need and
affection they often develop for one another can be overlooked because
their fights attract more attention. Ambivalence is characteristic of poor
as well as good relationships between young siblings. Most quarrels, even
those that look as if they would end in fratricide, are quickly forgotten
by the children, who make up wordlessly and resume their companionship while the parents are still pondering how they will manage the situation.

While difficulties in finding conflict-free space within the family and
desires for affection provoke rivalries, the similarities in how they are
raised and in their backgrounds can make siblings very much alike and
quite understanding of one another, and they are apt to be closer to one
another than to any other person. Their similar ways of regarding situations, and similar superego developments, may enable them to understand what the other thinks and feels without any verbal exchange. Indeed, a sibling's values may be as important as the parents' in the
formation of a child's superego. The need for a sibling's esteem and
affection can take precedence over strivings for parental love. A child
may cede priority with a parent rather than see his sibling unhappy or
disrupt their relationship. He may conceal or fail to develop some ability
rather than move into an area in which the other has gained recognition.
Siblings may divide roles between them as they find ways of sharing the
living space to avoid conflict. The division of a single place within the
family becomes most noticeable with identical twins who encounter the
special developmental problem of differentiating from one another as
well as from the mother.[19,20,22] Here, the sharing of ways of doing things
and the reliance upon one another for support create serious difficulties in
their learning to lead separate lives.

Ordinal Position and Development

The significance of the ordinal position of the child to various abilities, traits, and mental health has been studied in a variety of ways.
Statistical studies have limited value to the understanding of the individual because of the variations in circumstances and parental attitudes

from family to family. Apparently first-born children enjoy some advantages as far as achievement of intellectual superiority and eminence is concerned.[1] Oldest children clearly gain a different perspective from that of younger children, particularly in large families where they assume some responsibility for the siblings. The advantages may derive from the greater opportunity for contact with adults that they have while still small, and from their being the sole recipient of the parents' attention for a time. Whereas the first-born will often maintain a certain priority in the mother's affections, a youngest child may also have a special position in remaining her "baby" no matter how grown. Younger children benefit from the parents' experience with the older and from having an older sibling to provide an example. The middle child, particularly when all children are of one sex, is apt to be caught between the jealousies of the older and the envy of the younger who may form a coalition against the middle child.

Sibling Relationships and the Oedipal Transition

When the parents are particularly eager to have a son, the appearance of a second daughter can create poorly concealed disappointments. A second daughter may respond by tending to become boyish in order to compensate the parents; though the third daughter does not usually follow suit. Still, the long-awaited arrival of a son after several daughters (as one father commented, "After three zeros, finally a digit!") does not always place the boy in an enviable position. The older sisters become jealous of the parents' delight in the presence of a son and heir, and may be particularly envious of his prized penis. The boy grows up under the aegis of three or four mothering figures, not all of whom are completely benevolent, and in a family that is more attuned to feminine than masculine patterns of behavior. He may be pampered but at the same time be expected to have the manliness to become his father's successor and the carrier of the family name. Some such boys become very envious of the girl's role, with its freedom from great expectations and acceptability of continuing dependency, and develop strong castration wishes. The position in the family does not of itself establish definite patterns. One may also see a youth with three or four older sisters whose masculinity and independence has been properly fostered and with a suitable father figure to emulate who feels very comfortable in his favored position.

The sibling relationships, or more usually the parental attitudes toward the siblings, can decisively influence the child's oedipal relation-

ships as well as his gender identity. A girl born into a family in which the
parents had become emotionally estranged prior to her birth was confronted by a difficult situation. Her mother deeply resented her birth,
which she felt held her in a marriage that she had decided to dissolve
just before she found herself pregnant. The mother, feeling neglected by
her husband, had become very much caught up in her relationship with
her three-year-old son, and could find no room for a daughter. The
mother's own lack of self-esteem as a woman contributed to her disinterest in a daughter. The father moved into the gap, seeking to provide the
mothering the girl needed. The family soon divided into two hostile
camps. The mother, not caring for the father or the daughter, did not
furnish a model with whom the girl could identify nor did she impose
any obstacles to the father and daughter developing an intense relationship. The father, also feeling deprived, used the girl as a replacement for
the mother and formed a close and seductive relationship with her. The
way was prepared for the continuation of an incestuously toned relationship into the girl's adolescence.

A girl who feels displaced by a series of younger siblings may become
fixated upon a need to regain the mother's love and never properly develop oedipal strivings toward her father. She may prematurely decide
that if her mother has no room for her because of the needs of the
younger children, she will become her mother's helper, share the
mother's tasks and woes, and thereby gain her mother's approval and
affection. She then tends to become a little mother who never has a
proper childhood. Some such children continue to spend their lives seeking eventually to be appreciated and loved by the mother, even remaining at home unmarried, waiting until all the others have left.

The few illustrations that have been presented are intended only as
random examples of the diverse influences that sibling relationships can
exert on the oedipal situation. Common patterns may exist, but not
many have been clearly defined. Indeed, the whole question of the influence of sibling relationships upon a child's development beyond the relatively simple problems of sibling rivalry and twin relationships has received insufficient attention.

Siblings present so many difficulties to a child that he may well wish
that he were an only child, believing that life could unfold far more
smoothly without the competition. Yet, the only child is often lonely
and feels deprived of brothers and sisters. He does not have the opportunity to learn to cope with jealousy and envy of rivals within the home; or

to compromise with siblings and share adult attention; or to erect and strengthen defenses against feeling displaced. These may sound like very doubtful benefits, on the order of hitting oneself over the head so as to feel good when the pain stops, but they are important in the long run. The opportunity to share intimately in childhood, to know how someone close feels in various situations, to become familiar with the ways of the opposite sex, to assume responsibility for a brother or sister, to have a sibling show pride and happiness over what one accomplishes, are among the many benefits of having siblings. Basic experiences are properly gained within the shelter of the family.

The Resolution of the Oedipal Attachment

The child's attachment to the mother contains strong erotic components. The little child had required erotically motivated nurturant care from the mother which stimulated sensuous oral, anal, and tactile feelings which generalized to color the child's feelings toward his mother. As we have noted, genital feelings became connected to fantasies about the mother, stimulating feelings of possessiveness and love. The young child considers himself the center of his mother's interest and affection, just as she is central to his life. We have noted the egocentricity of the child's thinking, and nowhere is the child more clearly egocentric than in his view of his relationship with his mother. The mother is the child's source of comfort, nourishment, and protection, and she properly fills the role of a surrogate ego for the child, sorting out what is useful and harmful, and providing the direction that he does not yet know enough to provide for himself.

Changes have been occurring during the oedipal phase that alter both the child's way of life and his position in the family. The child seeks to avoid coming to grips with the changes, but inevitably reality closes in and forces the child to terms. The renunciation of his priority with his mother and repression of the erotic components of his attachment to her—the resolution of his oedipal attachment—seem to be the pivot about which many changes in behavior, thought, and personality organization occur.

Just how the oedipal conflicts are resolved will exert a major influence upon the pattern of all future interpersonal relationships and the structuring of the personality. How it is resolved depends upon prior experiences, the particular make-up of the individual, the family members, and the configuration of the family. For better or for worse, decisive changes will take place by the time the child enters school and the next developmental phase. Because of the central position of the oedipal conflict in personality development, and because Freud's discovery and exposition of the transition forms a landmark in the history of man's struggle to gain an understanding of himself, the classic psychoanalytic conceptualization will be presented, even though some aspects of the theory are no longer tenable.[6] We shall then consider a broader approach to understanding the oedipal transition.

●*The Classic Psychoanalytic Concept* ●

On the basis of his own self-analysis, the psychoanalysis of patients, and from Sophocles' *Oedipus* and Shakespeare's *Hamlet*, Freud recognized that the little child develops an intense sexualized love for the parent of the opposite sex; that the love arouses jealousy, guilt, and anxiety which leads the child to repress the feelings into the unconscious; and that in so doing the child comes to terms with his or her position in the family, identifies with the parent of the same sex, and gains a superego in the process. Freud explained the conflict and its resolution by following the vicissitudes of the child's libido. After the anal phase of development passes, the child's libido becomes invested in the genitals—in the penis in the boy and the clitoris in the girl. The shift of libido to the genitals causes or accompanies an upsurge of sexual feelings in the child, often with a marked increase in masturbation. The sexual feelings of the boy attach themselves to the mother, and those of the girl to the father. Freud offered various explanations of the shift of the girl's attachment from the mother to the father.* The child seeks erotic gratification from the parent who is the love object, and fantasies possessing this parent in marriage. The other parent is resented as an intruder, someone unnecessary and superfluous in the child's scheme of things. Those children who have witnessed parental intercourse, or who have developed fantasies based on noises they have heard, wish to replace the parent in the act. The child now wants to be rid of the rival parent, wishes that parent would die, and may fantasy killing the parent. The child's hostile and aggressive impulses are then *projected* onto the parent: if he can wish to be rid of the parent, the parent can want to be rid of him. He becomes anxious, and at night when his defenses are low and darkness and quiet foster fantasy, his dreams and nightmares bring terror. The little boy

---

* See S. Freud, "Some Psychological Consequences of the Anatomical Distinction between the Sexes" [7] and "Female Sexuality." [8]

who experiences the connection between his erotic fantasies and the sensations in his genitals may fear that his father will settle the matter by cutting off his penis. This "castration anxiety," Freud believed at times, was at the bottom of almost all anxiety, including anxiety over death. Unable to stand the anxiety he is experiencing, the little boy renounces his erotized wishes to possess his mother. Instead, he decides to grow up to become a person like his father who can gain the love of his mother. He now identifies with his father, seeks to take on his traits, and is impelled into a firmer masculine identity. The father's restrictions and prohibitions, whether real or imagined, are internalized and serve to bolster the ego's capacities to repress and to maintain the repression of the incestuous strivings. Freud considered that the superego is formed at the time of the resolution of the oedipal conflict by utilization of the libidinal energy that had been invested in the mother. As the libidinal energy is utilized largely in the service of repression of the id, the child then enters the latency period—a time relatively free from sexual strivings, preoccupations, and activities.

Freud was never quite satisfied with his understanding of the girl's oedipal situation and its resolution. The girl turns from seeking the mother as a love object because of inherent instinctual reasons, because she becomes hostile to the mother whom she feels deprived her of a penis, or because she feels that the mother who is also without a penis is not a worthy object of her love.

Freud finally emphasized that the girl's recognition of the anatomical differences between the sexes led her to desire a baby to compensate for the lack of a penis, and "with this purpose in view she takes her father as a love object. Her mother becomes the object of her jealousy." In the process the girl gives up her masculine orientation and becomes a little woman.* [7] As she already feels castrated, she cannot suffer castration anxiety that forces her to renounce her desire to possess the father. However, she comes to fear the mother's jealousy, or her projections of her own jealousy onto the mother, and fears the mother will kill or abandon her. She then accepts her identification with her mother and strives to become a woman who can gain a man like her father. However, Freud recognized that the girl does not usually repress her desires for the father so completely as the boy represses his erotic feelings for his mother.[9]

* Freud thus regarded the oedipus complex as a secondary phenomenon in the female, and gave the impression that it played a less important role in female development.[7, 8]

The question of the universality of the oedipus complex and, particularly, whether the boy's erotic attachment to his mother and the girl's to her father are inherent components of the human endowment became sources of considerable controversy. Understood in the terms just presented, it would be difficult to defend the omnipresence of the oedipal situation. However, the crisis that occurs can be understood in a way that makes the essence of the situation an almost inescapable and essential aspect of every person's development.

There is no evidence that the oedipal child experiences an upsurge of libido in the sense of an increased sexual drive such as occurs at puberty. The confusion of sensuous feelings with a sexual drive has created unnecessary theoretical complications. The child, particularly the boy, has shown genital masturbatory activity even earlier and, as we have previously noted, there are reasons why the child now tends to sexualize his feelings toward his mother. Biochemical assays of the hormones as well as observation discount the hypothesis of an increased sexual drive.[32] Gonadotrophic hormones are not detectable in children of this age, and only appear in detectable quantities a few years before the onset of puberty. Between the ages of three and five, seventeen ketosteroids which are considered to reflect secretions of androgen cannot be found in the blood. Estrogen secretion as measured by bio-assay is also negligible. The oedipal child may be preoccupied with erotic and sensuous ideas and feelings but he is not being subjected to the same type of biological sexual impulsion that occurs in adolescence.[15]

The Frustration of the Child's Erotized Bond to the Mother

The child must overcome the intense bond to the mother that has been essential to his pre-oedipal development. In the symbiotic relationship in which the little child and mother exist, the boundaries between them have been nebulous and the child's erotic feelings have been connected to both the mother and the self. The symbiosis must break down into two components: an identification, in which the child seeks to be like the mother and take on her attributes and abilities; and an object love, in which the child seeks to maintain a tender or erotized relatedness to the mother as a separate individual. Through identification, the child gains new attributes and inner strength; through object love, the child gains or retains a needed person. In general, the boy will retain the mother as a primary love object and the girl will retain her as a primary object of identification. The boy will seek to become a person capable of maintaining his mother's love and esteem. The girl will seek a love ob ject who will love a person who is like her mother.

The child relinquishes the mother as an essential erotized object for two reasons aside from fears of retribution by the father. First, the mother gradually frustrates the child's attachment as part of the diminishing care she provides as the child becomes increasingly able to do things for himself.[27] She knowingly or unknowingly places greater distance between herself and the child. The process is often aided by the birth of a younger child who pre-empts much of her attention. Second, the child suffers a serious blow as his egocentric view of the world diminishes. He learns that the parents do not consider his relationship to his mother in the same way he does. The mother's affectional attachments are divided between the child and her husband, and usually she gives love to other children as well. The child has difficulty realizing that love is not a quantity that is diminished by such division; he wishes to feel that he is central in his mother's life. The child has wished to marry his mother, and may have confided his wish and hope to her. "When I grow up, I'm going to marry you," he tells his mother and it has seemed to please her. Now, he realizes that she has not taken his wish seriously. She loves his father and the father has prerogatives that the child does not have. Although the child may be permitted in her bed, it is clearly a temporary matter whereas Father can stay. Mother will not wait for him to grow up to marry her. Indeed, she cannot, and will be as old as Grandma when he is old enough to marry. The child also begins to learn what marriage involves, and that parents have responsibilities as well as privileges, and the child becomes concerned over his capacities to handle responsibilities in reality. These concerns are part of the sorting out of reality and fantasy that occurs during this period, and perhaps a pivotal aspect of coming to terms with reality. Indeed, such enforced recognition of his position within the family and breaking up of his symbiotic relationship with his mother may well be an important factor in the diminution of the child's egocentricity that is essential to progression of his cognitive development to the stage of concrete operations.

The boy may become somewhat hostile toward his mother for turning away from him, but he also has reached a stage in which he, too, begins to feel the need for greater independence. The little boy often fears engulfment by the mother as much as he does castration by the father. He not only learns that his mother loves him differently from the way in which he loves her, but also that his father does not seriously take the child as a rival. Conversely, he finds that having a father has advantages. Such developments bring a release from "castration anxieties." He will wait until he grows up for fulfillment. He seeks to become a man like his father to be able eventually to gain a love object like his mother. He shifts from identifying with his mother to a firm identification with his father. He not only gains strength from the identification but also a model to follow into manhood. Further, rescinding immediate desires for more ultimate objectives strengthens his character as it helps give a long-term consistency to his behavior. The identification with the father may be said to strengthen the child's ego and also, through internalization of parental directives, the superego. Id impulses are being confined and repressed, and no longer are permitted as much direct expression. With better self-control, improved reality testing, and less need for gratification from his mother, the boy is ready to move into peer groups where he must make his way on his own. However, when the father is jealous of his son, resents the attention his wife gives the child, and punishes the boy to keep him away from his mother and assert his own authority, the boy's projected fears are reinforced by realistic concerns that aggravate the castration anxiety—and such behavior on the part of the father can produce lasting fears of sexual intimacy with any woman as well as other difficulties.*

The Girl's Oedipal Transition

The girl's oedipal transition is different and cannot be conceptualized as a mirror image of the boy's. She, too, must overcome her primary attachment to the mother in order to become a discrete individual. Freud emphasized the difficulties created for the girl because, in contrast to the boy, she must shift her basic love object from the mother to the father. However, she has the greater advantage of not shifting the parent with whom she identifies. Anger with her mother for not having created her a boy, or disappointment in the mother because she, too, is without a penis, may be significant in turning the girl's love from the mother to the father, but there are other important directives. As the girl emerges from her symbiotic existence with her mother and differentiates from her, she finds another love object within the family in the father, and is directed to him by his tendency to be close and affectionate with a daughter. She can be free of the primary bond with her mother and still have an ero-

---

* Sometimes including sadistic fantasies of revenge upon the father that can lead to the seeking of opportunities for sadistic outlets later in life.

tized love object within the family. Although she projects her rivalrous jealousy with her mother onto the mother and may fear reprisals, experience shows that the girl is likely to retain fantasies of becoming the father's sexual choice over the mother. Identifying with her mother, she is likely to assume something of a maternal role to her father. At about the time of puberty, however, she becomes frightened by the pressure of her desires and represses the erotic aspects of her attachment; or, as frequently happens, the father must place distance between himself and his nubile daughter. Many women feel and believe that they became unattractive to their fathers when they reached puberty because it was then that their fathers moved away from them.

Thus, the girl's oedipal transition is very likely to occur in two stages: the first is the oedipal period proper, when she differentiates from the mother and shifts to make her father her "object choice"; and then, the prepubertal or early pubertal period, when anxiety forces her to repress her feelings for her father.*

The girl's ability to retain the father as a love object keeps her major emotional investment within the home longer than the boy's, and appears to serve to prepare her for her greater emotional involvement in the home in adult life. It may also help account for the tendency, at least in our culture, for the girl to seek an older man as a mate, and often to select a person who clearly resembles her father.

Family Integration and the Resolution of the Oedipal Conflict

The fate of the oedipal situation depends upon a variety of factors, including some that are consequences of the child's maturation and some that depend upon the nature of the interaction between the child and one or both parents. However, the dynamic structure of the family here plays a major part in organizing the child's personality by guiding the way in which the oedipal conflicts are resolved. A properly structured family with a firm coalition between parents who maintain boundaries between the two generations and adhere to their respective gender-linked roles enables the child to grow into a relatively conflict-free place within the family. The reader is referred back to Chapter 2 for a discussion of the importance of the family's structure to the personality devel-

* In his later writings on the subject Freud considered the girl's attachment to her mother to be pre-oedipal and part of the girl's early masculine character associated with phallic (clitoral) sexuality. As the concept no longer seems satisfactory, the reader is referred to his writings[7, 8] for further discussion.

opment of its offspring. Here we are concerned only with the oedipal transition.

The desexualization of the parent-child relationship before puberty is one of the cardinal tasks of the family. It does not depend upon a subsidence of sexual drive as hypothesized in classic psychoanalytic theory, nor does it depend only upon the child's fear of retaliation from a parent, but primarily upon the child's coming to terms with the reality of the prerogatives of the parents and of the basic bond between them. A firm coalition between the parents does not permit the child's fantasies of separating the parents and gaining one for himself to continue on a realistic basis. A parent who turns to a child for gratification of his emotional or sexual needs instead of to the spouse or even extramaritally, moves the child across the generation boundaries. When there is a schism between the parents, the child can move into the breach and seek to replace one parent in satisfying the needs of the other. In either case, as commonly happens, it becomes difficult to repress the oedipal erotic fantasies. Similarly, when gender roles are not properly maintained by parents, as when the father is weak and ineffectual, or the mother cold and rejecting of sexual relations with her husband, the child can feel the lack and seek to assume the empty role. When the parents are united as spouses and parents, and complement each other's gender roles, the child does not have an opportunity to fill an empty place in the wrong generation, but grows into the proper position as a childhood member of his or her sex. The child properly enters the latency period after establishing a position as a boy or girl in relation to his parents. When he can identify with his family as a unit and feel secure in his dependency upon it, he can venture into the broader world with energies free to form new relationships and to invest in learning.

A harmonious relationship between the parents, in which the mother loves and respects her husband as a man and supports him in his masculine roles, permits the boy to develop a harmonious self-structure. The person with whom he identifies is desirable to the person who is his primary love object; and by following his paternal model he gains self-esteem in feeling that he can be loved and wanted. The same considerations apply to the girl. Unfortunately, such patterns are far more often an ideal rather than a reality. Not only are the majority of marriages far from fully satisfactory, but the child in his oedipal jealousy can find flaws in a parent and the parental relationships and readily magnify conflicts between parents.

There is an essential relationship between the oedipal situation and the incest taboo. While it has sometimes been assumed that the taboo which is virtually universal determines the resolution of the oedipal attachment, a need to evoke the taboo consciously is an indication that something is amiss in the family structure. The progression of the erotically toned child-parent attachment to an incestuous bond threatens the existence of the nuclear family, prevents the child from investing his energies in extrafamilial socialization, and blocks his emergence as an adult.* If conscious avoidance of incest becomes necessary, the family transactions and the personalities of the family members become further disturbed because spontaneous interactions become impossible, role conflict almost inevitable, and crippling defenses are often necessary. However, some transitory defenses against incestuous feelings' gaining consciousness are present in virtually all families; difficulties arise when defenses are necessary to stop overt activity.†

Oedipal Fixations

Fixations of development at the oedipal stage come in many configurations and intensities. Disturbances in the resolution of the oedipal conflicts enter into virtually all psychopathology. Fixations or serious difficulties in pre-oedipal development will also be reflected in oedipal difficulties. In a broad sense, the term "oedipal problems" refers to failures to emerge properly from the family, and to identify with the parent of the same sex and repress the sexual components in the love of the parent of the opposite sex. The common usage connoting a man's continuing dependency upon his mother often really refers to pre-oedipal oral dependency problems. The interference of sexualized feelings for a parent in later love relationships is a more central issue. Oedipal conflict is, as I trust has become clear, a normal aspect of development; it is the failure to find a suitable resolution of the conflict that creates ensuing developmental and personality disorders.

* Overt incest between mother and son is very uncommon, and rarely occurs unless the mother is psychotic and with very rare exceptions the son becomes schizophrenic. Father-daughter incest, which is not subject to as intense a taboo, is far more common. The father usually has been deprived of his mother early in life, and often the wife seems to have handed the daughter over to the father as a substitute in order to permit the wife to evade her wifely responsibilities. Severe hysterical symptoms are common in women who have had incestuous experiences with their fathers.
† As when the father of an adolescent girl moves away from the home, or becomes promiscuous to counteract more or less conscious incestuous impulses; or even when the father becomes overly critical of the way his daughter dresses lest he be tempted.

An Illustration of Unresolved Oedipal Problems

An excellent illustration of the disturbances that can ensue when oedipal problems persevere intensively into adult life can be found in the melancholic Dane with whom we all have at least a passing familiarity. Hamlet had remained unmarried at the age of thirty; he was an only child whose mother lived "almost by his looks."* He had identified strongly with his father, whose priority with his mother he had reluctantly accepted. When his mother remarried after his father's death instead of centering her attentions upon him, he was unable to accept the situation and became intensely depressed. When he then learns from his father's ghost what he has already unconsciously believed ("Oh, my prophetic soul, my uncle")†—that his mother had been seduced by his uncle, who had then killed his father—he can no longer tolerate the situation. He feels life is empty and worthless. Though he has sworn to avenge his father by slaying his uncle, he cannot act. Freud pointed out that he could not kill his uncle because his uncle had only done what he himself had wished to do as a child—kill his father and marry his mother.‡ However, Shakespeare also makes it apparent that Hamlet is enraged at his mother's betrayal of his father and of himself; and he is preoccupied with his mother's sexual activities with his uncle. He becomes intensely misogynistic, ranting at Ophelia and distrusting her for his mother's faults. If his mother is wanton, what woman can be trusted? It is only after he vents his rage upon his mother ("I shall speak daggers to her but use none"§) and insists that she leave his uncle's bed, that he becomes free and can move toward action. Instead of informing his mother that his father had been murdered, he admonishes her, "Go not to mine uncle's bed—not—let the bloat king tempt you again to bed; pinch wanton on your cheek; call you his mouse . . ." || What sorts of thoughts Hamlet had been having about his mother and stepfather seem fairly clear from the "closet" scene. His jealousy of a father figure is also noted in his discourtesies to Polonius, the father of his beloved, and whom he kills by accident as he may have in fantasy. Ophelia, an only daughter of a widower father, then loses her sanity and commits suicide, for she, even as Hamlet who loved his mother, is caught in a insoluble conflict—loving the murderer of her beloved parent.

* *Hamlet,* Act IV, Scene VII.
† *Hamlet,* Act I, Scene V.
‡ A theme elaborated by Ernest Jones in his famous essay, *Hamlet and Oedipus.*[18]
§ *Hamlet,* Act III, Scene II.
|| *Hamlet,* Act III, Scene IV.

A realistic version of the tale was found in a young man with homo-sexual proclivities and a great fear of women. His mother had showered affection seductively upon him as she felt neglected by her husband, who was preoccupied by his affairs of state—the direction of a large industry. When his father died following surgery, the young man fantasied that his mother had plotted with the surgeon to kill his father so that they could marry. His illusion was only partially resolved when the surgeon paid no attention to his mother. Indeed, when he was in psychiatric treatment several years later he managed to distort the events surround-ing his father's death, insisting that his father had died on the operating table when in fact his father had survived the operation for six months. He feared living alone with his widowed mother, at times (like Hamlet) fearing his incestuous impulses and at times his homicidal impulses. When she finally remarried, he made a serious suicidal attempt during the wedding reception, feeling both abandoned by her and disillusioned with her for capitulating to her sexual desires.

The resolution of the oedipal conflict terminates early childhood. The need to rescind the wish to pre-empt a parent brings with it a reorganiza-tion of the child's world and a re-evaluation of his place in it. Life will never again be viewed so egocentrically, and fantasy now yields priority to harsh reality. The child has taken a giant step toward becoming an independent and self-sufficient person, even though he has done so by recognizing the long road ahead before he can expect adult prerogatives. He has found peace with both parents by repressing the erotic aspect of his attachment to one. Nevertheless the erotic attachment survives in the unconscious and will become a determinant of later relationships. The precise manner in which the oedipal situation—sometimes called "the family romance"—has been worked through is likely to set a pat-tern that will later be relived in different settings.

References

1. William D. Altrus, "Birth Order and Its Sequelae," *Science*, 151 (1966), 44–49.
2. Gregory Bateson, Don D. Jackson, Jay Haley, and John Weakland, "Toward a Theory of Schizophrenia," *Behavioral Science*, 1 (1956), 251–264.
3. Mabel B. Cohen, "Personal Identity and Sexual Identity," *Psychiatry*, 29 (1966), 1–14.
4. Milton Diamond, "A Critical Evaluation of the Ontogony of Human Sexual Behavior," *Quarterly Review of Biology*, 40 (1965), 147–175.
5. Erik H. Erikson, "Growth and Crises of the 'Healthy Personality,' " in *Psychological Issues*, Vol. 1, No. 1, Monograph No. 1 (New York: International Universities Press, 1959).
6. Sigmund Freud, "Introductory Lectures on Psycho-Analysis" (1916–1917), in *The Standard Edition of the Complete Psychological Works of Sigmund Freud*, Vols. 15 and 16 (London: Hogarth Press, 1954).
7. Sigmund Freud, "Some Psychological Consequences of the Anatomical Distinction between the Sexes" (1925), in *The Standard Edition of the Complete Psychological Works of Sigmund Freud*, Vol. 19 (London: Hogarth Press, 1961).
8. Sigmund Freud, "Female Sexuality" (1931), in *The Standard Edition of the Complete Psychological Works of Sigmund Freud*, Vol. 21 (London: Hogarth Press, 1961).
9. Sigmund Freud, "The Psychology of Women," in *New Introductory Lectures on Psycho-Analysis* (New York: W. W. Norton, 1933).
10. Sigmund Freud, *New Introductory Lectures on Psycho-Analysis* (New York: W. W. Norton, 1933).
11. Hector Garcia, Digamber Borgaonkav, and Frederick Richardson, "XXYY Syndrome in a Prepubertal Male," *Johns Hopkins Medical Journal*, 121 (1967), 31–37.
12. Jane Goodall, "My Life among Wild Chimpanzees," *National Geographic*, 124 (1963), 272–308.
13. Jane Goodall, "New Discoveries among Wild Chimpanzees," *National Geographic*, 128 (1965), 802–831.
14. Radclyffe Hall, *The Well of Loneliness* (Garden City, N. Y.: Sun Dial Press, 1928).
15. David A. Hamburg and D. Lunde, "Sex Hormones in the Development of Sex Differences in Human Behavior" (to be published).
16. John L. Hampson and Joan G. Hampson, "The Ontogenesis of Sexual Behavior in Man," in William C. Young (ed.), *Sex and Internal Secretions*, Vol. 2 (3rd ed.; Baltimore: Williams & Wilkins, 1961).
17. Karen Horney, "Feminine Psychology," in *New Ways in Psychoanalysis* (New York: W. W. Norton, 1939).
18. Ernest Jones, *Hamlet and Oedipus* (New York: W. W. Norton, 1949).

19. E. Kent, "A Study of Maladjusted Twins," *Smith College Studies of Social Work*, 19 (1949), 63–77.
20. Helen L. Koch, *Twins and Twin Relations* (Chicago: University of Chicago Press, 1966).
21. Edmund Leach, "Anthropological Aspects of Language: Animal Categories and Verbal Abuses," in Eric H. Lenneberg (ed.), *New Directions in the Study of Language* (Cambridge, Mass.: M.I.T. Press, 1964).
22. Theodore Lidz, Alice Cornelison, Dorothy Terry, and Stephen Fleck, "The Transmission of Irrationality" (1958), in T. Lidz, S. Fleck, and A. Cornelison, *Schizophrenia and the Family* (New York: International Universities Press, 1965).
23. Theodore Lidz, Sarah Schafer, Stephen Fleck, Alice Cornelison, and Dorothy Terry, "Ego Differentiation and Schizophrenic Symptom Formation in Identical Twins," in T. Lidz, S. Fleck, and A. Cornelison, *Schizophrenia and the Family* (New York: International Universities Press, 1965).
24. A. A. Milne, *Winnie the Pooh* (rev. ed.; New York: E. P. Dutton, 1961).
25. John Money, "Psychosexual Differentiation," in John Money (ed.), *Sex Research, New Developments* (New York: Holt, Rinehart & Winston, 1965).
26. John Money, Joan G. Hampson, and John L. Hampson, "Imprinting and the Establishment of Gender Roles," *Archives of Neurology and Psychiatry*, 77 (1957), 333–336.
27. Talcott Parsons, "The Incest Taboo in Relation to Social Structure and the Socialization of the Child," in *Social Structure and Personality* (New York: Free Press, 1964).
28. Jean Piaget, *Play, Dreams, and Imitation in Childhood*, trans. C. Gattengo and F. M. Hodgson (New York: W. W. Norton, 1962).
29. Watty Piper (ed.), *The Little Engine That Could* (New York: Platt, n.d.).
30. Margaret T. Singer and Lyman C. Wynne, "Thought Disorder and Family Relations of Schizophrenics: III. Methodology Using Projective Techniques," *Archives of General Psychiatry*, 12 (1965), 187–200.
31. Margaret T. Singer and Lyman C. Wynne, "Thought Disorder and Family Relations of Schizophrenics: IV. Results and Implications," *Archives of General Psychiatry*, 12 (1965), 201–212.
32. James M. Tanner, *Growth at Adolescence* (2nd ed.; Oxford: Blackwell Scientific Publications, 1961).
33. Lev S. Vygotsky, *Thought and Language*, ed. and trans. Eugenia Hanfmann and Gertrude Vakar (New York: M.I.T. Press and John Wiley & Sons, 1962).
34. Heinz Werner, *Comparative Psychology of Mental Development* (New York: International Universities Press, 1948).
35. Benjamin L. Whorf, "Languages and Logic" (1941), in John B. Carroll (ed.), *Language, Thought, and Reality: Selected Writings of*

Benjamin Lee Whorf (New York: M.I.T. Press and John Wiley & Sons, 1956).

36. Cynthia Wild, Margaret Singer, Bernice Rosman, Judith Ricci, and Theodore Lidz, "Measuring Disordered Styles of Thinking in the Parents of Schizophrenic Patients on the Object Sorting Test," in T. Lidz, S. Fleck, and A. Cornelison, *Schizophrenia and the Family* (New York: International Universities Press, 1965).

37. Lyman C. Wynne and Margaret T. Singer, "Thought Disorder and Family Relations of Schizophrenics: I. A Research Strategy," *Archives of General Psychiatry,* 9 (1963), 191–198.

38. Lyman C. Wynne and Margaret T. Singer, "Thought Disorder and Family Relations of Schizophrenics: II. A Classification of Forms of Thinking," *Archives of General Psychiatry,* 9 (1963), 199–206.

39. William Young, Robert Goy, and Charles Phoenix, "Hormones and Sexual Behavior," *Science,* 143 (1964), 212–218.

Suggested Reading

Sigmund Freud, "On the Sexual Theories of Children" (1908), in *The Standard Edition of the Complete Psychological Works of Sigmund Freud,* Vol. 9 (London: Hogarth Press, 1959).

Sigmund Freud, "Introductory Lectures on Psychoanalysis" (1916–1917), in *The Standard Edition of the Complete Psychological Works of Sigmund Freud,* Vols. 15 and 16 (London: Hogarth Press, 1954).

Frank O'Connor, "My Oedipus Complex," in *Stories of Frank O'Connor* (New York: Alfred A. Knopf, 1952).

Margaret Mead, *Male and Female* (New York: W. W. Norton, 1939).

Jean Piaget, *Play, Dreams and Imitation in Childhood,* trans. C. Gattengo and F. M. Hodgson (New York: W. W. Norton, 1962).

CHAPTER 8

❀ ❀
❀ ❀ ❀ ❀ ❀ ❀

Childhood Integration

THE CLOSING of the oedipal period brings a consolidation of the child's personality. The child now first achieves a fairly firm integration as an individual. It would seem paradoxical to consider that the essential patterning of the child's personality has taken place even before he starts school. He has scarcely ventured beyond his home and the protection of his family; he must still accumulate most of the knowledge he will require to guide his own life, and he will remain dependent upon parental figures for support and guidance for many years to come. Yet, the Jesuits as well as the Communists have placed great emphasis upon these first six years of life, even venturing to say that if they can control these years they do not care who influences the child thereafter. Indeed, psychoanalytic psychology may convey the same impression because of its emphasis upon the events of childhood through the resolution of the oedipal conflicts and their pervasive influence upon all subsequent behavior. Even though the personality development is far from completed at five or six and many significant influences will still accrue before a firm integration and a stable identity are achieved, we must examine the paradox and the nature and extent of the organization that has occurred.

The Family Matrix

The fetus unfolds within the protected and relatively uniform intra-uterine environment which helps assure its proper maturation. The child is born into the womb of the family where conditions are far less predictable and stable, and it is within the microcosm of the family that the child's personality takes shape. Within it, the child is prepared to live in a specific society. Despite its shortcomings, the family forms a reasonably uniform social system that both shields the immature child from the larger society and also prepares the child to emerge into it. It forms a limited world, but the baby and small child are not ready to cope with complexity. The cast of persons with whom the child interrelates within the family remains fairly constant, which permits the child to develop expectancies and build up reasonably consistent behavioral patterns through reciprocal interaction. How the child learns to maintain his emotional equilibrium and a sense of well-being within the family sets a pattern for his behavior beyond the family. He will, at first, expect reactions from persons outside the family similar to those reactions learned from parents and siblings.* He will tend to change others into figures like his parents and to perceive them in familiar intrafamilial terms. The child has managed to find his place within the home, and now at the age of five or six must move on to learn to live in the wider world, a less stable and benevolent place where he does not occupy a specially favored position. The patterns acquired in the home form the foundations of his personality organization and will resist change: throughout his life his perception of significant persons and his ways of relating to them will be compromises between the expectations he developed within his family and the actual ways of persons he encounters.

As we have noted in the preceding chapter, the child's personality gained considerable organization with the closure of the oedipal period. He became much more firmly grounded in reality by the necessity of accepting his childhood position in the family, by rescinding or repressing desires to possess the parent of the opposite sex as a love object, and

---

* Piaget notes that many subsequent interpersonal relationships will be assimilated to the schemata established in adaptation to the parents, particularly the affective schemata of interpersonal relationships.[13]

by identifying with the parent of the same sex. In the process the child gained long-term goals toward which to strive and a model to follow into adulthood. The child's gender identity became reasonably firm through the identification with the parent of the same sex, and by his becoming directed toward seeking a love object of the opposite sex. The renunciation of hopes of possessing the parental love object in reality permitted the child to come to terms with both parents and to find a relatively conflict-free position in relation to them. The transactions between the parents enter into the child's self-concept and feelings of self-esteem. The boy whose father is loved and admired by his mother can gain a sense of worth in accordance with how he approximates the idealized father; and a girl can accept her femininity more readily when the mother is desired and esteemed by her father. The child also gains a feeling of the value of being a father or mother, a husband or wife, as well as of being male or female, from the parental interactions.

The Internalization of Parental Directives

The child, to function effectively outside of his family, must have become capable of delaying the gratification of impulse and wish and learned the essentials of socialization; he must also have learned many basic adaptive techniques, including language; and he must have internalized parental directives and standards. Although the parents will continue to provide guidance and delimitation for many years to come, they can no longer be with the child to serve as omnipresent counselors and protectors. We are interested, here, in the forces that direct and regulate behavior when the child is on his own. In attempting to consider the determinants of behavior in an abstract way, it is useful, as we noted in Chapter 3, to follow Freud's lead and symbolize the three sets of influences that enter into self-direction under the categories of *id, ego,* and *superego.**

The id concerns the influences of the basic drives produced by tissue tensions and which assure that the homeostatic needs for self-preservation, the aggressive drives that are important for self-defense, and the sexual drives that are vital to the continuity of the species will receive

---

* Attempts to define these constructs very precisely and to allocate just what should be included under each, rather than utilizing them as useful terms, leads to confusion rather than precision. Rapaport, who was one of the most scholarly, knowledgeable, and brilliant students of psychoanalytic theories, finally stated that the concepts were not indispensable to psychoanalytic theory[15] and gave up his efforts to clarify the theoretic confusions involved in their usage.

proper attention. The id, defined in a very general way, represents the bodily needs and desires. The tissue needs can be denied only with extreme difficulty, and ignoring them can lead to death. Still, it is possible to starve to death even among plenty for ideological reasons. However, the major concern of psychodynamic theory is with the sexual and aggressive drives which can be denied and require delimitation and channeling lest they interfere with the social systems that are essential for human existence. The child, as we have noted, has learned to delay the satisfaction of tissue drives such as hunger and thirst in accordance with the demands of reality and in order to gain parental approbation. Libidinal and aggressive desires and impulsions have also been repressed in varying degrees according to the standards of the culture and the parents.* Id impulsions are obviously of vital importance but socialization depends upon their control and proper channelling.†

The ego is characterized as that part of the personality or self,‡ that directs access to motility and has the function of decision making. Although the ego was originally considered an offshoot of the id, contemporary theory permits it to arise independently as part of the human endowment. The ego is concerned with language, memory, knowledge, reasons, etc., and we have been tracing how the child's gradually emerging ego gains scope as he identifies with others and as he takes into himself their ways of doing things, their roles, and their patterns of interrelating. The ego is dependent upon the capacities for categorization, memory, foresight, and choice that depend so much upon language functions. It depends upon the organization of an internalized, symbolized version of reality in which imaginative trials can be made without

* In some societies, as among the headhunters of New Guinea, the children are taught to be aggressively defensive at a very early age as is essential to their survival, but still it is aggression against enemies and not against fellow villagers that is condoned. The degree of sexual repression required also varies widely. Among some peoples, the young children masturbate openly and play at sexual intercourse, and in our society many parents seek to have the children refrain from masturbation only in public.

† In classic theory, the libido or sexualized energy was often considered the source of all "psychic" energy—and in extreme forms of theory, the ultimate source of all motivation. The untenable idea that such libido remained quantitatively constant, and that much of behavior and motivation was to be understood in terms of how quantities of this hypothesized energy were "cathected"—or invested in various parts of the body and in various objects (persons)—has been a major source of confusion in psychoanalytic theory.

‡ Confusions arise because psychoanalysts have sometimes used the term "ego" for the total self.

committing the self to the consequences of action. However, the ego has
the difficult task* of balancing the demands of the id, the demands of
reality, and the needs for self-approval and social approval that are internalized as superego.

The child internalizes some of his parental ways—and through them
the society's directives—as part of his ego, and some parental directives
as a reference system of what is desirable and undesirable, proper and
improper behavior. That is, some behavioral standards are internalized as
part of his basic ways of thinking, and some continue to be experienced
as externally imposed standards to which he conforms in order to remain
at peace with himself, very much as he had conformed with parental
wishes and edicts. The superego consists of internalized feelings of parental approbation or disapproval, and is very much like conscience but
includes positive as well as prohibitive influences. Everyone probably
conceptualizes and feels that certain parental and cultural ethical influences are added to one's own standards. Somehow, they do not seem to
be quite fully incorporated into the self.

Much of the supervisory activities of the superego are unconscious.
Many parental standards and societal sanctions are simply accepted as
the ways in which a person should behave and have never been thought
about consciously. A person feels euphoric when he has adhered to a
proper way of life and dysphoric when he has breached the accepted and
approved, and he may become self-punitive when he goes contrary to his
ethical standards but he may have no realization of what is affecting his
sense of well-being.

Just which influences are part of the ego and which are part of the
superego may be difficult to conceptualize. Indeed, the balance shifts as
the child grows older, when he feels less need for parental approval and
is less concerned with parental censure. Some ego syntonic standards
become more completely integrated into the core of the self.[11] A definite
differentiation between ego and superego functions may be an academic
matter but it reflects a basic attitude about self-regulation. Some principles continue to seem externally imposed and are regarded as reference
systems that serve to guide actions and feelings, and every person probably continues throughout life to imagine what his parents would sanction and what would cause them happiness. The concept of the superego

* The reader will note that in such discussions the author falls back on preoperational
patterns of thought and writes as if the ego were a decision-making person. It must
be taken metaphorically.

is very useful in work with patients, for it provides a simple means of symbolizing a major set of influences that enters into decision making and into feelings of self-esteem.*

Superego Formation

Freud considered that the superego formed at the time of the resolution of the oedipal conflicts; at times as a precipitate of the oedipal situation, with the libidinal energy that had been invested in the parent of the opposite sex turned to the service of repression. Superego formation can be understood without resorting to the notion of shifts in libidinal energy. The child now invests more in the identification than in his desire for the love object. The identification with the parent strengthens self-control because he has a model to follow. The child had internalized directives and prohibitions at an earlier age but now they are being strengthened as he seeks to become a person like one or both parents and also retain their love. Just as it is erroneous to think that the superego first forms at the age of five or six, it would be incorrect to believe that the child is now fully capable of self-regulation and that any shortcomings indicate a sociopathic future. The child may internalize parental directives but he is extremely dependent upon parental standards of right and wrong; and he still relies upon tangible adult authority. His views are now less egocentric but they are still family centered. He lacks judgment and tends to believe that rules are inherent parts of games or of life itself, and does not yet appreciate the more contractual nature of social behavior. God has ordained and the parents have taught what is right or wrong, and ethics are therefore likely to be considered in black and white terms. Such childhood rigor of evaluation is apt to continue into adult life. On the other side, he will first learn much of social values and particularly of peer-group values in the years ahead. Fortunately, time for consolidation and modification of the superego remains before the impact of puberty adds powerful new stresses.†

The child also has realistic reasons to relinquish immediate gratifica-

---

* Thus, the inability of a person to permit himself any sensuous gratification can be considered in terms of the ego's conformity to superego demands formed in terms of childhood perceptions of paternal prohibitions: some hallucinations can be understood as externalizations of threats from the superego for incipient infractions; depressive reactions are concerned with superego punishment—usually for hostile feelings and resentment toward significant persons.
† Changes that take place in the "superego" throughout life will be discussed in subsequent chapters.

tions. He has been learning that the pursuit of future objectives often requires renunciation of present pleasures. For instance, if he insists on dawdling in his mother's bed in the morning, he will miss going with his friend to the store. But he has also learned to forego many erotic and aggressive wishes because they will bring disapproval or punishment, and he has even learned to keep such thoughts from others. Now he is also keeping thoughts and feelings out of his own awareness because they provoke feelings of guilt, shame, or anxiety. The more definitive development of the superego at this phase of life also involves the child's realization that he will not necessarily continue to receive affection and protection as an ascribed right, but that it also depends upon achievement—in the sense of retaining affection by adhering to parental moral values. The balance between ascribed and achieved approval will gain importance as the child moves beyond the family, as will be shown in the next chapter.

We noted in Chapter 3 that the term "ego ideal" has often been used as a synonym for "superego," but it also has been given other meanings. One common and useful usage of ego ideal has been as the ideal image of what the child believes he should be, particularly in the form of the ideas the child forms of what the parents wish him to be and to become. The child measures himself by this standard and feels inadequate and perhaps depressed when he does not measure up to it. The ego ideal will usually contain large elements of the parent of the same sex whom the child wishes to resemble in order to become capable of gaining a love object like the parent of the opposite sex. Here again it becomes apparent that the organizing influences and the directive influences become confused when each parent negates the value of the spouse; or when they have conflicting values, standards, and ideals.*

* Thus, a girl whose father was a philanderer and who frequently left his wife and child and whose mother was a conscientious wife and overly solicitous mother was caught between irreconcilable parents with very divergent values. She needed her mother who was the only person upon whom she could depend, and sought to be a conscientious student and fastidious little girl, and when her mother chastised her for masturbating, tried to suppress all·sexual feelings. To satisfy her handsome and dapper father who made life seem carefree and easy, she fantasied becoming a woman like his attractive and sensuous mistress who seemed better able to hold him than her mother. Becoming a woman like mother seemed to have few advantages, and yet she needed her mother upon whom she could depend. Alternative and contradictory superegos formed that guided her into two different personality patterns, and eventually to an incipient dual personality.

Unconscious Mental Processes

An important aspect of the increased organization of the child concerns the sorting out of feelings, memories, perceptions, and ideas that are permitted to enter consciousness, or which the child lets himself think about. He cannot tolerate the anxiety caused by ideas and feelings which are unacceptable to the internalized parental standards and which, if expressed, would either produce rebuff or rejection by the parents or loss of self-esteem. It is safer not to permit temptation to occur than to be in danger of giving way to it. Yet, much of the temptation arises from within, from longings to have sensuous relationships and to give vent to aggressive feelings and from physiological drives that create tensions. The child can keep from recognizing the nature of these tensions, or having learned that such tensions are aroused by certain thoughts and perceptions he can keep such ideas from intruding. It is necessary to examine how this selection of what can enter consciousness occurs, and what happens to thoughts that are excluded.

The explorations of the unconscious processes have been a major achievement of psychoanalysis. Freud did not discover unconscious thought, but he discovered the dynamic force of unconscious processes and their far-reaching consequences; and through the study of dreams, the neuroses, the associations of patients in psychoanalysis, and the meanings of slips of the tongue, etc., went far in unraveling one of the most difficult and diaphanous topics ever studied. However, it is essential to keep in mind that the workings of the "mind" still present very much of a challenge, and many questions remain unanswered, if not, indeed, unasked.

In following the child's cognitive development and the progress of his linguistic abilities we have, for the most part, been examining his conscious processes concerned with problem solving and adaptation to the environment. We have, however, considered the development of fantasy and the problems that arise because of the child's difficulties in differentiating between reality and fantasy. Much of the child's mental activities are carried out in the service of the *pleasure principle*—in his seeking gratification more than in coping with reality—and in his gaining pleasure in fantasy when reality requires renunciation. Sometime around the age of five or six much of the fantasy is recognized as unacceptable to others, and even to the self, as it runs counter to superego dictates. Much of the oral, anal, oedipal, and aggressive fantasies are shut out and pushed down into the unconscious. We say that they are *repressed*, a term we have used before, but which now requires examination.

Origins of Unconscious Processes

Actually, from what we can determine, the oedipal child and young school child does not repress very effectively at first. Some of the forbidden material and fantasies are not unconscious but kept in separate compartments, so to speak, dissociated from his everyday activities. They are permitted to emerge under fairly specific circumstances, such as when he is falling asleep and is playing with his genitalia: a child of seven thus continues to fantasy seeing his mother undressed and putting his face against her breast. Another, while sitting on the toilet, has elaborate fantasies of an anal-sadistic and aggressive nature in which he imagines himself a superman bombing cities, visualizing the destruction of many little children each time his feces fall into the toilet. Such fantasies become more and more difficult to recall, and may eventually become "unconscious fantasies" that transpire automatically and cannot be recalled. The individual may become aware retrospectively that time has passed during which he does not know what he was thinking. However, in psychoanalysis, many adults realize that fantasies have persisted in isolation since childhood. A woman who hated her husband but still gained much orgastic pleasure from intercourse with him, realized that during intercourse she habitually fantasied sitting on an older man's lap and being masturbated—which she eventually traced to early childhood fantasies about her father.

Psychoanalytically oriented play therapy with children also indicates that many of their forbidden wishes and ideas have relatively simple access to consciousness. A six-year-old boy who started to stammer severely after a baby sister was born was watched playing with a family of dolls. He placed a baby doll in a crib next to the parent dolls' bed, and then had a boy doll come and throw the baby to the floor, beat it, and throw it into a corner. He then put the boy doll into the crib. In a subsequent session he had the father doll pummel the mother doll's abdomen, saying, "No, no!" At this period of childhood, even though certain unacceptable ideas cannot be talked about, they are still not definitely repressed. Indeed, even in adult life what can enter consciousness varies with the circumstances. Death wishes for a boss who has refused a raise are permitted, but they create guilt and are repressed when the boss becomes ill and may die. Sexual thoughts and even practices are permitted with a call girl that cannot occur with a fiancée. Superego standards vary with time and place and so does the division between what can be conscious and what must be unconscious.

One reason why unacceptable ideas can remain isolated, and can emerge in play and still not be clearly conscious, is that many of the little child's sensuous feelings, desires, and thoughts, as well as his primitive hostile feelings, originated before language was well developed and they were never properly linked up with words; and some were never precise or in a form that could be communicated. Consciousness is related to verbal symbolization if not dependent upon it. There are no simple words for many of the diffuse ideas and fantasies that the child has felt, or symbolized visually, and they are not a topic for discussion by elders or with elders.* They remain very much of a private world, and are thought about in an amorphous combination of feeling states and mental pictures.

As the child grows older he becomes more aware of which thoughts and impulses are acceptable. He is very dependent on the protection and care of parents and other significant figures. He has also become more sensitive to the possibility of losing them. Few children can reach the age of five or six without having experienced unbearable feelings of anxiety when parents have left, or the equally terrible depressed feelings that accompany their absence for a prolonged period. Efforts to avoid repetition of such feelings become fundamental motivations in the child's life. With the development of a superego, the child seeks to maintain himself as a person whom the parents will want and will not abandon, and still later as a person who is satisfied with himself and therefore can feel good. This requires control of id impulses and of hostile feelings toward loved ones. Paradoxically it also means finding ways of keeping out of consciousness any awareness of parental behavior or traits that would make them less desirable, less protective, or less dependable—as, for example, recognition that Father might not come back after one of the week-ends he spends in another house with some woman other than Mother.

The child has been developing ways of maintaining his equilibrium and avoiding distress by disregarding reality or by altering his perception of it; these include ways of keeping id impulsions from becoming conscious.

---

* In Piaget's terms affective schemata are not apt to be verbal schemata and new assimilations are made to them nonverbally. See also E. Schachtel, "Memory and Childhood Amnesia." [16]

These are the *mental mechanisms of defense* on the part of the ego against experiencing anxiety and which, stated symbolically, help the ego to satisfy the superego and withstand id impulses for immediate and unacceptable gratification. In the context of the physiological homeostasis of the organism, there are mental mechanisms that protect the individual from the physiological impact of anxiety and depression which can have deleterious effects upon the body's functioning (see Chapter 20). There are many different mechanisms of defense that influence thought, behavior, and character formation, as will be presented later in the chapter.

With the aid of various mental mechanisms of defense, various thoughts, impulses, and feelings that conflict with superego standards are banned from consciousness. Unconscious material cannot regain access to consciousness under ordinary conditions because defenses block associational pathways to it, or assimilation to schemata does not occur consciously; or, as we might put it in computer terms, the material is programmed out. The material or the impulses are not extinguished but merely contained, shunted aside, or, sometimes, altered to more acceptable form. Thus sidetracked, the unconscious processes and materials do not enter directly into decision-making functions or reasoning, but they continue in a more primitive, nonverbal type of activity that can exert potent influences upon conscious thought and behavior. The unconscious processes exert their influence in disguised and roundabout ways in order to assert the demands of the body's drives, the desires for sensuous gratification, or the pressures of aggressive feelings. The analogy can be made to a subversive organization that goes "underground" when it is banned by the government. It awaits and ferrets out opportunities to assert itself and influence the governmental procedures in hidden ways. It often utilizes individuals and organizations that do not even know that they are being used. Just as the government pays the price of not knowing what goes on beneath the calm surface, the individual does not know what is festering in him unconsciously. If repression in the service of a rigid or harsh superego is extreme and permits little pleasure or satisfaction of the body's needs, the unconscious force may upset the equilibrium. Inexplicable irrational behavior erupts or, in extreme instances, ego control gives way to dissociated experiences, or even to disorganized behavior.

The unconscious mental processes, then, do not generally serve reality testing and adaptation to social living, but *largely* the libidinal and aggressive drives that are unacceptable to the superego. They gain force from an individual's need for sexual outlets or for giving vent to unbearable feelings of hostility and aggression, and, in less demanding form from the intense desires to regain the sensuous gratifications and care of childhood that are denied to the older child and adult. The ego, having renounced such impulses and desires, can no longer control their unconscious derivatives and the uses they make of perception and memories. The ego is not free of them, for through influencing dreams, fantasies, and trends of associations, the unconscious processes often gain the upper hand. They may, so to speak, remain anonymous, but at the price of becoming the power behind the throne—that is, by gaining many of their demands from the ego provided they remain hidden or disguised.

Conscious, Preconscious, and Unconscious Mentation

The mind, according to psychoanalytic psychology, is divided into three layers rather than two: the *conscious, preconscious,* and *unconscious*. The preconscious, however, consists of material that has ready access to consciousness but simply is not in focus or the subject of attention at the moment. The conscious is limited to material which is being consciously thought about at the moment. The preconscious is not dormant but carries out activities in a fashion very much like that used by the unconscious, as will be explained presently.* Psychoanalytic psychology has been largely concerned with the dynamic unconscious—that is, the material that is denied access to consciousness. There are other sources of unconscious material. Ideas and ways of behaving that are inherent in the family or to the culture may be unconscious in that the individual never has reason to question them or even think about them. Egocentricity means, in a sense, unawareness that there are other, different ways of thinking or perceiving. Many of the unexpressed foundations of our belief systems and approach to living are unconscious.†

---

* Freud, at least at times, considered that the preconscious mind used "secondary process" thinking. Indeed, the preconscious is often included when one is talking about the conscious mind. However, "preconscious thought" is usually very different from conscious thinking.

† Another reason for maintaining material outside of conscious awareness requires mention even though it has received little if any attention in psychodynamic psychologies. As noted previously, each culture categorizes experiences differently. As experience tends to be continuous, what lies between these categories, between experiences and things that are recognized as entities and named—is kept from consciousness. Leach suggests that they are taboo; and as the separation of the self from the surrounding is particularly important, those substances that are ambiguously

The Primary and Secondary Mental Processes

Freud designated the type of thinking that transpires unconsciously as the *primary process,* contrasting it with the *secondary process* thinking that is reality-oriented and seeks to regulate behavior in terms of the future welfare of the individual. The primary process has been studied largely in terms of dream processes, which may differ from the primary process that goes on constantly during waking states. Freud tended to consider the primary process a forerunner of the secondary process. Secondary process rational thinking was a verbalization and organization of the diffuse primary process in accord with the demands of the superego and reality testing. However, it seems likely that the two types of thought processes which subserve different functions are carried out differently and that the secondary process does not simply reorganize more primitive material.* Transitional forms between the primary and secondary process are found in fantasies, semi-waking states, and in children's play.

Dreams are composed primarily of visual images. The *manifest dream* may derive from visual impressions of the preceding day and the associations they have unconsciously evoked translated into visual symbols. Thus, a female college student who has been rather promiscuous dreams of a young man she saw on the campus for the first time and thought attractive. In the dream she is lost in the country with him in an old auto. A sign points to her home town fifteen miles in the direction opposite to that in which she is driving. The dream is somewhat akin to a charade, but the meaning is masked from the dreamer. As Freud showed

---

self and non-self or which have been self but become non-self, such as excreta, hair cuttings, semen, are particularly subject to taboo in most societies. The same reasoning can be applied to nursing and sexual relations that blur the boundaries between the self and another.[10]

* Freud also described the functioning of the id in terms of primary process activity. When he formulated the *structural concept* (that is, the division of the mind into id, ego, and superego), he shifted much of his conceptualization of the unconscious as a division of the mind to the id, and thereby started the current confusions between the *topographical concept of the mind* (that is, the division of the mind according to layers of consciousness) and the structural concept. If, however, the structural division into id, ego, and superego is used as a means of conceptualizing the structure of the self or the personality rather than of the mind or psyche, much of the confusion is eliminated.

Piaget has presented a different conceptualization of unconscious processes and suggests a continuity between what Freud has termed "primary" and "secondary" processes. His cogent critique of Freud's approach to cognitive matters warrants careful study (see Chapter 7 in *Play, Dreams, and Imitation in Childhood* [13]).

in his study of dreams, it expresses a wish. She is on a date with the man who attracted her, and this is symbolized by driving with him in a car. The car also conveys much more, for she recalls that it is a car her family owned five years previously in which she first had sexual relations. She is lost in the country. She associates ideas of being a lost woman because of her promiscuity. She is fifteen miles from home. She had confided to a friend on the preceding day that she had had sexual experiences with fourteen different men: the fantasy concerns a fifteenth. She is, so to speak, fifteen men away from home, and going further away. She is driving. She is the seducer rather than the seduced, a factor which introduces her wishes to dominate men. There is an element of anxiety about being lost in the dream. It involves her sexual drives and aggression that have led her to run away from home symbolically. These are her primary associations, and it is apparent that each trend can be followed further, and in this respect the dream symbolizes a great many past experiences, current wishes, and problems that converge in this brief dream fragment.

The young woman's dream has expressed a great deal, but much concerns matters that she prefers not to think about and motivations which she has hidden from herself. It condenses a wish for intimacy with a specific man, but it also includes residua from previous sexual experiences. It condenses time, for it mingles elements of experiences that took place five years earlier with a depiction of her current wish. Similarly, places are symbolic rather than actual; she could not go on a date with the young man fifteen miles from home, as she is at college two thousand miles from home. Such apparent contradictions are not contradictory, for we see that morally she feels she is fifteen miles from home. The wish may also arouse anxiety, for its fulfillment is not only counter to her superego but she feels it would further separate her from her parents. The manifest content of the dream, which consists simply of her driving in a car with an attractive young man, neither runs counter to superego dictates nor creates anxiety; but the latent content—that is, the associated material symbolized in the dream—contains many disturbing elements. In order to express all of the material symbolized in the dream, the young woman would have had to tell herself a lengthy story about her life and desires, and it would have to have contained the contradictions and irrationalities that constitute so much of human behavior but are difficult to express in language. We may assume that even though the latent content had been hidden from consciousness it might have influenced her behavior, or indicated that she was in the process of reassessing her behavior—for she had just decided to seek psychotherapy because of her concerns over her increasing promiscuity.

Attributes of Primary Process Mentation

The study of <u>unconscious or primary process mentation</u> is a complex matter and highly conjectural.* We must be content here to note some of the salient aspects of dreaming, and then to examine some of the effects of unconscious processes on behavior. <u>The dream we have just examined briefly contained the following characteristics: thinking is carried out largely in visual symbols; the manifest content disguises and symbolizes a multitude of associations; it condenses many feelings and experiences and displaces ideas and feelings from one experience to another; it is timeless in the sense that old experiences have the same intensity as recent ones and connect to current experiences across time; opposites do not necessarily contradict but express a similarity between the apparently contradictory. The dream is also overdetermined; that is, the convergence of many related feelings and associations determines the</u> actual manifest content of the dream.

It is not known how much of the dream is organized during waking hours at the time some passing thought or perception is repressed and then unrolls during the night when conscious censorship is in abeyance, and how much is composed during sleep.† For example, the young woman's dream may be composed largely of repressed associations that unconsciously went on at the time she saw the attractive man and a fleeting thought of trying to meet him and seduce him was repressed.

Unconscious Processes and Behavior

Let us examine another example which can illustrate something of the influence of unconscious mentation upon behavior. A medical student becomes acutely anxious during a physiology seminar and feels forced to leave. While crossing a bridge on his way home he fears that he might

---

* The reader is referred to Chapter 7 of Freud's *Interpretation of Dreams*[4] and Lecture 10 in *A General Introduction to Psychoanalysis*.[6] A different approach to the topic can be found in Chapter 7 of Piaget's *Play, Dreams, and Imitation in Childhood*.[13] Erich Fromm's *The Forgotten Language*[7] presents still another approach to the understanding of dreams.

† Currently, there are indications that dreaming is an essential physiological process, carried out largely during those periods of sleep when rapid eye movements are going on (REM sleep); and depriving the sleeper of just this phase of sleep by awakening him when his eyeballs are moving causes emotional disturbances.[2, 17]

throw himself off of it. His anxiety increases and he hastens to the university psychiatrist, who manages to see him immediately. When he relaxes in the psychiatrist's office and tries to remember just what had been happening when he became so apprehensive in the seminar, he recalls that he had been looking at a fold in his trousers. The position of the fold led him to fantasy that he had a very large penis, and he went on to daydream of future sexual conquests. Then, with a shift in his position, the fold disappeared and the anxiety started. The trivial occurrence assumed importance because of the student's particular life situation. He had been crippled by poliomyelitis in early childhood and used crutches. He had been engaged to marry but his fiancée had died of meningitis during the preceding year. Because of his disability he found it difficult to form intimate relationships with girls, and he had felt very lonely and sexually frustrated since the death of his fiancée. He recognized that his feelings of physical inadequacy included concerns that his penis might be too small. The immediate reasons for the onset of the attack of anxiety when the fold in his trousers collapsed had been clarified, but in the next visit the student recalled a related episode that will serve to illustrate the workings of unconscious processes.

The incident that disturbed him had occurred a few months earlier while he was spending a week-end on a farm where he had previously vacationed on several occasions. While walking along a quiet road he had a transient vision, almost hallucinatory, of a bear coming out of the woods and menacing him. He fantasied defending himself with a crutch. When asked to give his associations to the occurrence without censoring them, he recalled that after his fiancée died he had spent a few weeks at this farm; and finding one of her handkerchiefs in his pocket he had, in a sentimental gesture, buried it precisely at the spot where he later had the vision of the bear. The psychiatrist, noting a similarity in the student's pronunciation of "bear" and "buried," simply commented that it seemed as though the buried had returned. The student then told of his despair after his girl's death, and thought perhaps he had tried to overcome his grief by burying the handkerchief. He then felt impelled to speak of another incident, even though he did not know why. It was about his last date with his fiancée. They had gone to dine in a Russian restaurant which, he suddenly remembered, displayed a Russian *bear* on its sign. After they had sat down, his friend had complained of a headache and he went out and bought her some *Bayer's* aspirin. After dinner they had gone to the girl's apartment, petted, and he had been *embarrassed* by the extent of her passion; as the psychiatrist suggested, *embarrassed* at being "bare-assed." The student went on to tell how they had undressed completely for the first time and he had been embarrassed by his deformity. Although a great deal more emerged, including concerns that his paralysis had been a punishment for masturbation, and that his girl had become ill because of their sexual activities, the material conveys how a series of associations about a bear—Russian bear, Bayer's aspirin, embarrassed, bare-assed, buried—had unconsciously been organized and reappeared as a single symbol of a threatening bear; a symbol which the reader may be able to grasp stood for an entire sequence of painful memories and which related to his current loneliness and deprivation, as well as to the feelings of genital inadequacy that had triggered his anxiety attack.

In the above illustration, one might consider that there is a type of logic in the associations that converged in the bear symbol. It had to do with connecting up a series of episodes about which the student felt guilt and for which he may have felt that he required punishment. He had tended to exclude these painful memories of his fiancée from his consciousness, but they clearly had been troubling him, and they became associated with the feelings of physical and sexual inadequacy that he had momentarily sought to resolve through fantasy during his seminar.

Preconscious Primary Process Thinking

The material that is subjected to primary process thinking may not be repressed but may be simply preconscious—that is, out of the focus of consciousness. Thus, a student who was reading Freud for the first time became convinced of the importance of unconscious mental activity by two episodes that happened in rapid succession while he was reading about unconscious determinants of behavior. Following an example in the book,[5] he asked his roommate to say the first number that came to mind. He wished to see whether he could learn why his friend had selected that particular number. The roommate promptly said, "Forty-three," but insisted that he could offer no ideas why he had made this random selection. The student of Freud, however, said that he believed he could follow the reasons and wondered whether his roommate had actually had the thoughts he now attributed to him. He reminded his friend that half an hour earlier, the last time they had spoken, he had told his roommate that he had just mailed a dollar bill to a friend to whom he had lost a seventy-five-cent bet on a football game. Had his roommate not thought, "Why are you sending a dollar, four quarters instead of the three that you owe him?" His surmise was correct, for his roommate had thought just that. The second episode that impressed the student occurred a few minutes later. His roommate had asked him to check a letter he had written to a book dealer in Germany with whom he was having a dispute over a bill. He had found his roommate's German letter grammatically correct except for the closing phrase. His roommate had intended to write *"Hoch Achtungsvoll,"* meaning "(with) great respect," but inadvertently had written *"Hoch Verachtungsvoll,"* or "(with) great contempt," which of course came closer to expressing his actual feelings.

Primary process mental activity is not pathological or even less useful than the secondary process. It not only helps assure attention to basic needs by transmitting drives to the thought processes, but we are dependent upon such unconscious and preconscious types of thinking for much of our creativity. If a person cannot trust his unconscious, he can have little spontaneity, intuition, or empathy.* Not only does artistic creativity rely heavily upon primary process organization, but problem solving can also occur without conscious awareness. Thus, the mathematician Poincaré described how he resolved problems concerning Fuchsian functions that had defied his conscious abilities only after he had ceased trying.[14] The answer came into his mind when he awoke in the morning; and subsequently another aspect resolved itself, so to speak, just as he was stepping onto a streetcar and was no longer consciously thinking of the problem. Awareness of problems can emerge in dreams in symbolic form, and answers to intellectual problems sometimes appear.† Some matters, such as with whom one falls in love, depend upon decisions that include factors that never even enter consciousness, as will be elucidated when we consider marital choice (Chapter 13).

The child relies upon primary process thinking far more than the adult, and the differentiation between the primary and secondary processes is not as yet so clearly drawn. The child is more intuitive in his likes and dislikes, more spontaneous in his decision making, and closer to his infantile experiences. The closing of the oedipal period does not sud-

---

* Friedrich Schiller, in response to a friend's complaints of his (the friend's) lack of creativity, warned the friend that he would never be truly creative rather than a critic because he could not remove the guards at the gates of his consciousness.

† I am, of course, not referring to the selection of race horse bets through the use of dream books, but rather to such things as Kekulé's discovery of the formula for the benzene ring in a dream of two snakes each with the other's tail in his mouth.

denly block off access to ideas and feelings that are more clearly drive derivatives. As the child grows older, just what material must be denied access to consciousness depends upon the nature of the superego and also upon the need to repress or exclude impulses that interfere with adaptive tasks. The screening or censorship occurs unconsciously and employs the various mechanisms of defense. Just how this sorting out occurs cannot be answered properly, but what answers can be given require consideration of the mental mechanisms of defense.

Anxiety and the Mechanism of Defense

The child has experienced anxiety and depressive feelings which are extremely unpleasant. He seeks means of preventing the recurrence of such feelings. Anxiety and depression both contain physiological components. Alterations in bodily function that accompany anxiety or depression serve as warning signals. For example, the slight speeding of the heart or the tightening of muscles that accompanies fear or anxiety unconsciously becomes a signal. The warning signal throws a switch, so to speak, and unconsciously one or more mechanisms of defense are brought into operation that serve to alter the perception of the danger or block out some temptation. As so much of anxiety derives from internal danger—that is, from the danger that the ego will give way to a forbidden desire—many defenses serve to block out awareness of the impulse, memory, or potentially dangerous train of associations. The use of a fragment of the physiological effects of anxiety as a warning is termed "signal anxiety." It takes effect without conscious awareness, and to some extent it is a matter of conditioning.

The mechanisms of defense are varied: some block out memories of disturbing experiences; some prevent the linkage of memories or experiences that would become disturbing if connected; some prevent emotions from linking with experience; some alter the perception of a drive or wish; some transform the drive into a form more acceptable to the superego.[3] Certain mechanisms of defense are more common in childhood than other, more sophisticated defenses. An examination of some of the more significant mechanisms will serve to illustrate how profoundly they can affect thought, behavior, and personality development.

Repression, by which a drive or forbidden impulse is barred from consciousness, has already been discussed. It includes the barring or banishment of memories, perceptions, or feelings that would arouse the forbidden. Thus, in order to prevent rearousal of some childhood sexual experience or the discomfort of remembering sexual desires for a parent, the entire period of early childhood may be repressed. Repression is unconscious in contrast to suppression, which concerns conscious efforts to keep memories or feelings from intruding. Repression has been considered a central mechanism of defense and, in a sense, the cause of the dynamic unconscious which theoretically is composed of repressed materials. Repression often requires the collaboration of other defenses to maintain its effectiveness.

Isolation is another basic defense that we have noted in connection with the separation of childhood fantasies from the remainder of consciousness. Material may be available in consciousness but it does not become linked up with other associations, at least not with material that would arouse anxiety. Thus, in the story of the young man, the memory of burying the handkerchief had not been repressed, but it had been isolated from memories of other experiences that would have brought painful memories of his last evening with his fiancée. It is not always clear whether something has been isolated or repressed.

Regression has also been noted. It can be considered a mechanism of defense in which the child falls back to an earlier phase of development at which he felt secure—in particular, secure in being cared for and having others assume responsibility for him. Some use of regression is a normal aspect of development—the falling back to regain security after overreaching for greater independence. It starts very early in life and is a major childhood adaptive technique. It can be anticipated in any person who becomes physically ill and is no longer capable of taking care of himself. It is almost a necessary accompaniment of placing oneself in the hands of a physician, and therefore it is important that all physicians recognize the phenomenon of regression and take it into account in caring for patients. A sick person can readily be misjudged, for he is commonly more childish, petulant, demanding, than when he is well. Further, regression is so tempting and so thoroughly patterned in childhood that many patients try to counter their tendencies to regress by refusing to become properly dependent when ill; and, conversely, an inability to overcome such regressions and again face the problems of living often complicates recovery. Regression to childhood stages of development is a major source of psychopathology.

Fantasy formation has already been adequately discussed as a major adaptive mechanism and defense of childhood. Creative fantasy is usually an asset and may prepare the child for future reality-oriented behavior as well as dull the pain of reality. Of course, some children will turn their backs on reality to a degree that interferes with adaptation. When it becomes a strong mechanism of defense, fantasy is accompanied by isolation.

Sublimation is often considered to be a more sophisticated defense. The original meaning was borrowed from chemistry—the transformation of a solid into a gas without its going through a liquid state—and connoted the unconscious alteration of a drive into something more sublime such as poesy. However, it now has a much broader connotation. Sublimation is an essential part of a child's development. He redirects drives and wishes into more acceptable channels but still has some outlet for them, as when aggression toward a sibling is transmuted into hammering on a toy, or when a wish to smear feces finds an outlet in finger painting. One might even say that a prizefighter who recognized in therapy that he had sworn as a child to beat his father to a pulp, had sublimated his aggression into a socially acceptable channel. Since the advent of psychoanalytic ego psychology the term *neutralization* has become important. It concerns the neutralization of a libidinal or aggressive charge with some counterenergy, thus permitting it to be used in the service of adaptation or intellectual functioning. The term bears a close relationship to sublimation. The concept of neutralization is useful and necessary only to those psychologists who are conceptualizing vicissitudes of libidinal energies. The cathexis of libido is neutralized by a *countercathexis*.

Denial simply refers to the ability to deny the existence of something disturbing, such as one's own anger or sexual feelings. The child may insist that he is *not* angry, and we have noted the tendency and ability of a little boy to deny that creatures without penises exist. Most commonly it is a denial of one's own responsibility with *projection* of blame onto a parent or another child. *Reaction formation* may accompany denial: an unacceptable feeling is turned into its opposite. The jealousy and hate of the newborn sibling may be *denied, undone,* and turned into its opposite. Reaction formation is apparent in individuals who turn anal impulses into overtidiness or scrupulous cleanliness.

Projection and *introjection* are defenses that are particularly important in personality development and character formation. Projection concerns the attribution to another of one's own impulses or wishes. The child cannot, for example, accept or tolerate his feelings of hostility for a brother but instead believes that the brother is hostile to him. The defense is related to the physiological efforts to rid the body of something

harmful as by vomiting or defecating—and, indeed, vomiting can symbolically represent efforts to be rid of an unacceptable feeling or wish.
Projection is a complicated defense that enters into much of psychopathology and cannot be discussed adequately here.* The following is a
clear-cut example of psychotic projection. A young soldier kept hearing a
voice threatening, "I'll kill you." At times he believed that a specific
friend was threatening him. In therapy he recalled that he had started
hearing the voice when his "buddy" had left him and become pals with
another youth. Then, his own inner voice had said, "Say I'm your best
friend or I'll kill you." His homicidal impulse was untenable to him, and
the threat was turned against himself by projection and the friend he
wished to threaten seemed to become the one who did the threatening.

Introjection, which is related to identification, has more to do with
the defense against disillusionment in a needed person. The child not
only needs his parents but needs good parents. He may blame himself, or
attribute to himself a parental trait, in order to preserve the worth of the
needed love object, or object of his identification. In simplified terms, he
says, "It is not his fault, he is not bad; I am." Or it may go, "They are
not hostile to me, they do not take care of me because I am hostile to
them, or because I am worthless."

Personality Constriction

There are many other mechanisms of defense, some of which will be
presented in specific contexts in later chapters. It is important, however,
to note the more sweeping result of an overly strict superego. The rigid
restrictions imposed on a child by his parents become self-delimitations
that require *constriction* of the personality and many defenses to maintain. Such restrictions lead the child to constrict his thoughts, feelings,
activities in order to continue to feel desirable. The child may be very
good, overly good, but his inner life becomes impoverished. Such constriction usually occurs gradually and unconsciously. A child may grow
up in a home in which he believes that such overconformity and neglect
of impulses is the only proper way. However, occasionally constriction is
more or less purposeful and seems the only means of preserving equilibrium and equanimity. Thus, a college girl who had grown up in a seriously disturbed home in which her parents were in constant discord, and

* The use of projection can also indicate that a person has failed to establish adequate
"ego boundaries," and still is unclear about what originates within himself and what
originates in others. A child who is closer to the original symbiotic tie with his
mother will be apt to blame her for what upsets him or what goes wrong with what
he plans—and it is not so pathological in a child.

whose only sibling had become psychotic, appeared to be reasonably well adjusted. However, she had given up having many friends, used few of her assets, and consciously strove to maintain acceptable relationships with both of her parents. She had taught herself not to think about her feelings toward her parents as well as never to express them, and indeed she had learned never to think back and recall disturbing events that had occurred during the day. She had learned that she could not tolerate having feelings, for they were almost always painful, nor could she have memories that would be certain to arouse hostility or despair. She maintained her emotional equilibrium but at the price of a relatively impoverished personality.

Mechanisms of Defense and Distortions of Perception

The various mechanisms of defense which we have been discussing may seem very complicated and beyond the capacities of a small child. In some respects we have outdistanced our slowly developing child in seeking to describe the organization of his personality. Still, the four- or five-year-old commonly experiences considerable anxiety, particularly at night when wolves and tigers invade his dreams and projected hostilities harrow his fantasies. These problems are within him and he requires mental mechanisms to counter them. The various defenses help him maintain equanimity and prevent the intrusion of forbidden, unacceptable, or otherwise disturbing impulses and ideas into consciousness. In the process they limit and distort the perception of reality. They change the view of the self, of motives, and of the significant others, and thereby can create difficulties in adaptation. However, some degree of self-deception is probably necessary for survival. As Goethe wrote, "who destroys illusion in himself and in others, nature punishes tyrannically." [9] As the same defenses or combinations of defenses tend to be used repeatedly by the same person, the defenses contribute to determining personality types and character. Whereas they help provide stability, they also create problems and foster some degree of neurotic behavior in everyone. An understanding of the defenses is paramount in understanding psychopathology.

We have been reviewing how the child's personality became organized within the shelter of his family, and have been considering constructs useful in discussing personality functioning. Now that the child is about to enter school, new important influences will enter into shaping his personality, and will build upon structures already organized within the family. The child's ability to function in his new environments and the ways in which he will utilize what they offer depend upon the emotional security and the intellectual equipment he has gained in the home. Although his parents will still provide, guide, and remain major formative influences for many years, the child has by now become sufficiently well integrated to emerge into less sheltered environments and expand his horizons. He has achieved something of a self-concept [12] through reacting to and internalizing the attitudes of family members to him, but such concepts of the self are limited because they derive largely from interactions with parents in intrafamilial situations. Still, they will form the basis of his ways of relating beyond the family. His ego functions have developed along with his linguistic and cognitive growth; and he has gained sufficient experience to begin to appreciate that others have somewhat different ways, including ways of understanding and believing, that must be taken into account in relating to others. He has completed his primary socialization and can control or contain wishes for sensuous gratification and outbursts of aggressivity. He is helped by his internalizations of parental standards and dictates which guide him when his parents are not about, and by his identifications with his parents which lead him to behave as they do. Concomitantly, his cognitive and emotional development has been channeled into appreciation of what he can consciously perceive, recall, and think about—in part in order to maintain parental approbation and his own self-esteem, and in part because the language and the parents have conveyed what is taboo, what is inconsequential, what can be noted, and what it is vital to perceive.

The psychoanalytic "structural concept" that divides the personality into id, ego, and superego; the "topographic concept" that divides mental functioning into conscious, preconscious, and unconscious processes; and a presentation of various mental mechanisms of defense have been utilized in order to summarize the integrative processes. These concepts contain various shortcomings, whether they are presented in classical form or as modified in this chapter,* but they provide useful constructs for conceptualizing and discussing the inordinately complex process of integration; and the literature on personality development and functioning is scarcely intelligible unless the reader is familiar with them.

---

* Three recent efforts to clarify psychoanalytic theory by leading psychoanalytic theoreticians serve to highlight the basic inconsistencies of psychoanalytic theory and the need for its thorough reorganization. See D. Rapaport,[15] M. M. Gill,[8] and J. Arlow and C. Brenner.[1]

References

1. Jacob A. Arlow and Charles Brenner, "Psychoanalytic Concepts and the Structural Theory," *Journal of the American Psychoanalytic Association* Monograph Series, No. 13 (New York: International Universities Press, 1964).

2. Charles Fisher, "Psychoanalytic Implications of Recent Research on Sleep and Dreaming," *Journal of the American Psychoanalytic Association*, 13 (1965), 197–303.

3. Anna Freud, *The Ego and the Mechanisms of Defence* (1936), trans. Cecil Baines (New York: International Universities Press, 1946).

4. Sigmund Freud, "The Interpretation of Dreams" (1900), in *The Standard Edition of the Complete Psychological Works of Sigmund Freud*, Vols. 4 and 5 (London: Hogarth Press, 1953).

5. Sigmund Freud, "The Psychopathology of Everyday Life" (1901), in *The Standard Edition of the Complete Psychological Works of Sigmund Freud*, Vol. 6 (London: Hogarth Press, 1953).

6. Sigmund Freud, *A General Introduction to Psychoanalysis* (New York: Boni & Liveright, 1916–1917).

7. Erich Fromm, *The Forgotten Language: An Introduction to the Understanding of Dreams, Fairy Tales, and Myths* (New York: Rinehart, 1951).

8. Merton M. Gill, "Topography and Systems in Psychoanalytic Theory," *Psychological Issues*, Vol. 3, No. 2, Monograph 10 (New York: International Universities Press, 1963).

9. J. W. von Goethe, "Die Natur" (1782), in *Schriften über die Natur* (Leipzig: Alfred Kroner Verlag, n.d.), pp. 15–17.

10. Edmund Leach, "Anthropological Aspects of Language: Animal Categories and Verbal Abuses," in Eric H. Lenneberg (ed.), *New Directions in the Study of Language* (Cambridge, Mass.: M.I.T. Press, 1964).

11. Hans W. Loewald, "The Superego and the Ego-Ideal. II. Superego and Time," *International Journal of Psycho-Analysis*, 43 (1962), 264–268.

12. George H. Mead, *Mind, Self and Society: From the Standpoint of a Social Behaviorist* (Chicago: University of Chicago Press, 1934).

13. Jean Piaget, *Play, Dreams, and Imitation in Childhood*, trans. C. Gattengo and F. M. Hodgson (New York: W. W. Norton, 1962), p. 207.

14. Henri Poincaré, "Mathematical Creation," in James R. Newman (ed.), *The World of Mathematics*, Vol. 4 (New York: Simon & Schuster, 1956), pp. 2041–2050.

15. David Rapaport, "The Structure of Psychoanalytic Theory, a Systematizing Attempt," *Psychological Issues*, Vol. 2, No. 2, Monograph No. 6 (New York: International Universities Press, 1960), p. 128.

16. Ernest G. Schachtel, "Memory and Childhood Amnesia," in *Meta-*

morphosis: On the Development of Affect, Perception, Attention, and Memory (New York: Basic Books, 1959).

17. Louis J. West, Herbert H. Janszen, Boyd K. Lester, and Floyd S. Cornelison, Jr., "The Psychosis of Sleep Deprivation," *Annals of the New York Academy of Science*, 96 (1962), 66–70.

Suggested Reading

Charles Brenner, *An Elementary Textbook of Psychoanalysis* (New York: International Universities Press, 1955).

Anna Freud, *The Ego and the Mechanisms of Defence* (1936), trans. Cecil Baines (New York: International Universities Press, 1946).

Sigmund Freud, "The Interpretation of Dreams" (1900), in *The Standard Edition of the Complete Psychological Works of Sigmund Freud*, Vols. 4 and 5 (London: Hogarth Press, 1953).

Sigmund Freud, "The Psychopathology of Everyday Life" (1901), in *The Standard Edition of the Complete Psychological Works of Sigmund Freud*, Vol. 6 (London: Hogarth Press, 1953).

CHAPTER 9

❀ ❀ ❀
❀ ❀ ❀ ❀ ❀ ❀

The Juvenile

THE CHILD'S DEPARTURE for school marks a long-awaited day. The mother leaves her child at the classroom or turns him over to the school bus driver, and breathes deeply to lighten the heaviness in her chest. She feels that she has handed her baby over to the world; she can no longer protect him and offer him guidance during the hours he is away from home. He must manage on the integration he has achieved during the years of domestic socialization, and on the security he feels awaits him at home which will still remain the center of his life. The child is buoyed by pride in joining the schoolchildren and leaving the "babies" at home. He enters the classroom and feels somewhat lost among so many strange children, uneasy over the unfamiliar procedures and uncertain as he seeks to follow the directions given by a strange woman. When the novelty wears off, he may decide that life at home was preferable.

The Crucial Issues of the Juvenile Period

The equilibrium the child gained at the closing of the oedipal period as he found his position within his family is disrupted when he moves off to school, where he will be judged on his merits, and into the neighborhood peer group, where he must find his place on his own. Neither the classroom nor the peer group forms a completely new environment. Most children have attended kindergarten, if not nursery school, and have played with children in the neighborhood. But new expectations accompany the role of schoolchild. He is no longer just a child within a family but a representative of the family, and his parents would like to be proud of him. The child compares himself to his classmates and playmates and wishes to measure up and be proud of himself. The critical aspect of the transition concerns the shift from ascribed to achieved acceptance and status.

Within his family, the child's position was determined largely by biological determinants: he was a member of the childhood generation of a given sex, age, and sequential position. Basically, he was loved or accepted because he was his parents' child. In school and with peers it matters little that he is a younger or older sibling, or a much loved or neglected child, except as such factors have influenced his personality and behavior. As part of a group of children of the same age, he is often treated as part of the collectivity rather than with the individualized attention to which he became accustomed at home. He must forego many of his desires and mask his idiosyncrasies in order to fit into the group. The teacher has an obligation to evaluate him on the basis of his achievement and, eventually, according to impersonal scales. Both in school and in the neighborhood his confreres are rivals—often harsh judges who are more likely to rub salt than salve in emotional wounds. In these altered circumstances, in these new environments, and in relation to new significant figures, the child's personality will undergo considerable reorganization and he will develop new abilities to prepare himself to live within the larger society rather than simply within his family.

Psychoanalytic psychology has relatively little to offer concerning the critical aspects of the period. Classic analytic theory considers the *latency period* a time of transition and consolidation between the closing of the oedipal period and the onset of puberty. Freud postulated that a biologically determined subsidence of libidinal drives permitted a period of relative calm. However, even as there is no evidence of a physiologically determined increase in sexual drive in the oedipal child, there is no reason to believe that a diminution in sexual drive occurs and accounts for the critical aspects of the latency period. There is little if any evidence that the child has less impulsion to masturbation or that sexual curiosity diminishes appreciably. However, the child has come to terms with his position in the family, repressed his sensuous desires for his mother, and internalized controls. He will now be investing his energies and interests outside the family, in his peers and in learning. With his attachments divided between parents, teachers, and peers, and with his many new interests, there is often less turmoil at home. Then, too, the child has completed his primary socialization and is less preoccupied with bodily functions, and requires and obtains less sensuous gratification from his parents.

Many psychoanalysts have recognized the need to reconceptualize this developmental period and its importance in personality development. Harry Stack Sullivan placed considerable emphasis upon the juvenile period and particularly on the child's social environment formed by his peer groups and on the "chum" relationship.[17]

Erikson has considered the development of a *sense of industry* the crucial theme of late childhood. Unless the child acquires a sense of industry he develops pervasive *feelings of inferiority and inadequacy.*[4] We can further recognize that the trait of industry is encompassed on the one side by the danger of habitual compulsive striving to excel in competition, and, on the other, by defeatist trends seen in an unwillingness to accept and face meaningful challenges. As striving to excel competitively is a highly valued American characteristic, its pathological aspects are readily overlooked.* The child during the latency period is faced by circumstances that can readily foster overcompensatory competitiveness or a pervasive sense of incompetence.

There are, however, other character traits that appear to have their roots in this period of life, and if not implanted firmly during it will never come to blossom. One is the *sense of belonging,* the assurance that one is an accepted and integral part of the group and of the broader

* Ruth Benedict astutely realized that there may exist in every culture a group of abnormals who represent the extreme development of the favored cultural type, and whom the society supports in their furthest aberrations rather than exposing them. They are given license which they may exploit endlessly—yet from the point of view of another culture or another time in history they are considered the most bizarre of the psychopathic types of the period.[1]

society, in contrast to feeling like an outsider. It involves more than social ease or anxiety; it concerns an identification with the society in which one lives and a commitment to its values and ethics. When alienation occurs, it usually becomes apparent toward the end of adolescence but it has precursors in the juvenile's relations with his peers. A *sense of responsibility* must also develop at this stage. It involves a willingness and capacity to live up to the expectations one has aroused. It is insufficient for a child to learn the technical skills and knowledge required for him to conduct his life tasks, for unless he can be relied upon, they are of little value to his fellow citizens. To gain approbation, a child needs to be trustworthy in the sense of being reliable rather than simply honest. Traits such as a sense of belonging and of responsibility are also basic to the quality of *leadership*. It is now, in finding his place among his peers, that the child begins to assume his place in society. He learns that he can lead and is expected to lead; that he is a supporter who helps the leader; simply a follower; or one who is habitually alienated or rebellious. The child places himself in part, and in part is placed by others.

In finding his place in a society of peers, and through being evaluated by adults, by schoolmates and playmates, the child develops a more adequate evaluation of himself than when he is relating primarily to family members, and forms a self concept that serves to regulate his ambitions and ways of relating to others. The ego, so to speak, contemplates and evaluates the self, but in so doing the ego is considering the reactions of others to him—to his self.* The child realizes that some hold him in esteem and seek him as a friend, as a member of a team, as a birthday guest. He evaluates who likes him and who avoids him and he notes how others respond to his critiques of these persons, and gains an evaluation of himself in the process. He recognizes that teachers praise his work, give him responsibilities, or consider him a dullard or a nonentity. He is learning who he is, and he is simultaneously learning his society's value system.

In the several environments in which the school-age child lives—the home, schoolroom, neighborhood play group—he begins to take on new sets of values and begins to view his social world from different perspectives, moving beyond the egocentric and family-centered orientations of

* G. H. Mead differentiates between the "I" and the "me" in his presentation of how a self concept arises through social transactions and recognition of how others evaluate the self.[10] It is of interest that Josiah Royce also emphasized how we achieve self-knowledge only through contrasting ourselves in many ways with other selves—in other words, how self-consciousness depends on social contrasts.

early childhood. As we shall see later in this chapter, the decline in ego-centricity is of paramount importance to both the child's cognitive and ethical development. As the child's orientation broadens, he moves into Piaget's period of *concrete operations,* in which he becomes able to classify through acquiring his culture's systems of knowing and thinking. In a similar manner his *moral judgment* matures, and he progresses from a *morality of constraint* to attain a *morality of cooperation,* if the setting permits.

Thus, although the juvenile period has not been generally considered a period when critical issues are decided, it becomes apparent that a number of important matters must be settled during these years. Indeed, where the sorting out of students for higher education occurs even prior to adolescence—as it does in most countries—the direction of the child's future will be determined by his personality and intellectual performance in grade school.

The Expanding Environment

As this chapter is concerned with a half-dozen years, we cannot describe with conciseness the change from kindergarten tot who has difficulty in differentiating play and fantasy from reality to junior high school boy or girl. Although at five and six the children's groups still are composed of both sexes engaged in playing "house" or "store" and in such activities as hide-and-seek and roller skating, between the ages of seven and eleven the two sexes are more completely separated than at any other time of life. Boys and girls may live as if in different worlds, coming together only within the home and in school, a state that is accentuated in large cities where they may also attend separate schools.

The child's environment varies greatly and accordingly influences his way of life differently. Life is different on farms, in suburbs, and in the city, but everywhere it is lived with playmates, though to a greater extent for the boy than for the girl. The social environment may consist of a few neighbor boys on the farm who go swimming together, play baseball in the town center, or turn the barn loft into a fortress. Or it may be a host of kids on a city street, seemingly a mixture of all ages and both sexes, but who are divided into subgroups within this agglomeration. Amidst the traffic of passers-by and cars the children are in a world of their own, excluding adults from their awareness, though always alert to the appearance of a policeman who might object to their activities.

These years are often among the happiest periods of life, particularly when the home is stable and relationships with parents are not a source of concern; but even when they are not, the child can often forget his domestic woes while he is with his gang. It is a golden period of freedom marred only by school, when hours can be spent with friends away from adult interference. The child has become sufficiently independent to be on his own, exploring new interests and moving into real or imaginary ventures while burdened with few responsibilities. The parents still provide for his essential needs and furnish a haven in the home to which the child can return when he is frustrated by his companions.

It is within this group of childhood companions that many essential traits develop and many of the patterns for social living are learned or consolidated. A considerable fantasy life is acted out in pairs and groups in which roles are enacted and rules are learned. Skills are learned in play, and fair play becomes a requisite; and team participation becomes a form of group identification and self-government. Here the child is judged by peers, learns value systems that differ from those learned at home and in school, and finds new heroes and models for identification. He is also being weaned from home, learning to feel comfortable and secure while interdependent with peers.

The Separation of the Sexes

The "gang" is more important to the boy than to the girl, and becomes more significant after the age of seven or eight. It draws him into a new subculture outside the home and school, one which is not directed or dominated by women. It has greater pertinence to male development as it helps train boys for future competitive careers and participation in the management of society. The exclusion of girls from the boys' juvenile peer group serves to help the boy become more secure in his gender identity and his masculine role. He is overcoming his dependency upon his mother but he is also divesting himself of residua of his identification with her and countering whatever envy he may have of the girl's prerogatives, particularly her socially ascribed right to remain more dependent. He adopts a contemptuous attitude toward girls and whatever is girlish. The epithet "sissy" can create strong leverage in motivating a boy to more aggressive and daring behavior. He convinces himself that being a girl is something he would want less than anything else. Indeed, there may be nothing he fears more—nothing that he fears wishing more because the wish is not far from the surface. Repressing such wishes into the unconscious is one task of the "latency" period. He does not reject all girls, girls who behave as boys—that is, who act out their wishes to be boys—are acceptable to him, for they reinforce the idea that no one would wish to be a girl. Those who first become interested in going with girls during adolescence are apt to be considered "deserters." They have gone over to the other side—not to the side of females so much as to the adult world in which women are desired and have prestige.

The Boy's Activities

Of course, boys' lives vary markedly, but rather typically they play the games of "cowboys and Indians" that turn into "cops and robbers" and various types of military games; "hide-and-seek," "red Rover," and "prisoner's base" are early organized games. They have a passionate interest in marbles, kite flying, bike riding, simple ball games; and then they begin to play games such as baseball, basketball, and football with poorly organized teams, countless fights about rules, arguments about cheating and lopsided scores. Hours indoors are spent playing checkers, cards, and other games or in constructing models and collecting almost anything. There is the fondness for wrestling and body contact; the dares to fight, the chip on the shoulder; the avoidance of the bully, the teasing of the poor sport. There are the quarrels between friends who will never talk to one another again but seek one another out within the day. There is the boasting, the importance of winning, the complete exhaustion by bedtime. There is the good life of the protected and happy child; but there are other lives that children lead as well. There is the slum child who returns to the empty flat after school with an empty stomach and an empty heart, who then ventures forth to find some companionship, looking at shop windows, snitching fruit from a stand, sharing a cigarette with a friend. There is the child of the migratory sugarbeet worker who never goes to any one school for more than a term, lives in a trailer or a series of shacks supplied by the farms, and works in the fields with his parents to help eke out a livelihood. There is the southern Negro child who must watch that he not overstep a thousand intangible boundaries and who is having inferiority woven into him. And then, of course, there are the children who for emotional reasons cannot move beyond the family into the peer group and remain very much to themselves, lonely and embittered.

The Girl's Activities

Girls' interests, values, activities, and group behavior differ from those of boys. Girls spend more of their free time at home, and usually continue to be closer to the parents. They are not likely to participate in group games except under supervision and therefore do not have the experience of learning to organize groups and to value themselves according to athletic achievement or leadership abilities. Jacks, hopscotch, rope skipping seem to be prerogatives of girls. Girls usually indulge in more quiet activities which do not interfere with their talking about people. They tend to make a great deal of sharing secrets and try to evoke curiosity or envy by exchanging them. The girl is permitted by the social mores to admit that she likes school, and at this age is more likely to enjoy it.* She tries on mother's dresses, jewelry, and make-up. In the country she has outlets for action in skating and bicycling. Girls also may become enamored of horses and horseback riding, sometimes developing a passionate interest in one horse: it seems likely that the feeling of power gained is a compensation for the absence of a penis and is fostered by the erotic stimulation of horseback riding. As the girl approaches ten and is almost prepubertal, she is likely to dress in blue jeans, walk in giggling groups, and have a need for almost constant companionship. She may leave her girl friends after several hours of chatter but find that by the time she reaches home there is so much to say that she must continue on the telephone.

The gender role patterning is continuing in various subtle ways. The girl remains closer to the home; she finds her interest in people and their interactions; she is less concerned with competitive activities. Her value system remains more like that of her parents and, perhaps, girls tend to develop less independent ways of thinking. Her self-image depends to some extent upon her girl friends' evaluations of her, but it will develop more definitely later in relation to boys. Some girls will become tomboys for a time, and gain acceptance by the boys and inclusion in their games. "She's O.K., she's not a girl," will be the boy's attitude and the girl finds this a high accolade. The tomboy ways usually fade in the prepubertal period when the girl begins to desire a different type of acceptance from

* Boys tend to have more difficulties in the early grades, and more frequently develop reading difficulties, tics, or mannerisms. Girls are developmentally more advanced, and also tend to be less restless. For reasons that have been presented, the boy is likely to be restive with mother figures, and, on the other hand, the woman teacher is likely to understand the girl's attitudes and behavior better than the boy's.

boys. Sometimes, of course, the tomboyish behavior reflects profound dissatisfaction with being female and forebodes serious gender identity problems. One girl insisted that she was a girl only because her mother dressed her as one, attempted to deny physical differences, and encountered profound problems when she started to menstruate which she sought to resolve by becoming a nun. Another learned to relate to boys as another boy, and eventually married a man who was unconsciously seeking a close relationship with another man as much as with a woman.

Cognitive Development

The Transition from Preoperational Thought to the Period of Concrete Operations

The child who enters the first grade is still in the preoperational stage of development described in Chapter 7, and even though he enters the period of concrete operations at about the age of seven or eight, the transition to logical ways of thinking occurs slowly. It is difficult for adults to realize the limitations of the juvenile's cognitive capacities and ethical evaluations, and unrealistic expectations by teachers as well as parents can be the source of many serious difficulties for the child. The second or third grader continues to confuse his fabulations with reality and is amazingly unconcerned about obvious contradictions in his statements and reasoning. Furthermore, he is likely to make false statements or answers with a conviction that seems to derive from the belief that something is so because he believes it so. Efforts to have him explain just how he sought to solve a problem indicate that he still cannot think about his thinking.

Thus, many eight- and nine-year-olds explained that placing a stone in a glass of water raised the level because the stone is heavy. However, to cite one example, when an eight-year-old was asked if wood was heavy, he said it was light. Still, he expected it would make the water rise—because it was light, and knew that it would make it rise more than the stone because it was bigger. Yet, when asked why a stone made the water rise, he again responded, "Because it is heavy." He cannot handle the several factors of heaviness, lightness, and size at the same time.* Although problems of egocentricity are fading, they still present notable difficulties. A child of nine or ten may have trouble realizing that if he traveled abroad he would be a foreigner, or that an American can be an

* J. Piaget, *Judgment and Reasoning in the Child*,[12] pp. 181–182.

enemy. As Piaget noted, even family relationships that seem so obvious are not altogether clear to a nine-year-old— "She has two sisters, she is not a sister" is a common type of confusion.* Names also cause perplexity. When a nine-year-old is asked whether a pencil knows its name, he is certain that it does "because it is written on it where it is made." † Further, the child explains why things have names— "It is called the sun because it shines." ‡—and not until some time between the ages of ten and twelve does the child appreciate that such names are arbitrary. There is still difficulty in judging what is alive—and life is often attributed to a river, the wind, the sun, for example, because they move, and such objects may be considered to be capable of feeling and perhaps perceiving.§

Piaget has emphasized the preoperational child's inability to carry out the essential operations of *conservation* and *reversibility*. Thus, after two identical glass beakers are filled with water to the same level, the water from one is poured into a wider beaker. The child is then asked which beaker, the wider or narrower, contains more water.The child either says that the wider beaker has less water because it does not rise as high in the beaker; or, focusing on the width, that it contains more water. He does not appreciate that if the operation were reversed the water would be at the same level in the two original beakers. He does not retain the original image in deciding the issue, or mentally reverse the procedure. He also is still unable to utilize two factors at a time. If he considers the width of the beaker, he does not simultaneously consider the height. Similarly, when a ball of plasticine is molded into a sausage shape, the child does not realize that it still contains the same quantity of the material. Piaget has tended to emphasize the importance of reversibility in analyzing this type of failure.|| The school-age child will gradually master problems at this level. At least some of the child's increased cognitive capacities on such tests relate to improved linguistic abilities which help him remember the earlier state and to keep one factor constant while considering the others, and so on.

* *Ibid.*, p. 75.
† J. Piaget, *The Construction of Reality in the Child*,[14] p. 79.
‡ *Ibid.*, pp. 80–83.
§ These are simply random illustrations of the child's limitations. The reader is referred to Piaget's *Judgment and Reasoning in the Child* [12] and *The Construction of Reality in the Child* [14] for a more organized presentation and analysis of his findings.
|| See J. Flavell,[5] Chapter 5, and J. Piaget, *The Psychology of Intelligence*,[15] for further discussion of a complex topic that is not essential to this presentation.

The Capacity for Concrete Operations

Piaget has analyzed several of the juvenile's new cognitive capacities which are basic to other achievements. The child becomes able to classify objects in groups according to one or another attribute, such as shape, color, or size. He can carry out such simple classification by inspection without having words to designate the categories but the process is helped by his having terms to use. More complex classifications require the use of appropriate terms. The child also becomes capable of arranging objects in series, according to increasing size, weight, or depth of color, etc. At a somewhat older age the child can either classify objects or serialize them using two attributes such as size and shape simultaneously. Piaget terms these three operations *classification, seriation,* and *multiplication* and has devoted considerable time to analyzing their development both experimentally and through formulating models in terms of mathematical logic.

A critical aspect of many of these abilities seems to lie in the fact that the child gradually learns an increasingly integrated cognitive *system* with which to organize and manipulate the world around him and into which he can fit his experiences. He becomes less likely to fall into contradictions or even to judge things egocentrically when he can fit things into an organized approach to understanding experience.* Now, the child goes to school to learn just such organized approaches to mental activities. He learns the meanings of the words that are the culture's labels for its categories—that is, its ways of classifying objects or experiences. He learns syntax—the rules for logical operations. He learns mathematics—an approach to concrete and formal operations. He is also taught in more explicit fashion various ways of solving problems, and to think causally—that is, to seek determinants in precursors of events. Children in other cultures are taught different systems of logic.

In an earlier chapter we considered the difficulties imposed upon the child when he had to assimilate his experiences, not only to the schemata that he had gradually built up through his own experiences, but also to the schemata that the culture had built up and conveyed to him through language. The school-age child is acquiring an ever increasing knowledge of the world, and the gap between what he experiences himself and what

---

* Representational acts that Piaget terms *operations* are an integral part of an organized network or system of interrelated acts. See also B. Inhelder and J. Piaget, *The Growth of Logical Thinking from Childhood to Adolescence,*7 Chapters 1, 2, and 3, for a systematic study of the schoolchild's developing intellectual abilities.

he hears or reads about lessens. He now not only accommodates his own schemata but his understanding of the culture's schemata, and what he learns "secondhand" becomes a more integral part of him. His schemata and those of the culture are being integrated. However, as we shall see, it is not until about the end of the grade school period that major confusions drop out.

The older juvenile is moving through this phase of concrete operations toward the stage of formal operations that he may reach early in adolescence.* A brief comparison of the concrete and formal operations will help convey the limitations of the juvenile's thinking. In the period of concrete operations the child can deal with systematic reasoning about situations which confront him or which he can imagine in a visual or tangible form. Concrete ideas are "internalized actions" according to Piaget. To carry out formal operations the child must become capable of thinking in propositions, using hypotheses and carrying out operations that are abstracted from concrete examples. It is a matter of carrying out "pure reasoning." Formal operations require considerable educational training, for only a very exceptional person can reach this stage of mental functioning on his own, if, indeed, it is possible for anyone. We can assert fairly definitely that the capacity for formal operations does not come simply with maturation, as a large segment of the population, even in industrial societies, does not reach this level.

The capacities for carrying out concrete operations may depend upon processes of maturation, but the school environment forces the child to recognize contradictions and to learn to think logically as well as supplying both information and techniques for reasoning. However, cognitive progress also requires gaining experience in new environments that overcome the child's egocentricity by making him realize that other children may regard things differently from the way he does, and that other adults, such as teachers, have different ideas and values than his parents. Although we cannot examine here what is taught in school, it is important to examine the classroom environment and its impact on the child's personality functioning.

The Classroom as a Socializing Agency

The school has the express function of teaching the child the knowledge and skills he will require in order to function as a reasonably self-sufficient adult in society. It is a major socializing agency, taking over from the family and implementing the family's functions. However, it

* The stage of formal operations will be discussed more fully in Chapter 10.

does not function simply through its expertise in educational matters. Because of the nature of the classroom as a social system, the school can carry out socializing functions different from those with which the parents are concerned, a process in which both teachers and classmates play a part.[11]

The Teacher's Role

The school serves as the first significant institution which differentiates children on the basis of achievement. The parents have accepted the child simply because he is theirs—an acceptance and affection through ascription which the child continues to need in order to feel emotionally secure. Status in the classroom is established by differences in performance on tasks set by the teacher, who is acting for the community's school system. This shift to being evaluated through achievement rather than ascription is fundamental to how the child learns who he is and what he can expect of himself. Although the child may be old enough to start finding his way in the world, he is far from ready to lose parental affection and protection if he cannot live up to expectations. Further, the parents are emotionally unsuited to evaluating the child on merit alone. They have a strong investment in him, and his well-being is a major factor in their own lives. The teacher, in contrast, has an obligation not to let the emotional needs of a child influence her evaluation of his achievement level. It is incumbent upon her to evaluate him fairly and serve as the agent for bringing about a differentiation of the children in the class on the basis of how well they can learn and assume responsibilities. The ethical development of the children, their willingness to accept the teacher's authority, and the children's evaluations of themselves depend upon the teacher's objectivity and fairness. Now, of course, the difference between parental and teacher roles is not so sharp as has been stated. The teacher, particularly in the early grades, often treats the children in a somewhat motherly manner and will take individual shortcomings into account; and the parents reinforce the school's influence by rewarding the child's school achievement and through conveying expectations that he will strive to do well. Many children soon learn that their mother's happiness and satisfaction with them fluctuate with their grades and class standings. Serious emotional problems and blocks to learning can follow when parents let their own affection and acceptance of the child depend on his school achievement.*

---

* Thus, a mother whose only way of feeling adequate and comparable with her peers had been to be the leading student in each grade, became very upset when

The Classmates' Role

The child's classmates also enter into the socialization process and the reorganization of the child's personality. The child is not only evaluated by his teachers in relationship to his fellow students and thus placed in competition with them, but he is also evaluated by classmates according to different standards. He learns to balance adult and children's values, seeking approval from both. He now also identifies with his age group in contrast to his identification with parents and teachers. It is a step that dilutes the intrafamilial identifications and starts a new group loyalty in which the child will identify with leaders of his own generation.* The peer group in school usually has a less personal relationship to the child than does the neighborhood group, and also differs in that it is supervised by an adult authority rather than being on its own. The child's personality gains complexity by his having to find ways of relating to three or more groups of which he is a member and still maintain an identity: to the family group; to the school group, both as student and as classmate; to the neighborhood peer group, free of adult presence.

The Stresses of Starting School

As eagerly as the child has looked forward to becoming a schoolchild, the new situation commonly places him under considerable emotional strain. He does not know how to respond to the teacher, who though a woman much like his mother is very different from her. He is not accustomed to being judged on his merits and being graded in relation to a large group of other children. He finds his individual needs are often ignored, and sometimes a trait that his parents have considered lovable or a reason to be lenient—such as a speech defect—is only an embarrassing handicap that the teacher strives to correct. He cannot evade rules by being cute or by crying. He finds himself in a secondary role to brighter children and may feel inadequate or stupid. The uneasiness reactivates wishes to regress, and his behavior can become more babyish for a time. The child may seek reasons to avoid going to school, and often illness becomes the only acceptable way out, so that he may use hypochondria-

---

her son had difficulties in learning to read and was in the lower half of his first- and second-grade classes. She sought to coach him, but became intolerant of his "stupidity" and conveyed rather directly that she could not love a poor student; and before long the boy had developed a serious learning block as well as a reading problem.
* Freud in "Group Psychology and the Analysis of the Ego" considers the unity of the group in terms of such common identifications.[6]

cal complaints, which need not be feigned, for anxiety creates feelings of dis-ease, and physical symptoms are a simple way of expressing a need for help. The problems usually pass as the child gains familiarity with the situation and makes friends with classmates. When a school phobia develops, the child is responding to his mother's anxiety that her child cannot manage without her; to fears that the mother will desert him while he is in school, or to jealousy of siblings still at home.

The Family Social Background and School Achievement

Children from deprived homes and even children from the lower socio-economic levels generally enter school with serious disadvantages; and, unless special efforts are made, the disadvantages can increase in school. The teachers are assessing and rewarding the child for cognitive abilities and for "citizenship"—reliability in meeting obligations and commitments as well as class conduct. Despite their efforts to evaluate and reward children on an egalitarian basis, teachers are human and usually become more involved with the intelligent, knowledgeable, and better-mannered children. The teacher's interest in a child and her expectations for higher performance levels appear to stimulate the development of intelligence as well as improve learning.* However, quite aside from the teacher's interest, the school system favors children who have been prepared in the home to be verbal, curious, motivated to learn, and to control distracting impulses.

Children from families of the higher socio-economic levels, which are also usually the better educated, have been exposed to more diverse information and to much more verbal interchange, although they often have had less experience with diverse situations.† Fluent verbal abilities do not simply reflect higher intelligence but enter into creating higher intelligence. How much intelligence level depends upon innate endowment and how much upon experience remains uncertain. Nature and nurture are both important, and experience, particularly experience in the first years of life, influences the intelligence levels markedly. Many intelligence tests tend to reward high verbal abilities and therefore help

---

* R. Rosenthal found that when teachers were told that certain students had unusual potential, these students showed a rise in I.Q., whereas a control series of matched students did not show a rise.[16]
† Whereas exposure to a wider range of families, to more street play, to seeing more of the "world" in slum areas may foster greater self-sufficiency and overcome an egocentric orientation, such premature exposure may deprive a child of the stability and relative freedom from tension that are conducive to learning.

select out children from educated homes as having better potential. Although tests can be utilized that minimize the influence of language skills and give a better index of the deprived child's potential capacities, they cannot eliminate the effects of early education completely.* It is becoming increasingly apparent that early experiences within the family strongly influence school achievement.

Intelligence and Family Background

The correlation between children's intellectual abilities and their parents' educational level or social status had formerly been widely accepted as an indication of the overriding importance of heredity in determining intelligence. Schooling was offered to all and the child would use as much of it as he was capable. There was concern that economic or emotional factors prevented some bright children from gaining as much edu-

---

* The Intelligence Quotient, or I.Q., is determined by giving tests that measure a person's mental age—how the problems he can solve match the median of an age group. The mental age, divided by the chronological age, multiplied by 100, yields the I.Q. (M.A./C.A. $\times$ 100 = I.Q.), which is supposed to remain fairly constant throughout life. If a child is ten years old and solves problems that a twelve-year-old is expected to solve, his I.Q. is 120. As the mental age does not increase very much after the age of fifteen or sixteen, an arbitrary upper limit of fourteen, fifteen, or sixteen is set for the chronological age (differing according to the standardization of the specific test) in calculating I.Q.'s of older adolescents and adults. As the I.Q. usually remains fairly constant throughout life, its use to predict the child's future potential for learning has been very successful despite occasional errors. Thus, I.Q.'s determined in the early school grades often influence teachers' appraisals of the child and advice given concerning the child's educational prospects. However, the child's I.Q. can often be modified by special educational efforts, particularly in the preschool years. The improvement may sometimes be maintained because of the child's improved abilities in school, but it may also be necessary to maintain a stimulating home environment or provide continued special tutoring. "Operation Head Start," the current effort to prepare underprivileged children for school by special education, depends upon such considerations, and experiences with the program will help solve many matters that currently are based partly on conjecture.

Stating the child's intellectual potential in terms of I.Q. has certain shortcomings —particularly of a statistical nature—and the results of tests are now often provided in terms of the percentile of children of the age tested into which the individual fits. A child in the fifth percentile is among the dullest 5 per cent, one in the ninety-fifth percentile is among the brightest 5 per cent. Other test results are given in terms of direct scores, sometimes arranged to approximate I.Q. levels.

I.Q.'s between 90 and 110 are considered normative. Children with I.Q.'s below 80 will have considerable difficulty keeping up with a normal class or in moving past the eighth grade. Children with I.Q.'s above 125 are apt to be bored with routine class work. Children who are idiots, due to a congenital abnormality or brain damage that affects cerebral functioning, fall outside of the bell-shaped distribution curves for intelligence found in the general population.

cation as they could utilize. Currently, however, there is a strong trend to consider that providing equal educational opportunity means instituting measures to develop the latent intellectual abilities of deprived children. Changes in the polity of the nation are involved. Efforts to raise the socio-economic and educational level of the Negro population and other impoverished groups relate to the rapidly diminishing need for unskilled labor as well as to democratic ideals. The task cannot be accomplished within a few years, and faces the difficulty that underprivileged families do not provide the necessary background.* However, unless we believe that it is possible to change the intellectual and educational level of the children of the underprivileged, no proper attempts to do so will be made.

The underprivileged child often enters school with other disadvantages. Unfamiliar with middle-class standards, he may be perplexed by the value systems he encounters. His parents do not provide models of intellectual achievement with whom to identify, and often have little interest in his achievement. Children from minority groups have difficulty fitting into the peer group and identifying with it. Neighborhood schools tend to lessen the impact when neighborhoods contain families of similar economic and ethnic backgrounds, but a school filled with children from deprived homes does not constitute a suitable environment for efforts to raise the cognitive level of the students. In any event, unless the school serves a very homogeneous community, the child now must come to grips with status problems based on social class and ethnic backgrounds. The attitudes toward the underprivileged child and toward his family enter into his self concept, into his evaluation of his parents as models, and his commitment to the values of the society.

The Development of Moral Judgment

The juvenile's moral and ethical values also change profoundly. The school influences him by introducing different and more impartial stand-

---

* The child's language and speech not only reflect his social background but constantly reinforce the social structure of which he is a part and which has entered into the formation of his personality. Lower-class speech patterns are limited verbally, relying heavily upon the common unspoken assumptions of speaker and listener, and they tend to deal with tangible concrete situations. The children are also apt to be taught obedience to rules without explanations in personal terms of why certain behaviors are desired or required, a training which does not encourage reasoning or promote curiosity. The child does not acquire the tools needed for intellectual achievement.[2]

ards than the home, and through being a more formalized representative of community values. However, the peer group and the neighborhood group in particular, the juvenile subculture, begins to exert a profound effect upon the child's value systems.

Adults commonly have difficulty appreciating the limitations of the child's understanding of right and wrong and the way in which he judges others as well as himself. The superego does not emerge like Pallas Athena, full-grown and -armed, out of the father's head at the closing of the oedipal period. The young child has neither the experience nor the intellectual capacities to use judgment rather than adhere to rules as he understands them. He tends to follow superego edicts in the form of internalized adult commandments which he reifies into immutable rules much more than he follows ethical values about which he can reason. In a sense, we are interested in noting how the child learns to make moral evaluations suited to circumstances rather than following relatively inflexible superego dictates. The superego and personal judgments will conflict throughout life: the superego will dictate at times and furnish reference points at others, but the ego gains the ability to make some ethical decisions on the basis of values gained through experience.

Ethical development, very much like intellectual growth, depends upon gaining experience and relating to different people in various settings, which gradually diminishes the child's egocentricity. Even within his home the child must learn that ethical values do not follow the "pleasure principle" but often require him to rescind immediate gratifications for future goals or to maintain the affection of parents. His desires are sadly not a criterion of what is "good" or "just." Later, he must move beyond simply accepting parental values as infallible guides. It is through interacting with adults whose values differ from those of his parents, and whose edicts he is less likely to consider immutable, and by learning to relate to peers and accept their very different perspectives that the child gradually learns to consider a person's intent and the specific circumstances in making moral evaluations.

The child of three or four does not have a real appreciation of rules when he tries to play games: he imitates using rules but he is apt to bend them to his need to win. The child of seven or eight not only learns rules and adheres to them reasonably well but is likely to consider the rules of a game immutable. They are inherent in the game, or imposed by a higher authority, and cannot be changed by mutual agreement. Thus, a boy of eight who moved to a different town complained bitterly that the neighborhood boys were stupid because their rules for playing marbles differed from those used in his former community. To the youngster, his new friends did not have different rules; they did not know the rules. A child at this age is also likely to judge culpability in terms of the damage done. The boy who accidentally bats a baseball through a store-front window is considered guiltier than a child who spitefully throws a stone through a windowpane in his friend's house. The child of eight or nine does not clearly know the difference between a lie and a mistake, and he will judge the guilt of a falsehood according to its magnitude. A "whopper" may be deemed a worse offense than a small lie told to cheat someone. By the onset of puberty the child considers rules as a type of contract capable of being changed by consent and that intent is important in evaluating guilt.[13]

From Morality of Constraint to Morality of Cooperation

The schoolchild exhibits what Piaget terms a *morality of constraint*. He usually has rigid standards about punishments, considering that the same punishment should be meted out for the same infraction regardless of circumstances. He believes that a four-year-old who breaks a dish should be reprimanded or punished in the same way as a ten-year-old; or that a hungry nursery school child should be expected to await his turn just like his older brother. This is a type of morality that develops because the immature and egocentric child accepts his position as inferior to the adult and accepts the adult's value system though he does not properly understand it. He usually must accept the adult edict or risk punishment. The adult, if challenged, is likely to bolster the rules he imposes by referring to essentially impersonal superordinate authorities such as the Deity, the police, or the school principal. From the child's vantage point, the consequences rather than the intent were important. It is not that what is bad is punished but what is punished is what is bad.* As the child passes his first decade, he begins to attain a *morality of cooperation* according to which the motivation and social implication of acts are appreciated. He also moves beyond seeking expiatory punishments in which the punishment fits the crime—a child is deprived of

* In a study of delinquents and their parents, the author and his colleagues noted that parents often had the attitude that a delinquent act was reprehensible only if the adolescent was caught at it; and they seemed to teach their children that what one says is more important than what one does. These adolescents seemed to regard laws and rules as arbitrary, and therefore a focus of rebellion against parents.

candy in proportion to the size of the dish he has broken or to the number of failing grades he received. He begins to comprehend punishment by reciprocity, as when a child who refuses to help his mother wash the dishes can expect his mother to refuse to drive him to the store when he wants to buy a comic book.[13]

The progression from a morality of constraint to a morality of cooperation depends upon the social environment in which the child lives. Rigid and arbitrary parents and teachers foster fixation at the earlier level. The teacher has the task of modifying the child's morality to a form that will enable him to use judgment and that will be of value in adult life, but schools with rigid disciplines prefer to maintain authoritarian standards. Progressive schooling encourages group activities and projects which require the children to formulate rules of procedure, and thus learn from experience why and how rules are made. It is clear, however, that the neighborhood peer group plays an extremely important role in the child's ethical development, for it is here that children must govern themselves, learn how to get along with one another, take the shortcomings of others into account, and where they wish to be judged in terms of intent rather than performance.[9] It seems very likely that peer-group activities during grade school are important preparation for democratic rather than authoritarian value systems.

The Society of Playmates

The society of playmates has a socializing influence as a subculture of its own. It is not a haphazard assemblage of children occupied with random activities. It is a subculture with mores that are transmitted relatively independently of either the family or the school, passed on from one age group to the next in a constant succession and with a turnover that is much more rapid than the generational cycle of the family. Each child remains in the juvenile period for a half-dozen years at the longest, and is replaced by another. There is constant movement of individuals into and out of the age group. The ways of the subculture are learned from the older children by the neophytes who hang on the periphery of the group, later assume fill-in roles, and then become members who gain increasing importance and responsibility over the next few years. The age roles are fairly well set and afford an opportunity to each child according to his ability, and acceptance according to his worth to the peer group. The task of learning how to get along with the group and be evaluated on his own merit sets a very real challenge to the child.

Childhood peer-group activities and mores may remain more stable over generations than the mores of the larger society, and they are a force for conservatism. It is known that some games, and probably the customs that accompany them, go back to antiquity. The checkerboards and marble holes used by Roman children can be found scratched into stone floors in the Roman Forum. Two paintings by Breughel show sixteenth-century children engaged in games most of which are readily recognized from their similarities to contemporary games. The jokes which each child thinks are new and hastens to tell his parents are usually much older than the parents. The child is engaged primarily in the task of learning to live with his peers, and the world of the juvenile group may change less than the adult world.

The Developing Self Concept

The manner in which the juvenile gains a clearer concept of the self in his peer group or neighborhood gang is complicated and often subtle. He learns to see himself as others see him and according to rather relentless standards. We have noted that at this age children have rigid standards of what is right and wrong, for they consider ethical values as fixed rather than suited to the circumstances, and believe individuals should be judged according to egalitarian standards and punished in an expiatory manner. The gang has standards of what makes a good companion and a good member. They are based upon the achievements and attitudes of the child and they are not concerned with exonerating reasons. At this age the children are concerned with how good a playmate or companion another makes, not with the reasons why he is or he is not. Important to the group are loyalty; a willingness to compromise and not insist on having one's own way; being a good "sport" in defeat; not being a "bully" who picks on smaller or weaker children; not being a "sorehead" who quits when decisions go against him, or a "crybaby" who runs home for parental help when teased or hit; not "snitching" on the gang even if others do something one thinks wrong. Honesty is a virtue, but the standards do not always agree with those of adults: "Finders keepers, losers weepers" is usually an acceptable guide for minor items; and "swiping" inexpensive objects from carts or chain stores, while considered dishonest, may not be deemed a real infraction. Such behavior is often a testing of limits, a response to taking a dare, a way of showing off; if one never goes beyond parental restrictions he is apt to be considered a "baby."

The threat of being called a "sissy," a term now partially replaced by "chicken," can force a boy to take a dare in order to prove himself to the gang. The child is in the process of learning for himself what challenges he can accept without coming to physical harm or suffering moral discomfort. Exclusion from the group brings intense unhappiness to most children, and a child will often prefer ridicule to being ignored, and will be the low man on the totem pole rather than feel unwanted. He will wear such nicknames as "Stinky" or "Dopey" in order to belong.

Athletic prowess is a very marked asset which may make a boy popular but not necessarily sought after as a friend. Athletics contribute to bringing more organization into the boys' groups as they grow older. The six- and seven-year-old cannot really play team games because he lacks the requisite coordination and ability to adhere to rules, but around nine or ten, groups may have more regular membership in order to be able to form teams. Regular teams and clubs require elected leaders and are usually very transient organizations until the boys gain enough maturity to be able to delegate authority and accept and provide leadership. The best athlete is not necessarily the leader. Even at this stage of life the leader must be able to forego his own interests for those of the group, and be fair in rendering judgments in order to preserve intragroup harmony. Reliability and responsibility—important assets in school—are also valued by the peer group, particularly when it reaches the stage of forming clubs and more permanent teams. Such peer evaluations may not only be of greater importance to the child than those of his teachers but his peers may also be more perceptive of values that count in the long run.

The Juvenile Peer Group or Gang

The term "gang" often has a bad connotation to parents. It conveys a vision of gang fights on city streets; of stealing, gambling, and narcotics peddlers. However, except in delinquent neighborhoods the gang is not an antisocial influence, nor does it provide a chaotic environment. It has an organization with rules and customs which have been transmitted by the juvenile subculture and which somehow are suited to the specific society to which the subculture belongs. Partly because of the erroneous conception of the children's peer groups conveyed by the term "gang," adults often seek to minimize peer-group influences by organizing Cub Scouts and Boy Scouts, and baseball teams supervised by adults in competitive leagues. Parents may send their children to private schools primarily to have them engage in the supervised play in the afternoons. Some supervision can be helpful, particularly in activities that require adult direction such as scouting or sailing, and there can be a pressing need for proper guidance in disorganized neighborhoods where children may readily come under delinquent influences. However, it is very important for peer groups to work out their own hierarchy and to set their own standards of behavior, learn to handle fights, deal with cheaters, and cope with less adaptable children. It is here that children gradually work out patterns of social interaction free from adult authority. They will make mistakes but they gain essential experience. It is here that they learn who they are, independently of adult evaluations.

Delinquent groups form problems in disorganized neighborhoods where children find acceptance and some center of loyalty in a gang which takes out its hostility toward a neglecting and untrustworthy adult world. Such gangs assume importance in adolescence, but the younger child mimics and hangs on to the gang members who are becoming his heroes through their defiance of adult authority. Although such antisocial gangs form subcultures that are antipathetic to adult society, the leaders are often following what they have been openly or covertly taught by their parents—to distrust others, to flout authority, to get the better of outsiders, to get away with what one can, to take out their unhappiness on other ethnic groups, etc. Members of such groups even in poor neighborhoods tend to be recruited from the more disorganized homes.[3] In better neighborhoods, children with antisocial tendencies often manage to find one another and form groups even when they form a very small minority and are without honor among their other age mates.

Sexual Interests

All juvenile peer groups are likely to carry out some activities which adults consider undesirable. The children will start using scatological words and engage in sex talk, progressing to telling stories that none of the group will admit not understanding. This is in part a penetrating into the mysteries of the adult world, in part a token of flaunting parental prohibitions as an indication of growing independence, and a means of gaining admiration by being more in the know than others. It is also a way of trying to share the fantasies of sex that the child experiences in private. The boys may have contests to see how far they can urinate, and compare the size of their genitals, an activity that may help overcome

feelings of inadequacy derived from seeing adult genitalia. Some indulge in masturbation in one another's presence or with one another.
Such sex play between boys or girls does not relate to homosexuality, as
parents often fear, but is usually a movement from narcissistic preoccupations to heterosexual interests through a phase of sharing with someone like the self. Some visual or physical exploration of children of the
same or opposite sex is fairly common during the so-called "latency"
period, but it is just as likely to happen in the home with siblings of the
opposite sex or the friends of siblings as in the gang. At any rate, the boy
who is not accepted in the neighborhood gang may have difficulty progressing to relate to girls in adolescence, or may gravitate to less desirable
groups composed of outsiders who are likely to indulge in more marginal
sexual and social activities. However, such undesirable activities usually
form a very minor part of the juvenile's life. The children are too absorbed
in all the new experiences available to them to become engrossed with
sex, and gang fights are a rarity except in disorganized neighborhoods.
The children have found a "moral equivalent for war" [8] by competing in
sports according to rules, and they are engaged in the process of learning
cooperative interaction.

Modification of Family Values

In these children's groups new sets of values are learned which may or
may not fit with those of the family. The child comes into intimate
contact with the value systems of his friends. He enters into other homes
and sees how they are conducted. The child learns how his friends are
treated by their parents and notes the different ways in which families
behave and compares the differing degrees of calm or friction within
other households to the atmosphere in his own home. He acquires a
basis on which he can judge his parents as individuals rather than continue his family-centered orientation toward them. He may learn better
to appreciate his own parents or may come to develop bitterness toward
them, but these experiences permit him to develop a perspective and
more realistic values and judgments.

There are limits to the broadening influences exerted by the child's
"gang." As the gang is usually formed in the neighborhood it is apt to
be constituted of children from families who are relatively homogeneous
economically and socially, and often also with respect to ethnic and religious backgrounds. The childhood peer groups thus continue to help
pattern and prepare the child for the type of life expected from persons

of a given family type. Even in heterogeneous neighborhoods children are surprisingly selective in the choice of companions, tending to pick friends who come from similar backgrounds and with similar levels of intelligence because they understand one another better.

The juvenile group has different ideals from those of the family, and the child idealizes new models whom he would like to emulate. One can say that the child's "ego ideal" becomes modified by incorporation of these new figures, or the term "ideal ego" can be used to signify the image of the person one would like to become. The new models are taken from both life and literature: the adolescent athlete in the neighborhood whom the child glorifies; the teacher, coach, scout leader whose achievements or kindness make him seem a more desirable model than a parent; the baseball hero one reads about in the papers; inventors, scientists, storybook heroes. A girl is likely to develop a crush on a teacher whom the girls all admire or on a girl friend of an older sibling who seems so glamorous. Occasionally one sees abrupt changes in a child's behavior when the boy or girl takes on a role as if donning a new garment and begins to act the part. More conventionally a boy will begin to eat and sleep baseball, insist on wearing the baseball cap and shirt, and mimic the gait of his hero, for this is a time of hero worship. The girl may assume the characteristics of a movie actress. The models are apt to disappear almost as rapidly as they are taken on, for the child is subject to the fads and whims of the group.

The Special Friend

At about the age of ten the center of the child's life moves from the group of peers to a special friend, the "chum" in Sullivan's terms, who is distinguished from all other friends by a special intonation when the child refers to "my friend."* It is an intense and important experience, for the relationship usually constitutes the child's first major realistic attachment outside of his family. The friend is of the same sex because sharing feelings and experiences with another and thereby achieving empathy can occur only with a person of the same sex at this age. The intimate exchange helps diminish feelings of uniqueness, enables each to learn how another person feels about and manages similar problems. It is an expansion of the self beyond one's own boundaries. There is a constant need to be with the chum, and an altruistic attitude develops in which the friend's welfare is almost as important as one's own. The

* Harry Stack Sullivan, *The Interpersonal Theory of Psychiatry*,[17] pp. 227–262.

friendship is the first movement toward intimacy that develops on the basis of common personality traits and ideals rather than through family relatedness. As psychoanalytic psychology has shown, this first close friendship contains homosexual components—a narcissistic quality of loving and sharing with someone like the self—but it is not an indication of homosexuality but of movement toward learning to relate intimately beyond the family. If a fixation occurs at this stage, it is more likely to indicate disturbances in the family relationships rather than that something is wrong in the friendship.

Growing Up without Playmates

Although the peer group and special friend are usually very important to the schoolchild's development, they are not a vital part of every childhood. Not all settings provide groups of peers as playmates; and some children are constrained from joining in the collective activities for reasons of health, because of parental restrictions, or because they are, for various reasons, "loners." The son of the school principal or the clergyman may feel that he is different and is treated as an outsider by his peers. The child from a minority group that is unwelcome in the community can be left very isolated though potential playmates abound. Such conditions are often trying for the child but they are not necessarily injurious to his development, particularly if he can maintain pride in himself and his family. The child does not learn to conform as rapidly or learn how to evaluate himself in comparison with his peers so readily, but most children can find ways of keeping occupied by themselves, utilizing their imagination and developing active fantasy lives, and perhaps special skills and hobbies. After all, it is difficult for a person to become truly creative if he has learned to be highly conventional and is so thoroughly grounded in the society's ways of regarding things, that all uniqueness of perception or reasoning is repressed early in life in favor of the society's norms. Fantasy is a precursor of creativity, and though fantasy activities can be shared by two or three it is not a group activity and usually flourishes on loneliness or isolation. Many a creative person feels himself something of an outsider because he has been subjected to two sets of cultural directives that prevent him from being as ethnocentrically oriented and as set in the cultural norms as most of his peers. The child who grows up without peers may have to lose his egocentricity later than other children; but he may not lose it to a degree that eliminates his individuality, which may flourish as originality or be noted as eccentricity. Still, only an occasional parent will purposefully promote a child's isolation for such reasons, as it entails some risk of leading to unhappiness and emotional instability, and instability occurs all too readily without being fostered.

New Ideals and Directives

One type of companionship is available to virtually all children who have had some schooling. The companionship of books and the characters who people them can fill the emptiness of lonely days and can transport the child from the isolated farm or fishing hamlet, or replace the dingy slum airshafts and alleys with prairie or castle. Books have furnished the vision of a different and more hopeful life that has motivated many; and have brought into a colorless or disorganized home the heroic models for identification that displaced the disheartening real models. They have taught the use of imagination and opened eyes to visions of beauty and ears to the sounds of beauty. The love of books and even the craving for books usually develops during the juvenile period. For most it is not a love of great literature, which is almost always beyond the child's comprehension of his limited world, and for many it starts with books of little merit beyond their inspirational and narrative values. The delight in reading and the enthusiasm for discovering new worlds in books is what counts. If children keep reading they will become bored with the tawdry and commonplace, and in proportion to their understanding progressively seek out books that provide new vision and perspective.

It is also during these grade school years when the child has gained a modicum of freedom from his home and family that other types of "rescue" operations sometimes alter the life of the child who has been raised in an unfortunate and distorting family environment. He now comes under the sway of new influences in school, in the neighborhood, and in his reading which can offset even though they cannot supplant the pervasive influence of parents and home. He may be included in the activities of a friend's family; a teacher, a social worker, a camp counselor takes an interest in him and becomes an ideal and a model. He spends summers with his grandparents or with an aunt or uncle.* In one way or another

---

* Samuel Butler, for example, after being pushed out of the frying pan of a rigid home with ununderstanding parents, was thrown into the fire of a boarding school that was intolerable to him; he was rescued by an aunt who happened to live near the school and who fostered his interest in music and playing the organ and engendered in him a confidence in himself that his parents had seemed bent on destroying under the guise of breaking his willfulness.

he learns that some path into the future exists, and confining gates can be opened and permit his entrance into a more hopeful world. If he is fortunate someone encourages him to start down the way and provides the emotional support he needs to move out and on. The family is the most important influence upon the child's development, but it is not the only influence and others can become increasingly significant.

Toward the end of the juvenile period, perhaps at a time when the girls are prepubertal, boys and girls may again gladly find companionship in mixed groups. The boys feel more secure in their male identity and will be able to enjoy girls with whom they are not competing. The groups can still be fairly spontaneous and provide an opportunity to gain some familiarity with the ways of the opposite sex before the shyness and tension that come with adolescence disrupt the ease of the situation.

New Sources of Anxiety and Despair

Although late childhoood is so often remembered nostalgically as a time of freedom and of outgoing activities, it contains ample sources of anxiety and discomfort. There are, of course, the problems that derive from unresolved difficulties at early developmental stages, such as the residues of the intrafamilial oedipal conflicts and sibling rivalries, but the juvenile period in itself contains sources of anxiety and sometimes of depression. The child wishes independence but can readily suffer from the insecurities of having responsibility for his own welfare. Whereas he becomes angered at parents who limit his activities, he still needs to be dependent. Now, he can become more upset than previously over his conflicting emotions toward his parents and needs to find a way of resolving them. Further, it now becomes apparent to him that even with the best will in the world his parents cannot provide certain security for him. They are not omnipotent or omniscient, and the child now knows that they may die and leave him. His death wishes, conscious and unconscious, become more frightening and anxiety provoking. The girl is often still caught up in her oedipal problems and as she grows older may become more guilt ridden by her rivalrous feelings toward her mother as well as her fantasies about possessing her father. Then, too, the parents have expectations concerning the child's achievement, expectations which he also holds for himself; and there are inevitable failures when self-esteem may be seriously threatened. He is afraid or ashamed to show his grades to his parents and ashamed that his friends will consider him stupid. There are bitter days when he feels left out by the gang for reasons he cannot fathom, or days of shame and self-reproach when he feels that he has behaved in ways that are unaccoptable to his friends, or when he has let his best buddy down. Even though it is a time of transition and trying out, the juvenile may become despondent about his prospects.

Juvenile Defenses against Anxiety

Just as at other phases of development, the juvenile is apt to defend against anxieties by regressing. He seeks ways of being cared for by his parents by being ill, suffering injury, or by invoking pity because no one seems to want him. He may spend more and more time at home, giving up his efforts to become a member of the peer group where he must be responsible for himself. Most children will more or less consciously avoid some stresses at school or with peers by finding ways of staying home on occasion, but some retreat more permanently and will then be confronted by adolescence without adequate preparation in relating beyond the family. The common defensive patterns used at this time of life are those related to obsessive-compulsive patterns. Ritualistic behavior carried out to ward off harm and undo unacceptable wishes appears in almost every child. It is a resort to magical thinking in order to control exigencies beyond the child's control. He must avoid stepping on cracks in the sidewalk, or he must touch every lamp post, or get up on the same side of the bed every morning, put on the right shoe before the left shoe. If he fails, some harm will befall him or his parents, or if he carries out the ritual correctly some wish will be granted—the home team will win or he will get the examination grade he needs. He is seeking a means of controlling his impulses and controlling nature, just as a primitive person seeks to control the weather or the outcome of a hunt by practicing a ritual which cannot be altered in any detail. The ambivalent feelings toward parents and siblings and the fear that harm may come to them because of hostile feelings are of particular importance. Reaction formation, undoing, and isolation are the mechanisms of defense used in such obsessive ritualization. *Reaction formation,* we may recall, concerns the tendency to repress an unacceptable impulse or wish and manifest its opposite—as when a child becomes oversolicitous of his father's health after having hostile feelings toward him. *Undoing* consists of rituals or prayers that have the magical property of undoing a wish. *Isolation* has to do with the separation of affect and idea; the idea is somehow deprived of its emotional impact, often by keeping ideas from linking up which would force recognition of consequences and therefore arouse anxiety. Thus, when combined with undoing and reaction formation, prayers that the father not be killed in an auto accident prevent recognition of wishes that the father be killed in an accident.

The rituals may seem less strange when they are a component of prayers. The child may say his prayers in a set sequence as part of his efforts at achieving magical control. The rituals may reinforce superego controls by reminding him of the need for proper behavior. However, there is also a strong tendency to seek dependency upon a Deity who can omnipotently control what the parents cannot control or provide. At this age the child may gain solace from severe anxiety by feeling that God will take care of him if he behaves and prays properly.

This is also a time when fantasy helps compensate for feelings of inadequacy and paucity of achievement. Fantasy also plays the more positive role of providing an imagined future greatness that spurs the child to achievement. The daydreams are not subjected to much reality testing and are often formed on the basis of the child's growing hero worship, but as he grows older they either reflect some of his real assets or serve more clearly as compensations for feelings of inadequacy. The juvenile has his "Dreams of Glory," which have been pictured so ably in cartoons by Steig. He is the football player who arrives just in time to dash onto the field and score the winning touchdown before the final whistle blows; he is the general who saves the war by flying an old decrepit plane to shoot down the enemy plane carrying an H bomb: he is the first man to land on Mars. The girl may be the trained nurse who refuses the blindfold when she is executed as a spy; the princess at King Arthur's court whose glove the knight carries on his search for the Grail; the beautiful young woman whom the high school football hero asks to the senior prom. *Identification* is also helpful and blends with fantasy. The boy or girl identifies with a hero or a greatly admired person and feels capable of becoming as able and thereby more secure in facing the future, or more able to stand present inadequacies. Somewhat similarly, the juvenile may gain security and comfort in the reflection of a leader and willingly follows and becomes subservient to an older child who is much admired; or he gains self-esteem from being a member of a group—a club, a team, a school with prestige.

Fixation at the Juvenile Level

The juvenile period also has importance because of the tendency to regress to it—a tendency which may be particularly common in the United States where children are permitted to lead relatively carefree and independent lives. Later, when one must do well in order to gain admission to college or find advancement in an occupation, the competitions of boyhood seem gratifying. When sexual problems occur in adolescence or when marital difficulties create anxiety, the old days before members of the opposite sex were so important are idealized. The adult retains some of the pleasures of the period by spending his free time in sports, competing for fun rather than for keeps; or in still glorifying the athlete and identifying with him; in sharing in fantasy the new record in auto racing. Some of the brutality shown in films and on television, some of the ever-present interest in westerns and in whodunits may not be so much an outlet for unconscious sadism as a fixation at playing cowboys and Indians, or cops and robbers—a regaining of the pleasant feelings of childhood. The hours spent in stag activities, the evenings at the club or corner bar, the afternoons the women spend in card games, may reflect the wish to again be free of the cares of a bisexual society and the obligations that it entails. Some individuals will, of course, remain fixated in the period of late childhood and early adolescence, seeking to maintain life as it was and occupied with games and with the members of their own sex.

The juvenile period ends with the new spurt in physical growth that precedes the onset of puberty when the child begins to turn into an adolescent. In the half-dozen juvenile years the relationships within the family and the personality integration achieved with the closing of the oedipal period have had time to consolidate and defenses have become strengthened, enabling the child to be better prepared for the emotional upsurges which accompany puberty and which threaten the established equilibrium. It is erroneous, however, to consider such consolidations as the major task of the juvenile period. While his life has still had its center within the family, the child's environment has broadened as he ventured off to school and into play groups consisting of his peers. Adapting to these new environments and finding his place in them has required a substantial reorganization of the personality.

The child has been faced by the difficult reorientation of having his status determined by his achievements rather than through ascription. In his teachers he has been confronted by significant adults who have related to him very differently from his parents. He has become part of a group of student peers and learned to identify with them and to measure himself against them. In the neighborhood peer group he has begun to learn ways of living and relating himself as a member of his society and with its ideals and value systems. In these broader environments the child has had the opportunity to strengthen his gender identity, to become less dependent upon his parents and their values, to learn how others evaluate his capacities and how much they care for him as a person. In the process he moves a long way in forming a self-concept on which his own evaluation of himself and his future potentialities will rest. He has learned that status rests heavily upon industriousness and reliability; and he has learned industry, perhaps becoming compulsively competitive, or he may have tended to withdraw and no longer accept challenges.

Usually the child has formed his first intense extrafamily relationship which, although it is with a member of the same sex, forms an important step toward ultimately forming an intimate heterosexual relationship. The experiences beyond the family, both in school and with peer groups, enable the child to overcome his egocentric and family-centered orientations, an essential step in both intellectual and ethical development; his ego capacities are greatly increased and he becomes prepared to be able to guide himself when he enters adolescence and begins really to emerge from his family, and to utilize his judgment when beset by sexual impulsions that urge him toward immediate gratification.

References

1. Ruth Benedict, *Patterns of Culture* (New York: Penguin Books, 1934).
2. Basil Bernstein, "Social Class, Speech Systems and Psychotherapy," *British Journal of Sociology*, 15 (1964), 54 ff.
3. Isidor Chein, Donald Gerard, Robert Lee, and Eva Rosenfeld, *The Road to H: Narcotics, Delinquency, and Social Policy* (New York: Basic Books, 1964).
4. Erik H. Erikson, *Childhood and Society* (New York: W. W. Norton, 1950).
5. John H. Flavell, *The Developmental Psychology of Jean Piaget* (Princeton: Van Nostrand, 1963).
6. Sigmund Freud, "Group Psychology and the Analysis of the Ego" (1921), in *The Standard Edition of the Complete Psychological Works of Sigmund Freud*, Vol. 1 (London: Hogarth Press, 1955).
7. Bärbel Inhelder and Jean Piaget, *The Growth of Logical Thinking from Childhood to Adolescence*, trans. Anne Parsons and Stanley Milgram (New York: Basic Books, 1958).
8. William James, *A Moral Equivalent for War* (Belmont, Mass.: Wellington Books).
9. Morris M. Lewis, *Language, Thought and Personality in Infancy and Childhood* (New York: Basic Books, 1964), pp. 203–228.
10. George H. Mead, *Mind, Self, and Society: From the Standpoint of a Social Behaviorist*, ed. Charles W. Morris (Chicago: University of Chicago Press, 1934).
11. Talcott Parsons, "The School Class as a Social System: Some of Its Functions in American Society," *Harvard Educational Review*, 29 (1959), 297–318.
12. Jean Piaget, *Judgment and Reasoning in the Child*, trans. Marjorie Wardin (New York: Humanities Press, 1947).
13. Jean Piaget, *The Moral Judgment of the Child*, trans. Marjorie Gabain (Glencoe, Ill.: Free Press, 1948).
14. Jean Piaget, *The Construction of Reality in the Child*, trans. Margaret Cook (New York: Basic Books, 1954).
15. Jean Piaget, *The Psychology of Intelligence*, trans. Malcolm Piercy and D. E. Berlyne (Totowa, N. J.: Littlefield, Adams & Co., 1960).
16. Robert Rosenthal, *Experimenter Effects in Behavioral Research* (New York: Appleton-Century-Crofts, 1966).
17. Harry Stack Sullivan, *The Interpersonal Theory of Psychiatry* (New York: W. W. Norton, 1953).

Suggested Reading

Talcott Parsons, "The School Class as a Social System: Some of Its Functions in American Society," in *Social Structure and Personality* (New York: Free Press, 1964), pp. 129–154.

Jean Piaget, *The Moral Judgment of the Child*, trans. Marjorie Gabain (Glencoe, Ill.: Free Press, 1948).

Harry Stack Sullivan, *The Interpersonal Theory of Psychiatry* (New York: W. W. Norton, 1953), pp. 217–262.

U. S. Children's Bureau, *Your Child from Six to Twelve* (Washington, D.C.: U. S. Government Printing Office, n.d.).

CHAPTER 10 ³⁰

❀ ❀ ❀ ❀
❀ ❀ ❀ ❀ ❀

Adolescence

INTRODUCTION

IT IS A DIFFICULT TASK to attempt to convey what transpires during these years in which the child blossoms into an adult beset by conflicting emotions, struggling to maintain self-control and to achieve self-expression under the impact of sensations and impulses that are scarcely understood but insistently demand attention. It is a time of physical and emotional metamorphosis during which the youth feels estranged from the self the child had known. It is a time of seeking: a seeking inward to find who one is; a searching outward to locate one's place in life; a longing for another with whom to satisfy cravings for intimacy and fulfillment. It is a time of turbulent awakening to love and beauty but also of days darkened by loneliness and despair. It is a time of carefree wandering of the spirit through realms of fantasy and in pursuit of idealistic visions, but also of disillusionment and disgust with the world and the self. It can be a time of adventure with wonderful episodes of reckless folly but also of shame and regret that linger. The adolescent lives with a vibrant sensitivity that carries to ecstatic heights and lowers to almost untenable depths. For some, the emotional stability achieved in childhood and the security of the family attachments contain the amplitude of the oscillations and permit a fairly steady direction; whereas others must struggle to retain a sense of unity and a modicum of ego control.

Adolescence can be defined as the period between pubescence and physical maturity, but in considering personality development we are concerned with the transition from childhood, initiated by the pre-pubertal spurt of growth and impelled by the hormonal changes of puberty, to the attainment of adult prerogatives, responsibilities, and self-sufficiency. It involves the discrepancy between sexual maturation with the drive toward procreation and the physical, emotional, and social unpreparedness for commitment to intimacy and for caring for a new generation. In industrial technical societies, in particular, the movement from childhood to the adult generation requires many years of experience. Although adolescence currently covers the teen-age period, its onset varies with constitutional differences in times of sexual maturation and its duration is influenced by socio-economic and other cultural factors. The youth whose father is a laborer and who leaves school at sixteen to take a semiskilled job and marries at eighteen has a very brief adolescence. In contrast, the graduate student who is still undecided about his career at twenty-three and has another three or four years of study ahead of him may be considered an adolescent in some respects, for he is still unprepared to assume adult responsibilities at the high level for which he is preparing.

The passage through adolescence forms a critical period. At the start the child is still at play, dependently attached to his family and with a future that is still amorphous; and at the end he becomes responsible for himself, his personality has assumed its patterning, his direction in life is settled. The period leading up to the closure of adolescence is particularly important, for now the personality must gel into a workable integrate. Achieving a successful integration depends upon a reasonably successful passage through all prior developmental stages, but also upon the solution of a number of tasks specific to adolescence which leads to a reintegration and reorganization of the personality structure to permit the individual to function as a reasonably self-sufficient adult. One of Erikson's major contributions to psychoanalytic developmental psychology was his emphasis upon the crucial importance of late adolescence. Now, the young person must gain an ego identity, an identity in his own right and not simply as someone's son or daughter, an identity in the sense of a unique consistency of behavior that permits others to have expectations of how he will behave and react. He will have, in a sense, answered the question "Who am I?" and therefore others will know who he is. The achievement of an ego identity usually requires the concurrent attainment of the capacity to move toward interdependence with a person of the opposite sex: an intimacy that properly encompasses far more than the capacity to have sexual relations, or even to enjoy orgastic pleasure in the act. It concerns an ability to dare to form a significant relationship without fear of loss of the self.* But adolescence is contemporaneously a lengthy developmental stage, and there are various other developmental tasks that must be carried out before an ego identity and a capacity for intimacy can be attained.

Whatever equilibrium had been established that permitted the relative calm of the latency period is upset by the biological changes that usher in puberty. First, the child finds himself growing away from his childhood as the prepubertal spurt of growth places an increasing distance between his eyes and his feet, and his size alone begins to proximate him to the adult world. Then, the maturation of secondary sexual characteristics tends further to estrange the child from his body, and soon thereafter an upsurge of sexual feelings that intervene in fantasy, dreams, thoughts, and behavior alters the young person's feelings about himself and those close to him. Even as his self-image and his perspective of the world is changing, and as his emotions and sensitivities come under the impact of new sensations and compelling drive impulses, equally profound changes in intellectual capacities occur, for the adolescent becomes capable of conceptual thinking, or in Piaget's terms, enters into the stage of formal operations. It is important that the tasks and conflicts imposed by biological ripening are usually accompanied by an increased intellectual potential to help cope with them.

Adolescence is a period during which the youth can prepare for self-sufficiency and independence while still gaining support, protection, and guidance from his family. The need to gain increasing independence from his parents creates serious difficulties both for the youth and for his

---

* Erikson considers the gaining of an ego identity as the primary task of adolescence and an essential precursor of the capacity for intimacy.[4] For reasons that will be presented in the discussion of late adolescence, I consider these two tasks as interrelated, moving ahead in steplike phases that alternate or provide support for one another, with the final phases of gaining a capacity for intimacy following the achievement of an independent identity.

family. The teen-ager's situation becomes increasingly paradoxical, for even as he is becoming a member of the adult generation, he remains a member of the childhood generation within his family where he lacks certain adult prerogatives and opportunities for self-completion. The movement beyond the family gains impetus from the upsurge of sexual drives. In contrast to the erotized and sensuous longings and desires of the oedipal period, sexual feelings are now driven by hormonal impulsions and are not easily repressed. The thoughts and feelings instigated by the drive naturally tend to attach to those who have been sources of love and affection, but run up against the generation boundaries, the incest taboo, and the guilt and fears that had been evoked earlier and brought closure to the oedipal phase. Now, however, repression cannot be as successful as earlier, and the sexual feelings must be redirected out of the family circle.

It seems essential to emphasize that the genital sexuality of adolescence is very different from oedipal and pre-oedipal sexuality. Freud tended to obscure the difference in order to accentuate the pervasive influence of sexuality before puberty. Prepubertal sexuality concerns erotic and sensuous aspects of affectional attachments, including the influence of stimulation of erogenous zones, upon general attitudes, thoughts and behavior, but it is not drive-impelled in the same sense as adolescent and adult sexuality; it does not involve increased hormonal secretions, a need to discharge sperm and semen, shifts in the menstrual cycle, or the increased erogenous sensitivity that follows the maturation of sexual organs at puberty. It is essential to any coherent theory and description of personality development to differentiate between pre- and post-pubertal sexuality.

Both the move toward independence from the family and the control and redirection of sexual impulsions require reorganization of the superego. Although the youth may continue to accept and adhere to parental standards in many areas, they should become his own standards rather than something imposed; they should become more completely internalized and, as far as some directives are concerned, become more ego functions rather than superego edicts.[9] The superego must also change to become suited to help direct adult rather than childhood behavior and to permit sexual gratification and intimacy.

An important aspect of finding an adult identity and becoming capable of intimacy involves the clarification and strengthening of gender identity. Gender identity, as we have noted, becomes established within the first few years of life and is strengthened by the resolution of the oedipal phase and by peer-group identifications during latency. However, during adolescence the choice of a love object of the opposite sex helps to settle residues of identifications with the parent of the opposite sex and desires for the physical attributes and social prerogatives of the other sex. The process involves different tasks for the boy and the girl. The boy, in preparation for his adult role, must more clearly overcome dependency upon his mother in order to become able to assume a protective role toward a wife and to fill his more instrumental role in his family and in society. The girl now completes the resolution of her oedipal attachment to her father and becomes motivated to find gratification and erotized attachments outside the family; but her social role permits more continued dependency upon parents. The dynamics of these vicissitudes in the choice of love objects, and their impact on the achievement of a firm sexual identity will be discussed more fully below.

The essential tasks of adolescence lead to conflicts with parents that are, in our society, almost an inherent part of adolescence. Readjustments are required of parents as well as the child, and a child's adolescence can provoke turmoil within a parent and conflict between parents as well as between parents and child. We shall seek to examine the relationship between the conflicts with the parents and the conflicts that rage within the adolescent. In considering the changes in the adolescent's personality according to the *structural concept*, we must recognize the profound reorganization required because of the increased force of the sexual impulsions; because of the new intellectual resources available to the ego; and because of the changes in the superego functions as well as the new ability to gain directives from ideals and ideologies. The inner conflicts between the new, intensified id drives and the superego provoke anxiety as the ego is, so to speak, squeezed between them, requiring new defenses. Anxieties also arise because the adolescent must sort out varient potential organization of the self and come to grips with how and where his life will be directed.

Adolescence is a time of particular significance to psychiatry, for it is then that the severe emotional casualties appear in appreciable numbers. Even though much of the damage may have occurred earlier in life, it is at this period that the severe failures that we term schizophrenia withdraw from social participation, cease trying to live confined by the culture's logic and language, and retreat into fantasy, guided by delusion rather than reality; and others rebelliously turn away from the restrictions required for social living and seek to live without the law.

Now, as these introductory comments indicate, the essential tasks of adolescence are complex and not readily summed up under the rubric of the attainment of an ego identity. The several requisite achievements are precursors of his integration into a reasonably independent individual about to launch on a course through life and to become intimately interdependent with another in order to gain completion as an adult man or woman. However, these complex tasks cannot be mastered rapidly. Adolescence is, currently, a lengthy period, lasting from five to ten years, and sometimes even longer. Properly, it is still a period of dependency, when the teen-ager is still trying out ways of living and of relating to others, testing out his capabilities and emotional limitations; he can still assume and shed roles, and bestow his love without expectation that it will lead to a permanent attachment. The period involves considerable trying out, with an implicit understanding that one is not yet playing for keeps. The adolescent is exploring his world and learning to know himself but the parents are still available to offer protection and guidance, and periods of regressive dependency upon them remain possible during recuperation from defeat or disappointment.

Three Subperiods of Adolescence

To bring some order to the description and discussion of the dynamics of this lengthy period, we shall divide it into three subperiods. However, these divisions cannot be considered as definitive separations because adolescents vary considerably in when and how they work through various aspects of adolescence. It is clear enough that the pubescent twelve-year-old differs markedly from a college sophomore, but there is considerable variation in how one turns into the other. Even though it has been fairly customary to focus separately on the prepubertal preparation for adolescence, and then divide adolescence proper into an early and late phase, we shall make different subdivisions. Three overlapping phases will be considered. *Early adolescence* will include the prepubertal phase when the spurt in growth initiates developmental changes and the onset of puberty which does not usually provoke a marked shift in orientation. The early teen-ager still continues many patterns established earlier, remaining in monosexual groups and with his home still very much the center of his life. Then, about twelve or eighteen months after pubescence, an expansive period of *mid-adolescence* sets in when movement toward the opposite sex breaks up peer groupings and intimate friendships. It is then that the period of revolt and conformity, so characteristic of adolescence, is apt to start—revolt from parental and adult dictates and conformity to peer-group standards, loyalties, and ideologies. There is often a beginning of sexual exploration, which is often concerned more with breaking through inhibitions and testing one's own limits rather than with an interest in intimacy; and love and sex may be kept quite separate. New horizons open which the youth wishes to explore. It is also a time of marked ambivalence and mood swings. Sooner or later a period of delimitation, *late adolescence,* sets in when the young person becomes concerned with the tangible tasks of coming to grips with his future. The boy becomes concerned about a career, and the girl more often with finding or preparing to find a husband. The reorganization of adolescence comes to an end; delimitation is accepted and guidence may be welcomed. The period of late adolescence carries the individual into occupational and marital choices which consolidate the ego identity and capacities for intimacy; and even though these are often partly adolescent problems they will be left for discussion in the chapters on the young adult period.

EARLY ADOLESCENCE

The gradual progression of the child toward maturity and independence is disrupted by the transformation of puberty which changes his physique, drives, intellectual capacities, and social milieu and requires profound intrapsychic reorganization. The child becomes impelled toward becoming an adult by the change in his size and contours; he must cope with a new inner pressure that creates strange feelings and longings, and adds an impulsivity and irrational force which the child has had little experience in managing but with which he must cope very much on his own—for it is an intensely personal matter which concerns the ties to the parents and provokes him toward breaking the attachments to them. It is a metamorphosis that brings about a new and definitive physical differentiation between the sexes, but also increases the attraction between them and prepares the individual for a search for a new type of intimacy and gratification which becomes a keystone in happiness and a loadstone in motivation.

The Prepubertal Spurt in Growth
The adolescent readjustment is set off even prior to pubescence when the gradual increase in size and weight that had prevailed since the age

of two abruptly shifts into high gear. The child had been gaining approximately four to six pounds a year, but about two years before the onset of puberty girls start to gain about eleven pounds and grow three to four inches a year; and boys gain thirteen to fourteen pounds and grow four to five inches a year for the next five to six years. The boy's muscle mass and strength double between the ages of twelve and seventeen, which has a profound influence upon his behavior and his self-image. The child's orientation and view of life begin to shift simply because of the change in his size; he is growing away from childhood and children, and adults are becoming less distant and awesome. Two factors in this upsurge in growth are important in changing the nature of the childhood society, and they are factors which carry over into puberty: one, girls mature about two years earlier than boys; two, there is considerable variation between individuals in the time of onset of the spurt in growth. In girls the median age of pubescence is at about thirteen; between eleven and fifteen in 80 per cent, "normally" between ten and seventeen, and with but rare exceptions between nine and eighteen.* In boys the onset cannot be determined as readily but puberty occurs about two years later with a median age of about fifteen. Thus, the upsurge in growth starts between ten and eleven in most girls and between twelve and thirteen in the majority of boys. In the sixth to eighth grades the girls tend to tower over the boys, some beginning to look like young ladies; while most of the boys are still immature. Movement of the two sexes toward one another is first impeded by the differences in size and then by the differences in the sexual maturity of boys and girls of the same age and educational level.

The Reshuffling of Peer Groups

The child can be upset when the spurt in growth and onset of puberty occur either particularly early or late. The girl who develops precociously worries about becoming a freakish giant, and then may become embarrassed by her changing contours as well as by her sexual feelings for which she has had little time to prepare. A mother described how she found herself becoming infuriated at men whose eyes lustfully followed her ten-year-old daughter whose bust and buttocks were rapidly taking on womanly proportions: "I want to scream at them that she is still only

* Figures vary from country to country: menarche has been found to occur in the United States at a mean age of 12.9 ± 1.4 years; in Florence, Italy, at 12.5; and in France at 13.5.[3]

a little girl." The tardy girl starts to wonder if she will ever become a woman and worries about her endocrine system. Early maturation is usually more pleasing to a boy than late development. This is a time of maximal interest in competitive sports, and late maturation may force the redirection of interests. Still, it is often the disruptions of close friendships due to differing rates of maturation that may be most upsetting to some children. The girl who has already started to menstruate and feels a physical attraction to boys has new interests and secrets that she does not confide in her former inseparable girl friend who is still "a child." In the reshuffling of groups and the formation of new close friendships, the less mature child may be left feeling lonely and neglected. Prepubertal girls tend to have a greater interest in sex than boys, perhaps because they undergo a more profound physical transformation in becoming a woman. They are apt to spend time in exchanging knowledge, beliefs, and misconceptualizations of menstruation, childbirth, and the fascinating topic of prostitution. The prepubertal boy having some friends who have matured also seeks knowledge, and is often fascinated by scatology which has a sexual connotation to him, and in telling stories he must pretend to understand to be one of the gang. More or less accurate information about sexual intercourse becomes common knowledge, but adult indulgence in erotic pleasures is difficult to comprehend for the child who does not yet know the drive of intense sexual urges. He may find it difficult to believe that his parents indulge in such unseemly conduct and fights off disillusionment in them.

The onset of puberty does not upset the monosexual peer groupings very noticeably. The shift in interest to the opposite sex that is driven by sexual impulsion usually lags a year or two behind pubescence. To some extent, the young adolescent's attention and energies are absorbed narcissistically, as he is directed toward gaining a new self-image by the rapid alterations in physique and feelings which lead to comparisons with friends of the same sex and to a need for a close attachment to a friend of the same sex. As the development of secondary sexual characteristics starts earlier in the girl and alters her more markedly than the boy, we shall consider her first.

Puberty in the Girl

Adolescence in the girl properly starts with an enlargement of the ovaries and the ripening of one of the Graafian follicles that will later produce an ovum, but the first visible manifestations are the elevation of the areola surrounding the nipple to form a small conical protuberance, or "bud," and the rounding of the hips due to broadening of the bony pelvis and the deposition of subcutaneous fat. The breasts also enlarge by disposition of adipose tissue and then by the development of the glands and their ducts. The legs lengthen, changing bodily proportions, and the thighs approximate one another. During mid- and late adolescence pubic and axillary hair appears, the labia and clitoris develop, and the clitoris becomes erectile. The skin secretions change, becoming more sebaceous and contributing to the development of that bane of most adolescents, acne. Sweat glands become hyperactive with ensuing hyperhidrosis, which creates an odor which can embarrass the girl when she starts dating. Although seemingly trivial, acne and perspiration become matters of considerable moment to adolescents of both sexes.

Then, some time after the first changes in her physique have occurred, the girl starts to menstruate and she feels herself a woman. A few periods of spotty and almost unnoticeable discharge may precede menarche, and the periods are apt to be scanty and irregular for a year. These first periods are not accompanied by ovulation, and the girl is rarely able to conceive during a year or two following her menarche.

It is usually the onset of menstruation rather than the profound change in her appearance that is most disturbing or satisfying to the girl. Although nowadays most girls are prepared for menarche by their parents, who often convey considerable misinformation, it is not unusual to find a girl who was terrified by the flow of blood, and some who concealed it believing that it was a sign of some dread disease or a result of masturbation. Of course, despite precautions, a girl may be seriously embarrassed when her first period stains her dress at school, or blood drips to the floor at a party. Menarche is a critical moment in a girl's life, and the frequency of menstrual difficulties of emotional origin indicates that it is often a source of a marked disturbance. Efforts are usually made to prepare the girl in a manner that makes her feel proud that she has become a woman and possesses organs that will enable her to become a mother. Some schools now instruct the prepubertal girl in the meaning and physiology of menstruation, as it has become obvious that many mothers are either insufficiently informed or emotionally blocked and are unable to inform their daughters properly. The term commonly used by women for their menses, "the curse," tends to express, however jocularly, the notion that menstruation forms a symbol of woman's burden and inferior status. Despite such feelings, however, it is also an important badge of womanhood. When the author engaged in a study of a group of women who had a virilizing pseudohermaphroditic syndrome at a time when the condition first could be reversed by cortisone therapy, he found it of interest that these women who had no breast development or other secondary sexual characteristics, and had deeply pigmented skins and kinky hair that conferred a somewhat Negroid appearance, expressed the hope that the new treatment would enable them to menstruate, even if it could do nothing else for them.

Menarche, and in some individuals each recurrence of menstruation, can reactivate a girl's pervasive dissatisfactions and concerns over being a female. The early childhood notion that mother had deprived the girl of a penis may regain consciousness. The secret fantasy of really being a boy, which occurs with varying force in very many girls, must now face the challenge of reality.* Some girls are so blocked by feelings of being physically deprived that they learn little if anything about their own sexual organs; and many women maintain a profound ignorance of their own bodies even after marriage and childbirth.

Acceptance of Femininity

How the girl accepts the change in her physique and menstruation depends, of course, on the stability of her gender identity: upon the firmness of gender allocation by her parents within the first few years of life; upon passing through the oedipal period in a positive manner that leads to a firm identification with her mother; upon the group identities she achieved during the latency period. But during early adolescence when she is learning to feel at home with her woman's body and with woman's role in society, the parents' attitudes are particularly important —their attitudes toward their daughter but also toward one another. When a mother not only accepts her life as a woman but finds fulfillment in it, and when a father admires and appreciates his wife, a girl can welcome the signs that she has become a woman and feel secure that she will be loved and desired as a woman. Even though a girl need not feel as

* Thus a young woman described previously who was seriously ill with ulcerative colitis considered that her menarche formed a trauma she had never been able to assimilate. Throughout childhood she was her father's "pal" and insisted that she was really a boy, and that she had only been a girl because her mother insisted on dressing her as a girl. With menarche she finally capitulated and shed her blue jeans, but experienced bitter hostility toward her mother for having made her a girl. She later tried to achieve a compromise with her sexuality and overcome her feelings toward her mother by becoming a nun.

confined and limited because of her sex as in former eras, she may still resent the boy's greater freedom to explore his world, and the societal expectations that she grow up to be a housekeeper and nursemaid. Still, serious resentments usually derive from a feeling that anyone without a penis is a cipher. Whereas cultural change has greatly modified the feminine position in society, conferring advantages over the male in some areas, it has also diminished the tendency toward fatalistic and unconscious acceptance of being a member of the "second sex," and has opened the way for more conscious ambivalence and for more acceptable strivings toward masculine roles in life.

Though such potential dissatisfactions with being female may exist, they are usually overshadowed by the adolescent's pride in her new status as a woman, the acquisition of a physique that attracts attention, and the value of the capacity to bear children. If she does not possess a penis, she can have an attractive body which she begins to groom with an unconscious compensatory narcissism. She becomes motivated to have a baby at some future time, particularly a son. Although probably every girl has some regrets over being female, and must find ways to come to terms with it and compensate for it that have a profound influence upon her psychological make-up, most will recognize some of the advantages and gain contentment through building upon these potential assets. In recent years it has become clear to many psychoanalysts that many men have deep but more hidden wishes to have been a woman, and in the past decade the dress and behavior of many adolescent boys has made this rather obvious.*

The Influence of the Menstrual Cycle

With the menarche the girl's life comes under a new influence that is often puzzling to her as well as to those who live with her. The cyclic changes in the hormonal balance each month either directly or indirectly influence her mood and behavior. Benedek and Rubenstein[1] carried out hormonal studies of women who were in psychoanalysis, and followed the nature of their dreams at various phases of the menstrual cycle. They reached the conclusion that during the first phase of the cycle, when the ovarian follicle is ripening, estrogen secretion mobilizes heterosexual

* It has been fairly acceptable for a woman to wish to be a man, but shameful for a man to wish to be a woman. Nevertheless, many more men seek to be turned into a woman operatively than vice versa. The Plains Indians institutionalized the "berdache"—men who chose to live as women, but who were also unusually brave in battle as members of the Crazy Horse societies.

tendencies and outgoing behavior, the sexual desires reaching a height at the time of ovulation—usually about twelve days after the start of the last menses; then, following ovulation, the progestin secretion favors a more passive receptive attitude and an inner-directedness, as if preparing the woman emotionally as well as physically for pregnancy; then, shortly before the start of the next period, progestin secretion drops sharply and the woman is apt to feel empty, irritable, and moody.*

Such cyclic changes have long been considered as an inner tide that influences the woman's life and exerts some degree of control over her conscious and unconscious behavior and thought. The study by Benedek and Rubenstein has never been replicated and, as far as the author knows, no systematic attempt has been made to do so; and although other authorities place the time of heightened sexual excitement at some other point in the cycle, it is apparent that many women are profoundly affected by the course of the menstrual cycle—both by its physiological influences and by the unconscious attitudes provoked by menstruation. Among other influences, the increase in interstitial fluid premenstrually, which is quite marked in some women, can produce discomfort and irritability, but this is not usually an adolescent problem. The girl's attitudes toward her menses may reflect her mother's warnings that a girl must remain inactive during her period and put up with this burden in life, but more often will reflect her mother's own behavior. It is natural enough for a girl who has seen her mother become incapacitated for several days each month to anticipate her menarche with foreboding, and then perhaps to utilize her periods in order to obtain a secondary gain of attention and concern from those about her. Incapacitation during menses often runs in families, without demonstrable physical cause. Even without such disturbances, the menstrual cycle provides a periodic-

---

* Although in very many women the cyclic changes in behavior and mood are scarcely noticeable, in some they almost dominate the women's life and the shifts in their behavior are almost incomprehensible without regard to the cycle. Thus a woman in intensive psychotherapy, albeit a very disturbed woman, exhibited very different attitudes toward the therapist as well as toward her husband and children in the different phases of the cycle, month after month. In the postmenstrual phase she dressed carefully and tended to be seductive and outgoing—striving to please her therapist by what she brought to the sessions; during the second half of the cycle she would neglect her dress, become very discontented with life, and carry a chip on her shoulder, often attacking the therapist verbally; then premenstrually she would feel despondent and express her hopelessness, at times thinking of running away to find a new life, at others behaving like a helpless child and becoming dependent upon her husband and children as well as her therapist.

ity to a girl's life and an awareness of the passing of months accompanied by increasing and decreasing feelings of worth which form a major distinction between male and female psychology.

Her Changing Appearance

Concern with the continuing transformation of her figure naturally preoccupies the adolescent girl. She knows that her popularity and her chances of attracting a desirable husband will be markedly influenced by her changing facial configuration and her emerging bodily contours. Only an occasional girl can appreciate that attractiveness is not primarily tied to physical configurations, and if she is not pretty seek to become attractive through fostering other assets rather than by trying to mask what cannot be hidden. To a very large degree the girl, despite her careful attention to what she sees in the mirror, and despite her constant comparisons of her own physique with those of friends and movie starlets, does not achieve an estimate of her charms by what she sees as much as through how she perceives others regard her; and at this age her father's reactions to her are particularly significant. The father is very likely to draw away from a daughter entering her teens, feeling that he should no longer be as physically close as previously, and he is often withdrawing from the sexual feelings she induces in him. The daughter often feels that her father now finds her unattractive or is actually repelled by something about her.* It requires considerable tact on the part of a father to convey somehow that he considers that his daughter has become attractive and likes the way she looks and yet assume a proper distance. The changes in the way in which boys and men relate to the girl can also cause anguish, embarrassment, or pleasure. A girl may become flaming red when boys emit low whistles as she walks by, or become upset when they whistle at another girl but not at her. A typical feminine dilemma sets in. The girl will be upset if boys do not seek her out because of her appearance but becomes angered because they like her for her looks and not for "herself," and later because they are interested or not interested in her sexually rather than in that indefinable self.

* Women in intensive psychotherapy or analysis are often astounded when they develop the insight that their father's withdrawal was in reaction to attraction and sexual stimulation rather than because of disappointment in their daughter's appearance—an insight that sometimes marks a significant turn in therapy.

Puberty in the Boy

The physical maturation of the adolescent boy is also striking, even though it does not involve as much of a metamorphosis as the girl's. The alterations in size and muscular strength prepare him for the primal role of guardian and food gainer. It would appear that such changes move him into a period of heightened athletic activity and competitiveness in contemporary society, and contribute to his difficulties in remaining a child in relationship to his parents. The size of the genitalia remained unchanged throughout childhood, but now at about the age of twelve or thirteen the testes begin to increase in size and the scrotal skin to roughen and redden; these changes are soon followed by an increase in the size of the penis. The appearance of pubic hair is followed by growth of axillary hair. The prostate and seminal vesicles mature, and spermatozoa form. The beard and body hair appear and the voice deepens, usually about four years after the first pubertal changes and when bodily growth is almost completed. The indentation of the temporal hair line is among the very last changes and indicates that adolescent maturation has been completed. Most boys are fully mature at seventeen or eighteen, but some complete maturation at fifteen and others not until twenty.[11]

Most youths have been masturbating before adolescence, but the activity generally increases after puberty. Ejaculation occurs after maturation of the prostate and seminal vesicles, but spermatozoa are neither numerous nor motile, so that the adolescent remains sterile for a year or longer after ejaculation first occurs. Nocturnal emissions usually start between fourteen and sixteen and can cause considerable concern if the boy has not been properly prepared by his parents, though most youths will have learned about the phenomenon from friends. A boy may think that something is drastically wrong, perhaps that masturbation has damaged him. However, even the informed may experience anxiety because of the nature of the vivid dreams which precede and accompany the nocturnal emission and which seem more real than most dreams. The repressed sexual wishes of the adolescent may find undisguised expression in the accompanying dream and, at this time of life, are likely to contain homosexual and incestuous elements.

The force of sexual drives begins to exert its potent influence upon the thought and behavior of the adolescent, and whatever innocence existed in childhood requires strong defenses to maintain, and gives way in thought and fantasy if not in action before the internal pressures that refuse to be completely denied. In general, boys seem to experience urgency concerning sex sooner after puberty than girls and must find ways of coping with it. Stimulation from the seminal vesicles adds to the hormonal influences. Genital sensations cause restlessness, direct his thoughts to sexual objects, and urge him toward relief. Although he has experienced erections since infancy, they now occur with greater frequency, heat, and even pain; and unexpected erections can cause embarrassment as he seeks to hide them from others. The thoughts that come unbidden and the fantasies in which he finds himself lost also cause embarrassment and feelings of shame which contribute to the frequency of blushing during this time of life. Masturbation becomes an almost universal practice in boys and, indeed, psychiatrists consider the absence of masturbation during adolescence a cause for concern as it indicates a need for intense repression—or self-deception. However, in some social groupings masturbation is so frowned upon that early premarital intercourse is fostered.*

Masturbatory Concerns

Although masturbation is not as common in the adolescent girl, Kinsey's figure that 40 per cent of girls masturbate during adolescence seems a low estimate;[8] many girls can masturbate by pressing their thighs together, and some are unaware that they are masturbating. Girls have less immediate physiological tension that drives them toward relief, as there is no female equivalent to local pressure from the seminal vesicles. The girl is more likely to be aroused by external stimuli and may not masturbate until after she has been sexually aroused by actual experiences with another person.

Masturbation usually provokes guilt and concern, particularly in the young adolescent. Such feelings may derive from the fantasies that generally accompany the act, but also from the spoken and unspoken indications from adults and peers that it is shameful and harmful. There has been a pervasive folk belief that masturbation causes insanity; it is a belief that was not only shared by the educated but promulgated by

* Kinsey has pointed out the marked differences between social classes in the United States at the time of his study. A policeman stemming from the lower class might arrest a boy he finds masturbating, but the judge would not consider it a notable offense—whereas finding youngsters having intercourse might provoke reverse judgments. (See Chapter 10 in Kinsey *et al., Sexual Behavior in the Human Male.*[7])

psychiatrists and almost accepted as a fact during the Victorian era.*
Both boys and girls are likely to believe that continued "self-abuse" carries the danger of impotence, sterility, general debility, poor eyesight,
and baldness, and that it forms a prime cause of acne. Although contemporary teen-agers are likely to be more sophisticated and are less confused and misinformed by the literature on the subject, masturbation
continues to be a source of much anguish to many adolescents. A cycle
often develops in which the boy or girl determines to renounce the practice, struggles with himself to overcome the urge for relief and gratification, but fails to abide by his vow and suffers a loss of self-respect, considering himself a weak person and a wastrel; this can have a notable
effect upon the youth's personality development and character. Still,
such concerns are usually weathered and only contribute to major
difficulties when other forces lead to asocial behavior. Although decisions
about the future are often made because of these unnecessary concerns
—such as a resignation never to marry, or to prepare to become insane at
an early age—the decisions vanish as the youth becomes more certain of
his normality. On the positive side, the ability to gain relief from sexual
impulses through masturbation often permits the relative quiet needed
for study or for delaying marriage in order to prepare for a career.†

Within a year or two after puberty the sexual urges have added a new
force to id impulses and are consciously and unconsciously beginning
to become an urgent directive force with which the young person must
learn to cope in some manner or other. We shall return to a discussion
of some of the influences of puberty upon the family relationships and
social life of the teen-ager and upon the reorganization of his psychic
structure, but first we must note the changes in his intellectual capacities
which are occurring concomitantly.

* Among the more prominent psychiatrists, Freud at first attributed neurasthenic
symptoms to excessive loss of sexual fluids, and Adolf Meyer, even though somewhat
skeptical, stated that he had never seen a patient with schizophrenia who had not
masturbated—which was probably correct. The literature concerned with child rearing
as well as that presenting youths with "the facts of life" both emphasized the dangers
of masturbation to one's moral and physical well-being.
† Kinsey found that whereas masturbation is more common in children from educated circles, even lower-class children who manage to gain a higher education have
masturbated more than peers from their social class. (See Chapter 14 in Kinsey et al.,
Sexual Behavior in the Human Male.⁷)

The Adolescent's Cognitive Development

It is of particular interest that at just about the time the child is beset by an awakening of sexual impulsions that demand attention and can lead to impulsive activity that disrupts a life pattern and his basic relationships, he also acquires a new scope in his intellectual functioning that enables him to cope with his drives and feelings more effectively. He not only becomes capable of reasoning more logically and to consider imaginatively the effect of what he does upon his future welfare, but he also begins to evaluate his behavior in terms of ideals and ideologies. Of course, we might consider the matter conversely—that is, to note that just as the child becomes capable of thinking far more effectively and directing his life reasonably toward future goals, a new force that invites irrationality and fosters impulsivity enters his life. The body's demands for sexual fulfillment that must be contained and at least partially repressed increase the domain and power of unconscious processes and motivations. It has been said that an adolescent is a person with two heads and it is often the head of the penis that guides his behavior.

Piaget's Period of Formal Operations

The change in the adolescent's cognitive abilities is not simply a matter of increased intelligence. As Inhelder and Piaget [5] and Vygotsky[12] have clearly demonstrated, the gradual increase in intellect leads to a qualitative change at about the time of puberty and the individual enters into a new stage of cognitive development—the period of *formal operations* in Piaget's terms. The stage starts at about the age of eleven or twelve but the capacities will develop for several years, consolidating at about the ages of fourteen or fifteen; and, indeed, the process of "decentering" through gaining perspective will continue into early adult life.

What is the nature of formal operational thought? The child becomes capable of propositional logic, a second-order type of thinking about concepts abstracted from reality. It is a capacity for hypothetical-deductive thinking, an ability to make logical deductions from imagined conditions. The youth can reason, "If x is true, then y must follow," and also, "Had x been true, y would have been a possibility." His use of language develops to a point where concepts can be abstracted from reality and then be manipulated imaginatively—not simply as fantasy but with concern about figuring out solutions to real problems and the course of future events. Inhelder and Piaget emphasize that the critical attributes of formal operations are both the ability to think about thoughts and a reversal of relationships between what is real and what is possible. The child in the phase of concrete relationships could move from the real to the possible (as when after placing objects in series according to size, he could imagine continuing the sequence beyond the objects he had available); the adolescent, however, comes to have a wide range of possible operations ready into which he can fit the particular situation. He has ways of reasoning worked out in advance which he will try on the task at hand.*

Ideas, Ideals, and Ideologies

The adolescent has moved beyond childhood in his capacity to think beyond the present. He can orient himself to thinking about and directing himself toward a future he has conceptualized, or even toward alternative potential futures that are contingent upon his own actions as well as upon contingencies he cannot control. He also begins to form systems and theories into which he fits his perceptions and conceptions of reality. He becomes interested in ideas, ideals, and ideologies, and these serve to lift him beyond the present moment, his body's demands, and desires for hedonistic gratification. He can be motivated by goals that even surmount his lifetime. He may well walk through these years of adolescence with his eyes riveted on an unattainable star even as his body is demanding relief from the sexual tensions that possess it. The adolescent conceptualizes social systems as well as logical systems. Behavior can be directed by the values of the social systems rather than simply through interpersonal relations and values, and he begins to place his family, his parents, and himself in a broader social context in which the societal values are superordinate to the family value systems.†

* Inhelder and Piaget have carefully analyzed the nature of formal operations in terms of symbolic logic and in terms of the mathematical logic of lattices and groups. These contributions to both formal logic and mathematics as well as to epistemology go beyond the scope of the present book and the reader is referred to their joint study, The Growth of Logical Thinking from Childhood to Adolescence,[5] and also to Piaget's Logic and Psychology.[10]

† Inhelder and Piaget (The Growth of Logical Thinking from Childhood to Adolescence,[5] p. 337) consider that the transition to the stage of formal operations is made possible by a further maturation of the central nervous system at about the ages of eleven or twelve, but they recognize that the relationship is "far from simple, since the organization of formal structures must depend on the social milieu as well. . . . A particular social environment remains indispensable for the realization of these possibilities. It follows that a realization can be accelerated or retarded as a function

The development of the new cognitive abilities of formal operations cannot be understood simply as a development of the mechanism of defense which we call *intellectualization* in the sense that it is used as a defense against experiencing emotions or as a means of sublimating sexual drives; it must be understood rather as a general expansion of the individual's intellectual horizons, including the potentiality for greater ego controls.

The extent of the development of formal operations varies greatly from individual to individual and particularly from social class to social class, depending notably upon the educational level achieved. Perhaps no one in certain preliterate societies ever reaches the level of formal operations;* but it is also clear that there are many persons in our society, particularly those who do not have more than a grade-school education, whose capacities for formal operations such as concept formation and the proper consideration of future goals are but feebly developed. The new cognitive capacities bestow many of the essential characteristics of adolescence, but they involve a very complex development that occurs over a period of several years. The new abilities enable youths to embrace ideologies, to challenge the status quo, to envision a better world, to gain gratification through fantasy while waiting to become able to achieve in reality, and in general to soar above the prosaic world with its plodding inhabitants. These abilities will also enable him eventually to envision a more realistic world into which he must fit himself and to understand orientations other than his own concerning what is meaningful in life. His superego will become modified not only by incorporating new ego ideals but also through embracing the arbitrary but socially accepted standards that are essential to the regulation of any social system. We shall later examine some of the more important derivatives of the adolescent's new cognitive facilities as they interrelate with other forces that

---

of cultural and educational conditions. . . . The growth of formal thinking . . . remains dependent on social as much as and more than on neurological factors." Actually they produce no evidence that the capacity for formal operations depends upon a further maturation of the cerebral cortex rather than upon the steplike development of the intellectual processes, the stage of formal education achieved, and the demands of moving toward adult responsibility. A similar line of reasoning would lead to the conclusion that the type of scientific thinking that started during the late Renaissance had awaited the further genetic evolution of the brain, rather than man's cultural evolution and his acquisition of some new and essential tools for thinking, such as the decimal system and algebra.
* The idea that primitive peoples are incapable of abstract thinking is being redefined in terms of their lack of the conceptual tools needed for abstract thinking.

are reshaping his life and restructuring his personality in preparation for adult behavior and responsibility. In early adolescence these capacities are not yet striking, for they are still emergent and the young adolescent is still only preparing to develop his own ideas and to try them out. Nevertheless, the new intellectual resources are important in increasing his ability to cope with the heightened sexual impulsions, to consider future objectives, and to enable him to become interested in new adventures into the world of imagination that offer alternative as well as substitute activities and gratifications. The young adolescent's intellectual development is part of the entire process of adolescent awakening in which new horizons open before him and he begins to see the world in which he is going to live with an exciting and poignant freshness.

Early Adolescent Crushes

The onset of adolescence does not produce any striking changes in the youth's behavior or way of life for a year or longer. It is a time of inner stirring from sexual arousal, but the boy or girl is not yet ready to act upon the impulsions and much of the sexual arousal is absorbed by fantasy and by preoccupations with the changes that are occurring in the body and in one's own feelings. The adolescent continues to go around in the same monosexual groupings as he did in latency but with the group membership shifting because of the differing rates of maturation and as close friendships give way to crushes. This is a time of intense crushes; most of which, but not all, are directed toward persons of the same sex. The young teen-ager's life may be filled with thoughts of the person he admires, about whom he wishes to know more, and with whom he wishes to spend his time. In general, girls have more intense and outspoken crushes than boys and feel freer to manifest them. The adored person is someone very much like the self or someone whom the youth would like to be. In a sense there is still no clear division between identification and object choice: the young teen-ager loves a person he wishes to be like rather than someone who would complement his existence. He is still involved in trying to find himself, to become accustomed to his changing body, to become someone, and he is very much preoccupied narcissistically with his own feelings and longings. In the process of moving from self-love to the love of another person, the love of someone like the self is a way station. The youth is not yet sure enough of himself to move toward a person of the opposite sex and the attachments are part of the process of self-completion. The current trend in which teen-age girls form intense crushes for long-haired musicians, and even the admiration of boys for long-haired musicians, is part of the transition to finding love objects of the opposite sex. Girls are apt to have crushes on boys earlier than boys seek after girls, not only because they become pubescent at an earlier age but also because they seek a love object who possesses what they do not have—and because the boy, even as during latency, is fighting against his dependency upon mothering figures and fears losing his identity through engulfment by a female.

The crushes commonly move toward older persons—a teacher, camp counselor, Scoutmaster, older sibling of a friend whom the teen-ager at first admires from afar but seeks to be near. Such crushes can be embarrassing to the older person, for the teen-ager can find all sorts of ways to seduce the teacher or counselor into bestowing special attention and affection on him, and then becomes hurt and even depressed when the older person purposefully or unwittingly neglects or rebuffs the advances. The young adolescent's tendency to have such intense feelings for older persons contains some danger of homosexual seduction because persons who are homosexually attracted to the young adolescent—that is, to a person who is not too definitively either a boy or girl—often take up occupations or activities that permit them to have close relationships with youngsters of this age group. However, these attractions generally fill important functions in personality development. They are part of the process of movement away from dependency on parents, and the new object of attachment forms an ideal that the youth seeks to emulate, and in the process the youth gains new ego ideals that modify the superego originally based on parental models, directives, and dictates.

Sublimation of Sexuality

The sexual impulses of boys are largely drained off into other activities, or at least efforts at sublimation of sexuality are pursued intensively. The boy seeks to gain repute among his friends and to emulate his heroes by means of his athletic prowess. His efforts to achieve security as a man and prestige as a masculine figure are still more important to him than the pursuit of love objects. He is still seeking recognition and admiration from his male peers to affirm his own worth, and only later will he perform athletically in order to gain the admiration of girls.

There is, of course, considerable daydreaming about the other sex and often important secret crushes. The girl, in particular, may begin to spend hours by herself daydreaming of the hero who will rescue her, still able to transform herself and her hero into a knight and lady re-enacting tales of chivalry.

Society usually provides means of strengthening ethical standards as children approach and pass through puberty. The Scouts mobilize the idealistic strivings of youths and provide a code of ethics while seeking to interest the young adolescent in nature, as well as providing a favorable group setting to offset antisocial gang formation. Religious feelings become important and churches provide confirmation ceremonies with preparatory classes that reinforce ethical values. The adolescent with his new interest in ideals and ideologies can now find an interest in religion, although it may have only bored him previously. He has need for such strengthening of his superego and he is beginning to seek reasons and meanings in life. Puberty rites in primitive societies served to lead directly from childhood to adult status, whereas confirmation ceremonies seek primarily to designate to the youth that he has reached a time of life when he must become responsible for his moral and religious behavior. The youth now often experiences a closeness to God and feels that he has support and guidance in countering the temptations that are besetting him. The attachment to the church will form an indirect continuing bond to the parents whom he may now be starting to deny.

The Resurgence of Oedipal Feelings

Although the adolescent's relationships to his family are beginning to change, he is still very much family centered, accepting his role as a member of the childhood generation even though he is beginning to feel uneasy in it. Along with the upsurge of sexual feelings there is some reawakening of oedipal attachments. The sensuous and affectional attachments to the parent of the opposite sex, even though under the ban of repression, are the obvious channels into which the sexual feelings can flow. The work of the oedipal period has to be carried out once again but at a different level, and this time the sexual feelings will not be repressed so much as redirected away from the parent. The boy may now begin to idealize his mother and find nothing wrong in commenting on how beautiful she is and seek ways to please her and gain her affection. The girl's situation differs, as has been previously noted, for either just prior to the onset of puberty or early in adolescence she turns from her father and her father turns away from her. It usually constitutes the primary renunciation of her attachment to her father rather than a repeat performance.

Then, as the real upsurge of sexual feelings gets under way, the youth begins to turn away from his or her attachment to the parent, unconsciously and sometimes consciously concerned by the sexual aspects of the attraction. He begins to find fault with the parent, criticizing him or her, convincing himself that the parent is not attractive and not an object worth seeking. The criticism also spreads to the parent of the same sex, for the youth is beginning to try to free himself from the domination of a superego formed in large part by introjection of the parents and their dictates. He does so by devaluating the worth of the introjected parent. This process will pick up intensity as adolescence progresses and we will examine it in greater detail in our discussion of mid-adolescence. The girl is apt to dream of being a woman more capable than her mother, a person more attractive to her father, and may begin to talk to her mother in rather condescending tones, sorry for this "has-been" who has passed her prime. It is generally helpful to the girl and her development if the mother is not angered by the condescension and can allow her daughter to indulge in such fantasies of being a more desirable female and potential sexual partner than her mother. It helps the girl gain self-esteem and enables her to feel capable of relating successfully to boys. As the problems of adolescence focus around problems of becoming an adult and gaining emancipation from the family, intrafamilial difficulties are an almost inevitable concomitant of adolescence and they will be discussed in some detail below.

The young adolescent is about to start the process of emancipation; he is beginning to experience feelings that are difficult to contain, and he is required to relate to people more as an adult than as a child. It is a difficult time, and during the beginning of adolescence he is not yet ready to assume responsibility for himself and to be capable of containing his drives and fantasies on his own. He still requires direction and protection; and even though he is beginning to be rebellious, he is apt to feel unloved and unwanted unless the parents place limits upon his behavior and provide safeguards against his venturing beyond his depth.

MID-ADOLESCENCE

A year or two after pubescence the increase in sexual drive adds impetus to the movement toward adulthood. After the brief recrudescence of oedipal attachments, the intensity of the feelings creates a need for the youth to gain emotional distance from his parents. He will be motivated to form and maintain affectional and sexual relationships to persons outside of the family; to have, for the first time, both affectional and sexual strivings consciously focused upon the same individual. He cannot continue to feel himself a child dependent upon his parent and must begin to feel capable of directing his own life. The change requires a profound inner reorientation as well as a change in the actual relationships with his parents. As the tasks of this phase of life primarily concern gaining independence from parental supervision and from the youth's own emotional attachment to the parents, it is natural that the family commonly becomes an arena of conflict. Although the youth may need to overcome his parents' concerns about granting him sufficient latitude, much of the conflict involves his own ambivalences as he is caught between a need to free himself and his longings for the security and affection he is leaving behind.

Overcoming Family Attachments and Controls

Mid-adolescence is a pivotal time of life when the youth turns his face away from the family that has formed the center of his existence for some fourteen or fifteen years. His having the security to move through it depends, as always, on the successful and harmonious passage through the earlier developmental phases—particularly the oedipal phase, for he must once again overcome his erotized attachments to a parent in order to feel free and secure from danger. However, earlier it had involved finding a relatively conflict-free position within his family, whereas now it concerns freeing himself from his family. The youth will not only be overcoming the repression of sexual expression, breaking his oedipal ties and modifying his superego to provide reliable inner directedness when he becomes free of parental supervision, but he must also be gaining a knowledge of his own capacities and limitations in terms of the adult world, and a familiarity with the ways of the opposite sex in order to help himself overcome residual inhibitions to sexual intimacy. The odyssey is rarely calm; it includes passages between Scylla and Charybdis, times when the youth needs lash himself to the mast to resist the sirens' singing, and when he can be bewitched by Circe and turned into a swine.

Revolt and Conformity

It is a time marked by revolt and conformity; a strange and interesting admixture that characterizes the height of the adolescent period. The parents and their standards must be denied as the youth tries things out in his own way. The parents with their conservative concerns for their child's future do not seem to understand him; adolescents have never been able to believe that parents can grasp the problems of the new generation. Indeed, the conflict between generations is inherent in social living and essential to social change. The turn from parents as models and authorities spreads to relationships with teachers and often to all adults, but creates uncertainty and a degree of recklessness as the adolescent tests his own capabilities and limitations.

The rebels are at the same time among the most consistent conformists, conforming to the ways of the adolescent group from which they fear to deviate lest they find themselves outcasts and isolates. Currently it is often a conformity to a pattern of nonconformity that proclaims a freedom from, and even a contempt for, the useless conventions of society while also displaying loyalty to the youth group and its culture. The adolescent society provides standards that furnish considerable guidance as well as the milieu in which the individual can feel that he belongs to something while seeking to renounce his attachments to his family. The youthful adolescent is likely to conform rigidly with the outer tokens that proclaim membership. The way he dresses, talks, flirts, become identification marks for the person who still has no secure inner identity. Customs and clothing vary for differing socio-economic and ethnic groups and from decade to decade: there are "hoods" who may indulge in gang fights and flaunt a degree of sexual promiscuity along with their black leather jackets and duck-tail hair cuts that mark them as tough characters; there are youthful "hippies"—the "teeny-boppers" somewhat prematurely following or aping the older alienated adolescent; and various other adolescent subgroups, including those headed for admission to superior universities, who consider themselves an elite and also wear distinctive clothing arranged with meticulously studied carelessness. Even as other subcultures, the adolescent culture tends to have a distinctive language with many terms that are understandable only to themselves; they are contemptuous of those who do not understand, but discard expressions as they become known to younger groups or to adults. Fraternities and sororities also provide places where adolescents belong and feel accepted, conveying status and self-esteem simply through the fact of belonging, making the youth a member of an "in" group who can look down on those who do not belong. There are also the unorganized fraternities with less formal initiation procedures that hang around certain street corners where regulars can always be found for a game of cards or pool; or the more demanding city gangs in which membership requires participation in antisocial activities in preparation for later membership in criminal and semi-criminal groups, though fortunately most will withdraw after a few brushes with the law and not progress to criminal careers.

Overcoming Sexual Repression

The individual's inner equilibrium as well as the family homeostasis is upset by the intense impact of libidinal drives with which the child has had little experience. The urgency and autonomy of the sexual impulsions are strange and can be frightening. In contrast to other needs provoked by basic drives the parents cannot help their offspring very much in managing or satisfying the sexual needs. The parents may prepare, discuss, and advise them, but a great deal must remain intensely personal, particularly because it involves separating and differentiating from the parents. The early childhood erotic strivings had been directed toward a parent but had been repressed in the resolution of the oedipal phase through fear of loss of love and retributive hostility, and often in the boy through fears of castration. Now, the repressive ban on the expression of sexuality must be raised while the interdict on linking sex with affection for family members is retained; and the fusion of erotized and affectional feelings toward companions of the same sex must be disconnected in order to permit the fusion of sex and affection in heterosexual attachments.

During later childhood the repression of sexual impulses had been sweeping and was reinforced by many ego defenses. The prohibition cannot be raised simply by turning away from parental injunctions or even by parental permissiveness, because it has become firmly incorporated in the superego. The lifting of the repression requires both changes in attitudes toward parental authority and modification of the superego to permit more latitude for sexual expression. We can conceptualize the situation by saying that the id, having gained additional strength from sexual maturation, pushes the ego to challenge the superego restrictions and standards that were suited to the less driven child. However, much of the ego's strength and security in the ability to take care of and direct the self was gained by identifying with the parents and accepting their authority. Attempts to deny the superego mean turning away from identifications that had provided strength and stability. A precipitous break with the source of identification can undermine the self, provoke intense guilt, and a loss of self-esteem in this process of achieving greater freedom for expression. Efforts to deny the superego can provoke severe anxiety that the ego will completely lose control to the id without the superego's support. After years in which the child has accepted if not admired the parent and during which he has felt guilt when disobedient, his achieving success in surmounting either parental authority or the internalized authority in the superego can provoke intense feelings of guilt and depression. The hostility toward the parental figure is considered synonymous with a hostile act for which the child feels he must be punished and he tends to punish himself. The adolescent must usually shift his position slowly, build up security and confidence in his ability to cope with the sexual drives, gain standards to protect himself realistically, test his own limits of tolerating anxiety and guilt, modify his superego through interacting with peer groups with similar problems, and learn in actuality that sexual expression will not lead to catastrophe—before he can negate the standards taken over from his parents.

Reactivation of Oedipal Attachments

In moving away from the family, which had formed the matrix of his life, it is natural for the adolescent to become involved in numerous conflicts with his parents; but many of the expressed causes of conflict are but surface manifestations, rationalizations, and displacements of the sexual struggle that simultaneously attracts him to them and repels him from them. Since much of what is going on is under the ban of repression and is carried out unconsciously and therefore contains irrational and contradictory trends, any effort to discuss the developments of the period in reasonable and logical terms cannot convey the ambivalences, vacillations, and contradictions so characteristic of mid-adolescence.

With the onset of puberty, as has been noted, the former oedipal attachments become reactivated and the adolescent may indulge in considerable fantasy that is but thinly disguised about gaining the parent of the opposite sex and somehow gaining acendancy over or being rid of the parent of the same sex. The fantasies usually concern parent substitutes or fictional characters but the youngster's behavior may clearly reflect the renewed attraction to one parent and the resentment of the other. Sometimes an awareness of the sexual attraction breaks through the repression or the clear revelation of a sexual dream creates alarm, but usually it is an inchoate awareness of discomfort aroused by the sexualized feelings toward the parent that leads the adolescent to seek to erect a barrier and to place distance between himself and the parent. There are many similarities with the closing of the oedipal period, and the manner in which the young child resolved the intense attachment to the mother established a pattern that tends to be repeated in adolescence. However, the adolescent is not a five-year-old child and knows that children cannot marry parents but must find partners in the outside world. Nevertheless, the extent of the fantasies that seek to circumvent such realistic considerations can be extensive, and an adolescent's behavior may be directed toward living out such fantasies. Thus, an adolescent girl not only fantasied that she could stop her father's alcoholism by being more understanding than her mother and more interested in his work and hobbies, but she began to pattern her life to become her father's savior after her mother divorced him. A boy prepares for the day when he will be able to support his mother and thus enable her to throw his philandering father out of the house. The youth's physical development since childhood also leads to differences from the oedipal period. The adolescent boy may not only fear his father's retribution but may also fear his own hostile feelings toward his father now that he is as strong or stronger than his father. Both the girl and her father can be aware of the dangers of their mutual attraction and seek to desexualize the relationship. In one way or another the oedipal attraction is again repressed. Temporarily the need for repression creates guilt over sexuality and reinforces the ban on sexual expression, but ultimately it is the attraction to the parent as a sexual object that is repressed. Freedom of sexual expression will eventually be gained after sexuality is directed toward persons outside of the family and the erotic components of the attachment to the parent are again securely repressed, which is often a lengthy process. When it is necessary for family members to more or less consciously move away from one another in reactive efforts to escape from their sexual feelings for one another, the spontaneity of family life suffers and the totality of the intrafamilial relationships is apt to become seriously strained. Optimally a stable coalition between parents who maintain proper boundaries between themselves and their child guides the adolescent to an unconscious and satisfactory resolution of his attraction to parents even as it had helped bring about the earlier oedipal resolution. Then, as the child recognizes the finality of the loss of his primary love object within the family, he is apt to experience an emptiness and depression which motivate him to seek a more permanent love relationship outside of the family.

Overcoming Family Dependency

Needing to free himself from the attraction to a parent, the adolescent usually begins to deny the attractiveness of the parent by devaluing the parent's attributes, but he has other unconscious reasons for derogating his parents. Movement toward adulthood requires the youth to overcome his desires to remain dependent, as well as his feelings that his parents are more capable of directing his life than he is himself. He must prove to himself that he is capable and does not need to rely upon his parents' judgment and advice. Nevertheless, his own inner directives derive largely from internalizations of his parents and their standards and directives. Such inner restrictions must be overcome as much as, or more than, the actual limitations set by the parents. The superego must be reconstituted in order to become suited for directing adult rather than childhood behavior; loosened to permit greater latitude but at the same time strengthened to become capable of directing the self with less supervision from parents.

Although modification of the superego is an intrapsychic matter, it usually involves altering the perception and evaluation of the parents whose value systems had been internalized as superego. The youth sets out to establish that his parents neither always know what is correct nor are they paragons of virtue beyond emulation. They have sinned and they have erred. Even if their values and standards were once correct they were suited to that primordial era prior to World War II when the world was inhabited only by squares. The youth is in the process of convincing himself as much as his parents that both they and he are very different from the way they were when he was only a child. Before long he often talks and behaves as if nothing his parents do is acceptable. He must convince himself, for he is beset by ambivalences, both wanting his parents and wanting to be rid of them. The pendulum swings from one side to the other and episodes of denial of the parents are countered by periods of regression during which he seeks surcease from turmoil through regaining peace with the parents he loves. Commonly the force of the revolt indicates the violence of the wrench necessary for the adolescent to free himself rather than a basic hostility toward the parents. His arguments may become blindly irrational in order to help him overcome the contradictions and the longing to remain attached. The inability of parents to understand him is magnified; grudges are reinstated. The turmoil is within; the pulls are in both directions. Adolescence is the proper time to want to be—and to be—both dependent and independent.

Typically, the youth begins to search out flaws in his parents. The process may start with a basic disillusionment in learning about their sexual life—their hypocrisy in practicing what they have forbidden—but he seeks shortcomings that he can attack openly and resent rationally. The criticisms of the parents' behavior and even more the attacks upon their character constitute a serious blow to the parents' authority and self-esteem. They may turn upon the ingrate upstart with a vindictiveness that leads into a cycle of misunderstanding and bitterness. Now, although the teen-ager wishes to free himself from his parents' domination and direction, he does not wish to demolish them. He still needs them as objects of identification and as objects whose admiration and affection are worth seeking. His own self-esteem remains closely linked to the esteem he has for his parents. Late in adolescence, after he has divested himself of constricting inner controls and begins to see his parents from a more adult perspective, he will again return to accepting many of their standards as part of his own ego and superego.

Youth is apt to have unusually severe standards. In trying to contain his importunate sexual impulses and to stop the id incursions that are forcing abandonment of his former ways of maintaining security, the adolescent often magnifies superego injunctions in order to bolster the forces of repression. He tends to judge his parents by the same standards that he creates for his own defense, and no one is able to live up to his expectations. Still when the teen-ager later becomes more tolerant of himself, he will become more tolerant of his parents. The criticisms of his parents and his misunderstandings with them usually diminish as the adolescent finds himself capable of independence and when his perception and judgment of others becomes less egocentric.

Real Disillusionment with Parents

Unfortunately, serious and permanent difficulties between parents and child sometimes develop when the adolescent's search for flaws in his parents' behavior and character leads to the discovery of a disillusioning reality. The youth gains a pyrrhic victory, so to speak, that shatters his image of his parents and concomitantly disturbs his own development. A teen-age girl was brought for psychiatric help after becoming promiscuous. She had tended to idealize her mother who had seemed a model of both glamour and efficiency. Her mother had provided her daughter with winter vacations in Florida and unusually fine clothing by owning a flourishing insurance business. The girl came to realize that the mother's business was not what it seemed to be. The trips that kept her mother away from home one or two nights each week were spent with a wealthy industrialist who was her sole insurance client. When the girl had accompanied her mother on two vacations, it had just happened that the industrialist was staying at the same hotel. She also realized that her father, who could not maintain the family in the manner in which his wife expected him to, was managing not to realize that his wife was being unfaithful to him even though it was obvious to many others in the small community. The inevitable and necessary loss of unrealistic childhood idealizations, or the failure of parents to live up to the excessive standards of the adolescent, is very different from the disillusionment that cracks the parental image and with it the adolescent's superego.

At this developmental stage, when the oedipal resolution must be reconfined, and when the young person needs tangible models to follow into adulthood, who the parents are and how they interrelate is particularly important to their child's harmonious development. The adolescent is becoming aware of the parent as a real person and model rather than as a fantasied image; and who the parent is, influences whom the child seeks to become. The coalition between the parents, the support they give one another, the admiration they have for one another greatly influence the youth's transition through the adolescent period.

Parental Tribulations

Adolescence is a time of considerable difficulty for the parents as well as for the developing child. Their trust in the child they have raised and in their own capacities to raise a child undergoes its most severe test. The child in whom they have invested so much love and effort is moving away from them. They can no longer supervise and fully protect him but must place their reliance on what they have already inculcated in the child. Yet they know that their offspring lacks experience and his judgment cannot be fully adequate to new situations that will confront him. They fear that a single careless moment or a rash judgment will undo their years of effort and permanently blight the child's life. Excessive concerns are apt to reflect a parent's desire to prevent his child from repeating his own tragic youthful mistakes. Still there are few parents who do not experience restless nights when their son starts driving a car, or when they must first entrust their daughter to some oafish-looking, pimply-faced boy over whom she has lost whatever sense she had formerly possessed. Limits must be set somewhere, but where are the boundaries? Adolescents are bound to resent delimitation and restrictions, considering them indications of lack of confidence if not an absence of trust; but they are just as likely to resent failures to set limits, taking such permissiveness as evidence that the parents are not sufficiently concerned or interested. The adolescent may begin to test his parents' limits and in the process move beyond his own. The adolescent is not yet an adult and when the parents rescind their parental responsibilities prematurely, the adolescent is left without the support and protection he needs—albeit sometimes from his own desires and impulses.

The adolescent is apt to take out his unhappiness upon his parents, vent his dark moods upon them, express irritation over trivia. When they try to offer the affection their child seems to need, they may be rebuffed angrily, for it is at just such times that the youth cannot let himself continue to be babied and must tear himself away from what he would like so much to have. He needs something to rebel against and, at times, life seems to go easier for the adolescent if the parents become more strict and give him something to be angry about. Wide mood swings may occur that puzzle the youth as well as his parents. He feels expansive and elated after having proved to himself that he does not need his parents, only to plunge into despair when he is unconsciously concerned about surpassing his father or when feelings of hostile resentment toward his parents create remorse—the youth reacting as if death wishes toward them were equivalent to murder. He surmounts his superego and feels elated; he is punished by his superego and becomes depressed. It is part of the crucial struggle to come to terms with his superego and re-establish an equilibrium between the id, ego, and superego.

It is unfortunate but often an inherent part of the life cycle that the crisis of adolescence in the child occurs contemporaneously with a critical period in his parents' lives. The child's adolescence in itself tends to create a crisis in the parents' lives because of the impending change in the family composition, the loss of the child's admiration, and an awareness of the child's sexual attractiveness and vigor at a time when their own sexual power is waning. However, most parents have problems of their own in facing middle age and the realization that their own lives have reached a climax; that they must come to terms with what they will be able to achieve in life, with menopausal problems, with declining abilities. Such problems will be considered in the chapter on middle life, and here we can only note that the teen-ager is markedly affected by how the parents as individuals and as a couple are coping with the very consequential problems in their own lives. It may be of particular significance that the parents are coming to final terms with the limitations imposed by the "realities of life" just at the time when an adolescent offspring's imagination is beginning to soar and he is becoming impatient with the limitations that adults and their society impose by their stodginess and conservatism; the differences between the generations and the age-old ideologic conflict between them reach their zenith.

The Youth Group and Its Culture

As the adolescent moves away from his parents, the adolescent peer group gains in importance. The peer group changes into a youth group that carries the youth culture, and differs from the childhood peer group in having an anti-adult orientation and in becoming heterosexual. It is no longer simply a neighborhood group and may even span several high schools and communities, tending to be composed of youths with common interests and ambitions who, therefore, usually come from reasonably similar backgrounds. They band together for mutual support as well as companionship. The core is formed by a few close friends—pairs, and small groups of individuals who are extremely important to one another. Here the youth feels accepted because of friendship and finds some respite from judgment and the acceptance on the basis of achievement that is becoming increasingly important in school and to himself as well as to his parents. Within his group he feels free from parental controls and can try out more adult behavior, which at first may mean daring to carry out things that had been forbidden in childhood. Here he finds others who admire him and show a liking for him and who replace the loss he suffered in withdrawing from his parents. The others are in very much of the same situation as he and they support one another and learn to manage without parental supervision. The group serves an important function in modifying superego controls, for through observing others in the group, the group's reaction to the self and others, through accepting its standards and by means of constant discussions with these friends, the adolescent gains new guiding principles.

The adolescent group at first continues to be formed of members of the same sex, and throughout mid-adolescence friendships with members of the same sex are apt to take precedence over heterosexual attachments. Identification and object choice are still intertwined, and the teen-ager can be closest to those with whom he can identify. There is still considerable narcissism in the admiration of another. They also band together because they are coping with similar feelings of strangeness in moving toward the opposite sex. Friends are sought not only for support and in order to like and be liked, but also to have someone whom one respects to measure oneself against. There is considerable rivalry in most adolescent friendships, for even though direct competition for the same objectives is avoided, there is competition in collecting achievements. Who one is, is partly a matter of whom one has for friends. The youth feels he is not so well defined by his family name, for he simply happened to be born into the family, but he has formed his friendships and has been accepted by the group. Here, in his group, the youth learns to know who he is in the world beyond his family, to judge his capacities, and then, from the security of the group, he will begin to gain experiences with the opposite sex. Such needs for self-definition and for finding security take precedence over desires for actual sexual outlets. This process of freeing oneself from the family in order to find oneself and of moving into the proper group as a step toward independence is usually a more important task of mid-adolescence than forming love relationships and finding heterosexual outlets.*

The Youth Group Mores

The "gang" increasingly becomes the arbiter of appropriate behavior, a transition that often causes the parents considerable concern. Although the group's mores are likely to move toward the limits of what is acceptable to the parents, it usually serves as a modifying and restraining influ-

* The youth group and its culture probably plays a more important role in the life of the adolescent and his development in the United States than in European countries. Perhaps nowhere else is there such definite preparation in childhood peer-group activities for autonomous youth groups. Peer-group activities both in childhood and in mid-adolescence are under much closer family supervision among the middle class in European countries, perhaps leading to a more definitive and precipitous break from adult guidance when independence is finally gained in late adolescence. Moving away from the family at an earlier age, the American adolescent tends to be more dependent upon being popular to maintain a modicum of self-esteem. Even though the emphasis on group loyalty and decision making in the youth groups may well be part of the preparation for democratic living, it also contributes to a marked dependency upon the opinion of peers to provide motivation and direction for behavior.

ence upon the individual while fostering a less family-centered orientation and an expansion of activities beyond what parents might condone.
The peer group usually has a code that does not differ greatly from the
basic mores of the families of its members, even though it fosters adventuresome behavior that might be imprudent. Although in this rebellious
period an individual might well engage in activities that he considers
unacceptable to his parents, he will hesitate to risk serious censure from
friends, or do something that could lead to ostracism from the group.
Thus he may gamble but not cheat; a girl may go with a boy of whom
her parents disapprove but would be reluctant to be seen with a type of
boy who would lower her friends' esteem for her. The need for conformity is a major safeguard. Although delinquent gangs are most commonly
found in slum areas, even here the core members come from seriously
disturbed families. When a youth living in a better neighborhood or
from a "good" home joins together with others who have delinquent
tendencies, he almost always comes from a home that somehow fosters
antisocial tendencies, or in which rigid demands for obedience permit no
latitude for the instrumental behavior appropriate to his age which is
necessary for him to develop into an adult.

The movement toward the opposite sex starts from the security of the
monosexual adolescent peer group. The boy and girl must first become
more secure in their own sexual identity before daring to engage with the
opposite sex. The interest does not arise from sexual drive alone; the
narcissistic supplies needed to maintain and increase self-esteem are not
as likely to come from friends of the same sex as from the opposite
sex. At first the activity patterns do not change markedly but tentative
brief meetings take place with groups of the other sex. They engage
in a collective teasing banter which seeks to hide interest while still
showing it. "Whom one teases, one loves." Neither boy nor girl is likely
to show more than a casual interest in the person who is actually the
center of fantasy and consumes so much of daydreams.

In the insecurity concerning his worth, the adolescent seeks attributes
that make one enviable or popular. There is an increased consciousness
of the father's occupation, the neighborhood one lives in, the prestige of
a sporty car, etc. Security comes with wearing just the right shoes, tie, or
hairdo. Both sexes may spend considerable time in front of a mirror
examining their faces, the girls working on their make-up, but also in
practicing the proper face to wear under certain circumstances, and how
to shift facial expressions in a sophisticated manner. The boys now wish

for athletic prowess to be a hero to the girls. They join clubs and run for office in high school. To know that one is someone requires recognition by others.

Male and Female Patterning of the Personality

The boy is gaining experience and finding out what he can accomplish on his own, indirectly preparing for a career, but he is following the pattern that has been noted since early childhood in which the boy does things and intrudes himself into activities while the girl is more passive and becomes occupied and preoccupied with relationships between people. The girl may become a "big wheel" in high school, though usually not by actively seeking office but because of her willingness to assume responsibility and because she has become popular through being interested in people. Both sexes are indulging in a great deal of fantasy, but the girl's daydreams occupy more of her life. The girl uses her newly gained intellectual capacities to contemplate the subtleties of interpersonal relationships more than for purely intellectual matters or in considering how to change the world. The ways of thinking of the male and female begin to diverge more definitely during the middle of adolescence, and the girl is less likely to deal with abstract topics or to be an innovator. The greater amount of time spent in fantasying how she feels about others and how other people may feel in various situations ultimately leads to the development of "feminine intuition" and an ability to empathize with others. Of course, such attributes are not limited to girls, but we may say that boys who have such tendencies have something of a feminine quality that softens their edges and their ways of relating. Occasionally, the girl's fantasy life becomes so important during this phase of waiting for real experiences with boys that she tells herself long tales of romantic encounters which may occasionally spill over into outright fabrications that seem more real than reality, and can hold her friends spellbound until they become aware that she is telling them about her dreams rather than reality. However, such fantasies are often a type of preparation for romantic engagement; the imaginary conversations, encounters and embraces have an impact that permits her to feel desirable and glamorous and are something of a rehearsal for what is to come. As these fantasies may mask the still dominant interest in the father and concern an older man with whom she is secretly in love, she may experience difficulty in stepping down into the reality of dating younger, less romantic boys of her own age. Such relatively isolated adolescent experi-

ences on the part of girls whose major gratifications come from daydreams seem to be more common in European cultures than in the
United States where peer-group activity is so very important. In many
European countries the girl moves directly from such fantasies to marrying a man who is a generation or almost a generation older than she.

The Merging of the Sexes

The movement toward openly falling in love proceeds slowly, and
achieving real sexual intimacy takes even longer. At first the male and
female peer groups are apt to mingle primarily in reasonably public
places, often in some hangout frequented by older mixed groups whose
ways they watch and mimic. Then the groups may grow smaller, offering
opportunities for couples to pair off in the dark but with the protection
of having other couples close at hand, while starting tentative explorations of the mysteries of the other sex. The "necking" or "petting" at
this age is as much a matter of exploring one's own feelings and learning
to gain control of one's impulses as it is a matter of gaining sexual
gratification. It is a matter of exciting exploration and stimulation rather
than a means of gaining release from sexual tensions. It may have very little to do with being in love and be much more an expression of eagerness
to begin to live out one's fantasies and enter into the mysteries of sexuality. Usually the more complete loss of the self in sexuality that leads to
"heavy petting" with orgastic experience awaits late adolescence when a
person feels reasonably secure with the self, understands the desires of
another, and feels certain that limits can be set when necessary.

The group parties will change into double dating, which permits each
person to feel more secure with another couple around to provide sanctions concerning what is permissible. Many boys are likely to gain their
first experiences in sexual exploration with casual acquaintances such as a
blind date or with a girl from another community who is more experienced and will take the initiative. The need to get away from girls whom
they think about in more personal terms can be very great. The girl may
first overcome her inhibitions on a date with an older boy who is more
daring and whose attraction to her arouses assurances that she can be
attractive to a boy in sexual terms. Of course there is no set pattern, and
how persons overcome their inhibitions and repressions is a very personal matter. In all eras and cultures, some youths are unable to contain
their impulses and have sexual intercourse at an early age. Others, particularly during the past two decades, seek to avoid the insecurities and the

emptiness that comes with breaking the bonds with the parents by forming more permanent attachments as early teen-agers, trusting that their first infatuation or "puppy love" will ripen into a more mature love relationship. Such early pairing off on a more or less permanent basis will naturally occur more readily in suburban communities where children of both sexes have attended school together and the mingling of the peer groups of the two sexes occurs more easily. Although individual personality characteristics exert an important influence, the customs of the country, social class, and the particular period in which people are living exert very powerful directive forces. Customs and mores vary greatly from country to country, and generalizations to all youths must be avoided.

Blocks to Early Sexual Relationships

In our contemporary society it usually takes a number of years before the sexual drives that have started soon after puberty can achieve expression and fulfillment. Probably not more than a quarter or a third of male college students have had sexual intercourse before the age of nineteen or twenty. Our culture has taught that premarital intercourse is immoral, particularly for the girl. It has been only during recent decades that the double standard has broken down, that standard which permitted boys to have sexual relations because of the urgency of their drives but insisted that girls retain their virginity. However, it is more than morality that is involved in creating the delay between the capacity for sexual relationships and their realization.

The adolescents of both sexes must overcome the repression of sexuality that had become so firmly entrenched and they must disengage the drive from the earlier incestuous choices involved. The boy in particular must manage to overcome unconscious fears that sexual activity can lead to castration by his own father or the girl's father, or at least arouse dangerous hostility in his or the girl's father. He must also overcome his feelings that females in the image of the mother are powerful and enveloping and he will be lost if he gives in to his need for them. Confusions of castration fears and fears of mothering figures can also arouse unconscious concerns that the boy may lose his penis in the vagina, unconsciously considered as a biting organ with teeth—a fairly universal fantasy that sometimes emerges into consciousness. The girl, too, has special fears to overcome: fears of penetration and injury, fears of annihilation that come with orgasm, feelings that without a penis she is nothing and cannot be desired, feelings of disgust and shame with her own genitalia which she feels must be similarly repulsive to any male. The superego also gains support in repressing the id impulses by marshaling the dangers that can come from such sexual indulgence. There are more or less realistic fears of pregnancy and venereal disease which have become less important only during the past decade or two. Even though venereal disease is still sufficiently common to cause concern, gonorrhea no longer imposes a threat of sterility, nor does syphilis mean years of treatment and perhaps a need to forego marriage and having children. The changes in adolescent sexual practices which are developing with reasonable security from pregnancy and the ravages of venereal disease are just unfolding at the present time. However, these are matters that are usually of more concern to the late adolescent. The girl, too, often pauses before losing her virginity, and in some ethnic groups intactness of the hymen remains a requisite at the time of marriage. A girl may have fears, too, of becoming a lost woman, unable to control her impulses and lust after she has once given way to her desires; and the boy may also take pause in feeling that the intensity of the experience will be overwhelming and more than he can contain.*

The intermingling of the sexes brings about an expansion of the adolescent's social awareness more than of sexual knowledge and experience. Members of the other sex are perceived in more realistic terms of appreciating that they have similar problems, uncertainties, and desires. Desires for recognition shift more definitively to the opposite sex; and behavior becomes directed toward being more attractive to the other sex. There is a constant building up of illusion and return to reality. The more basic patterns of the personality characteristics of the two sexes begin to interrelate, with the more active intrusive behavior of the male fitting into the more passive receptive behavior of the female. The girl does not form a direct rival to the boy and can provide him with satisfac-

* There are also more irrational fears that are utilized to buttress the superego. We have already observed that the male's fear of a vagina with teeth has been noted in virtually all parts of the world. Less obviously, the adolescent is also apt to be fascinated by fictitious stories of couples who were unable to separate after having intercourse and had to be taken to the hospital in the embarrassing position in which they were locked. It is of interest that this myth was utilized to preserve the sanctity of the dark medieval church, in the lore that this situation would occur when couples had sexual relations in the church. It was further fortified by the legend that such unions would lead to the birth of a werewolf. Perhaps a werewolf would be the proper product of the "black mass," an anti-Christian witchcraft rite during which couples copulated on the altar.

tion and assurance by enjoying his achievements and prestige and sharing them with him; she thus bolsters his narcissistic needs while she
spurs him onward. The girl also finds that she need no longer compete so
actively with other girls now that she finds boys can like her or love her
the way she is—as a girl. She can turn more fully to the development of
the feminine characteristics of making herself likable and desirable
through taking an interest in the achievements of another and through
understanding others.

Early Love and Sexual Identity

Sometime during late mid-adolescence or early in late adolescence the
youth is likely to fall in love. It is quite likely that the first heterosexual
love will contain narcissistic components. The boy may well fall in love
with a girl whom he unconsciously recognizes as someone he would like
to have been, had he been a girl. The girl may fall in love with the boy
she might have been. These early loves can be important in fostering
a more secure gender identity. While there are still some narcissistic and
homosexual components in this type of object love, for it is a stage in the
movement from narcissistic love to heterosexual love, something significant happens for identity formation; the boy is placing the feminine
components of himself—the residua of his identification with his mother
—onto the girl whom he loves. He no longer needs to contain these
elements, these introjects, in himself because he can have them in the
girl he loves and whom he seeks to possess. In this manner the early
object love for the mother is transferred to his heterosexual object
choice. His masculinity is solidified and confirmed and he becomes ready
to achieve an ego identity of his own and to move toward intimacy with
another. The same process is likely to happen with the girl and perhaps
in an even more dramatic manner. In falling in love with a boy and
finding herself lovable to a boy, she need no longer fantasy having a
penis or regret not having the prerogatives of a male. She can be satisfied
with loving the boy who has the penis and who may be all too willing to
share it with her. She again feels complete and is ready to progress toward interdependence and the further completion of her life through
having a child.

Unfulfilled Sexuality and the Unconscious

Being in love, a state which cannot be fully explained or analyzed,
seems to be a state of existence in which the boundaries between the self

and another are again loosened and one's sense of well-being depends on being of utmost importance to the chosen person. It is a condition that will be discussed again in later chapters. During these years, even though the physiological drive toward sexual expression is probably as intense as at any time in life, particularly in the male, in our contemporary industrial society—at least in the middle and upper classes—it does not lead to fulfillment in heterosexual love. The adolescent is going through the necessary phases in preparation for later fulfillment. Some relief is gained through masturbation, which in turn is apt to cause considerable conflict in some and little if any in other youths; and there is a greater or lesser amount of sexual play, which often serves to heighten tension rather than relieve it. Even though sexuality often preoccupies the adolescent, much of the sexual thought and fantasy takes place at the borders of consciousness when he is somewhat cut off from the world of reality, as when he is in bed falling asleep or he is awakening in the morning—at times when ego functioning is in abeyance. Even more is censored, repressed, and remains unconscious, becoming manifest only in dreams but still exerting a powerful influence upon behavior. The high school boy who barks at his mother and criticizes her bitterly and somehow finds a reason why he must be away from home whenever his father has to spend an evening in his office has no awareness that he is combating his attraction to his mother. The girl who has started running around with a fast crowd and lets herself be seen engaged in heavy petting only realizes during psychotherapy that she has been trying to demonstrate her heterosexuality to others as well as prove it to herself, whereas her most fundamental attachment and the subject of her half-waking fantasies is a female teacher.

The new force of the sexual impulsions, together with the repression necessary to keep the sexual urges under control, increases the scope of unconscious mental processes considerably. The increased drive, so to speak, directs the individual's perception and interests toward what is forbidden, and like a magnet among iron filings draws more and more associations into its sphere of attraction. Further, the earlier childhood pregenital erotic and sensuous strivings that have long been banned from consciousness join together with the new unconscious sexual motivation. Oral and anal erotic desires and fantasies, masochistic and sadistic imaginings, voyeuristic and exhibitionistic strivings, homosexual attractions and concerns, imagining of the parents in the primal scene, etc., are reawakened during this period of unfulfillment as if the strivings motivated by the sexual impulsion flowed into all of these old outlets in the search for some way of achieving gratification.

Adolescent Mechanisms of Defense

The newly gained capacities for conceptualization and abilities to deal with ideas abstracted from concrete reality not only permit the greater intellectual control that comes to the aid of the ego but they also make possible a greater elaboration of the mechanisms of defense. At this age the adolescent may not gain much sexual gratification in reality, but his active fantasy helps him ward off impulsive activity that might create realistic dangers or generate "instinctual" anxiety of complete loss of control in the sexual act. Masturbation is usually accompanied by fantasies that relieve the emptiness and the loneliness of the act. Such fantasies can serve a variety of purposes such as permitting a safe linkage of genital activity with the desired love object, providing a mental preparation for future activity, affording an imaginary outlet for pregenital or polymorphous perverse erotic strivings that are residues from earlier developmental phases. Other fantasies which are less directly connected with sexual stimulation can help drain off the unconscious associations through the elaboration of romantic daydreams of loving and being loved as well as of future achievements that will bring greatness and renown and thereby admiration and love.

Fantasy formation relates to the defense of *sublimation*, in which sexual impulses are redirected into less earthy and more "sublime" activities. The sensitive adolescent who cannot yet fall in love with a specific person on a realistic basis, or at least gain sexual release through such love, can experience a more diffuse love of nature or of mankind in which there is a vague seeking for expression and fulfillment of the feelings that are surging within him. He feels that he must lose himself in nature or find ways of giving himself to the service of mankind. Poetry bubbles within him and flows from his lips, or he seeks to contain nature on a canvas. These and similar activities are pushed by the sexual drive and made possible by the increased cognitive ability to deal with things imaginatively.

The adolescent is also entering a time when he *intellectualizes*, utilizing his capacity to think and reason in order to control his impulses, not necessarily by reasoning out rational solutions of his problems, but through diverting his interests into intellectual channels. The common manifestations of such intellectualization are the prolonged discussions and arguments about the nature of things, the purpose of life, the errors in the parents' ideas. He is also likely to attach himself to an ideal or an ideology in order to find an outlet for his energies, including his sexuality and aggressivity, but also to achieve new guidelines through having a more meaningful way of life. The ideology may now take precedence over parental teachings and modify the examples of parental behavior that have guided him, notably modifying the superego. The youth may embrace the new ideology with a fervor that consumes his energy and directs his attention, forcing aside any ideas that conflict with it as well as any of his personal needs that interfere with its pursuit. He is, in Piaget's terms, more or less in the egocentric phase of formal operations, in which he does not appreciate that other persons can start from different premises or can reasonably believe that other ideals have even greater importance. There is often a touch of fanaticism in his behavior which both political and religious movements have often utilized. The Children's Crusade, the Hitler Youth, and currently the Chinese Red Guard are examples of how the ideological selflessness of youth can be mobilized into mass movements.

Asceticism, related to such abnegation of the self for ideologic purposes, is another common means used to control the upsurge of sexual and aggressive impulsions. It is as if the strength of the erotic drives were turned against themselves and the superego injunctions that the id seems on the verge of overthrowing were strengthened to deny any pleasures. The ascetic adolescent denies all types of sensuous gratification and through such mortification of the flesh seeks to bury the erotic needs and be rid of the difficulties they are causing. Still the eroticism in this mortification of the spirit and flesh is often apparent even when it leads to the extreme of masochistic flagellation.

Although the adolescent needs to find means of containing the sexual drives until he is better prepared to cope with them realistically, the drives help push him toward seeking and gaining adult prerogatives. He is motivated toward exploring his world and those in it and expanding his horizons. This is a time of expansion, expansion beyond the home, beyond the neighborhood peer group, beyond learning the fundamentals and into gaining knowledge of his own society and other societies to an appreciation of ways of life other than those carried out by the persons with whom he is intimate and which he might decide to follow.

Although many adolescents are now beginning to help the family earn a living even if they continue at school, this is by and large still a time when responsibilities are not too great. The youth does not yet need to confine his restless energies to the prosaic step-by-step surmounting of realistic problems that later will limit his daydreams, bring pause before risk, and lead him to understand the adult's inability to change the world into what the youth thinks it should be. It is still difficult for the young person to understand why people do not "do" things about injustices; why their lives are so prosaic; why they refuse to take a chance. It is a time in which the youth can float above the world, secretly glorying in beauty, being in love with love, and dream of future greatness. There is also the loneliness of feeling deserted by friends who have now found new loves. The world at times is too much to bear. The adolescent is filled with potentiality and hovers in it. Whether he will continue to expand in late adolescence or begin to pull in his tentacles and start to consolidate his efforts depends on many contingencies.

LATE ADOLESCENCE

The major tasks of late adolescence concern the achievement of an ego identity and capacities for intimacy. When the young person has liberated himself from his family sufficiently and gained enough latitude and security to permit sexual expression, he pauses before undertaking definitive commitments. The expansiveness of mid-adolescence gives way to the need to consolidate and to try out imaginatively and realistically various ways of life, including trials at relating meaningfully to persons of the opposite sex. It is often an uneasy pause, for he feels that time is running out in that he will soon be expected to assume adult status and direct his own life and find ways of supporting himself. His life requires a more definitive integration than previously so as to provide him with an identity as a person in his own right and to enable him to move beyond independence to gain completion in intimate interdependence with another.

The Identity Crisis

"Who am I?" is a theme repeated in countless variations by late adolescents. It is a question that troubles them unconsciously even more than consciously. The youth is in the process of finding himself even when he gives it little thought. The boy needs to know now what to do with his life and the girl may focus more upon whom she shall marry, but neither can answer such questions without knowing who he or she is. In some, the recognition that a turning point in life has been reached when decisions of a fairly irrevocable nature must be made precipitates a crisis. The individual realizes dimly or with anxiety-provoking acuteness that if he does not make decisions, the passage of time will make them for him. Friends move on, move past, embark on careers, prepare to marry. The pause can lengthen into a paralysis of indecision. The responsibility of independent choice and its consequences can bring a period of perplexity, turmoil, and sometimes profound despair. The adolescent may fly from his surroundings, leave college, leave home—as if distance will resolve his problems. The change may bring respite and though it is unlikely to solve what he carries within him, a moratorium during which he can gain additional experience, a broadened perspective, or increased emotional maturity can help him find direction.

Identity crises of late adolescence have received considerable attention both in novels and in psychiatry. Novelists have frequently passed through serious identity crises themselves, and psychiatrists are involved with patients many of whom had difficulties in emerging from adolescence. Most individuals, however, manage the transition with reasonable calm as a natural progression into an acceptable identity. The college student who knows that he will enter his father's business is only disturbed intellectually by the various problems aroused by his studies but they have not altered his tangible objectives. The girl who has found her future spouse has no doubts about entering teachers' college to learn to teach until her boy friend can afford to marry and support her. The muscular young man who finds that he is not good enough for the freshman football team, and has no other reason to continue in college, joins the police force at Christmas vacation, content to have realized a lifelong ambition. A girl who cannot remain in her large and very unhappy family after completing high school but who is too insecure to venture forth on her own, enters nursing school where she will be financially independent in a protected environment. Nevertheless, with increased education and with rapid social change, there has been an increasing need for the individual to find his own identity relatively independently of his family; the young adult is less likely to remain somewhat dependent upon his family or to follow in a family tradition than in previous eras, and identity problems have become increasingly common and difficult.

Identity Formation

The transition from adolescent to adult involves becoming a person in one's own right, not simply someone's son or daughter, and one who is recognized by the community in such terms. It involves the drawing together and resynthesis of a process that has been going on since birth and the crystallization out of an individual who will tend to preserve his identity despite the vicissitudes of life that are yet to come. The individual has passed through a series of developmental phases, and at each level there has been an identity and there has been a relatedness between the identities at each phase. Still, these identities always had a tentative quality, for each was a phase in becoming; but now it is time to be. The concept of ego identity was formulated by Erikson to emphasize that the developmental phases of childhood are not ends in themselves but stages in the progression toward developing into an integrated and reasonably self-sufficient person capable of filling an adult role in life and fitting into the social system in which he lives. The integration is not achieved simply by passing through successive stages of psychosexual development without traumata and undue fixations, but depends on constant reorganization during the process, and then, during adolescence, a reintegration to permit moving from childhood dependency to adult responsibility.* It is concerned not simply with inner organization but also with how that organization permits the individual to move properly into the social roles permitted an adult and expected of him in a given society and its subsystems.

The concept of ego identity is not definable in very precise terms and a degree of vagueness is preferable, for it is still simpler to delineate the area of interest than define it in terms of critical attributes. It concerns the consistency that characterizes an individual despite the changes that occur over time, and as he moves into the many different roles he fills at any one period in his life.† We might say that by the end of adolescence

---

* "The process of identity formation emerges as an evolving configuration, a configuration which is gradually established by successive ego syntheses and resyntheses throughout childhood; it is a configuration gradually integrating constitutional givens, idiosyncratic libidinal needs, favored capacities, significant identifications, effective defenses, successful sublimations, and consistent roles" (E. Erikson, "The Problem of Ego Identity," [4] p. 116).

† The concept of ego identity also implies the attainment of a homeostasis of the self or the personality which absorbs the impact of influences upon the personality and tends to resist radical change and perpetuate itself, so to speak. The homeostatic mechanisms within the personality are extremely complex, and involve matters beyond

the individual's name—as should be the case with all nominal words—provides a degree of predictability concerning how he will behave and what others can anticipate from him under a variety of circumstances. Equally important is that the individual also has some idea of how he will behave, relate, and feel under varying conditions. Of course, human behavior is so complex and subject to so many contingencies, as well as conscious and unconscious influences, that prediction of how a person will react and interact in unfamiliar situations remains limited (except, of course, to a psychiatrist).

Identity formation has much to do with the person's past identifications and their fusion into a new integrate. The identifications with the parents remain basic despite the many vicissitudes they have undergone, but to them have been added the identifications with various ideal figures and both friends and enemies,* for something remains of all. Various significant persons who have been lost—or more or less abandoned—particularly the parents, are preserved within the self. Identity formation also involves identifications with groups as well as individuals: the family as a unit with its traditions and specific mores; the social class into which one is raised; ethnic and religious groupings; and one's nation and time in history, which are usually taken for granted, as well as one's gender, which, as we have emphasized, forms a keystone in stable identity formation. To gain coherence of personality functioning and a sense of unity, aspects of identifications that are inconsistent with the total pattern,

---

current knowledge. While the sorting out of identifications is very important, it involves many other matters, some of which I shall indicate here: (1) What a person perceives and how he perceives it influences markedly the further development of personality traits; yet it involves a process that is circular, for perception depends in part on the projection of personality characteristics—as we know from the utility of projective personality tests. (2) Patterns of relating within the family now come to a closure, but will continue to influence all further interpersonal and group relationships. (3) Parental directives have now been internalized into the superego; but even more important, many have moved closer to the ego "core" and become ego rather than superego functions and thus are fundamental and rather spontaneous determinants of behavior. (4) The patterns of the defensive mechanisms utilized to avert anxiety and depression as well as cognitive styles and patterns of emotional reactivity have become fairly set. (5) The individual has assimilated into the self both cultural instrumentalities and norms as well as much of the social system in which he lives, and thus gains a stability in behaving, perceiving, relating, according to these norms. (6) The assumption of a major life role—such as the role of a physician or future physician, lawyer, or even profligate—contributes to consistency and resistance to change.
* Identification with the aggressor is often an important defense in which one takes on strengths and attributes of a feared and hated object.

which are ego-alien, must be discarded or repressed. "Identity formation," as Erikson has pointed out, "begins where the usefulness of
identification ends. It arises from the selective repudiation and mutual
assimilation of childhood identifications, and their absorption in a new
configuration, which in turn, is dependent on the process by which a
society (often through subsocieties) identifies the young individual, recognizing him as somebody who had to become the way he is, and who,
being the way he is, is taken for granted."*

The adolescent is seeking consistent ways of relating to others, for
finding his way through life and for solving problems. He needs and
seeks reference points. He feels, like Archimedes, that if he has a place
on which to stand, he can move the world—or at least he can face it.
Although finding guidance into the future depends upon the stability of
previous identifications and their resynthesis, it also requires standards
for judging behavior and directives. We have seen that the adolescent
moves beyond superego injunctions taken from the parents; the parental
injunctions have been modified through fusion with ego ideals, and
through the assimilation of standards of peer groups and the mores of
the community; and in an effort to find a definite way of life, he is likely
to embrace a cause which not only tells him what to do with his life, but
also provides standards for judging what is right and wrong, what is pertinent and what irrelevant. Still, only a small minority find that their
major problems will be solved by joining a political party, a religious
movement, or a social movement. Politics is not a way of life for most,
nor is religion. Joining the Peace Corps or becoming involved with racial
equality movements usually lends direction to a life for but a few
years. Direction is more apt to come from reaching a decision about a
career. When a youth makes the choice about his future occupation, he
has settled many problems, for he can direct his attention and exert his
energies in preparing for it. What he will do with his life helps answer
the query "Who am I?" †

Identity and Delimitation

Yet, one of the functions of adolescence is to keep pathways into the
future open, to prevent premature closure before the youth has gained
sufficient experience to judge properly what he wishes to do with his life.
One of the reasons for attending a university is to broaden horizons be-

* E. Erikson, "The Problem of Ego Identity," 4 p. 113.
† A topic that will be expanded in the chapter on occupational choice.

yond the occupations known at home or in the local community; to introduce new ways of considering the world and how one may live in it. He had been expanding, sampling, so to speak, but now in late adolescence matters change as he realizes he must consolidate, weighing whether or not he wishes really to pursue some particular field of endeavor. He may find it difficult to renounce one potentiality to follow another, yet he knows that he has only one life to lead. Now, more than ever before, he must delimit himself in order to gain organization. He becomes weary of the indecision, and seeks a future objective which will do away with vacillation and the constant need to make decisions. He may feel, and believe correctly, that everything hangs in the balance— and that if, by chance, he takes one road and not another, it will decide much of his future. This is a time when a single decision can greatly influence his entire life, whereas later, after he has embarked on a set course, it will require a major reorientation to alter his life pattern. He can become paralyzed with indecision when any decision seems so important. A college senior had entered the university some three years before, fairly certain that he would follow his father and become a physician. He had been responding to expectations for him rather than his own interests. He became increasingly engrossed in courses in literature and history, and found that the natural sciences were tolerable but uninteresting to him. His father died, and soon thereafter he decided not to become a physician; but now he found himself torn between following an academic career or entering the government's foreign service. He did not have difficulty finding something he wished to do with his life, but rather found himself unable to decide what not to do with it. Some in this predicament can, like Goethe, decide that it does not really matter whether they make pots or pans, or plant peas or beans, but can trust to their genius to make whatever they do turn out well.*

The achievement of an identity includes recognition by others, and such recognition, even when tentative, often helps the youth find a place in society that he can occupy without inner conflicts. The recognition by a teacher who suggests or persuades him to enter a given field can help settle problems of finding an identity. To some, such experiences come quietly and unexpectedly while they still consider themselves junior de-

* Developmental novels—*Erziehungsroman*—usually deal with the crisis the author passed through in finding a way of life and are of particular interest to the study of personality development. Noteworthy examples are Goethe's *Wilhelm Meister*, Samuel Butler's *The Way of All Flesh*, Somerset Maugham's *Of Human Bondage*, Strindberg's *The Red Room*, James Joyce's *A Portrait of the Artist as a Young Man*.

pendent members of society. A college sophomore spends his summer vacation working as a surveyor, enjoying the work with a crew in the woods. When the foreman becomes ill, the student takes charge of the crew and gains their respect despite his youth. At the end of vacation the head of the engineering firm suggests that he remain in a more responsible position, assuring him that he can have a good future with the firm. Although he continues college, he has definitely decided to become a civil engineer and has the assurance of an excellent position after he is graduated. He had started the summer still carefree and without feeling pressed to decide about a career; his life and future were still amorphous, but when he returned to college he could envision a pattern of life and he had a plan to follow that solved many problems for him.

The youth seeks outward to find a way of life that will satisfy. The searching also turns inward as he seeks resources and weighs liabilities. What are the talents, and what are the desires that need fulfillment? Comparisons with others are searching, and he may mercilessly take into account only the strongest assets of the person to whom he is comparing himself. He casts aside attributes he possesses that will not lead to perfection. He holds up a mirror to his soul and unconscious processes well up and threaten to bring chaos. When the forward flow of the stream is halted, much old debris can float to the surface. He may recognize and become disturbed by the erotic nature of his love for his mother, by sadistic impulses, or by worries about his masculinity that make him wonder if he might be homosexual. He may achieve profound insights into unconscious processes, but they are often of little help at this juncture of his life. For many adolescents, the solution to many sources of anguish, to much of the self-doubting, lies in finding direction and starting toward a goal rather than in further introspection.

Adolescent Turmoil and Ego Diffusion

Such problems are so common at the end of adolescence that they are often considered as an inherent part of the period. Late adolescence is a time of conflict, and some neurotic suffering is almost inevitable. The seriousness of the problems may be difficult to assess. The dangers lie not so much in failure to reach an immediate solution and find an identity and way of life—for many persons will take several years until they find themselves—but in finding a negative solution: the youth gives up, feels defeated and suffers an "ego diffusion" in which he virtually ceases to try to direct his life consciously, leaving himself prey to unconscious motivations, and he drifts, perhaps becoming more or less schizophrenic; or he becomes embittered about the ways of society and the adults who inhabit and direct the Establishment, and becomes alienated refusing to become committed to a way of life; or he embraces alienation itself as a way of life, to become "beat" or to assume the way of life of an artist without being an artist.*

Although the inability to find a positive identity and a way of life may seem to be a matter of decision, insofar as it depends upon decision rather than chronic indecision the choice rests upon unconscious determinants that reflect profound problems. A bright college student who "drops out" to join the fringe Bohemian groups in Greenwich Village or Berkeley, experimenting with marijuana or even with heroin, is not only unable to identify with his father—or any paternal figure—but must prove to himself that he is different from his father; he may also be unable to relate to women, who are experienced as engulfing, overwhelming figures who are untrustworthy, and he may be moving into or reactively fighting against a homosexual identity. Study reveals serious family and developmental pathology. As Keniston has elucidated through his studies of alienated students,† the young man may have been profoundly disillusioned in his mother, who had been seductively close to

* The current trend toward the use of marijuana and LSD as a means of finding oneself and discovering a new truth and meaning through more immediate access to the unconscious is clearly related to the Dionysian religion in ancient Greece. Dionysus was the "liberator"—the god who through the use of wine and the ecstasy of the bacchanal enabled a person to stop being himself for a brief period, thereby setting the person free from feelings of responsibility and the burden of being himself. It was a flight from the Apollonian spirit, which sought self-understanding through experience, an attempt to gain insight through revelation. Dionysus was thus a god of illusion with a welcomed way of release from planning and control. He appeared at a time when the individual began to emerge from the solidarity of the family for the first time, and "found the burden of individual responsibility hard to bear." The aim of the cult was the achievement of ecstasy, a losing of oneself, and its psychological function was to "satisfy and relieve the impulse to reject responsibility, an impulse that exists in all of us and can become under certain social conditions an irresistible craving." LSD is used for similar purposes, primarily by late adolescents and young adults who find the burden of achieving an ego identity too great. The illusion of profound insight into the self and the meaning of the universe so often experienced under the influence of the drug makes it particularly tempting and dangerous. The taker has the illusion of finding himself through losing himself. The use of the drug is often bound to group ritual in which the individual feels freed from responsibility for his own behavior and can be carried away as were the participants in the bacchanalia. It is of interest that some devotees seek to ritualize the use of LSD into a religious rite. (See E. R. Dodds, *The Greeks and the Irrational*,[2] pp. 76–77.)
† See K. Keniston, *The Uncommitted*.[6] Such tragic situations are dramatized effectively and realistically in Arthur Miller's *Death of a Salesman* and Eugene O'Neill's *Long Day's Journey into Night.*

him, when she betrayed him by adhering to his father; and disillusioned
in a father who despite external appearances turned out to be weak,
relatively ineffectual, and perhaps effeminate. Others have been disillusioned in recognizing that one or both parents are dishonest, promiscuous, deceitful toward spouse and child.

The Girl's Identity Problems

The identity crisis of late adolescence affects young men more often
than young women. The girl is likely to become concerned over whether
she should pursue a career or prepare for marriage. When a girl experiences a serious identity crisis, it is apt to involve security of gender identity and her unpreparedness to forego her claim to masculine prerogatives. Contemporary society places a high premium on achievement,
upon making something of oneself, and girls are influenced by such
values, and higher education prepares a girl to pursue a career. She
knows that she may be a superior student, musician, or architect—better
than most of her male colleagues—and she is reluctant to give up the
possibility of having a career. Still, when the chips are down, so to speak,
in late adolescence, she usually reconsiders and redirects her interests
toward marriage. There are several interrelated reasons for the change in
perspective. As we have shown in earlier chapters, the entire pattern of
the girl's development has directed her to seeking fulfillment in marriage
and child rearing. In many, if not in all girls, there is an unconscious
belief in having been born deprived and incomplete which leaves
them feeling instrumentally inadequate despite protestations and displays of competence. In school and college a girl may have sought unconsciously to show that her intellect was as good as a boy's, sometimes
to use her intellect aggressively—phallically. Her intentions often change
when, as has been noted, she can displace her masculine identifications
onto a man whom she loves, and feels that she can gain satisfaction
through his achievements. The contemporary role expectation for the
girl is early marriage, and she may well be influenced by the expectations
others hold for her. She is almost certain to be affected by friends and
classmates who never held serious career aspirations and who are now
engaged in seeking a suitable husband. As a superior student she is accustomed to receiving praise, but now the plaudits are going to the girls who
are finding husbands. Intellectual abilities and achievements attract a
limited number of men, and she becomes afraid that she will be left at
the post in the dash for a husband. It may be important that, just like

the male, she take pause before entering the competition of the adult
world. She not only must make decisions about what career to pursue
but also wonders about her chances of success in a male environment.
But, in contrast to her male colleagues, she has no obligation to pursue
a career. The female prerogative of remaining dependent and gaining
status through the husband's achievements becomes more enticing. Her
previous contempt of the woman's role in life, and of women who were
content to fill it, turns into an appreciation of its advantages. Furthermore, if her development has been more or less normative for the society,
and if her family has provided an example of the benefits of marriage and
of the roles of wife and mother, she feels that her eventual sense of fulfillment rests upon having a husband and children and investing her
energies in them. Her sense of completion depends so very much upon
such goals that she tends to direct herself toward assuring them earlier
than does the male. The girl, of course, may continue her studies or preparation for a career, but for most it loses its central importance as her
future does not depend upon it.

Identity and the Capacity for Intimacy

The discussion of the problems of achieving an ego identity separately
from the consideration of gaining a capacity for intimacy has been arbitrary, required for clarity, for the two processes are closely interrelated,
particularly for the girl. The answer to the query "Who am I?" depends,
in part, upon knowing that one can love and be loved as an individual,
and even more specifically upon whom one loves and from whom one
desires love. Ego identity involves the feelings of completion that come
from feeling loved and needed, from being able to share the self and the
world with another. Still, the capacity of intimacy can develop only as
feelings of self-assurance and of being an integrated and reasonably independent individual gradually consolidate. Concerns over sexual capacities, over gender identity, and then over the ability to be close and gain
closeness markedly influence the adolescent's developing ego identity.

The girl, in particular, seeks to learn who she is in terms of whom she
needs and who admires and needs her; and her capacities for intimacy are
an essential part of gaining a stable and cohesive identity. The problems
are not so very different from the boy's, but the emphasis and sequence
differ. In a sense, the question "Who am I?" has a more specific connotation for the girl. She is concerned with who she is, in herself, and less
in terms of success in a career. The basic aspirations have been more

definitively provided by her biological make-up as the child producer and child rearer, and the accompanying role allocations have marked similarities for all women in all societies. Her major interest lies in finding an intimate relationship suited to her needs, for so very much of her life will depend upon just whom she marries. A great deal goes into the exploration of her own attributes and what sorts of boys and men can engender a sense of completion in her. As the average age at which women marry is currently about twenty, her concerns about intimacy properly are more pressing than the male's, though we might also consider that because her concerns about intimacy are so dominant, she moves toward marriage earlier and more decisively than does the boy. Her attention, both consciously and unconsciously, centrally and peripherally, is directed toward acquiring a suitable husband. As the mores of our society dictate that she remain passive and receptive rather than actively pursue this major objective, she learns varying degrees of artifice, cultivates wiles that attract boys, and ways of appearing passive while actively pursuing them. It is a difficult and trying role to balance; and often enough the aggressiveness shines through and her behavior becomes ensnaring, which can frighten away a youth who has just managed to free himself from his mother, and who dashes away more rapidly than a deer who has picked up the scent of the hunter.

Although most young women will prepare for and enter into an occupation, it is usually a secondary matter, a means of filling time or supporting her husband during his training years and augmenting the family income when she is not caring for children. The selection of an occupation will not be concerned with gaining prestige, wealth, or power but will more commonly be directed toward finding a job in which she can be an assistant, a helper, or in which she can fill a nurturant role, as in nursing, teaching, social work, and medicine. There are, of course, a number of women who will pursue more masculine careers for a variety of reasons, sometimes because they cannot come to terms with their feminine identity and wish to compete with and surpass men, but also often from fears of marriage and childbirth, or of the dangers of dependency.

The capacity for intimacy, then, is an inherent part of the identity formation in most girls; and readiness for intimacy requires acceptance of and security in a feminine identity. The girl may enter late adolescence quite firmly established in her identification with womanhood, wishing primarily to complement the life of her husband and find happiness in her family. She may not feel unduly masochistic in accepting the more passive role. Usually, though, she may still need to discover the positive values of being a woman through experience. Some shifts in her conscious and unconscious attitudes must still take place, and these often occur as she falls in love. The unconscious envy of the penis can vanish when she learns that she can be loved and admired without one, indeed because she does not have one. Though she may feel burdened by being forced to wait for a husband and by the limitations on self-expression, she also can sympathize with the young man's problems of needing to prove himself constantly.* She can realize, in a more mature way, the satisfactions her mother gained in loving and being needed, which may earlier have seemed only a burden to her. She is learning from her own experiences and those of her friends that sexual behavior is not only permissible, but that the female role can be enjoyable, indeed that the woman can gain as much sexual satisfaction as the man.†

* A young woman who married in late adolescence and found that neither she nor her husband was really ready for married life spoke with considerable understanding of her young husband's situation—how he could no longer rely on his athletic prowess to bolster his self-esteem; how he had to shift to more covert ways of competing with peers; how he was constantly judged and judging himself on the basis of achievement in his new occupation; and how when he felt a failure, he had difficulties with the sexual act, when he would feel even less of a man, and tend to move away from her. In contrast, she felt that she did not have to strive constantly, had time to relax and pursue old interests, and when she was not really up to the sexual act or did not gain pleasure from it, could always fake it.
† The comparison of the relative satisfaction gained by each sex in the sexual act is, of course, impossible. The only person who has ever been deemed capable of so judging was the mythical Tiresias. According to legend, Tiresias had been turned into a woman when he saw snakes copulating, and had then lived as a courtesan for many years, but eventually regained his masculine anatomy. It seems that once when Hera was upbraiding Zeus for one of his many infidelities, he told her not to complain for as a woman she gained far more pleasure when they did have sexual relations. Hera did not accept her spouse's infinite knowledge and insisted that the remark was ludicrous, that everyone knew that the man gained more pleasure from the act than the woman. The quarrel thus turned from the particular to the universal, but neither one could convince the other. Finally they remembered Tiresias and called upon him to settle the argument, admitting that for once a mortal could know something hidden even to a god. Tiresias stated that if the pleasure of the sexual act is divided into ten parts, nine parts are the woman's. This assertion so angered Hera that she struck Tiresias blind. Zeus could not undo Hera's act, but sought to compensate Tiresias by conferring upon him inner sight, thus making him the greatest of all seers; and he bestowed on him seven life spans, which accounts for the appearance of Tiresias in myths that took place in different eras.

Intimacy and Love

Even though the adolescent may have had various sexual experiences, usually he is not ready to become involved in intimate relationships until late adolescence; and even then, they are apt to be tentative. He has been seeking release, knowledge, excitement, and has been engaged in exploring his feelings and those of persons of the opposite sex, more than in seeking completion of the self through a permanent relationship with another. Indeed, a stable love relationship in the mid-teens often indicates an inability to tolerate independence from essential persons and can block the development of a firm ego identity. Even though the sexual drives are as imperative as earlier, the late adolescent is often less upset by them. He has usually found some means of coming to terms with his sexual needs, even though on a temporary basis, and his super-ego is more tolerant. The mystery is no longer so tantalizing and he feels more certain of his capacities; defenses against the drives have been found and strengthened, and he permits himself some outlets without too much conflict.

Gradually the youth begins to have a less self-centered and narcissistic orientation to his sexual and affectional needs. He becomes involved in love relationships in which the welfare of the partner is also important, and the satisfaction that the other obtains becomes a source of pleasure to him. He feels, even if he does not consciously realize it, that he is incomplete alone and that a member of one sex cannot feel complete without joining with a member of the opposite sex. He wishes to share and find someone whose roles and ways of loving are complementary to his, who gains satisfaction from what he does, who is not a rival, and to whom he is necessary. He is no longer seeking someone like himself, or even someone of the other sex in whom he finds attributes he might have liked to possess, but someone who completes him and admires him. When an adolescent persists in pursuing an unrequited love, the romantic striving has a pathological character as if the boy or girl feels fated to repeat the frustrations of the oedipal situation rather than to find situations that can bring fulfillment.

Now that the individual has begun to come to terms with who he or she is, and has a fairly definite ego identity, he often falls in love in a serious fashion. The meaning and intensity of being in love varies with the maturity of the person, but even the "puppy loves" of early adolescence can have considerable impact. Now, couples are drawn together and the life of each encompasses the other. There is an impelling need to be together and share experiences. Things done separately are carried out with thoughts of the partner. Separation can be painful, and thoughts of being replaced by another engender real suffering. The lover invests the representation of the loved one intensely, and even though it may be painful at times, the experience of being drawn beyond one's own confines and beyond one's own life into such intimate concern and involvement leads to a loosening of boundaries of the self, to a release that is ecstatic. Now, an intense attachment to another that combines the affectional and erotic can for the first time replace the intense attachment to a parent that had to be renounced. The psychic intimacy usually blends with a physical and sexual intimacy, but the emotional and psychic investment can become more irresistible than the sexual urges from which such feeling may derive.

I cannot don the poet's mantle to write of the bliss of early love when the self is partially lost in devotion to another, and when the awkwardness of self-consciousness shifts into a grace of being desired. Even though most early loves break up sooner or later, they form important omens for the future. They indicate that disappointments over frustrations within the family can be overcome, that repressions of sexuality are not too great, that defenses are not too rigid. The relationships may be disrupted because the choice resembles a parent too closely or, conversely, is too dissimilar; or because the boy and girl are not yet ready to relinquish their newly gained independence; or because too many tasks toward achieving security and a career remain. Sexual frustrations may produce too may frictions. Such relationships are an important part of developing into an adult, a proper trying out of how one relates to another on intimate terms. They are part of the expansion of adolescence but also a coming to terms with the need to delimit and share, and such courtships should be trial periods rather than firm commitments.

The Changing Sexual Mores

The changes in adolescent sexual mores have permitted many in recent decades to include sexual intercourse as part of their experimentation with intimate relationships. It is possible that there has not been a great change in the number of late adolescents who currently have intimate sexual experience in comparison with previous generations, but there is probably more intercourse than petting to orgasm than earlier in the century,* and more openness about cohabitation. There is probably consider-

* It should be realized that university students in many other countries had prolonged sexual affairs even prior to World War II, and, in particular, Scandinavian sexual

ably greater freedom, particularly for the girl to have sexual relationships without a serious commitment to the partner; sometimes with only sufficient commitment for her to assure herself that she is not promiscuous. A great effort has gone into making premarital sexual relationships more casual and less focal. The changes in the parietal rules in college dormitories reflect students' insistence that they are sufficiently mature to make their own decisions concerning sexual relationships, and that sexual intercourse and immorality are not synonymous.

It is also apparent that the adolescent can permit himself to feel bolder and require less in the way of protection from parietal rules because the sexual act encompasses far less danger and is far less threatening to the continuity of his development and career than formerly; and there is less threat of a girl's being forced into an undesirable marriage. Improved contraception and a decrease in the seriousness of the consequences of venereal infections are important factors in producing this change; but even many progressive religious leaders no longer equate sexual abstinence with morality, and some even believe that greater freedom of sexual expression may lead to a lessening of unconscious motivations toward unethical behavior. The concept, stemming originally from psychoanalytic teachings that sexual repression can be harmful to the harmonious development of the individual, has had considerable influence upon teachers, clergy, doctors, and parents. The greater acceptance of sexuality by elders permits more open discussion in adolescence; and it is the openness of talk about sexual relationships rather than the frequency of premarital relationships that represents much of the change over the past few decades. It is natural enough for the boy to desire sexual release with a girl whom he likes rather than with either a prostitute or someone who does not matter, and for the girl to wish to share sexually with her boy friend rather than have him turn to another for gratification. It makes sense to many to explore and try out how things work with different partners; and not to feel impelled to marry in order to have a sexual relationship. The new freedom can have the salutary influence of lessening the import of sexual desire as a dominant motivation for marriage and the choice of marital partners; and in diminishing sexual repression

---

mores have long differed markedly from those of the United States. The practice of "heavy petting" that had been considered more permissible in contrast to sexual relationships has something of a perverse character, in that forepleasure becomes the goal, and this seemed very bizarre to many Europeans.

during late adolescence to permit more rational decisions concerning other matters aside from marriage, including career choice.

There are, however, some difficulties inherent in the contemporary situation. They devolve from problems of emotional maturity more than from questions of morals or ethics. Adolescents of both sexes tend to engage in sexual relationships of either a transitory or more involved nature before they are ready. The group mores no longer tend to support refusal or delay, and the individual must be willing to maintain a stand concerning what is right for himself or herself. When a young couple has a sexual relationship, one member is apt to invest more of the self in it than the other, and not be able to accept the other's casualness. Actual sexual difficulties are apt to occur more commonly among adolescents who are still not properly disengaged from their oedipal attachments, and who cannot cope with the dependency needs of a partner when they are far from independent themselves. Of course, similar problems occur in young married couples. It is not a matter of age but of readiness, and couples are more apt to be ready when they must also consider the life-long involvements of marriage. The solutions are not readily available, for there cannot be generalized answers. Here we are simply noting that the adolescent often considers such matters in terms of standards of morality and propriety, which they are willing to change, when questions of maturity may be more pertinent.

Variant Uses of Sexuality

The adolescent may start to use his or her sexuality for purposes other than either gaining sexual release or moving toward intimacy. Compulsive sexuality that enables the boy to believe that he is a real man, or the girl to think that she is irresistibly sensuous—or at least to lead others to believe so—is often a defense against fears of homosexuality or deep feelings of worthlessness, or a flight from loneliness and emptiness. Some will use sexuality as a means of sadistically dominating the partner, or of humiliating the opposite sex; or to make the other feel sexually inadequate or worthless. Then, there is the potentiality that the pleasures of the sexual act can lead a person with a shaky identity into finding solace and diversion through it, and sexuality becomes something of a game. The use of sex as a game or a diversion in late adolescence and early adult life is common enough; it can be part of a competition with peers of the same sex, or seduction through various tactics and strategies becomes a game in itself. Some consider such activities an inherent part of late adolescence and early adulthood in the male, a diversion that need not be deleterious unless it ultimately becomes a substitute for seeking after real intimacy.

The End of Adolescence

Sooner or later adolescence ends for most (but not all) persons, and it can end in many different ways. Still, we may generalize and consider that a person enters maturity and becomes an adult after he feels independent enough and has explored the horizon enough. He begins to feel that the world is too large and he can become lost in it. He realizes all too keenly that success in his chosen career depends upon the effort he puts into it, for he is competing with others who seem as capable as he is. An obsessive quality may develop in a youth who formerly had been carefree; it is an obsessiveness deriving from efforts to overcome anxiety about the future through thinking through and working out solutions in advance, mingled with compulsive strivings to satisfy expectations. He cannot afford to fail. Such concerns can lead to overdelimitation, to a constriction of interests and of the personality. It is the danger opposite to that of ego diffusion—an outcome that is not so devastating and chaotic, but narrowing and sometimes paralyzing.

Now the loss of bonds to his family is no longer pleasing, particularly as his newer relationships are being cut into as friends pair off and marry. The need for interdependence with another and for intimacy asserts itself and gains dominance as a motivation. He cannot keep seeking after some indefinite ambition but must settle down to conquer a specific section of the vocational world. The youth begins to believe, albeit often unconsciously, that striving after fame or wealth, or the pursuit of some ideology is less important than coming to mean something to some specific individual. He realizes that life will gain in meaning through his being meaningful to another person and having the other person need him. Thus the strivings for intimacy and identity come together, for much of his feelings of having a specific identity will come from his being needed and wanted by another person, and from the meaning he has to the other person. Even as the self first took form in childhood through a feedback from significant others, now one particularly significant person helps define the self. Intimacy comes when an individual is capable of balancing giving and receiving and can seek to satisfy another rather than simply seek self-fulfillment and achievement.

It is now, at the end of adolescence, that the youth often moves out of a child-centered perspective of the world. He begins to see himself moving through a complex world and a maze of people rather than having others pass through his world.* He realizes that he is living in a brief span of history isolated in an infinity of space. If he is fortunate he finds meaning in what the world is, and does not get lost in his insignificance. He appreciates that there are ways of regarding the world which are very different from his. Reluctantly, he may decide that although ideologies are worth pursuing, he must first look out for his own future. The egocentricity of the early stage of formal operations is now behind him. He also begins to see his parents as individuals with lives of their own, caught up in their own marriage and occupations, rather than simply as parents. He now begins to understand their foibles and deficiencies and sometimes even to hope that he will be able to do as well. He may begin again to accept components of his parents as conscious objects of identification and their standards as part of his superego. As he leaves his youth, he may have lingering regrets that he has not dared more or that he has not been able to stick to the ideals that but so recently fired his life. In a way, it is always regrettable when the youth becomes as conservative and conventional as his parents at an early age.

* A nineteen-year-old, after revisiting the town in which he had spent his first summer vacation during college and where he had made many friends, recalled his thoughts and feelings while walking to the railroad station when he left. "I was in something of a daze; the people hurrying through the streets looked different to me than people ever looked before. I realized in a way that I had never before that all of this had remained while I had come and gone: my friends were pursuing their lives, falling in love and out again, changing their studies, finding new interests, and I was only peripheral to it, indeed scarcely mattered. Of course, I had *known* this before but I had never *felt* it."

References

1. Therese Benedek and Boris B. Rubenstein, "The Sexual Cycle in Women: The Relation Between Ovarian Function and Psychodynamic Processes," *Psychosomatic Medicine* Monographs, Vol. 3, Nos. 1 and 2 (National Research Council, 1942).
2. Eric Dodds, *The Greeks and the Irrational* (Berkeley: University of California Press, 1951).
3. D. J. Duche, W. Schonfeld, and S. Tomkiewicz, "Physical Aspects of Adolescent Development," in G. Caplan and S. Lebovici (eds.), *Psychiatric Approaches to Adolescence*, International Congress Series, No. 108 (New York: Excerpta Medica Foundation, 1966).
4. Erik H. Erikson, "The Problem of Ego Identity," *Journal of the American Psychoanalytic Association*, 4 (1956), 56–121.
5. Bärbel Inhelder and Jean Piaget, *The Growth of Logical Thinking from Childhood to Adolescence*, trans. Anne Parsons and Stanley Milgram (New York: Basic Books, 1958).
6. Kenneth Keniston, *The Uncommitted: Alienated Youth in American Society* (New York: Harcourt, Brace & World, 1965).
7. Alfred Kinsey, Wardell B. Pomeroy, and Clyde Martin, *Sexual Behavior in the Human Male* (Philadelphia: W. B. Saunders, 1948).
8. Alfred Kinsey, Wardell B. Pomeroy, Clyde Martin, and Paul Gebhard, *Sexual Behavior in the Human Female* (Philadelphia: W. B. Saunders, 1953).
9. Hans Loewald, "Ego and Reality," *International Journal of Psycho-Analysis*, 32 (1951), 1–9.
10. Jean Piaget, *Logic and Psychology* (New York: Basic Books, 1957).
11. William A. Schonfeld, "Primary and Secondary Sexual Characteristics: Study of Their Development in Males from Birth through Maturity, with Biometric Study of Penis and Testes," *American Journal of Diseases of Children*, 65 (1943), 535–549.
12. Lev S. Vygotsky, *Thought and Language*, ed. and trans. Eugenia Hanfmann and Gertrude Vakar (New York: M.I.T. Press and John Wiley & Sons, 1962).

Suggested Reading

Peter Blos, *On Adolescence: A Psychoanalytic Interpretation* (Glencoe, Ill.: Free Press, 1962).
Helene Deutsch, "Selected Problems of Adolescence," *Psychoanalytic Study of the Child*, Monograph No. 3 (New York: International Universities Press, 1967).
Anna Freud, "Adolescence," *The Psychoanalytic Study of the Child*, Vol.

13 (New York: International Universities Press, 1958), pp. 255–278.

Irene M. Josselyn, *The Adolescent and His World* (New York: Family Service Association of America, 1952).

Kenneth Keniston, *The Uncommitted: Alienated Youth in American Society* (New York: Harcourt, Brace & World, 1965).

Sandor Lorand and Henry I. Schneer (eds.), *Adolescents: Psychoanalytic Approach to Problems and Therapy* (New York: Paul B. Hoeber, 1961).

CHAPTER 11 [3]

❀ ❀ ❀ ❀ ❀
❀ ❀ ❀ ❀ ❀ ❀

The Young Adult

THE LENGTHY DEVELOPMENTAL PROCESS as a dependent apprentice in living draws to a close as the individual attains an identity and the ability to live intimately with a member of the opposite sex, and contemplates forming a family of his own. He has attained adult status with the completion of physical maturation, and hopefully he has become sufficiently well integrated and emotionally mature to utilize the opportunities and accept the responsibilities that accompany it. He has reached a decisive point on his journey. He has dropped the pilot and now starts sailing on his own—but he has been taught to navigate and he has been provided with charts, albeit they are charts that can be only approximately correct for the currents and reefs change constantly. He has practiced under more or less competent supervision, taken trips in sheltered waters, and now he assumes responsibility and must accept the consequences of his decisions. Usually he asks another to share the journey, and soon others join them, bidden and unbidden, and their welfare depends upon his skills and stability.

The young adult's energies and interests can now be directed beyond his own growth and development. His independence from his natal family requires that he achieve an interdependence with others and find his place in the social system. Through vocation and marriage he is united to networks of persons, finds tasks that demand involvement, and gains roles into which he fits and is fitted which help define his identity. He is virtually forced to become less self-centered through the very pursuit of his own interests.

The time when adult life starts is not set chronologically, for a person may have entered upon his vocation and selected a spouse some time in adolescence: but if he is still uncommitted, he must make an occupational choice early in adulthood, as must virtually all men. Most individuals will also give up their much sought independence to share with another in marriage. Then the life cycle rounds to the point at which the young adult is again confronted by the start of life, but now as a member of the parental generation, and he often undergoes a profound personality reorientation as he becomes involved in the unfolding of a child's life. The period ends at a somewhat indefinite time, approximately when children's needs no longer form a major focus of attention, and usually around the age of forty when he has attained a stable position in society or, at least, when he realizes that he must come to terms with what he will be able to make out of his one and only life.

The young adult is at the height of his physical and mental vigor as he launches upon making his way and establishing his place in the world; and his energies are usually expended more effectively than they were during adolescence. The expansiveness of adolescence had usually given way to efforts at consolidation in late adolescence, but the young adult must focus his energies and interests even more definitively as he commits himself to a specific way of life and usually to marriage with its libidinal investment in a single significant person. Now, more than ever, alternative ways of life must be renounced to permit the singleness of purpose required for success and to consolidate his identity; and his intimacy becomes reserved for a single person to make possible meaningful sharing with a spouse. Although commitment to another person entails the danger of being carried along in the other's inadequacies or misfortunes, its avoidance carries the penalty of lack of opportunity to be meaningful to others and have others become meaningful to the self.

Vocational choice and marital choice are two of the most significant decisions of a lifetime. Although they are sometimes made easily and even seemingly casually, they are both extremely complex matters that are resultants of the individual's entire personality development. They are two cardinal resultants of the lengthy process of achieving adulthood that we have been tracing; and now these decisions will become major determinants of the course of the individual's further personality development, of the satisfactions that will be gained from life, and of the trials and problems that will ensue and strain the integration of the personality and perhaps even warp it. The individual's own capacities and integration markedly influence his choices of occupation and spouse, and then influence how he can cope with and gain fulfillment from both—and subsequently from being a parent. We shall, in the following two chapters, scrutinize the choices of vocation and spouse and then consider the tasks involved in adjusting to marriage and being a parent.

The Integration of the Young Adult

What does the young man or woman require within the self to make these essential decisions and have a reasonable chance of gaining strength and finding satisfaction from them? Fortunately, perhaps, the psychiatrist is not required to sit in judgment and only very few persons seek his opinion and permission. We have followed the phasic preparation since birth for the assumption of adult status, and we shall not attempt to summarize here the steps by which a person integrates, achieves an ego identity and a capacity for true intimacy. We shall but attempt to state briefly some of the essential and some of the desirable aspects of a person's integration at this stage of life—concepts which will be amplified in subsequent chapters. Although it is simple to illustrate how deficiencies in achieving such capacities can lead a person into serious difficulties, we hesitate to call them requisites rather than desiderata, for few, if any, persons have all of these attributes, and the attainment of any of them always remains a matter of "more or less." We are considering an ideal, so to speak, to convey how a mature young adult might be integrated.

The young man or woman has, as we discussed in the preceding two chapters, become reasonably independent of his parents. He has established fairly clear boundaries between himself and his parents; properly, he has not been burned in the process and become wary of ever relating intimately again, but he recognizes that his own and his parents' paths now diverge because they are moving toward different goals. If his early development went well, the revolt through which he gained his own identity has subsided and he can appreciate his parents on a fairly realistic basis. He no longer needs them as essential objects who support and direct him, for they have been internalized and are thus a salient part of his identity; and now he will continue to take into himself their characteristics as spouses and parents as he becomes a spouse and a parent himself. His identity also includes derivatives from other significant figures, including those he has sought to reject. When his early family environment had been unfortunate, later relationships with teachers, friends, or friends' parents may have furnished stabilizing forces, more suitable objects for identification and more hopeful objectives. He does not confuse new significant persons in his life with his parents or siblings to the extent of repetitively re-enacting old intrafamilial problems. He does not, for example, awaken at night uncertain whether he is sleeping with his wife or mother, as did the son of a highly seductive woman; or repeat with his son and his wife an old rivalry with his brother for the mother's affection and esteem.

As a result of the reorganization accomplished during adolescence, those components of the superego derived from internalization of the parents and their directives are less important. The individual may still follow his parents' dictates, but because they have been incorporated into his own ethical system rather than because of fear of displeasing the parents. Indeed, as we have previously noted, much of what had been reasonable and useful in the superego now becomes part of the ego, and becomes more and more fully incorporated into the core of the ego— that is to say, into the basic orientation upon which decisions are made. The directives which help the individual to decide what is acceptable and unacceptable behavior now concern social and cultural norms and ideologic standards that are superordinate to parental dictates. The parents are no longer seen from the perspective of the child and, concomitantly, the superego permits latitude for sexual outlets which, in turn, can help diminish the urgency of id impulsions. Although certain impulses, desires, and behavior arouse guilt, shame, or anxiety, these emotions are more likely to become signals to alter behavior or attitudes rather than leading to self-punitive depressions.

The ego tends to have greater control, considering one's ultimate well-being before giving in to immediate gratifications. A mass of data garnered from personal experience as well as from the person's cultural heritage can be utilized in reaching decisions. It can be manipulated imaginatively in an effort to try out alternative courses and their probable consequences, and also for fantasied gratifications; but the person distinguishes between pure fantasy and what it might be possible for him to realize. Magic and wishful thinking have given way before the need to turn fantasy into action so as to be able to gain the realization of wishes. The young adult now knows enough about himself and the world to decide whether the realization of a wish or a fantasy is a possibility worth pursuing.

A major aspect of the ego's ability to carry out adaptive behavior concerns the capacities to tolerate tensions and the inevitable anxieties of life and still adhere to objectives and work through difficulties. The ability to adhere to commitments is usually taken as an index of "character," for it permits consistency and the avoidance of distraction by each attractive opportunity—whether it is an opportunity at work extraneous to one's own goals or a sexual distraction. The adult cannot be like Harpo Marx and whirl away from what he is doing to follow each pair of shapely legs that pass. Whereas at some periods in adolescence each fork in a road seems to require a decision, as the course of a life may be changed by following one path rather than the other, now that commitments have been made, the objectives determine the ultimate direction and it matters little if one route or the other is followed for a stretch in progressing toward the goal.

Tensions and frustations create anxiety and depressive spells but do not lead too often to a search for regressive solace in sensuality, in sleep, or in loss of self-awareness through the use of alcohol or narcotics. Frustrations are recognized as a part of life and, although avoided, they are accepted when necessary without mobilizing undue hostility and aggression—and such aggression as is aroused is directed toward overcoming the frustration rather than in vengeance or in hurting the self or those whom one needs. Various mechanisms of defense help control anxiety, but they are not called into play to an extent that markedly distorts the perception of the world or blinds one to realistic difficulties which must be faced and managed.

Now that problems of dependency and symbiotic strivings have been worked through, the boundaries of the self are secure enough for the young adult no longer unconsciously to fear losing his identity when he seeks after intimacy. He does not fear that a needed person will devour, engulf, or annihilate him; or that the loss of the self in orgasm will lead to obliteration; nor will he confuse the self with a child, as does a mother who feeds her child when she is hungry. The individual is also now se-

cure enough in his or her gender identity not to need to prove his masculinity or her femininity to the self and others by repetitive compulsive
sexual activity, or in undue masculine aggressivity or feminine seductive-
ness.

It has been customary in psychoanalytic literature to evaluate the stability and maturity of the progression to adult life in terms of the capacity for genital sexuality—properly, not simply the capacity for pleasure
from orgasm in heterosexual relationships, but to enjoy sexuality in a
meaningful intimate relationship. Originally, the progression to genital
sexuality was considered to depend on freedom from fixations at pregenital—oral, anal, or purely phallic—levels of development because of constitutional factors or traumatic occurrences. As has been emphasized in
previous chapters, an understanding of the development of the capacities for intimacy provides a more meaningful conceptualization of genital sexuality.

The developmental achievements that we have been considering as
necessary for proper behavior in early adult life have been presented in
black and white terms. In actuality no one outgrows childhood needs
and dependency strivings so fully; no one progresses to adulthood un-
scarred by emotional traumata and more or less injurious relationships;
no one manages to avoid being caught up in trying to solve some old
problems; everyone continues to be somewhat motivated to gratify residual pregenital strivings; and we all utilize defenses of our ego that are
no longer really necessary, and transfer characteristics of parents onto
other significant persons. These are the things that color personalities and
provide a distinctiveness and human frailty to all.

Still, such deficiencies, to sum up, should not lead a person to invest
too much energy and effort in repetitively seeking after solutions to old
problems poured ever again into new bottles, and should not prevent him
from seeking completion in the present and the future rather than
through the impossible task of remaking the past. The adult, too, should
be capable of accepting the realization that many of the ways and rules
of society are arbitrary, but that people need such regulations in order
to live together—and he does not feel deceived and cheated by the
arbitrariness of the rules; and he finds his place in the social system, accepting it while hoping to improve it. Nor is he so readily disillusioned
by other individuals, for faced by the difficulties in living he has become
more tolerant of the failures and even deceptions of others.

Whatever his preparation, the time has come for the young adult to make his own way in the world; he can delay and linger in the protection of his home, or in the halls of his alma mater where the storms of the world are filtered and refined, but he cannot tarry too long without commitment and the direction it provides. The choice of an occupation and the choice of a mate are the decisions that start him on his way. While both of these choices are often made as a rather natural progression in the path that a life has been taking, they are both highly *overdetermined,* tending to be resultants of the total developmental process together with the realistic opportunities available at the critical time of life. Although a single factor may clearly predominate in leading to a decision, a variety of factors virtually always enters consideration; and the conscious motives are often only rationalizations of unconscious forces that are exerting an indirect and disguised but powerful influence. The decisions may be no less useful and no less wise because of such unconscious influences, for unconscious motives may direct a person to significant and essential needs that are neglected or denied consciously, and because unconscious decisions can include repressed memories and intangible and nebulous perceptions and associations that may have considerable importance.

CHAPTER 12

Occupational Choice

AN OCCUPATION REPRESENTS much more than a set of skills and functions; it means a way of life. It provides and determines much of the environment, both physical and social, in which a person lives; it selects out traits that are utilized most frequently and strengthened; and it usually carries with it a status in the community and provides social roles and patterns for living. Through determining with what sorts of persons one spends much of his life, a vocation markedly influences value judgments and ethical standards. Occupation and personality traits are intimately related.

We find ourselves forming judgments about people according to their vocations. The physician asks his patient, "What do you do?" and the response not only helps him decide what sort of person he is taking care of, and what sort of fee he can charge, but also may help him reach a diagnosis and formulate a plan of therapy.* A bartender is not only a

* Jeremy Morris, for example, in his epidemiologic studies of coronary occlusion found that London bus drivers were significantly more vulnerable than conductors.[5]

different sort of person from a soda jerk but also more likely to suffer
from cirrhosis of the liver; a male dress designer, an actor, a teacher in a
prep school is more likely to be homosexual than is an engineer, a hockey
player, or a university professor. Even though we have difficulty in defin-
ing the reasons for our anticipations, we expect a lawyer to be more
aggressive and argumentative than a minister and we are apt to relate
differently and present different aspects of ourselves to them. We may
appreciate that taxi drivers and long-haul truckers, even though they are
in closely related occupations, tend to different personalities and have
very different ways of living.* Such preconceptions aroused by the name
of an occupation are usually tentative and are sometimes erroneous, but
there are good reasons for such "snap judgments" that psychological
studies are tending to validate.† Is it that similar personalities tend to
select given occupations, or is it that the pursuit of a specific vocation
leads to the development of certain traits? Both factors operate. Occupational choice is usually a function or a reflection of the entire personality;
but then the occupation plays a part in shaping the personality by providing associates, roles, goals, ideals, mores, and a life style.

Despite the importance of occupational choice in determining the further course of personality development and of the functions of an occupation in the emotional and physical well-being of those who pursue it,
relatively little can be found on the topic in the psychiatric literature.‡
The neglect of the topic is even more surprising because a person's
choice of vocation brings into focus much of his developmental dynamics as well as many unconscious forces influencing his life. Perhaps
the topic has received so little attention because it has been only in re-

---

Was this because of differences in the amount of physical activity, of emotional stress,
or was it a reflection of the different personalities of drivers and conductors?
* In my experience taxi drivers in large cities are often attracted by a job requiring
minimal skills in which they can be reasonably independent. Subjected to constant
stress, they often suffer from gastric disturbances including peptic ulcer. The long-
haul truck driver is more fiercely independent and aggressive, often carries a chip
on his shoulder and finds an outlet in driving his huge truck. Severe and intractable
headaches related to the tension of driving and his aggressivity are not uncommon.
The cab driver is also subject to frequent sexual stimulation by the behavior of his
passengers and by suggestions from women that coming into the apartment for a few
minutes will be more rewarding than finding another passenger.
† See, for example, E. K. Strong, Vocational Interests of Men and Women.[6]
‡ The first dynamically oriented study, which still remains one of the most significant,
combined the efforts and skills of an economist, psychiatrist, and other social scientists.[3]

cent years and in a relatively few countries that the opportunity to select an occupation has been available to any sizable proportion of the population. In most countries well over 50 per cent of the people are engaged in farming; the differences between laboring jobs available to the poorly educated are scarcely worth considering; and skills, crafts, and small shops are traditionally passed from parent to child.* In most countries (and even in the United States during the economic depression of the 1930's) a young person starting to work feels fortunate to find any sort of worth-while, interesting position and many are simply glad to be able to earn a livelihood. In most countries the type of schooling a child will follow is decided early in adolescence, or even earlier, in accord with expectations of the occupation he will pursue. In many societies, perhaps in most, parents consider it rather foolish to consider that a child or even a youth can make a career decision for himself better than can his more experienced parents.

Overdetermination of Vocational Choice

In contrast, in the United States vocational choice currently constitutes a major problem of adolescence. This chapter, therefore, even more than other chapters, applies primarily to the contemporary American scene. A youth has probably never been so conscious of how much his future welfare depends upon the length and quality of his education, and of how the maintenance or advancement of his social and economic position involves pursuing a suitable vocation. The late adolescent, particularly the college student, often lives with the problem as a background against which he samples courses, tries out jobs, and evaluates people he meets as models he might wish to emulate. The youth worries and cogitates about his future vocation and although his conscious evaluations and decisions are important, he is often motivated to make a final decision by determinants of which he is unaware; not that unconscious factors are all important but rather that they are frequently the decisive element in a matter that is so highly overdetermined.

If, for example, we consider a class of medical students, we find that the reasons for their selection of medicine as a career are not only varied but often very private. Indeed, there is probably less frank discussion even among close friends about career choice than there is about sexual problems. Many students have considerable difficulty thinking through

---

* In the Middle Ages, parents placed their children as apprentices with another family at the age of seven.[1]

and conveying the reasons for the decision or how it was reached, and many of the reasons they give and accept themselves are clearly only part of the story. One is emulating his father; another is living out his pharmacist father's thwarted ambition; someone is responding to his mother's idealization of the obstetrician who delivered him—influences of which the student is only partially aware because they were simply part of the atmosphere in which he grew up. There may be a student who has secretly vowed to himself to combat cancer, which robbed him of a mother, or to learn to treat schizophrenia, which permanently removed his sister to an institution. Some consider medicine as a means of earning a secure livelihood that assures prestige in the community, and some as a means of social advancement. Others may have in childhood feared death and decided to meet the problem counterphobically, head on, as a foe to fight and at the same time to learn to tolerate death as a familiar. Another may have simply agreed with Philip Carey in Maugham's *Of Human Bondage*, who decided that if he could not be great he could at least be useful. Indeed, he may find it difficult to admit that he is following his idealism and finding a meaning in life by seeking to help others. These are all acceptable motivations, but rarely the only significant influences. Although it has been said that a surgeon may be a sublimated sadist who might have been a butcher if he had been less well educated, or that a psychoanalyst is only a refined variant of a voyeur, such sorts of pseudoanalytic statements are usually oversimplifications of characterologic influences that will be discussed later (see Chapter 19). Still, the author once studied three prizefighters and could not fail to note that all three had brutal fathers whom they had vowed to beat up when they were old enough and strong enough. And it appears fairly obvious from his autobiographical narrative that one of our greatest explorers almost lost his life seeking to overcome once and for all his childhood anxiety over separation from his mother.[2]

To convey something of the complexity that can enter into a vocational choice, let us turn to a specific example which may serve to illustrate the fusion of childhood residues, characterologic factors, and realistic determinants that contributed to a decision. It is somewhat atypical, at least in being concerned with an unusual person whose capacities permitted a fairly wide choice.

A young internist, R., consulted a psychiatrist on his return from military service. He had been assigned to Japan, where he had enjoyed the aesthetic properties of the country and of many of its inhabitants, but found himself becoming depressed and increasingly dissatisfied with his life as a physician. At the age of thirty-five, R. had already published several significant contributions to science and success in his career seemed assured. After he had been away from his practice for a year, he began to doubt that he was gaining satisfaction from medicine. He resented the demands that required him virtually to forego other interests. R. had shown considerable talent as a painter while in college, and now he was wondering whether he should abandon medicine and enter upon some artistic career; but as he had a wife and child, a radical shift in his vocation would be difficult, if not impossible.

To clarify his predicament and discomfort, R. reviewed the steps that had led him into medicine, recalling incidents and determinants that he had virtually forgotten until he had reviewed his life while inactive in Japan.

During his junior year in college R. had been unable to decide what to do with his life. His father, a successful architect, had suggested that R. follow in his footsteps, as had his older brother, and join the flourishing family firm. R. had expected to become an architect but had been reluctant to abandon his hopes of becoming an artist; though on the other hand, he was concerned about risking his future on his artistic talent. He had been raised amid reasonable affluence and would not enjoy penury. He decided to take a year off to study at an art school in New York in order to gain a better estimate of his abilities and interests, but also to get away from his home and his friends to think things out on his own. He was taking a moratorium before making a career choice. Although he enjoyed painting and the life he was leading in Greenwich Village, R. found himself becoming even more indecisive as the year passed, and he became intensely anxious and somewhat depressed. Then, at the end of the year, much to the surprise of his family, R. announced that he was going to study medicine.

Now, with a psychiatrist some fifteen years later, R. was trying to reconstruct the events of that year in New York and examine how he had reached his decision. He was certain that when he had left home to go to New York he had no thoughts of studying medicine. Indeed, if he had been asked what he might become, medicine would not even have been included among the potentialities. He had, however, determined to reach a decision by the end of the year and adhere to it, for he feared that endless vacillation could lead him to drift into an unsuitable vocation.

THE PERSON

In thinking about his early connections with medicine, R. recalled that he had suffered from an episode of rheumatic fever just before starting school which had kept him in bed for some months and had left him with a slightly damaged heart valve. For several years his parents had been overly protective whenever he had a respiratory infection and they had limited his activities. He remembered how close he had felt to his mother during these periods of incapacitation. During high school, he experienced some envy when the family physician had suggested to his studious older brother that he study medicine and eventually take over his lucrative general practice—but this had been envy that his brother had been preferred rather than due to an interest in medicine.

During the year in New York, R. had shared a couple of rooms with a fraternity brother who was doing graduate work in physiology. He became intrigued by a subject about which he had been completely ignorant, fascinated by the intricate and complex balance of the human organism. A fellow art student contracted jaundice, and having little money became a patient on the public wards in a municipal hospital, where R. visited him and deplored the circumstances. R. recalled how as a child he would wonder how grownups could manage when ill without a mother to care for them; indeed, he had dimly considered the ability to care for oneself alone when ill as a sort of measure of maturity. As he talked, R. recalled his pervasive concerns about illness throughout his childhood and adolescence, which may have reflected his parents' unexpressed anxieties over his rheumatic fever. Perhaps, he reflected, learning that physicians received free medical care from their colleagues had influenced his choice of a career.

He had first consciously thought of studying medicine during a discussion of physiology when his roommate had talked about a friend who, after two years in law school, had changed his mind and was taking premedical courses. He realized that he, too, could still make a radical shift in his plans and perhaps escape from his indecision concerning the choice of art or architecture.

When Easter came and went, he started to experience episodes of acute anxiety and found himself worrying that he might have cancer. He could not decide about his future—but slowly he reached the conclusion that it did not really matter what he did, provided he pursued it enthusiastically. He could learn to like and even enjoy anything that really challenged him. The next step carried the matter further when he decided, masochistically, that perhaps he should do what he liked least and prove

that aptitude and liking for a particular occupation made little difference. Such ideas virtually led to the choice of medicine, but there were
other influences, too, several of which will be mentioned. R. felt, in retrospect, that he had been rebelling against his parents' expectations that
his artistic abilities would define his future, and that he had been reacting against the praise he received for his paintings which let him doubt
that his parents liked or loved him "for himself."

Then, with considerable embarrassment and uneasiness, R. suddenly
remembered something he felt certain had been of considerable moment
in his shift to medicine. When he was fifteen, he had gone camping with
friends, his first extended stay away from home. He had become ill,
suffering from nausea and feelings of malaise which may only have been
the resultants of fatigue and nostalgia. Still, he had been convinced that
he had cancer, probably because a cousin had died a lingering death
from leukemia a few months earlier. His concerns mounted, and in his
anxiety R. prayed and made a vow that if God would let him live for
another twenty years, he would devote his life to the welfare of mankind. As usually happens, after he recovered, his pact with God was forgotten. But during the year of decision in New York when he became
anxious, depressed, and hypochondriacal, his vow returned to plague
him. He doubted that the life of either artist or architect would redeem
his pledge of self-sacrifice; one would be too enjoyable and the other too
lucrative. The recurrent anxiety contained fears that he might soon die
and recalled his earnestly given pledge, which helped explain his curious
decision to launch into doing what he least wanted to do. It was a means
of redeeming his vow and saving his life. R. was further shaken when the
psychiatrist pointed out to him that the twenty years of life he had
sought from God had been completed just at the end of his tour in
Japan and that now he was again uncertain about his future.

The negation of a specific talent in making an occupational choice and
the appeasement of God through altruistic choice may be somewhat unusual, but the complexity of the decision-making process may not be so
extravagant as it seems. The residua of childhood anxieties over separation from the mother; the concerns over trying to compete with a father
and older brother whom R. felt he could surpass; the influences of a
serious childhood illness; the control of impulses through ascetic strivings are among the influences that coalesced to guide this individual into
an acceptable path into the future.

The Developmental History of Occupational Choice

The choice of an occupation does not usually take place abruptly, but tends to be the product of a long process that starts early in childhood and changes as the individual develops, and it reflects the nature of the personality integration. The earliest considerations of a future vocation are diffuse and unrealistic, reflecting the little child's preoperational thinking and his egocentric, narrow view of the world. The three-year-old boy may state that he will be a mommy when he grows up; the little girl will have skaty-eight children and live with her mommy and daddy. The child may wait in suspense as someone counts the buttons on his clothes to find out whether he will be a "doctor, lawyer, Indian chief," or less fortunately "poor man, beggarman, thief."

As the child enters into dramatic play with his peers, his fantasy choices are abundant and shift from hour to hour. He not only decides to become a fireman or a doctor, but becomes one in his imaginative activities. The play contains elements of his trying out various occupational roles, but possibility, feasibility, ability, or the steps that must be taken to achieve the role in reality are not considered. Occasionally, a role that is somehow reinforced sticks, becomes a favored game and fantasy, and may eventually lead to an occupation, as when a little girl plays nurse with dolls, progresses to helping an overburdened mother care for younger siblings, and thereby gains approval and attention that offset the shift in her mother's attention to the babies and establishes a pattern for gaining praise and affection that eventually leads to a choice of nursing as a career.

In the latency period the child plans to follow in the path of his various idols and heroes: space pilot, baseball player, movie star, probably more often someone known through television or reading than a person in his own environment. Gradually, consideration of ability and realistic limitations enter the picture; the baseball star becomes a sports announcer, the general becomes a simple marine sergeant.

As the child reaches high school he may have some awareness of whether he will seek to emulate a parent or seek some parent surrogate or other ideal figure to follow. Tentative choices are made that may guide him for a time but the youngster knows neither himself nor the world well enough. During his high school vacations, he may take jobs to see if he likes them, steps that can be decisive in his finding a vocation if his education does not go beyond high school. During the period of adolescent expansiveness, as previously noted, there is often both a turning away from parental models and guidance and an upsurge of idealistic goals.

A college education brings new careers into consideration as the student's world broadens and he comes in contact with teachers with whom he may identify. Here, he also finds opportunities to measure himself against others with similar aspirations. Eventually, a *realistic* phase starts in which the youth takes stock of his capacities, his needs, and the potentialities that open before him. The young man will take into account what is most important to him, how much he hopes to earn, how long he can delay earning a living, when he expects to marry, etc. He will try to consider where the world is going; currently he may decide that computers, physics, and city planning offer particularly good opportunities. If he considers that a war is imminent, he may plan a military education or, conversely, seek a field that will keep him out of military service.

In a general sense, there are two major ways of thinking about a career. Some consider it most important to seek out an occupation which will provide satisfaction and enjoyment and from which they can hope to gain a full and interesting life. Others will consider an occupation primarily as a means of gaining security or power, whereas satisfactions will come from a family, prestige in the community, sports, an avocation, or from something made possible by money, such as collecting paintings or girls. A shift from the first of these approaches to the second is likely to occur as the time approaches for reaching a definite decision and the young adult becomes concerned with providing security for himself and the family he is about to start.

To *crystallize* goals and firmly commit himself to a vocation, one must find a way of entering upon the career and gain a pattern to follow. The absence of a known pattern, usually in the form of one or more persons with whom to identify, can divert the youth from a field of interest. Crystallization requires commitment with acceptance of the ensuing uncertainties, but firmness of commitment is essential to prevent veering into new attractive areas that appear en route: some premedical students may be tempted into biochemistry or physiology through fascination with such fields or through identifications with teachers, whereas others will shed such temptations, having committed themselves to medicine. The crystallization often engenders regrets over the loss of former important interests, and such a loss may become particularly hard to accept if attainment of the goal involves relatively uninteresting preparation, as, for example, some future physicians find the preclinical medical sciences.

The final phase in occupational choice concerns the *specification* of interest within a field through the acquisition of specialized skills. It means further renunciation of diversified interests and activities, and often a willingness to delay gratifications such as income, marriage, and recognition. On the other hand, it can also permit the utilization of specific assets and personality traits as well as the cultivation of special areas of interest. A person who is fully committed to being a psychologist can through specialization make use of an aptitude for mathematics by concentrating on statistical methodologies; or return to the humanistic considerations which had led him into psychology but which had been caught in the blind alley of a rat-maze, by moving into clinical psychology or school counseling; or bring into his occupation his knowledge of art and liking for artists by studying the creativity or the visual and verbal imagination of painters. Such increased delimitation and specialization is often essential for reaching the higher levels of achievement and recognition, but it may come simply as an outgrowth of an occupation on which a person has already embarked, as when an attorney gradually moves into a specialized field such as dealing with corporate tax matters. Often, of course, the crystallization of a vocational choice, made with such effort, is but the first of a series of specifications. Medicine and psychology are fields of interest that require certain basic training, but further decisions must still be made: medicine; surgery, specific field of surgery; length of training; private, group, institutional practice; teaching; research, area of research; etc. Even after specification or specialization, further occupational decisions will be required throughout life which can markedly influence personality functioning: will the investigator accept a promotion that makes him a research administrator; will the clinical teacher turn from the care of patients to try to solve some problem that puzzles him in the laboratory?

Personality Traits and Vocational Choice

Occupational choice reflects the development and integration of the personality. A special genetically determined trait may be essential for some careers: for example, the capacity for a musical career may depend on a specific inheritance, and color blindness closes off some careers. It is often difficult to follow just how specific career choices are determined, but personality traits which we term characterologic play a significant part in the selection of a type of occupation. We can note that fixations

in psychosocial or psychosexual development will contribute to the decision: "anal" characters with tendencies to obsessive meticulousness are
likely to enter careers that deal directly with money, such as banking,
bookkeeping, accounting—or with collecting and assembling. "Oral"
characters may be attracted toward becoming chefs or dieticians, or may
seek security by becoming wealthy in order to be assured that oral supplies will always be available. The "phallic" character may seek some
occupation in which he can assert power, or gain admiration for his physique.

It is apparent that certain types of personalities are better suited for
some occupations than others, and that some are unsuited for certain
occupations. The human race can be categorized in various ways to take
note of such compatibilities and incompatibilities (see Chapter 19). Introverts are not apt as pitchmen, nor are they likely to try to be; extroverts would be unhappy as art critics. Occupational counselors and
psychologists utilize such characterologic groupings as aids in placing persons in suitable occupations.* Such categorization is usually made on the
basis of expressed occupational interests, personality traits, including intelligence and aptitudes, and noting whom a person would like to emulate.

The Influence of Occupation on Personality Development

We have been examining how the personality enters into the choice
of an occupation, but we must now turn to consider how a person's
occupation becomes a major influence in the sort of adult he becomes. If
he has been able to select his vocation, he has tended to choose a social
environment in which he feels comfortable, composed of persons with
whom he likes to associate and whose regard he seeks. It will act to
preserve personality traits he has developed or it creates strains that provoke change, or it may warp his personality if he cannot change. The
person's identity gains solidity through his identification with a group of

---

* Holland has found it most useful to divide persons into the following categories:
realistic, intellectual, social, conventional, enterprising, and artistic, or into combinations of these categories; but some are virtually exclusive of another, such as realistic
and artistic. He has also placed occupations in the same categories. He considers that
inventories of interests are personality inventories; that members of a vocation tend
to have similar personalities and developmental histories; that persons in a vocational
group having similar personalities will create characteristic interpersonal environments;
and that vocational satisfaction, stability, and achievement depend upon the con-
gruency between one's personality and the environment in which one works.[4]

people pursuing similar objectives and with its group mores. Although an occasional individual maintains his own standards relatively independently of what those around him believe and do, most persons' superego standards bend toward the group values and to the ideals and demands of the group leaders. We can note exaggerated forms of such group influence upon behavior. A soldier who accepted his officer's direction and shot helpless prisoners of war cannot comprehend such behavior after he has returned to his family. The Nazi SS troops contained many who could not have sought to eradicate all Jews and Poles had the group and national mores not condoned such behavior. The person who enters the advertising business may not have been overly scrupulous about truth, but he enters an environment in which the truth is pilloried for sales. He comes to value the capacity to deceive and mislead and his personality alters,* for he gains the esteem of those he esteems by his ability to mask the truth.

Some occupations support more conventional and acceptable superego standards and may, of course, be selected for such reasons. The clergy, police, and others attach themselves to the maintenance of ethical standards. The physician selects a profession in which his own welfare is supposed to be secondary to the well-being of his patients. Value systems and goals are reinforced or redirected.

In the process of learning a trade or a profession, the novice learns a way of life along with the knowledge and skills of the occupation. It will shape or help shape many facets of his personality. The first-year medical student may wonder how a physician behaves under a variety of circumstances and how he will reach decisions concerning life and death, and he unconsciously gains the answers from observing his teachers and colleagues and assuming their ways of behaving and styles of living before the end of his training. Whatever his traits before he entered medical school, he develops a degree of obsessive meticulousness; he assumes a benevolent protective way of relating to people that becomes a part of him; he expects a type of deference from his patients; he intellectualizes as a defense and learns to hide his feelings or even repress them to a marked degree; and he takes into himself an acceptance of responsibility for making critical decisions. He also learns to eat at irregular hours, forego sleep, not to anticipate uninterrupted evenings. He realizes he must choose a wife who will not expect him to provide companionship

* A current study suggests that such traits also influence his children, who learn that what they say and can get away with is more important than what they really do.

for her during the evenings. The man who enters a scientific career develops an allegiance to honesty of reporting and to intellectual effort, and concomitantly may tend to use intellectualizing defenses against anxiety that would not have been so well developed had he become a travel agent.

One can note how friends or brothers who have been close friends because of common interests, traits, and ideals begin to change and differ after more or less chance—or seemingly arbitrary—selection of different occupations. The factory worker spends his evenings out at the corner tavern, playing cards and spinning yarns, while his wife stays at home tending the children; but his brother who has become a priest acquires a very different set of interests, standards, and ways of relating to people. They have developed a very different ego functioning—different intellectual assets, areas of competence, ways of relating—and they also have different outlets of id impulsions, with the priest requiring sublimation and asceticism to satisfy his superego. Here is a banker in a small New England community, a pillar of conservatism, married to a puritanical wife; he gains little sexual gratification in his marriage and expects little but would not consider divorcing his wife who is a "good" woman. His childhood neighbor, who had similar beliefs and ways in childhood, lives among his Madison Avenue public relations colleagues a little further west in New England, and now considers that his life would be blighted were it not sexually exciting, and tries analysis and divorce, or, more likely, divorce and then analysis after his second marriage is also not fully satisfying. Such comparisons cannot be made properly because no individuals are alike, and there are no "if's" in life, but it appears from experience that the way of life dictated by a career influences personality functioning very profoundly.

The physician whose occupational choice was discussed earlier in the chapter might have become an artist or an architect except for certain chance occurrences that tipped the balance when the decision was being weighed. Life is aleatory and contingencies can make a difference. The life and personality of R., the physician, is different from what the life and personality of R., the artist, would have been. He leads a more regular life; he is a member of a medical school faculty; he has tended to suppress his fantasy and shift his creative urges into disciplined research; his colleagues admire responsibility and accepting the responsibility for others; he has learned scientific ways of thinking that permeate his domestic life and child rearing; he has married a social worker who also has a highly developed sense of social responsibility, etc. R., the artist, would seek gratification through what he painted, and acclaim through his paintings. If he were properly creative, he could innovate at the behest of his fantasy, unconcerned with the impact of his experiments on the future of science. He could and probably would work at irregular hours, and follow the direction of his creative impulses rather than his sense of responsibility. The people with whom he associated would cherish the free spirits who lived as they liked without too much concern for social conventions. Success would not depend as much upon effort alone as upon his creative capacities. Whereas he might have a sense of responsibility, it would not be an obligatory part of his life; and his ways of thinking would be less organized and scientifically trained, and perhaps free from intellectualizations that might hinder his artistic creativity; he would not have been likely to date a social worker, and if he did, they would probably have had too few interests in common to marry, etc. The occupational roles, the institutions to which one belongs, the style of life, the education in preparation for the occupation, the ideals and ideal figures one follows, the values of one's peers—all will greatly influence who one will be in later years.

The Mores and Morals of Various Occupational Groups

The understanding of the ways in which people of varying occupations lead their lives, and the perspectives and goals they are likely to hold, is essential to the therapist, who must overcome the tendency to understand patients in terms of his own mores and morals. An illustration may serve to indicate how such understanding can increase a therapist's skills. During World War II two young officers were promoted to the rank of captain and sent to an antiaircraft weapons unit defending a beautiful South Sea island well away from combat. One was delighted by his good fortune and thoroughly enjoyed the life on the island of his dreams. The other soon complained of intractable headaches that led to extensive medical studies until an experienced army physician sized up the situation. This second officer was a West Pointer whose life ambition was to become a general. His chances of ever becoming a general were minimal unless he found an opportunity to display his abilities—and preferably also heroism—and he became a colonel by the end of the war. He felt that he had been sidetracked into an unimportant position by a prejudiced senior officer and he could scarcely contain his hostility toward that officer and the army. In contrast, the captain who was pleased by the assignment was a reserve officer who, though a conscientious patriot, had little interest in military life or in becoming a hero, preferring the life among the Polynesian girls—which he had never really hoped to experience.

Occupational Choice in Women

Problems of vocational choice are more significant to men than to women, for whom, by and large, marriage and child rearing take precedence over a career. The future of most women depends to a frightening degree upon whom they marry. Unless she remains single, a woman's status in life and that of her family will almost always depend upon her husband's career even if she works, and her hopes for the future rest more in the lives of her husband and her children than in what she can accomplish vocationally.

Still, many will give considerable thought to the choice of a suitable and interesting occupation. Currently, a very large proportion of women work before they marry and after their children are grown, and frequently even when the children are young in order to increase the income of the family. However, except for highly educated women, there is a general difference from men in the type of career sought and pursued. The young woman is very likely to choose an occupation in which she fills a helping, ancillary position or a more or less maternal role. The office worker may seek a good wage but usually she is not so concerned with what she can achieve in a career as with the person for whom she works; and she may prefer aiding a man with his business and career to having one of her own. Nursing, teaching, social work are conventionally women's career jobs and all have a maternal as well as a helping function. There is, of course, a marked difference between a nurse who cares for patients and an executive administrative nurse. Medicine in Russia and some other countries is also predominantly a feminine career—and it certainly provides outlets for nurturant interests.

Women do not usually need to prove themselves through accomplishment and achievement, and gain more satisfaction from being admired and loved because of who they are, or because of what they can give. However, the need to gain satisfaction from admiration leads some women into careers such as ballet dancing, acting, and other performing arts which furnish such admiration as well as the development of talents.

Although some women enter adulthood with a fairly firm decision to pursue a career come what may, eventually marriage usually takes precedence and a career becomes secondary. Most women recognize, even if the colleges they attend do not, that being a good wife, and even more, being a good mother, requires many refined abilities and skills and forms a career in itself. Dissatisfaction with this limiting career will often arise; this will be discussed in the chapter on marital adjustment (Chapter 14). The woman's career choice leads us into the significant topic of marital choice.

Occupational choice, then, forms one of the crucial decisions of a lifetime. Such choices are usually highly overdetermined, reflecting much of the entire prior personality development, and the conscious reasons usually are but part of the determinants of the decision. The occupation selected and pursued, then, becomes a major influence in the subsequent personality development, the persons with whom one interrelates, and the type of life that is led. Vocational choice is usually more significant to the man, for with the vast majority of women the choice of occupation is less critical than the choice of husband.

References

1. Phillipe Ariès, *Centuries of Childhood* (New York: Alfred A. Knopf, 1962).
2. Richard Byrd, *Alone* (New York: G. P. Putnam's Sons, n.d.).
3. Eli Ginzberg, S. Ginzberg, S. Axelrod, and J. Herma, *Occupational Choice: An Approach to a General Theory* (New York: Columbia University Press, 1951).
4. John L. Holland, *The Psychology of Vocational Choice* (Waltham, Mass.: Blaisdell Publications, 1966).
5. Jeremy Morris, J. A. Heady, P. A. B. Raffle, C. G. Roberts, and J. W. Parks, "Coronary Heart-Disease and Physical Activity of Work," *Lancet*, 265 (1953), 1111–1120.
6. Edward K. Strong, Jr., *Vocational Interests of Men and Women* (Stanford, Calif.: Stanford University Press, 1943).

Suggested Reading

Eli Ginzberg, S. Ginzberg, S. Axelrod, and J. Herma, *Occupational Choice: An Approach to a General Theory* (New York: Columbia University Press, 1951).
John L. Holland, *The Psychology of Vocational Choice* (Waltham, Mass.: Blaisdell Publications, 1966).

CHAPTER 13

Marital Choice

THE COUPLE who are about to marry realize, as on few other occasions in their lives, that they are making a decisive commitment. The ceremony culminates their lives to that moment, and their choice of a partner is a resultant of their total experience. It marks the start of a new way of living and the achievement of a very different status in life. They are aware that their future happiness will depend in large measure upon the relationship being established. They may also feel, though they usually do not consciously recognize it, that the direction of their future personality development and their entire manner of adapting to life hang in the balance. While the marriage ceremony has been considered by some primarily as providing permission and social sanction for sexual intercourse, such views when not facetious are alarmingly superficial. The union that is formed changes, or at least should change, the ego structure of both persons, so that it henceforth concerns the direction and welfare of two lives rather than one; and new superego directives are taken over from the partner which together with id impulses and basic drives of the spouse will henceforth influence behavior. Along with the hazards and the need for realignment of personality functioning, the marriage brings with it new opportunities for self-fulfillment and completion.

The bride and groom have reason to experience anxiety for, as with any commitment, consequences must be accepted in advance. It is, however, a special commitment to intimate interdependence. In their relationships with their parents, they had no choice of the objects of their dependency, but now a voluntary choice is being made and the responsibility for consequences must be accepted. The potential sources of disturbance and danger are overshadowed by the recognition of marriage as a new source of strength and support. In finding an occupation or career, the individual gains solidity through the pursuit of a definite goal, by limiting his strivings, by taking into himself the way of life, the roles and value systems that accompany it. In marrying, one gains a partner who shares and supports and upon whom one can rely, for the well-being of each is bound up with the fate of the other. Further, the person assumes the pattern of living of a married person for which there are traditional directives, and he also acquires a definite place in the social system. Again further delimitations of the numerous potential ways of living have occurred; and while limitations may seem onerous, they also promote cohesiveness and can open new ways of expressing one's potentialities.

The problems of marital adjustment and family living are of paramount importance in understanding the emotional difficulties of patients, and cannot be considered separately from the choice of the partner. While this may seem a platitude, many marital problems are largely dependent upon the personality characteristics of one member which might well create difficulties no matter who was the spouse. One might consider, for example, a man who appeared to have made an excellent choice of a beautiful and very wealthy young woman who understood his difficulties with his own family and was willing to help him overcome a number of anxieties that interfered with his ability to work. However, even though his wife bore no noticeable resemblance to his mother, he was so fearful of all women because of his experiences with an overbearing, directive, and demanding mother, that any proximity to women that might lead to sexual relationships provoked intense anxiety in him. He could scarcely remain in the same house with his wife after supper, and was soon too removed from her to enable her to try to be helpful to him. Still failures of complementarity create many other problems.

It becomes apparent during the psychiatric treatment of many married persons that the choice of the spouse for neurotic reasons ties the individual to an untenable way of life which leads to the mobilization of deleterious traits and prevents the development of more favorable characteristics. While it is usually true that the partner selected fills some basic need and in some respects forms a suitable choice, the concept can be overemphasized, as will be considered later in the chapter. It is quite apparent that many people do not really know the person whom they are marrying and do not realize how greatly the partner's personality will influence their own. In considering marital problems, one is no longer concerned with an individual but with a dyad, and how the marriage works out relates clearly to the question of the partner selected. It must also be recognized, however, that even pathological needs may properly be managed if a suitable partner is selected, as when a woman who has a morbid fear of childbirth finds a man who wishes to be the center of his wife's life without any interference from children.

We wish to consider why people marry, whom they marry, and when, examining how the decision to marry and the choice of a mate fit into the pattern and sequence of the life history and influence further development. The emphasis upon the family as the primary socializing agency for the child means that particular consideration must be given to the marital union that forms the milieu in which the children will be raised. There is also the practical everyday need of the therapist who, when he becomes aware of it, finds that marital problems often form a focal point in the unhappiness and the emotional disturbances that bring many patients to him. While patients at times come directly seeking advice about marital situations, more commonly the resultant distress has produced physiological dysfunctioning that creates symptoms or leads to displaced substitutive complaints. It is a common experience that the complaint of chronic backache in a woman may relate to her wish to refuse sexual relations that she finds repulsive; or the obesity that complicates a medical ailment depends upon the need for a person who feels starved for affection to gain satisfaction from overeating, etc. A man complaining of intractable headaches soon vents his rage which arises because he believes his wife married him only for his money and constantly expresses contempt for him because of his lower social status. He also expresses his feelings of hopeless frustration because she is unapproachable and unresponsive to his sexual needs, considering them an imposition and making him feel he is being indecent.

Although interest here does not lie in the pathological but the unfolding of the personality through marriage, any discussion of marital choice and adjustment must take into account shortcomings and failures, for these pertain to the majority of marriages rather than the exception in contemporary society. Although the majority outcome cannot be considered as the norm, it indicates the difficulties of attaining a satisfactory marital choice and adjustment. Approximately one out of six first marriages formed at the present time in the United States will terminate in divorce, the rate having fallen and leveled off since the postwar high of about one in three in 1946.[8] About half of the divorces will take place during the first ten years of marriage and fortunately about one half before there have been any children. Such figures must not be taken as an indication that marriage is becoming less important. Indeed, almost three-quarters of the people who divorce will remarry within five years and it is particularly noteworthy that the proportion of the population that marries each year is higher than ever: eleven to twelve per thousand as against nine per thousand in 1900.[8] Further, a larger proportion of the population is married than ever before as the diminution in the deaths of partners has more than offset the dissolution of marriages by divorce. Divorce rates in general reflect the ease of obtaining a divorce rather than the success or failure of marriage in general. On the other hand, they do not indicate the extent of marital unhappiness, for many marriages that formally remain intact are seriously disturbed. There are various figures concerning successful marriage and they are difficult to interpret. Perhaps the optimal estimate has been that somewhat less than 25 per cent of marriages are fully satisfactory to both partners, but other studies cut the figure to anywhere between 5 and 25 per cent. It has also been estimated that considerably less than half are deemed reasonably adequate by the couple. Still such figures do not mean that many more marriages do not subserve some essential functions for both partners who might be even unhappier if unmarried or married to someone else.

Marital Choice: Love and Unconscious Processes

The basis of marital choice in the United States today reflects the individualistic, democratic society in which decision and responsibility rest primarily upon the two persons who are marrying. While the reasons for the specific selection of a partner are elusive, the reason usually given and generally though not always believed is that they have fallen in love; and love is a state that has eluded philosophic and scientific definition throughout the ages. Freud, like others, drew an analogy between being in love and being sick when he said that "this sexual overestimation [of the love object] is the origin of the peculiar state of being in love, a state suggestive of a neurotic compulsion," [4] but he did not underestimate its importance, calling love "the highest form of development of which object—libido—is capable," [4] and he defined normality in terms of the "ability to love and to work."

Falling in love is largely an irrational matter, dependent upon unconscious determinants that trail back into infancy. However, as has been noted in other connections, the unconscious processes may be more suited than intellectual assessments for drawing together the diffuse needs of an individual, the incoherent judgments of people, the feeling-tone memories, the pleasing and displeasing in the expression, vision, feel, smell of another, and many other such factors that enter into personal attraction. The intellect could scarcely cope with so many variables, even if they were consciously available to weigh. While the unconscious processes designate whom one loves, they are apparently less capable of judging properly with whom one can live in harmony. It is of more than passing interest that one of the most decisive steps in a person's life rests largely upon unconscious processes which are at best checked by logical appraisal of the chances for success or failure.

Anyone who has had the unpleasant task of suggesting to a couple who are prepared to marry that they at least postpone a marriage which seems unwise because of the serious emotional instability of one of them, has learned that reason has little chance against the erotically driven impulsion with its capacities to blind. It is also important to note that the choice of partners by the couples themselves on the basis of romantic love forms a custom that is fairly unique to modern civilization and is probably more prevalent in the United States than anywhere else. Indeed, some authorities consider that romantic love in itself is a phenomenon of Western culture which only started with the troubadours, who even then were not singing of love in connection with marriage. Although ancient literature from many countries appears clearly to negate this theory and indicate that "love," whatever this connoted at the given time and place, has always tended to draw people together, and lead them to desire marriage, still it has usually not been a major determinant of marital choice: partners have been chosen by parents, by kin groups, according to prescribed relationship patterns, and for economic and social reasons.

There is little if any evidence that the contemporary freedom to select partners has led to happier marriages; but the functions that marriage seeks to fill today are vastly different and are not easily equated with marriage under different traditions. Attention here can only be directed to the contemporary scene, with recognition that the nature of marriage and the way in which partners are chosen is an integral part of the society in which it exists. While young people in particular are apt to confuse a passionate attraction for mature love, it must also be recognized that currently many young adults are very staid in their judgments and marry only after a lengthy period of "going steady" with one another. Indeed, the trend has been to exchange the range of potential choice for the security of early permanent attachment. Further, the love attraction is usually tempered by the couple's own concern for their parents' approval, even though they no longer feel it to be mandatory.

The Place of Marriage in the Life Cycle

The understanding of why people marry and, perhaps, the meaning of the intangible but very real and pertinent force of love appear to require a scrutiny of the place of marriage in the developmental sequence of a person and of the biological and social forces playing upon the young adult when he decides to marry. While we cannot hope properly to define love and explain why a specific person is selected, the whole process may be clarified if we view it in the total developmental setting rather than as an isolated phenomenon. The fusion of biological and social determinants demands attention, for reference to only the sexual drives or the societal functions of marriage leads to an inadequate and confusing view of the institution.

We have followed the young adult as he achieved reasonable emancipation from parental control and started on a search for a way of life of his own. The unmarried young man and woman find themselves in anomalous positions in the parental home. They are adults, no longer requiring care or wishing to be children, but they are still members of the childhood generation. The attachment to the home derives largely from former needs and abiding affections, but the home is no longer the real center of their lives or the focus of their hopes and desires. The family must function as a unit and requires a leader, and it becomes increasingly likely that clashes will occur between the parents and the adult child who has different attitudes, goals, and desires. The erotic bonds and dependent needs that helped foster harmony have been severed or negated. The path toward fulfillment as an adult does not lie in the parental home. In particular there can be no fusion of sexual and affectional needs or completion of generative desires within the family of origin. Emotional independence has been gained but freedom does not bring fulfillment, it simply opens the doors to permit the individual to seek it. The young person is likely to feel at loose ends as part of a home in which he no longer fits: an adult with few prerogatives, an heir apparent awaiting his own domain. Waiting will not suffice, for he cannot inherit his father's family, or the girl her mother's, though the desire to do so often enough gains the upper hand and leads to a frustrated life.

Usually the major attachments that provide direction to the person's life and the meaningful relationship now lie outside the family. There are a group of friends of the same sex who have common interests and with whom activities and confidences are shared. The occupation and activities related to it gain prominence whether a person is already started on a career or is still a student. The wish and need to satisfy and please the boss or teachers become as important as satisfying parental wishes. There are friends of the opposite sex who provide passing or more permanent companionship, partial or complete outlets for sexual drives, admiration that bolsters self-esteem, and from whom one seeks and may find affection and love.

The variations are manifold, but usually the peer group, including members of the opposite sex, forms the major source of interpersonal satisfaction. Customarily for the man, and in recent decades for many girls, life as an unmarried young adult is considered a period during which he or she can enjoy freedom before assuming the responsibilities and restrictions of matrimony. Often this is a time of sexual adventure that is more direct and less hesitant than it was during adolescence and a time when sexual excitement and the challenge and intrigue of conquest become ends in themselves. Others give up this period of freedom and the search for just the right partner by growing into adulthood as a couple. During the period the young woman will be more likely to be assessing potential husbands while the man will be more concerned with adventure, gaining experience and proving his masculinity to himself and others. The freedom from parental edict permits a freer and more conscious pursuit of sexuality. The intensity and extent of the occupation or preoccupation with sexual conquests relate to such factors as inability to tolerate loneliness, the need for physical contact to feel desired or desirable, and the search for reassuring experiences concerning sexual capacities, rather than to any quantity of sexual drive. Often the young man or woman leaves home and establishes bachelor quarters in order to assert and enjoy the freedom from his family that he has gained. The adult who has been away from home during the transition from adolescence attending a university, employed in a different community, or in military service, often finds it difficult to return home to live. When he does, it becomes a period of waiting during which he feels something of a stranger within his own family. It is often easier for the young woman to remain at home, for she is more able to accept the prerogatives of the father and has been educated to remain more dependent. She also may find it useful to have a home where she can await and entertain suitors, and feel more secure than she would be on her own.

Of course, life as an unmarried adult may not exist at all, marriage following the closure of adolescence, or with the marital choice already made and simply awaiting consummation, and the period may terminate abruptly any time when the person falls in love and decides to marry. For some, the hesitancy concerning marriage may be overcome only as friends pair up and marry, leaving the single individual feeling out of place with friends whose major emotional investments now lie in their own homes and their young children. The pressures of parents and married friends, who feel that life can be completed only in marriage, increase. Loneliness becomes a greater problem and the person begins to wonder about his own rationalizations for not marrying. The entire social system pushes young men and women toward marital status, for the life of a single person, particularly for a woman, becomes increasingly limited. Motives other than romantic love gain more importance in the decision to marry and in the choice of a partner.

The Nature of the Impulsions to Marry

The impulsion to form a lasting marital union rests upon the biological nature of man and the requisite lengthy period of nurturance in the family setting. The two sexes are obviously different and have different biological functions and are suited to each other for satisfactory release of sexual tensions and attainment of the complete orgastic pleasure on which nature through the evolutionary process has set a high premium to assure perpetuation of the species. Sexuality in itself, however, does not explain the institution of marriage nor does sexual attraction suffice as a reason why people marry. Sexual gratification is scarcely considered a primary function of marriage in many societies, occurring independently of marriage, particularly for men, and it may be pertinent to marriage only in regard to procreation. It is apparent that even in the contemporary scene the satisfaction of sexual drives does not necessarily wait upon marriage. While it is commonly stated that about 80 per cent of men and 20 per cent of women have experienced sexual intercourse before marriage, the figure is clearly skewed. It would mean that a small proportion of women have intercourse with many different men, showing a greater promiscuity than occurs among men. However, prostitution is so markedly on the wane in the United States that according to Kinsey it does not even provide as much of a sexual outlet as homosexuality.[7] Other figures would indicate that approximately 50 per cent of women engage in sexual relations prior to marriage.* Still, it must be recognized that much of such sexual activity may provide release but relatively little emotional satisfaction.

The desire to propagate, which may well have instinctual components particularly in women, but which also arises through the desire of both sexes for a sense of completion through parenthood, more clearly fosters a reasonably permanent relationship. The children require protective nurturance for many years. The roles of the two parents are divided according to biological determinants and complement one another. As elaborated in Chapter 2, the woman, while providing for the immediate nurturant needs of the offspring, requires protection and the support of a provider. Along with the biological division of abilities to propagate and the child-rearing roles, further divisions of role functions emerged that are transmitted by cultural institutions which have a great deal to do with the desire to marry.

We have noted throughout the process of development the consistent training, which is often unconscious and unnoted, toward the filling of male or female roles. The divergent preparation leads to a need for interdependence with a member of the opposite sex in order properly to carry out the activities of life. These sex-linked roles and skills go beyond the care of offspring. The two genders are trained to possess different abilities and focus on different interests. A man, for example, does not usually possess various homemaking skills and even if he does he is unlikely to gain satisfaction from them. The differences extend beyond such tangible matters to differing ways of regarding and relating to people, and to finding different sources of satisfaction so that neither a man nor a woman has a rounded approach and grasp of life alone. Although the

* But a noteworthy proportion only with their future husbands.

adolescent and, at times, the young adult may be more at ease with members of his own sex whose ways are more familiar because they resemble his own, when the adult becomes independent it is far more likely that a man and woman will complement one another and fill out each other's interests and needs than will a person of the same gender, quite aside from the sexual needs.

The incompleteness of the individual, however, is particularly telling because each person grew up as a member of a family in which tasks and roles were shared, which provided support during immaturity and which formed a place where he was accepted for affectional reasons rather than for his abilities or achievement. During infancy and childhood intangible bonds to others were formed that provided warmth and security, and gave meaning to life. In particular, primary love relationships were established first with the mother and later with the father. We have seen that the child starts life in symbiosis with the mother and gradually gains an independent self. The movement toward separation and increasing independence had always been ambivalent, containing an urge toward freedom for self-realization and a regressive pull toward dependent relatedness with its comfort and security. Throughout development there had been a strong impetus, largely unconscious, toward regaining a total relatedness with another person.

It has also been noted, particularly in the discussion of the resolution of the oedipal attachment, that the sensuous or erotic components of the relatedness to parents had to be frustrated within the family in order to foster proper independent ego development. The upsurge of sexual feelings at puberty not only remained unfulfilled but led to further movement away from the parents. A major aspect of development, the strong attraction to the parent of the opposite sex, after having been formed and having served a useful purpose, was frustrated and left hanging. It was sublimated and displaced, but unconsciously left a sense of incompletion that required closure. These structured but unsatisfied longings and patterns provide the foundation for the later love relationships.

The young person had to overcome a variety of feelings of inadequacy before being ready to lose himself in a total relationship again. The unconscious memory of the disappointing frustration remains in him. The boy needed to gain security against being overwhelmed and lost in a relationship with a woman. The forbidden incestuous connotation of sexuality had to be overcome in both sexes, the dangers of rivalry with parents set aside, and independence from parents achieved. The independence from family, however, increases the feelings of incompletion and aloneness. The sexual drive, however, now is free to find expression and adds compelling moment to the forming of a new union which will more fully, sexually as well as affectionately, complete the strivings and pattern that had been forcibly renounced in childhood. The person who falls in love again transcends himself but this time as an adult who can take care of the other as well as be cared for. The welfare of the other becomes synonymous with one's own welfare. The libidinal strivings are again focused but also shared. Though the two persons are still physically separate, the act of falling in love forms a union between them.

The libidinal drives play a major role in the finding of a love object. The passionate needs pervade intellect and color perception. The wish for the desired object transcends reality. It attaches to some desired and needed fragment in another person, to a physical characteristic or behavioral trait, and around it fashions the idealized person of one's desires. In a sense, every lover is something of a Pygmalion.

It is a time-worn adage that love is blind. It is blind in proportion to the intensity of one's needs. There is an old story told by Petrarch, I believe, of a youth who fell in love with a one-eyed girl and was sent away by his parents who opposed the marriage. After he returned several years later, when he asked his former love how she had lost her eye during his absence, the girl replied, "I have lost none, but you have found yours."

What is the image the lover sees? Some trait produces a resonance of the primary parental love model. It may be quite apparent or because of residual incestuous fears be hidden under markedly different characteristics such as a different physical appearance or divergence of race or religion. Although an attempt by Hamilton[5] to trace such a similarity between marital partners and parents led to a negative conclusion, psychoanalytic work is more likely to uncover one. It is not always present or at least not observable even with careful scrutiny, and it would seem that women tend to marry a man more obviously related to the father than a man is likely to choose a wife resembling his mother. The person in love also sees an admiring person, noting in the eyes of the other the devoted attraction which may well relate to the infant's fixation on the eyes of the loving and admiring mother. He finds someone who supports and increases his own self-esteem and turns the admirer into the person whose admiration and love he wishes. While a person is desired who will complement the self, the loved one may be selected narcissistically in the image of the self whom one loves. However, the resemblance of a spouse to the self, which is often so noticeable, is not this simple, for the choice is apt to fall on someone who resembles a parent through the urge toward regaining the primary parental love object; and as a person is apt to resemble a parent, the spouses may bear resemblances to one another. The choice of a love object seen as the source and possessor of total erotism which re-creates fantasy images of adolescence is apt to be based on an evaluation even less close to reality than other types. There are, of course, many other specific determinants of the choice of the precise partner which are elusive and can be traced only in extreme instances when the determining factors are unusually clear.

Readiness for Marriage

In some respects the question of whom a person chooses to marry must be related to the question of when a person becomes ready to marry, for when conscious and unconscious preparation for marriage has been completed the proper person often mysteriously appears. While it is romantic to believe that true lovers will eventually meet though separated by continents, the facts show that 12.5 per cent of five thousand couples in Philadelphia lived at the same address prior to marriage and over 50 per cent within twenty blocks of one another.* Proximity of residence is clearly a major factor in selection, while attendance at the same schools and churches accounts for another large proportion. The choice is basically not of one person from among the inhabitants of the world but from the relatively small number of persons met under favorable circumstances at a very specific time in life.

The Developmental History of Marital Choice

The process of marital choice has a developmental history much like that of occupational choice and this history influences the outcome, for the choice may take decisive form at different stages in the process. The various phases have already been noted as we followed personality development from early childhood. The earliest choice is the incestuous wish to marry a parent which occurs before the child recognizes that the parent also grows older while he grows up, a choice retained until the

* See J. Bossard, "Residential Propinquity as a Factor in Marriage Selection." [1] The topic has been reviewed by A. M. Katz and R. Hill, "Residential Propinquity and Marital Selection: A Review of Theory, Method, and Fact." [6] The figure given for similar address is higher than that found in other studies, perhaps because it did not take into account a tendency for engaged couples to move close to one another.

resolution of the oedipal phase takes place, when it is banished into the unconscious where it continues to exert its influence. There is a period when fantasy choices are fairly clearly parental substitutes, friends of parents, teachers, and the like, who can approximate a realistic choice as the child's age comes closer to that of the parental substitutes, as when a high school student falls in love with a teacher, or the student nurse with the physician who teaches her. Eventually, the possibility of marrying an older person who remains something of a parental figure becomes realistic. It is a common pattern of marriage in some countries where the woman marries an older, paternal man. Although it is not the commonly accepted pattern in the United States, it occurs often enough. More commonly, the adolescent moves from the fantasy of a romantic storybook ideal divested of sexuality to form a crush on an older adolescent who is an idol of the peer group. During adolescence there may be considerable daydreaming of the perfect person one will find, and, for the girl, of a man who will pursue her and sacrifice himself for love of her. In late adolescence desirable sexual characteristics enter into the image.

Eventually fantasy choices give way to courtship experiences which involve the actual trying out of the suitability of potential partners. At present, particularly in suburban societies where adolescent peer groups are mixed, the trying out starts long before actual courtship through the gaining of familiarity with members of the opposite sex and the sorting out of what types of persons one likes. In contrast to societies where the girl cannot go out unchaperoned, the courtship period will usually include "going steady" as a trial of compatibility in consideration of future marriage, or simply as an experimental run. There may also be a pre-engagement understanding between the couple that is a semiformal consideration of future engagement and marriage. Such pledges accompanied by the presentation of a fraternity pin or the exchange of significant tokens have varying degrees of meaning, but are more readily broken than a formal engagement which is publicly announced and usually involves the meeting and sanction of the two families.

With the achievement of adult status, dating often assumes the significance of courtship, particularly at times when marriage occurs early as at present. By then the person has had an opportunity to take stock, not only forming opinions concerning the type of mate desired but also what sort of person he is likely to gain. Who has shown serious interest provides some measure of prospects. Still, the chance meeting or unexpected interest of a person may upset fantasies, expectations, and self-assessment at any time. Thus a young woman of twenty who became engaged to a man twelve years her senior tried to explain her decision which was as unexpected to her as to her family; she said, "I had always expected to marry someone who I was sure would amount to something, but also liked to have fun, to go dancing, play tennis, and enjoy the things I did. Then suddenly he came along and asked me to go out with him. I didn't think I'd be interested and I wasn't sure I'd know how to behave with an older man. I made excuses several times until I didn't know what to say. Then on our first date I found I was comfortable with him and felt taken care of. It was clear he wanted to get married. He isn't what I'd thought I wanted, he's just an insurance salesman and doesn't want to be anything else, he just wants to have a good home and a nice life. Still now I know I love him and want to be with him as I never wanted anyone before." Indeed, in falling in love seriously the young adult is apt to descend from romantic dreams to reality, but through falling in love he or she magnifies the reasonably prosaic choice into the most important and wonderful person in the world. The shift involves the more mature realization that the other need only be the most wonderful person in the world for the self.

The Engagement

The decision to marry is conventionally marked by the formal engagement. Although in some societies the engagement or betrothal is virtually a contract to marry, it currently forms a period prior to marriage that permits the couple to associate intimately and fairly constantly and to make certain that they are suited to one another. The engagement, particularly among younger people, involves getting parental approval. While the right of the girl's father to forbid the marriage carries less weight than formerly, the very prospect of having to confront the parents with someone of whom they will not approve deters girls from accepting some proposals as well as men from venturing them. Realistic considerations are forced to the forefront, such as the compatibility of the families, financial prospects, and the desire to retain the esteem and affection of parents. It should be noted, however, that the final proposal seems to be becoming less and less common and often a couple cannot clearly say just when they decided to marry and how the matter came up. Despite the insistence on self-determination by the couple, parental opinions as well as those of friends are often heeded and probably serve as a useful check against impulsive or inappropriate marriages.

The engagement is more than a trial period. It provides time prior to the actual sharing of living and the assumption of responsibilities to fuse interests and identities and for each to accommodate to the other in a movement away from the romantic attraction to a more conjugal relationship. It is usually a period of more intense sexual intimacy, which helps prepare the couple for intercourse and for physical familiarity in the marriage. It often forms a difficult and frustrating time if the couple decides to wait until marriage to have sexual relations, for the sexual play and love naturally heighten the desire for immediate consummation. In the 1920's in particular, when a number of authorities considered sexual compatibility to form a primary foundation for harmonious marriage, some believed that a planned period in which the couple tried out their sexual relationship should precede marriage; as in the concept of companionate marriage. Concepts have changed with the recognition that trial situations are usually not conducive to sexual satisfaction and the realization that a good sexual adjustment is not something that is dependent upon the physical make-up of the partners as much as upon their emotional maturity and that sexual satisfactions may come only with experience and familiarity. However, at least one survey of college graduates indicates that about half of engaged couples will have intercourse with one another.* There is some vagueness about the figures, which stand as a striking measure of the reliability of questionnaire statistics. In one study, each member of the married couple was asked if he or she had engaged in premarital intercourse with the spouse. It seems that approximately 50 per cent of the husbands had engaged in intercourse with their wives, but only 16 per cent of the wives had premarital intercourse with their husbands.

It is clear from various sources that a reasonably lengthy engagement safeguards against later divorce. Impulsive marriages without any waiting period are notably unsuccessful, which forms one reason why many states require a waiting period or at least three days between obtaining a license and the actual wedding ceremony. Trends concerning optimal length of engagements cannot be clearly established. Some couples, particularly childhood sweethearts or college couples, may have a brief formal

---

* See A. C. Kinsey, W. B. Pomeroy, C. Martin, and P. Gebhard: *Sexual Behavior in the Human Female,*[7] p. 336. Data vary, depending upon the type of survey and social class of respondents. Whereas premarital intercourse increases inversely to socioeconomic class, marriage occurs earlier among men and women who have not gone to college. Among women who have had premarital intercourse 40 to 72 per cent (differing from study to study) state they had premarital intercourse only with their husbands.[3]

engagement though they have been informally engaged for many years. Three different studies indicate that the chances for excellent marriage adjustment are greatest when the engagement has lasted more than two years, but few advisors would suggest such prolonged formal engagements. As a survey of married college graduates indicated that about one third of the women and one fourth of the men had previously been engaged to another person, it is clear that engagements serve a useful purpose as a trial period.[2]

Aside from testing the compatibility of the couple, and permitting closer assessment by each of the other, the engagement also provides a person time to ascertain his own ability and readiness for marriage. As the actual event approaches, concerns about one's ability to accept responsibility, of sexual competence, and of less conscious fears of genital injury promote anxiety. The feelings of inadequacy may be displaced or projected onto the partner. The narrow margin between anxieties which will blossom into incapacitation in marriage and those which will fade when the period of waiting is over may be difficult to assess. Those who approach the psychiatrist, clergyman, or marital counselor may wish someone else to make the decision for them, but usually they come too late for anyone to help them work through an adequate assessment of themselves and the partner, and only under extreme conditions can a third person assume responsibility. It is of interest that a notable proportion of those who break an engagement will break more than one.

Various Motivations to Marry

There are many reasons for marriage and the choice of a partner other than falling in love. They may be ancillary and only contributory factors or they may be dominating motivations, adequate in themselves; or they may, because of their force, almost preclude a lasting, satisfactory marriage. Some are clearly negative motivations in the sense that they cause a person to seek marriage in order to compensate for some unhappy life situation rather than because of strong desires for married life with the partner. It would be naïve to consider marital and family problems on the assumption that the marriage arose through love, and without being ready to hear and understand what led each spouse into the unhappy bond. Yet, as with many other life situations, what might be favorable or unfavorable for the success of a marriage can rarely be stated in categorical terms, for the chances of success depend upon the balance of factors involved in the specific situation. Some reasons aside from love of the specific partner that enter to a greater or lesser degree into any marriage are the desire to have a home of one's own, to gain completion and complementation with a person of the opposite sex, to find sexual outlets and settle problems of sexuality, to have children, to gain security, to acquire status and a place in society. Yet each of these may contain distortions that will interfere with the relationship, as will be discussed and illustrated.

While the desire for a home of one's own properly emerges with the change in the young adult's relations with his own family, it can also arise primarily as a need to get away from unhappiness in the parental home. The parents' quarrels, their domination, the breakup of the parents' marriage after the children have grown, and countless such reasons can impel a young person to seek a spouse hastily. Statements that one hears from unhappily married people such as, "After that fight with my father, I would have married the first man that came along, and I suppose I did," may overlook the fact that the young woman seduced the first man she went out with and made him feel obligated to marry her. In a different context the youth who is away from a small community for the first time, as for example after he is inducted into the army, feels intense loneliness without a home and may find a girl in the nearby town who behaves much more forwardly than any he knew before to be most desirable, and he cannot wait to marry her.

Sexual attraction and the impulsion of sexuality form a desired component of the decision to marry. Marriage not only provides an outlet for sexual expression but it permits a settling of sexuality so that it need no longer be a preoccupation or finding a partner a constant occupation. While sexual needs can be satisfied outside marriage, such experiences or affairs rarely blend with affectional needs, desires for a lasting union, and wishes for a home and children. Still, sexual need can lead to impetuous choice or unwittingly into a relationship that has few if any other virtues. The selection of a partner simply because of his or her sexual attractiveness to others not uncommonly derives from a need to gain prestige or bolster self-esteem through having an enviable partner. Anxieties concerning sexual adequacy can lead to a marriage undertaken primarily to assure the self of one's adequacy as a man or woman, or occasionally simply to conceal impotence or homosexuality from the world. A young woman who has considerable guilt over masturbation and who has some intermittent concerns that she might be homosexual because she recognizes her competitiveness with men and her jealousy of their friendships with each other, starts having casual affairs. Before long she compulsively sleeps with any college classmate who makes advances to her. When she finds a passive young man whom she can dominate and with whom she assumes a masculine role in intercourse, she seduces him into marriage in the hope that it will stop her promiscuity. She does not recognize that he seeks to marry her because of his need to find a boyish girl in order to feel aroused, and soon after marriage she resents being treated as a boy rather than a girl. A college professor finds that his homosexual interests are creating suspicion on the campus and seeks to shield himself. He selects a woman he meets at a religious conference whom he believes has no interest in anything but spiritual matters. His inability to tolerate any physical closeness becomes unbearable to the wife, particularly as she married largely to have children. Such conscious use of marriage for self-protection or for selfish motives is not a rarity among disturbed persons.

The wish for security and to have someone who will provide support financially and emotionally is not only an appropriate part of marriage but can be an acceptable reason in itself, particularly when it is openly or tacitly understood by both persons, as when a widower with children marries a woman who wishes a home and to make a home for someone. It is less favorable when a girl becomes fed up with her work in a factory or with being the target for the foreman's expectations that she sleep with him and decides that marriage to the young man she has been trying to avoid is preferable to the insecurities and burdens of unmarried life. Ambition also often takes precedence over other motivations; and sometimes it is the ambition of the parents rather than of the person who is marrying. After all, marriage for wealth, career, opportunity, or social advancement has the sanction of ages when such motives were considered natural and proper, with each family or individual seeking the best opportunity and with love a secondary factor. While such reasons in themselves need not be injurious to a good marriage, especially when they are clearly the dominant motive, the partner whose wealth or prestige is being acquired may all too readily feel unwanted for himself or the spouse may feel obligated to act deferential or subservient.

The wish for children, too, can form a primary rather than an adjunctive reason for marriage, with the choice of the spouse a secondary matter, and may eventually leave the spouse feeling neglected after the arrival of the child. A woman in her thirties who has had little opportunity to marry because she is contemptuous of men spends much time in fantasy about a son who will become a great musician such as she would have been if she had been born a male. She is intensely rivalrous with her sister, and when the sister has a child she attaches herself to a younger man and for the the first time in her life becomes very seductive. The man's personality matters little except that she rightly feels she can lead him to the altar. Soon after the birth of the son this woman became very discontented with her husband's passivity and sought a divorce, feeling she had no need for him and resenting his attachment to her son.

Marriages are often enough precipitated by pregnancies. It has been estimated that in England about one out of six brides is pregnant,* though no definitive data are available in the United States, it is probable the figures would not be very different. In many instances the pregnancy only determines the time of a marriage between a couple who have already decided to marry or simply serves to chase away the last hesitancies of one or the other partner. Marriage is, of course, not a necessary outcome of impregnation. There are about 100,000 illegitimate births in the United States each year, and a sizable proportion of the million or so illegal abortions carried out each year in the United States pertain to unmarried women. However, it is not favorable if the woman feels that the man has married her only because she is pregnant, and often feelings of shame and guilt are apt to persist and disturb the initial relationship. At times, of course, such marriages are carried out with the expectation of divorce after the baby has been legitimatized. Pregnancy has been a more or less customary—for one cannot say conventional— way for a girl to secure the man she wants but who avoids proposing or ignores her proposals. While surely leading to some satisfactory marriages when the girl knows her mind and perhaps her boy friend's better than he does, the resentment over being forced to marry can place a lasting blight over a marriage.

The Hostile Marriage

The expression of hostility through the act of marrying forms a common source of disastrous marriages. It is usually as destructive to the person who is being hostile as to the relatively innocent partner who has become involved. The hostile persons use themselves as weapons for gaining revenge, wishing others to suffer because they suffer. In the process they become the targets of their own animosities. The most obvious

* The percentage is considerably higher in Sweden, where premarital intercourse is socially condoned.

instances are marriages on the rebound, after the desired partner rejects or marries someone else. The hasty step may be carried out in order to regain self-esteem by feeling wanted and needed by someone, but it usually contains the intention of showing the rejecting person that he or she is not needed; and it contains the fantasy that the true love will realize his error and dash in at the last moment and insist he cannot live without her. The hostility over being rejected takes precedence over love and the woman (or as commonly a man) punishes herself for the hostility by making an inappropriate marriage, in a sense wishing the true love to suffer because she is unhappy. Even when hostility does not dominate the picture, the marriage made hastily, before the disappointment has been worked through and assimilated, leaves the person dissatisfied with the spouse, and involved often for years with fantasies of the first true love whom the spouse can never match. A young woman who married hastily primarily to get away from home after her fiancé was killed in combat, insisted on wearing the engagement ring from her first fiancé until the moment she entered the church for her wedding. She lived through her first pregnancy fantasying that the dead man was the father of her child. A similar situation arises when a youth marries to spite parents who have objected to a marriage he desires. He takes the attitude, "I'll show them," and selects a girl with attributes they have suggested but with obviously undesirable traits in addition, or he maneuvers into a position in which his parents must approve an even less favorable marriage. A woman who became depressed after the birth of her child had married on the rebound and to spite her father. Her father had refused for over a year to approve a marriage she had desired and her boy friend had stopped waiting and married another. She started an affair with a man, largely to arouse jealousy in her former boy friend and to bring him back to her. She became pregnant and her father was now forced to approve her marriage to a very dependent, weak man for whom she had little feeling other than contempt. She could not desire her infant or feel maternal toward the child whom she felt tied her to a marriage she had never wanted and whose care interfered with her search for solace in fantasy.

A different type of hostile marriage involves the expression of diffuse antagonisms toward members of the opposite sex, often provoked by envy. The person marries a dependent person and seeks to treat a subservient spouse sadistically. The marriage takes the form of a misplaced triumph over the hated enemy. A young woman had been aggressively homosexual during adolescence and in her early adult years. Her homosexuality had been determined in large part by her envy of her brothers who were obviously preferred by her mother. She eventually learned she could seduce and dominate some men by being a sexual tease just as easily as she could dominate certain women. She married a masochistic man whom she constantly teased and belittled sexually and she gained great pleasure in being able to use him sexually in perverse acts that were humiliating to him. In a somewhat similar manner a man who was bitterly hostile toward his mother became a specialist in wooing many girls until they seemed desperately in love with him and were willing to abase themselves sexually, and then rejected them. When he finally married he repeatedly stimulated and frustrated his wife sexually but expected her constantly to derogate herself and admire him.

Rescue Fantasies and Sado-Masochistic Marriages

It may be useful to note the place of rescue fantasies in the choice of a partner, for they are particularly pertinent to the medical and nursing professions. Perhaps eliciting sympathy because of unfortunate life circumstances creates a particular attraction, engendering in the other the fantasy that he can undo the harm and save the person from an unfortunate fate. A man feels impelled to rescue a girl from a home that is miserable because of an alcoholic father. He sees the girl's faults but believes that they are not really part of her and that he will change matters by providing love and care. Doctors are apt to confuse caring for patients with the desire to take care of them personally. A nurse may seek to marry a schizophrenic patient in the belief that her care will cure him. Such desires may often grow out of a lack of security in one's own attractiveness or sexual ability accompanied by the feeling that he or she has a right to marry only if it is a sacrifice to save the spouse.

Some of the types of marital choice that we have been discussing in the past few pages are often designated as sado-masochistic. The spouses unconsciously select partners whom they can hurt and who, in turn, will hurt them. They may argue, quarrel, fight, repeatedly injure each other's self-esteem and be chronically unhappy, but because of the interdigitating psychopathology they could not live intimately in any other type of relationship—one might almost say, could not be happy in any other sort of marriage. In most such marriages, a sadist does not select a masochist, but rather both are sado-masochistic in varying proportions. One may behave sadistically under certain circumstances, and the other under different conditions. Each has his vulnerabilities which the other rapidly uncovers and uses as a target for his or her barbs and sallies. Frequently each is preoccupied with hurting the other to get even. The patterns usually do not involve sadistic perversions, and need not include physical violence, and the sadistic pleasure can even be gained through moral righteousness. A fundamentalist minister brought his wife to a psychiatric clinic because of her drinking. It soon became apparent that the minister habitually and sanctimoniously caused his wife to consider herself a sinner because of her sexual desires, and because she had not been "saved" by an inner revelation as he had been. He had, indeed, treated her very much like a servant. The wife in turn hurt him and gained vengeance by being "ill" with "alcoholism," which she manifested primarily by attending services and church socials in an intoxicated state. Her behavior permitted her husband to feel even more pious and self-sacrificing because of his tolerance of her illness, which he dealt with, however, as if it were a visitation of Satan that marked his wife as selected for damnation whereas he had been elected for salvation.

Largely because of such sado-masochistic marriages, in which the conflict and hurt really serves the unconscious needs of both partners, there has been a strong tendency on the part of psychiatrists to consider that virtually all such marital choices serve some fundamental personality needs of the persons who make these seemingly unfortunate selections. The partners find their complementary mate intuitively; through their interaction during courtship; or perhaps most commonly because of resemblances to parents who had been involved in such sado-masochistic relationships throughout the person's childhood. Indeed, one may gain the impression that for some persons marriage means a sado-masochistic relationship because of the homes in which they were reared, and that they seek a spouse who will fill the necessary role to create a marriage similar to those of their parents.

Nevertheless, as noted earlier in the chapter, the concept that all unhappy marital choices serve the unconscious needs of the spouses can be overdone and applied inappropriately. The marital choice serves a purpose, but as we have been saying, there are factors other than unconscious needs that can lead into an unhappy marriage.

Young people, in particular, are apt to disregard the family of the intended spouse, insisting that they are not marrying the family. While this is true enough, it is also clear that one of the best indicators of a future happy marriage is whether or not the person comes from a stable and happy home. Divorce runs in families as much as certain hereditary illnesses. In a sense, of course, one is marrying the family insofar as the spouse is the product of the parents and the way in which he has been raised in the family.

The choice of the suitable partner clearly presents difficulties, and it has been possible only to indicate the importance of a suitable choice and some of the types of difficulties that commonly arise. The choice of the partner constitutes the major decision of a supposedly voluntary nature that can complement and alter the personality make-up and afford opportunities for self-completion before the production of a new generation. In contemporary society the marriage leads to the fusion of two persons necessary to produce offspring and to furnish the family milieu in which they grow up. While offering opportunities that should help them to mature, the decision and selection rest upon the outcome of each person's development in a family. They are impelled by sexual feelings and other needs for affinity. The frustrations of the oedipal bonds in the family of origin leads to the search for completion in marriage, and the marital choice is apt to reflect the many unconscious problems of the intrafamilial oedipal situation. It turns backward as well as into the future and thus is particularly prone to regressive or neurotic determination. It can include such motives as the effort to undo and redo childhood unhappiness; to live in the present in terms of infantile and childhood situations that are no longer appropriate; the holding of expectations from a spouse that are more suited to a parent; the search for narcissistic gratification as an admired child rather than wishing to share and to direct the life for mutual satisfaction. The entire matter of choice of a marriage partner is so closely linked with the entire personality development that the choice forms a distinctive measure of the total outcome of the process. Perhaps it was simpler when the decision did not rest upon the individual partners and less was expected of marriage and the blame for its shortcomings did not fall so heavily upon the couple itself.

References

1. James H. S. Bossard, "Residential Propinquity as a Factor in Marriage Selection," *American Journal of Sociology*, 38 (1932–1933), 219–224.
2. Ernest Burgess and Harvey Locke, *The Family: From Institution to Companionship* (New York: American Book Co., 1945), p. 390.
3. Winston Ehrmann, *Premarital Dating Behavior* (New York: Dryden Press, 1952).
4. Sigmund Freud, "On Narcissism" (1914), in *The Standard Edition of the Complete Psychological Works of Sigmund Freud*, Vol. 14 (London: Hogarth Press, 1957).
5. G. Hamilton, *A Research in Marriage* (New York: Boni Publications, 1929).
6. Alvin M. Katz and Reuben Hill, "Residential Propinquity and Marital Selection: A Review of Theory, Method, and Fact," *Marriage and Family Living*, 20 (1958), 27–35.
7. Alfred C. Kinsey, Wardell B. Pomeroy, Clyde Martin, and Paul Gebhard, *Sexual Behavior in the Human Female* (Philadelphia: W. B. Saunders, 1953).
8. United States Government, *Population, Marriages, Divorces and Rates with Percent Changes from Preceding Year. United States 1920–1959. Vital Statistics of the United States, 1959* (Washington, D.C.: Government Printing Office).

Suggested Reading

Lee G. Burchinal, "The Premarital Dyad and Love Involvement," in Harold T. Christensen (ed.), *Handbook of Marriage and the Family* (Chicago: Rand McNally, 1964).

Winston Ehrmann, *Premarital Dating Behavior* (New York: Dryden Press, 1952).

P. Jacobsohn and A. P. Matheny, "Mate Selection in Open Marriage Systems," *International Journal of Comparative Sociology*, 3 (1962), 98–123.

CHAPTER 14

Marital Adjustment

THE TOPIC OF MARITAL ADJUSTMENT is often taken to refer to the couple's sexual adjustment. Even though the sexual adjustment is of vital moment to the future of the marriage, the subject has much broader ramifications. It involves the requisite shifts within each person—within the personality of each—that make possible the necessary interrelationship that proximates a coalition; it concerns the finding of reciprocally interrelating roles that permit the meshing of activities with minimal friction; it includes the reorganization of the family patterns which each spouse learned at home, and which may involve differing ethnic and social class patterns, into a workable social system; it concerns how the childhood family romance of each partner can find consummation. The achievement of a sexual union that satisfies the erotic needs of both partners fosters mutuality and can lessen the tensions that mount in each partner and the strains in the relationship that must inevitably arise. In general, it can be the lubricant that eases friction. It often serves as a sensitive indicator of the maturity of each partner and of their capacity to interrelate on an intimate and adult level.

Yet it is but part of the total relationship, and it will pall if it is not emergent from a satisfying and completing interpersonal relationship.

When a marriage gets off to a good start, it forms a stabilizing influence for both spouses and a new opportunity for self-realization. Life becomes a new adventure filled with opportunity to live out what has long been imagined. Each partner relishes having another person so interested in his or her well-being and feels secure in being the center of the spouse's interest and love. Activity, thought, and fantasy have a new tangible and legitimate focus which gives a new coherence to one's life. The companionship banishes loneliness, and sexual satisfaction brings a sense of release and fulfillment that mobilizes energies for the pursuit of incentives derived from the marriage. Many new tasks provide novelty. During separation between breakfast and supper, which can seem very long, the thoughts of each turn toward the other, sharing in fantasy until rejoined. The freedom of sexual intimacy and mutual exploration lends excitement which, in turn, leads to a new-found calm. Each partner makes mistakes and is apt to misunderstand, but evidence of love negates any intent to hurt. The glow of the first months of marriage, with its romantic and even unrealistic overassessment by the spouses of each other, can provide an opportunity for the couple to gain a true familiarity with one another, to gain reciprocal roles, to learn how to share their lives.

However, even the best-matched couples encounter difficulties in adjusting to the new life together. The harmonious transition from honeymoon to ordinary life is often hampered by various disagreements and disappointments that can mount to resentment and regrets over the commitment. Most couples are well aware that such difficulties are likely to arise and feel determined that they will not happen in their marriage. The potential sources of friction are legion, and there seems no reason to try to catalogue these common sources of irritation which can mount to chronic disappointment or discord when one or both partners feel the other is selfish and does not reciprocate in investing effort and showing concern for the other. Topics that the couple have difficulties in discussing because they seem so intensely personal, such as sexual desires and dissatisfactions (which will be discussed later in the chapter), personal hygiene, or jealousies of parents-in-law, can become serious sources of resentment. These early months can contain periods of trial when each spouse may wonder about the wisdom of the marriage and experience anxiety about the future.* Even when things go very badly the newly-

* J. Landis[7] classified the major areas that are likely to be divisive as "religion, social life, mutual friends, in-laws, money, and sex relations," which seems fairly inclusive;

weds are reluctant to let others know of their plight, and will suffer in quiet resentment and despair before falling back on parents for advice as they might desperately wish to do.

The marriage ceremony is not the end of the story as it is in so many romantic novels, and most couples are very aware that it only marks the beginning of a new stage in life in which happiness or contentment must be achieved rather than simply expected as a consequence of the marriage. However, for many adolescent girls and young women finding a suitable husband has been so much of a preoccupation, so much of a major goal, that the married woman may forget that it is but a means toward achieving a rounded life. The woman who stops her vocational and educational activities simply to be a married woman may soon become bored, irritated that her husband does not continue to provide excitement, and worried about the emptiness of her days; these feelings may lead to somewhat premature desires for a child to bring meaning to the marriage rather than as a product of marital fulfillment.

The Effect of Marriage on Personality Structure

A successful marriage will usually both lead to and require a profound reorganization of the personality structure of each partner that will influence the further personality development of each. The marriage necessitates forming a union in which certain functions are shared, others undertaken by one spouse, and in which some aspects of individuality are renounced. Certain facets and traits of the personality will be developed further and others fade, for the personality configuration changes in relation to a new most significant person. Even as occupational choice influences the further development and configuration of the personality, the marital adjustment can change how a spouse unfolds. The nature of such reorganizations is difficult to state coherently but may be elucidated through considering the changes in personality somewhat schematically in terms of the *structural concept*.

The directive agency of the person, the ego, must expand at marriage to consider the spouse as well as the self and also the marriage as an entity. Optimally, the spouse becomes an alter ego whose desires, needs, and well-being are considered on a par with one's own, and whose opin-

---

but W. Goode[5] also considers as important: drinking, triangles, gambling, helling around, value differences, etc. Many of these are symptomatic difficulties—either of the emotional instability or immaturity of one or both partners, or of failure to achieve compatibility, and a mutually satisfactory reciprocity and sexual adjustment.

ions and ideas are taken into account in the reaching of decisions affecting spheres of common interest. The wife usually replaces her own ambitions with a concern for her husband's career, which she seeks to abet. The husband is seeking to improve or maintain his wife's position in society as a part of his own. The change involves small matters as well as major decisions, and indeed becomes an inherent part of a way of life. The wife cooks the hamburgers her husband likes rather than the artichoke salad she would prefer. The choice of a movie involves weighing the intensity of the preferences of each. The purchase of a house and the selection of a neighborhood in which to live cannot be the sole decision of one partner without creating difficulties. The couple realize that they have become interdependent in many areas and that the well-being of each is bound up with the contentment of the other. It is not a matter of the willingness of one to sacrifice for the sake of the spouse. Self-sacrifice leads to masochistic attitudes that can slip over into punishment of the other through suffering. In the intimate relationship of marriage, each member finds a major reward in the comfort, absence of tension, and warmth of affection achieved when the spouse feels relaxed and happy; and each strives, consciously and unconsciously, for this reward. The situation is analogous to the process through which the infant and mother achieve mutuality, discussed in Chapter 5. The process requires more than intent and the desire to please, for it cannot transpire without an understanding of the needs and preferences of the other, recognition of what is crucial to the happiness of the other as well as to one's own, and an ability not to confuse the other's preferences—which can be set aside —with the other's needs. As might be anticipated from the lifelong "training" of men and women, the wife is usually more sensitive to the ways and needs of the spouse than is the husband. It is when one or both partners give up efforts to achieve such satisfaction from the marriage that difficulties become serious; and when efforts to gain one's way through bargaining, the use of various wiles, by gamesmanship or deceit become prominent.[1]

The superego of each partner also changes to meet the superego standards and cope with the id impulsions of the spouse. Each partner grew up with differing parental and societal directives that have been internalized as superego. A husband may be placed under new standards by his acceptance of his wife's aspirations for him; or modify his drinking patterns because of his wife's attitudes about alcohol which she assimilated from her mother; or his wife's superego may permit him to overcome repressions fostered by his own superego and engage in sexual behavior which previously had been barred even from his fantasy. We may note that the tragedy of Macbeth unrolls as Macbeth's superego injunctions against regicide are overcome by his wife, who has fewer conscious scruples in the way of her ambition; and her taunts of his weakness and cowardice vanquish his conscience. Indeed, a spouse's value system, particularly a husband's, will usually markedly modify the value systems derived from parents which initially formed the foundations of the superego. Discrepancies between these two major sources of behavioral guidance can create considerable conflict within the individual, between spouses, and between a spouse and in-laws.

Alterations in the expression permitted to id impulses follow as a consequence of modification of the superego; but other influences are also effective. Consideration of the partner's sexual urges are clearly basic to a satisfactory sexual adjustment. A person will, at times, be motivated to sexual activity by the spouse rather than by his or her own urges. A new freedom in giving vent to sexual drives follows the availability of a sexual outlet that is not only permitted by society and parents but is even an obligation. The release of interests tied up in conjunction with sexual repression extends beyond the area of sexuality and provides new energies that can be turned to constructive uses and permit the development of a more harmonious and rounded personality. The aggressive and self-preservative drives of the spouse are also important; it is obvious that both minimizing a spouse's aggression and coping with it are important aspects of marital adjustment. The *ego defenses* that the partner utilizes in order to control id impulses must also be respected lest the partner's ensuing anxiety create serious problems. Of course, certain defenses—such as a wife's obsessive cleanliness or a husband's projections of blame onto his wife—can create considerable marital difficulty. Still, a husband or wife frequently accepts a spouse's peculiarities as well as defenses as perfectly reasonable in order to maintain harmony. Thus, a young wife was willing to adhere to a rigidly restrictive diet even though she was not obese in order to placate her husband, who needed her to have a boyish figure to stimulate him sexually. Many married persons rapidly learn what they must do or not do in order to avoid enraging the partner, even if the partner's need seems very unreasonable.

The personality may also change gradually after marriage because of a shift in identification models, notably by taking on characteristics and standards of a parent-in-law. A young attorney whose father had been a farmer married the daughter of a federal judge. He soon began to resemble his father-in-law in many ways, in his gestures and intonations as well as in his politics and ambitions. His admiration of his father-in-law may have been a determinant in his marriage, but his wife had probably been attracted to him because she saw in him characteristics that resembled her father's—and she unconsciously fostered the development of these traits in her husband. In the process the young attorney acquired an identification that began to direct his career. Indeed, there is a German adage according to which a man's career is commonly continued by his son-in-law—recognizing the woman's tendency to fall in love with a man who is like her father.

Some women, however, ambitious for themselves through having competent husbands, may have had to compromise and marry men who do not live up to their aspirations; and others, who wish to shape their husbands, marry less forceful and more malleable men. Difficulties can then ensue because the wife sets out to remake her husband in the image of her own ideal, which may be difficult for the husband to tolerate, for directly or indirectly his own sense of adequacy is being undermined, and his potency may decline as well, either because of his feelings of inadequacy or as a means of passive rebelliousness by which he indicates that he is the possessor of the male genitals and they do not belong to his wife.

The Transference of Parental Traits to the Spouse

Almost everyone tends to "transfer" parental attributes to a spouse because the relatedness to the parents forms the foundations for relationships with other intensely significant persons. These transferences lead to some blurring of the marital relationship when the spouse is seen more in the image of the parent than as he really is. Indeed, herein lies the source of many neurotic marital conflicts, and it is often complicated by the choice of a person who actually fills the shoes of the parent. On the one hand, a person may be upset when the spouse does not remain true to the needed image and breaks the illusion; on the other, undesirable traits of a parent are attributed to a spouse erroneously. A newly married woman, for example, became upset and punitively withdrawn whenever her husband took a cocktail before dinner and infuriated when he took two. She expected her husband to become abusive after a few drinks, drift away from home after dinner, and come home intoxicated late at night. Only during psychotherapy did she realize that nothing in her husband's past or present behavior warranted her fears and anger. She had married a man who had some resemblances to her father. She had thought he had her father's good traits without the passive-dependent characteristics and tendency to go on alcoholic sprees that had created many anxiety-filled days for her mother and for herself as a child. The husband's taking of a cocktail had mobilized concerns about the imminence of divorce that neither she nor her husband had been able to understand. A common source of impaired communication lies in such misinterpretation of even minor signs in terms of parental behavior. A man accustomed to his mother's resentment whenever he was late for supper, enters his own home with a chip on his shoulder whenever he is late and starts counterattacking as he opens the door. He has no chance to find out that his wife has been awaiting him calmly and cheerfully, for having grown up as the daughter of a general practitioner whose hours were very irregular she did not, like his mother, expect her husband to appear on schedule.

The narcissistic needs of a husband or wife for unceasing admiration also usually reflect ways of relating to a parent of the opposite sex. A husband may need his wife to support his masculinity by admiring his athletic prowess or his charm with women as had his mother. A wife who had been her father's favorite, who had been pampered and praised for her beauty, and had usually been able to "twist her father around her finger" by her seductive behavior, expected her husband to continue to admire her beauty and stop whatever he was doing to fondle her whenever she flirted with him as he had done during their courtship. She felt hurt when he criticized her poor cooking and lackadaisical house-keeping and when he could not be sidetracked by her pouts and seductive twirls. Further misunderstandings arose when her husband failed to real-ize that his wife's display of her nude body before a mirror was for her own admiration or to elicit praise from him rather than an invitation to him to have sexual relations.

The Parental Roles of Spouses

Such examples of difficulties that may result from transferrring paren-tal attributes to a spouse should not be misconstrued to indicate that wishing a spouse to fill something of a parental role is necessarily neu-rotic or otherwise detrimental to a marriage. Indeed, a marriage encom-passes desires to complete the family romance that had to be frustrated in the family of origin. Even mature persons seek something of a parent in a spouse. It is a matter of the proper balance of such needs. Even a husband who can be decisive on his own and unhesitatingly accept the responsibility for his wife and family will welcome a maternal nurturant attitude from his wife when he is ill or disheartened. The capacity of a spouse to be protectively and affectionately parental and conversely to be able to permit the other to provide solace can be particularly important during times of stress, disappointment, or loss, when the disturbed spouse can feel his troubles dissolve through receiving tangible evidence of being loved or wanted. The ability of a couple to sustain one another and give of themselves during times of difficulty is a critical aspect of any marriage.

We have been examining how the personality of a person alters in marriage and how the "structures" change through the interrelationship. The changes involve something of a fusion of the personalities in which each gives up some aspects of independence for the benefits of a new interdependence. Of course, unless individuality and individual interests remain, there can scarcely be a meaningful and lasting interrelatedness. Still, in forming the coalition each person leaves himself vulnerable to feeling incomplete if the spouse is lost, and accepts the risk of giving himself in expectation of receiving in return; a commitment that can lead to profound hurt.

Mechanisms of Defense of the Marriage

The coalescing of personalities and dependence upon the spouse often lead to a remarkable inability to perceive a spouse's faults and mistakes. We frequently find a wife—or a husband—constructing defenses to cover a spouse's weaknesses rather than to defend her own ego. When the attachment is needed greatly one partner may construct a whole array of defenses against the recognition of something that could disrupt the relationship. A woman who had waited three years for her husband's return from overseas combat duty during World War II blossomed when she had news that he was finally en route home. Yet within two weeks of his return she was suffering from an agitated depression and was profoundly delusional. She had been orphaned early in life and had fallen in love with her husband and idolized him while still in her early teens. She had never recognized that he could be difficult, stubborn, and insensitive, even though he was brilliant, competent, and a strong father figure. In the hospital she castigated herself for not feeling adequate love for her husband. She could think of no sources for her current unhappiness until she was urged to re-create in detail just what had happened upon her husband's return. Then she recalled that his first words when they met on the pier were "My, but you've grown older," and after their first sexual union he remarked, "Is this what I've been waiting three years for?"

The need to defend the partner and accept his beliefs can extend to become a *folie à deux*, which in minor forms is far from uncommon among married couples. An attorney, after losing a local election which he considered critical to his career, believed that the mayor who had been his close friend was responsible for his defeat. His friends and relatives could not persuade him that the mayor had extended himself to try to secure his election. His bitterness reached delusional proportions when he believed that the mayor was sabotaging his legal practice. His wife, otherwise a very sensible woman, shared his animosity and became enraged at her relatives when they tried to convince her that her husband was in error and that they were being unjust and hurting themselves in defaming the mayor.

The Fusion of the Families of Origin

The interrelationship of two persons to form a marital unit involves the reorganization and fusion of the influences of both of their families of origin. The families in which they were reared have been incorporated into their personalities and every person retains many attitudes originating in his family concerning marital roles, marriage as an institution, and the value of family life. Further, the family of origin incorporated the values, mores, and sentiments of its ethnic, religious, and social class origins and each spouse carries such cultural values and mores into the marriage. Such considerations are particularly important in the United States where marriages often cross the various cultural boundaries and where the new family gains cohesion and form through the blending of the two personalities rather than through merging into a network of kinfolk (see Chapter 2). The greater the divergency of backgrounds, the greater difficulty the couple may find in achieving a satisfactory reciprocal relationship.*

The couple share the tasks of the marriage and the roles they fill according to their own dispositions, particularly before they have children,

* However, in some respects persons from educated backgrounds from different countries and cultures may have more in common than persons of widely differing socioeconomic classes within the same country.

but they have expectations of how to move into reciprocally interrelating roles which derive from the patterns in their families of origin
which each is likely to believe is the natural and proper way of doing
things. The man assumes what he considers to be the husband's role,
and the woman assumes the wife's role, and each expects the spouse to
fill the converse role. Even though there are similarities in a husband's
and wife's roles in all societies, there can still be marked discrepancies
that lead to role conflict. Many personality clashes in marriage are basically clashes between such role expectations. A marriage between a midwestern Lutheran man and a Catholic woman of Irish and German extraction encountered serious difficulties from its inception despite the
husband's premarital agreement not to interfere with his wife's Catholicism and to permit their children to be raised in her faith. He later
insisted that having grown up in a small farming community composed
entirely of Protestants, he had no idea that Catholicism was a way of life
as well as a religion. In seeking to follow his own Germanic family pattern in which his father had completely dominated the family, he became infuriated when his wife placed the dictates of the Church above
his wishes. He was angered when she went to confession, considering
that their life was no concern of the priest's, and he resented her insistence on attending morning Mass when he expected her to be serving
breakfast to him. Even though the wife was willing to modify her religious practices, she soon found that she felt uncomfortable and insecure
when deprived of the pattern.

Reciprocal versus Collateral Marital Roles

There are some fundamental differences in families that can be very
difficult to bridge, particularly if the spouses are unaware of the great
differences in their orientations to family life. In somewhat simplified
form we may consider that the contemporary urban American family
tends to rest upon companionship between the spouses and finds its stability from the couple's finding reciprocal interactional patterns agreeable to
both; but other families, including many in lower socio-economic groups,
tend to find stability in an institutional pattern of many cultural groups
in which the roles of husband and wife are parallel or collateral rather
than interactional. In the collateral type of family the husband and
wife each have sets of functions and roles to carry out, and the marriage
is more concerned with a way of sharing the tasks of life and having a
home in which to rear children than with providing companionship for

the spouses. Such nuclear families are likely to be part of a more extended family system (see Chapter 2 and E. Bott[2]). In these families the spouses gain support and definition for their lives by having rather clear-cut roles to fill and tasks to carry out and from interrelating with the larger family group rather than from the companionship and personal support of the spouse. Even when persons who have emerged from collateral families have modified their views by contacts with the more common companionship type that is portrayed in motion pictures and stories, residues are likely to remain that can interfere with their finding harmonious relationships with spouses raised in isolated nuclear families.*

Autonomy of the New Family

The highly mobile self-sufficient family made necessary by contemporary industrial society requires that the primary allegiance of each marital partner shift from the parental to the marital family; that the center of gravity, so to speak, be established within the nuclear family; and that decision-making functions be assumed by the couple. However, in the kinship type of family close attachments to families of origin are retained, and loyalty and obedience to parents may continue as long as the parents live. Still, the interference of parents in a marriage and the use of parents as a major source of security are common disruptive forces in marriages. A family in an Eastern city had not really become a unit even after fifteen years of marriage and the birth of three children. The husband complained that his wife placed more importance on her mother and sisters than on him. She refused to move away from an apartment house in which her mother and married sisters lived, even though this required the husband to travel two hours to work each morning. The sisters spent a large part of the day together and it was a rare evening when one of the sisters was not in the apartment. The wife discussed each family quarrel with her sisters and consulted them before any major family decisions were made. The wife agreed with her husband's account but insisted that his devotion to his mother was largely responsible for the situation. He spent two evenings a week with his mother and usually expressed his mother's views rather than his own when they argued. She

* A young woman from a New England Protestant family married a man of Greek Orthodox extraction who considered himself liberated from the old traditions. However, the wife became upset when he took it for granted that he would spend much of his free time in coffeehouses with male friends, whereas he objected to her passing an evening with a bridge club rather than with his sisters.

complained that because of her husband's neglect she could not have tolerated the marriage without her family's company and help in raising the children. Fortunately, with professional help, both managed to see that their attention and loyalty to their original families had never permitted their own marriage to become firmly established.

Marriage as a Support

The capacities to adjust to marriage and the potential for growth through marriage depend upon the successful passage through prior development stages, particularly upon having gained during adolescence a suitable identity as an individual reasonably independent from parents, and capacities for intimacy. Nevertheless, many marriages between persons who have not had an unblemished passage through prior developmental stages, and who may even be rather seriously impaired, are adequately successful. "An arch," wrote Leonardo, "is a strength built out of two opposing weaknesses." Couples who are fortunate have unconsciously sought out and found partners with complementary needs. A woman who feels unable to empathize with babies and make decisions about children's needs finds a man with strong maternal tendencies and who, as an oldest child, has had considerable experience in helping raise his younger siblings. Some partners know that they each have shortcomings and try to help one another manage. Indeed, even marriages between mature persons are helped when each knows that he or she is far from perfect and does not expect perfection from the spouse. Some persons marry knowing that the marriage will be difficult, but believe that it will be better than life alone. Marriage provides an integrating force, not only because of support from the partner, but also because it provides tangible tasks to cope with, rather definite roles to take on, and a position within society. However, even though personality problems can be helped by marriage, they more commonly create difficulties, for marriage presupposes reasonable independence, a secure ego identity, and capacities for intimacy from each partner.

The Sexual Adjustment

A mutually satisfying sexual relationship, while not essential to a satisfactory marriage, is usually critical to marital happiness. Currently, in marriages that rest on the interaction between spouses and on companionship, the sexual goal of both partners is to experience orgasm, which not only offers relief from tension but ecstatic pleasure enhanced by the

providing of a similar experience for the spouse. The release and enjoyment of a good sexual relationship smooths away the rough edges of the
minor incompatibilities that occur in every marriage and the frictions
that arise in daily living. Sexual incompatibility will usually reflect disturbances in other areas of the marriage that have engendered resentments, anxieties, fears, and even loathing that virtually eliminate the potentialities of achieving sexual harmony. Various personality disturbances may interfere with participation in the sexual act or enjoyment of
it; some of these problems have been discussed in previous chapters
under the following topics: achievement of capacities for intimacy, attainment of a secure gender identity, and the gaining of adequate independence from parental authority.

Sexual Difficulties of Newlyweds

Many of the sexual problems of married couples require consideration
of psychopathological patterns and cannot be considered here. Commonly, however, some of the difficulties in sexual adjustment arise in the
early days of the marriage as reflections of inexperience, ignorance, sensitivities, and difficulties in communication that can be overcome by collaborative effort when pertinent advice is available. If uncorrected, such
early maladjustments can freeze into chronicity or deepen into serious
incompatibilities, spilling over and blighting any chances for a happy
marriage. The husband who has had difficulty with his potency becomes
fearful of rebuff, resentful of his bride who does not or cannot help him,
and worried about his masculinity, and withdraws; the bride who is
tense and finds intercourse painful and disappointing seeks to avoid
coitus. The topic of sexual adjustment in marriage has endless ramifications; here, we shall be concerned only with difficulties which frequently
arise early in marriage and which are not necessarily due to severe individual personality disturbances or which are reflections of notable incompatibilities in other areas of the marital relationship.

The physician, nurse, clinical psychologist, and social worker require
knowledge of the sexual act and the problems that interfere with its
satisfactory consummation. People may go to the clergyman or the attorney with other problems arising in marriage, but they tend to turn to the
physician, nurse, or marital counselor for help with sexual problems.
Further, the alert physician finds that many physical complaints that
bring patients to him are essentially displacements of sexual problems.
All too frequently, the physician is not an authority on sexual matters,

and may give advice according to stereotyped concepts, or according to what he and his particular socio-economic and ethnic group deem proper and satisfactory. Sexuality in practical, everyday marital terms has rarely been taught as part of the medical curriculum, but patients are very likely to regard the physician as someone who has learned all about such mysteries.

The Victorian Heritage

I have, however, some hesitancy in writing about sexual adjustment in marriage, which has been the subject of many popular treatises, because recent studies have made it clear that even widely recognized authorities have offered considerable erroneous and even harmful advice based upon folklore and pet preconceptions rather than upon scientific foundations. Sexuality is not a topic that benefited greatly from the scientific revolution, remaining under the extensive repression that had been our heritage of the Victorian period. Havelock Ellis and Freud sought to sweep away the barriers, but even they promulgated erroneous concepts which their reputations have helped perpetuate.

The emergence from the peculiarities of Victorian morality has taken over half a century—and we now find that even much of the enlightenment that started in the 1920's continued many errors that arose in reaction to the excessive prudery of the Victorian. The Victorian mores were probably unusual with their notions that a proper "lady" would not be interested in sex: that she would not think about it and certainly would not talk about it. Indeed, there was the connotation that enjoyment of sex would be improper. She would accommodate herself to her husband and would wish to have children, but she would not expect fidelity from him but be relieved if he had a mistress who provided for his sexual needs.* Residues of this morality still linger in current mores; and though it still influences the formal ethics, it has been pretty well shattered as far as upper-middle-class society is concerned, and is about to be pulverized by the "pill." However, white lower socio-economic groups still are affected by it. Sexual mores vary widely with socio-economic class and ethnic grouping.

* Ibsen's *A Doll's House* and *Ghosts* cannot be understood out of the context of this morality, nor Strindberg's *A Madman's Defense*. It is also inherent in Shaw's early play *Misalliance*.

Intimacy and Sexuality

Sexual compatibility forms a critical measure of two persons' capacities to achieve true intimacy. It forms a test of the security and stability of personality development. Here, an individual must perform very much on his own and achieve without the support of his parents. He—or she—may blame parents for difficulties, but it will help little; but the ability to turn to the spouse for help, or for both to work through problems together, can be decisive. The person feels that sexual abilities are somehow a reflection of something very basic in him; and each spouse feels revealed as well as naked before the other.

The proper carrying out of the sexual act and the enjoyment of it involves an ability to give way to the irrational, the timeless, the purely animal in one: it includes a loss of individuality in a temporary fusion with another. It contains the potentiality of leaving behind the tensions of civilization as one loosens the bonds to reality to float again in the purely sensuous. Here, one needs to be unabashed by the nakedness of impulse and drive, by recrudescence of the infantile and the revealing of much that one has sought to hide from others. The woman in particular requires a capacity to rescind control and give way before an ecstasy that threatens to overwhelm and annihilate her by its very intensity. The sexual act contains a definite and direct relationship to infantile relatedness to the mother, with a renewed interest in sucking, in odor, in skin eroticism; and a reawakening of old forbidden desires to explore and play with orifices. So very much that has been learned needs to be undone; much that has been forbidden and long repressed and kept unconscious but that haunted dreams and masturbatory fantasies needs to be released to permit sexual intimacy and enjoyment and to allow fulfillment rather then provoke shame and guilt. The very good sexual adjustment demands such abilities to reverse the socialization process—and yet to permit the individual to be secure in the feeling that the regression and reversal will be only temporary and not reclaim the self.

Fortunately, the strength of the sexual drive is great, and to some extent the movements used in the sexual act are inherent, firmly built into the organism. When the partners are reasonably mature and desire one another, they can usually work through the difficulties and with patience find a unique source of profound pleasure as a shared experience that heightens their love. It provides relief from tensions and a total absorption that obliterates concern and can lead a couple to believe that no other pair has experienced similar pleasure and that they are uniquely matched. The fulfillment binds them closer, whereas frustration tends to separate them as their urges crave satisfaction.

Although traditionally the husband was expected to be experienced sexually and to introduce the virginal wife to the joys of conjugal bliss, matters are now usually otherwise—although a substantial number of husbands and wives and even couples have their first coital experience after marriage. According to a survey carried out in the late 1950's a sizable proportion of wives in a low socio-economic bracket had little experience or knowledge of sex before marriage.[12] A college education and even a modicum of sexual experience premaritally are, however, no assurance that the individual is knowledgeable or has had any experience that was remotely satisfactory; and sometimes a person who has functioned well premaritally experiences difficulties with a spouse. A couple who had lived together before marriage for two years among Bohemian friends and had a highly enjoyable sexual relationship encountered difficulties almost immediately after legalizing the relationship when the husband frequently was unable to have an erection with his wife, and then sought to reassure himself about his masculinity by having extramarital relationships. He could no more consider his wife as a sexual object than he had been able to think of his mother as having sexual relations.

The Marriage Night

The bridal bed of the marriage night is frequently far from an optimal place for the consummation of the marriage. The long anticipation, the fatigue, intoxication, and anxiety can interfere with the act, and set off a chain of unfortunate consequences. According to medical and psychiatric tradition, the bride may be so pained and shocked by the trauma of having her hymen ruptured that she can become bitterly resentful toward her husband and fearful of further sexual experiences.* Such concerns have led virginal brides to have hymenectomies and dilatations prior to marriage—sometimes upon the urging of the gynecolo-

---

* A Greek epitaph reads:
> At the bridal bed of star-crossed Petale
> Hades, not Hymen, stood: for as she fled
> Alone through the night, dreading love's first stroke
> (as virgins will), the brutal watchdogs seized her.
> And we, whose morning hope had been a wife,
> Found scarce enough of her body for burial.
>   Antiphanes the Macedonian

(Translated by Dudley Fitts in *Poems from the Greek Anthology*.[3])

gist from whom they sought a contraceptive diaphragm. However, other factors are more likely to impede adequate performance and undermine the confidence of either in his or her capacities.

The husband's concerns over his adequacy turn toward his ability to have an erection and maintain it sufficiently long to satisfy his wife, and often, about whether or not he will be able to have coitus frequently enough. Stories of impotence and premature ejaculation may trouble him, particularly as many men have had such difficulties on some occasions. The wife will be concerned with her responsivity—with whether or not she will be frigid, whether she will be able to have an orgasm and even if she will behave in a proper manner, not knowing just what a proper manner should be.

Physical Sources of Sexual Frustration

Indeed, an inexperienced couple may have difficulties with penetration; and even if they do not fail, the coitus may be painful to the wife and afford neither any satisfaction. Let us consider the sources of such difficulties.

The young male becomes fully aroused sexually more rapidly than the woman, even without actual physical stimulation. With an erect penis and concerned about carrying out the act, he may seek to penetrate his wife long before she is physically ready. The woman has the task, which may at first be difficult, of being able to relax her perineal musculature in the time of excitement. She may experience spasm of the muscles at the orifice and in the lower third of the vagina, that will block penetration or cause pain. While she may become sexually excited, proper preparation for an orgasm often requires considerable physical stimulation, particularly until she has learned or becomes enabled to experience orgasm readily.

Arousal in the Woman

Although the woman can experience an initial sexual excitement almost instantaneously by either psychic or physical stimulation, it does not prepare her for intercourse. A secretion in her vagina by transudation is the source of the wetness women feel and recognize as an indication of psychic stimulation, and the nipples and clitoris may become erect and more sensitive. These phenomena can serve as a signal that stimulates desire for arousal or form the first phase of progressive arousal. Only with some further psychic or physical stimulation does the vagina become lengthened and widened and does it open into a receptive organ by vascular engorgement of the vaginal walls, very much as the penis expands and hardens by vascular engorgement. Only somewhat later, and in most women only after there has been physical stimulation and the entire perineal area becomes congested and highly sensitive, does the external third of the vagina become markedly congested and narrow through its thickening to form what Masters has termed the "orgasmic platform," [10] a soft but firm and lubricated canal that properly envelops and stimulates the penis during its thrusting movements; and simultaneously permits the penis indirectly to exert mechanical traction on the clitoral hood that stimulates the clitoris and heightens the woman's excitement.* Until the vagina and perineal region are thus prepared, intromission of the penis will not only be difficult, but may also be unpleasant, if not painful, to the woman and unsatisfactory to the man. Now although there are many similarities between the male and female preparation for coitus and orgasm, the man is more likely to attain a full erection from psychic stimulation and be prepared for the act sooner than his wife. In many marriages, the man learns to delay and becomes capable of greater delay with relaxation, security, and experience; and the woman becomes capable of more complete arousal with less physical stimulation, and may gain an ability to reach orgasm more rapidly.

The wife, particularly early in marriage, may be unable to achieve orgasm unless she has experienced considerable physical stimulation; her arousal is heightened by precoital play with her breasts, kissing, caressing of her body, and stimulation of her mons and clitoris prior to intromission. She may be able to be fully prepared for intromission only after considerable stimulation of her external genitalia. Then, after intromission, she may not be able to have an orgasm unless her mate can delay— or continue his thrusting movements after his orgasm. A discontinuance of the stimulation is very apt to disrupt the progression to orgasm; but when the husband cannot continue intromission, stimulation of the mons area or perineal region in general can rapidly revive the arousal and lead to orgasm unless strong psychic factors cause repression of the excitement.

---

* The research of Masters and Johnson[11] on the mechanics and physiology of the sexual act has brought much needed information to a subject that had remained in the prescientific era, if not in the Dark Ages. They have also dispelled a number of serious misconceptions, as will be noted in the text.

Clitoral or Vaginal Orgasm?

The clitoris serves as the primary center for sexual arousal in the woman; and it is necessary specifically to negate several common misconceptions that have gained wide acceptance. The most drastic and widespread misconception concerns the notion that there is a difference between a clitoral and a vaginal orgasm, and that one of the difficult developmental tasks of the woman is to progress from immature clitoral orgasm to experience vaginal orgasm and that childhood and adolescent clitoral masturbation serves to fixate the clitoris as the focal area of libidinal excitement. Freud, for example considered that the vagina displaced the clitoris as the focus of libidinal excitement after puberty unless fixations occurred or a congenital abnormality existed.[4] Indeed, many women have continued in psychoanalysis or psychotherapy because they considered their orgasms remained "clitoral."*

The recent studies of Masters and Johnson appear to have demonstrated conclusively that the orgasm is essentially the same, no matter where the stimulation is applied, and that during coitus it is still the clitoris that is the major site of stimulation and sexual excitement. When the vaginal mucosa is thoroughly engorged to form the "orgasmic platform," the engorged clitoris has retracted against the symphysis pubis and is covered by its "hood" or prepuce. The labia minora

---

* It is difficult to know just how this concept arose and just what it was supposed to mean. It properly meant that a woman who was able to have an orgasm only through direct stimulation of the clitoris and not from penile stimulation within the vagina was not able to experience or enjoy intercourse properly. However, it also seems to have meant that some women could not experience a generalized, deeply felt total bodily orgastic response but only a rather localized erotic heightening of tension and release that left her incompletely satisfied. But beyond this it often led women to believe that because they required preliminary stimulation of the clitoris to become properly aroused, or because excitement was felt primarily in the clitoral area rather than intravaginally, they were not experiencing a proper orgasm; and women have completed psychoanalysis resigned to the fact that they would simply have to make do with a "clitoral orgasm," which even though it seemed fully satisfying was just not the real thing that more completely feminine and mature women experienced.

Although doubts were expressed that the vagina could properly become the primary erogenous zone as it does not have genital corpuscles (sensory nerve endings of a type found in the clitoris and labia minora and in the glans of the penis), the idea was so firmly entrenched in psychoanalytic theory that even major investigators of female sexuality have had difficulty in discarding it. The first decisive disagreement was presented by Marmor in 1954,[9] who insisted that the clitoris must remain the major area of sexual excitement and that this function could not transfer to the vagina.

are also engorged and highly sensitive. When the penis distends the vaginal outlet it also distends the labia minora which, in turn, pulls upon the clitoral hood. The thrusting movements of the penis thereby indirectly cause the clitoris to be rhythmically stimulated by its hood, which leads to heightened excitation and properly to orgasm. Sensory sexual excitation within the vagina does not occur. The failure of sexual arousal by the penile thrusting during intercourse occurs when the clitoris is not stimulated indirectly because of lack of proper vascular engorgement of the vagina and other perineal tissues—a failure that usually is due to emotional blocking, but sometimes to inadequate preparation. Damage to the area in childbirth can impede the necessary mechanical traction, but this is not usually a problem of newlyweds. The intensity of the orgasm does not depend upon whether the clitoris or vagina is stimulated: some women experience more intense orgasm through clitoral masturbation and others through coitus; and for many women it is the circumstances rather than the site of stimulation that makes the difference.

The Female Orgasm

The orgasm properly involves a general bodily response for both sexes. For the woman after a period of mounting muscular tensions that may involve involuntary contortion of the face and spasms of the long muscles of the arms and legs, the orgasm starts with a sensation of intense sensual awareness in the clitoris that radiates upward into the pelvis followed by a sensation of warmth spreading from the pelvic area through the body. The woman then experiences a feeling of involuntary contraction in the lower vagina, followed by a throbbing that unites with the heartbeat. At the onset, the outer third of the vagina may or may not go into a brief spasm; there are then rhythmic contractions at 0.8 second intervals for the first three to six contractions (the periodicity is the same as that of the penile emissive contractions), and then another three to six contractions occur somewhat more slowly and less intensely. The uterus also undergoes spasmodic contractions during orgasm, as do the rectal and urinary sphincters. The attainment of the orgasm requires a continuation of the stimulation—in coitus, of the penile thrusting. Cessation or interruption of stimulation will disrupt the heightening of excitement to orgasm.

The Male Orgasm

The male orgasm starts with the expulsion of the contents of the seminal vesicles, prostate, and ejaculatory duct into the prostatic urethra, giving the man the feeling that ejaculation is now inevitable: but it will take several seconds before ejaculation occurs (an interval utilized in the practice of coitus interruptus). Then, in the second phase of the orgasm, the semen is propelled through the penile urethra by the perineal muscle contractions and expelled in forceful spurts into the vagina. After several ejaculations the force lessens and the timing lengthens for several more contractions. During the experience, the extended penis is exquisitely sensitive, which tends to impel the man to seek further stimulation and leads to a pleasure-pain tension for which relief is sought (the continued intense erection can even be painful while simultaneously pleasurable); and during coitus the man, usually together with the woman, is impelled to move the penis in rhythmic thrusts in the vagina, which heightens the excitement of both—and eventually leads to the intense orgastic release. The phase leading to orgasm is usually accompanied by increased muscular tension in many parts of the body, with considerable involuntary contractions as well as voluntary, which heighten during the ejaculation, after which relaxation occurs abruptly.

There are many similarities between the male and female orgastic behaviors and, as would be expected, they are suited to one another and to foster preservation of the species by placing a high sensuous reward on seeking copulation rather than masturbatory gratification. Aside from the male's more rapid preparation for the act, one other difference requires comment. The wife can experience multiple orgasms during a single sexual act, or after a brief interval, whereas the husband has a longer refractory period, requiring at least several minutes between acts, and he has a more limited capacity to have repeated orgasms within a given period.* This discrepancy, however, has little practical significance in

* Masters and Johnson have found that below the age of thirty many males may be able to ejaculate several times after relatively brief refractory periods of a few minutes. Some young men may also be capable of experiencing orgasm ten times during a night, but few would have any urge to do so except upon some special occasion to prove or test their capacities. Whereas women may be capable of virtually unlimited orgasms, this is merely a technical matter because a woman will not desire such unlimited experience after participating fully in the sexual act. Discussions of far-reaching effects upon society of the recognition of woman's unlimited capacities to experience orgasm, such as can be found in M. Sherfey, "The Evolution and Nature of Female Sexuality in Relation to Psychoanalytic Theory," [13] are unrealistic and confuse what

marriage, where the quality of the experience is what matters and rapidly repeated sexual intercourse is not usually deemed necessary or even desirable.

The Wife's Potential Difficulties

The newlywed woman may be unable to experience orgasm during coitus. If she chronically continues to become excited and physically prepared without progressing to orgasm, she will usually feel tense and irritable from the frustration of unresolved sexual excitement. The condition can, of course, be relieved by masturbatory activity, unless the woman is also psychologically blocked from achieving orgasm under such conditions. The danger is that the couple gives up trying to have the wife experience coital orgasm. According to the Masters-Johnson studies, the woman is more likely to reach orgasm when her tissues are thoroughly engorged because the indirect stimulation of the clitoris will then be more successful; and they also believe that learning to have an orgasm is necessary for many women; and that after a woman has experienced an orgasm several times, she will progressively have less difficulty and reach it more quickly, thereby increasing the physical compatibility between the couple.*

From Rainwater's studies of women of lower socio-economic status, it is clear that many women have had little or no sexual experience at marriage, and that many husbands teach them only enough to gain their participation but with little or any regard for the wife's satisfaction. The investigation indicated that when the husband was solicitous and interested, the wife was far more likely to enjoy the act and share it, whereas those wives whose husbands taught only "the bare essentials necessary to perform the act" [12] are apt to regard coitus as something for a husband's

is possible for a woman with what she would desire and enjoy. Sherfey seems to confuse satisfaction, satiation, and exhaustion.

* Thus, the following measures may be helpful. Although the husband obviously cannot continue the single act indefinitely, repetition several times over a few hours may help because the wife's genital area becomes increasingly engorged with repetition of frustrated excitation. Then, too, the husband often can continue the act longer after his initial orgasm has relieved the acuteness of his desire and because of the decrease in volume of the seminal fluid that enters the prostatic urethra prior to ejaculation. As the woman's pelvic organs tend to be engorged during a week or so prior to her menstrual period, efforts to produce orgasm may be more successful during this phase. Finally, relaxation of concern can be extremely helpful—it is difficult for a concerned woman, but perhaps more possible if the problem can be shared with her husband and his cooperation in overcoming it gained.

pleasure alone, feel used, and resent it. Thus, the husband's way of proceeding and the effort that goes into making coitus a mutually satisfying experience can be very important. However, many of the 40 or 50 per cent of women who are essentially frigid have profound blocks to the enjoyment of intercourse because of the intensity of the repression, oedipal fantasies, fears of damage or of pregnancy, resentment of male prerogatives, etc., that may require skilled psychotherapy to overcome, and attention to the precise physical aspects of intercourse are unlikely to alter the situation markedly or permanently.

Common Problems of Husbands

The young husband not infrequently has difficulties early in the marriage. He may find that his erection fails when he tries intromission, or that he ejaculates so quickly that neither his wife nor he can enjoy the act. He is usually aware that he is expected to delay until his wife is prepared and becomes too preoccupied with efforts at control. He may have unrealistic ideas of how potent he is supposed to be. It is not uncommon that the wife may be the more sexually experienced person, and he becomes concerned with how he will measure up to her previous partners. An understanding and patient wife can help overcome difficulties before they become set or even multiply. Efforts to enter the vagina prematurely greatly increase the difficulties, for not until the woman has become properly aroused can the penis move into the vagina easily. Even then, the husband may need his wife's help in guiding the penis properly. When there are difficulties in maintaining the erection, stimulation by the wife will usually correct the situation. Premature ejaculation tends to become less of a problem as the man gains confidence. Repetition of coitus for a second or third time within an hour or two can help the man gain control and confidence in his performance. Here, the ability to discuss problems rather than conceal them, and planned efforts to better the sexual relationship, help a great deal. Concerns over loss of the penis or damage to it when it is in the vagina, fears of damaging the wife's internal organs, fear of impregnating her, residual incestuous concerns, and other such difficulties can all create problems. Some such concerns are usually present, consciously or unconsciously, and when not profound are likely to vanish or become relatively unimportant when confidence is gained and as familiarity with the wife develops. The more serious problems will require psychiatric help.

Many men are concerned with the size of their genitalia—perhaps often as a carry-over from childhood when the father's genitalia by comparison seemed enormous to the child, and concern was heightened by the many remarks boys and young men make about genital size as an index of virility and of desirability to a woman. Although the size of men's penises varies notably in the flaccid state, Masters' measurements show that the size of the flaccid penis makes relatively little difference, for small penises expand more than large ones—and even though differences may remain they are relatively slight. Further the vagina, unless damaged in childbirth, accommodates itself to the penis, and size is rarely a factor in a man's ability to satisfy his spouse, and it is no indication of his virility or sexual capacities.*

The husband's abilities to satisfy his wife should not depend upon a capacity to have sexual relations with great frequency, but more upon the way in which the sexual act is carried out. When the wife experiences a deeply felt orgasm during coitus, she can feel relaxed and satisfied. Her potential capacity to have many more orgasms is not particularly pertinent. Desire varies from person to person and according to circumstances. Differences in frequency of desire, however, are one of the most commonly reported problems of sexual adjustment.[1] It is likely that the frustrated male is less able to set aside feelings of arousal and tension than the woman. However, such matters are difficult to judge as they have been influenced greatly by the cultural tradition. Couples who are interested in one another's happiness can almost always manage to regulate the sexual relationship so that it is mutually satisfactory.†

Achieving Mutual Sexual Gratification

The communication of desire can, of course, present problems, particularly to the inhibited. For most couples most of the communication of desire is nonverbal and wives rapidly learn to recognize when their husbands are desirous, but husbands are less likely to be as sensitive to their wives' signals. Wives also learn how to refuse to recognize signals when

---

* A woman may also be concerned that her vagina will not be large enough. The vagina can distend enormously—as is required in childbirth. The size of the penis or the vagina is important in cases of developmental failure when the organs remain infantile or anomalous—but these are very uncommon.

† Of course, a variety of difficulties or misunderstandings can arise. Thus, a woman who had been married for ten years consulted a psychiatrist because her husband still sought to have relations three to four times each day and returned home from work at lunchtime primarily in order to have intercourse. Such frequency of the need for intercourse is not a matter of unusual potency but an indication of a sexual compulsivity, often to reassure the self against concerns about homosexuality.

they are not feeling responsive or to find means of sidetracking the husband's demands.[12] An ability to talk about desire can help the adjustment, and discussion may be essential to the improvement of the act to attain mutual gratification. However, some couples, particularly well-educated couples, engage in considerable discussion prior to each sexual experience or during it, which often indicates some lack of proper mutuality. Talk about desire is often kept minimal because it can only be accepted or openly refused, and a spouse may wish to feel out the situation rather than impose his or her own wishes on the other, or risk rebuff. Still, in some marriages, the failure to discuss lack of satisfaction leads to continued misunderstandings.

The desirability of simultaneity of orgasm has also received considerable attention in literature on sexual adjustment, where it has sometimes been considered a major measure of a satisfactory marital adjustment. Most couples find that such simultaneous experience heightens the pleasure of both partners and the feelings of unity and loss of boundaries, but some women may prefer to have an orgasm and then more quietly enjoy the husband's pleasure in orgasm. In any event, such simultaneity is not something that must preoccupy a couple, for it is likely to occur after the spouses are familiar at a preconscious level with the way in which the partner acts and reacts—and the signs of impending climax in one serve as a trigger for the other.

Some Common Misconceptions

The occurrence of menses can also lead to some minor difficulties. Some husbands will wish to have intercourse during their wife's menstrual period, but the wife feels that it is dangerous. Some women are not only more sexually excited during the menses but find coitus more satisfying, yet find their husbands reluctant for aesthetic reasons. In any event, there are no reasons, other than aesthetic or religious, why couples cannot have coitus during the menses.

Norms for marital sexual behavior do not exist, and indeed what is considered normal or abnormal behavior varies widely among ethnic groups and socio-economic classes, and from couple to couple. As discussions of sex are not only apt to promote misconceptions but often contain much boasting and banter, young persons may have marked misconceptions of what might be considered abnormal or perverse. Young men listening to their confreres may consider themselves inadequate if they do not have intercourse four or five times a night, or their wives to be cold if they do not wish to participate on retiring and awakening each day. One such young man had serious qualms about his right to marry and experienced great surprise and relief when he learned from his fiancée that she thought sexual relations once or twice a week would be more than adequate and hoped that he would be tolerant of her efforts to learn to participate properly. It is not uncommon to hear among laboring groups in particular that intercourse is regarded by both husband and wife as something the man needs to have nightly for his health, very much as he is supposed to move his bowels, and it is carried out in a routine perfunctory manner without any relationship to affection. The wife who considers intercourse little more than a duty expresses her satisfaction with a husband who is thoughtful and "doesn't bother me too often." Alert physicians and therapists are aware that a woman who responds to inquiries about her sexual life with "It's all right" or "He's pretty considerate" is getting little if any enjoyment from it.

Divergent Sexual Mores

Sexual practices vary greatly. Some couples raised in certain European traditions or as members of fundamentalist religious sects may never have seen one another in the nude in many years of married life.[6] Others will consider any masturbatory foreplay as shameful or disgusting, and some will be shocked at the idea of deviating from the customary face-to-face position with the man above the woman.* Many will maintain that whatever a couple wish to do in the privacy of the marital bed that is mutually satisfactory and injurious to neither is acceptable. For many persons, in any case, the private and shared intimacy of the sexual act is a time when various repressed fantasies and desires are indulged. Various types of precoital play are considered proper preliminaries. According to various surveys and on the basis of psychiatric experience, it is clear that many couples practice oral-genital relations on occasion without causing concern to either partner. In some respects what occurs during or before sexual intercourse in marriage bears a resemblance to preconscious fantasy life and tends to be dissociated from what occurs in the workaday world or even from what goes on between a couple at other times. It involves a sort of sharing of preconscious and unconscious strivings as part of the intimacy and fusion. However, the insistence of one partner

---

* It may be of interest that according to Malinowski[8] the Trobriand Islanders find it a source of great amusement to mimic this position, which they term the "missionary position" and which they find very unsatisfactory.

on a practice that is repugnant to the other, such as anal or oral relations or some other perversion, can create difficulties, and can cause symptoms such as vomiting or intestinal upsets that a person has difficulty revealing even to a doctor.

The physician and marital counsellor must not be naïve about marital practices. He will encounter newly married women who consider their husbands perverts for trying to have normal coitus; women who believe it indecent to have an orgasm; men or women who soon wish to invite another man or woman to share the marital bed; men who rarely if ever wish to have relations. The variations and permutations of sexual desires and practices are so great and concerns about them are so frequently displaced onto other complaints that it is necessary to be able to hear what patients may have difficulty in conveying, to listen without personal prejudice and with emotional equanimity. The therapist must also recognize that sexuality can be used as an expression of hostility as well as love, and as a means of domination or degradation of the spouse, or to express deep resentments toward the opposite sex. Sex can also mean little to one spouse other than being a means of bargaining to have his or her own way in other matters—such as the right to purchase a new dress, or to go fishing for a week-end. It is also something that some spouses prefer to have the partner indulge outside of the marriage, and not all infidelity is motivated primarily by the unfaithful partner.

Marriages Without Sexual Relations

Marriages can survive without sexual activity and even provide satisfaction for both partners; and though usually one will feel seriously deprived if not cheated, other factors including deep admiration or love for the impotent or invalided partner may be compensatory. Marriage is a relationship that is broad enough to find stability on varied foundations. In some marriages both partners are happier when sex is not in the picture. In others, the couples find other interests that furnish adequate self-realization. However, difficulties that block sexual intimacy will usually affect other areas and, if they do not create friction, at least limit the mutuality the couple can achieve. Yet, when it is necessary and when a decision can be made that abolishes constant expectation, indecision, frustration, and self-pity, the marital bond can transcend disappointments in the sexual sphere.

Sex and Emotional Maturity

While the achievement of "genital sexuality" has been considered a major indicator of mature personality development in both psychoanalytic theory and practice, as discussed in the chapter on adolescence, it is a concept that confuses as much as it clarifies. If the concept is to be meaningful it must involve more than a capacity to achieve and induce orgasm in heterosexual coitus. In such terms it has often been pursued by immature persons and accepted as a reassuring token of normality. The concept of "genital sexuality" properly contains the implications of the capacity to relax defenses through having sufficient security in the self to let a truly intimate relationship develop that fuses affectionate and sensuous love in a lasting relationship; to be sufficiently autonomous not to fear the loss of boundaries in being joined to another, or being overwhelmed in giving way to id impulsions, or becoming lost amid unconscious fantasies of childhood years when indulging sexuality; or being dominated and used by another if one shows the intensity of one's needs.

Theoretically, at least, it helps the solidification of a marriage when the couple have time to learn to know one another intimately, find reciprocal roles, and achieve a satisfying sexual relationship before children arrive on the scene. Gaining a satisfactory marital adjustment prior to parenthood helps the couple share the offspring, to enjoy them as a mutual product, and to maintain a coalition as parents.

The experience of marriage offers opportunities for more complete fulfillment and the rounding out of the life cycle. The living out of adult patterns in the relatedness to another as a mature man or woman, the experiences of producing a new generation and gaining a vital connection with the future, the giving of oneself to children and living as a parent are virtually closed to the unmarried. The changes in the personality that develop as the intimate interrelationship forms, in themselves tend to stablize the personality, establish firmer bonds to others, provide a completion through complementarity with another, and lessen the sharp edges of egocentricity. The sexual interchange permits reasonable mastery of libidinal strivings that may otherwise be primarily diverting, in both senses of the word, and turns them into a force that promotes unity and cohesiveness.

The Single Life

While living through adult life in marriage must be considered the desirable course, a fair segment of the population remains single either through conscious choice or through unconscious choice more often than from lack of opportunity. While bachelorhood and spinsterhood close many doors, there are still countless ways available that can lead to a rich and meaningful way of life. Though many persons will prefer to venture into a marriage that offers little chance of happiness rather than remain single, others can rightfully feel that an unhappy and conflictful marriage is more confining than completing and can be destructive of such integrity as the person has obtained. The life development of many persons does not lead to the potentiality of further growth through marriage or for the assumption of the intimate relatedness and the responsibilities of parenthood. Many such persons correctly realize that their future will be more secure and complete if it is pursued in some other direction.

The formation of a stable and satisfying marriage is probably the most crucial factor in assuring the emotional stability and security of the next generation, as well as a favorable subsequent personality development of the spouses. The outcome of the marriage depends to a very great extent upon the choice of the spouse, as has been explained in the preceding chapter. What the ultimate success of a marriage depends upon goes beyond the objectives of this chapter and the capacities of the author. Spouses can complement one another and live together harmoniously in a wide variety of ways. Some of the requisites for married life as parents will be discussed in the next chapter. In general, a good marriage in our contemporary society usually depends upon the achievements by both spouses of sufficient independence and firm integrations as individuals to enable them to live interdependently rather than with one partner dependent on the other; and upon the ability of both to continue to grow after marriage and develop new interests so that the marriage is constantly being renewed. Such continued renewal is important to the stability of the marriage and the satisfaction of both partners, and goes beyond settling down and trying to find a way of living together harmoniously. Children and interest in their constant change is one important means by which such renewal can be achieved.

References

1. Jessie Bernard, "The Adjustments of Married Mates," in Harold T. Christensen (ed.), *Handbook of Marriage and the Family* (Chicago: Rand McNally, 1964).
2. E. Bott, "Urban Families: Conjugal Roles and Social Networks," *Human Relations*, 8 (1955), 345–384.
3. Dudley Fitts (trans.), *Poems from the Greek Anthology* (New York: New Directions Paperbook, 1938).
4. Sigmund Freud, "Three Essays on the Theory of Sexuality" (1905), in *The Standard Edition of the Complete Psychological Works of Sigmund Freud*, Vol. 8 (London: Hogarth Press, 1953).
5. William Goode, *After Divorce* (Glencoe, Ill.: Free Press, 1956).
6. Mirra Komarovsky, *Blue Collar Marriage* (New York: Random House, 1964).
7. J. Landis, "Length of Time Required to Achieve Adjustment in Marriage," *American Sociological Review*, 11 (1946), 666–677.
8. Bronislaw Malinowski, *Sex and Repression in a Savage Society* (New York: Meridian Press, 1955).
9. Judd Marmor, "Some Considerations Concerning Orgasm in the Female," *Psychosomatic Medicine*, 16 (1954), 240–245.
10. William Masters and Virginia Johnson, "Orgasm, Anatomy of the Female," in Albert Ellis and Albert Abarbanel (eds.), *The Encyclopedia of Sexual Behavior*, Vol. 2 (New York: Hawthorn Books, 1959).
11. William Masters and Virginia Johnson, *Human Sexual Response* (Boston: Little, Brown, 1966).
12. Lee Rainwater and Karol Weinstein, *And the Poor Get Children* (New York: Quadrangle Press, 1960).
13. Mary Jane Sherfey, "The Evolution and Nature of Female Sexuality in Relation to Psychoanalytic Theory," *Journal of the American Psychoanalytic Association*, 14 (1966), 28–128.

Suggested Reading

Jessie Bernard, "The Adjustments of Married Mates," in Harold T. Christensen (ed.), *Handbook of Marriage and the Family* (Chicago: Rand McNally, 1964).

William Masters and Virginia Johnson, *Human Sexual Response* (Boston: Little, Brown, 1966).

Lee Rainwater and Karol Weinstein, *And the Poor Get Children* (New York: Quadrangle Press, 1960).

John P. Spiegel, "The Resolution of Role Conflict within the Family," *Psychiatry*, 20 (1957), 1–16.

CHAPTER 15

❀ ❀ ❀ ❀
❀ ❀ ❀ ❀
❀ ❀ ❀ ❀ ❀

Parenthood

THE ARRIVAL OF THE FIRST CHILD transforms spouses into parents and turns a marriage into a family. The endless drama has curved around to face again the beginning of life; but now the players are taking the parents' nurturant and supportive roles that they learned while they were ingénues playing the children's parts; but the old lines do not quite fit and constant improvisation is required.*

In becoming parents, the marital partners enter into a new developmental phase.[1] The tasks with which the parents must cope, the roles they occupy, their orientation toward the future alter profoundly. They

---

* Many aspects of parenthood have been discussed elsewhere in this book. The requisites that a married couple must fulfill in order to provide a family proper for raising reasonably well-integrated children have been presented in Chapter 2; some of the changes that take place in the wife when she becomes a mother in Chapter 4. The parental tasks of coping with the child's changing needs have formed a major portion of the chapters on infancy through adolescence. This chapter does not attempt to repeat such material. It is concerned with how becoming and being a parent influences the personality of the parent.

are offered opportunities for new satisfactions, to achieve a greater sense of completion, and to live through experiences which had been fantasied but frustrated since early childhood. They need no longer play at being "mommy and daddy"—they are. However, this simple step into parenthood, so often taken as an inadvertent misstep, provides a severe test of all preceding developmental stages and the consequent integration of the individual parent. The inevitable changes in the husband and wife will, in turn, alter the marital relationship and place strains upon it until a new equilibrium can be established.

The birth of a child, perhaps actually the awareness of conception, changes the marital partnership by the need to make room—emotional room—for a third person. The product of their unity can be a strong bond, a source of common interest and shared identification, but children are also a divisive influence—in varying proportions in each marriage, a unifying and separating force. The spouses who properly have transferred their major object relationships to each other, and each of whom wishes to be the focal point of the partner's emotional and affectional investment, now find the other intensely investing a newcomer. Further, a family unit is not as plastic as a marital union. A childless couple can relate to each other in a great variety of ways and the marriage remain adequate if but both partners are satisfied or even if they simply believe it more satisfactory than separating would be. The preservation of the equilibrium of a family, however, and even more clearly the adequate rearing of children, requires the achievement and maintenance of a dynamic structuring of the family in which each spouse fills fairly definitive role allocations. Deficiencies of the marital partners in filling their requisite roles leads to conflict and family imbalance. On the other hand, the structure and role allocations that are an inherent part of family life can provide greater security to the spouses and increased stability to the marriage.

Let us first consider the changes in the individual spouses and their capacities to move into the phase of parenthood, because it is the immaturities, fixations, and regressions uncovered by the need to be a parent that usually interfere with a spouse's acceptance of his or her respective parental role allocation or with the capacity to fill it adequately.

Parenthood and Personality Development

Speaking of the ideal which reality occasionally approaches, the partners who married have each achieved an individual identity, shown themselves capable of intimacy, and have given up independence for the benefits of interdependence with its security of knowing that his welfare is as important to the spouse as his own. They have found the completion that could not be gained within their own natal families where sexual satisfaction could not be permitted and in which they must have remained children. Each spouse seeks resolution of his own particular version of his frustrated and incompleted family romance. The incompleteness of the male or female roles and skills is balanced by those of the mate. The task of self-creation is more or less over for most. The energies that went into sexual repression or in seeking ways of satisfying sexual drives, and into the search for the partner who could bring completion to the imbalance of being a man or a woman, are released for investment in a creativity that transcends the self. While the child does not always oblige and wait, a person properly becomes a parent only after he is reasonably launched as an adult, when he is at the height of his physical and intellectual capacities and well settled in his marital relationship. He can feel himself an adult because the incompleted oedipal strivings which indicated his junior status—his membership in the childhood generation—have now found indirect expression and fulfillment. The spouses have been freed from the basic restrictions of childhood, and are ready to become parents themselves.

The conception of the child is an act of mutual creativity during which the boundaries between the self and another were temporarily obliterated more completely than at any time since infancy. One can grasp the symbolic validity of the common but erroneous notion that a woman must have an orgasm in order to conceive. The infant is a physical fusion of the parents, and their personalities unite within the child as they raise him. The child can become a continuing bond forged by that creativity for he is their common product, a focus of mutual hopes, interests, and responsibilities. Whereas each parent grew up a product of different family lines with differing customs and identifying with different parents, they are now united by a child whose experiences they will share and with whom they both identify. We must also recognize that whether they have willingly or unwillingly been turned into parents, here as in other spheres of life many persons grow through finding the abilities to meet responsibilities thrust upon them.

The Woman and Procreation

Particularly for a wife, a sense of fulfillment comes with the creation of a new life. Her biological purpose seems to require completion through conceiving, bearing, and nurturing children, and strong cultural and educational directives have added impetus to the drive. Her generative organs seem meaningless unless her womb has been filled and her breasts suckled. Her sexual desires are less satisfied by copulation alone than the man's. Feelings of incompletion and deprivation in being a girl have been compensated for by realization of her innate capacities for creativity, but the realization has required actualization. The woman's creativity as a mother becomes a central matter that provides meaning and balance to her life. Vestiges of envy of the man lead many women to desire strongly to have a son through whom they can unconsciously live out a life closed to them because they are women. Childhood fantasies of displacing mother and providing a child for father are now symbolically realized. The birth of a child turns a wife into a woman by setting her on a par with her mother. Her love for the husband who has made such completion possible deepens. She does not wish the child just for herself but as a meaningful outcome of her relatedness to her husband, pleasing him with a gift that is part of him that he has placed in her to nurture but also something of herself that the husband will cherish. To some extent, the baby is herself loved by a benevolent father. The process carries residua of the little girl's envy of the mother who could produce a child with and for the father. The husband who is loving permits the woman to complete an old but very important fantasy.

The strength of some women's drive to procreate is shown most clearly by those who prefer to risk death rather than remain barren. A physician who observes such situations gains the impression that the desire to produce a new life forms a drive that takes precedence over self-preservation. A woman in the days prior to antitubercular chemotherapy became ill with tuberculous pneumonia shortly after her marriage and verged on dying for several months. The disease was finally arrested after several years of sanatorium care but a threat of breakdown of the healed lesions remained. After continuing in good health for several years after resuming married life, she insisted the time had come for her to have a child. Her physician sought to dissuade her lest the pregnancy and delivery reactivate the disease, and her husband reassured her that she was more important to him than a child. Eventually both husband

and physician realized that she would never be content without a child. Perhaps the strong maternal desires were a good omen, for she blossomed during her pregnancy and neither the delivery of the child nor caring for it affected her tuberculosis.*

The Desire for Paternity

The husband—the idealized husband we are considering—also has strong desires for an offspring and can be transformed by it. The child provides a continuity into the future that mobilizes ambitions. An offspring forms an important sign of virility—even though it does not require much virility to impregnate a wife (one father replied on being congratulated, "Don't congratulate me, it was the easiest thing I ever did—and besides I wasn't even trying"). The child's admiration and adulation of him will provide him with narcissistic supplies. Paradoxically, even as paternity secures and heightens his masculine self-esteem and permits realization of the masculine instrumental functions of protecting and providing, it also provides him with an opportunity to express the feminine nurturant qualities derived from his early identification with his mother that previously had few acceptable outlets and required repression. More clearly, however, he now gains the position and status of "father" that he had envied and desired to attain since his earliest childhood.

Fears of Paternity

There are also forces that promote jealousy of a child, particularly of a son, and antagonisms to the child. The husband may resent his wife's attention to the child, and old sibling rivalries may thus be rekindled. There may exist more deeply buried fears that his son will grow up and wish to get rid of him, even as, in the oedipal phase of his childhood he had fantasies of killing his father.†

* Even though a woman's desires to have a child are firm and decisive, they are often mixed with concerns, some conscious and many unconscious. Some are residual from early childhood fantasies about oral impregnation, fears of the baby's growing as a parasite in the stomach, fears of being mutilated when the baby is delivered, etc. Some derive from her having observed the martyrlike suffering of her pregnant mother, or from listening to old wives tales from her grandmother or from not so old wives of her own generation.

† Some of the earliest Greek myths concern this cycle of fathers seeking to be rid of their sons, and indicate impulsions or wishes that are subject to the strongest taboos. The myths serve as reminders of the hideous penalties that follow infractions of the taboo. Uranus, the primeval Greek deity, having married his mother, Earth, banished

The Reorientation of Parents' Lives and Marriages

A young wife's readiness to become pregnant is often marked by "nesting procedures" which signal that she feels settled in the marriage and is ready for the next major event of her life. If the couple have been living with parents, or in some transient manner, she wishes a home of her own. If she is employed, the job begins to pall. There may be a flurry of interest in fixing up the home with thoughts of preparing a room and play space for the baby. Sexual intercourse now carries a context beyond love and passion. Her thoughts may focus more on the possibility of conceiving than on the mutuality with her husband. The husband, noting the change, may feel hurt, believing that he is no longer sufficient for his wife. Menstrual periods bring disappointment and feelings of emptiness. If the woman has difficulty in becoming pregnant, she may stop work and focus her interest on the home, believing that it will help her conceive—and it may.

The knowledge that she is pregnant changes the woman's life, for she now feels free to indulge her fantasies about a tangible future with the child. She daydreams of the child, plans her future in terms of him, and makes provision for his care. Her life has found a new center which is within her and she enjoys feelings of self-sufficiency. For many years to come the center of her existence will be her children. She requires the capacity to include both husband and children as her major investment rather than dividing her interest and affection between them.

When the spouses are both emotionally ready for parenthood, the arrival of an offspring stabilizes and deepens their relationship, and different ideas about family and parental roles, or of child-rearing techniques, are not likely to become disruptive. The child provides new sources of interest which both share, and which no one else will find as

---

his sons, the Titans, to Tartarus, but the youngest, Kronos, aided by his mother Gaia, eventually castrated Uranus. Kronos ate his first two sons, but the third, Zeus, saved by his mother Rhea, eventually overthrew him and started the era of the Olympian gods. The legend of the accursed House of Tantalus which eventually led to Agamemnon's death and then to the slaying of Aegisthus and Clytemnestra by Orestes who became mad after the matricide, started when Tantalus fed one of his children to the Gods. The myth of Oedipus also unfolds from the same theme. Laius in seeking to save himself from the prophecy that his infant son would grow up and slay him, ordered the infant Oedipus exposed on a mountain side. Such fears and antagonisms can perpetuate themselves from generation to generation, and removing such dangers to family life required the emergence of myths that emphasized the penalties—the myths serving as something akin to a cultural superego.

absorbing. Any slack in their lives that permitted boredom now disappears; and doubts about the marriage, which may have arisen after the initial ardor had passed, vanish.

Some young married couples are surprised to find that the birth of the first child changes their lives even more than did their marriage. There are many satisfactions in watching the baby change from day to day, and in having such a tangible focus to one's life, but there are also tribulations. The carefree days of early married life are gone, and the young mother spends most of her time at home. As much as she loves her baby, the need to care for him constantly becomes wearisome as a steady regimen. The daily routine is arduous, and can require real management skills when there are two small children. The mother who had worked misses adult companionship. She begins to count the days until the weekend when her husband can share the duties, and she begins to await the time when a child can be off to nursery school or kindergarten. It may not be a good omen when a mother feels too guilty to admit that she feels burdened at times and would like an occasional respite from the household chores and care of children.

The presence of a child also requires reorganization of the marriage and can upset the equilibrium that the spouses had established as a couple. In a marital relationship harmony depends essentially upon the couple's finding reciprocally interrelating roles, but one spouse may forego his or her desires or needs in order to support the partner and avoid conflict. The wife may fill male roles while the husband cooks and cares for the house. But a father cannot properly "mother" the child, and even less skewed role divisions are bound to distort the child's development even if they do not provoke disharmony between the couple. The distribution of roles and tasks within the family and how they derive from male and female characteristics were presented in Chapter 2; and the importance to the children of the formation of a parental coalition by the spouses, and of their maintaining generation boundaries and their respective gender-linked roles, has been emphasizd repeatedly. When the unity of the parents as a couple had been established before the arrival of a child and can be retained the complexities of the relationships among three or more family members are simplified, and the tendency of small groups to break down into dyads is minimized. The parents have a definite division of responsibilities and each respects and supports the functions of the other. The gender difference between the parents properly designates and provides different tasks for each and different types of relationship to the child that should complement rather than interfere with each other. The mutuality of parenthood fosters a supportive interdependence between the spouses.

Still the unexpressed but essential demands for parents to fit into specific roles and carry out role-bound fuctions can cause serious strains on the individuals and the marriage. The stresses can be particularly insidious as the spouses may be only dimly aware of the functions and obligations of their roles, and that the acquisition of a child has imposed a need for more definite structuring of their relationship and for more rigid adherence to their respective roles. Indeed, the need to fill these parental roles in which demands are made by the child and the spouse while the rewards of parenthood are still nebulous can set a stern test of the marriage and the stability of the parents. A child can almost as readily provoke conflict as promote greater closeness and sharing. Whereas the wife usually wishes to share the child with her husband and feels hurt if he does not share her enthusiasm, her essential preoccupation with the baby and her own feelings about the baby can leave the husband feeling excluded.

The Impact of Children on Parents' Personalities

While the parental influences on children seem obvious and the relationship of parents' difficulties to the children's personality problems have been discussed in various contexts, the child, in turn, can profoundly affect one or both parents. The influences are reciprocal—a child's needs or specific difficulties uncover a parent's inadequacies. A mother can lose her self-esteem when she finds herself unable to cope with her baby. A woman who had been highly successful in business and had helped her husband in his career by her perfectionistic attention to detailed problems, became frustrated when she could not seem to help her baby. The baby developed colic at three weeks of age, and as a sophisticated person she knew that some pediatricians attributed such difficulties to the mother's way of handling the baby. Intensity of effort could not help, and feeling herself a failure she became angered by the infant who unwittingly frustrated her and she began to suffer from episodes of incapacitating migraine. A rather common pattern has been noted in men who develop peptic ulcer soon after the birth of a child. They had always been anxious about the security of sources of food and support and married women who worked and provided additional security against poverty and starvation. When the wife can no longer work and there is an additional family member to provide for, the anxiety becomes serious and chronic.

The woman's capacities to provide maternal nurturance to her infant are related to the quality of the nurturant care she herself received in her infancy and childhood. If her needs then were met with reasonable consistency and she did not experience chronic frustrations and rage, she now has confidence that she can properly satisfy her own child. We might hazard that her own feelings and responses were properly programmed in her childhood and she can now empathize with and understand the needs and feelings of her children. The mutuality established between herself and the child increases her self-esteem, her pride in her motherliness, and her assurance of her femininity. She can transcend the inevitable difficulties and periods of frustration without self-derogation or distorting defenses against loss of self-esteem. In contrast, the woman who was deprived in early childhood responds to a child's dissatisfactions and refusals to be placated with increased feelings of inadequacy. Regrets at having married and hostile feelings toward the child are disturbing and must be undone. A vicious cycle sets in between a frustrated child and frustrated mother. The mother's inadequacies and despair soon spill over into the marital relationship; she may become depressed, place unrealistic demands upon her husband for support, or erect defenses, including projection of blame, that upset the family equilibrium.

A woman whose concerns about her capabilities as a wife were heightened by a long period of sterility, had her pleasure in having a baby turn into desperation when she found that she could not quiet her infant who would become rigid and shriek when she picked him up to try to comfort him. Her husband's attempts to be helpful were taken as criticism of her adequacy. Her mother had been an aloof woman who had avoided physical contact with her children and had never been able to convey a sense of warmth and protectiveness. The young wife now felt herself even more inadequate than her mother, whose attitudes she had resented. As becoming a more adequate wife and mother than her own mother had formed a major motif of her life, the foundations of her integration were being undermined. She turned the old hostilities toward her mother against herself—she had not rid herself of the resented internalized mother—and became convinced that her husband wished to be rid of her.

Although the topic cannot be discussed at this juncture, we must remember that the need for a parent to adjust and for the marriage to readjust is not confined to the time of the birth of the first child or to the first few years of its life. As we have noted in following the child's development, each transition into a new developmental phase requires an adaptation by the parents, and one or another of these required adaptations may disturb a parent's equilibrium. The child's going off to school may reawaken the fears the mother experienced in her own childhood when she was separated from her mother; a father's jealousies become aroused when his daughter starts dating; the parents have difficulty being left without children in the home, etc. A highly intelligent woman, who had been terrified in her own childhood that her mother would abandon her if her mother learned that she continued to masturbate despite warnings of dire consequences, could not tolerate her son's playing with his penis in his bath and would frantically warn him that he would become an idiot if he continued, even though intellectually she knew differently. As her own childhood had been lonely and she had felt unwanted by her peers—largely because her parents never remained in one neighborhood for more than a year or two—she would become very upset whenever her son had a quarrel with playmates, or if he were not invited to a party. She would scold him for not being more affable and more popular, which made him self-conscious and less able to seek companionship.

We have been considering how the personality changes, emotional difficulties, and regressions of a spouse that occur in response to some phase of parenthood can upset the marriage. The manner in which either one of the parents relates to the child can in itself create problems. A wife, whose beauty flattered the husband's pride and whose vivaciousness delighted him, turns into an ogress to the husband who empathizes with the son whom she treats as a nuisance and mistreats when she feels annoyed with his need for attention. Ethnic or social class differences in role expectations which had been inconsequential in the marital partnership become more troublesome when they concern child-rearing practices. A woman of Irish descent accepted and even admired her Polish-American husband's domination of her and his decision making for both of them; but she could not tolerate his expectations that their three-year-old son would be strictly obedient or else receive a thrashing, or his insistence that she docilely accept his decisions concerning the child's upbringing.

The Child Conceived to Save a Marriage

The stresses of being parents are great enough to challenge the harmony of a fairly secure marriage, yet many children are born in an effort to salvage one that is threatening to disintegrate. The very immature young wife who married after her first fiancé had died in combat and spent most of her pregnancy fantasying about him (see page 405 above) remained intensely bound to her mother and spent many evenings with her and even slept with her mother one or two nights a week. She resented her husband's refusal to take her dancing two or three nights a week as he had during the courtship. When he threatened to leave because he could not tolerate her immaturity and inability to stay home, she decided to have a second child, even though she could not properly care for the first, believing that two children would keep her so busy that she would not have time or energy for dancing and would certainly be unable to leave her husband. Although a child can help a marriage that is not working well by producing a new interest for one or both partners, it is not likely to repair a really unhappy marriage. The baby then simply binds the partners in a relationship they cannot tolerate and the child can be severely resented for holding them together. However, the baby often does dissipate boredom in a wife and dispel the feelings of emptiness that may come after the initial phase of marriage has passed and expectations that marriage would profoundly change life are unrealized. The husband may also gain new self-esteem that changes his behavior and even modifies his personality. The man who married only after his girl friend assured him that she did not expect great potency from him (see page 435), annoyed his wife by his lack of self-confidence and his desire for her to make the important decisions. The birth of a son set aside his insecurity, fired him with ambition to provide for his son better than he had been provided for, and he began to assert himself at work and with his wife—much to her satisfaction.

The Parents' Identifications with Their Child

Children not only identify with parents, but parents also identify with their children. The baby is immediately part of the mother's life, for he has grown in her and only gradually separates from her. Some fathers will require time before they can spontaneously enjoy the baby, sometimes not until the child is old enough to be considered something of a person. The experience of parenthood makes possible a sharing of another life reciprocally to the way the parent as a baby shared feelings with his mother. Again, as in infancy and as in some fortunate marriages, there exists a type of unique closeness and pleasure that comes of being empathically related, with the boundaries between the self and another lowered in a positive rather than a pathological manner. The parents take pleasure in the child's joy and suffer with his pains more than in almost any other relationship. The child's development and achievements are experienced with pride and increase the parents' self-esteem. In certain respects the parent lives again in the child. The parent reexperiences many of the joys of childhood simply through observation and has permission to regress in time and behavior in playing with the child. The parent often lives in the child for whom he establishes a more favorable situation than the one he experienced himself in childhood. Such feelings provoke efforts that are commonly overdone in an attempt to provide the child with what the parent lacked in childhood. It usually fills the parents' needs rather than the child's. The son must have the carpentry set the father had wanted so badly and the father is usually so impatient that he gives it before the child is ready, which permits the father to indulge himself with the toy for a time, and the child to tire of it before he can use it properly. When overdone, such needs of a parent to live through a child interfere with the child's development, particularly when he properly feels he cannot become an individual but must live primarily to complete a parent's life. The converse situations also hold. The parent who had been indulged and who resented the lack of direction and firmness may provide the restrictions he considers desirable for the child.

Through the process of identification the child can also provide one of the two parents with the opportunity to experience intimately the way in which a person of the opposite gender grows up. The sharing of the vicissitudes in the life of a child of the opposite sex, almost as if they pertained to the self, provides a broadening perspective even if it is not needed to fill some residual childhood wishes. Such living through the child is probably more significant for a mother with a son and does not assume importance until he is a boy rather than an infant. The use of a son by the mother and occasionally of a girl by the father to live out a life the parent would like to have lived as a member of the oppoite sex has been noted by many as a source of potential difficulty for both child and parent. However, one cannot consider such patterns to be detrimental or useful in themselves for it is rather a matter of balance. The inability for the mother to empathize and enjoy the experiences of a son as a son interferes with the development of the necessary reciprocal identifications between them. Parenthood also provides the opportunity to be loved, admired, and needed simply because the person is a parent and as such, a central and necessary object in the young child's life. The many potentialities for emotional satisfactions from parenthood manage to outweigh the tribulations and sacrifices that are required.

The Change in the Couple's Position in Society

Aside from directly influencing the parents and their marriage, the child exerts an indirect effect through changing the parents' position in the society. New sets of relationships are established as the parents are drawn to other couples with children of the same age. The mother seeks out other young mothers with whom she can compare notes and exchange advice and admiration of the children. They are later drawn together to share supervision in order to gain some free time. As the child grows older the parents are brought together with other families through interest in nursery schools, parent-teacher's organizations, cub scouts, and in gaining suitable recreational pursuits for the children. They join organizations and clubs and plan vacations for the benefit of the children. The way in which the parents conduct their lives alters and may include a change in residence to assure the proper advantages, physical and social, for the children. A new impetus toward economic and social mobility often possesses the parents. The family's position in society becomes more definite and includes a general pattern of how parents should live in order to raise children properly. Frequently the couple's relatedness to their own parents improves and grows firmer once again. They have achieved a new status in their parents' eyes and in focusing upon their children have a new common interest and can bypass areas of friction which may have existed between the two generations.

The Changing Satisfactions and Tribulations of Parenthood

Parenthood, the satisfactions it provides and the demands it makes, varies as life progresses; and changes with the parents' interests, needs, and age as well as with the children's maturation. There are phases in the child's life that the parents are reluctant to have pass, whereas they tolerate others largely through knowing that they will soon be over. The changing lives of the children provide many satisfactions that offset the tribulations, uncertainties, and regrets. The little girl that the mother nourished as a baby becomes a helper about the home, following the mother's model; she matures into adolescence and becomes a companion who shares and understands as well as requiring understanding; she becomes a wife and mother herself and has a new appreciation of her mother's life. The father finds his son experiencing many things that had long before absorbed the father, and he is fascinated to note how alike boys and their games remain over a generation. They share interests in sports and athletic teams, but eventually the son develops an interest in matters that are more meaningful to the father—hobbies, music, literature, a career. Although rivalries can pervade the father-son and the mother-daughter relationships, usually the parent can share with a child without rivalry, for the child's achievements are regarded by his parents very much as accomplishments of their own.

The parents change. The young father, who was just starting on his career when his first child was born, settles into a life pattern. He becomes secure with increasing achievement and interacts differently with his youngest child and provides a different model for him than for his oldest. Or, he becomes resigned to falling short of his life goals, pursues them with less intensity, and focuses more attention on his children's future than on his own. The mother may have less time for a third or fourth child than for her first, but she may also be more assured in her handling of them. The birth of a baby when the parents are in their late thirties will find them less capable of physical exertion with the child and less tolerant of annoyances, but they are less apt to be annoyed. The parents become accustomed to the child's increasing independence; and though they are concerned because they provide less guidance, they are also relieved by the greater freedom from responsibility. Yet according to an adage that is virtually a platitude, a parent's concerns about a child never cease but only change. Eventually the children marry and leave home. The couple do not cease to be parents; but with their major responsibilities for their children over, a way of life to which they had become accustomed and which provided much of the meaning to their lives comes to an end. They pass through another major demarcation line in life which we will consider in the next chapter.

The Child-Centered Home

Parenthood is something of a career as well as a phase of life. The consciousness that the children's personalities, stability, and happiness are influenced profoundly by how they are nurtured and reared has altered the tasks of parenthood profoundly. Parents are currently much less likely to rely upon time-honored techniques, the methods by which they were reared, or biblical injunctions than they were in former eras. The common desire of American parents is to wish their children to have opportunities that were not available to them; and to become more significant, more learned, more prestigious, happier, or wealthier than they have been; and the belief in the malleability of mankind through better techniques has combined with such hopes to make parenthood a self-conscious activity. The emphasis on improving the children's opportunities has contributed to the child-centered home, which has been considered one of the outstanding characteristics of American society. The term properly implies a home in which the ultimate welfare of the children takes precedence over the convenience and comforts of the parents. The child-centered home, however, becomes a travesty when the wishes and whims of the children dominate the home; or when parents fear to carry out the parental functions of delimiting and guiding their children's behavior. Teachings and misunderstandings of teachings concerning dangers that arise from frustrating a child's self-expression or his "instinctual drives" serve to suppress proper parental functioning. The insecurity thus engendered in parents often offsets the potential advantages of their being parents who seek to adjust to their child's needs. Few things are as important to a child as a parent's self-assurance and security. Self-assurance does not mean rigidity or dogmatism. Perhaps only a parent with self-assurance can properly elicit his child's opinions and foster the child's self-expression before reaching some decision pertaining to the child. However, a home in which the parents can find no calm because of their children's "prerogatives," or in which the mother constantly feels harassed in her efforts to do the right thing without taking her own needs and desires into account, can be detrimental to the children through making the parents unhappy in their lot as parents. The parents require satisfaction if they are to be able to give of themselves to the child; and their happiness as individuals, and as a couple, is just as important as anything they may be able to do for a child or that they can give him.

Many things are required from persons to be competent parents and from a marriage to be suited for family life. Some of the most salient considerations have been discussed in the chapter on the family when we considered the requisites of the milieu in which the child develops. If one reviews these desiderata a central theme can be noted. The parents need to be persons in their own right with lives and satisfactions of their own, firmly related in marriage and gaining satisfaction from it, rather than having their individuality and the marriage become subordinated to their being parents. All too commonly child rearing is discussed in terms of techniques—of what parents do for a child and how it should be done; or in terms of the mother's nurturant capacities and emotional stability. Who the parents are and how they relate to one another, and the nature of the family they create are also fundamental influences upon the child. The parents as models for identification, their interaction as an example of mutuality, the importance of the family structure in integrating the children's personalities are among the topics that demand careful scrutiny if we are to learn what produces stable and unstable children. Perhaps, when parents learn that their behavior as individuals and as a married couple is of prime importance in determining their children's personality development, they will be in a better position to raise happy and stable children.

A psychiatrist tends to think of his patients, and therefore of unhappiness in marriage and of difficulties created for children and also for parents by children. The rewards of parenthood are, by and large, great. The recent trend toward larger families despite excellent contraceptive methods indicates a renewed appreciation of the importance of children. In an era that has been called "the age of anxiety," and in which insecurities about the future are rife which individual effort cannot counter, people turn to the tangible reward of close interpersonal relationships. Couples are willing to give hostages to fortune by having children. Children provide objects whom parents can feel free to love and from whom they gain the satisfactions of being needed. The Japanese use a concept in discussing interpersonal relationships which is expressed by the term *amaeru*, which means both a person's need for another to be dependent upon him, the satisfying of another's need to be needed, and also the wish for such dependency upon another.[2] It is of the essence of parenthood, and may well be fundamental to satisfaction in life, even when it causes pain and requires sacrifice.

References

1. Therese Benedek, "Parenthood as a Developmental Phase: A Contribution to the Libido Theory," *Journal of the American Psychoanalytic Association,* 7 (1959), 389–417.
2. L. T. Doi, "Amae—A Key Concept for Understanding Japanese Personality Structure," *Psychologia,* 5 (1962), 1–7.

Suggested Reading

Therese Benedek, "Parenthood as a Developmental Phase: A Contribution to the Libido Theory," *Journal of the American Psychoanalytic Association,* 7 (1959), 389–417.

Hilde Bruch, *Don't Be Afraid of Your Child: A Guide for Perplexed Parents* (New York: Farrar, Straus & Young, 1952).

Theodore Lidz, "The Effects of Children on Marriage," in Salo Rosenbaum and Ian Alger (eds.), *The Marriage Relationship: Psychoanalytic Perspectives* (New York: Basic Books, 1968).

CHAPTER 16

The Middle Years

IF WE THINK OF A LIFE as a play, <u>middle age is the period leading up to and away from the climax of the story.</u> The characters have all been on stage, the theme and countertheme introduced, and as the third act ends the play reaches its denouement and the fourth act moves on toward an inevitable conclusion. The critical transition may not have been recognized at the moment, and alternative outcomes still seem possible—some hoped for and some feared—and restitutional measures are instituted. <u>In the middle years an individual learns how his life will turn out. Can the themes draw together, goals be achieved and satisfaction attained? Will the relationships that have been established provide fulfillment and happiness? Or must one come to terms with getting by, or with disappointment and disillusionment?</u> At the start of middle age there still seems time to start anew, to salvage the years that are left, and many will try.

The turn from young adulthood to middle life involves a state of mind rather than some specific bodily change such as marked the onset of adolescence and adulthood. Although middle age contains the menopausal period, the "change of life," the woman is usually well into middle age when it occurs. Middle age is initiated by awareness that the peak years of life are passing. A person realizes that he is no longer starting on his way, his direction is usually well set, and his present activities will determine how far he will get. We might also consider that middle age starts when children cease to be a major responsibility; they have married, are away at college, or at least they are late adolescent and are largely responsible for themselves. A man had been occupied and preoccupied with making his way in a career, and with providing for his wife and children. A woman's life had centered around the care of her children and in making a proper home for them. Now it is time to look where their lives have been going, for new patterns of living are required. Then, too, parents have died or retired; and the person realizes that he is one of the older, responsible generation. He has moved to the center of the stage.* The consciousness of the critical transition is abetted by awareness that the body is slowing down. It is no longer the well-oiled machine that quietly responds to the demands placed upon it; it creaks and groans a bit. The woman sees the menopause looming before her when her generative capacities will come to an end. What has been achieved? And what do the years ahead still hold?†

A Time of Stock Taking

This is the time of fulfillment, when years of effort reach fruition. This is autumn when the fruits are harvested and colors are brilliant

* I recall an occasion when several medical school professors in their mid-forties received the news that a department head had died of a stroke; it was the third death of a senior faculty member within the year. They sat silently, a bit stunned, and then one looked at the others and quietly said, "Now it is up to us."
† While writing this chapter I chanced on the following passage from a book review written by James Baldwin which expresses something that I had been groping to say.

> Though we would like to live without regrets, and sometimes proudly insist that we have none, this is not really possible, if only because we are mortal. When more time stretches behind than stretches before one, some assessments, however reluctantly and incompletely, begin to be made. Between what one wished to become and what one *has* become there is a momentous gap, which will now never be closed. And this gap seems to operate as one's final margin, one's last opportunity, for creation. And between the self as it is and the self as one sees it, there is also a distance, even harder to gauge. Some of us are compelled, around the middle of our lives, to make a study of this baffling geography, less in the hope of conquering these distances than in the determination that the distances shall not become any greater.

(From a review of *The Arrangement*, by Elia Kazan, in *The New York Review of Books*, Vol. 8, No. 5, March 23, 1967, p. 17.)

though mellow. Not all reap the harvest, and for some the regrets and disillusion mount, often mixed with a bitter resentment that life has slipped through their fingers. Still, even for the fortunate, the balance of life is upset by awareness of the passing of time and the limits of life's span. There is a recrudescence of a type of existential anxiety; an awareness of the insignificance of the individual life in an infinity of time and space. Now, in middle life, a stock taking and a re-evaluation occur. Two of the world's literary masterpieces start on this note. Dante opens the *Divine Comedy* with the line "Midway in the journey through life, I found myself lost in a dark wood strayed from the true path." Goethe's Faust finds that although he has studied philosophy, medicine, and law thoroughly, he is fundamentally no wiser than the poorest fool,* feels his life wasted despite his achievements, and makes a pact with Mephistopheles in his attempt to salvage it. The lives of ordinary mortals beyond this juncture are more prosaic than the ways in which these two giants attained salvation; but in a personal rather than a universal context, the path often leads through hell and to pacts with the devil before a resolution can be found. For some, middle age brings neither fruition nor disappointment so much as angry bewilderment as they find that their neglect of meaningful relationships in the frenetic striving for success now makes life seem like "a tale told by an idiot—full of sound and fury, signifying nothing." †

Although the usual course of life continues along a well-trodden path, with ample satisfactions and rewards found on the way, with hopes and ambitions tempered by experience, and doubts and concerns countered by religion or philosophy—summing up and reassessment are characteristic of middle age, even when they do not lead to any notable changes.

The Physical Changes

Middle age is a period of considerable significance both for medicine and for psychiatry. Whether a person admits it or not, although he may be in the "prime of life," he has passed the peak of his physical abilities. Hair is growing gray or sparse, wrinkles appear, the abdomen gets in the

---

* *Habe nun, ach! Philosophie,*
   Juristerei und Medizin,
   Und leider auch Theologie!
   Durchaus studiert, mit heiszem Bemühn
   Da steh ich nun, ich armer Tor!
   Und bin so Klug als wie zuvor
              (*Faust*, Part I, Opening scene.)
† *Macbeth*, Act V, Sc. 5.

way when he bends. The paper must be read at arm's length and then bifocals become a necessity. The wear and tear of life add up and begin to be felt. The knee injured in youth stiffens at times and aches in bad weather. A back injury may be incapacitating every now and again. The drink before supper is no longer taken simply to enliven one, but to counter the dull fatigue felt after a day's work. The slow increment in weight requires reluctant attention to diet, for a gain in weight at this age is considered hazardous to health.

Changes in the various organ systems occur as processes of repair and renewal lag and lead to degenerative changes that increase the proneness to illness and dysfunction. For the man, the years between forty and fifty hold the threat of sudden death from coronary occlusion. Such heart attacks are less likely to be fatal later in life after a gradual narrowing of the coronary arteries leads to development of anastomatic arterial pathways by which the heart muscle can receive blood after a large vessel occludes. Malignancies take their toll and women are advised to check their breasts for masses regularly and have annual gynecological examinations. Even a person who remains healthy becomes familiar with hospitals through visiting friends, and finds that he can no longer avoid scanning the obituary columns if he wishes to keep track of his acquaintances. He may gain some secret satisfaction from surviving enemies, or even friends, and noting that he is lasting longer or that his achievements surpass theirs. The middle-aged individual becomes aware that ill health and even death are potentialities that hover over him and those close to him. Such awareness consciously or unconsciously influences the pattern of his life. Some slacken the pace of their activities to keep in step with the body's capacities or infirmities, whereas others are provoked to renewed exertions in order to get more or further before it is too late. Psychologically disorganizing illnesses become less common, for the personality has become more firmly integrated and an ego identity established; but depressive reactions become more frequent, and they are related to regrets over the way life has gone, accompanied by resentment toward those who have caused frustration and by anger against the self for failing to meet expectations.*

* Concerns over the meaningfulness of life in general, and of the course of one's own life, are not confined to intellectuals. A coal miner who was hospitalized because he was becoming increasingly incapacitated from arthritis expressed some suicidal ruminations. He was deeply disappointed because he realized that his life's strivings would amount to nothing. Raised in poverty by immigrant parents, he had entered the pits at twelve. He had become resigned to spending his life in the mines but swore that

Satisfactions of the Middle Years

When life has gone well, when ambitions and expectations have not exceeded potential, or when modifications of goals either downward or upward have been made in accord with reality, the middle years can bring great satisfactions. An adolescent or even a young adult commonly considers that his parents' lives are over; that they have had their day in a remote past, but now, in their forties or early fifties, the "heyday in the blood is tame";* that their lives are without passion and without a future. Some middle-aged persons feel the same way about themselves. But each period of life differs from the others, offering new opportunities and new ways of experiencing as well as tasks to be surmounted. The more mature can accept the advantages and pleasures of middle life together with the limitations it imposes. A person becomes pathetic and sometimes even ludicrous when he insists on seeking the rewards appropriate to a younger age. Some fear displacement by the next generation; some now begin to live through their children; but others are still very much engaged in pursuing their own careers and life patterns and may well feel that with responsibility for children gone they have a new freedom to focus on their own lives and interests.

The man is now established in his work. For some, particularly in executive circles, the period between forty and fifty, or even fifty-five, may involve intense striving to capture the elusive top positions or properly to climax a career by amassing the wealth or prestige that has come within grasp. Demonstrated capacities may lead to greater demands, expectations, and responsibilities, and open new opportunities. Others become involved in political jockeying to win out over a competitor. The strain of the competition can be wearing. However, as far as the vast majority is concerned, if the individual has not yet reached the peak of his achievements, he can see how far he will get, and moves toward it as

---

his children would become educated and lead a better life. Both his wife and he had scrimped and taken extra jobs whenever any were available. Now, at the age of forty-five he was an old and disabled man and had not saved enough to send his two sons to college. Even more disappointing, neither of his boys wished to continue beyond high school; neither was interested in their father's ambitions for them—that one become an engineer and the other a doctor. In actuality, it seemed apparent that neither had the capacity for a higher education; but the hopes that had given meaning to the miner's life had collapsed. He was resentful toward his sons, but he also blamed himself for having been an inadequate father.

* *Hamlet*, Act III, Sc. 4.

part of the career pattern. In the factory, he has become a foreman, or at least an old and experienced hand with security and some special prerogatives. In a profession, he is an established member whose experience is valued by younger colleagues. He is no longer in direct competition with younger men, but can take a parental attitude in guiding the next generation. He need no longer prove himself from day to day, for he is credited with past accomplishments. Those whom he directs or supervises respect him and seek to satisfy him. He sees the realization of his efforts and he can relax occasionally and depend upon his experience.

The Critical Problems

For the man, a critical aspect of middle age concerns coming to terms with his accomplishments; but, at times, also with accepting the responsibilities that have come with his achievements. Soon after a much desired promotion or some specific recognition of his abilities he becomes depressed—the "promotion depression" that catches all by surprise. Classically, he is caught in an outgrowth of a pattern that had its origins in his childhood—he feels vulnerable in surpassing his father. It is a version of the childhood fantasy of displacing the father with his mother; and old fears haunt him that father will take vengeance, and he punishes himself for his hubris. Commonly, however, the man resents being burdened with a new load of responsibilities. He had striven to reach the goal, but the goal turns out to be something of an illusion. It is no haven but requires more work, more decision making, more responsibility. He cannot turn from it without loss of self-esteem, but he resents the expectations others have for him, the demands of the boss or the organization, or his wife's ambitions that carried him beyond his limits.

The changes in a woman's life are more tangible than those in a man's, and, in general, middle age is a more critical and difficult period for her. The end of the children's dependency, which has been taken as one of the significant indications of the start of middle age in the parents, affects a mother more than a father. The nurturant functions, which have constituted her cardinal interest and shaped her activity for two or more decades, come to an end. Concerns for her children may remain a dominant interest, but they are in the form of thoughts and feelings and no longer take up much of her time and effort. She feels that her major life function has been completed. Though she may be pleased and even relieved at the release from so much work and responsibility, she usually also has regrets and feels an emptiness in her life. A mother may feel that the children to whom she has given so much have become neglectful and ungrateful, and misunderstandings can easily arise with children whose dominant interests are now their own spouses, children, and careers.* The mother whose children no longer require her care must find a new way of life, or expand old interests so that they fill out her days.

The middle-aged woman is usually confronted by very different problems from those her husband faces. Even as the man's life will change abruptly at retirement, the woman must often make a profound shift in her way of living in middle life. She is still young enough to start on a new career, re-enter an old one, or devote herself more fully to some activity she had pursued part time while occupied with her children. Although she may work to help finance the children's higher education, she will often pursue an avocation to bring new interest into her life rather than primarily to supplement the family income. She may study to be a practical nurse or social worker, or resume teaching. This is a period of life when time can be devoted to humane activities or to local politics; and, seemingly, an ever increasing number of women become artists or skilled craftsmen. Of course, grandchildren can occupy a woman's life, particularly when she cares for the children while her daughter works or continues her education. The woman's life will change again when her husband retires and their days can be spent together and he wishes to have her companionship.

The Menopause

The loss of nurturant functions is compounded by the loss of generative capacities, the other function that has been so much a part of the woman's existence and so fundamental to her self-esteem. The menopause looms before her as a major landmark in her life; and she feels that she will be an elderly woman after it occurs, and unconsciously—or consciously—an empty woman. The menopause occurs at a mean age of forty-eight or forty-nine; but often in the mid-forties and occasionally even earlier. Most women are psychologically preparing themselves for it as they turn forty. It is common for women to believe that the menopause comes in the early forties or even the late thirties, and some women oblige by suffering from appropriate symptoms ten or fifteen

* The "empty nest" syndrome can contribute to depressive illnesses in middle-aged women. The problem is likely to be most severe in divorced or widowed mothers, and particularly by immigrant or first-generation women who have not become well acculturated and whose families were, therefore, particularly important to them.[2]

years ahead of time. The difficulties ensue both from the physiologic changes that occur with the cessation of estrogen secretion and from the emotional impact of the "change of life."

The changes in hormonal secretions, with a marked decline in estrogen secretion as the climacteric starts, upsets the physiological homeostasis and produces an array of physical discomforts that vary in degree and duration from individual to individual. The menses may cease abruptly or taper off over a year or longer, with periods missed or coming irregularly; the flow may be sparse or unexpectedly profuse. The woman may become uneasy, for the irregularity can interfere with plans, lest she be caught unawares. Although an occasional woman may experience no discomfort during the climacterium, vasomotor instability often causes considerable trouble during the menopause and occasionally for some years thereafter. Waves of hot feelings that sweep over the woman, termed "hot flashes" or "hot flushes," are most common, but unexpected sweating, blotching of the skin, and feelings of being unpleasantly warm much of the time can also be annoying. Episodes of faintness or dizziness make some women feel insecure, and headaches can become troublesome. Some women are simply uncomfortable and uneasy, but others are severely upset. Indeed, emotional disturbances, primarily depressive, are a common concomitant of the menopause; and whereas the emotional lability may be provoked by the hormonal changes, it is clear that the menopause requires a realignment of attitudes about the self that cuts deeply into the personality and its defenses. It is a time of major emotional vulnerability when neurotic difficulties often flare into symptoms and incapacitations can occur. After menstruation ceases and a hormonal equilibrium is re-established, the physical symptoms usually cease. Although an emotionally stable and adaptable woman may experience only physical discomfiture, even she will feel changed by the event and will have readjusted her inner balance to maintain emotional equilibrium.

Neither the physical nor the emotional aspects of the climacteric are caused by the endocrine changes alone. Some of the difficulties derive from fears of the effects of the menopause that provoke anticipatory concerns. The folklore handed down among women engenders the belief that the menopause causes serious emotional and mental instability and that a woman is fortunate if she does not become seriously depressed or insane: the physical symptoms are amplified into an almost unbearable suffering, another burden to which the deprived sex is subjected. A relationship frequently exists between the difficulties experienced during menstrual periods, childbirth, and the menopause; they are difficulties that relate to attitudes toward womanhood. The tradition that the climacteric is a time of suffering serves to foster difficulties, which in turn perpetuates the tradition. A common belief, held by men as well as women, that the woman loses her sexual responsivity and ability to enjoy sex with the menopause, may lead a woman to feel that she will become an undesirable old woman whose husband may properly seek gratification elsewhere. Such concepts have no basis in fact. Indeed, there is now ample evidence that, in general, the woman's potential for sexual responsivity throughout middle age is greater than the man's.

The woman's self-esteem is often closely related to her capacities to bear children. We have already emphasized sufficiently that the girl's feelings of deprivation were compensated for at puberty by the development of her female physique and appreciation of her procreative capacities. We noted that menstruation, even though resented as a burden, constituted a desired symbol of femininity (Chapter 10). The woman feels the loss of this badge of womanhood—an indicator of her capacity to reproduce—that has provided feelings of worth. In contrast to the situation in childhood, she now has no prospects of a future flowering to offset feelings of emptiness and deprivation. Unless her self-esteem as a woman and a mother has become ingrained within her, she suffers with the loss of the physical tokens of her femininity. She knows, indeed, that she will lose more than her menses and fertility: her breasts grow flabby, the subcutaneous adipose tissue that softens her contours gradually disappears, her skin becomes wrinkled and sags, and pouches appear under her eyes. Ultimately she will again assume a rather sexless appearance which she may be better able to conceal from others than from herself. Her narcissism suffers, for she will no longer be able to use her physical charms to attract. She will mourn for the person she had been. As Helene Deutsch commented, "almost every woman in the climacterium goes through a shorter or longer period of depression." [1] It may be scarcely noticeable in a woman who feels that her life has been productive, who finds new sources of fulfillment and pleasure in middle life and who no longer bases her attractiveness primarily on physical charms, or it may be apparent only in bursts of frenzied activity utilized to ward off recognition of the changed status; but many women will experience a downswing before they reorganize themselves and find new ways of living and new sources of self-esteem.*

* The relationship of a woman's pride and self-esteem to the intactness of her body and particularly to her generative organs is often overlooked by gynecologists who can cause considerable unhappiness by expecting patients to assume a logical attitude to-

Fortunately, the physical discomforts of the menopause can be largely dissipated by replacement therapy with estrogens. The woman no longer need fear incapacitating or even distressing symptoms. At the present time the medical management of menopausal symptoms varies according to the opinions of the gynecologist or internist: some prefer to let mild or moderate symptoms continue without replacement in order to permit a new balance to become established as soon as possible. However, discomforts can easily be checked if deemed necessary.

Currently, an increasing number of gynecologists institute permanent estrogen replacement therapy at the start of the climacterium. They not only consider that it is unnecessary for women ever to experience menopause, but that various other manifestations of aging can be prevented. The subcutaneous tissues do not atrophy, protein loss is countered, the breasts remain firm, the genital tissues do not atrophy, and the loss of calcium from the bones that leads to bowing of the spine and loss of height is prevented. As such measures have been undertaken only in recent years, the long-term results and possible dangers cannot yet be assessed.* At present, it appears that the increasing longevity of women can be accompanied by preservation from many aspects of aging.

The Security of a Good Marriage

A good marriage provides great security, for each spouse is certain of the affection of the person most important to him or her. They do not have to pretend, or extend themselves, or find new meaningful relationships but can feel settled with one another. The children are now more likely to be sources of pleasure than concern. If the spouses have one another, the disappointments of life are buffered. If others do not regard the husband as a successful man, at least his wife appreciates what he has

---

ward the removal of the uterus or the ovaries in middle life. When the gynecologist finds a benign uterine tumor that requires removal, he may insist upon removing one ovary at the same time: the woman does not need it, one ovary supplies sufficient hormone, and the chances of developing cancer of the ovary is halved. However, many women cannot take this attitude and feel that they are being mutilated. All too often more radical procedures are carried out when they are not absolutely essential; the woman is "cleaned out" of her uterus and both ovaries, the gynecologist assuring her that menopausal symptoms can be avoided by estrogen replacement therapy. Somehow male surgeons tend to have relatively little regard for ovaries because in contrast to testes they are not visible. A rational approach recognizes how much a woman's uterus and ovaries are related to her feelings of worth.

* However, no evidence of carcinogenic effect has been found in the seven or more years that this kind of therapy has been used—and there is some evidence that such treatment lessens the chances of cancer of the genital tract and breasts.

done or tried to do. If the children seem to neglect their mother or have become hostile during their adolescence, her husband still loves her. Even if there had been friction earlier in the marriage, middle-aged spouses often come to terms with one another. Each knows that his or her way of life and well-being depends upon the other. Each has become accustomed to the ways of the other, and would feel uneasy with another. For many couples the sexual adjustment is more satisfactory than when they were young; perhaps it is less frenzied but they know the other's needs and tacit signals, and have found ways of satisfying each other. With greater control, skill, or artistry, the sexual act can bring more subtle pleasures.

However, some problems in sexual adjustment can arise. The wife may experience a heightening of sexual drive with the menopause; particularly if concerns over impregnation had interfered with her spontaneity she now feels a release to enjoy sex without worry. Then, too, the relative freedom from concerns about her children and from the fatigue caused by looking after them permits relaxation and renewed interest in sexual pleasures.* The husband whose sexual drive has been declining may not respond to the wife's increased interest. After the age of fifty, the man's sexual adequacies may decline rather notably, but he remains interested and capable under proper circumstances. However, the failures of potency that occur on occasion may upset him considerably and lead him to avoid further attempts except when he feels certain of success, and because of the psychic factors involved in male potency, self-consciousness can augment his difficulties. Such problems can lead a husband to seek extramarital relations in which he finds new stimulation and in which he may be less embarrassed by failure. But a harmonious and affectionate married couple can usually manage the shifts in sexual interests and capacities between themselves.

Restitutive Efforts

The man who is satisfied with where he is getting in his career, the woman who feels that she has provided a good home for her husband and children, the husband and wife who enjoy a harmonious marriage

---

* In contrast, as Masters and Johnson have noted, a woman who has never gained pleasure from the sexual act may use the menopause as an excuse to avoid frequent sexual relations. These investigators have also found that sometimes the post-menopausal woman will experience pain on urinating after intercourse—a result of the thinning of the vaginal wall. They note that unless replacement therapy is used, a woman must have intercourse with some regularity after the menopause to maintain an adequate vaginal outlet and to prevent shrinkage of the vagina.[3]

and have the affection and respect of their children—such persons can meet their middle age wisely and complacently and seek simply to round out a full life in the years that lie ahead. Still, the person who has few regrets or who has acquired sufficient wisdom to absorb the disappointments must be considered fortunate. It is not so simple to continue to meet life with dignity and integrity when envy, regret, and bitterness gnaw at one. Life is a one-time matter and it is difficult to cope with the feeling that the chance has been wasted. There may yet be time before old age brings infirmities, time to realize the life dreamed of in youth, to love and be loved, to gain the pleasure one has had to forego, to win the fame and fortune one has envied—or, perhaps, simply to feel wanted by someone who cares, or to be free of carping criticism and blame for past mistakes. Middle age is notably a time when restitutive efforts are made. For some the grasping after the gold ring succeeds, but more often impetuous attempts bring further unhappiness. The final fling before the gates close* can disrupt a family and fill the last half of life with bitterness. The spouse becomes resentful and the children disillusioned and unforgiving. The wife who is striving to ward off feelings of emptiness and of being unlovable after her menopause becomes hostile and depressed when her husband has an affair with a younger woman. More marriages would be wrecked if many wives did not anticipate such behavior from their husbands in middle age and, biding their time, try to feel secure enough of themselves while awaiting the husband's return.

The narcissistic person, whose equilibrium has rested upon the admiration of others and in pride in youthful attributes, seems most prone to seek to regain adolescent capacities. A woman who was admired for her beauty and whose self-esteem derived largely from the glow of desire she could light in men's eyes felt displaced when her daughter was pursued by many suitors and when she was praised for having an extraordinarily beautiful daughter. The mother had her face lifted, spent long hours at the beautician's, and began to dress more and more youthfully. She intruded upon the young men who called upon her daughter, and sought to captivate them with her wit and physical charm. At times, it was hard to tell whether the young men were courting the mother or the daughter.

* *Torschluss* is a syndrome recognized in the German language and literature in which a middle-aged person seeks gratification while it is still possible, and the term *Torschlusspanik* is used to describe the frenzied anxiety-driven efforts of a man to make the most of his waning potency by pursuing young women.

Strains Upon the Marriage

These years can present a severe test to a marriage. With the children no longer a major focus of attention, the spouses are on their own again, largely dependent upon one another to keep their marriage alive and their lives meaningful after a lapse of twenty or thirty years. The children no longer provide diversion or activity, or serve as scapegoats for the conflict between the spouses. The couple have more time together, which can be either a burden or an opportunity for increased closeness. Boredom comes easily after all these years together, and a number of persons will return to adolescent and early adult patterns of using sexual adventure as a way of averting ennui and loneliness. There is some increase in the divorce rate in middle age. However, a fair number of such divorces are not caused by new infatuations, or middle-aged flings, but rather because the couple had decided to wait until their children were grown before dissolving an unsatisfactory marriage. Although friends are often reluctant to see a marriage that had endured for so many years break up, and though it usually causes considerable unhappiness for one of the partners, such shifts of marital partners in mid-life work out well for many. One or both partners have matured sufficiently to select a spouse with better judgment than he or she used in the impetuousness of youth. However, the tendency for repetition in the marital choice is striking. Often friends observe that the new spouse has characteristics very similar to the first. Then, too, the older man who finds a young wife whom he feels appreciates his virility, may well be marrying a woman who is seeking a father figure and who is relatively disinterested in the sexual aspects of marriage. Because of the imbalance caused by the higher death rate among men than women in middle age, more divorced women than men are likely to remain unmarried, particularly as they are much less likely to marry a younger spouse. A man is also less likely to remain unmarried after a divorce—or the death of a wife—because he is less capable of taking care of himself and a home.

Vocational Problems

Even as some persons will seek to salvage their lives by changing spouses, some will decide to change jobs. It is too late to change one's vocation, but a man may now seek a new position in which his good qualities and efforts are appreciated and will lead to promotion. Such a change comes at a time in life when he should be getting settled in what he has been doing rather than moving into a spot where he must prove himself anew. There are many opportunities, of course, for the successful man who may be much sought after, but there are few good places available for one who has not yet made the grade. Indeed, blue- and white-collar workers will at this time of life be more concerned with maintaining the position and security they have attained than in seeking a better opportunity. They rely upon the union to protect them from displacement by younger persons and to defend their seniority rights when unemployment threatens. They learn to control feelings of resentment toward employers, to swallow their feelings when they are passed over for promotion, and find virtue in patience. As age increases, future security progressively takes precedence over opportunity. Other sources of self-realization must be found. Still, not all are wise or able to contain themselves. To some who have sought wealth, the stock market beckons —or the races or gaming table where luck may succeed when effort has failed.

Although when all goes well a person experiences relief from the need to prove himself constantly, success does not necessarily bring surcease from striving. Indeed, many successful men tend to be compulsive, becoming anxious when they are not giving their best, while others have succeeded because they find and enjoy challenge in what they are doing. Still, it is easier to continue strenuous efforts when they are not taken as a test of worth. Some cannot accept being bested by youth or admit that age brings some limitations. A man who was invalided by a heart attack, and soon died of a second, described how his first heart attack occurred. He was a sandhog, extremely proud of his strength and his independence since early adolescence. He had been unable to accept the banter of the young crew he supervised and who referred to him as Grandpa even though he had just passed forty. He felt that to retain their respect as a foreman he must show himself as capable as any. When his crew was confronted by a particularly difficult task in moving a boulder in a tunnel, he insisted on showing how it could be done. Their entreaties to him to desist and let them do it only infuriated him. As he tugged and shouted directions, he experienced a sudden sharp pain in his chest and collapsed. In the hospital he vowed that he would never live as an invalid and rely on his wife's support—and he never did. The industrialist may continue to expand his business as if his livelihood depended upon it. Indeed, some "oral" characters can never feel that their future supplies are secure. At first, they feel they will be haunted less by the specter of insecurity after they have made a million, but the million then seems peanuts and not security, and failure of an important business venture creates as much anxiety as if they could no longer feed the family. However, the pursuit of unnecessary riches even to the hurt of others brings high esteem in Western civilization.

Ill Health

The problems that arise from ill health in middle age form realistic difficulties often enough to require at least passing comment. Illness can temporarily disrupt the course of a life or require reorganizations of a life plan. The blood pressure rises insidiously and indicates a need to slow the pace; diabetes that starts after forty is relatively common and not usually serious but requires attention to diet. Some such moderate incapacitations can bring compensations. Sir William Osler is said to have remarked that one of the best ways of assuring a long life is to suffer a mild heart attack in middle age. The man gains a sufficient reason to cease driving himself and permit himself to enjoy living. He may have played golf only for the companionship, and now he can limit himself to a few holes and then sit at the nineteenth hole sipping a highball while he chats with friends. The wife of a man who had once been a prominent attorney considered that a mild heart attack had saved him from a serious depression. His practice had fallen off precipitously after the death of his partner, but he could not admit his inability to manage the firm and gain new clients. The family lived largely on his wife's inherited wealth, but without openly recognizing the situation. Her income would not have been able to offset his business deficit much longer, but he had been unable to give up his office and disclose the poor state of his practice to his friends and colleagues. His wife had helped maintain the pretense lest he become depressed and suicidal. The heart attack brought relief for both of them. His physician agreed with his wife that he was unable to continue his work, and he retired, occupying himself with legal research at home. The tendency to fall back upon ill health, either real or imagined, as a means of resolving serious difficulties presents a very real problem to physicians. The prop of ill health should not be removed incautiously. The reasons why a person needs it must be ascertained, evaluated, and removed before a physician insists that there is no need for the patient to refrain from his usual activities. On the other hand, a person can be made to despair and feel that his life is worthless by overly cautious efforts to preserve his life.*

* The point is illustrated by a story which, I believe, was told originally about the distinguished Baltimore internist Dr. Louis Hammond. A patient consulted with

Children and Grandchildren

Even though children cease to be a major responsibility for the middle-aged couple, they are usually not lost to the parents and continue as a major center of interest. The parents who have given of themselves while fostering their children's growth and gradual emancipation from them now have children who feel free to return to them, and even to turn to them for help, for they have no reason to fear losing their independence when they do. The couple acquire new children when their children marry. The arrival of the first grandchild will usually evoke some feelings of strangeness and perhaps something of a shock at becoming a member of the third generation. Grandparents are supposed to be old, but middle-aged grandparents do not yet feel old. The grandchildren furnish a new major source of interest; and if the grandparents can participate in raising them, they often behave differently from the way they did in rearing their own children. They feel more free to give and indulge, for they seek to be loved and needed by the grandchildren—sometimes to their children's despair.

Middle Age for the Unmarried

However, not all persons marry. Some consciously prefer to remain single and others remain single unwillingly but, as we considered the matter in an earlier chapter, they usually have unconscious deterrents to marrying or unadmitted reasons for remaining single. There are many ways in which a single life can be satisfactory and even happy; but as the middle years pass, the advantages are apt to diminish. The daughter who has been the dutiful child and remained unmarried to look after her parents may have persevered in the hope of becoming the most favored child who would be properly appreciated after her siblings all married and left home; or perhaps the strength of the oedipal attachment prevented marriage: her parents absorbed her entire emotional life and she seems content to remain with them. Eventually, she finds herself saddled with the care of infirm or even senile parents who can no longer

Dr. Hammond after recovering from a coronary occlusion. After Dr. Hammond had examined him thoroughly, the patient said, "My doctor told me that I must give up smoking, business, golf, sexual relations, and go to bed each night before eleven— is that correct?" Dr. Hammond agreed that it was sound advice. "If I follow it," the patient then asked, "will I live longer?" "That," Dr. Hammond replied, "I can't say, but it will seem longer."

give her anything in return. The reward for being a dutiful child turns into a resented burden. When the parents' deaths eventually sever the relationship, she is unprepared to live on her own. Although it is easier for a bachelor to find a wife in middle life, he has often become too set in his ways to share his life with another. Moreover, according to Kinsey about 50 per cent of men who have never married by the age of thirty-five are actively homosexual, in the sense that they have had some homosexual relationship within the year—a finding confirmed by clinical experience—which makes it even less likely that a middle-aged bachelor will be able to make a satisfactory adjustment to marriage. The widow and widower have better chances of marrying than the spinster and bachelor. Reasons for marrying and remarrying in middle age are likely to be different from reasons for marrying earlier: though the desire for a companion with whom to share life remains a major motivation, the need for a wife to care for the tasks of living and for a husband to help provide the necessities become more important and acceptable grounds for marriage.

The passage over the crest of life is a particularly critical period, a time of summing up in preparation for the second half of adulthood, and as such, a time of further integration or reintegration. In the transition from adolescence to early adulthood, the individual had become committed to a way of life. He has now lived it and is now mature—or is unlikely ever to become mature. Now, approaching the divide, he looks back and also tries to prognosticate on the basis of his experience. Perhaps he will try to climb still higher, change course while he still can, or decide upon which path of descent is safest. Whether a person makes the most of the opportunity available or whether he begins to die slowly depends upon a wide variety of personality factors, but they continue to include attitudes related to the confidence, trust, and initiative inculcated in the earliest years. The realization that the turn toward the end of life has been rounded awakens anxiety and despair in proportion to feelings that one has never really lived and loved.

As the middle years pass, the likelihood of reorganizing and reorienting diminishes. It becomes time to make the most of the way of life that has been led. Regrets cannot be waved away but they are futile: what life has brought must be accepted if the closing years are not to be wasted or become unendurable. Dignity, perhaps shaded by resignation, protects an individual against despair. When he is not caught up in efforts to undo or redo, or to search after what has been missed in earlier years, or in wallowing in self-pity, he can often find and use the benefits that come with maturity, enjoy the opportunities it presents, and move toward bringing closure and completion to his life in the years that still lie ahead.

References

1. Helene Deutsch, *The Psychology of Women*. Vol. 2: *Motherhood* (New York: Grune & Stratton, 1945), p. 473.
2. Eva Deykin, Shirley Jacobson, Gerald Klerman, and Naida Solomon, "The Empty Nest: Psychosocial Aspects of Conflicts Between Depressed Women and Their Grown Children," *American Journal of Psychiatry*, 122 (1966), 1422–1426.
3. William Masters and Virginia E. Johnson, *Human Sexual Response* (Boston: Little, Brown, 1966).

Suggested Reading

Therese Benedek, "The Climacterium," in *The Psychosexual Functions in Women* (New York: Ronald Press, 1952).

Helene Deutsch, *The Psychology of Women*. Vol. 2: *Motherhood* (New York: Grune & Stratton, 1945).

Barbara Fried, *The Middle-Age Crisis* (New York: Harper & Row, 1967).

CHAPTER 17 ⁹

Old Age

OLD AGE IS CONSIDERED, somewhat arbitrarily, to start at about sixty-five, the time when most men retire. Retirement may mean a well-earned surcease from work which permits the individual to enjoy his declining years, or it may connote being discarded to the slag heap, worn out and useless to industry and society. The difference is conveyed, in part, by the contrast between the active, "I am retiring," and the passive, "I am being retired." Many of the contemporary problems of the aged involve this dichotomy between a desirable unharried, unhurried, and dignified closure of life and a hollow survival, feeling useless, unneeded, and burdensome. The problems that come with retirement, with facing the end of life, with the encroachment of physical and mental infirmities, combine with the difficulties of the age in coping with the aged to create serious difficulties for the large majority of the elderly. We have promoted the "old man" and "old woman" by coining the euphemisms "senior citizen" and "golden age," but in the United States we are just beginning to make it possible for the vast majority to live out these penultimate years with a modicum of security, independence, and dignity.

The biblical threescore years and ten have currently become the life expectancy of the child who survives the neonatal period rather than the life span of the few fortunate survivors. The person who reaches sixty-five still has a life expectancy of over twelve years and must plan accordingly. If a person survives to reach eighty, as many will, he will still have an expectation of another ten years. The persons who enter old age form something of a select group,* and with advancing age the body's decline seems to slow down.

The Crucial Problems of the Aged

Although I would not wish to push the analogy too far, the aged person goes through a reversal of some of the critical developments experienced during adolescence. The force of the sexual drives diminishes, which lessens the id impulsions; although some desires motivated by hormonal secretions remain, a major portion of the sexual strivings again arise from desires for affectionate and sensuous sharing and from dependency needs as in childhood. The capacities for ego control diminish as the abilities to conceptualize gained in adolescence fade with the senile changes in the brain. The aged will again become increasingly dependent, but now upon their children or other members of a subsequent generation. Concomitantly, their independence diminishes; and at times the aged must again become virtually obedient to the caretaking persons or they will be rejected, even as in childhood. Then, as the secondary sexual characteristics and the physical strength attained in adolescence shrink away, the pride and confidence derived from such attributes diminish; and the physical differences between the sexes lessen. Finally, whereas the adolescent was moving toward sharing his or her life intimately and interdependently, the aged person must sooner or later absorb the loss of the person with whom he has shared his life, and who had virtually become part of him.

After a paragraph that conveys so distressing a picture, it may be use-

---

* The increase in life expectancy derives largely from the decreased mortality of young children. After the age of sixty or sixty-five there has been little if any increase in life expectancy over the past fifty years. As has often been pointed out, the best way of having a long life is to select long-lived parents and ancestors. Whereas the life expectation of nonwhites is lower than for the white population probably because of the latter's better nurture, after the age of sixty-five the life expectancy of nonwhites is greater.

ful and necessary to remind the reader that old age also has, or can have, compensations and pleasures. The pleasures derive largely from experiencing the rewards of fulfillment and the successes of those whom one created, or of institutions one helped create. Contentment comes from relief from impassioned strivings and struggle, and to some extent from resignation. There is also time, time to enjoy and experience what had to be put off or renounced during periods of greater demand.

It seems useful to consider three phases in the latter years of life; however, they may neither be discrete nor occur in all persons. The time of retirement at about the age of sixty-five will be taken as the start of old age. Many persons remain essentially unchanged from their middle years except for the differences in their way of life created by retirement. The person is *elderly* but considers himself capable, complete, and competent to take care of his needs and affairs. Sooner or later changes in his physical condition or in his life circumstances force the elderly person to become reliant upon others and he is considered *senescent*. The last phase, which many are spared and which may not occur even in advanced age, is *senility*, when the brain no longer serves in its essential function as an organ of adaptation and a person enters his second childhood or dotage, during which others must look after him almost completely. The process of aging varies greatly and some will be senescent and occasionally even senile by the time they reach sixty-five, whereas others are reasonably independent at ninety. However, in almost everyone physical decline begins to cause appreciable limitations in the decade divided by the seventieth birthday.

Whatever other changes may occur, the elderly person's life is altered by retirement, and then by a return to a dependency on others. Retirement from an occupation that had provided a pattern to living and focal interests forms a greater transition for the man and working woman than for the housewife. The days can now be filled according to desire and require a new type of planning. The woman's life is affected largely through changes in the pattern of her husband's life and in the economic situation. The impact of retirement on people varies. Some feel that life is over, whereas others consider that they have earned a respite from earning a living and can devote themselves to other activities. The period of aging as a whole may be considered by the person to be the end of the line where he is left standing at the outskirts of life, waiting at the edge of nothingness, or as a time of relaxed closure of life which still contains much to experience and enjoy.

The elderly person may have mixed feelings about his prospects of reaching a very advanced age. His hopes for the years ahead are usually reasonably modest. He wishes to live out his life with dignity, to remain capable of caring for himself and his wife, or rather that together they will manage for themselves. He hopes to find ways in which he will be useful to others even if not essential, but particularly that he will not become a burden to anyone. The retiring person hopes to find enjoyment and interests and that as he grows still older he will be able to find serenity and contentment. There is concern lest he become invalided or senile and hope that death will intervene before such eventualities. Completing life in an old-age home or a mental hospital, separated from family and friends, is a dreaded possibility, but even this often seems preferable to burdening those one loves.

A couple have by now become extremely closely related and interdependent. Their major interests center in one another and they often hope to end their lives at the same time, believing it too late to again achieve a sense of completion without a spouse. The elderly person wishes to see his children well established in life and his grandchildren well on their way. The family and descendants assume increasing importance for the elderly person who, expecting little from his own future, finds major satisfactions from their achievements and happiness and increasingly lives more and more through their lives. Friends are dwindling and as those who remain become limited in their activities, the family members—brothers, sisters, and children—assume increasing importance. Less immediate relatives may also be seen more frequently, for their common backgrounds furnish topics of interest and form new bonds between them.

Many marriages have already been broken by the death of one partner by the time a person becomes elderly. Because of the higher death rates among men and the tendency for husbands to be older than wives, 50 per cent of the wives and 20 per cent of the husbands have lost their spouses.[2] When both partners continue into old age, sooner or later the invalidism or death of one brings the need for another major adjustment. It often forms a critical juncture, for the couple have managed through their interdependence upon one another; and their familiarity and devotion have eased the way. The old person must not only assimilate the loss of a partner who has become an integral part of his life, but he must often also adjust to becoming dependent on others. The woman is usually better able to manage by herself than the man who has not learned domestic skills. Both retirement and the loss of a spouse provoke periods of stress when it appears that an elderly person is particularly prone to incapacitation or death.

The Aged Population as a Social Problem

Various societies have dealt with the aged in various ways.[5] Economic considerations are a potent factor in shaping the traditional position of the elderly in a society. The Eskimo of the far north, who live an arduous existence in an environment that scarcely supports their small, isolated families, cannot afford to provide for the infirm. When the aged person—and people age early under the demanding conditions—feels that he has become useless, he goes off by himself to freeze to death on the ice.* In the tropics, where nature's abundance makes the care of an additional person no hardship, the society can afford to be more benevolent. The elderly can lead a simple life helping to care for the young children. The Chinese have—or had—tended to revere the aged, who carry the responsibility for making the important decisions for the extended family. They have learned in their ancient civilization that they cannot afford to neglect the accumulated experience and knowledge of how life should be conducted, particularly during periods of stress. In the United States we have done rather poorly with our aged, and hundreds of thousands have been rather unnecessarily herded into institutions largely because no other provisions for them existed. The wisdom of the past is less valuable in our changing society, but the family structure with the isolated nuclear family that is geographically and socially mobile leaves little room for the dependent aged. Homes have little surplus space and rents are often paid in terms of the number of rooms. It is also important that there are few clear-cut roles for the elderly to provide them with a sense of being useful. Still, before we blame ourselves too readily we must recognize that no society has previously been confronted by an equivalent problem. In 1963 over eighteen million, or about one tenth of the population, were over the age of sixty-five. The responsibil-

---

* An anecdote related in the book *The Top of the World* [4] indicates that the stoic measure is not carried out gladly. The grandmother in the story goes out to sit on the ice when a grandchild is born and there is another mouth to feed. Just after she leaves, the parents, who had never before seen an infant, as can well happen in their isolated existence, came to believe that their toothless newborn was defective and incapable of survival. They ran out to give the infant to the grandmother to take along with her. She realized that she was still necessary to the naïve couple and, telling them that she knew how to make the child get teeth, returned to live a few years longer.

ity for those below sixteen and over sixty-five falls to just about the equivalent number of persons between these ages.

The increasing size of the aged population presents one of the major social problems of contemporary society. It has developed more rapidly than measures designed to meet it. In 1840 the life expectancy of an infant was forty years. By 1900 it had increased seven years, but by 1930 it had risen abruptly to sixty and by 1950 to sixty-eight years. In 1950 there were ten million people over sixty-five, but in 1963 there were nine million over seventy-five. It is a problem created largely by the advances in medicine.

Medical science has not only changed the nature of the practice of medicine but the structure of society itself. Still, organized medicine has been more than reluctant to turn its attention to the problem it has created, either through preparing physicians to care for the aged patient properly, or through supporting measures to provide suitable medical care for the aged as a group. Although the major interests of students who enter medicine continue to be in curing patients, they find that they are engaged in a task of caring for more and more patients whom they will not cure but must seek to help. Medicine has become increasingly caught up with problems of invalidism, disabilities due to chronic illnesses, with problems of the aged and the prevention of the infirmities that come with age. The task, of course, transcends the problems of medicine, and many liberal policies of government concerned with social security measures have not been brought about by increasingly liberal beliefs on the part of politicians but through the need for measures to cope with the changing age distribution in the population. The older voter, who has never been considered radical or even liberal, has managed to mobilize the collective power of the elderly to make it possible for retired persons to have a means of living without having to fall back on family or institutional charity.

The expansive prosperity of the United States has not yet benefited the majority of the elderly. For the year 1962 the median income for the unmarried, who make up approximately half of the population over sixty-five, was a paltry $1,130; and for the married couples, who generally are younger, but $2,875. Almost 30 per cent of married couples over sixty-five had an income of less than $2,000.[2] Not even graduate students can manage on such incomes!* Medicare is now helping to provide for health needs; and social security benefits are being increased gradually.

* These incomes include the benefits that 70 per cent of the aged population received under old-age, survivors', and disability benefits in 1962.

As retirement insurance and various pension funds instituted in labor contracts become more effective with the accumulation of benefits, the current dire situation will be eased for a sizable segment of the population.

The Elderly: Retirement

At the start of old age, the impairments of health do not usually form a dominant problem. The man who is retiring may still be perfectly capable of continuing at work for some years. The retirement ages of sixty-five or sixty-seven have been set arbitrarily, and the wisdom of such inflexible policies, both for industry and the individual, has often been challenged. They provide assurance that persons who are failing do not impede progress by their presence, and they eliminate the need for individual decisions that may seem unjust to the person affected. The questions of moment concern how the person will afford the imposed retirement and how he will find interests that make life meaningful to him. Many observers have been struck by the frequency with which sudden deaths occur soon after retirement, particularly in persons whose entire way of life had been bound up in a specialized occupation and who found little satisfaction in other areas of living. Sudden complete retirement appears to be a menace for many, to be avoided when possible in favor of a gradual transition. Many business firms and other institutions provide for such partial retirements, but the decision is not open for many to make. An alternative lies in proper preparation for retirement many years in advance through gaining interests and hobbies or even preparing for a second and less demanding occupation to pursue after retirement. One of the best assurances of good health for an elderly person comes through keeping occupied with matters of some real interest.

Many persons look forward to retirement, particularly if their economic needs are assured, as a time when they will be free of responsibility, routine, or a job that has become drudgery. The person feels certain that he will not be bored, but will have time to fish, go to ball games, visit, and travel. Soon the days are empty or lead nowhere and the purposelessness of life weighs heavily on him. The couple who had never before spent so much time together now find a dearth of things to say and do. The wife is unaccustomed to having her husband hang around, often disrupting her activities. The life is unimportant and the person feels unimportant to himself. He is apt to grow touchy, feeling neglected and unwanted. He becomes depressed and resentful but blames himself for having little to offer, or irritable and paranoid, believing that others do not want him around. He grows annoyed by his wife and annoying to his wife, whose way of life has not changed markedly as her major readjustment took place when her children left home. Fortunately, many people now are paying more attention to how they will spend their old age long before they retire. They set aside very specific things to do and ventures to undertake. They travel and become involved in community organizations. It can be a good time of life if a person keeps busy but does not feel pushed. There is time to be sociable, to see the grandchildren, to read, and to garden. Money has been saved for trips to some of the many places a couple has long wished to visit. Yet it goes best if there is a schedule and when somehow there is never quite enough time to fit in all of the things that one would still like to do.

Satisfaction after retirement concerns more than finding ways of filling days, and it involves a general attitude toward the end of life. For some it is not just a period of decline and waiting, even though they recognize their waning abilities and increasing limitations. It is still a period of growth when the experience and wisdom they have accumulated can be used and there is time to contemplate, observe, and join the many strands together. One gains an impression that persons who continue some sort of productive activity remain alert longest. Some persons, either because of their inner capacities or their fortunate heredity, seem to go on forever; Chief Justice Holmes, for example, remained a brilliant and active jurist into his nineties, even as his father, Oliver Wendell Holmes, the physician and poet, remained a productive writer. Some men, such as Titian, Frank Lloyd Wright, Picasso, and Somerset Maugham, seemed to become more productive as they aged, perhaps because they felt freer to express themselves. Winston Churchill first really came into his own and achieved greatness at an age when most men are retired. A medical scientist and medical school dean kept busy with national medical affairs for fifteen years after his retirement. When he was almost ninety the dean assured a colleague who had not seen him in two years that his health was good, adding that of course he had had a small coronary occlusion and a bit of cancer removed from his gut in the interval, but that a few things remained to be done before he would be ready to call it quits. Such men have lived fully and continue to make the most of what life offers until the end. However, they form a tiny minority, for very few have their assets and inner resources. Yet many who are less well endowed will still seek to experience life actively and enjoy it rather than fall into despair. Even in old age there can be no standing still; waiting or not utilizing one's resources leads to stagnation and regression.

It is difficult to change patterns established throughout a lifetime, particularly when there is little need to keep pace. The habitual ways do not suit the changing conditions. The old person becomes anxious about new untried methods and grows increasingly conservative, wishing to use the ways that have proven adaptive but which now make him less capable of mastering new tasks. The need to do things differently grows burdensome. There is a desire for respite from change, and enjoyment is sought with old friends in remembering the old days when the world was sane, or more adventuresome, according to the person's disposition.

Increasing Dependency and Senescence

Retirement with its benefits and disadvantages usually requires the first major readjustment, but the elderly person eventually becomes increasingly dependent on others. He becomes old rather than elderly. The change in status is difficult for many to assimilate. The person who had provided for his children and guided them now becomes dependent on them. Self-esteem derived from self-sufficiency is undermined. While little difficulty arises when firm family relationships exist, the dependency commonly provokes anxiety and friction. The old person may react by increasing assertiveness, or with feelings that his children are ungrateful, and is eaten by resentments. Some become so insistent upon not becoming a burden that their family worries about their well-being. Indeed, as a person progresses into advanced age, his care becomes a burden, even though it may be willingly accepted by children who provide for a loved parent. It can, however, be a time when old injuries are consciously or unconsciously repaid. Not all children feel devotion to their parents and many give grudgingly and gain satisfaction from dominating a parent who once dominated them. Children who were glad to get away from home because of unhappiness with their parents will not be pleased to have the parents rejoin them. Shakespeare's keen portrayal of the problems of advanced age in *King Lear* offers a dramatic example of the woes that can follow dependency upon hostile children; and of how the failing judgment of a proud and rigid man can lead him into such a dilemma. The elderly person is rightfully concerned over losing his autonomy and becoming financially dependent. When independence goes, some individuality soon follows.

The change toward a more restricted, conservative, and rigid pattern of living is complicated by the increasing limitations imposed by the changes in the brain that are part of the process of aging. When the loss of cortical cells and brain tissue occurs gradually, it imposes limitations but it also helps protect the individual against the impact of the inevitable misfortunes that come with age and the concerns over the approach of death. In a way, the dropping out of the brain cells parallels the dropping out of the ties to important persons that had made life meaningful and helps life taper off gently.

Improved living conditions and advances in medicine, particularly in the use of prosthetic aids, have made it possible for an increasing proportion of the elderly to enjoy their remaining years. Physical deficiencies eventually occur in everyone. The presbyopic diminution in visual accommodation that occurs in the forties is offset by eyeglasses. The cataracts of old age can be removed and adequate vision restored. Some loss in auditory acuity occurs in all, and deafness can become an extremely serious problem. In some respects, deafness is a greater handicap than loss of vision, as it cuts off communication, turns the person more and more inward, and increases misunderstandings. Deaf people can be particularly troublesome to others and arouse more annoyance than the blind. The person feels left out and, characteristically, any tendencies toward suspiciousness increase. The electronic hearing aid has provided a major advance in maintaining pliability in the aged and in permitting them to relate to others. Still, it is not simple for an elderly person to adjust to a hearing aid, and it properly requires education before the hearing impairment becomes severe and while the person is not too rigid to accept the new appliance. The use of dentures has become so widespread that currently it is difficult to realize how the absence of teeth can not only impair the pleasures derived from eating but also affect health by provoking nutritional deficits. The prostatic enlargement that led many men to end their lives in misery can now readily be remedied by surgery even in advanced age. The common occurrence of osteoarthritic changes in the joints brings some limitation to virtually all elderly people and in some becomes a major source of invalidism which unfortunately cannot be helped appreciably and thus becomes a major cause of dependency on others.

Senility

Health can fail in many ways and can provoke rather striking changes in the person who finds limitation difficult and dependency hard to bear. Still, it is the inevitable changes that occur in the brain that are most pertinent here because of their impact upon the critical integrative functions.

Senile and arteriosclerotic changes lead to a gradual loss of cells in the cerebral cortex. Large blood vessels may occlude, causing apoplexy or a "stroke"; and if an area essential to symbolic activities is damaged, intellectual capacities are seriously affected. Indeed, some decline in intellect begins in the thirties, but it is relatively insignificant until the sixties and becomes marked in the seventies. However, the extent of the decrement varies widely; some individuals suffer appreciable deterioration even before reaching sixty, whereas in others special tests must be used to demonstrate the deficits even in advanced age. Knowledge learned in the past and even habitual ways of solving problems tend to be retained, whereas abilities to think out new solutions to problems and new techniques are more clearly impaired.* As many persons in their prime seldom learn new ways of solving problems and tend to rely on what they learned earlier in life, the intellectual impairment in old age may not be apparent. Suggestions that an elderly person is mentally limited are often angrily refuted by relatives. One may note, though, how a man in his seventies who can take care of himself capably is unable to help his six-year-old grandson piece together a simple jigsaw puzzle. The child finally masters the task while the grandfather finds means of hiding his failure. The difficulties are usually most apparent in memory functions. Although it is often said of an elderly person that he is intact except for memory failures, careful testing will demonstrate a more general limitation even before memory deficiencies become obvious.†

Memory Impairments

Elderly people, as is well known, spend an increasing amount of time thinking and talking about the past. It seems natural that as they feel out of the run of things, they should turn back to the days when life was

---

* Kurt Goldstein, in explaining why certain capacities are retained and others lost in brain-damaged persons, including many aged persons, considered that the brain-damaged person can no longer take an abstract approach to problems but could still think concretely.[1] However, a more clear-cut difference exists between retention of what was previously learned and the diminution in abilities to solve problems at the present time. The general vocabulary and general information tend to be retained and form a measure of former intellectual capacities, and new tasks that must be solved with minimal reliance on past learning (such as the block design test or digit symbol test) offer a measure of current intellectual capacities.[3]
† The Wechsler Adult Intelligence Scale (WAIS) takes this anticipated decline into consideration in providing a measure of what an elderly person's intelligence level had been.

more rewarding and enjoyable, and when events had a deeper impact upon them. When the future holds little, and thinking about it arouses thoughts of death, interest will turn regressively to earlier years. Still, in most persons who become very old, the defect is more profound. The person becomes unable to recall recent events and lives more and more in the remote past, as if a shade were being pulled down over recent happenings, until eventually nothing remains except memories of childhood. This type of memory failure depends on senile changes in the brain and is perhaps the most characteristic feature of senility. We do not properly understand why earlier memories are retained while more recent happenings are lost.

If a person lives long enough, the time may come when he not only lives in the past but acts as though he were in the past, and then he is no longer capable of caring for himself and must be considered psychotic. Thus, a man in his eighties talked about little except events of his boyhood in a rural community. The failure of his memory was obvious. When a friend who had been a history professor visited him, the old gentleman, remaining a proper host, turned the conversation to the American history he had learned in a one-room schoolhouse. However, he would stop and ask the former professor, "You know who Abe Lincoln is, don't you?" and "You have heard of Ben Franklin, haven't you?" He could not put together his appreciation of his visitor's profession and his realization that the professor obviously knew the rudimentary facts he could still recall. Yet, after his guest departed, he was able to take a bus to another part of the city, get a hair cut, buy his cigars, and find his way home without difficulty. In contrast, an ancient lady in a mental hospital behaves very differently. A doctor who has looked after her for several years visits her. She greets him by offering him a chair and saying, "My father will be right down. Yes, he is the minister and will be glad you've come to talk about building the new church." She sits down, waits, and wonders if her visitor would like some tea. After he declines, she waits a few minutes longer, goes to the door and says, "I don't know what's keeping Father. I'll go and call him again." She walks out and with the change in scene completely forgets about her physician, who must fetch her from another room, where she sits looking at a magazine. This woman does not just talk about the remote past but lives in it and is therefore disoriented as to time and place and requires constant supervision.*

* However, one may be fooled by one's preconceptions. An elderly man of seventy-six was brought into the hospital in heart failure and was completely disoriented.

Diminution in Impulse Control

The failing intellectual abilities may also become manifest in diminished control over impulses and emotions; frequent displays of anger or distrust may make it difficult for others to get along with the aged person. Sexual drives or sexual sensations may no longer be properly controlled. The old person may indulge in masturbatory activity, which can embarrass others. Occasionally, an old man makes sexual advances to women, perhaps more frequently to young children. Though such sexual activity usually has a childlike character consisting of exhibitionism, voyeurism, or attempts to be masturbated, it can create serious difficulties. Elderly women may also be troubled by sexual sensations and avoid situations that arouse them. Such feelings may be heightened by irritation in the vaginal area that comes with senile atrophy of the mucous membranes. Their sexual urges are rarely expressed aggressively, but may create shame and concern over masturbation.

The change from old age to senility, if it occurs, may take place gradually as brain cells drop out, or the break may come suddenly. During an illness such as pneumonia or heart failure the diminished oxygen supply to the brain, which would have no permanent effect upon a younger person, sounds the death knell for degenerating brain cells. Or a drug given for an illness affects the brain but instead of causing a transient toxic dysfunction destroys cells and the person never recovers; or the margin of adjustment had been so narrow that once mental disorganization takes place the person cannot regain his equilibrium. Such senile breaks are often precipitated by an emotional crisis or a change in the life situation that requires readjustments beyond the old person's capacities. A man's wife dies and he cannot care for himself and grows confused in the attempt; or after moving into a new home he cannot orient himself to the strange surroundings; or the children with whom he lives quarrel, or turn against him and blame him for their difficulties, and he cannot cope with the conflict and emotional turmoil around him. Kurt Goldstein[1] has emphasized the importance of "catastrophic reactions"

After the heart failure had subsided and his brain again received sufficient oxygen, he appeared to be oriented and rational. However, since he kept insisting that as he was ready to return home his mother would drive over and pick him up, his physicians decided to keep him a few weeks longer to see if his mental state would improve further. Then one day, somewhat to their chagrin, his mother of ninety-five drove over from a town some hundred miles away, accompanied by her ninety-seven-year-old sister, and took their little boy home.

in the behavior of brain-damaged persons, including the senile. When such persons are confronted by a task beyond their capacities, the resultant frustration causes mental disorganization that carries over into subsequent efforts. The confusion can perpetuate itself as the disability spreads to other capacities. The reaction can be halted by simplifying the environment and the tasks demanded of the person.

The Need for a Stable Environment

An old person requires a reasonably stable environment in which he feels secure; and as he grows still older, calm and simplicity in surroundings where things remain in familiar patterns. Shakespeare recognized such factors in his portrayal of King Lear's insanity. Although Lear displayed poor judgment, he functioned reasonably well until he was cast out of his home by the daughters he had favored and trusted. When he became enraged and found himself in strange surroundings, he became disorganized and behaved in a senile, confused manner. Typically, when the weather turned fair again and he found shelter in the love of his faithful daughter, Cordelia, he again became reasonably well integrated.

It seems necessary to emphasize again that not all persons become senile, even at very advanced ages. A person of ninety can be alert and keep himself usefully occupied, even though he can rarely remain self-sufficient. Still, those who are mentally intact are likely to grow somewhat depressed as the relationships to others that made life meaningful are broken by the deaths of relatives and friends, and they come to feel unnecessary, even if not unwanted. However, not all such feelings that death would be welcome are indications of depression. Death is usually less feared by the very old, who may regard it as a haven from the efforts required to continue enfeebled living, and preferable to the senescence that looms ahead. A man of eighty, who started to distribute his possessions in expectation of dying, was still alert and cheerful. At the family's request, his physician reassured him about his health and advised him that as he might well live another ten to twenty years he should not give away so much of his wherewithal. He told his doctor that were it not sinful he would pray to die soon: he was not downhearted but he had led a full life, his children were all married, and as almost all of his generation were dead, he could wish for nothing more except to escape becoming a burden to himself and those he loved.*

* A young physician, social worker, or clinical psychologist may believe that very little can be done to help persons of advanced age with emotional or social prob-

The Need for Adequate Social Measures

It is estimated that by 1980 there will be twenty-five million persons in the United States over sixty-five.[6]

For a large proportion of them, life will finally end in a twilight stage after some years that are neither happy nor unhappy. Many will move beyond feelings of despair at critical losses. Their lives narrow as relatives and friends die and they feel themselves anachronisms without a proper place or purpose. Thoughts and interests increasingly become directed backward into the past. A new egocentricity develops as concerns over security and prestige engender pettiness and miserliness. Without interests that draw outward, concerns over bodily functions increase in importance. Health becomes a major topic of conversation, and feelings of being neglected can lead to an increase in complaints over failing health. Release from striving turns into stagnation in those who were not prepared when they were younger to pursue interests of their own. Even as life draws to a close a person still requires self-esteem and a purpose that provides meaning beyond the day, week, or month. An ability to look forward to a meaningful future, for others if not for the self, helps counter apathy and promotes alertness. The time-honored means of finding purpose in age has been offered by religions. They teach either hope in a life after death or the subordination of the individual to a higher and ultimate good. Religion, when meaningful, has provided solace, hope,

---

lems. However, because many elderly persons expect so little and because their needs are limited, a great deal can often be accomplished briefly. Such efforts are not directed toward profound personality changes. Thus, a seventy-six-year-old man who was hospitalized for intractable bronchial asthma was found to be sensitive to dog and cat dander. When he was told that he would be able to return home if he got rid of his two dogs and four cats, he exploded and insisted on seeing a psychiatrist. He told the psychiatrist that the recommendation was nonsense. He had known he was allergic to cats and dogs for many years, always had these animals in the house, but had not suffered from asthma since he was fourteen. At fourteen he was allergic to horses but more to the riding master who was having an affair with his widowed mother. He stopped being asthmatic when he left home and went to live with his aunt. Now he was allergic to alcohol—to his wife's drinking, for when intoxicated she would start cursing him, make suicidal attempts, and leave him feeling desperate. He was too old to cope with her, and too old to live by himself. He needed her. It turned out that his wife, who was twenty years younger than he, was now very upset because she feared her husband's death and being left alone, even as she had felt abandoned when her father had died shortly before she married. Some psychotherapeutic work with the wife, but also bringing a housekeeper into the home, changed the entire situation.

and a way of life in old age; but if it is mere form rather than a vital part of a person's life it may do little more than teach resignation to an unhappy lot. Religion appears to serve best, even in old age, when it continues to be a way of life rather than becoming a way of dying.

The elderly will increasingly form one of medicine's and society's major problems. The preservation of life and lengthening of the life span by medical science become dubious achievements unless the added years can be reasonably satisfactory. Still, many measures have been instituted to help alleviate the situation; and an understanding of the elderly person's assets, needs, and difficulties can help guide the expansion of such measures. Retirement insurance, private, industrial, and governmental, has started to alter the situation. It is no longer necessary for the employed to support the retired as completely as formerly. Although social security measures lag behind those of most other industrialized nations, a firm start has been made. In providing for the later years while he is still working, a person helps assure his security and his future independence from charitable help. Still, for many it is better to work as long as possible, and it became amply clear during World War II that many useful roles can be found for the aged. Permitting the elderly person to work by choice is a very different matter from having him burdened by a need to work out of necessity, plagued by fears that disability or failing skills will leave him impoverished. Despite efforts in the direction of permitting voluntary continuation of work, the increasing automation of industry augurs earlier rather than later retirement. There is, however, increasing awareness that along with providing financial security for later life, it is also necessary to foster interests while one is still young that will enable life to be more meaningful in old age. Still, if it is difficult to interest educated groups and executives in such preparation, it is far more difficult with the factory worker whose life has been narrowed by performance of rather routine work over many years.

The changing family structure presents another major problem. It is very difficult for three, or sometimes four, generations to live in the shrinking contemporary house. Here again retirement and social security payments have helped the situation, for many families welcome the additional income that the elderly can provide. They do not, however, furnish a real place in the home. The couple who provide a parent or grandparent with a home may find their lives limited by so doing. Even though the elderly woman can be more useful in a home than the elderly man, many families find that having two women trying to run a household is one too many, particularly when the older one cannot give up her prerogatives to the younger.

Several developments that increase the opportunities of the elderly will serve as examples of future potentialities. The migration of persons of all economic levels to Florida and the Southwest has been meaningful.* They seek a climate where they are not restricted by winter weather and where housing can be less expensive. In the process, cities like St. Petersburg have found it economically advantageous to make special provisions for the aged, and furnish examples of how to foster their comfort and happiness. The hotels and the community as a whole find ways of keeping these guests or residents active and well occupied. The hotels provide movies and entertainment, foster collective activities, and see that the guests are introduced and brought together. Doctors in attendance can be readily obtained at night. The sidewalks are built without curbs, benches are provided for those who tire, and wheelchairs are readily available. New friendships develop to replace those that have vanished. As lessened mental agility also means less initiative, stimulation to activity needs to be provided by others. There is good reason, aside from the climate, for the elderly to move to St. Petersburg.

Golden age clubs exist in many communities. Here elderly persons have a meeting place where they find companionship which does not require individual initiative to establish. Hobbies and various activities are fostered and taught. Many old people, unfortunately, are reluctant to give in and let others assist them in finding friends and activities, or to admit that they have reached a stage where they need to change their habitual patterns. Many who do, find new sources of interest and an escape from increasing loneliness.

The good modern home for the aged can be turned into a welcome haven for those who no longer have a home, who can no longer fend for themselves, or who do not wish to burden their children. It need not be a last resort of outcasts. A modern home provides room in which individuals or couples can retain some of their own possessions and have a place of their own. As long as they are able, the elderly people participate in housekeeping and cooking, which gives them a sense of being useful; and recreational and occupational activities are provided that are suited to

---

* However, many find that such moves to more congenial climes deprive them of old friends and haunts. Firm, congenial relationships are usually more important than climate to happiness and contentment, and reliable friendships are not easily made in old age.

their abilities. When they become ill or bedridden and must be removed to an infirmary, they are not cut off from the friends they have made in the institution. There has been a trend to construct hotels in northern cities resembling those in St. Petersburg that are particularly designed for the elderly, but they are few in number and costly. Federally aided housing for the aged, designed with suitable facilities, is now developing rapidly. However, congregation of elderly people into special homes or communities has at least two major shortcomings. It tends to separate them from their children and other relatives who form their strongest link to a meaningful life, and it segregates them from younger people. The elderly can carry out many useful functions if they are not segregated. They baby-sit, or care for the homes, animals, and plants of people who go away for week-ends; or help cook or garden, make children's clothes, etc. However, living in special facilities for the aged is far better than exile into outmoded mental hospitals and bleak old-age homes.*

The way of life of the elderly reflects the personality configurations established in earlier years, but it is greatly affected by how adaptive capacities are reduced by physical infirmities and mental limitations, as well as by the potentialities afforded by the society to persons as they age and become less able to manage for themselves. The aged person has passed the stage of being procreative and is often beyond being creative, but the type of life he leads and is afforded by others will still profoundly influence those who come after him. His welfare creates concern for his children and grandchildren. His presence in a child's home may cause disturbances and conflict that create stresses in the child's marriage and affect how his grandchildren are raised. He may serve as a beneficent figure for identification to grandchildren, and liaisons between grandparents and grandchildren frequently form important influences that convey traits and interests over an intervening generation. The way in which he leads his last years provides an example and a warning to his descend-

* The allocation of thousands upon thousands of the aged into mental hospitals forms one of the more disgraceful chapters in American social history. Although it is probably correct that few if any were sent to mental hospitals who were not seriously depressed or disorganized, many became incapacitated largely because of lack of suitable places to live and of means of support. Once they are hospitalized, the lack of personal attention, the barren surroundings, and the depressing atmosphere impede recovery, and often lead to apathy and progressive deterioration. In contrast, in a good home for the aged in which socialization and activity is carefully fostered, only a very occasional person has to be sent to a mental hospital, even when many are in their nineties.

ants and influences how they provide for their own later years. Further, how the old people are treated by their children commonly furnishes an illustration to grandchildren of how persons treat parents. The aged may be close to the end of life, but the way in which they live and let live will continue to influence life.

References

1. Kurt Goldstein, *The Organism* (Boston: Beacon Press, 1963).
2. Group for the Advancement of Psychiatry, "Psychiatry and the Aged: An Introductory Approach," Report No. 59, 1965.
3. Theodore Lidz, James R. May, and Christopher Tietze, "Intelligence in Cerebral Deficit States and Schizophrenia Measured by Kohs Block Test," *Archives of Neurology and Psychiatry*, 48 (1942), 568–582.
4. Hans Ruesch, *The Top of the World* (New York: Pocket Books, 1959).
5. Leo W. Simmons, *The Role of the Aged in Primitive Society* (New Haven: Yale University Press, 1945).
6. United States Bureau of the Census, "Current Population Reports," Series 25, No. 241, Interim Revised Projections of the Population of the United States by Age and Sex, 1965 and 1970 (Washington, D.C.: U. S. Government Printing Office, 1962).

Suggested Reading

Maxwell Gitelson, "The Emotional Problems of Elderly People," *Geriatrics*, 3 (1948), 135–150.

Alvin I. Goldfarb, "Patient-Doctor Relationship in Treatment of Aged Persons," *Geriatrics*, 19 (1964), 18–23.

Group for the Advancement of Psychiatry, "Psychiatry and the Aged: An Introductory Approach," Report No. 59, 1965.

Paul H. Hoch and J. Zubin (eds.), *Psychopathology of Aging* (New York: Grune & Stratton, 1961).

Sidney Levin and Ralph J. Kahana (eds.), *Psychodynamic Studies on Aging: Creativity, Reminiscing, and Dying* (New York: International Universities Press, 1968).

Edward J. Stieglitz, *Geriatric Medicine* (3rd ed.; Philadelphia: J. B. Lippincott, 1954).

CHAPTER 18 ⁴

Death

IT MAY SEEM STRANGE for an unconsidered moment to conclude this guide to the life cycle with a chapter on death. But death is part of the life cycle, an inevitable outcome of life that brings closure to a life story; and, because the human from early childhood is aware of his ultimate death, it influences his development and his way of life profoundly. Then, the physician—as also the nurse and medical social worker—has intimate relationships with death: he confronts death as the immortal antagonist against whom he shields his patient for a time; but when the outcome becomes inevitable the physician again turns midwife to ease the passage through the gate of life, this time to return his patient into the dark womb of oblivion where he will find surcease from pain and striving.

The topic is large, the subject of countless religious and philosophic treatises and, of late, of psychological and sociological studies.[1,5] Here, we shall but briefly direct attention to the importance of considering death when seeking to understand a person's life. Traditional psychoanalysis has considered concerns over dying as manifestations of either separation or castration anxieties; and Freud believed that a death instinct [3,4] draws man toward death and the cessation of all striving. He came to consider the struggle between Eros and Thanatos fundamental to understanding behavior—a view that attained limited acceptance.*

Changing Attitudes toward Death through the Life Cycle

Death has a different meaning and impact on a person at different periods of life. The child usually becomes aware in a meaningful way of death as the end of life at about the age of four or five. His concerns are clearly an aspect of separation anxiety; and fears that his mother will die arouse as much concern as his own death. It is a fear of being isolated without a protecting and nurturing person and reflects the child's incompletion and the lack of clear boundaries between himself and his mother. It can mount to become a serious problem in the insecure child, perhaps particularly in a child whose mother has left him for a prolonged period in his second or third year. But many children will also puzzle about death, and experience any uncanny feeling in trying to grasp its essence—the beginnings of an "existential" anxiety.† Many children find solace or release from such anxieties through belief in a life after death in which they will continue to have their parents. A patient recalled what he believed was a milestone in his maturation. Shortly after his marriage, war had broken out and his native country was attacked; on his way into combat he found himself wishing to believe in a life after death but not, as in childhood, from anxiety, but rather because of his love for his wife and the intensity of his desire to be certain he would again be with her.

The interpretation of fears of death and dying as a form of castration anxiety seems, at times, an attempt to handle a pervasive source of con-

---

* An excellent discussion of the confused concepts of aggression, destructiveness, and the death instinct in psychoanalytic theory can be found in Robert Waelder's chapter "Destructiveness and Hatred" in his *Basic Theory of Psychoanalysis*.[8]

† Thus, a patient recalled how at the age of six he suddenly stopped playing with a construction set while his mother was singing a melancholy tune; he felt confronted by an intangible but impossible something as he suddenly thought to himself, "Death—what does it feel like, what happens?" After a time he asked his mother, but felt that her remarks about God were simply evasive, and he went about in something of a daze, seeking to avoid thinking about it. Similar episodes returned upon occasion later in childhood and still had repercussions in his adult life. The interpretation of these episodes in terms of an earlier separation anxiety does not explain away the phenomenon.

cern by changing it into an immature and needless childhood oedipal fear, to consider an ultimate reality by saying, in effect, "Death is no more real than fears that father will castrate you and you are really only suffering from guilt over wishing that your father were dead." Of course, such wishes are sources of anxiety that one will be castrated or die, but they do not explain why death is feared. Death can also seem like castration when a man is cut down in the prime of his life, thereby rendered impotent to carry out his strivings and hopes, and to find fulfillment in love. Death is the reaper with a scythe who cuts off life. Death also provides a challenge and a test, particularly to men who must prove to themselves that they can face death and not run or flinch—the essence of bravery. Perhaps a person feels that he must conquer death through flaunting it, or at least through looking straight into its hollow eye sockets before he can feel man enough to live.

With marriage and parenthood, concerns over death transcend the self, even as do concerns in other areas. A father—or mother—will be concerned over what will happen to his spouse and children should he die, and take precautions for their sakes as much as for his own. We also see how despite self-preservative drives parents readily give up their lives to save their children. Indeed, anyone with combat experience soon realizes that men will die for their group; and many will seek to preserve their group's good opinion of them at the risk or sacrifice of their lives. Moreover, many men are willing to fight in wars because they consciously or unconsciously believe that preserving a way of life takes precedence over preserving a life.

A person's attitude toward death usually changes as he ages. To the old person, death becomes a familiar. He has had much experience with it, has thought a good deal about it, and eventually expects the final visitor and may even await his call. Whether the desire for death can be considered an "instinct" is a moot question. The elderly often tire of life and simply wish to drop out of the circle of the dance.*

---

* Freud believed during World War I, when life was growing burdensome, that although man could desire the death of an alien, and even unconsciously wish for the death of one he loves, he has profoundly repressed ideas of his own mortality. He asked if it would not "be better to give death the place in actuality and in our thoughts which properly belongs to it—it has the merit of taking somewhat more into account the true state of affairs, and of making life again more endurable for us. To endure life remains, when all is said, the first duty of all living beings. Illusion can have no value if it makes this more difficult for us . . . If you would endure life, be prepared for death." [2] A somber note and view of life, but one that can fortify.

The Choice of Life and Death

Of the essence is that man alone is aware of death and can make the decision whether he wishes to live or die. Indeed, he repeatedly faces the decision unless he makes it once and for all as part of his abiding ethic, as most persons do. Still, human behavior and attitudes can never be comprehended properly unless one realizes that death is often tempting, and that fears of giving way to the desire despite wishes to live are a source of anxiety and various neurotic defenses.* When life grows burdensome, particularly when significant persons are lost, or when resentments become pervasive, death can become tempting.† Religions have dealt with the problem in various ways. The Christian or Mohammedan is assured of a heavenly life after death if life is lived properly or if he dies protecting the religion; but he is threatened by far greater torment than he can possible suffer in this life if he commits suicide. Some, like the Swedenborgians, consider that we are living through purgatory in this life, and must endure it for the sake of the salvation that assuredly follows—for how else can the torments on earth have meaning? The Hindu is tied to the wheel of life, and will be punished for his sins, including suicide, by having lower status in human or animal form in future metamorphoses. He hopes ultimately to achieve Nirvana, an oblivion of absence of stimulation and striving which is akin to our concepts of death. Some consider that the essence of Judaism concerns the affirmation of life despite suffering and tribulations.

The Influence of Death on Ways of Living

The belief in some type of existence after death clearly influences how most persons live. Man is directed by future goals as well as impelled by

---

* The fear of giving in to suicidal impulses as a source of anxiety is perhaps seen most clearly in combat situations where the temptation to have it over with and no longer suffer the anxiety, deprivation, anger, and loss of comrades can become great. The temptation is usually repressed but the wish reappears in nightmares—or is projected in the form of heightened danger from the enemy.[6] Similar conditions arise in civilian life. Suicide is the tenth leading cause of death, and accidental deaths which are not always so "accidental" are another leading cause of death.

† As the most popular soliloquy in the greatest Western drama reflects:

> To be, or not to be, that is the question;
> . . . 'tis a consummation
> Devoutly to be wish'd, to die, to sleep;
> But that dread of something after death,
> Makes us rather bear those ills we have . . .
>   (*Hamlet*, Act III, Sc. 1.)

drives—the carrot motivates as well as the stick. The ethos of Christian beliefs blends with superego dictates and makes conflicts over giving in to unacceptable impulses more poignant by stretching the punishment into eternity. The converse attitude which accepts the death of the mortal body as the end of the individual leads some to "take the cash and let the credit go" and seek what pleasure they can while there is still the chance; or to learn to fortify themselves stoically against inevitable contingency. Although which religious or philosophic attitude a person embraces is determined partly by the culture, the family, and the formal education, it is also influenced by basic attitudes concerning trust and distrust, anxiety and security, hopefulness and pessimism, passivity and aggressivity, etc., established in the early years of life. Nevertheless religion, and philosophy, either explicitly or tacitly, usually concern mortality and contribute to a way of life and personality development.*

The desire for some type of continuity into the future is pervasive, particularly in societies in which the person is an individual rather than primarily a member of a collectivity.† The individual seeks many ways "to cheat drowsy death" and somehow perpetuate himself—that is, his name, his ideas, his ways of doing things, his "flesh and blood"—from oblivion. The desire for descendants in whom one lives, who will carry the name or keep alive even a spark of memory of one's existence, has been a significant directive in virtually all societies, and influences marriage and divorce as well as extramarital procreation. Some seek to leave their tangible imprint on the world through the structures they build, be they indestructible pyramids or more useful bridges, dams, or buildings; some leave behind the children of their fantasy in poems and story; some strive to insure that posterity will know that the course of history changed because they lived and conquered, and some because of what they discovered or invented. Others will seek a type of immortality through joining their lives to a more abiding organization, a church, philanthrophic movement, or library or orchestra; or by playing an active part in the conquest of a specific disease or some other scientific problem. The infinitesimal grain in the cosmos becomes part of a visible body and a significant force. The ways of seeking some semblance of immortality are diverse, but how the individual strives for it provides a key to

* As Montaigne expounded in his essay "To Study Philosophy Is to Learn to Die," [7] and concerning which Freud comments in "Thoughts for the Times on War and Death." [2]

† In more collectively oriented societies, the continuity and reputation of the family, the city, or the nation may take precedence over individual life.

understanding many aspects of his behavior. Some individuals clearly and loudly proclaim how they seek to perpetuate themselves, but others almost hide it from themselves, yet still it can be detected from their actions and from what they hold most significant.

The realization of mortality also influences the life pattern by provoking a desire to bring it to a close. The sense of closure may involve finishing a single important job or a more general life task such as building up an estate for one's children or completing an area of scientific investigation to which much of a lifetime has been devoted. It may concern achieving some final years of relaxed living in order to observe the world or enjoy the fruits of a lifetime of effort; or the conscious rounding out of a life story as if it were a novel being told. The finite lifetime provides delimitation that directs an individual toward specific and limited objectives and counters diffusion and unbridled strivings. Death hangs as a reminder to man of his limitations—which he may strive against but with which he must somehow come to terms. It provides the foil for contrasting classical and romantic approaches to living. Life, we may consider, is provided with a frame by death. Death not only influences how the course of life is run, but it lends incisiveness to the meaning of events, sharpens our appreciation of the transitory and of the beauty we would like to hold. Perhaps, above all, it heightens the preciousness of those we love because of their mortality.* It requires of each a willingness to risk pain in committing himself to a meaningful attachment to another, but it also augments the value of such relationships.

To those who reach old age and have attained some wisdom in the process, death often assumes meaning as the proper outcome of life. The world and those who inhabit it have changed. The loved ones are dead or scattered. New ways of doing things have replaced the familiar. The new generation places little value on what is most important. The government piles up debts, encourages the idle, forgets the heroes of the war before the last. Girls act like boys and men dress like women. Life can never contain a moment of inertia, but the ways of the individual begin to congeal. The need to understand differently from earlier in life and to alter standards, ideas, and techniques is resented. Then, too, life brings sorrow and tribulations which are apt increasingly to outweigh the happy occasions. It is time for others to take over, and the old person feels in the way. He has had his run of it, now it is time for others to take the

* Freud considered that man invented ghosts in his desire to preserve loved persons who die.[2]

field. He may appreciate life and living, and his hours may be crowded with fond memories that block new experience, but he grasps that death is nature's way of making possible much life and assuring constant renewal.

Then, too, there is a significant reversal from the child's anxiety about death as some unknown state of separation from parents which would leave the child isolated and intensely alone. The aged person becomes increasingly lonely as he is separated from those who have been most meaningful to him. Death now is no longer perceived as an ultimate loneliness, but rather as an assurance that sooner or later he need no longer feel alone—whether because he believes he will be reunited with others or because it will simply bring an end to all experience.

However, people for the most part and under most circumstances do not wish to die, but cling to life as their most precious possession. They will face death and accept it for the sake of what they cherish—for companions and to preserve honor; but they may also cling to life in concentration camps as long as the faintest glimmer of hope remains. Paradoxically, but understandably, it is those who have never been able to live, either because others have restricted them or because of their own neurotic limitations, who may fear death the most. There are some, even some elderly persons, who not only suffer anxiety but become agitated when they know they are going to die, and who may not only suffer but cause others to suffer with them. Still, people are almost always able to accept the inevitable. It is uncertainty that creates anxiety. Few who know that their death is inevitable and close do not accept the knowledge with resignation.

The Dying Patient

It is an integral part of being a physician to face the dying and to help the patient and his family meet the situation. By and large, physicians have in recent years sought to protect the dying from becoming aware that their fate is sealed. Perhaps, as has been suggested, many who enter medicine are particularly afraid of dying and transfer their own concerns to their patients. A considerable literature has appeared to point out that the physician, in seeking to protect the patient, often overprotects him and creates serious difficulties, and may sometimes be protecting himself rather than the patient from an unpleasant and painful situation.

The care of the dying patient is a large topic that is not really germane to the subject of this book, but it seems worth devoting a few paragraphs to it because of its importance to physicians and paramedical workers, and because of the pathological way in which it is so frequently carried out. The physician cannot find a general rule about whether or not to inform a patient that he has a fatal illness,* for each patient is an individual. He cannot properly cope with the patient's problems in terms of his own fears or of his own religious (or nonreligious) beliefs. An alert physician can usually tell when a patient does not wish to know that he has a fatal condition; and if he is uncertain, he can test out the patient's defenses against recognizing the fact or hearing it. Patients can have strong mechanisms of defense against perceiving what may seem obvious.†

However, all too frequently, attempts to protect the patient have unfortunate and sometimes disastrous effects. A wall of deception is constructed between the patient and his family and friends that keeps them from really communicating at a time when they may wish to be closer than ever before. The patient is prevented from setting his house in order, and commonly he is more concerned about the continuing welfare of his spouse and children than about whether he lives for another few years. Some dying persons also feel that efforts to hide their condition almost succeeded in depriving them of properly experiencing their last experiences, and of understanding what dying is like—something they had wondered about since childhood. Even more unfortunately, the insistence to a patient with a terminal illness that he is not so ill and will recover can confuse the patient, provoke profound distrust, and even lead to disorganization and delusion. The patient is not permitted to believe what he consciously and unconsciously knows to be a fact. A middle-aged woman, who was suffering from metastases in her bones from cancer of the breast, was told that she was suffering from severe

---

* Physicians usually have greater difficulty telling patients that they have a malignancy—that is, a neoplastic illness—than other, even more definitively fatal conditions. Perhaps cancer seems more final and seems to conjure up greater suffering.
† Thus a young physician who had caught a very serious infectious illness from a patient verged on dying for a week. He was aware that he had relatively little chance of recovery but fortified himself by preparing himself for the next week when, he convinced himself, the illness would first reach its height. After recovering, he wondered why he had never been afraid he was about to die. He then recalled that one night when he was most ill, he had been afraid that someone was going to come through the window and shoot him. He had projected the danger from the illness within him to the environment that could be controlled; and at the same time it was a regression to early childhood when he had had such fears of burglars coming in the window to kill him.

arthritis; and when she asked if she did not have metastases, the truth was denied. Eventually, she developed delusions of persecution—in part because she was being persecuted in having the extent of her suffering denied and her knowledge negated, supposedly to spare her unnecessary suffering.

The patient with a terminal illness can usually accept what those around him can accept—albeit sometimes with periods of depression and unhappiness—but he wishes to be assured that he will not undergo prolonged suffering, and this is an assurance that can almost always be given honestly today because of the availability of tranquilizers and narcotics.

The author recently had an experience that will serve to close the discussion of this involved topic. I was asked by friends to see their mother, aged ninety-three, who was slowly dying of a malignancy. They asked that she not be told the diagnosis because their aunt, her favorite sister, had died a slow and painful death from cancer some forty years earlier, and their mother had for many years feared a similar end. The relationship between the mother and her children had been unusually good, but now she was angry and did not even wish to see them. I requested permission from both the family and the attending physician to use my own judgment in managing the situation.

As soon as the amenities were over, and the old lady realized my visit was professional, her anger toward her children burst out. She had thought that she had been a pretty good mother and had always considered her children before her own wishes—but now that she was really helpless, her children had abandoned her. Not one of the three had offered to take her into his home! What would she do? She was well-to-do but how long could she spend $250 to $300 a day for room, nurses, physicians! Apparently they thought she might live for years, but she wished she could die now and have it over with.

This was a sorry ending for a congenial family. The patient was told that her children had not abandoned her, but that she had but a month or two to live and they knew that she could not leave the hospital. She could feel certain that we would not let her suffer unduly, and it was time to prepare for her end. The patient calmed down immediately and asked why in the world her doctor or her children had not told her. Did they think she was a child? She knew she would soon die even if she were not ill. Why not now? Her relationship with her children and grandchildren changed immediately as they could again talk about their past days together, and about plans and hopes for the future. I stopped in to see the patient from time to time during the month she lived. She would tell me tales about New York in the 1880's and 1890's, about her travels in various parts of the world, and about interesting people she had known. She enjoyed reminiscing, as if she were going through a final review of a reasonably happy life.

During one of my visits, she fell asleep for less than a minute and awakened with a start and a puzzled smile. She had been dreaming, a vivid and realistic dream. In the dream her aged mother was living with her, and she was sitting in her rocking chair just as she had sixty years before. Her mother had a set of false teeth for appearances but they were not good for chewing. In the dream the patient and her husband were going to dine at her sister's house. She told her mother she would prepare supper for her and in the dream scraped an apple and made a gruel for her—perhaps just as she once had done in reality—and then she had awakened. The patient was not asked to associate to the content of the dream; but it seemed clear it was the manifestation of a wish, a wish fulfillment. Perhaps it was a wish to be young, or to have her mother again; perhaps it was a wish to be treated by her children as she had treated her mother; but I think it also expressed a desire to be able again to be the useful, nurturant woman she had so long been. In any event, it is the only dream I have heard from a ninety-year-old, and it is a very important and informative dream to me.

References

1. Herman Feifel, *The Meaning of Death* (New York: McGraw-Hill, 1959).
2. Sigmund Freud, "Thoughts for the Times on War and Death" (1915), in *The Standard Edition of the Complete Psychological Works of Sigmund Freud*, Vol. 14 (London: Hogarth Press, 1957).
3. Sigmund Freud, "Beyond the Pleasure Principle" (1920), in *The Standard Edition of the Complete Psychological Works of Sigmund Freud*, Vol. 18 (London: Hogarth Press, 1955).
4. Sigmund Freud, "Why War?" (1933), in *The Standard Edition of the Complete Psychological Works of Sigmund Freud*, Vol. 22 (London: Hogarth Press, 1964).
5. Group for the Advancement of Psychiatry, "Death and Dying: Attitudes of Patient and Doctor," Symposium No. 11, 1965.
6. Theodore Lidz, "Nightmares and the Combat Neuroses," *Psychiatry*, 9 (1946), 37–49.
7. Michael E. de Montaigne, "To Study Philosophy Is to Learn to Die," in *Complete Essays of Montaigne*, trans. Donald M. Frame (Stanford, Calif.: Stanford University Press, 1958).
8. Robert Waelder, *Basic Theory of Psychoanalysis* (New York: International Universities Press, 1960).

Suggested Reading

Herman Feifel, *The Meaning of Death* (New York: McGraw-Hill, 1959).
Group for the Advancement of Psychiatry, "Death and Dying: Attitudes of Patient and Doctor," Symposium No. 11, 1965.

PART III

Patterns and Perspectives

CHAPTER 19

Life Patterns

WE HAVE FOLLOWED the human life cycle, examining the critical tasks of each developmental stage, and how different persons tend to be confronted by similar problems at the same phase of life. We have sought to emphasize the continuity of the process in which progression depends upon how the preceding developmental tasks were surmounted; but also the continuity that arises because the mastery of the tasks of each stage is not an end in itself but subordinate to the goal of the development of a reasonably self-sufficient individual capable of living cooperatively with others and properly rearing his offspring while assuming some responsibility for the welfare of the society. In focusing upon each phase of the life cycle in turn, we have noted that themes or patterns develop in each individual that color and sometimes virtually determine the way in which he responds to the phase-specific tasks and tries to cope with them. In the inordinately complex task of seeking to understand an individual, we can be guided, by finding such repetitive patterns and leitmotifs. We strive to grasp their origins and to perceive the variations in the themes as they recur in differing circumstances.

Out of the multiplicity of factors that enter into the shaping of a life, resultant patterns of living and relating emerge. A theme, or a group of interrelated themes, appears that can be modified and adapted to the stage-specific tasks or to the exigencies that arise. Sometimes the dominant theme results from an early childhood fixation and reiterates itself, unable to develop and lead onward, remaining in the same groove like the needle on a flawed phonograph record. The basic themes are more readily detected in emotionally disturbed persons because they are more set, more clearly repetitive, and perhaps more familiar to the practiced ear that has heard similar themes so often before. Still, repetitive ways of reacting and relating occur in all lives. The meaning of an episode in a life can often be grasped properly only through understanding how it furthers, impedes, or disrupts essential themes.

Understanding a Repetitive Pattern

● Let us consider a woman's behavior that seems absurd as well as pathetic. She had grown up in a home that was miserable as well as impoverished because of her father's severe alcoholism. In late adolescence, she had married an older man, an alcoholic who had been killed in an automobile accident just as she was about to divorce him after ten unhappy years. Now she spends her evenings trying to take care of a man who flees from her into the oblivion of an alcoholic stupor every week-end. She cleans him, bathes him, nurses him back to face the work week, and she is distressed because she has failed to convince him that he needs her and should marry her. She knows that she is foolish, but she feels certain that she can make him happy, satisfy his needs, and wean him from the bottle.

We can seek to understand her repetitive involvement with alcoholic men in a variety of ways. In terms of the structural concept, we might consider that she needs punishment by a strict superego because of her rivalry with her mother for her alcoholic father. In terms of fixation of libidinal investment, we might consider her masochistic behavior to be a reaction formation to anal-sadistic impulses against her father, or we might weigh the oral components of her fixation and emphasize that she identifies with the oral addictive behavior of her alcoholic men and provides the care that she would like to have received from a mothering person. However, focusing upon oral or anal character traits, or upon an abstract balance between superego, ego, and id, provides little specific understanding of this woman and why she is seriously upset because an alcoholic man will not marry her. The term "masochistic" is useful in summarizing some of her basic characteristics, but it is also necessary to note that she behaves masochistically only in the fairly specific context of her need to be made unhappy by alcoholic men.

The woman's compulsion to repeat an unhappy experience with a second alcoholic husband becomes specifically meaningful when the theme is traced back to its childhood origins in her family. In psychotherapy, she recalled the hours she had spent as a little girl with her father, who would tell her wonderful stories of his childhood and of leprechauns while he was repentant and sober between alcoholic bouts; these wonderful hours were disrupted by her mother's scoldings of her father for his idleness and unworldly dreaming. As a girl she had believed that her father was an alcoholic because of her mother's coldness and shrewishness. Her late oedipal fantasies dwelled on what her father would have been like with a different wife: herself, grown up into a sensuous and sensitive woman who could care for his needs. She came to despise her mother as an embittered harridan. Differentiation from her mother became a major developmental motive. She sought to be warm and nurturant, the only person who understood and appreciated her father. In therapy she recalled having had vague fantasies in early adolescence in which her mother would desert the family and leave her to care for it; but her mother remained while her father became a hopeless invalid. The theme developed through her marriage to a man who resembled her father both emotionally and physically. She would prove in the marriage that, had she been her father's wife, her father would have been a very different person. She would demonstrate to herself that she was unlike her mother. Despite her efforts and resolve, she found that her nurturant, protective, and sensual efforts failed. Indeed, in retrospect, she thought it likely that her attempts to be particularly close and protective precipitated her husband's episodes of drinking.

Shortly before her husband's death, she had been forced to recognize that she could no longer tolerate the situation. Her husband was neglecting and mistreating their children, and when drunk he often turned against her and struck her. She was not even as capable as her mother, who had managed to remain with her father and nurse him during his years of chronic illness. Much of the hostility she had felt toward her mother was now directed against herself. She had not only mourned her husband but had become depressed after his death, tending to blame herself for his hapless life and premature end. She emerged from her depressed and somewhat apathetic state when she again became involved with an alcoholic whom she hoped to marry and sought to save. She entered therapy in part because she found herself becoming upset because he avoided marriage, and in part because her priest sized up the situation and urged her to seek help. The priest had recognized her compulsion to repeat a pattern that would lead her into another hopeless and desperate situation. She would continue to try to solve the old problem of proving to herself that she, in contrast to her mother, could have prevented her father's alcoholism. A primary task of psychotherapy was to release the patient from her bondage to such unconscious repetitive and frustrating efforts to solve old problems in the wrong generation, and, through viewing her parents from a more adult and realistic perspective, enable her to gain a new self-image and more mature motivations. The therapeutic task was to overcome a fixation involving a failure to resolve the oedipal situation adequately, but the designation of the problem in such terms means little without the more specific knowledge of the repetitive pattern, how it arose, and how it reappeared in new situations. •

Repetitive Patterns and the Nature of Trauma

Without an appreciation of the nature and force of the life pattern, it often is difficult to grasp the emotional impact of events on a person, or even what is beneficial and what traumatic. A brother's marriage is usually considered a happy event, but a young woman became severely upset when her older brother's marriage upset her lifelong pattern of security operations. As a child of six she had suffered from desperate anxiety when her mother died and the family almost broke up. She had thrown herself into the task of helping her father care for the home and her brothers in order to make it possible for the family to remain together. She feared that unless she constantly proved her usefulness she would be unwanted and sent to an orphanage.

As she grew older she developed little faith in obtaining security through marriage—for as a Negro woman she had seen many men desert their wives. She felt that only relationships between a parent and a child provided security that could be trusted. Her father would never desert her because she was essential to him, caring for him and his household. Still, her father was growing old and death would eventually take him from her. She developed two safeguards against feeling lost and deserted after he died. Marriage was not one of them. Indeed, she refused to marry a persistent suitor, for marriage would take her away from her home. But she sought to have a baby by him out of wedlock, a child to whom she would give so much love that the child would never leave her. In addition, she made a home for her older brother and worked to supplement his income. She filled all of his needs, other than sexual, so that he had no reason to marry. He needed her and would remain with her after her father died. However, her plans went awry. She failed to become pregnant by her boy friend; and while considering finding another who might be more fertile, she had herself examined and found that it was she who was sterile. Then, soon after her father's death, her brother decided to marry—perhaps because her intense solicitude, which included unconscious seductive behavior, frightened him into marriage. Suddenly, the pattern she had developed to insure against the recurrence of being deserted collapsed, in part because of the intensity of her defense.

Repetitive Patterns, Personality, and Ego Functioning

Freud's major contribution, among his many contributions to the understanding of human functioning and malfunctioning, was his elucidation of the limits of man's conscious decision making and of the rationality of his behavior. He clarified the force and scope of unconscious determinants in the service of sexual and aggressive impulses and desires, and demonstrated how the avoidance of anxiety leads to the construction of mechanisms of defense that limit or distort the perception and understanding of reality. The directive capacities of the self that we term ego functions are never free from repressed unconscious influences. At times, the ego is little more than a front serving to maintain self-esteem by transforming underlying irrational motives into an acceptable form. For a time during the development of psychoanalytic theory and practice, the pendulum swung far in the direction of underestimating the role of rational, reality-oriented decision making. Currently, a new theoretic balance has been achieved by an assimilation of studies of cognitive development into psychodynamic theory. However, in studying the limits of reality-oriented behavior—of the capacity of the ego to direct the self by balancing reality needs, id demands, and superego injunctions—we must be concerned with the limits set by the personality configurations and life patterns that emerge during the developmental years.

Psychosexual Fixations and Character

Psychoanalysis has developed two interrelated approaches to the study of personality types and how such personality patterns limit the adaptive range of the individual but at the same time make his ways of reacting and relating more comprehensible and predictable. The first approach is based upon fixations of psychosexual development—originally conceived in terms of libidinal fixation at one or another erogenous zone. Failures to work through the essential developmental tasks of the period result in fixation of interest and attention on these tasks or regressively on those satisfactions gained in an earlier period before the frustrations occurred. Fixation can be taken to mean, as in this volume, that when the tasks of a developmental phase are not mastered adequately the child is unprepared to cope with subsequent developmental tasks and continues to seek fulfillment of the frustrated needs in a repetitive manner. Such fixations can be major determinants of basic life patterns. The major traits of "oral" characters were discussed at the end of the chapter on infancy, and of "anal" characters in the chapter on the toddler. These are the two best-developed categories, but a "urethral" character and a "phallic" character have also been described.* The concept of the "genital" character is not used to describe a personality type but rather to designate more or less normative development in which no serious fixations occur at pregenital phases. Originally the term connoted that the libido was free for mature investment in a gratifying sexual relationship, with pre-

* The concept of the "urethral" character is not well developed. It is related to fixation at a level of urethral erotism—the sexual excitation felt when urinating, perhaps accentuated by irritation from chronic childhood masturbatory play. It relates such burning sensations to burning ambition; and also to the excitement of lighting fires and wishing to extinguish them by urination. Bed wetting is thus related to sexual excitement. The "phallic" character, whose development is related to fixations at the oedipal period, is overly masculine, tending to be a Don Juan, boastful and reckless. The reactive nature of the masculinity becomes apparent after a little study. Incestuous drives are not far beneath the surface, and perverse activities or fantasies are common. The character configuration has been related to fixations caused by castration fears which block the proper resolution of the oedipal conflicts; but it seems more clearly related to a boy's relationship with a mother who focuses her admiration and love on her son's genitalia, which she prizes highly. The penis, so to speak, remains the mother's possession, and the man repetitively seeks admiration through overly masculine behavior, considering his penis a prize that women cannot resist. Women may be termed "phallic" when they habitually use their bodies exhibitionistically as a substitute for the penis they lack; or sometimes the term is used for aggressive women who fantasy and act out fantasies of being dominant masculine persons, either subjugating men or dominating other women homosexually.

genital investments subserving forepleasure to sexual intercourse rather than remaining a goal of sexual desire. In terms of Erikson's concepts of psychosocial development, the attainment of genital sexuality is approximately akin to the capacity for intimacy after an ego identity has been achieved. The concept of the genital character emphasizes the deficiencies of a characterology based on phases of libidinal development. It pays little if any attention to the developmental tasks of adolescence, and it has required profound modifications to include interpersonal and intrafamilial influences on character formation.

Characterologic Syndromes

The second common way of characterizing persons used in psychoanalytic psychiatry is borrowed from clinical syndromes. A person is termed "hysteric," "phobic," "obsessive," "schizoid," "paranoid," "sadomasochistic," etc., but these terms do not necessarily designate obvious psychopathological conditions. The usage rests upon the recognition that there is no sharp line of demarcation between the normal and abnormal, and that psychopathological syndromes are essentially aberrations of personality development rather than discrete illnesses. Each of these terms derived from pathological states also designates a characteristic combination of mechanisms of defense that gives a particular pattern to the person's ways of thinking, relating, and behaving—a pattern which is found in more exaggerated and more rigid form in persons suffering from the clinical syndrome. The way in which these designations are used depends somewhat upon the user's conceptualization of the psychiatric disorders. A proper discussion requires careful consideration of psychopathology, and thus extends beyond the province of this book; but we shall define several terms briefly, simply to illustrate the usage of terms which not only is common in the psychiatric literature but has entered the general vocabulary of the language.

Paranoid personalities utilize *projection* as a major defense against recognition of unacceptable impulses and motives. There is a failure in establishing proper boundaries between the self and others, and one's own motives are ascribed to others. Persons who constantly feel belittled, misjudged, and who bear grudges because they feel thwarted by others whom they believe are against them are often termed paranoid. *Hysterical* personalities readily *repress* upsetting situations and impulses, particularly sexual desires, and bolster the repression by *conversion* into some physical symptom and through *displacement* of affect. The failure to recognize motives that seem obvious to others may create an impression of prevarication or malingering—as in a soldier who emerges from a harrowing combat experience without awareness of having experienced any fear but suffering from an inability to walk. The term "hysterical" is often used to refer to women who are unaware of their habitually seductive behavior and who are upset or insulted when men respond and make advances to them. Such personality traits are related, with some justification, to fixations at the oedipal phase. The term may also refer to persons who are emotionally labile because of uncontrolled outbursts of repressed feelings or impulses in a disguised or displaced form. Obsessive personalities tend to seek to control their impulses and also the contingencies of the future by being meticulous, by carefully following routines and perhaps by being particularly neat and orderly, and by the use of the defenses of isolation, undoing, reaction formation, and intellectualization. The relationship to the "anal character" has been noted in the chapter on the toddler. The term *compulsive personality* is sometimes used almost as a synonym for "obsessive personality," but it may also indicate persons who need to satisfy or placate the needs of others in order to feel secure though unconsciously resenting the demands they believe others place upon them. The relationship to rescinding initiative in order to comply with parental demands during the period of ambulation can be noted. The use of these terms in categorizing persons is approximate, and in general they serve primarily as means of communicating some concepts about a person's characteristic ways of behaving and relating.*

* There are many other ways of categorizing personality types, all of which have serious shortcomings. Some seek to relate personality types to some physiological process or to physique. Thus, Hippocrates divided people into choleric, sanguine, phlegmatic, and melancholic types, a personology which brought various body fluids into the language as adjectives describing persons and states of emotion. Kretschmer[5] related personality characteristics to body structure, classifying individuals as leptosome (asthenic), pyknic, athletic, or dysplastic types—a typology that gained a considerable following in both medicine and psychiatry. Sheldon[10] pursued a related but more complex classification based on physique. Jung's division of people into extroverts and introverts[4] has probably been the typology most widely followed. In brief, the extrovert's energy and interests are directed toward activities, interpersonal relationships, and objective facts and actions, whereas the introvert is more interested in ideas, subjective states, spiritual values, etc. Such classifications have some utilitarian value, but most persons refuse to fit clear-cut categorizations. Their usefulness has also been limited because of the attempts to link character or personality with some inborn physical characteristics in a rather simplistic manner. As Stern[11] pointed out, most typologies tend to divide persons on the basis of inward and outward

Life Patterns and Fixations

In the study of life patterns or basic life themes, we are concerned with a type of fixation, but it is usually not a fixation that can be defined in terms of developmental stages alone. The fixation is to a pattern of gaining security that is more specific and usually relates to a way the child found security within his family. The fixation may, however, be to a life pattern that was developed in order to defend against the recurrence of a situation that caused severe or intolerable anxiety or depression—as in the case of the woman who found a major guide and motivating force in securing her relationships to her father and brother in order to prevent a re-experience of the unbearable separation anxiety that followed her mother's death. Such clearly defensive patterns will usually have their origins in the family because that is where the immature child is usually most vulnerable. It may be difficult to decide whether a life theme is basically adaptive, in the sense of being concerned with the development of assets, or defensive—that is, adaptive in defending against a trauma. Perhaps adaptation and defense, in this context, are never clearly separable.

Defensive Life Patterns

Defensive life patterns are not the same as patterns of mechanisms of defense of the ego against anxiety. The mechanisms of defense operate by repressing awareness of a disturbing impulse or experience or through altering the proper perception of it. The defensive life pattern seeks to avoid the recurrence of an unbearable threat. It will usually include mechanisms of defense, but the pattern may sometimes prevent the establishment of satisfactory defense mechanisms. Thus, a person who finds means of always remaining dependent upon a parental figure may not develop defenses against experiencing separation anxiety or gradually gain confidence in his capacities to manage on his own. Then if the defensive pattern is undermined—as occurred when the woman's father died and her sibling substitute for him married—the person is left relatively defenseless and prey to severe anxiety.

---

directedness. Riesman's use of inner and outer directedness has become an integral part of the American intellectual scene.[8] A different approach to classifying people can be found in Chapter 12. The reader is also referred to the review of the topic of personality types by D. W. MacKinnon, in Chapter 1 of Volume 1 of *Personality and the Behavior Disorders*,[6] and to A. A. Roback, *The Psychology of Character*.[9]

The satisfactory development of defensive life patterns enables many persons to compensate for serious traumatic occurrences in childhood or chronically disturbed childhood environments and lead satisfactory lives despite them. The outstanding assets of some individuals are developed as part of such defensive or compensating patterns. The psychiatrist, however, is likely to see people as patients after the defensive patterns of their lives have been undermined and collapsed, or when frantic restitutional efforts are being made. Indeed, the understanding of the nature of an emotionally traumatic occurrence requires a grasp of how such life patterns are threatened or demolished by the occurrence. The topic will be elaborated further in the next chapter when we discuss physiological functioning, for the disruption of defensive life patterns can place serious strains on the body's physiological defenses.

The Family and Life Patterns

The family occupies a central position in the understanding of life styles and life patterns because the family is everywhere the essential agent that provides the nurture, structure, and enculturation needed by the infant to survive and develop into a person capable of adapting to his physical and social environment; but also because the child develops through internalizing his parents' ways and their interactions with each other, and because he gains motives and directives by his need and desire to relate harmoniously to them. Further, it is in the family that patterns of emotional reactivity develop and interpersonal relationships are established that pattern and color all subsequent relationships. The family is also central because for most persons, if not all, it is the intimate relationships in both the natal and marital family that provide much of the fulfillment and meaning in life—and because, as we have considered elsewhere, an individual's satisfaction with himself and his sense of self-esteem continue to depend to some degree upon internalized parental values, even though the parents may be dead for many years.

In Chapter 7 we examined how the child's transition through the oedipal phase and how he comes to terms with what Freud called "the family romance" [1] helps to crystallize his personality and to establish basic patterns of interpersonal relationships. The oedipal situation sets a basic pattern for the human condition, not because it is "instinctual" but because all babies are dependent and form erotized attachments to the nurturing person or persons which must be frustrated to a greater or lesser degree in order to permit the development of autonomy and later the achievement of an ego identity and a capacity for intimacy. It is also virtually inevitable that the small child who regards his mother egocentrically will struggle against surrendering his prerogatives and accepting the importance of other family members to her and will become jealous of his father and siblings; and, commonly enough, the father and older siblings resent the young child's arrogation of the mother's time and attention. Freud's genius in recognizing and elucidating the oedipal complex and how it colors subsequent relationships and patterns repetitive conflicts opened the way for a new type of understanding of human behavior and its pathology. However, if something is common to virtually all individuals it does not clarify the reasons for differences in life patterns. The oedipal situation transpires and resolves somewhat differently for every individual, but common patterns recur and lead to relatively similar life patterns. A major task in becoming a psychiatrist lies in gaining familiarity with these various ways of resolving the oedipal situation and the ensuing life patterns, and then from knowledge of developmental dynamics and familiar themes to be able to formulate useful conjectures about new and unfamiliar patterns.

The term "oedipal situation" is used with varying degrees of specificity. The child establishes life patterns not only through how his erotized attachment to the parent of the opposite sex is resolved, but also through how he finds or seeks to find his place within the family, with parents, siblings, and any other significant persons in the home. He is not reacting only in response to his own egocentric appreciation of the situation and his fantasies about it, but also to the way in which the other family members relate to him—which very often is far different from the more or less ideal circumstances presented in the chapters on childhood in this book. The way in which the parents relate to the child and to each other may guide the child into various patterns. Thus a boy or girl may be led to identify strongly with the parent of the same sex in order to gain the affection of the parent of the opposite sex, and later become capable of marrying a person like the parent of the opposite sex to form a union in which each supports the other and both have a major interest in rearing the next generation, etc. Or it may, as in the case of the woman with the alcoholic father and husband, lead to efforts to be very different from the parent of the same sex—to differentiate rather than identify. Or it may foster a reversed oedipal resolution in which the child identifies with the parent of the opposite sex and seeks a love object of the same sex. It may lead to efforts to relate to two parents who differ so profoundly that the child has an impossible task. There are many such general patterns, and the common variants are too numerous to designate here, for they are properly learned in clinical work with patients.*

The sibling patterns within a family may be regarded as offshoots of the oedipal situation, and they can also be fundamental in establishing life patterns. Sibling rivalries can establish a pattern of relating to peers in a hostile, aggressive competition for supremacy. In contrast, when siblings provide strong support to each other in extrafamilial settings they may tend to rely on teamwork in sports and seek cooperative coalitions in occupational ventures. An oldest daughter may develop maternal attitudes toward younger siblings that virtually direct her life efforts into teaching and then toward having a large family of her own. Though they have not been emphasized particularly in this book, sibling relationships can be almost as profoundly influential as the relationships with parents, and a person's relatedness to a brother or sister is often closer and more meaningful than that to his parents.†

Myth and Life Patterns

Legend and myth are important to the psychiatrist and to the understanding of man because tradition filters out and deposits into such tales significant and commonly experienced patterns; and they are often patterns that can be considered only in myth or dream because they deal with drives and wishes that have been taboo in the society and repressed in the individual. The myth may deal with ancestral figures who lived

* Not only because the topic is beyond the scope of this chapter and book, but because many such patterns have not been specifically delineated in the psychiatric literature—and still remain part of the more or less conscious knowledge of the experienced clinician.

† Freud, in "Totem and Taboo," [2] postulated that brothers in the "primal hoarde" envious of the father's prerogatives with their mother banded together to kill the father. The Joseph saga of the Old Testament suggests another basic configuration in which the youngest son of an elderly father does not become involved in clear-cut oedipal rivalry but is favored by the father and identifies with him. The older siblings become resentful and seek to be rid of the favored intruder who is identified with the father and seek to kill him. The story also suggests how a younger child may be able to fare well in a distant land where he is free of the danger of the envy of the older siblings.

The Joseph story is also a story of death and rebirth that relates to the Adonis and Tammuz myths—as well as to the story of Jesus in which the favored son of God is killed and resurrected; the Joseph story is also, in essence, the story of the "chosen" Jewish people who are repeatedly being exterminated and reborn.

before cannibalism, incest, parricide, matricide, and the like became taboo, and it may concern fantasies of such behavior that are repressed in
the developing child. The myth holds before us, as a sort of cultural
superego, the horrors that follow upon such unthinkable behavior.* The
Greek tragedies and the plays of Shakespeare and Strindberg survive in
part because they are concerned with variations on basic life themes or
patterns that transcend individual experience and even eras and differences in cultures. *Hamlet* is not simply the story of an oedipal conflict; it
is rather a particular variant of a faulty resolution of an oedipal conflict
that sheds light upon the emotional consequences of many variants of
the theme. It is related not only to the Oedipus saga through Hamlet's
parricide[3,7,12] and incestuous preoccupations about his mother but
even more closely to the Orestes myths in which Orestes kills his mother
because of her infidelity to his father and collusion in his murder. Because he committed matricide, Orestes becomes insane, whereas Hamlet,
who has an impulsion to kill his mother upon which he cannot act, verges
on insanity and is preoccupied with suicide. Freud gained some of his
most telling insights from Shakespeare and Sophocles, and these writers'
works remain excellent sources from which understanding of various
basic life patterns can be gleaned.

* The myths of the accursed house of Tantalus, for example, move across the generations to tell of the punishment of Tantalus by the gods because he fed them his son,
an act which once may have been the essence of piety; of the punishment of Thyestes
for seducing his brother Atreus' wife; of that of Atreus for serving a stew of Thyestes'
children to Thyestes in vengeance; of the fate of Agamemnon because of his father
Atreus' vengeance and for sacrificing his daughter Iphigenia to help recover his
sister-in-law from Troy; of the death of Clytemnestra, Agamemnon's wife, at the
hand of her son Orestes for killing her husband and virtually abandoning her son;
of the insanity of Orestes that followed his matricide.

THE PERSON

References

1. Sigmund Freud, "Family Romance" (1909), in *The Standard Edition of the Complete Psychological Works of Sigmund Freud*, Vol. 9 (London: Hogarth Press, 1959).
2. Sigmund Freud, "Totem and Taboo" (1912–1913), in *The Standard Edition of the Complete Psychological Works of Sigmund Freud*, Vol. 13 (London: Hogarth Press, 1955).
3. Ernest Jones, *Hamlet and Oedipus* (New York: W. W. Norton, 1949).
4. Carl Jung, *Psychological Types* (New York: Harcourt, Brace, 1938).
5. E. Kretschmer, *Physique and Character* (New York: Harcourt, Brace, 1926).
6. Donald W. MacKinnon, "The Structure of Personality," in J. McV. Hunt (ed.), *Personality and the Behavior Disorders*, Vol. 1 (New York: Ronald Press, 1944).
7. Gilbert Murray, *Hamlet and Orestes: A Study in Traditional Types*, The Annual Shakespeare Lecture of the British Academy (New York: Oxford University Press, 1914).
8. David Riesman, *The Lonely Crowd* (Garden City, N.Y.: Doubleday Anchor Books, 1954).
9. Abraham A. Roback, *The Psychology of Character. With a Survey of Temperament* (New York: Harcourt, Brace, 1927).
10. W. Sheldon and S. Stevens, *Varieties of Temperament* (New York: Harper & Bros., 1942).
11. William Stern, *General Psychology from the Personalistic Standpoint* (New York: Macmillan, 1938).
12. Frederick Wertham, *Dark Legend* (New York: Duell, Sloan and Pearce, 1941).

Suggested Reading

Helene Deutsch, *Neuroses and Character Types* (New York: International Universities Press, 1965).
Ernest Jones, *Hamlet and Oedipus* (New York: W. W. Norton, 1949).
Carl Jung, *Psychological Types* (New York: Harcourt, Brace, 1938).
Donald W. MacKinnon, "The Structure of Personality," in J. McV. Hunt (ed.), *Personality and the Behavior Disorders*, Vol. 1 (New York: Ronald Press, 1944).
Otto Rank, *The Myth of the Birth of the Hero*, trans. E. Robbins and S. E. Jelliffe (New York: Robert Brunner, 1952).

CHAPTER 20

Personality Development
and Physiological Functions

IN THIS PENULTIMATE CHAPTER we must direct our attention, albeit but briefly, to what has been called "the mysterious leap from the mind to the body." Despite the obvious influence of thought upon the body's functioning—the sudden cold sweat, the pounding heart, the penile erection, the urgent defecation—it has been difficult for the philosophically oriented to pass beyond the barrier of the mind-body dichotomy to grasp how the intangible idea or an emotional state can influence something real and composed of matter such as the heart or the even more prosaic intestines. We are not, however, primarily concerned with the resolution of an age-old metaphysical dilemma, but enter upon the topic because we cannot understand human functioning without a clear appreciation of how emotions and physiology are inextricably interrelated, and how the nature of an individual's personality development influences his body structure and can even determine what constitutes stress for him and creates strains on his physiological apparatus.

The student of medicine's primary interest in personality development may properly derive from the impact of personality functions on physiological functioning, and on the etiology and treatment of disease. The good physician has always been aware that the majority of patients come to him because of emotional disturbances. It has become increasingly apparent that personality and emotional disorders are not only a major factor in the etiology of the so-called diseases of stress—such as peptic ulcer, ulcerative colitis, asthma, essential hypertension, hyperthyroidism —but may also contribute to the causation or chronicity of almost any illness.* Nonmedical persons who are involved in the care or treatment of personality disorders require constant awareness of the physiological concomitants and potential bodily repercussions of emotional disturbances. The topics of psychophysiological disturbances and psychosomatic medicine form disciplines in themselves.† As the reader is not expected to be versed in physiology and neuroanatomy, we shall seek to present here merely a general orientation that will permit a grasp of the essentials of the topic and of its importance.

Personality development influences the physiological processes in many different ways. There is essentially nothing different about the gastric apparatus of a Hindu and a Mohammedan, and yet the appetite of the Hindu may be stimulated by pork but not by beef, whereas his Mohammedan neighbor may even become sick if he finds that he has inadvertently swallowed some lard.

Although the sight of a friend at mealtime may stimulate gastric secretions and improve the appetite, it is not expected to cause one to drool. Yet the author encountered some persons in the South Seas for whom

---

* Including fractured bones because of "accident-proneness," and acute infectious diseases such as pneumonia through style of life, unconscious neglect of reasonable precautions, etc. Thus, a man who suffered from lobar pneumonia three times in one year had almost courted such illnesses after serious family arguments. He would emerge from the very hot furnace room in which he worked all day, go to a bar and take three shots of whiskey, which dilated his peripheral blood vessels still further as well as dulled his feelings about his enraged wife, then would walk for hours in freezing weather rather than go home, occasionally stopping for another drink of whiskey, which would interfere further with his body's ability to conserve heat.

† At least three journals in English are specifically devoted to studies in the field, *Psychosomatic Medicine, Journal of Psychosomatic Research,* and *Psychosomatics.* For a more physiologically oriented introduction, the reader is referred to the author's chapter in the *American Handbook of Psychiatry.*[9] *Psychosomatic Medicine,* by Franz Alexander,[1] furnishes a good general approach to clinical problems. *Recent Developments in Psychosomatic Medicine*[12] provides an excellent survey of many of the essential areas in the field, even though it is not quite up to date.

the sight of a stranger entering their village started them salivating even as the ringing of a bell stimulated Pavlov's dogs. Such changes in appetite are, of course, not simply ideas but also alterations in the physiological functioning of the stomach, which is very sensitive to the emotional state of the person of whom the stomach is a part.*

Personality and Physique

A person's physique is commonly considered a product of his heredity, his physical environment, and his nutrition during his developmental

---

* Scientific studies of the effects of emotion on gastric physiology started when one of the heroes of American medicine, William Beaumont, made direct observations of the interior of the stomach and of its secretions; he concomitantly demonstrated that a good scientist can function under almost any circumstances or find material for study wherever he may be.

As an army surgeon stationed on the frontier in 1829, Beaumont saved the life of a trapper, Alexis St. Martin, who had suffered an accidental gunshot wound in the abdomen. St. Martin was left with a fistula between the stomach and the exterior abdominal wall, which permitted direct observation of the interior of the stomach, its activity, and the sampling of its secretions. Beaumont hired St. Martin and carried out careful studies of his unique subject for many years, which included observations of the effects of emotional states on gastric physiology.[2]

Another series of classic studies of the stomach, carried out by Stewart Wolf and Harold Wolff [13] on another man with a gastric fistula, was directed specifically at elucidating the effect of emotions on gastric functioning. The experimental subject, known only as Tom, suffered from atresia of the oesophagus—not from ingestion of lye as is usually the case, but, as a good Irishman, from inadvertently swallowing a cup of scalding chowder. Since he was unable to eat, a fistula into his stomach was created surgically. The researchers gave Tom a job doing chores around the laboratory so that they would have him available for their studies. They observed their subject's stomach as he spontaneously experienced a variety of emotional states and they learned how to induce various emotional states in him to further their studies. The proper digestive functioning of the stomach depends upon the harmonious integration between acid and pepsin secretion, motility, the degree of dilation of the blood vessels in the mucosal lining, and the proper opening of the entrance to the duodenum. In brief, they found that when Tom was anxious or fearful the motility of the stomach decreased, the mucosal lining of the stomach became pale, but acid secretion continued; when he was angry the mucosa became engorged, the acid secretion might double, and the stomach which could be overactive was also friable and easily injured. Both patterns disrupted the harmoniously integrated patterns of motility, acid and pepsin secretion, and vascular engorgment of the mucosa conducive to proper digestion. Other investigators disagree with these precise findings, but all have found significant alterations in motility, secretions, and vascularity with various types of emotional stress.

Another highly significant study has been carried out by Engel and Reichsman[7] on a young child, Monica, who was born with an oesophageal atresia and had a gastric fistula made surgically. The study has particular importance in relating the effects of apathy and depression to gastric functions.

years. Yet his personality development is also involved. A critical study that changed the conceptualization of Fröhlich's syndrome provides an excellent illustration. The syndrome, which consisted of obesity and small genitalia in boys and often also sluggishness or somnolence, had usually been considered to result from some unknown dysfunction of the pituitary gland. Bruch[4] noted, however, striking similarities in the personalities of the mothers of these children and in the ways in which they reared their sons. These mothers were unable to bestow any real affection but gave their sons food instead. To these mothers, who had grown up in deprived homes, food formed a symbol of affection and security. They felt insecure and inadequate as mothers unless the child overate and appeared healthy and well provided for by being obese. In addition, these women were reactively concerned about their sons' safety and needed to keep them in the home and away from play with other children lest they get in trouble or danger. The combination of stuffing a child by making him feel guilty if he did not overeat and preventing expenditure of energy was sufficient to explain the obesity and sluggish inactivity; the genitalia were in fact not small but only appeared so because of the child's obese abdomen and thighs.

The syndrome of anorexia nervosa in which the person is chronically emaciated, sometimes to the extent of being a "living skeleton" of fifty or sixty pounds, was once thought to be due to a pituitary deficiency. It is, however, due to self-imposed starvation of emotional origin; and, when it starts in early adolescence, the person often fails to develop secondary sexual characteristics. Oskar Mazareth, the hero or anti-hero of Günter Grass's *The Tin Drum*,[8] who stopped growing at the age of three, is only a fictional symbol, but in recent years clear evidence has been found of emotionally induced dwarfism.[3] Somewhat less dramatic but more common are the decrements in rates of growth and weight gain in children after they are institutionalized, despite the availability of ample nourishment and excellent physical care.

The development of an athletic physique can also depend upon the individual's self-concept and his defenses. A youth of seventeen was slight, poorly developed muscularly, and had a small frame when he entered college. He sought psychiatric help early in his freshman year because of phobic symptoms. During his therapy he soon became aware of intense feelings of rivalry with his father and his wishes and fears of attacking and injuring him. As he worked through his hostile feelings toward his father, and in seeking some expression for his aggressive impulses that previously had been repressed, he became a member of the college wrestling squad. Exercising daily with various apparatus in the gymnasium as well as wrestling, he became one of the strongest and most massive students in the university by the time of his graduation.

Personality Development and Physiological Functioning

Let us turn now to consider the influence of personality development on physiological functioning. It will be recalled that in discussing the endowment with which the infant enters this world, we noted that relatively early in the evolutionary process the organism developed automatic means of spontaneously preparing for flight or fight when confronted by danger. These emergency responses are part of the organism's patterns of fear and aggressivity. They are not simply emotional states but pervasive changes in the functioning of the entire organism in preparation for coping with the danger and to minimize the effects of any consequent injury. Although the neurophysiological mechanisms that set off and mediate these reactions are very complex, for our present purposes it will suffice to note that they involve secretion of the hormones epinephrine and norepineprine by the adrenal medulla, and the activation of the autonomic nervous system—of which the adrenal medulla is, in a sense, a part.* Almost instantaneously, the person becomes more alert and sensitive to stimuli because of changes in the reticular activating system in the brain; blood flow is shunted to the muscles and brain from the peripheral vessels and digestive organs, and the heart rate increases the better to supply oxygen to the muscles and brain, and to remove waste products; the coagulability of the blood increases to counter bleeding; the peripheral blood vessels constrict not only to shunt blood to the muscles but also to lessen blood loss; sweating helps dissipate the heat generated by muscular activity and makes the body slippery; the pupils dilate, either the better to see in the dark or to make the animal appear more frightening—the list of physiological changes is great and still not fully known. They include mobilization of blood sugar from depots in the liver to provide energy; changes in kidney function to lessen

* It has often been considered that epinephrine primarily prepares for flight and norepinephrine for fight. It has been suggested that animals who tend to flee secrete more epinephrine than norepinephrine and the opposite occurs in those more apt to fight than flee. More recent evidence as summarized by Engel [6] suggests that epinephrine is the major secretion during the period of alarm and anxiety without action; but that with action, be it either flight or fight, norepinephrine secretion becomes greater, automatically shifting the physiological patterns for action.

blood volume; alterations in respiration to increase the oxygen-carbon dioxide exchange; a series of changes in the stomach and intestines, including a tendency for immediate evacuation of the bowels. In addition the adrenal medullary secretions may trigger secretion of adrenocorticotrophic hormone by the pituitary that sets off another major defense system of the organism that will be considered later in the chapter.

Now all of these responses can be highly useful and life-saving when an animal, including the human animal, confronts an enemy from which he must flee or engage in mortal combat, or when all possible resources must be marshaled in overcoming some environmental hazard as in running from a forest fire, but they are not always useful in mastering the enemies and hazards of a civilized world, such as in combating a business opponent, or the need to make a good impression when being interviewed for admission to a graduate school. The physiological responses to danger contribute little toward countering the hostility of a rival for promotion, or to finding a job by means of which a person can indirectly feed himself and his family. These physiological responses are of even less value in situations that arouse anxiety, anger, or resentment. Yet, anxiety, as noted in Chapter 8, is related to fear, and anger and resentment to aggression, and these emotions are accompanied, to a greater or lesser degree, by the same fundamental bodily defenses against impending danger. The more acute the anxiety or severe the anger, the more likely that the physiological changes will be severe and diffuse. But anxiety occurs in relation to danger from one's own impulses, or to concerns over loss of significant persons, or to apprehensions about future contingencies—and these can rarely be solved by either flight or physical combat. Similarly, hostile feelings and resentments can rarely be overcome by fighting and vanquishing the person with whom one is angry. Still, these physiological states create unpleasant and even unbearable feelings, and anxiety impels an individual toward ridding himself of its source. These states serve useful functions primarily in motivating a person toward changing the conditions that may be inducing them—if the person consciously knows what they are. As anxiety is most commonly brought about by unconscious factors, it can serve only as a very diffuse type of motivation.

Functional Symptoms

The physiological accompaniments of anxiety and hostility, however, particularly when they are chronic, are major sources of so-called "functional symptoms." These psychogenic complaints are not imaginary but usually have a firm physiological basis. The man who suffers from severe headaches for which no "organic" cause can be found—no brain tumor, eyestrain, sinus infection, arthritic vertebrae, or migraine—is not imagining the pain. He usually suffers from a "tension headache," caused by the tensions of the muscles that accompany increased alertness. The pain from the tense neck muscles is felt over the occiput, and from the frontal and oculomotor muscles in the forehead. The pounding heart, the sudden abdominal cramps, the drenching sweat can all be part of the physiological response to danger. A syncopal attack—a faint—can occur when the blood vessels in a person's muscles dilate suddenly in preparation for flight; but when the person merely stands instead of running or fighting, the muscles do not pump blood as they do during activity, and insufficient blood reaches the brain. In a state of inaction the individual becomes aware of such physiological responses and may consider them to be symptoms.*

It will be recalled (Chapter 9) that the mental mechanisms of defense may be unconsciously brought into operation at the first physiological signal of anxiety. Either the signal leads to cognizance of the threat of danger and directs the person to do something about it, or a mechanism of defense such as repression, isolation, projection, prevents perception of the threat or changes it into something that does not threaten self-esteem or require self-punishment. The mechanisms of defense, then, do not simply help a person to maintain self-esteem—or to alter id impulsions into a form acceptable to the superego—but they help to keep the body from responding to potential anxiety-provoking situations. These responses would serve little but would disturb the body's physio-

* Although the physiological responses to anxiety and hostility are diffuse, individuals usually become conscious of one or more specific manifestations, and these seem to become the primary symptoms of anxiety or fear for the individual. It is not clear how this occurs. In World War I, for example, many soldiers, particularly in the British Army, were incapacitated by the "effort syndrome" or "neurocirculatory asthenia"—the heart beat very forcefully and rapidly and the soldier became short of breath with very slight exertion. Considerable attention was paid to the syndrome. In World War II, during the Solomon Islands campaign, numerous soldiers had similar symptoms but together with the full gamut of physiological responses to danger—hyperalertness, sweating, diarrhea, slightly elevated blood pressure, etc.—and when special effort was made to prevent them from focusing on their heart symptoms rather than on their anxiety, only a very few developed the "effort syndrome," which clearly seemed a residue of the more diffuse anxiety state and could be relieved by blocking the sympathetic nerves to the heart.

logical equilibrium and thus produce unnecessary strains on the organism. They are thus a means of protecting the body's integrity from the physiological concomitants of anxiety, anger, and resentment.

Emotions and Bodily Damage

Although the physiological responses to anxiety are usually brief and produce discomfort rather than damage to the organism, an inability to resolve the anxiety-provoking situation or failures of the ego's mechanisms of defense to conceal the threat can lead to untoward effects. A clear and dramatic though unusual example was provided by a twenty-year-old college student who was admitted to a general hospital for intensive study because of a puzzling, life-threatening ailment. Although his blood pressure was generally normal, on three distinct occasions it had soared to extremely high levels and had remained elevated for several days. On one of these occasions a hemorrhage of a retinal blood vessel had temporarily blinded him in one eye. Such abrupt and transitory episodes of hypertension can be caused by a tumor of adrenal medullary cells that pours epinephrine or norepinephrine into the blood stream when the tumor is squeezed by an abrupt change in posture, as in bending. However, very careful studies eliminated the possibility that the patient had such a tumor. He was referred to a psychiatrist, and was pleased to have an opportunity to discuss some serious personality problems and the situations in which his hypertensive episodes had occurred.

He related that he had been engaged in a homosexual relationship with a classmate for five or six years; but during the past year they had both determined to terminate the sexual aspects of their relationship. His home life had been unfortunate. His parents, who had been markedly incompatible, had divorced when he was ten, and he had been sent to boarding school. During his vacations he was shifted from one parent to the other, feeling happy with neither one. His father was a highly successful surgeon who held rigid and high expectations for himself and his son but who was given to violent rages during which he sometimes broke furniture and windows. The patient recalled imagining his father's surgery as brutal and sadistic assaults on people. His mother was over-solicitous, worrisome, and conveyed a lack of confidence in herself and her son. Without attempting to portray his complicated and unhappy childhood, it will suffice to say that he was not averse to homosexual seduction in boarding school, and after indulging in such activities with several boys he formed an intense relationship with a classmate who became the only important person in his life.

The first episode of high blood pressure occurred when he was eighteen. When he was examined for induction into the military service, his blood pressure was found to be so high that he was hospitalized immediately. No cause could be found for the elevation, which disappeared after a few days. The patient knew that he had been extremely upset at the time, indeed had been suffering from almost unbearable anxiety. He did not believe, in retrospect, that he had been anxious about induction but rather was intensely fearful of being separated from and eventually losing his homosexual partner. The second episode might seem humorous were it not for the dire consequences. The patient and his friend, having become concerned about their homosexuality, had decided to end the sexual aspects of the relationship and make heterosexual adjustments. When resolve did not lead to results, they made a substantial wager about which one would first have sexual relations with a girl. The college year ended with the wager unclaimed. During the summer vacation the young man met a girl who gave ample indication that she was not averse to going to bed with him. After vacillating for several weeks, he mobilized his courage and decided upon a specific date and place. During the day prior to the chosen night, he suffered from severe tension, was unable to eat, and occasionally felt faint. He was determined not to back down from his resolve, and he forced himself to drive to the girl's home despite feeling nauseated and unbearably anxious. Just as he rang the doorbell he lost the vision in his left eye. A physician found his blood pressure to be extremely high and discovered a hemorrhage in his retina. He went to the hospital instead of to a motel and once again his blood pressure receded after two or three days and he soon regained his vision.

The student then made no attempt to win the bet for several months, but when he returned to college in the fall his friend also could not claim the money. Then the young man noted that a park near his college was frequented by women of a professional character, and he decided that he might be able to "make out" with one of them. He again steeled himself for the venture, and finally sat down on a park bench with a woman and arranged to go to her room. When he stood up he became acutely dizzy and could scarcely walk. He took a taxi to his doctor and was again placed in the hospital. On this occasion his pressure was extremely high and his condition became even more serious when his kidneys shut down and did not produce any urine for several days. Once again his blood pressure returned to normal, but then, partly at his suggestion, a psychiatric consultant was asked to see the patient.

The genesis of this young man's homosexuality need not be considered here beyond noting that it constituted a pattern established to ward off fears of being overwhelmed and engulfed by women but which also partly masked his incestuous fixations which were terrifyingly dangerous because of his fantasies of mutilating reprisals by his violent father. His homosexuality eventually became socially unacceptable and threatened his self-esteem. His attempts to change to heterosexuality by determination and his refusal to be stopped by his anxiety and symptoms of fear, and his failure to overcome the problems and fears that had directed him toward homosexuality, left him prey to an intense physiological concomitant of anxiety.

Such devastating effects of the physiological responses to fear, anxiety, or hostility are uncommon.* The more lasting bodily disturbances related to these emotions usually occur when the physiological defenses against threat and danger chronically interfere with the homeostatic functions mediated by the autonomic nervous system.

The Dual Functions of the Autonomic Nervous System

Let us look at the problem a little more closely. The reader will recall that the entire evolutionary process has had to do with finding new ways to preserve the cell and assure its reproduction (Chapter 1); and that when higher and more complex forms of life arose, complex mechanisms were required to make certain that the tissue fluids surrounding the cells retained their chemical composition with the remarkable constancy needed for maintenance of the cells. It may seem eccentric and even cynical to suggest that all of the complexities of personality development and the human life cycle that form the subject of this book are concerned with a unique way of preserving the germinal cell—at least when regarded from an evolutionary perspective. The body fluids must remain very constant, for slight change in the acidity of the

---

* How uncommon remains uncertain. In any event, hyperthyroidism or Graves' disease sometimes follows directly upon a terrifying experience about which the person can do little.[10] Thus, a Negro man who was raised in the deep South was terrified after he killed a white man in an auto accident. He had nightmares of a lynching he had witnessed as a child and soon become hyperthyroid. Another man became hyperthyroid after watching his farmhouse burn with his wife and child in it, being restrained from attempting to rescue them because it was hopeless. The thyroid hormone sensitizes to epinephrine and has something to do with mobilization for severe chronic stress as well as the regulation of metabolism. Sudden death after acute fright has also been reported by various observers. The author believes that he knows of coronary occlusions, including several deaths from such heart attacks, that followed upon the patient's experiencing unbearable anger and frustration.

blood, the oxygen and carbon dioxide tensions, the concentrations of sodium, potassium, calcium, and other ions, or in the body temperature are incompatible with proper physiological functioning and the survival of cells, tissues, and the life of the individual. The internal environment is maintained relatively constant by means of complicated chemical buffering systems and various checks, balances, and feedback systems. Man must rely upon what Walter Cannon termed "the wisdom of the body" [5] to handle itself, for it far surpasses conscious human intellectual abilities. Now what concerns us here is simply that a great deal of the nervous control of these homeostatic mechanisms is mediated by the autonomic nervous system, the same system and pathways that are involved in the preparation of the body to flee or fight when the person is confronted by danger or, as we have seen, when he becomes anxious or hostile.* When, for example, the body temperature begins to fall, the autonomic nerves carry impulses that cause constriction of the peripheral blood vessels to conserve heat loss from radiation. If the carbon dioxide tension in the blood rises, respiration automatically deepens. Heart rate and constriction of various blood vessels vary in accord with the needs of exertion and the maintenance of a proper blood pressure. The secretions of the digestive juices in the stomach, the state of the blood vessels in the lining of the stomach, and the motility of the stomach are influenced by the autonomic nervous system. There is no need to attempt to convey the sweeping and important homeostatic functions of the sympathetic and parasympathetic nervous systems.

What ensues when these two functions of the autonomic nervous system conflict? As the reactions to danger are emergency functions, they are usually short-lived and usually do not interfere for long. When fear, anxiety, aggressivity, or hostility become chronic, or occur repetitively, then the smooth regulation of the body's maintenance of its homeostasis can be impaired. Under some conditions such disturbances can lead to more permanent changes, including illnesses such as peptic ulcer, hyperthyroidism, or bronchial asthma.† A middle-aged woman is sent into the

---

* A great deal more is involved than the autonomic nervous system, of course, including virtually all of the endocrine glands, but the secretion of epinephrine plays an important role in triggering some of these secretions, and the autonomic nervous system is intimately connected with the various visceral centers in the brain.
† In some of the diseases of stress it is clear that other factors are essential. Peptic ulcer, for example, occurs predominantly in persons who constitutionally tend to have high levels of pepsin secretion—as well as emotional problems. Most persons with bronchial asthma are severely allergic, yet some are not allergic at all but have

hospital with a severe skin condition, an atopic dermatitis, that has affected her face particularly severely. The condition started a month after her second marriage and steadily worsened over the ensuing two months despite various therapeutic regimens. She is clearly depressed and when the resident physician, in seeking to learn what might be disturbing her, inquires about her recent marriage, the woman begins to cry. She reluctantly relates that she made a serious mistake in marrying again. Soon after the marriage, it became clear that her new husband was interested only in a type of perverse sexual relationship. When she had refused to participate, he had asked why she would not, saying that her sister had always enjoyed it. The patient had complied but felt humiliated and ashamed—and perhaps even more ashamed and angry to learn that her sister, who was married, had been having an affair with her new husband for many years. She did not know what to do or how she could even continue to see her sister. As she discussed her problem and eventually decided on what she might do about it, her skin healed and remained normal. The vascularity of her skin apparently had been chronically affected by her reactions of shame and buried rage.

Life Patterns and Physiological Imbalance

The life pattern of a person and particularly the repetitive ways of reacting and relating can have much to do with creating a state of physiological strain or imbalance. It will be recalled that in our discussion of the influence of oral fixation on character formation at the end of the chapter on infancy, we presented the problems of a man suffering from peptic ulcer. He had remained closely tied to his mother, insecure of his capacity to support and feed himself, and fearful of re-experiencing a traumatic episode in his childhood when his family had been threatened by poverty and starvation. He was an obese man who habitually overate when he felt insecure and suffered from frequent episodes of heartburn. He had married a motherly woman when he realized his mother was getting old. He suffered his first attack of bleeding from a peptic ulcer while awaiting induction into the army, and a second serious episode

---

only a certain type of emotional difficulty; many will have asthma only when exposed to the proper allergen, and the severity of the asthma depends on both the severity of the exposure to the allergen and the degree of emotional upset. Asthmatic patients often cease being asthmatic when they are removed to the hospital, away from a difficult home situation. Similarly, the blood pressure of patients with essential hypertension usually becomes lower after they are placed in the hospital and without any other therapeutic measures.

when his wife unexpectedly became pregnant. The theme that ran through his life, and which was repeated in many variations according to his age and the specific circumstances, concerned the need for assurance of "oral supplies" of food and nurturing protection. Never able to venture beyond his dependency on maternal figures, this man found even the ordinary course of life to be filled with threatening, anxiety-provoking situations that could upset his physiological functioning—and perhaps because of his oral fixation his gastric functioning in particular.* Any threat of separation from his mother and any need to become self-reliant provoked anxiety which he never overcame because a phobic defense against traveling kept him from leaving his small native town. He needed to earn more money as a married man in order to feel secure. He had the intelligence and training to hold a far better position than the one he had; he often thought of changing jobs or starting a business of his own, but when he did he became anxious and suffered from stomach upsets and convinced himself that his health did not permit him to change jobs. But then, he would become resentful that his boss did not appreciate his abilities and promote him, and he would suffer from indigestion again. A new job could not offer him an enjoyable challenge and a sense of accomplishment; going into the army could not provide new adventure; his marriage provoked as much anxiety as it did happiness despite finding a considerate and nurturant wife; the prospect of becoming a father was an ordeal rather than an anticipation of fulfillment. The minor, almost daily upsets that helped keep his gastric functioning disturbed can readily be imagined. As the defensive pattern of his life was concerned with an unrealistic and unattainable search for complete security, it contained in it the sources of repetitive episodes of anxiety and frustration.

Sometimes the defensive pattern of life opens the way for serious

---

* The influence of life patterns, particularly defensive life patterns, is particularly important in the study of the "psychosomatic disorders." Many investigators in this field strongly believe that each of the major psychosomatic disorders occurs in persons who are sensitized to similar types of problems and perhaps whose life patterning leads to specific types of conflict. The patient being discussed is rather typical of many patients who suffer from peptic ulcer. Patients with ulcerative colitis are even less mature and more childishly dependent and have grave difficulties in making decisions; hypertensive patients may well show a different configuration which leads them to feel chronically enraged but rarely able to express their feelings, and so on. The "specificity" of such configurations is a matter of considerable dispute. A good presentation of this general orientation can be found in Franz Alexander's, *Psychosomatic Medicine*.[1]

emotional trauma that can have a devastating effect upon the person's emotional stability and on his physiological functioning. The impending induction into the army of the man we have been discussing was more than an anxiety-provoking episode. It threatened the core of his security operations. He would no longer be able to have a mother or mothering wife at hand; his phobia of traveling would be unable to protect him from being removed from them; he would be cast out on his own into a hard world that did not supply sustenance. As he had neither gradually gained confidence in his ability to care for himself, provide for himself, and survive on his own nor had he developed various mechanisms of defense that could serve to buffer the anxiety and perhaps change the perception of the danger into a more containable form, he reacted to the threat of induction with all of the physiological intensity of a child who loses his mother or who is faced by some overwhelming danger. However, his system was no longer as resilient as it was when he was a child. It was at this juncture of his life that he developed his peptic ulcer and bled from it. Similarly, a woman who seeks security against feelings of abandonment by her mother by becoming the essential loyal child who will care for her mother after the other children leave, eventually loses her mother by death or finds herself resentfully burdened with a helpless old person. If, as a part of the pattern, she seeks to bind a child to her by lavishing on it an overprotectiveness she believes she would have liked as a child, then the child is likely to rebel in a desperate effort to gain his freedom and his own identity, and flee from his mother rather than remain in a filial relationship to her. Then, when this trauma that has been feared since childhood occurs, she, too, responds with a profound and even devastating physiological reaction as if to an overwhelming danger: perhaps as she did in childhood when the sensitizing event originally occurred. Indeed, it was at this juncture in her life that a woman in this situation developed hyperthyroidism.

Misfiring of Mechanisms of Defense

We must note, too, that although the mechanisms of defense usually serve to lessen the physiological impact of situations that are potentially anxiety-provoking, they can also increase the person's vulnerability. If, for example, a defensive mechanism prevents awareness of a situation that is actually dangerous, reality may eventually force recognition of the serious dilemma and the physiological response to the shock of recognition of danger can be profound. A man whose entire way of life rested upon his devotion to his wife and children managed to forgive his wife when she confessed to having an affair, but stated definitely that any further infidelities would lead to a divorce. Several years later he managed to use various mechanisms of defense to keep himself from realizing that his wife was proving La Rochefoucauld's epigram, "There are many wives who have never been unfaithful but none who have been unfaithful once." When he was abruptly and unexpectedly forced to recognize the actual situation, he suffered a serious coronary occlusion.

Furthermore, mechanisms of defense can go astray, so to speak, and become sources of severe anxiety. Thus, a woman managed to repress her hostility toward her husband and her wishes to be rid of the child who tied her to the marriage with the aid of various mechanisms of defense including undoing, reaction formation, and obsessive oversolicitude for her child. She eventually worked herself into an unbearable position. She became fearful of ever leaving her child alone, unable to sleep unless the child was sleeping beside her, fearful when he walked to school, and she could scarcely bear the anxiety of waiting for his return, fearing some harm had befallen him. She was unable to tolerate any prolonged separation from her son, which led to difficulties with her husband. When it became necessary for her to remain in the hospital, she insisted on leaving to accompany her son to a picnic, for he might drown while swimming unless she were present to watch, even though she could not swim. Such decompensated defenses are not uncommon, and when chronic they can become a major factor in the etiology of psychosomatic disorders.

The Alarm Reaction and the General Adaptation Syndrome

There are various other ways in which adverse life situations and serious emotional distrubances affect physiological functioning and the integrity of the body which do not depend so greatly upon dysfunction of the autonomic nervous system. One major set of interrelated physiological responses to severe stress involves the defensive activity of the adrenal cortical hormones. Rather than preparing the organism for action against danger as by flight or fight, these hormones provide a strengthening of physiological defenses against bodily injury, but the reactions also come into play following emotional stress, at least after severe emotional trauma. Epinephrine triggers the secretion of adrenocorticotrophic hormone (ACTH) by the pituitary, which in turn stimulates secretion of the adrenal cortical hormones (cortisone and related hormones). A continuation of the trauma can overstimulate the physiological defenses and lead to permanent changes in various organ systems, or exhaust the defenses, which can also cause profound structural damages. The physiologist Hans Selye, who has been a primary investigator of these types of responses to stress, has termed one set the *alarm reaction* and certain of its more continued physiological consequences the *general adaptation syndrome*.* The changes that occur seem to help explain the etiology of some illnesses such as rheumatoid arthritis, some types of kidney ailments, and various types of "collagen disease." Although the adaptation syndrome may primarily be a defense against physical injury, it can also occur in response to severe emotional trauma. Thus, Selye found that the entire reaction leading to death from adrenal cortical exhaustion could be produced in rats by tying their legs—a procedure which produces extreme fright in these animals. Death ensued with typical changes in many organ systems, even though the animals were carefully shielded against injuring themselves during their struggles. The endocrine, neuroanatomic, and neurophysiological interrelationships involved in the adrenal cortical defenses are under intensive study by many investigators.

Although emotional factors appear to influence the individual's resistance to illness, including infectious illnesses, the area has been very difficult to investigate carefully.

Physiological Responses to Hopelessness and Helplessness

Engel and his coworkers[7] have focused their investigations upon physiological reactions accompanying a person's withdrawal of emotional

* Selye[11] became interested in the physiological responses that are common to many illnesses and may also accompany injury: such as the shifts in the number and types of white cells circulating in the blood, fever, changes in blood pressure and volume, changes in vascular permeability, etc. Many such responses hinge upon the secretion of adrenal cortical steroids. In a general way, a primary response to trauma is the alarm reaction, in which increased corticoid secretion decreases vascular permeability and diminishes fluid loss from blood vessels into the tissues, which together with other measures helps prevent shock. Following the alarm reaction, a state of resistance follows, accompanied by tissue changes, and when trauma is severe may eventually lead to death. The type and extent of these defensive tissue changes depends upon such factors as severity, spread, and duration of the trauma as well as constitutional factors. However, even relatively early in the adaptation response, growth can be inhibited, the gonads can undergo involution, lactation in nursing mothers ceases, and ulcerations occur in the gastrointestinal tract. Later, tissue changes such as are found in the various "collagen diseases" occur. The total reaction involves a profound shift in balance of the entire neuroendocrine system and cannot be presented here.

loss of a significant person, and
he reactions of helplessness and
,ered means of conserving energy
ysiological impact of unbearable
erns are related to those of apathy
,e evidence of profound physiologi-
of the changes remains uncertain.

npact of emotions on physiological
opment influences the physiology of
ne aspect of the involved and highly
ntion particularly on the automatic
,y the autonomic nervous system, and
is can conflict with the homeostatic
em and produce a variety of dysfunc-
,s, particularly a defensive life pattern-
.ng of the physiological defenses against
, life patterns can create overwhelming
,y severe strains on the integrity of the
sms of defense serve not only to defend
eem but also to protect against anxiety
al defenses against danger; but at times,
such in, y and provoke emotional states that create
strains on the physiologica. fenses.

References

1. Franz Alexander, *Psychosomatic Medicine: Its Principles and Applications* (New York: W. W. Norton, 1950).
2. William Beaumont, *Experiments and Observations on the Gastric Juice and the Physiology of Digestion* (Plattsburgh, N. Y.: F. P. Allen, 1833).
3. Frederic M. Blodgett, "Growth Retardation Related to Maternal Deprivation," in Albert J. Solnit and Sally A. Provence (eds.), *Modern Perspectives in Child Development* (New York: International Universities Press, 1963).
4. Hilde Bruch and Grace Touraine, "Obesity in Childhood: V. The Family Frame of Obese Children," *Psychosomatic Medicine*, 2 (1940), 141–206.
5. Walter B. Cannon, *The Wisdom of the Body* (rev. ed.; New York: W. W. Norton, 1963).
6. George Engel, *Psychological Development in Health and Disease* (Philadelphia: W. B. Saunders, 1962).
7. George Engel and Franz Reichsman, "Spontaneous and Experimentally Induced Depressions in an Infant with a Gastric Fistula: A Contribution to the Problem of Depression," *Journal of the American Psychoanalytic Association*, 4 (1956), 428–452.
8. Günter Grass, *The Tin Drum* (New York: Pantheon, 1963).
9. Theodore Lidz, "General Concepts of Psychosomatic Medicine," in Silvano Arieti (ed.), *American Handbook of Psychiatry*, Vol. 1 (New York: Basic Books, 1959).
10. Theodore Lidz and John C. Whitehorn, "Life Situations, Emotions, and Graves' Disease," *Psychosomatic Medicine*, 12 (1950), 184–186.
11. Hans Selye, "The General Adaptation Syndrome and the Diseases of Adaptation," *Journal of Clinical Endocrinology*, 6 (1946), 117–230.
12. Eric Whittkower and Robert Cleghorn (eds.), *Recent Developments in Psychosomatic Medicine* (Philadelphia: Lippincott, 1954).
13. Stewart Wolf and Harold G. Wolff, *Human Gastric Function* (New York: Oxford University Press, 1943).

Suggested Reading

Franz Alexander, *Psychosomatic Medicine: Its Principles and Applications* (New York: W. W. Norton, 1950).
Association for Research in Nervous and Mental Diseases, *Life Stress and Bodily Disease* (Baltimore: Williams & Wilkins, 1950).

Walter B. Cannon, *The Wisdom of the Body* (rev. ed.; New York: W. W. Norton, 1963).

Leon J. Saul, *The Bases of Human Behavior: A Biologic Approach to Psychiatry* (Philadelphia: Lippincott, 1951).

Hans Selye, *The Stress of Life* (New York: McGraw-Hill, 1956).

CHAPTER 21

The Therapeutic Relationship

THIS CHAPTER will move beyond the dynamics of personality development to consider some essential aspects of the therapeutic relationship. The practice of medicine or psychotherapy, or relating properly to a patient or "client" as a nurse, social worker, or clinical psychologist, requires profound knowledge of people, and this book has sought to provide a guide for studying people and learning from relationships with them. Knowledge about persons and their development, however, does not assure a capacity to relate effectively and therapeutically with them. A major difficulty in the practice of medicine, and particularly in the related disciplines which are concerned with the treatment of people's problems in living, is that the therapist's major instrument is himself. The good physician, even before his differentiation from medicine man or priest, relied upon his personal powers to help promote healing, and has ever needed to be a student of people. The advances of scientific medicine that have eradicated so many diseases during the past century have not diminished the importance of the physician as a person; and they have made possible the turning of more time and attention to problems of living rather than to the preservation of life. The focusing of increased attention on personality functioning and malfunctioning during the past decades permits a more rational attitude in working with the irrational, and has provided guidelines for assuring more useful therapeutic relationships. As we are not here concerned primarily with pathology or its therapy, attention will be directed only toward an essential aspect of the therapist's relationships with patients that rests upon the understanding of personality development. We shall consider the *transference* relationships between patient and therapist and how they are critical to clinical work in all fields of medicine and form the core of psychotherapeutic activities.

"Transference"

The term "transference" refers to the unconscious tendencies to relate to another person in terms of a prior relationship, basically in terms of a childhood relationship with a parental figure, transferring to the person attributes of the parental figure or another significant individual with whom he is being identified. Although such transferences occur in all important relationships, coloring and obscuring the characteristics of the person with whom one is interacting, they are of particular moment in medicine where the physician has a unique importance to the patient, and in relationship with any therapeutic figure upon whom a person depends and toward whom he is apt to behave dependently.

Before discussing the transference relationship, let us consider some rather typical and clear-cut episodes that occurred on the medical service of a university hospital. A third-year medical student has just started his clinical clerkship in internal medicine. His position, in essence, is that of assistant to the intern, learning through active participation under close supervision in the work of the medical service. He is assigned a young woman patient and he elicits a detailed history of her current illness and past health record; he draws blood from her veins for various laboratory tests; and he performs a physical examination. Like all students at the start of their clerkship experience, he is uneasy and rather insecure because he is still hesitant and awkward in carrying out his duties. Nevertheless, after a few days he notes, or others remark, that his young woman patient seems to have improved; at least she has perked up and gained sufficient energy to apply eye shadow and lipstick and arrange her hair carefully each morning. She has her sister bring in her silk nightgowns and a new dressing robe. She always greets the student with a pleasing smile, and recalls some additional information to impart to him. She asks his advice concerning the operation on her heart that is being considered. When the student asks her what the professor has advised, the patient imparts her lack of confidence in the professor's opinion because he is so very busy that he can have little time to think about her and her heart; she places the most weight on the student's judgment. The student tries to stifle his joy at having been assigned a patient who is so astute as to recognize ability when she encounters it. He sits down and offers his considered opinion, based on his experience with one other similar case and his reading in the textbook (written by the professor).

Another student is not so fortunate in the assignment of patients. He helps with the care of a truck driver admitted late in the evening with severe liver disease. The student stays up most of the night with the house staff testing urine specimens, drawing samples of blood, helping to give intravenous fluids, holding the patient's head when he vomits, etc. The next morning he wearily drags himself from bed after a couple of hours' sleep and rushes to the ward, where he is pleased to hear that the patient is doing nicely. He happily walks into the patient's room to draw some blood, and is taken aback when he is assailed by a series of choice invectives from the patient, who wishes to be left alone, and who accuses the student of having collected sufficient blood during the night to support himself for a month. Every friendly approach is met by a renewed outburst in which the patient makes it clear that he despises the student and his canine forebears. The student begins to feel that the efforts of the previous night had been a mistake, for the man was not worth saving, and he lets the patient know it.

Although these examples may seem to gild the lily, they are actual occurrences that may perhaps have become a bit polished in the telling. It is sometimes difficult for the physician to follow Osler's advice and retain his equanimity,[1] but recognition of the transference nature of both the young woman's admiration and the truck driver's hostility could have helped each student keep his feet on the ground and use such situations to gain better understanding of the person he was treating. Neither of these patients knew much about the students, and the woman had little reason to become enamored of one or the man to hate the other. They were relating primarily to symbolic figures in terms of earlier relationships to some significant persons. The young woman with the damaged heart valve was unconsciously seeking security, when she was dependent and rather helpless, by seductively wooing a man to look after her even as she had learned to gain her way with her father. The truck driver carried a chip on his shoulder, for he felt that if he had to be dependent and rely on any man he would be used and victimized even as his father had forced him to work when he was a boy and had appropriated his earnings until he ran away from home. Neither of these patients' responses was suited to the students' behavior, but being sick and dependent had provoked old patterns of reactivity. If a therapist recognizes the tendency of a patient to identify him with an earlier significant figure in the patient's life, he need not take such reactions personally, but can more dispassionately observe the patient's ways of relating to him and utilize the understanding he gains in the management of the patient.

The ability to utilize the self as an instrument for comprehending and gaining insight into the patient's ways of reacting and relating and for influencing treatment, requires an objectivity about one's own feelings and behavior and knowledge that comes only with experience. It is among the most difficult skills required of a therapist. Still, in the illustrations we have used, it was fairly obvious to anyone other than the students involved that the woman had no logical reason to consider her student-clerk the best physician available, and the student should have been able to realize that he was neither Sean Connery nor Rex Morgan, and not even Sir William Osler; and that the man had no grounds for such violent antipathy toward a person seeking to help to save his life.

All relationships, particularly new relationships, contain elements of earlier ones. The judgment of a new acquaintance is based upon experiences with others of whom they remind one. We size up the new person by consciously and even more unconsciously fitting him into the pattern of someone we have known, or a class of persons we have known. Stereotypes can, of course, save considerable energy and even keep us from knowing persons as individuals. If, however, the observer is astute, he may gain considerable knowledge about a person by recognizing subtle similarities to others. Transference situations are usually more loaded emotionally. The intense relationships with parental figures in childhood become an integral part of the personality and influence the entire behavioral pattern of a person. Various childhood distortions of the relationship with parents and feelings about them are usually partially corrected as an individual gains maturity and a secure ego identity; but some childhood feelings and perceptions remain, and others are very likely to become reactivated during periods of intense emotional insecurity. The life patterning established by the transactions within the family of origin strongly directs an individual toward fitting new significant persons into the pattern, changing them to fit, or persons are selected to be significant who fit into the life patterning. As has been discussed in the two preceding chapters, there is a fundamental tendency throughout the course of life to pour the new into an old mold; to deal with persons according to past experiences. Such repetitive tendencies are usually more prominent in emotionally disturbed persons or during times of emotional disturbance.

The Therapist's Position and Role

A therapist is not simply another person to a patient, and the relationship is not a casual matter to him. The patient comes to a physician with a need he cannot manage by himself, no matter how mature and self-sufficient he may be about nonmedical matters; and persons come for psychotherapeutic or casework help because they can no longer cope effectively. The difficulties are usually worrisome, interfering with patterns of living and threatening the person's well-being. The patient expects that when he places himself in a therapist's hands, his health and welfare will be of primary importance to the therapist. The therapeutic relationship rests upon the tradition of the doctor-patient relationship; and the physician long held an especially prestigious place in society because along with the clergy he was expected to place the patient's welfare on a par with his own. Indeed, he was expected to risk his life regularly in caring for the sick; and until the serious infectious diseases were brought under control during recent decades, he could give but little thought to his own safety while caring for the ill. He continues to do whatever he can for a patient—whatever lies within his abilities, not because of his own needs, or because of some personal relationship to the patient, but simply because the patient comes to him in his role as a physician. As other professions have moved into the healing arts, or become adjuvants to medicine, they have to a greater or lesser degree assumed a similar role. One of the problems has been that few such professions, aside from nursing, have been taught in a similar life and death relationship which emphasizes the difficulties and burdens of assuming responsibilities. The patient, however, expects any therapist to consider his well-being as a physician would—or should.

The Transference Relationship

The conventions inherent in the physician's role and status help pre-determine the nature of the transference relationship in therapy. The patient must place the therapist in a position of authority if he is to feel secure, and he tends to make him as omniscient and omnipotent as possible. He seeks to endow the therapist with the qualities of a parental figure who will care for him and protect him. Thus, to a much greater extent than in most relationships, the therapist is regarded as a parental person and the characteristics of one or both parents are often transferred to him, a process which reactivates patterns of interrelating that were used with them. The age and sex of the therapist make relatively little difference. The most virile physician may be perceived by a patient very much in terms of his mother, and an aged woman may regard the young intern as she would a father figure. Recognition of such general trends which so often enter into the therapeutic relationship provides the therapist with an orientation that guides him in using himself helpfully. Blindness to the nature of the relationship engenders trouble.

Let us consider an example that is not so gross as the problems encountered by the medical students. A woman who is seriously ill requires considerable attention from the physicians and nursing staff. She is appreciative and complains little despite intense suffering. Then, as her illness comes under control, her complaints increase rather than subside. At times she resembles a whining child and the ward personnel have trouble containing their annoyance and begin to avoid her. The physicians become concerned and repeat several expensive procedures to make certain that she is recovering properly. The head nurse, however, notes that her complaints fluctuate during the day in a way that relates to changes in personnel rather than in her fever chart. One particular older staff nurse had spent much time with the patient during the critical phase of her illness. If, when this nurse comes on duty, she first sees the patient and spends a few minutes with her, everything goes well; but if she carries out some procedure with another patient first, the woman has many complaints by the time the nurse reaches her. The circumstances become fairly apparent to the perceptive head nurse when this patient occupies a double room with a very ill patient. If the particular nurse pays more attention to the roommate, difficulties arise and the patient become petulant and childish. Indeed, she reacts badly when she receives less attention than the other patient from any of the staff, but it is most obvious with her favorite nurse. The patient, as subsequent discussions with the psychiatrist revealed, had again become a child, having regressed markedly as do many seriously ill persons. She again had in the nurse a benevolent mother who was concerned about her and carefully nursed her; she became an envious child as she had many years before when her mother seemed more interested in her younger sister who had been in bed for many months with a chronic illness and required considerable attention. The patient now as in childhood sought to regain maternal attention by emphasizing her own needs in a hypochondriacal manner.

Misuse of Transference Phenomena

Knowledge of the transference aspects of patients' behavior, particularly a little knowledge about transference phenomena, can lead to its misuse by a therapist in order to protect himself from a patient's criticisms. Not all of a patient's misapprehensions, antagonisms, desires to change therapists, or to leave treatment derive from transference problems. Transference difficulties should not be blamed for resentfulness induced by failures to understand, thoughtlessness, mistakes, or neglect. Hospitals, for example, can provoke considerable aggravation in the bedridden patient. A patient can become annoyed by senseless hospital routine, lengthy waiting when he needs a bedpan, cold and scarcely edible hospital food. A therapist may usefully wonder with the patient why these inconveniences produce such excessive reactions, but time and aggravation can usually be spared by reserving consideration and discussion of transference problems for significant situations for which the therapist's behavior or current circumstances are probably not responsible and the patient's reactions seem inappropriate. In most situations in medical practice, transference difficulties are considered primarily when a patient's behavior appears out of place, exaggerated, or based on misunderstandings.

Transference in Psychotherapy

In medical practice, general social casework, and in other situations where the therapist is not specifically trained in the utilization of transference phenomena, they serve primarily as a guide to more effective use of the therapist-patient relationship. But in psychotherapy, transference serves as a major means of gaining understanding of a patient's basic attitudes and his ways of relating, and often as a major therapeutic lever in bringing about changes in the patient's attitudes and ways of understanding others.

• A psychiatrist who practiced psychoanalytically oriented therapy became ill and canceled his appointments for a day. The following morning, his first patient told him that she was glad to have had the extra hour, for she had been extremely busy at her job and would have needed to remain overtime had he kept the appointment. In fact, she continued, missing the session may have been more helpful as it gave her time to talk to her boss about some of her difficulties and he was very understanding and gave her some sound advice. As the psychiatrist had returned to his practice before he was fully recovered because he believed that this particular patient might become upset if he were ill, he could have become annoyed to hear her say that she was glad he had missed an hour with her and that her boss was able to give advice that the psychiatrist withheld or could not give. However, he simply listens and it soon becomes apparent that the patient is trying to tell herself and her psychiatrist that she will not let herself be hurt by needing someone badly and then be left in the lurch by him. She will make it clear to her psychiatrist that he is not so very important to her. This is an old pattern that has kept her from forming any close relationships and one of the reasons she is still single and turning into a spinster. The psychiatrist eventually comments in an offhand way that he recognizes that she is not angry because he stayed home on the preceding day and it does not matter if he or anyone else is really interested in her or not. Tears begin to trickle down the patient's cheeks, and when she tries to talk she finds herself sobbing that she did not really mean that; and, now, she feels for the first time the importance of her denial of her wishes and needs to be cared for and to be taken care of, a recognition which she has managed to evade in therapy except in intellectual discussions which were kept isolated from emotional context. She then goes on to consider her loneliness as a child and how her father was only interested in her brothers, with whom he could fish and hunt. •

• Another patient had heard that the psychiatrist had been ill. She starts her hour by expressing her concerns about his health and then tells of a fantasy she had that morning in which she told the psychiatrist that she loved him. In her daydream the psychiatrist was very ill, worried about dying, and needed the solace of the love she could express for him. The psychiatrist does not believe that the patient really loves him, nor does he think he must reassure the patient that he had been home with a relatively inconsequential viral infection. He notes to himself that although the patient has been in treatment for over a year, only in these circumstances has she been able to let herself fantasy being close to her therapist. It is only when she feels she is needed and can be useful because the man is weak and helpless that she can dare to experience affection. As she is married to a semi-invalid, the psychiatrist wonders whether this is a repetitive pattern and just how it had originated. He becomes alert to how the situation may be utilized and simply asks, "You felt that I needed you?" which starts the patient talking about her need to be needed before she can feel affectionate. •

• As elsewhere in psychotherapy, insight into a patient's misapprehensions or unconscious motives does not call for immediate interpretation; indeed, many experienced therapists rarely give intellectual interpretations at all, but seek to guide the patient to reach an understanding himself, and largely through feelings and thoughts engendered in the transference relationship with the psychiatrist. Transference misconceptions may be utilized most effectively by letting them be worked through against reality. •

• A psychiatrist who had his office in his home received an urgent call from a woman graduate student who asked for an emergency consultation because of her suicidal preoccupations. Although it was evening, he arranged to see the patient immediately. When she arrived, the psychiatrist's sixteen-year-old daughter opened the door and showed her to the waiting room. After several sessions, the patient started psychoanalytic therapy with him. Somewhat to his surprise, the patient referred to his daughter as his beautiful young mistress. He did not correct her misapprehension, which of course led to a rather distorted view of the psychiatrist and his way of life. The references to the imagined mistress gradually became more frequent and central to the young woman's problems. They were transferred from her disillusion in her father, her envy of his mistress, her disappointment in her mother, and many other such matters that had long directed much of the patient's fantasy life and distorted her image of herself. After about eighteen months, she suddenly realized that her idea that her analyst had a young mistress was without basis and she began to understand how profoundly a central theme from her childhood was affecting her life. •

Countertransference

The patient's transference affects one side of the therapeutic relationship; the *countertransference*—the therapist's tendencies to react to the patient in terms of his own earlier significant relationships—is, in many ways, even more important. Clearly, a therapist needs to view his patients as realistically and as free from distortion as possible. The patient properly must be treated for his own problems and not for some other person's difficulties, including the therapist's. If, for example, a therapist had an alcoholic father who made his family life miserable, old resentments toward his father may deleteriously color his relationships with alcoholic patients. If a therapist has idealized his mother and mother figures and been willing to sacrifice himself to gain a token of affection from motherly women, his judgment in his treatment of older women may be faulty.

Countertransference phenomena enter into a therapist's attitudes toward patients in many ways simply because the therapist is human and his early interpersonal relationships can never be fully excluded from them. Insofar as countertransference enters the relationship, the actuality of the situation is obfuscated. Yet, some countertransference feelings are advantageous, for without such connectedness to prior significant relationships, the therapist might be too aloof and be unable to empathize with his patients. Psychoanalysts must be thoroughly analyzed themselves, in large part to gain sufficient insight into their own lives and to become aware of the unconscious components of their ways of relating to and understanding others in order to provide assurance that countertransference problems will not seriously influence their work with patients. Knowledge of the self, however gained, is of the essence to anyone engaged in treating people psychotherapeutically. Whether analyzed or not, a good therapist continues to learn something from virtually every patient he treats, about his own foibles and his tendencies to misperceive patients and what they communicate. Psychoanalysis is purposefully carried out in a manner that seeks to heighten the use of the transference attitudes and to minimize the distortions stemming from the countertransference. The patient on the couch does not see the analyst who sits behind him, and does not receive direction from the analyst's expressions, or from his comments, which are, particularly during the early phase of analysis, sparse and non-directive, seeking to increase the free flow of associations from the patient. The patient, thus, with little knowledge about the analyst and his attitudes tends to transfer to the therapist ideas and feelings derived from earlier significant relationships, which eventually become the topic of analytic scrutiny. The analyst's minimal activity lessens the impact on the therapy of countertransference; for after the patient becomes a more distinctive individual to the analyst, countertransference phenomena are less likely to interfere.

Relatively few analysts, however, adhere rigorously to the style of making themselves a "blank screen" for the patient's transferences and projections. Many analytically oriented therapists seek to serve as what Sullivan termed a "participant observer," listening to the patient's associations and past and present experiences,[2] while trying to guide the patient into more objective and less distorted perceptions and understanding by commenting briefly and inserting questions or questioning sounds at appropriate moments. Such psychotherapeutic interventions as a participant observer properly require even greater self-knowledge and ability to manage countertransference phenomena than do more classical psychoanalytic techniques. Perhaps, most analysts work in a style between these two models, varying their techniques to suit the patient and the phase of therapy. Whereas a thorough psychoanalysis is the most effective way for a therapist to gain self-understanding, unfortunately it does not assure it; and there have been gifted therapists, including Freud and many of the early analysts, capable of proper empathy and with deep insights into their own natures and foibles who were not formally analyzed.

Countertransference phenomena cannot be completely avoided or excluded. In customary relationships between a physician, a nurse, or social worker, and a patient, it is the countertransference excesses that require checking. A therapist becomes alert when, for example, he finds the patient's difficulties provoking strong emotions in him; or when he begins to realize that he is strongly involved emotionally as when falling in love with a patient, or when he feels hostile to a patient. At such times, the danger arises that the treatment will be influenced or even directed toward alleviating the therapist's feelings rather than the patient's problems. Equanimity does not mean disinterest, but it implies that the therapist can maintain a suitable perspective, and that the patient's problems rather than the therapist's emotional needs will guide their relationship.

Countertransference phenomena are, in a sense, part of the larger problem of a therapist being caught up in his own needs in treating a patient. They may involve the reasons for the choice of a career. A physician, or any therapist, may seek power and an opportunity to display it and be unable to countenance any interference with his decisions; or he may seek the love of his patients, leading him to sacrifice himself excessively; or he may unconsciously seek to make his patients feel dependent upon him and indebted to him, thus interfering with his purpose of fostering the patient's development of autonomy. He may desire the plaudits of colleagues more than the well-being of his patients; or he may make authoritarian use of his position in order to gain vengeance on mother or father figures. The therapist strives constantly to achieve a reasonable equanimity and objectivity that permits optimal use of his knowledge and skills for the benefit of the actual patient. He requires an ability not only to learn to know the patient as a specific individual and to recognize the patient's transference problems, but also to know himself, his strengths, weaknesses, needs, and repetitive patterns as well as he can.

It is often difficult for a physician to keep his feet on the ground when he holds the responsibility of dealing with life and death, and also for any therapist who can rightly believe that he can often change the course of a life. When patients idealize him, he can lose perspective and begin to believe he is the person whom patients think they see. Such exaltation of the self can rebound and bring him misery if he expects the impossible from himself and finds it difficult to forgive his own errors. The failure to recognize the transference attitudes of patients breeds trouble, but when the therapist sees himself in terms of his patients' transference reactions to him, he is courting disaster.

Although the ability to assess countertransference attitudes competently is essential for psychotherapists, such insights concerning the self cannot be expected from other physicians or from those in related professions. Still, an illustration of how countertransference can be kept from interfering excessively with a therapeutic relationship may be useful. A resident psychiatrist, well along in his training, started to treat a new patient under supervision. He spent a considerable portion of the first supervisory hour discussing his initial encounter with the patient and the feelings and memories it had aroused in him. When he first saw the patient, he felt his heart start to speed up. He noted the reaction and realized that her appearance had surprised him. He had expected a young woman who was seeking help because of marital difficulties, but he had not anticipated the pretty, vivacious, and extremely well-dressed woman who stood before him. He realized that she was a type he had liked to date while in college and bore some resemblance to his wife in the way she walked and talked. When he contemplated his reaction to her, he realized that a connection existed between something in her appearance and his older sister, whom he had idolized in his early childhood. But he also recognized that something in the patient created an unpleasant feeling in him which he could not fathom but which he believed would eventually lead him to dislike her. In retrospect he thought it had to do with a smug self-satisfaction which conveyed an assurance that everyone admired her beauty and that any person would be lucky to have her about. The resident felt annoyed, because he did admire her appearance and feel attracted to her. The details are not so important as the therapist's awareness of the feelings that had been aroused in him, and his efforts to alert himself from the very onset of the therapeutic relationship to potential sources of countertransference distortion, of both a positive and a negative character.

The Use of Transference Relationships Outside of Psychotherapy

In the practice of general medicine and in other relationships that contain a therapeutic intent or implication, transference relationships are not used so pointedly and purposefully as in psychotherapy; but they often influence the relationship for better or worse even though the therapist may not realize it. Clearly, the therapist can use himself and the relationship more effectively when he is aware of its importance and how it can affect his patient. The simple recognition by the therapist that he is, or can be, a parental authority figure and a potential source of support to the dependent, often regressively dependent, patient can help the patient surmount crises. As a person who is capable of countering the internalized superego, the therapist, by the power vested in him by the patient's transference, can help offset patients' losses in self-esteem. When illness has fostered regressive needs for dependency, a physician can permit the patient to gain security through dependency upon him until the circumstances change. A patient confronted by a serious operation may feel far more secure if the general practitioner whom he has known for years is present in the operating room. He may know that the surgeon and his assistants are far better equipped than the general practitioner, who could do little if anything to help, but the practitioner is a parental figure who, he feels, will be protecting him. It may be irrational, but it is an understandable and an emotionally useful irrationality. Persons who become dejected because they are invalided and no longer self-sufficient may regain self-esteem because of a therapist's interest in them and respect for them. The ramifications are many, and it is such transference phenomena, whether evoked purposefully or accidentally, that account for many unexpected transitions back to health akin to those documented by faith healers.

· Sometimes a patient's needs can be met by the controlled use of a transference relationship when little more specific can be done and with unexpected salutory results. A young woman with severe acute arthritis lay in the hospital feeling hopeless and lost without any family to whom she could turn. Her father, if she had a legal father, had abandoned her mother when the patient was still an infant. Her mother had been a prostitute, but a rather unusual woman with an interest in literature that she had conveyed to the patient, but she was now in a mental hospital, chronically psychotic. The patient had spent her adolescence in foster homes and institutions, but because of her attractiveness, superior intellect, and drive, she had been provided with a college education by a church group. She had repeatedly sought to attach herself to one or another mothering woman attempting to become the favorite child by working inordinately hard to become essential to the mothering person. However, she either became too involved in the woman's family or involved with homosexual women whose advances she rebuffed, so that she never managed to find a permanent home. She had become ill with arthritis while working in a missionary school in the southern mountains after she had been displaced as the woman missionary's favorite and was no longer permitted to live in her home. It had been a severe blow, as she had believed that she had finally found a haven, a mother, and her proper calling..

- The attending physician took an interest in the patient and suggested that she become an occupational therapist or nurse. He visited her daily and would chat briefly with her about her life and her many interesting experiences. A rapid shift occurred in the course of the illness, and somewhat to the surprise of the hospital staff she made a complete recovery without any residual deformities. The physician then fostered a long-term relationship in which she came for "check-ups" at regular intervals, during which she told him about her progress in nursing school and discussed her plans with him. He was demonstrating that someone was interested in her, and indeed he had become interested in her. As he had consciously developed the relationship to foster the patient's self-sufficiency rather than to permit her to become permanently dependent upon him, he was surprised neither by her seductive efforts to attach herself to him nor by her suggestions that she could be very useful to his wife if permitted to live with his family as a mother's helper. He could retain interest without being frightened away by her attempts to become part of his life, for he had anticipated such efforts from her life story; and he could seek gradually to redirect her energies into channels that held promise for her future. •

Indeed, a physician or any other therapist can sometimes be very helpful because of his transference position, even when he does little more than permit the person to come to his office where he listens attentively and empathically to what the patient wishes to convey. A man who finds little understanding from his wife and children, or an aged person who no longer has any significant person left, may gain much from a therapist's interest, and from being able to talk to someone who listens dispassionately and does not place blame vindictively. All too often a physician believes that he is wasting his and the patient's time when he simply listens to a patient, and thinks that he must *do* something—prescribe medicine, a diet, a vacation, or stop the patient from wasting his money on unnecessary visits. He may feel uncomfortable because he cannot offer useful advice concerning the patient's insoluble problems. The patient, however, knows that his problems cannot be resolved and is grateful for the opportunity to ventilate feelings that must be hidden from others, and gains support of his self-esteem because the therapist considers him a person worth listening to.

An understanding of transference and countertransference phenomena provides directives that can greatly improve the therapist's relationships with his patients, but more precise guidelines are gained through interviewing skills with which the therapist helps the patient tell about himself. The patient's anamnesis—his account of his illness and relevant material from his past life—constitutes the most important diagnostic tool in medicine, and it forms the foundation of any type of psychotherapeutic relationship. The various techniques that help elicit information from patients form a major topic in themselves, and are not part of the subject matter of this volume. However, the capacity to listen and be able to hear and understand what a person seeks to communicate and to note what he does not or cannot say are major aspects of skillful interviewing. A patient's recognition that the therapist listens, hears, and understands provides an incentive to him to communicate what he considers meaningful. Such capacities to hear and understand what is meaningful in an individual's life rest upon knowledge of psychodynamics: upon knowledge of the epigenetic nature of personality development, of the crucial tasks of each phase of the life cycle and what is likely to be most significant to a person at his stage of life, of the critical importance of interpersonal relationships to everyone; and upon the ability to detect life themes and repetitive patterns. This book has sought to provide a guide for gaining such knowledge; but it cannot be learned from books alone, for it requires responsible involvement with people and a readiness to learn to know the self. What the therapist hears from patients about themselves can be disturbing because some of it will surely also apply to him. Yet much of the satisfaction gained from the practice of medicine and from conducting any type of therapy derives from a willingness and ability to hear and understand. It enables the therapist to gain and grow from each relationship, which in turn makes each patient a new adventure. As the therapeutic relationship ceases to be something given to the patient but rather a situation in which the therapist also receives, he can give of himself without resentment or feeling deprived.

References

1. William Osler, *Aequanimitas and Other Papers* (New York: W. W. Norton, 1963).
2. Harry Stack Sullivan, *The Interpersonal Theory of Psychiatry* (New York: W. W. Norton, 1953).

Suggested Reading

Michael Balint and Enid Balint, *Psychotherapeutic Techniques in Medicine* (Springfield, Ill.: Charles C Thomas, 1962).
Carl Binger, *The Doctor's Job* (New York: W. W. Norton, 1945).
Frieda Fromm-Reichmann, *Principles of Intensive Psychotherapy* (Chicago: University of Chicago Press, 1950).

Index

Aberle, David F., 16 n., 48 n.
Abraham, Karl, 161 n.
accident-proneness, 524 n.
accommodation, in cognitive development (Piaget), 83
acculturation, and personality, 52–53
ACTH (adrenocorticotrophic hormone), 528, 537
adjustment, marital, see marriage; sexuality
adolescence, 73 n., 76, 80, 84 n., 85, 275, 298–361; conflicts of, 302, 322, 325; defense mechanisms of, 317, 340–342; early, see early adolescence; ego in, 302, 324, 325, 328, 330, 340; and ego diffusion, 348–350; end of, 358–359; and family, overcoming attachments to, 322, 327–328; id drives in, 302, 314, 324, 325, 328, 330, 337; identity crisis of, 342–343, 350; late, see late adolescence; mid-, see mid-adolescence; peer relationships of, 305–306, 331–334; personality development in, 299; sexuality in, 301, 302, 312–313, 333, 335–340, 355–358; sub-periods of, 303–304; superego in, 301, 302, 317, 320, 321, 322, 324, 327, 328, 330, 331, 337 and n., 341; see also puberty
adrenal cortical hormones, 537
adrenal-neural system, 32
adrenocorticotrophic hormone (ACTH), 528, 537
adult: anal character traits in, 379; concept formation in, 202 n.; oral character traits in, 152–155, 379; young, see young adult
agenesis, gonadal, 211 and n.
aggression, 30, 31, 32 and n., 33 and n., 185, 240, 241 and n., 249, 497 n., 533
Ainsworth, Mary Satter, 149 n.
alarm reaction (Selye), 538 and n.
alcohol, 366, 413, 415, 416, 510, 511, 512
Alexander, Franz, 524 n., 535 n.

alienation, 267, 323, 349
aliment, in cognitive development (Piaget), 83, 84, 170
amaeru, 455
amaurotic family idiocy, 38 n.
ambivalence, 181, 221; in toddler, 177
American Handbook of Psychiatry, 524 n.
anal characteristics, 181–182, 379, 514, 516
anal phase, of psychosexual development (Freud), 77, 161, 179
androgen, 210, 212, 227
anger, 528, 532 n.
animism, 201, 202, 203, 205 n.
anorexia nervosa, 27 n., 526
anthropoid apes, 8 n., 30, 32 n.
anxiety, 33, 74 n., 225, 226, 244, 245, 248, 253, 365, 502, 517, 528, 533, 539; in adolescent, 340; castration, 215–216, 216 n., 226, 228, 229, 336, 497; and defense mechanisms, see mechanisms of defense; "existential," 497; in juvenile, 291–293; within marriage, 387; physiological responses to, 529 n.; in preschool child, 195–196; separation, 207, 497 and n., 517; in young adult, 365, 366
apathy, 36
apes, anthropoid, 8 n., 30, 32 n.
apoplexy, 486
Ardrey, Robert, 32 n.
Ariès, Phillipe, 82 n.
Arlow, Jacob A., 261 n.
arthritis, 538, 555
artificialism, 202, 205 n.
asceticism, 381; adolescent, 341
assimilation, in cognitive development (Piaget), 83
asthma, 490 n., 524, 533 and n., 534 n.
attachment behavior, between mother and child, 130–131
automation, industrial, 491
autonomic nervous system, 32, 527, 537; dual functions of, 532–534

"promotion depression," 462
prosthetic aids, 485
prostitution, 394
Provence, Sally A., 147 *n*., 148, 149 *n*.
pseudohermaphrodite, 211, 308
Psychoanalysis of Children, The (Klein), 124 *n*.
psychoanalytic approach to study of personality types, 514–515
Psychoanalytic Studies of the Personality (Fairbairn), 88 *n*.
Psychology of Character, The (Roback), 517 *n*.
Psychology of Intelligence, The (Piaget), 273 *n*.
psychosexual development, phases of (Freud), 76–80, 81; *see also* personality development; sexuality
Psychosocial Analysis of a Hopi Life-History, The (Aberle), 48 *n*.
psychosocial phases of life cycle (Erikson), 80–82
psychosomatic disorders, 535 *n*.
Psychosomatic Medicine (Alexander), 524 *n*., 535 *n*.
psychotherapy, transference in, 548–550
puberty, 72, 73 *n*., 78, 85, 230, 243, 300, 303, 305, 306, 314, 315, 320; in boy, 312–313; in girl, 306–311; *see also* adolescence
pygmies, African, 38

racial physical endowment, 37–38
Rainwater, Lee, 431
Rapaport, David, 240 *n*., 261 *n*.
rapid eye movements (REM), 252 *n*.
reaction formation, 220, 258, 292, 293, 510, 516
Read, Grantly Dick, 104, 105
reality principle, 87 *n*.
reality testing, 205, 229, 250
reasoning, and formal operations, 275, 315–316, 316 *n*.
Recent Developments in Psychosomatic Medicine, 524 *n*.
reflex: Babinski, 97; gastro-colic, 179; grasp, 96–97, 133, 134 *n*.; plantar, 97; startle, 97; sucking, 124, 133, 134
regression, 74 and *n*., 75, 154, 257, 292, 294, 484, 548

Reichsman, Franz, 525 *n*.
religion, 320, 490–491, 499, 500; Dionysian, 349 *n*.
REM (rapid eye movements), 252 *n*.
repression, 101, 241, 248, 256–257, 326, 339, 515; sexual, overcoming during mid-adolescence, 324–325, 336
responsibility, sense of, 267, 285
reticular activating system, 24 *n*., 35 *n*., 527
retirement, 476, 478, 482–484, 491
reversibility, and preoperational child, 273
Ribble, Margaret, 129 *n*.
Riesman, David, 517 *n*.
Rights of Infants, The (Ribble), 129 *n*.
Roback, Abraham A., 517 *n*.
Rosenthal, Robert, 278 *n*.
Royce, Josiah, 267 *n*.
Rubenstein, Boris B., 309, 310

sadism, 33 *n*., 209, 229 *n*., 406, 407
St. Martin, Alexis, 525 *n*.
Saussure, Raymond De, 112 *n*.
Schachtel, Ernest G., 247 *n*.
Schaffer, H. R., 139
schema, in cognitive development (Piaget), 83–84
Schiele, B. C., 27 *n*.
Schiller, Friedrich, 255 *n*.
schizophrenia, 207 *n*., 302, 314 *n*.
school: juvenile in, 264, 265, 271 *n*., 274, 275–279; as socializing agency, 275–279
Schur, Max, 139 *n*.
Sears, Robert S., 143 *n*.
secondary process thinking, 249 *n*., 250 and *n*.
secondary sexual characteristics, 300, 306, 477
Seitz, Philip F. D., 140 *n*.
self, basic trust in, 81, 123, 160
self-absorption (Erikson), 81
self-concept, 261, 267 and *n*., 526; development of, 284–285
self-demand feeding, 128–129
self-esteem, 243, 261, 293, 328, 402, 451, 465 and *n*., 484, 513, 529, 539, 555, 556
Selye, Hans, 538 and *n*.